THIRD

EDITION

Drugs, Society and Criminal Justice

Charles F. Levinthal

Hofstra University

Prentice Hall

Boston   Columbus   Indianapolis   New York   San Francisco   Upper Saddle River

Amsterdam   Cape Town   Dubai   London   Madrid   Milan   Munich   Paris   Montréal   Toronto

Delhi   Mexico City   São Paulo   Sydney   Hong Kong   Seoul   Singapore   Taipei   Tokyo

Editorial Director: Vernon R. Anthony
Senior Acquisitions Editor: Eric Krassow
Assistant Editor: Tiffany Bitzel
Editorial Assistant: Lynda Cramer
Director of Marketing: David Gesell
Senior Marketing Manager: Adam Kloza
Senior Marketing Coordinator: Alicia Wozniak
Marketing Assistant: Les Roberts
Senior Managing Editor: JoEllen Gohr
Project Manager: Steve Robb
Senior Operations Supervisor: Pat Tonneman
Operations Specialist: Pat Tonneman

Creative Director: Christy Mahon
Art Director: Diane Y. Ernsberger
Cover Designer: Suzanne Duda
Cover Art: Habman/Fotolia
Media Editor: Michelle Churma
Media Project Manager: Karen Bretz
Full-Service Project Management: Nancy Kincade, PreMediaGlobal
Composition: PreMediaGlobal
Printer/Binder: RR Donnelley & Sons
Cover Printer: Lehigh-Phoenix Color/Hagerstown
Text Font: 10/12 ElectraLH-Regular

Credits and acknowledgments for content borrowed from other sources and reproduced, with permission, in this textbook appear on page xix.

Library of Congress Cataloging-in-Publication Data
Levinthal, Charles F.
  Drugs, society, and criminal justice / Charles F. Levinthal.—3rd ed.
    p. cm.
  Includes bibliographical references and index.
  ISBN 978-0-13-512048-4 (hardcover: alk. paper)
  1. Drug abuse. 2. Drugs of abuse. 3. Drug abuse and crime. 4. Drug abuse—Prevention. I. Title.
  HV5801.L493 2012
  363.290973—dc22

                                                                                2010048456

10 9 8 7 6 5 4 3 2 1

Prentice Hall
is an imprint of

www.pearsonhighered.com

ISBN-10:   0-13-512048-9
ISBN-13: 978-0-13-512048-4

**For
My Family**

CONTENTS

CHAPTER 15
Nicotine and Tobacco Use   348

PREFACE

New to This Edition

- The chapter on Drugs and Crime and the chapter on Drugs and the Criminal Justice System, now shifted to earlier placements in the text (Chapters 5 and 6), thus providing a clearer focus on issues of drug-taking behavior as they pertain to the criminal justice system.
- Information about recent legislative and regulatory developments having an impact on drug-taking behavior. Examples include the Family Smoking Prevention and Tobacco Control Act of 2009 (giving the FDA authority to regulate the sale and manufacture of tobacco products) and Mental Health Parity and Addiction Equity Act of 2008 (allowing reimbursements for substance abuse treatment to be on a par with the treatment of physical disorders).
- New updated Portraits of individuals who have impacted or been impacted by drug use and abuse in America. Examples include From Oxy to Heroin: The Life and Death of Erik (Chapter 1), Ryan Haight and the Ryan Haight Act of 2008 (Chapter 2), and Dr. A. Thomas McLellan—Reframing National Drug Policy (Chapter 16).
- New Drugs . . . in Focus features, including Understanding Drug Names (Chapter 1), Measuring the Impact of Drugs on our Society (Chapter 2), and Abraham, Depression, and "those little blue pills" (Chapter 3).
- New text discussion on odds ratios with regard to risk and protective factors (Chapter 4), changes in mandatory minimum sentence guidelines and implementation of the RICO statute in the prosecution of drug traffickers (Chapter 6), and the nonmedical use of stimulant medications in baseball (Chapter 12).
- Drug Trafficking Update features with the latest information about trends in the international drug trade as they impact upon drug-taking behavior in America. Sources include the 2009 and 2010 Drug Threat Assessment Reports, published by the Drug Intelligence Center, U.S. Department of Justice.
- Updated statistical information from the 2009 Monitoring the Future survey of drug use among secondary school and college students as well as young adults. There is also information from the 2008 Drug Abuse Warning Network survey and 2008 National Survey on Drug Use and Health.

- Expanded discussion of concepts, such as odds ratios in the understanding of risk factors and protective factors for drug-taking behavior (Chapter 4), sensitivity and specificity in the understanding of drug testing (Chaper 12), and criteria for evaluations of substance abuse prevention and treatment interventions (Chapter 16).
- Inclusion of current information about *Salvia divinorum* abuse among high school students. According to the 2009 Monitoring the Future survey, six percent of high school seniors reported using Salvia in the past year. The Drug Enforcement Administration (DEA) has considered recommending that Salvia, presently a legal commodity, be classified as a Schedule I controlled substance.

Drugs, Society, and Criminal Justice, Third Edition, is specifically designed for students who want to learn about drug use, drug misuse, and drug abuse from a criminal justice perspective. The goal is to introduce the basic facts and major issues concerning drug-taking behavior in a straightforward, comprehensive, up-to-date, and reader-friendly manner. A background in biology, sociology, psychology, or chemistry is not necessary. The only requirement is a sense of curiosity about the range of chemical substances that affect our minds and our bodies and an interest in the challenges these substances bring to the public health and public safety of our society—as well as to our daily lives.

As you proceed through this textbook, a central theme will be apparent: The array of social problems associated with drug-taking behavior in America today extends beyond the use of illicit street drugs such as heroin, cocaine, amphetamines, hallucinogens, and marijuana (Chapters 7–10). It is important also to address the problems associated with legally available drugs such as alcohol and nicotine (Chapters 13–15), as well as a variety of depressants (Chapter 11), performance-enhancing drugs (Chapter 12), and (when used for nonmedical purposes) prescription and nonprescription (over-the-counter) drugs such as Adderall, Ritalin, Vicodin, and OxyContin (Chapters 1, 7, and 8). *Drugs, Society, and Criminal Justice* addresses the entire range of drugs used and abused in our contemporary society. The complex relationship between drug-taking behavior and crime as well as the challenges of contending with drug-taking behavior within a system of criminal justice will be covered in Chapters 5 and 6, respectively.

In the third edition, a particular emphasis has been placed on the impact that new laws and regulations have had on drug-taking behavior and drug policy in the United States. The effects have been significant for millions of Americans. As a result of the Ryan Haight Online Pharmacy Consumer Protection Act of 2008, there are strict regulations over access to prescription drugs via the Internet. It is far more difficult now to obtain prescription drugs through unregulated and unsupervised online services. As a result of the Family Smoking Prevention and Tobacco Control Act of 2009, the Food and Drug Administration (FDA) now has regulatory authority over the manufacture and sales of tobacco products. As a result of the Parity Act of 2009, drug-abuse treatment expenses are now reimbursed on a par with the reimbursement of expenses for the treatment of physical disorders. As a result of the Fair Sentencing Act of 2010, the gap has been reduced between the federal penalties for the possession of powder cocaine and possession of crack cocaine. All of these developments will have a significant influence on drug-taking behavior in the decades ahead.

Features of the Third Edition

The structure of chapters in *Drugs, Society, and Criminal Justice*, Third Edition, has been changed in order to enhance the dialogue and discourse through which we can effectively grapple with the issues of drug-taking behavior and criminal justice. I have listened to reviewers who wanted the chapter on Drugs and Crime and the chapter on Drugs and the Criminal Justice System positioned earlier in the text. They are now Chapters 5 and 6, respectively. The third edition has a clear focus on drugs and criminal justice in America. The chapters are now organized in four major sections:

- Part 1 (Chapters 1–6): Drugs and Society: The Criminal Justice Perspective
- Part 2 (Chapters 7–12): Legally Restricted Drugs in Our Society
- Part 3 (Chapters 13–15): Legal Drugs in Our Society
- Part 4 (Chapter 16): Drug Abuse and Drug Policy

As has been the case in earlier editions, a number of special features will enhance your experience as a reader and serve as learning aids. Many of them have been updated for maximal educational impact in the third edition.

Quick Concept Checks

Sometimes, when the material gets complicated, it is very handy to have a quick way of finding out if you understand the basic concepts being explained. Each chapter of this book includes from time to time a **Quick Concept Check**, where you can see in a minute or two where you stand. Some of the Checks are in a matching format; others involve interpreting a graph or diagram. In some cases, you will be asked to apply the principles you have learned to a real-world situation.

Portraits

Sixteen **Portrait** features, one in each chapter, take you into the lives of individuals who have either influenced our current thinking about drugs and society or have been influenced by circumstances of drug use and abuse. These stories offer an engaging insight into the impact of drug-taking behavior on history and on contemporary life in America. Some of the subjects of the Portrait features are known to the public at large, but many are not. In any case, the Portraits put a human face on the discussion of drugs, society, and criminal justice. They remind us that throughout this book we are dealing with issues that affect real people in all walks of life, both past and present. Here are some examples:

- From Oxy to Heroin: The Life and Death of Erik (Chapter 1, page 8)
- Ryan Haight and the Ryan Haight Act of 2008 (Chapter 2, page 46)
- Pablo Escobar—Formerly Known as the Colombian King of Cocaine (Chapter 5, page 101)
- Barry Tuttle and Russell Fitch—The Two Sides of OxyContin (Chapter 7, page 162)
- Robert Downey Jr.—Cleaning Up His Life after Cocaine (Chapter 8, page 177)
- Bill W. and Dr. Bob—Founders of Alcoholics Anonymous (Chapter 14, page 339)
- Sigmund Freud—Nicotine Dependence, Cigars, and Cancer (Chapter 15, page 367)

Drugs . . . in Focus

There are many fascinating stories to tell about the role of drug-taking behavior in our society, along with the important facts and serious issues surrounding drug use. Some of the **Drugs . . . in Focus** features summarize information that you can refer to at a later time when the need arises; others provide an interesting look at a question or issue that you might have wondered about. Here are some examples of the forty-one Drugs . . . in Focus features that you will find in the third edition:

- Understanding Drug Names (Chapter 1, page 6)
- Acute Toxicity in the News: Drug-Related Deaths (Chapter 2, page 32)
- Abraham Lincoln, Depression, and Those "Little Blue Pills" (Chapter 3, page 54)
- A Wave of Narcoterrorism in Mexico (Chapter 5, page 97)
- What Happened to the Coca in Coca-Cola? (Chapter 8, page 169)
- Stimulant Medications as "Smart Pills" (Chapter 8, page 188)
- Strange Days in Salem: Witchcraft or Hallucinogens? (Chapter 9, page 197)
- Is There Any Truth Regarding "Truth Serum"? (Chapter 11, page 245)
- THG and the War on Performance-Enhancing Drugs (Chapter 12, page 284)
- Smoking in Movies and Movie Ratings (Chapter 15, page 364)
- Alcohol 101 on College Campuses (Chapter 16, page 395)

Help Lines

Useful information regarding the effectiveness and safety aspects of particular drugs, specific aspects of drug-taking behavior, and new medical applications can be found in fifteen **Help Line** features throughout the third edition. At the end of each Help Line, there is a Website that can be of further assistance to you. Here are some examples:

- The Possibility of a Drug–Drug or Food–Drug Combination (Chapter 1, page 15)
- Cocaine after Alcohol: The Risk of Cocaethylene Toxicity (Chapter 8, page 168)
- Emergency Guidelines for a Bad Trip on LSD (Chapter 9, page 202)
- MDMA Toxicity: The Other Side of Ecstasy (Chapter 9, page 208)
- The Dangers of Rohypnol as a Date-Rape Drug (Chapter 11, page 252)
- The Symptoms of Steroid Abuse (Chapter 12, page 280)

- Emergency Signs and Procedures in Acute Alcohol Intoxication (Chapter 13, page 308)
- The TWEAK Alcoholism Screening Instrument for Pregnant Women (Chapter 14, page 332)
- Ten Tips on How to Succeed When Trying to Quit Smoking (Chapter 15, page 369)

Drug Trafficking Updates

When you are reading about drugs and criminal justice, it is important that you understand the global economics and global politics that form the context of today's illicit drug trade. **Drug Trafficking Update** features provide important up-to-date information about the illicit trafficking of heroin, cocaine, methamphetamine, LSD, MDMA (Ecstasy), PCP, and marijuana—direct from Drug Enforcement Administration reports and those of other governmental agencies engaged in the struggle against international as well as domestic drug trafficking.

An Invitation to Readers

I welcome your reactions to *Drugs, Society, and Criminal Justice*, Third Edition. Please send any comments or questions to the following address: Dr. Charles F. Levinthal, Department of Psychology, 135 Hofstra University, Hempstead, NY 11549. You can also fax them to me at (516) 463-6052 or e-mail them to me at charles.f.levinthal@hofstra.edu. I look forward to hearing from you.

Acknowledgments

In the course of writing the third edition, I have received much encouragement, assistance, and expert advice from a number of people. I have benefited from their sharing of materials, knowledge, and insights. I am particularly indebted to Dr. Elizabeth Crane, Substance Abuse and Mental Health Services Administration, U.S. Department of Health and Human Services; Charles F. Miller of the Office of Policy and Interagency Affairs, National Drug Intelligence Center, U.S. Department of Justice; Dr. Patrick M. O'Malley, Institute for Social Research, University of Michigan, Ann Arbor; and Lawrence Payne of the Office of Public Affairs, Drug Enforcement Administration, U.S. Department of Justice.

I am quite fortunate to have worked with a superb team at Pearson Prentice Hall. I am especially indebted to my editors, Tim Peyton and Eric Krassow, and to my project manager, Steve Robb. Their professionalism and friendship are greatly appreciated. I also want to acknowledge the efforts of project editor Nancy Kincade and photo researcher Megan Lessard, who have contributed so much to the editorial excellence and production quality of this book.

I thank the manuscript reviewers who made suggestions that proved invaluable as I worked on the third edition of *Drugs, Society, and Criminal Justice*. They are: C. Randall Eastep, Brevand Community College; Tricia Klosky, Saint Mary's University of Minnesota; Patricia L. McDiarmid, Springfield College; and Carleen Vincent-Robinson, Florida International University. On a more personal note, there are others who have given me their support over the years and to whom my appreciation goes beyond words. As always, I thank my mother-in-law, Selma Kuby, for her encouragement and love.

Above all, my family has been a continuing source of strength. I will always be grateful to my wonderful sons, David and Brian, and to my daughter-in-law, Sarah, for their love and understanding. I am especially grateful to my wife, Beth, for her abiding love, support, and complete faith in my abilities. The third edition is dedicated to my family.

Charles F. Levinthal

Supplements

- Instructor's Manual with Test Bank
- PowerPoint Presentations
- CourseSmart

Download Instructor Resources from the Instructor Resource Center

To access supplementary materials online, instructors need to request an instructor access code. Go to **www.pearsonhighered.com/irc** to register for an instructor access code. Within 48 hours of registering, you will receive a confirming e-mail including an instructor access code. Once you have received your code, locate your text in the online catalog and click on the Instructor Resources button on the left side of the catalog product page. Select a supplement, and a login page will appear. Once you have logged in, you can access instructor material for all Prentice Hall textbooks. If you have any difficulties accessing the site or downloading a supplement, please contact Customer Service at **http://247.prenhall.com**.

Photo Credits

PART ONE
Drugs and Society: The Criminal Justice Perspective

chapter 1

Understanding Drug-taking Behavior

After you have completed this chapter, you should have an understanding of

- Basic terminology concerning drugs and drug-taking behavior
- The ways drugs enter and exit the body
- Factors determining the physiological impact of drugs
- The distinction between physical and psychological dependence
- The psychiatric definitions of substance abuse and substance dependence
- The five-schedule classification of controlled substances in the United States

Mike was seventeen, a high school junior—an age when life can be both terrific and terrifying. He looked at me with amazement, telling me by his expression that either the question I was asking him was ridiculous or the answer was obvious. "Why do kids do drugs?" I had asked.

"It's cool," he said. "That's why. Believe me, it's important to be cool. Besides, in my life, drugs just make me feel better. Smoking a little weed, mellowing out with some Perks or a little Vicodin, spinning with some Addies—it's a way of getting away from 'stuff.' And you know that everybody does it. At least all of my friends do it. It's easy to get them. All you need to know is where to go."

The meeting was over. But as he started to leave, Mike seemed to notice the concern on my face. "Don't worry about me," he said. "I can handle it. I can handle it just fine."

There is no question that drugs are all around us. Thousands of Internet web sites offering information about drug use are just a click away. It seems difficult at times to pick up a newspaper, watch television, or listen to popular music without seeing or hearing some reference to drug use. We are continually bombarded with news about drug-related arrests of major drug dealers and ordinary citizens, news about the most recent drug involvement among popular celebrities, and news about drugs intercepted and confiscated at our borders and in the towns and cities of America.

It is also difficult to avoid the reality of drugs in our personal lives. Seven out of ten adults surveyed in the United States describe the nation's drug problem as either extremely or very serious; one out of four Americans report that drugs have been a cause of trouble in their family. In school, you have been taught the risks involved in drug use, but it is likely that you have had to contend with the social pressure to engage in some form of drug-related activity with your friends. According to a national survey, about one in five males and about one in eight females between the ages of twelve and seventeen have been approached in the past month by someone selling drugs. For fifteen- or sixteen-year-old youths, the number is approximately one in four. In light of your own experiences, these official statistics might appear to be underestimates.[1]

Two central facts should be kept in mind as we begin an exploration of present-day issues regarding drug use and abuse. First of all, the challenges we face with respect to drug-taking behavior today include not only the availability of illegal drugs such as cocaine, amphetamines, heroin, LSD and other hallucinogens, and marijuana, but also the availability of legally sanctioned drugs such as alcohol and nicotine. The decision

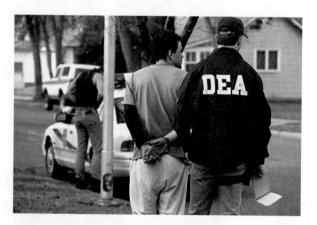

An accused drug user is led away by an agent in a DEA wind-breaker on a residential street in Billings, Montana, far away from the urban communities usually associated with drug use.

to use drugs of all types and forms, legally sanctioned or not, has become one of life's choices in the United States as well as in nations around the world. Second, the problems associated with drug-taking behavior encompass every segment of society; it is not just a "young people's issue." The potential for drug abuse and drug dependence exists for people of all ages, from the young to the elderly. The adverse impact on our society can be seen in the workplace and retirement communities as well as on street corners, in school yards, and college campuses. The social and personal problems associated with drug use extend in one way or another to men and women of all ethnic and racial groups, geographic regions, and socioeconomic levels. No group or individuals should believe themselves exempt.[2]

Finally, we should recognize the heavy price that we pay. The direct and indirect monetary costs of drug abuse in our society are enormous, amounting to hundreds of billions of dollars each year.[3] The costs are traditionally classified in four major areas:

- The economic costs of lost workplace productivity due to absenteeism, industrial accidents, and premature death of workers.

- The health-care expenditures required to treat individuals with illnesses related to drug use, particularly with respect to the abuse of tobacco and alcohol.

- The costs of drug-related crime borne by the victims of criminal behavior and the community in which the criminal activity occurs.

- The expense of maintaining a criminal justice system devoted to the control of illegal drugs.

Most importantly, there are costs that cannot be calculated in monetary terms. They include the decline in our collective sense of social order, the diminishment of personal dignity and self-worth, and the devastating effect on relationships we have with our families and individuals around us.

The purpose of this book is to answer your questions and address your concerns about drugs and behavior in our society today, particularly as they pertain to criminal behavior and the criminal justice system in America. In the chapters that follow, the complex issues of legal and illegal drugs in the United States will be viewed from a number of perspectives. As we will see, it is important to understand the biological, psychological, and sociological foundations of drug use. It is also important to understand the history of drug use in order to understand why drug-taking behavior has been so pervasive a phenomenon over the many centuries of human history and the reasons why drug-taking behavior remains so compelling for us in our society today. Finally, we need to understand the ways our society has responded to the problems of crime and violence associated with drug use. A particular focus will be on the criminal justice system in the United States that has been created to reduce the negative impact of drug-taking behavior.

Social Messages about Drug Use

Unfortunately, we live in a social environment that sends mixed messages with respect to drug use. The images of Joe Camel, the Marlboro Man, and the Virginia Slims Woman in print advertisements for cigarettes are increasingly distant memories, but at one time they were iconic anchors for marketing campaigns designed to convey the attractiveness of smoking to the public, and particularly to young people. They are gone now as a result of federal regulations established in 1998. For decades, warning labels on cigarette packs and public-service announcements have cautioned us about the serious health hazards of tobacco use. Yet cigarette smoking is still often portrayed in a positive light in movies and other forms of entertainment media.

Beer commercials during telecasts of football games and other athletic events are designed to be fun and engaging, to associate beer drinking with a desirable lifestyle filled with friendship, sex, and romance. But we are expected to "drink responsibly" or to "know when to say when." The social messages about alcohol drinking inherent in these commercials extend beyond

The pills and capsules shown here represent only a small portion of the thousands of medicinal drugs that are available in our society today. The potential for abuse and misuse of many of these legal drugs is significant; the impact of such drug-taking behavior continues to be a major social problem.

simply the selling of a product. It has been established that positive expectancies (such as gaining social acceptance) that these commercial engender predict the onset age of drinking and the transition to high-risk alcohol use over time.[4] Experiences with alcohol abuse and alcoholism abound, and we fully recognize the potential for injuries and death as a result of driving while intoxicated. At the same time, we hear reports that moderate alcohol drinking (unless contraindicated) is actually beneficial to our health.

Prominent political figures, including a former U.S. president (Bill Clinton) and a former U.S. vice-president (Al Gore), as well as a host of public officials on local and national levels, have admitted their experiences with marijuana earlier in their lives. Yet the position of the U.S. government on marijuana is that it is an illegal substance, officially classified since 1970 as a drug with a high potential for abuse and no accepted medical use—in the same category as heroin (see page 24).

Anti-drug campaigns in the media are created to discourage young people from being involved with drugs in general. At the same time, we observe a continuing stream of sports figures, entertainers, and other high-profile individuals engaging in drug-taking behavior. Even though their careers are frequently jeopardized and, in some instances, lives are lost as a result (see Chapter 2), powerful pro-drug-use messages continue to influence us. These messages come from the entertainment industry and traditional media sources, as well as from web sites on the Internet.[5]

As confusing and often contradictory as these messages are, they represent the present-day drug scene in America.

Looking at Drugs and Society

There are two basic ways in which we can look at the subject of drugs and society. First, we can examine the biological, psychological and sociological effects of consuming certain types of drugs. The focus is on the study of drugs that alter our feelings, our thoughts, our perceptions of the world, and our behavior. These substances are referred to as **psychoactive drugs** because they influence the functioning of the brain and hence our behavior and experience. Examples that often receive the greatest amount of attention are officially defined in the

psychoactive drugs: Drugs that affect feelings, thoughts, perceptions, or behavior.

United States as **illicit** (illegal) **drugs:** heroin, cocaine, and marijuana, along with club drugs such as methamphetamine (meth), Ecstasy, LSD, PCP, ketamine, and GHB. Other equally important psychoactive substances, however, are **licit** (legal) **drugs,** such as alcohol, nicotine, and caffeine. In the cases of alcohol and nicotine, legal access carries a minimum-age requirement.

Second, we can focus on the social circumstances that lead to drug-taking behavior. We will examine the possibility that drug use is, at least in part, a consequence of how we feel about ourselves in relation to our family, to our friends and acquaintances, to our life experiences, and to the community in which we live. An exploration into the reasons why some individuals engage in drug-taking behavior, while others do not, will be an important topic in Chapter 4.

Ultimately, understanding the interplay between drug-taking behavior and society (Figure 1.1) is essential when we consider the dangerous potential for drug use to turn into **drug dependence.** As many of us know all too well, a vicious circle can develop in which drug-taking behavior fosters more drug-taking behavior in a spiraling pattern that can be extremely difficult to break. Individuals showing signs of drug dependence display intense cravings for the drug and, in many cases, require increasingly greater quantities to get the same desired effect. They become preoccupied with their drug-taking behavior and eventually feel that their lives have gotten out of control.

Current research on drug dependence points to the need for us to examine the issue on a biological level, psychological level, and sociological level. On a biological level, the use of psychoactive drugs modifies the functioning of the brain, both during the time when the drug is present in the body and later, when the drug-taking behavior stops. Drug dependence, therefore, produces long-lasting brain changes. As one expert has put it, a "switch" in the brain seems to be thrown following prolonged drug use. It starts as a voluntary behavior, but

FIGURE 1.1

Understanding the interplay of drug-taking behavior and society through the biopsychosocial model of drug use.

once that switch is thrown, a pattern of drug dependence takes over. On a sociological level, drug dependence can be viewed as the result of a complex interaction between the individual and his or her environment. We cannot fully understand the problem of drug dependence without being aware of the social context in which drug-taking behavior occurs. As we will see in Chapter 16, the recognition that drug dependence can be defined in terms of biological and social components has important implications for designing effective treatment programs.[6]

Which drugs have the greatest potential for creating drug dependence? How can someone escape drug dependence once it is established? What factors increase or decrease the likelihood of drug-taking behavior in the first place? What is the relationship between drug-taking behavior and crime? What impact have social policies and our system of criminal justice had on drug-taking behavior? These are some of the important questions we will consider as we examine the impact of drugs and drug-taking behavior on our lives.

illicit drugs: Drugs whose manufacture, sale, or possession is illegal.

licit drugs: Drugs whose manufacture, sale, or possession is legal.

drug dependence: A condition in which an individual feels a compulsive need to continue taking a drug. In the process, the drug assumes an increasingly central role in the individual's life.

A Matter of Definition: What is a Drug?

Considering the ease with which we speak of drugs and drug use, it seems that it should be relatively easy to explain what we mean by the word **drug.** Unfortunately, there are significant problems in arriving at a clear definition.

The standard approach is to characterize a drug as *a chemical substance that, when taken into the body, alters the structure or functioning of the body in some way.* In doing so, we are accounting for examples such as medications used for the treatment of physical disorders and mental illnesses, as well as for alcohol, nicotine, and the typical street drugs. Unfortunately, this broad definition also could refer to ordinary food and water. Because it does not make much sense for nutrients to be considered drugs, we need to refine our definition by adding the phrase, *excluding those nutrients considered to be related to normal functioning.*

But we may still be on slippery ground. We can now effectively eliminate the cheese in your next pizza from being considered a drug, but what about some exotic ingredient in the sauce? Sugar is safely excluded, even though it has significant energizing and therefore behavioral effects on us, but what about the cayenne pepper that burns your tongue? Where do we draw the line between a drug and a nondrug? It is not an easy question to answer.

We can learn two major lessons from this seemingly simple task of defining a drug. First, there is probably no perfect definition that would distinguish drugs from nondrugs without leaving a number of cases that fall within some kind of gray area. The best we can do is to set up a definition, as we have, that handles most of the substances we are likely to encounter.

The second lesson is more subtle. We often draw the distinction between drugs and nondrugs not in terms of their physical characteristics but rather in terms of whether the substance in question has been *intended to be used primarily as a way of inducing a bodily or psychological change.*[7] By this reasoning, if the pizza maker intended to put that spice in the pizza to make it taste better, the spice would not be considered a drug; it would simply be another ingredient in the recipe. If the pizza maker intended the spice to intoxicate you or quicken your heart rate, then it might be considered a drug (see Drugs … in Focus).

The problem is that we are trying to reach a consensus on a definition that fits our intuitive sense of what constitutes a drug. We may find it difficult to define pornography, but (as has been said) we know it when we see it. So it may be with drugs. Whether we realize it or not, when we discuss the topic of drugs, we are operating within a context of social and cultural values, a group of shared feelings about what kind of behavior (that is, what kind of drug-taking behavior) is right and what kind is wrong. As we will see in Chapter 3, these values have manifested themselves over the years in social legislation and a criminal justice system for the purpose of regulating the use of specific drugs and specific forms of drug-taking behavior.

The judgments we make about drug-taking behavior even influence the terminology we use when referring to that behavior. When we speak of "drug misuse" and "drug abuse," for example, we are implying that something wrong is happening, that a drug is producing some harm to the physical health or psychological well-being of the drug user or to society in general.

But what criteria do we use to decide whether a drug is being misused or abused? We cannot judge on the basis of whether the drug is legal or illegal, since the legality of a psychoactive drug may depend more on historical and cultural circumstances than on its chemical properties. Tobacco, for example, has deeply rooted associations in American history, dating to the earliest colonial days. Although it is objectionable to many individuals and harmful to the health of the smoker and others, tobacco is nonetheless legally available to adults. Alcohol is another substance that is legal, within the bounds of the law, even though it can be harmful to individuals who become inebriated and potentially harmful to others who may be affected by the drinker's drunken behavior. The difficulty of using a criterion based on legality is further complicated by cultural differences in communities around the world.

Instrumental and Recreational Use of Drugs

Given the differences in attitudes toward specific drugs across cultures and societies, it is useful to look closely at the relationship between drugs and behavior in terms of the intent or motivation on the part of the user. Based upon on the intent of the individual, drug use can be categorized as either instrumental or recreational.[8]

> **drug:** A chemical substance that, when taken into the body, alters the structure or functioning of the body in some way, excluding those nutrients considered to be related to normal functioning.

Drugs... in Focus

Understanding Drug Names

The names we give to a particular drug can range from a tongue-twisting generic or chemical term, to a catchy commercial word selected for marketing purposes, to often-colorful street slang. It is important to keep straight the different circumstances in which a drug name might be used. We will focus on four major categories of drug names: brand names, generic names, natural-product names, and street names.

Brand names

Once a pharmaceutical manufacturer receives official governmental approval to hold a patent on a new drug, it has exclusive rights to sell the drug under a name referred to as its brand name. The brand name is a registered trademark of the manufacturer and cannot be used by any other manufacturer for the life of the patent. As examples, while the drugs are on patent, the stimulant drug Adderall, used in the treatment of attention-deficit disorder (ADD), is marketed under that brand name exclusively by Teva and Barr Pharmaceuticals, and the cholesterol-lowering drug Lipitor is marketed under that brand name exclusively by Pfizer, Inc. Illicit drugs do not have brand names.

Generic names

The chemical name of a drug is its generic name. Physicians will often write prescriptions for a particular drug using its generic name (if available), since it is less expensive than its brand name. Once a drug patent has expired, a drug formerly available under its brand name is now available under its generic name, sometimes alongside its brand name equivalent. For example, the nonprescription analgesic drug Tylenol is marketed by McNeil Consumer HealthCare in North America and its "sibling" Panadol is marketed by GlaxoKlineSmith in the United Kingdom and other countries outside North America under their original brand names. Since the patents have long since expired, they are also marketed as generic drugs under their generic names, acetaminophen and paracetamol (para-acetylaminophenol) respectively. Illicit drugs are referred to by federal and state authorities by their generic names, unless they are botanical products (see below). Examples are cocaine hydrochloride, heroin, dextroamphetamine, methamphetamine, lysergic diethylamide (LSD), phencyclidine.

Natural-product names

In some cases, drugs names refer to (1) plants from which the drugs originate (examples: marijuana, opium, coca, amanita mushrooms), (2) chemical entities isolated directly from plants (examples: morphine and codeine from opium poppies, cocaine hydrochloride from the coca plant, THC from marijuana, psilocybin from psilocybe mushrooms, mescaline from peyote cactus), or (3) chemical entities derived directly or indirectly from plants through a specific process (example: alcohol created as a result of the fermentation of grains, free-base cocaine and crack cocaine created from a chemical modification of cocaine hydrochloride).

Street names

Street names refer to slang terms generated by a subculture of drug users for a particular illicit drug or combination of illicit drugs. Any listing of street names is bound to be incomplete, as the slang is continually changing. Nonetheless, some street names have been around for a long time. Examples are "speed" for methamphetamine, "smack" for white heroin, "black tar" for Mexican heroin, "speedball" for a combination of heroin and cocaine, "grass" or "weed" for marijuana, and "coke" for cocaine.

By **instrumental use,** we mean that a person is taking a drug with a specific socially approved goal in mind. The user may want to stay awake longer, fall asleep more quickly, or recover from an illness. If you are a medical professional on call over a long period of time, taking a drug with the goal of staying alert is considered acceptable by most people as long as the drug does not interfere with one's duties. Recovering from an illness and achieving some reduction in pain are goals that are unquestioned. In these cases, drug-taking behavior occurs *as a means towards an end that has been defined by our society as legitimate.*

The legal status of the drug itself or whether we agree with the reason for the drug-taking behavior is not the issue here. The instrumental use of drugs can involve

instrumental use: Referring to the motivation of a drug user who takes a drug for a specific purpose other than getting "high."

prescription and nonprescription (over-the-counter) drugs that are licitly obtained and taken for a particular medical purpose. Examples include an antidepressant prescribed for depression, a cold remedy for a cold, an anticonvulsant drug to control epileptic seizures, or insulin to maintain the health of a person with diabetes. The instrumental use of drugs also can involve drugs that are illicitly obtained, such as an amphetamine that has been procured through illegal means to help a person stay awake and alert after hours without sleep.

In contrast, **recreational use** means that a person is taking the drug not as a means to a socially approved goal but for the purposes of experiencing the effect of the drug itself. The motivation is to experience a pleasurable feeling or achieve a positive state of mind. *Whatever happens as a consequence of recreational drug-taking behavior is viewed not as a means to an end but as an end unto itself.* Drinking alcohol and smoking tobacco are two examples of licit recreational drug-taking behavior. Involvement with street drugs, in that the goal is to alter one's mood or state of consciousness, falls into the category of illicit recreational drug-taking behavior (Figure 1.2).

Although this four-group classification scheme is helpful in understanding the complex relationship between drugs and behavior, there will be instances in which the category is less than clear. Drinking an alcoholic beverage, for example, is considered as recreational drug-taking behavior under most circumstances. If it is recommended by a physician for a specified therapeutic or preventative purpose (see Chapter 13), however, the drinking might be considered instrumental in nature. You can see that whether drug use is judged to be recreational or instrumental is determined in no small part by the attitudes of the society in which the behavior takes place. As mentioned earlier, these attitudes have a direct influence on the establishment of drug-regulation laws.

Misuse and Abuse of Drugs

How do the misuse and abuse of drugs fit into this scheme? **Drug misuse** typically applies to cases in which a prescription or over-the-counter (OTC) drug is used inappropriately. Many instances of drug misuse involve instrumental goals. For example, drug doses may be increased beyond the level of the prescription in the mistaken idea that if a little is good, more is even better. Or doses may be decreased from the level of the prescription to make the drug supply last longer. Drugs may be continued longer than they were intended to be used; they may be combined with some other drug; or a

recreational use: Referring to the motivation of a drug user who takes a drug only to get "high" or achieve some pleasurable effect.

drug misuse: Drug-taking behavior in which a prescription or nonprescription drug is used inappropriately.

	Licit	Illicit
	Legal Status	
Instrumental use	Taking Valium with a prescription to relieve anxiety	Taking amphetamines without a prescription to stay awake the night before a test
	Taking No Doz to stay awake on a long trip	Taking morphine without a prescription to relieve pain
Recreational use	Having an alcoholic drink to relax before dinner	Smoking marijuana to get high
	Smoking a cigarette or a cigar for enjoyment	Taking LSD for the hallucinogenic effects

Goal

FIGURE 1.2

Four categories of drug-taking behavior, derived from combinations of the user's goal and the drug's legal status.

Source: Expanded from Goode, Erich (2005). *Drugs in American Society* (6th ed.). New York: McGraw-Hill, p. 16.

prescription drug may (in violation of instructions) be shared by family members or given to a friend even though the medical conditions may differ among them.

Drug misuse can be dangerous and potentially lethal, particularly when alcohol is combined with drugs that depress the nervous system. Drugs that have this particular feature include antihistamines, antianxiety drugs, and sleeping medications. Even when alcohol is not involved, however, drug combinations can still represent serious health risks, particularly for the elderly, who often take a large number of separate medications.

drug abuse: Drug-taking behavior resulting in some form of physical, mental, or social impairment.

This population is especially vulnerable to the hazards of drug misuse.

In contrast, **drug abuse** is typically applied to cases in which a licit or illicit drug is used in ways that produce some form of physical, mental, or social impairment. The primary motivation for individuals involved in drug abuse is recreational. *We should remember that drugs with abuse potential include not only the common street drugs but also legally available psychoactive substances such as caffeine and nicotine (stimulants), alcohol and inhaled solvents (depressants), as well as a number of prescription or OTC drugs designated for medical purposes but used by some individuals exclusively on a recreational basis.* In Chapter 7, we will examine recent concerns about the

PORTRAIT

From Oxy to Heroin: The Life and Death of Erik

Erik lived in a suburban Long Island, New York community, and heroin killed him in 2008 at the age of 19. His mother, Linda D., never imagined what she was up against. "You worry," she has said, "about them smoking pot. You worry about them driving recklessly. You worry about them not using their seat belt. You worry about that phone call in the middle of the night. You don't worry about heroin. Because it didn't exist in my mindset."

In the last few years, the reality of heroin in the suburbs and small towns of America, previously considered to be immune from its deadly reach, has hit home with a sudden and unexpected vengeance. As a director of a local drug-counseling center has expressed it: "They're starting younger, they're starting with more substances, they have better access, everything is cheaper, and they have more money." You would call it a perfect storm. Heroin arrests have doubled; rehabilitation-facility admissions of those 21 and under for prescription pain reliever dependence have tripled or quadrupled in many cases.

In the case of Erik, it began after an emergency appendectomy with a prescription for Vicodin. Erik gradually entered into a shadowy world of

drug-taking behavior. Finding new supplies of Vicodin, then shifting to OxyContin, was easy. "It sounded grimy and sleazy," a teenager would say in reference to her own dependence on prescription pain relievers, "but at the time it was just what I did. Everyone knows someone who can get them for you."

At some point in early 2008, according to Linda, "The oxys dried up." Erik turned from pills to heroin. "It started at a party," she has said, "Someone said to him, 'Oh, try this.'" By May, Linda and her husband realized Erik was using heroin. In the weeks that followed, they tried to convince him to get help. The family's insurance covered Erik's first trip to a rehabilitation facility in upstate New York, but when Erik left after three days, they told the family that he had used up their insurance company's "once in a lifetime" rehabilitation coverage. They tried to convince public hospitals to admit Erik, but he was denied. In the meantime, Erik's parents were finding injection needles around the house and discarded rubber tubing. They desperately tried to cobble together funds to pay for rehabilitation, but they didn't succeed in time. Erik died in July.

If Erik had rejected his parents' efforts to get him help, they would have faced considerable legal obstacles. In New York State, no one, even a minor, is required to get treatment for substance abuse. Parents can petition a county probation department to have a drug-abusing child designated as a Person in Need of Supervision (PINS), but a court order has to be issued by a judge for a PINS child to be admitted for treatment. Even then, the child may leave at any time regardless of medical advice to stay.

In the meantime, medical examiner statistics indicate that there have been 173 heroin-related deaths from 2006 to 2009 in a county with a population of approximately one million. One out of ten deaths have involved an individual under the age of 21, with the youngest being 14.

Sources: Alterr, Stacey (2009, November 12). Push for heroin help. *Newsday*, p. A5. Lefrowitz, Melanie (2009, June 14). Heartbreak of addiction hits home. *Newsday*, pp. A4-A6. Archibold, Randal C. (2009, May 31). In heartland death, traces of heroin's spread. *New York Times*, pp. 1,24.

abuse of prescription pain-relievers that contain synthetic opiates or opiate derivatives and are marketed under such brand names as Vicodin, OxyContin, Percocet, Demerol, and Darvon. In these particular cases, the distinction between drug misuse and drug abuse is particularly blurry. In the chapters that follow, when there is no intent to make a value judgment about the motivation or consequences of a particular type of drug-taking behavior, we will refer to the behavior simply as *drug use*.

Inevitably, decisions over whether a particular form of drug-taking behavior is categorized as drug use, abuse, or misuse take into account the potentially harmful physiological effects of the drug in question. It is important, therefore, to begin with an examination of the ways in which drugs have an effect on the body. What is the impact of the manner in which a drug is administered? What is the impact of timing factors on the overall effect of a drug? How do we measure its potential harmfulness? These are some of the questions we will now address.

How Drugs Enter the Body

Some of you might have heard of the classic public-service announcement, which aired frequently on television in the late 1980s:

> *This is your brain (view of egg held in hand).*
> *This is drugs (view of sizzling frying pan).*
> *This is your brain on drugs (view of egg frying in pan).*
> *Any questions?*[9]

Giving the viewer considerable "food for thought," its impact was immediate and unmistakable: Don't do drugs because they fry your brain. The creators of this message were speaking metaphorically, of course. In effect, they were saying that there are certain classes of drugs that have a devastating impact on the human brain. Therefore, stay away from them.

Clearly, psychoactive drugs affect our behavior and experience through their effects on the functioning of the brain. Therefore, our knowledge about drugs and their effects is closely connected with the progress we have made in our understanding of the ways drugs work in the brain. A reasonable place to start is to answer the question: How do drugs get into the body in the first place?

There are four principal routes through which drugs can be delivered into the body: *oral administration, injection, inhalation,* and *absorption through the skin or membranes*. In all four delivery methods, the goal is for the drug to be absorbed into the bloodstream. In the case of psychoactive drugs, a drug effect depends not only on reaching the bloodstream but also on reaching the brain.

Oral Administration

Ingesting a drug by mouth (later digesting it and absorbing it into the bloodstream through the gastrointestinal tract) is the oldest and easiest way of taking a drug. On the one hand, oral administration and reliance upon the digestive process for delivering a drug into the bloodstream provide a degree of safety. Many naturally growing poisons taste so vile that we normally spit them out before swallowing; others will cause us to be nauseated, causing the drug to be expelled through vomiting.

In the case of hazardous substances that are not spontaneously rejected, we can benefit from a relatively long absorption time for orally administered drugs. Most of the absorption process is accomplished between five and thirty minutes after ingestion, but absorption may not be complete for as long as six to eight hours. Therefore, there is at least a little time after accidental overdoses or suicide attempts to induce vomiting or pump the stomach.

On the other hand, the gastrointestinal tract contains a number of natural barriers that may prevent certain drugs that we *want* absorbed into the bloodstream from doing so. One determining factor is the degree of alkalinity or acidity in the drug, measured by its pH value. The interior of the stomach is highly acidic, and the fate of a particular drug depends upon how it reacts with that environment. Weakly acidic drugs such as aspirin are absorbed better in the stomach than highly alkaline

Orally consumed drugs are absorbed into the brain relatively slowly, though for a liquid beverage containing alcohol, the opposite applies: It is easily absorbed.

drugs such as morphine, heroin, or cocaine. Insulin is destroyed by stomach acid, so it cannot be administered orally, whereas a neutral substance such as alcohol is readily absorbed at all points in the gastrointestinal tract.

If it survives the stomach, the drug needs to proceed from the small intestine into the bloodstream. The membrane separating the intestinal wall from blood capillaries is made up of two layers of fat molecules, making it necessary for substances to be *lipid-soluble,* or soluble in fats, to pass through. Even after successful absorption into blood capillaries, however, substances still must pass through the liver for another "screening" before being released into the general circulation. There are enzymes in the liver that destroy a drug by metabolizing (breaking down) its molecular structure prior to its excretion from the body. There is a further barrier separating the bloodstream (circulatory system) from brain tissue, called the *blood-brain barrier,* which determines a drug's psychoactive effects.

As a result of all these natural barriers, orally administered drugs must be ingested at deliberately elevated dose levels to allow for the fact that some proportion of the drug will not make it through to the bloodstream. We can try to compensate for the loss of the drug during digestion, but even then we may be only making a good guess. The state of the gastrointestinal tract changes constantly over time, making it more or less likely that a drug will reach the circulatory system. The presence or absence of undigested food and whether the undigested food interacts with the chemical nature of the drug are examples of factors that make it difficult to make exact predictions about the strength of the drug when it finally enters the bloodstream.

Injection

A solution to the problems of oral administration is to bypass the digestive process entirely and deliver the drug more directly into the bloodstream. One option is to inject the drug through a hypodermic syringe and needle.

The fastest means of injection is an **intravenous** (i.v.) injection, since the drug is delivered into a vein without any intermediary tissue. An intravenous injection of heroin in the forearm, for example, arrives at the brain in less than fifteen seconds. The effects of abused drugs delivered in this way, often called *mainlining,* are not only rapid but extremely intense.

---

intravenous (i.v.): Into a vein.
intramuscular (i.m.): Into a muscle.
subcutaneous (s.c. or sub-Q): Underneath the skin.

In a medical setting, intravenous injections provide an extreme amount of control over dosage and the opportunity to administer multiple drugs at the same time. The principal disadvantage, however, is that the effects of intravenous administration drugs are irreversible. In the event of a mistake or unexpected reaction, there is no turning back unless some other drug is available that can counteract the first one. In addition, repeated injections through a particular vein may cause the vein to collapse or develop a blood clot.

With **intramuscular** (i.m.) injections, the drug is delivered into a large muscle (usually in the upper arm, thigh, or buttock) and is absorbed into the bloodstream through the capillaries serving the muscle. Intramuscular injections have slower absorption times than intravenous injections, but they can be administered more rapidly in emergency situations. Our exposure to intramuscular injections comes early in our lives when we receive the standard schedule of inoculations against diseases such as measles, diphtheria, and typhoid fever. Tetanus and flu shots are also administered in this way.

A third injection technique is the **subcutaneous** (s.c. or sub-Q) delivery, in which a needle is inserted into the tissue just underneath the skin. Because the skin has a less abundant blood supply relative to a muscle, a subcutaneous injection has the slowest absorption time of all the injection techniques. It is best suited for situations in which it is desirable to have a precise control over the dosage and a steady absorption into the bloodstream. The skin, however, may be easily irritated by this procedure. As a result, only relatively small amounts of a drug can be injected under the skin compared with the quantity that can be injected into a muscle or vein. When involved in drug abuse, subcutaneous injections are often referred to as *skin-popping.*

All injections require a needle to pierce the skin, so there is an inherent risk of bacterial or viral infection if the needle is not sterile. The practice of injecting heroin or cocaine with shared needles, for example, promotes the spread of infectious hepatitis and HIV. If administered orally, drugs do not have to be any more sterile than the foods we eat or the water we drink.

Inhalation

Next to ingesting a drug by mouth, the simplest way of receiving its effects is to inhale it in some form of gaseous or vaporous state. The alveoli within the lungs can be imagined as a huge surface area with blood vessels lying immediately behind it. Our bodies are so dependent upon the oxygen in the air we breathe that we have evolved an extremely efficient system for getting oxygen to

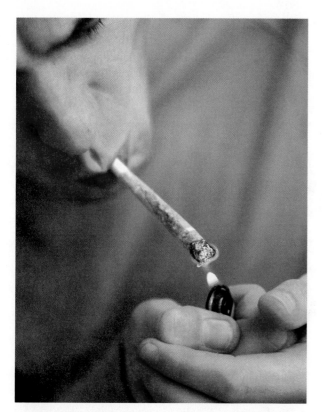

Drugs consumed by inhalation, such as marijuana (shown here) and tobacco, are absorbed extremely quickly, aided by a very efficient delivery system from lungs to brain.

its destinations. As a consequence of this highly developed system, the psychoactive effect of an inhaled drug is even faster than a drug delivered through intravenous injection. Traveling from the lungs to the brain takes only five to eight seconds.

One way of delivering a drug through inhalation is to burn it and breathe in the smoke-borne particles in the air. Drugs administered through smoking include nicotine from cigarettes, opium, tetrahydrocannabinol (THC) from marijuana, free-base cocaine, crack cocaine, and crystallized forms of methamphetamine. Drugs such as paint thinners, gasoline, and glues also can be inhaled because they evaporate easily and the vapors travel freely through the air. In medical settings, drugs that produce general anesthesia are administered through inhalation, since the concentration of the drug can be precisely controlled.

The principal disadvantage of inhaling smoked drugs, as you probably expect, arises from the long-term hazards of breathing particles in the air that contain not only the active drug but also tars and other substances produced by the burning process. Emphysema, asthma, and lung cancer can result from smoking in general (see Chapter 15). There is also the possibility in any form of drug inhalation that the linings leading from the throat to the lungs will be severely irritated over time.

Absorption through the Skin or Membranes

Drug users over the ages have been quite creative in finding other routes through which drugs can be administered. One way is to sniff or snort a drug in dust or powder form into the nose. Once inside the nose, it adheres to thin mucous membranes and dissolves through the membranes into the bloodstream. This technique, referred to as an **intranasal** administration, is commonly used in taking snuff tobacco or cocaine. Prescription medications are becoming increasingly available in nasal-spray formulations, avoiding the need for needle injections or difficult-to-swallow pills.

Snuff tobacco, chewing tobacco, and cocaine-containing coca leaves also can be chewed without swallowing over a period of time or simply placed in the inner surface of the cheek and slowly absorbed through the membranes of the mouth. Nicotine chewing gums, available for those individuals who wish to quit tobacco smoking, work in a similar way. Nitroglycerin tablets for heart disease patients are typically administered **sublingually**, with the drug placed underneath the tongue and absorbed into the bloodstream.

At the opposite end of the body, medicines can be placed as a suppository into the rectum, where the suppository gradually melts, and the medicine is absorbed through thin rectal membranes. This method is less reliable than an oral administration, but it may be necessary if the individual is vomiting or unconscious.

Another absorption technique involves a **transdermal patch,** which allows a drug to slowly diffuse through the skin. Transdermal patches have been used for long-term administration of nitroglycerin, estrogen, motion-sickness medication, and more recently, nicotine. Newly developed procedures to enhance the process of skin penetration include the promising technique of administering low-frequency ultrasound, which allows large molecules such as insulin to pass through the skin. Insulin administration is an especially interesting application because, until now, the only effective way of getting it into the bloodstream has been through needle injection.

intranasal: Applied to the mucous membranes of the nose.

sublingual: Applied under the tongue.

transdermal patch: A device attached to the skin that slowly delivers the drug through skin absorption.

Alternative methods under development include small silicon chip patches containing a grid of microscopic needles that painlessly pierce the skin and allow the passage of large molecules into the bloodstream. Other future techniques may involve the application of ultrasound waves to increase skin permeability or the combining of medication with special compounds that help the medication slip through skin pores.[10]

Drugs… in Focus summarizes the various ways drugs can be administered into the body.

Drugs… in Focus

Ways to Take Drugs: Routes of Administration

Oral Administration (by Mouth)

- Method: By swallowing or consuming in eating or drinking
- Advantages: Slow absorption time; possibility of rejecting poisons and overdoses
- Disadvantages: Slow absorption time; no immediate effect
- Examples: Medications in pill form, marijuana (baked in food), amphetamine and methamphetamine, barbiturates, LSD (swallowed or licked off paper), PCP, opium, methadone, codeine, caffeine, alcohol

Injection (by Hypodermic Syringe)

Intravenous Injection

- Method: By needle positioned into a vein
- Advantages: Very fast absorption time; immediate effects
- Disadvantages: Cannot be undone; risks of allergic reactions
- Examples: PCP, methamphetamine, heroin, methadone, morphine

Intramuscular Injection

- Method: By needle positioned into a large muscle
- Advantages: Quicker to administer than an intravenous injection
- Disadvantages: Somewhat slower absorption time than an intravenous injection; risk of piercing a vein by accident
- Examples: Vaccine inoculations

Subcutaneous Injection

- Method: By needle positioned underneath the skin
- Advantages: Easiest administration of all injection techniques

- Disadvantages: Slower absorption time than an intramuscular injection; risk of skin irritation and deterioration
- Examples: Heroin and other narcotics

Inhalation (by Breathing)

Smoking

- Method: By burning drug and breathing smoke-borne particles into the lungs
- Advantages: Extremely fast absorption time
- Disadvantages: Effect limited to time during which drug is being inhaled; risk of emphysema, asthma, and lung cancer from inhaling tars and hydrocarbons in the smoke; lung and throat irritation over chronic use
- Examples: Nicotine (from tobacco), marijuana, hashish, methamphetamine, ice, free-base cocaine, crack cocaine, PCP, heroin, and opium

Vaporous Inhalation

- Method: By breathing in vapors from drug
- Advantages: Extremely fast absorption time
- Disadvantages: Effect limited to time during which drug is being inhaled; lung and throat irritation over chronic use
- Examples: Surgical and dental anesthetics, paint thinners, gasoline, cleaning fluid

Absorption (through Skin or Membranes)

- Method: By positioning drug against skin, inserting it against rectal membrane, snorting it against mucous membranes of the nose, or placing it under the tongue or against the cheek so it diffuses across bloodstream
- Advantages: Quick absorption time
- Disadvantages: Irritation of skin or membranes
- Examples: Cocaine, amphetamine, methamphetamine, nicotine, snuff tobacco, coca leaves

How Drugs Exit the Body

Having reviewed how a drug is absorbed into the bloodstream and, in the case of a psychoactive drug, into the brain, we now will consider the ways in which the body eliminates it. The most common means of elimination is through excretion in the urine after a series of actions in the liver and kidneys. Additionally, elimination occurs through excretion in exhaled breath, feces, sweat, saliva, or (in the case of nursing mothers) breast milk.

The sequence of metabolic (chemical breakdown) events leading to urinary excretion begins with a process called **biotransformation,** chiefly through the action of specific enzymes in the liver. The end-products of biotransformation, referred to as **metabolites,** are structurally modified forms of the original drug. Generally speaking, if these metabolites are water-soluble, they are passed along to the kidneys and eventually excreted in the urine. If they are less water-soluble, then they are reabsorbed into the intestines and excreted through defecation. On rare occasions, a drug may pass through the liver without any biotransformation at all and be excreted intact. The hallucinogenic drug *Amanita muscaria* is an example of this kind of drug (see Chapter 9).

A number of factors influence the process of biotransformation and urinary excretion and, in turn, the rate of elimination from the body. For most drugs, biotransformation rates will increase as a function of the drug's concentration in the bloodstream. In effect, the larger the quantity of a drug, the faster the body tries to get rid of it. An exception, however, is alcohol, for which the rate of biotransformation is constant no matter how much alcohol has been ingested (see Chapter 13).

The activity of enzymes required for biotransformation may be increased or decreased by the presence of other drugs in the body. As a result, the physiological effect of one drug may interact with the effect of another, creating a potentially dangerous combination. An individual's age also can be a factor. Because enzyme activity in the liver decreases after the age of forty, older people eliminate drugs at a slower pace than do younger people. We will look at the consequences of drug interactions and individual differences in the next section of this chapter.

Finally, it is important to point out that drugs are gradually eliminated from the body at different rates simply on the basis of their chemical properties. In general, if a drug is fat-soluble, the rate will be slower than if a drug is water-soluble. On average, we can look at the rate of elimination of a particular drug through an index called its **elimination half-life,** the amount of time it takes for the drug in the bloodstream to decline to 50 percent of its original equilibrium level. Many drugs such as cocaine and nicotine have half-lives of only a few hours; marijuana and some prescription medications are examples of drugs with much longer half-lives.[11] Understanding the variation in the elimination rates of drugs and their metabolites is extremely important in the development of drug-testing procedures to detect drug-taking behavior, a topic to be examined in Chapter 12.

Factors Determining the Behavioral Impact of Drugs

The type of delivery route into the bloodstream, as has been discussed, places specific constraints upon the effect a drug may produce. Some drug effects are optimized, for example, by an oral administration, whereas others require more direct access to the bloodstream.

Other factors must be considered as well. If a drug is administered repeatedly, the timing of the administrations plays an important role in determining the final result. If two drugs are administered close together in time, we also must consider how these drugs might interact with each other in terms of their acute effects. Repeated administrations of a drug may produce a diminished physiological or psychological effect.

Finally, it is possible that two identical drugs taken by two individuals might have different effects by virtue of the characteristics of the drug user at the time of administration.

Timing

All drugs, no matter how they are delivered, share some common features when we consider their effects over time. There is initially an interval (the **latency period**) during which the concentration of the drug is increasing

---

biotransformation: The process of changing the molecular structure of a drug into forms that make it easier to be excreted from the body.

metabolite (me-TAB-oh-lite): A by-product resulting from the biotransformation process.

elimination half-life: The length of time it takes for a drug to be reduced to 50 percent of its equilibrium level in the bloodstream.

latency period: An interval of time during which the blood levels of a drug are not yet sufficient for a drug effect to be observed.

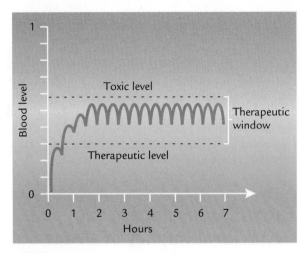

FIGURE 1.3

The therapeutic window. Time-release drugs are formulated to administer the drug in small amounts over time to stay between the therapeutic level and the toxic level.

in the blood but is not yet high enough for a drug effect to be detected. How long this latency period will last is related generally to the absorption time of the drug. As the concentration of the drug continues to rise, the effect will become stronger. A stage will be reached eventually when the effect attains a maximum strength, even though the concentration in the blood continues to rise. This point is unfortunately the point at which the drug may produce undesirable side effects. One solution to this problem is to administer the drug in a time-release form. In this approach, a large dose is given initially to enable the drug effect to be felt; then smaller doses are programmed to be released at specific intervals afterward to postpone- up to twelve hours or so- the decline in the drug's concentration in the blood. The intention is to keep the concentration of the drug in the blood within a "therapeutic window," high enough for the drug to be effective while low enough to avoid any toxic effects. When drugs are administered repeatedly, there is a risk that the second dose will boost the concentration of the drug in the blood too high before the effect of the first dose has a chance to decline (Figure 1.3).

synergism (SIN-er-jih-zum): The property of a drug interaction in which the combination effect of two drugs exceeds the effect of either drug administered alone.

potentiation: The property of a synergistic drug interaction in which one drug combined with another drug produces an enhanced effect when one of the drugs alone would have had no effect.

Drug Interactions

Two basic types of interactions may occur when two drugs are mixed together. In the first type, two drugs in combination may produce an acute effect that is greater than the effect of either drug administered separately. In some cases, the combination effect is purely *additive*. For example, if the effect of one drug alone is equivalent to a 4 and the effect of another drug is a 6, then the combined additive effect is equivalent to a value of 10. In other cases, however, the acute combination effect is *hyperadditive*, with the combined effect exceeding the sum of the individual drugs administered alone, as in the two drugs in the first example combining to a value of 13 or more. Any hyperadditive effect produced by a combination of two or more drugs is referred to as **synergism.** In some synergistic combinations, one drug may even double or triple the effect of another. It is also possible that one drug might have no effect at all unless it is taken simultaneously with another. This special form of synergism is called **potentiation**; it is as though a drug with no effect at all by itself, when combined with a drug having an effect of 6, produces a result equivalent to a 10. The danger of such interactions is that the combined effect of the drugs is so powerful as to become toxic. In extreme cases, the toxicity can be lethal.

In the second type of interaction, two drugs can be *antagonistic* if the acute effect of one drug is diminished to some degree when administered with another, a situation comparable to a drug with the effect of 6 and a drug with the effect of 4 combining to produce an effect of 3. Later chapters discuss drugs that are totally antagonistic to each other, in that the second exactly cancels out, or neutralizes, the effect of the first. Help Line provides some examples of drug–drug combinations and food–drug combinations that can present significant problems.

Tolerance Effects

Legend has it that in the first century B.C., King Mithridates VI of Pontus, a region of modern-day Turkey near the Black Sea, grew despondent following a series of military defeats by the Romans and decided to commit suicide by poison. The problem was that no amount of poison was sufficient, and the grim task had to be completed by the sword. It turned out that Mithridates, having lived in fear of being poisoned by his rivals, had taken gradually increasing amounts of poison over the course of his life to build up a defense or immunity against this possibility. By the time he wanted to end his

Help Line

The Possibility of a Drug–Drug or Food–Drug Combination Effect

It would be impossible to list every known drug–drug interaction or food–drug interaction. Nonetheless, here are some examples. Any adverse reaction to a combination of drugs or a combination of a drug with something eaten should be reported to your physician immediately. An awareness of adverse interactions is particularly important for elderly patients, who tend to be treated with multiple medications. The best advice is to ask your physician whether alcohol, specific foods, or other medications might either increase or decrease the effect of the medication that is being prescribed.

Hyperadditive Effects

Alcohol with barbiturate-related sleep medications, cardiovascular medications, insulin, anti-inflammatory medications, antihistamines, painkillers, antianxiety medications

Septra, Bactrim, or related types of antibiotics with Coumadin (an anticoagulant)

Tagamet (a heartburn and ulcer treatment medication) with Coumadin

Aspirin, Aleve, Advil, Tylenol, or related painkillers with Coumadin

Plendil (a blood pressure medication) and Procardia (an angina treatment), as well as Zocor, Lipitor, and Mevacor (all cholesterol-lowering medications), with grapefruit juice

Lanoxin (a medication for heart problems) with licorice

Lanoxin with bran, oatmeal, or other high-fiber foods

Antagonistic Effects

Morphine/heroin with naloxone or naltrexone

Norpramin or related antidepressants with bran, oatmeal, or other high-fiber foods

Soy products and certain vitamin K–rich vegetables such as broccoli, cabbage, and asparagus with Coumadin

Possible Toxic Reactions

Internal bleeding by a combination of Parnate and Anafranil (two types of antidepressants)

Elevated body temperature by a combination of Nardil (an antidepressant) with Demerol (a painkiller)

Excessive blood pressure or stroke by a combination of Parnate, Nardil, or other monoamine oxidase inhibitors (MAOIs) used to treat depression with cheddar cheese, pickled herring, or other foods high in tyramine

Agitation or elevated body temperature by a combination of Paxil, Prozac, Zoloft, or related antidepressants with Parnate, Nardil, or other monoamine oxidase inhibitors (MAOIs) used to treat depression

Irregular heartbeat, cardiac arrest, and sudden death by a combination of Hismanal or Seldane (two antihistamines) with Nizoral (an antifungal drug)

Note: The hyperadditive effects of grapefruit on certain medications can be dangerous or useful under certain circumstances. If grapefruit enhances the effect of the cholesterol-reducing medication Lipitor, for example, it is possible that drinking grapefruit juice might allow the patient to take less Lipitor (reducing costs and possible side effects) and still receive the same level of benefit. Combinations of this kind, however, should be administered only under the close supervision of one's physician.

Where to go for assistance:

www.drugs.com/drug_interactions.php

Check out any combination of prescription or OTC drugs for potential adverse interactions.

Sources: Graedon, Joe, and Graedon, Teresa (2000, October 16). Say "aaah": The people's pharmacy; drugs and foods can interact adversely. *Los Angeles Times*, p. 2. Graedon, Joe, and Graedon, Teresa (1995). *The people's guide to deadly interactions.* New York: St. Martin's Press. Sørensen, Janina M. (2002). Herb–drug, food–drug, nutrient–drug, and drug–drug interactions: Mechanisms involved and their medical implications. *Journal of Alternative and Complementary Medicine, 8*, 293–308.

life by his own hand, he could tolerate such large doses that poisoning no longer presented any threat to his life. This royal case is the first recorded example of drug tolerance. In fact, the phenomenon originally was called *mithridatism,* and several celebrated poisoners of history, including the notorious Lucretia Borgia in the early sixteenth century, were later to use the same defensive strategy.[12]

The concept of **tolerance** refers to the capacity of a drug dose to have a gradually diminished effect on the user as the drug is taken repeatedly. Another way of

tolerance: The capacity of a drug to produce a gradually diminished physiological or psychological effect upon repeated administrations of the drug at the same dose level.

Having overdosed on pure heroin, the driver in the car had already died, and the passenger would die soon afterward. The police found a needle injected through the driver's pants leg. The two men had just cashed their paychecks and bought the drugs.

viewing tolerance is to say that, over repeated administrations, a drug dose needs to be increased to maintain an equivalent effect. A common illustration is the effect of caffeine in coffee. When you are first introduced to caffeine, the stimulant effect is usually quite pronounced; you might feel noticeably "wired" after a 5-ounce cup of coffee, containing approximately 100 mg of caffeine. After several days or perhaps a few weeks of coffee drinking, the effect is greatly diminished; you may need to be on the second or third cup by that time, consuming 200 to 300 mg of caffeine, to duplicate the earlier reaction. Some individuals who drink coffee

behavioral tolerance: The process of drug tolerance that is linked to drug-taking behavior occurring consistently in the same surroundings or under the same circumstances. Also known as *conditioned tolerance.*

regularly have developed such high levels of tolerance to caffeine that they are able to sleep comfortably even after several cups of coffee, whereas individuals with more infrequent ingestions of caffeine end up awake through the night after a single cup.

Tolerance effects, in general, illustrate the need for us to look at the *interaction* between the actual amount of the drug taken and other factors involved in the drug-taking behavior. For example, as already noted, the number of previous times the drug has been used is crucial; repetition is what tolerance is all about. Another important factor, however, is the setting within which the drug-taking behavior occurs. There is strong evidence that tolerance is maximized when the drug-taking behavior occurs consistently in the same surroundings or under the same set of circumstances.[13] We speak of this form of tolerance as **behavioral tolerance**.

To have a clear idea of behavioral tolerance, we first have to understand the processes of Pavlovian conditioning, upon which behavioral tolerance is based. Suppose that you consistently heard a bell ring every time you had a headache. Previously, bells had never had any negative effect on you. The association between the ringing bell and the pain of the headache, however, would develop to such an extent that the mere ringing of a bell alone would now give you a headache, perhaps less painful than the ones you had originally but a headache nonetheless; this effect is Pavlovian conditioning at work.

Pioneering studies by the psychologist Shepard Siegel showed a similar phenomenon occurring with drug-taking behavior. In one experiment, one group of rats was injected with doses of morphine in a particular room over a series of days and later tested for tolerance to that dose in the same room. Predictably, they displayed a lessened analgesic effect as a sign of morphine tolerance. A second group was tested in a room other than the one in which the injections had been given. No tolerance developed at all. They reacted as if they had never been given morphine before, even though they had received the same number of repeated injections as the first group.

In a more extreme experiment, Siegel tested two groups of rats that were administered a series of heroin injections with increasingly higher dosages. Eventually, both groups were surviving a dosage level that would have been lethal to rats experiencing the drug for the first time. The difference in the groups related to the environment in which these injections were given. One group received these injections in the colony room where they lived. When the second group was receiving the injections, they were in a room that looked quite different and were hearing 60-decibel "white noise." Siegel then administered a single large dose of heroin, normally a level that should have killed them all. Instead, rats administered this extremely high dosage in the *same room* in which they had received the earlier heroin injection series showed only a 32 percent mortality rate. When the room was different, the mortality rate doubled (64 percent). In both groups, more rats survived than if they had never received heroin in the first place, but the survival rate was influenced by the environment in which the heroin was originally administered.

Siegel explained the results of his studies by assuming that environmental cues in the room where the initial injections were given elicited some form of effect *opposite* to the effect of the drug. In the case of heroin, these compensatory effects would partially counteract the analgesic effect of the drug and protect the animal against dying from potentially high dosage levels.

The phenomenon of behavioral tolerance, also referred to as *conditioned tolerance* because it is based on the principles of Pavlovian conditioning, explains why a heroin addict may easily suffer the adverse consequences of an overdose when the drug has been taken in a different environment from the one more frequently encountered or in a manner different from his or her ordinary routine.[14] The range of tolerated doses of heroin can be enormous; amounts in the 200- to 500-mg range may be lethal for a first-time heroin user, whereas amounts as high as 1800 mg may not even be sufficient to make a long-term heroin user sick.[15] You can imagine

how dangerous it would be if the conditioned compensatory responses a heroin addict had built up over time were suddenly absent.

Behavioral tolerance also helps to explain why a formerly drug-dependent individual is strongly advised to avoid the surroundings associated with his or her past drug-taking behavior. If these surroundings provoked a physiological effect opposite to the effect of the drug through their association with prior drug-taking behavior, then a return to this environment might create internal changes that only drugs could reverse. In effect, environmentally induced withdrawal symptoms would increase the chances of a relapse. The fact that

Quick Concept Check 1.2

Understanding Behavioral Tolerance through Conditioning

Check your understanding of behavioral tolerance as proposed by Shepard Siegel by answering the following questions.

1. Suppose that you have a rat that has been placed in an environment where it had been repeatedly injected with morphine. You now inject that rat with a saline solution (a substance that has no physiological effect). Assuming that morphine will make a person less sensitive to pain, how will this animal react to the saline injection? Will the rat be less sensitive to pain, more sensitive to pain, or will there be no effect? Explain your answer.

2. If King Mithridates VI had changed palaces from time to time during his reign, what would have been the effect on his eventual level of drug tolerance to poison when he chose to attempt suicide?

Answers: 1. The rat will now be more sensitive to pain. The exposure to an environment associated with morphine injections will have induced a conditioned compensatory effect: a heightened sensitivity to pain. The saline injection produces no physiological effect of its own; however, because it is given in that same environment where the morphine was administered, the conditioned effect will remain, and the rat's reaction will be hyperalgesia. (The experiment has been performed, by the way, and this predicted outcome does occur.)
2. Most likely, the king would have died. He would not have been able to develop a sufficient level of drug tolerance to protect himself from succeeding in his suicide attempt.

conditioning effects have been demonstrated not only with respect to heroin but with alcohol, cocaine, nicotine, and other dependence-producing drugs as well makes it imperative that the phenomenon of behavioral tolerance be considered during the course of drug abuse treatment and rehabilitation.[16]

Cross-Tolerance

If you were taking a barbiturate (a sedation-producing drug that acts to depress bodily functioning) for an extended length of time and you developed a tolerance for its effect, you also might have developed a tolerance for another depressant drug even though you have never taken the second one. In other words, it is possible that a tolerance effect for one drug might automatically induce a tolerance for another. This phenomenon, referred to as **cross-tolerance,** is commonly observed in the physiological and psychological effects of alcohol, barbiturates, and other depressants. As a result of cross-tolerance, an alcoholic will have already developed a tolerance for a barbiturate, or a barbiturate abuser will need a greater amount of an anesthetic when undergoing surgery.

Individual Differences

Some variations in drug effects may be related to an interaction between the drug itself and specific characteristics of the person taking the drug. One characteristic is an individual's weight. In general, a heavier person will require a greater amount of a drug than a lighter person to receive an equivalent drug effect, all other things being equal. It is for this reason that drug dosages are expressed as a ratio of drug amount to body weight. This ratio is expressed in metric terms, as milligrams per kilogram (mg/kg).

Another characteristic is gender. Even if a man and a woman are exactly the same weight, differences in drug effects still can result on the basis of gender differences in body composition and sex hormones. Women have, on average, a higher proportion of fat, due to a greater fat-to-muscle ratio, and a lower proportion of water than men. When we look at the effects of alcohol consumption in terms of gender, we find that the lower water content (a factor that tends to dilute

the alcohol in the body) in women makes them feel more intoxicated than men, even if the same amount of alcohol is consumed.

Relative to men, women also have reduced levels of enzymes that break down alcohol in the liver, resulting in higher alcohol levels in the blood and a higher level of intoxication.[17] We suspect that the lower level of alcohol biotransformation may be related to an increased level of estrogen and progesterone in women. Whether gender differences exist with regard to drugs other than alcohol is presently unknown.

Another individual characteristic that influences the ways certain drugs affect the body is ethnic background. About 50 percent of all people of Asian descent, for example, show lower than average levels of one of the enzymes that normally breaks down alcohol in the liver shortly before it is excreted. With this particular deficiency, alcohol metabolites tend to build up in the blood, producing a faster heart rate, facial flushing, and nausea.[18] As a result, many Asians find drinking to be quite unpleasant.

Ethnic variability can be seen in terms of other drug effects as well. It has been found that Caucasians have a faster rate of biotransformation of antipsychotic and antianxiety medications than Asians and, as a result, end up with relatively lower concentrations of drugs in the blood. One consequence of this difference is in the area of psychiatric treatment. Asian schizophrenic patients require significantly lower doses of antipsychotic medication for their symptoms to improve, and they experience medication side effects at much lower doses than do Caucasian patients. Since other possible factors such as diet, life-style, and environment do not account for these differences, we can speculate that these differences have a genetic basis.[19]

In some cases, differences in the physiological response to a particular drug can explain differential patterns of drug-taking behavior. For example, researchers have found recently that African Americans have a slower rate of nicotine metabolism following the smoking of cigarettes relative to whites. This finding might be the reason why African Americans, on average, report smoking fewer cigarettes per day than whites. If we assume that an equivalent level of nicotine needs to be maintained in both populations, fewer cigarettes smoked but a higher level of nicotine absorbed per cigarette will produce the same effect as a greater number of cigarettes smoked but a lower nicotine level absorbed per cigarette. Consequently, African American smokers may be taking in and retaining relatively more nicotine per cigarette and, as a result, not having to smoke as many cigarettes per day.[20]

cross-tolerance: A phenomenon in which the tolerance that results from the chronic use of one drug induces a tolerance effect with regard to a second drug that has not been used before.

Psychological Factors in Drug-taking Behavior

It is clear that certain physiological factors such as weight, gender, and race must be taken into account to predict particular drug effects. Yet, even if we controlled these factors completely, we would still frequently find a drug effect in an individual person to be different from time to time, place to place, and situation to situation. Predictions about how a person might react would be far from perfect.

> *A good way of thinking about an individual's response to a particular drug is to view a drug effect as essentially a three-way interaction of (1) the drug's pharmacological properties (the biochemical nature of the substance), (2) the individual taking the drug (set), and (3) the immediate environment within which drug-taking behavior is occurring (setting).*

Whether one or more of these factors dominate in the final analysis seems to depend upon the dosage level. Generally speaking, the higher the drug dose, the greater the contribution made by the pharmacology of the drug itself; the lower the dose, the greater the contribution of individual characteristics of the drug-taker or environmental conditions.[21]

Expectation Effects

One of the most uncontrollable factors in drug-taking behavior is the set of expectations a person may have about what the drug will do. If you believe that a drug will make you drunk or feel sexy, the chances are increased that it will do so; if you believe that a marijuana cigarette will make you high, the chances are increased that it will. You can consider the impact of negative expectations in the same way; when the feelings are strong that a drug will have no effect on you, the chances are lessened that you will react to it. In the most extreme case, you might experience a drug effect even when the substance you ingested was completely inert—that is, pharmacologically ineffective. Any inert (inactive) substance is referred to as a **placebo** (from the Latin, "I will please"), and the physical reaction to it is referred to as the *placebo effect*.

The concept of a placebo goes back to the earliest days of pharmacology. The bizarre ingredients prescribed in ancient times to treat various diseases were effective to the extent that people *believed* that they were effective, not from any known therapeutic property of these ingredients. No doubt, the placebo effect was strong enough for physical symptoms to diminish. During the Middle Ages, in one of the more extreme cases of the placebo effect, Pope Boniface VIII reportedly was cured of kidney pains when his personal physician hung a gold seal bearing the image of a lion around the pope's thigh.[22]

It would be a mistake to think of the placebo effect as involving totally imaginary symptoms or totally imaginary reactions. Physical symptoms, involving specific bodily changes, can occur on the basis of placebo effects alone. How likely is it that a person will react to a placebo? The probability will vary from drug to drug, but in the case of morphine, the data are very clear. In 1959, a review of studies in which morphine or a placebo was administered in clinical studies of pain concluded that a placebo-induced reduction in pain occurred 35 percent of the time. Considering that morphine itself had a positive result in only 75 percent of the cases, the placebo effect is a very strong one.[23]

Unfortunately, we cannot predict with certainty whether a person will react strongly or weakly to a placebo. We do know, however, that the enthusiasm or lack of enthusiasm of the prescribing physician can play a major role. In one study that varied the attitude of the physician toward a particular medication, negative

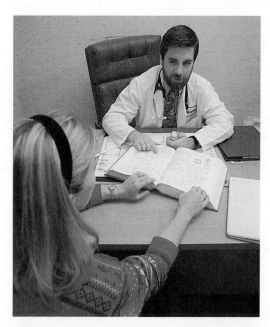

The likelihood of a placebo effect is maximized when the patient highly regards the expertise of the physician prescribing a drug. This placebo effect will often increase the benefits of a drug with known therapeutic properties.

placebo (pla-SEE-bo): Latin term translated "I will please." Any inert substance that produces a psychological or physiological reaction.

attitudes toward the medication resulted in the least benefits, whereas positive attitudes resulted in the most.[24]

It is not at all clear how the placebo effect is accomplished. In the case of pain relief, there is evidence that we have the natural ability to increase the levels of endorphins (internally-produced opiates) in the bloodstream and the brain from one moment to the next, but the nature of our ability to alter other important substances in our bodies is virtually unknown. Recent studies have documented a 33 percent increase in lung capacity among asthmatic children who inhaled a bronchodilator containing a placebo instead of medication and the development of skin rashes in people who have been exposed to fake poison ivy, to name a few examples of placebo-induced physiological reactions. Placebo research forces us to acknowledge the potential for psychological control over physiological processes in our bodies.[25]

Drug Research Methodology

Given the power of the placebo effect in drug-taking behavior, it is necessary to be very careful when carrying out drug research. For a drug to be deemed truly effective, it must be shown to be better not only in comparison to a no-treatment condition (a difference that could conceivably be due to a placebo effect) but also in comparison to an identical-looking drug that lacks the active ingredients of the drug being evaluated. For example, if the drug under study is in the shape of a round red pill, another round red pill without the active ingredients of the drug (called the *active placebo*) also must be administered for comparison purposes.

The procedures of these studies also have to be carefully executed. Neither the individual administering the drug or placebo nor the individual receiving the drug or placebo should know which substance is which. Such precautions, referred to as **double-blind**

---

double-blind: A procedure in drug research in which neither the individual administering nor the individual receiving a chemical substance knows whether the substance is the drug being evaluated or an active placebo.

physical dependence: A model of drug dependence based on the idea that the drug abuser continues the drug-taking behavior to avoid the consequences of physical withdrawal symptoms.

---

procedures, represent the minimal standards for separating the pharmacological effects of a drug from the effects that arise from one's expectations and beliefs.[26] We will return to the issue of interactions between drug effects and expectations when we consider alcohol intoxication in Chapter 13.

Physical and Psychological Dependence

When we refer to the idea of dependence in drug abuse, we are dealing with the fact that a person has a strong compulsion to continue taking a particular drug. Two possible models or explanations for why drug dependence occurs can be considered. The first is referred to as physical dependence, and the second is referred to as psychological dependence. The two models are not mutually exclusive; the abuse of some drugs can be a result of both physical and psychological dependence, whereas the abuse of others can be a result of psychological dependence alone.

Physical Dependence

The concept of **physical dependence** originates from observations of heroin abusers, as well as of those who abuse other opiate drugs, who developed strong physical symptoms following heroin withdrawal: a runny nose, chills and fever, inability to sleep, and hypersensitivity to pain. For barbiturate abusers in a comparable situation, symptoms include anxiety, inability to sleep, and sometimes lethal convulsions. For chronic alcohol abusers, abstention can produce tremors, nausea, weakness, and tachycardia (a fast heart rate). If severe, symptoms may include delirium, seizures, and hallucinations.[27]

Although the actual symptoms vary with the drug being withdrawn, the fact that we observe physical symptoms at all suggests strongly that some kind of physical need, perhaps as far down as the cellular level, develops over the course of drug abuse. It is as though the drug, previously a foreign substance, has become a normal part of the nervous system, and its removal and absence become abnormal.

From this point of view, it is predictable that the withdrawal symptoms would involve symptoms that are *opposite* to effects the drug originally had on the body. For example, heroin can be extremely constipating, but eventually the body compensates for heroin's intestinal effects. Abrupt abstinence from heroin leaves the processes that have been counteracting the constipation with nothing to counteract, so the result of withdrawal is diarrhea. You may notice a strong resemblance between the action–counteraction phenomena of withdrawal and the processes Siegel has hypothesized as the basis for behavioral tolerance.

Psychological Dependence

The most important implication of the model of physical dependence, as distinct from psychological dependence, is that individuals involved in drug abuse continue the drug-taking behavior, at least in part, *to avoid the feared consequences of withdrawal.* This idea can form the basis for a general model of drug dependence only if physical withdrawal symptoms appear consistently for every drug considered as a drug of abuse. It turns out, however, that a number of abused drugs (cocaine, hallucinogens, and marijuana, for example) do not produce physical withdrawal symptoms, and the effects of heroin withdrawal are more variable than we would expect if physical dependence alone were at work.

It is possible that drug abusers continue to take the drug not because they want to avoid the symptoms of withdrawal but because they crave the pleasurable effects of the drug itself. They may even feel that they need the drug to function at all. This is the way one heroin addict has expressed it:

> I'm just trying to get high as much as possible.... If I could get more money, I would spend it all on drugs. All I want is to get loaded. I just really like shooting dope. I don't have any use for sex; I'd rather shoot dope. I like to shoot dope better than anything else in the world.[28]

Many heroin abusers (between 56 and 77 percent in one major study) who complete the withdrawal process after abstaining from the drug have a relapse.[29] If physical dependence were the whole story, these phenomena would not exist. The withdrawal symptoms would have been gone by that time, and any physical need that might have been evident before would no longer be present.

When we speak of **psychological dependence**, we are offering an explanation of drug abuse based not upon the attempt of abusers to avoid unpleasant withdrawal symptoms but upon their continued desire to obtain pleasurable effects from the drug.

Unfortunately, we are faced here with a major conceptual problem: The explanation by itself is circular and tells us basically nothing. If I were to say, for example, that I was taking cocaine because I was psychologically dependent upon it, then I could just as easily say that I was psychologically dependent upon cocaine because I was abusing it. Without some *independent* justification, the only explanation for the concept of psychological dependence would be the behavior that the concept was supposed to explain!

Fortunately, there is independent evidence for the concept of psychological dependence, founded chiefly upon studies showing that animals are as capable of self-administering drugs of abuse as humans are. Using techniques developed in the late 1950s, researchers have been able to insert a catheter into the vein of a freely moving laboratory animal and arrange the equipment so that the animal can self-administer a drug intravenously whenever it presses a lever (Figure 1.4). It had been well known that animals would engage in specific behaviors to secure rewards such as food, water, or even electrical stimulation of certain regions of the brain. These objectives were defined as positive reinforcers because animals would learn to work to secure them. The question at the time was whether animals would self-administer drugs in a similar way. Could drugs be positive reinforcers as well?

The experiments showed clearly that animals would self-administer drugs such as cocaine and other stimulants despite the fact that these drugs would not ordinarily produce physical symptoms during withdrawal. In one study, rats pressed the lever as many as 6,400 times for one administration of cocaine; others were nearly as eager for administrations of amphetamines.[30] Interestingly, a number of other drugs were aversive, judging from the reluctance of animals to work for them. Hallucinogens such as LSD, antipsychotic drugs, and antidepressant drugs were examples of drugs that animals clearly did not like.[31]

By connecting the concept of psychological dependence to general principles of reinforcement, it is possible for us to appreciate the powerful effects of abused

psychological dependence: A model of drug dependence based on the idea that the drug abuser is motivated by a craving for the pleasurable effects of the drug.

FIGURE 1.4

A simplified rendition of how drugs are self-administered in rats. The rat's pressure on a lever causes the pump to inject a drug through a catheter implanted into its vein.

drugs. When an animal is presented with a choice of pressing a lever for food or pressing a lever for cocaine, cocaine wins hands down—even to the point of the animal starving to death.[32] When the effects of heroin are compared with those of cocaine, the differences are dramatic:

> *Those rats that self-administer heroin developed a stable pattern of use, maintained their pretest weight, continued good grooming behavior, and tended to be in good health. Their mortality rate was 36 percent after thirty days. Those self-administering cocaine . . . exhibited an extremely erratic pattern of use, with "binges" of heavy use alternating with brief periods of abstinence. They lost 47 percent of their body weight, ceased grooming behavior, and maintained extremely poor physical health. After thirty days, 90 percent were dead.[33]*

In the final analysis, from the standpoint of treating individuals who abuse drugs, it might not matter whether there is physical dependence or psychological dependence going on. According to many experts in the field, the distinction between physical and psychological dependence has outgrown its usefulness in explaining the motivation behind drug abuse. Whether the discontinuation of an abused drug does induce major physical withdrawal symptoms (as in the case of heroin, alcohol, and barbiturates) or does not (as in the case of cocaine, amphetamines, and nicotine), the patterns of compulsive drug-taking behavior are remarkably similar. If the pattern of behavior is similar, then there can be common strategies for treatment.[34]

A Final Note: Two Perspectives on Drugs and Drug Use

In order to understand the societal problems associated with drug use and abuse, it is necessary to examine these problems in terms of two major perspectives. The first perspective, adopted primarily by psychiatrists, psychologists, drug-abuse counselors, and other health professionals, focuses on the adverse effects of drug-taking behaviour on one's physical health and psychological well-being. In this regard, no distinction is made with regard to the specific drug involved, only its behavioural consequences. Legality or illegality is not at issue. The second perspective, adopted primarily by professionals in the area of criminal justice, focuses on the specific drug being used. In this regard, drugs are examined in terms of their accepted medical benefits, their potential for abuse, and their legal status. The implication for viewing drug-taking behavior from a criminal-justice perspective is that drugs with the fewest medical benefits and the greatest potential for abuse should be the drugs with the most stringently restricted availability, as established by law.

Drug-taking Behavior: The Health Perspective

Most health professionals use guidelines published by the American Psychiatric Association as an official standard for defining problems associated with drug-taking behavior. Generally speaking, these problems, which

TABLE 1.1

Criteria for substance dependence and substance abuse according to the DSM-IV

SUBSTANCE DEPENDENCE	SUBSTANCE ABUSE
At least three out of the following must apply within a twelve-month period:	At least one of the following must apply within a twelve-month period:
1. Tolerance. The person has to take increasingly large doses of the drug to get the desired effect. Or else the person experiences a diminished effect from the same amount of the drug.	1. Recurrent substance use resulting in a failure to fulfill major role obligations at work, school, or home. Examples include repeated absences from work, suspensions or expulsions from school, or neglect of children or one's household.
2. Withdrawal. When the drug is stopped, there are psychological or physiological withdrawal symptoms. Or else the substance is taken to relieve or avoid these symptoms.	2. Recurrent drug use in situations in which use is physically hazardous.
3. Unintentional overuse. The person repeatedly takes more of the drug or takes it over a longer period of time than he or she intended.	3. Recurrent substance-related legal problems, such as an arrest for disorderly conduct or drug-related behavior. Symptoms of the disturbance must have persisted for more than a month or occurred over a longer period of time.
4. Persistent desire or efforts to control drug use. The person tries to quit and repeatedly relapses into further drug use.	4. Continued drug use despite the knowledge of persistent social, occupational, psychological, or physical problems that would be caused or made more difficult by the use of the drug.
5. Preoccupation with the drug. The person spends a great deal of time in activities necessary to obtain the substance, use it, or recover from its effects.	*Important:* The person must have never met the criteria for substance dependence for this particular drug.
6. The reduction or abandonment of important social, occupational, or recreational activities in order to engage in drug use. A person quits a job, neglects a child, or gives up other important activities.	
7. Continued drug use despite major drug-related problems. A person repeatedly arrested for drug possession still maintains the drug habit, or a person with serious lung disease continues to smoke cigarettes, for example.	
Symptoms of the disturbance must have persisted for more than a month or occurred repeatedly over a longer period of time.	

Source: Adapted from the *American Psychiatric Association: Diagnostic and statistical manual of mental disorders. Text Revision.* (4th ed.). Washington, DC: American Psychiatric Association, 2000. Reprinted with permission from the *Diagnostic and statistical manual of mental disorders* (4th ed.), Text revision. Copyright 2000. American Psychiatric Association.

range from the ingestion of a drug of abuse (including alcohol) to the experience of side effects of a medication, are collectively referred to as *substance-related disorders.* The fourth edition (text revision) of the association's *Diagnostic and Statistical Manual of Mental Disorders* (DSM-IV-TR or simply DSM-IV, for short), published in 2000, identifies two specific behavioral conditions: **substance dependence** and **substance abuse** (Table 1.1).

substance dependence: A diagnostic term used in clinical psychology and psychiatry that identifies an individual with significant signs of a dependent relationship upon a psychoactive drug.

substance abuse: A diagnostic term used in clinical psychology and psychiatry that identifies an individual who continues to take a psychoactive drug despite the fact that the drug-taking behavior creates specific problems for that individual.

Two features of the DSM-IV guidelines are worth noting. First, the guidelines consist of a listing of behavioral criteria to be used for the diagnosis (identification) of substance dependence or substance abuse. There is no discussion of *why* these problems have arisen or what circumstances produced them, only an account of their behavioral features. The position of the American Psychiatric Association is that a judgment of whether a person has a problem of dependence or abuse should depend on the behavior of that person, not on the chemical that is being consumed or the legal status of that chemical. Second, the broader term "substance" has been substituted for the word "drug" in the guidelines primarily because there is often confusion in the public mind about what is defined as a drug and what is not, particularly in the instance of alcohol or nicotine use.[35]

Drug-taking Behavior: The Criminal-Justice Perspective

The criminal-justice profession views the range of problems associated with drug-taking behavior primarily in terms of a five-category system, established as a result of the 1970 Comprehensive Drug Abuse Prevention and Control Act (popularly known as the Controlled Substances Act). Under this system, psychoactive drugs considered to be more dangerous and presenting greater potential for abuse are more stringently restricted in their availability to the public. Guidelines for federal prosecution of drug possession and/or drug trafficking are adjusted accordingly (see Chapter 6). Alcohol and nicotine are not included in this classification system.

Schedules I and II refer to drugs presenting the highest level of abuse potential, and Schedule V refers to drugs presenting the least. All drugs, except for those included in Schedule I, are available legally or on either a prescription or nonprescription (over-the-counter) basis. In the case of Schedule I drugs (heroin, LSD, mescaline, PCP, and marijuana, for example), no acceptable medical use has been authorized by the U.S. government, and availability of these drugs is limited to research purposes only.[36]

The five schedules of controlled substances, shown in Table 1.2, reflect the official stance of the U.S. government with respect to licit and illicit drug use and form the basis for present-day federal enforcement activity. In some cases, the classification can be controversial. The current designation of marijuana, for example, as a Schedule I controlled substance (defined as having no accepted medical use), as opposed to a Schedule II controlled substance (defined as having some accepted medical use), has been and continues to be hotly debated (see Chapter 10).

TABLE 1.2

Summary of Controlled Substances Schedules under the Controlled Substance Act

SCHEDULE I

High potential for abuse

No accepted medical use

Research use only; drugs must be stored in secure vaults

Examples: heroin, LSD, mescaline, and marijuana

SCHEDULE II

High potential for abuse

Some accepted medical use, though use may lead to severe physical or psychological dependence

No prescription renewals are permitted

In cases of medical use, drugs must be stored in secure vaults.

Examples: cocaine, amphetamines, opium, morphine, hydrocodone (Vicodin), oxycodone (OxyContin, Percocet), codeine, methadone, some barbiturates, phencyclidine (PCP)

SCHEDULE III

High potential for abuse

Accepted medical use, though use may lead to low or moderate physical or psychological dependence

Up to five prescription renewals are permitted within six months.

Examples: codeine, some barbiturates, anabolic steroids and other testosterone-related compounds, ketamine

SCHEDULE IV

Low potential for abuse

Accepted medical use

Up to five prescription renewals are permitted within six months.

Examples: Phenobarbital, antidepressant medications, antianxiety medications, sleep medications

SCHEDULE V

Minimal potential for abuse

Widespread medical use

Minimal controls for selling and dispensing

Examples: cough-control medications containing small amounts of codeine and diarrhea-control medications containing small amounts of opium or morphine

Source: Drug Enforcement Administration, U.S. Department of Justice, Washington, DC.

Summary

A Matter of Definition

- Psychoactive drugs are those drugs that affect our feelings, perceptions, and behavior. Depending on the intent of the individual, drug use can be considered either instrumental or recreational.

- Drug abuse refers to cases in which a licit (legal)or illicit (illegal) drug is used in ways that produce some form of impairment. Drug misuse refers to cases in which a prescription or nonprescription drug is used inappropriately.

How Drugs Enter the Body

- There are four basic ways to administer drugs into the body: oral administration, injection, inhalation, and absorption through the skin or membranes. Each of these presents constraints on which kinds of drugs will be effectively delivered into the bloodstream.

How Drugs Exit the Body

- Most drugs are eliminated from the body through urinary excretion. Drugs are broken down for elimination by the action of enzymes in the liver. An index of how long this process takes is called the elimination half-life.

Factors Determining the Behavioral Impact of Drugs

- The physiological effect of a drug can vary as a factor of the time elapsed since its administration, the possible combination of its administration with other drugs, and finally the personal characteristics of the individual consuming the drug.

- Some characteristics that can play a definite role in the effect of a drug include the individual's weight, gender, and racial or ethnic background.

- Two important issues need to be understood in looking at the physiological effect of drugs: the extent to which drugs pass into the bloodstream and from the bloodstream to the brain and the extent to which tolerance effects occur over repeated administrations of a given drug.

Psychological Factors in Drug-taking Behavior

- Although the physiological actions of psychoactive drugs are becoming increasingly well understood, great variability in the effect of these drugs remains, largely because of psychological factors.

- The most prominent psychological factor is the influence of personal expectations on the part of the individual consuming the drug. The impact of expectations on one's reaction to a drug, a phenomenon called the placebo effect, is an important consideration in drug evaluation and research.

Physical and Psychological Dependence

- Drugs can be viewed in terms of a physical dependence model, in which the compulsive drug-taking behavior is tied to an avoidance of withdrawal symptoms, or a psychological dependence model, in which the drug-taking behavior is tied to a genuine craving for the drug and highly reinforcing effects of the drug on the user's body and mind.

Drug-taking Behavior: The Health Perspective

- The American Psychiatric Association currently recognizes two major conditions associated with drug-taking behavior: substance dependence and substance abuse. The broader term "substance" is used instead of "drug," because there is often confusion in the public mind in deciding what is defined as a drug and what is not. The focus is on the behavioral aspects of drug use, making no distinction with regard to the specific drug involved.

Drug-taking Behavior: The Criminal-Justice Perspective

- The range of problems associated with drug-taking behavior can be viewed in terms of five categories or schedules of controlled substances, as established by the 1970 Comprehensive Drug Abuse Prevention and Control Act (popularly known as the Controlled Substances Act). Schedules I and II refer to drugs presenting the highest level of abuse potential, and Schedule V refers to drugs presenting the least. This classification system is the official position of the U.S. government with respect to licit and illicit drug use and forms the basis for present-day federal enforcement activity.

Key Terms

behavioral tolerance, p. 16
biotransformation, p. 13
cross-tolerance, p. 18
double-blind, p. 20
drug, p. 5
drug abuse, p. 8
drug dependence, p. 4
drug misuse, p. 7

elimination half-life, p. 13
illicit drugs, p. 4
instrumental use, p. 6
intramuscular, p. 10
intranasal, p. 11
intravenous, p. 10
latency period, p. 13
licit drugs, p. 4

metabolite, p. 13
physical dependence, p. 20
placebo, p. 19
potentiation, p. 14
psychoactive drugs, p. 3
psychological
  dependence, p. 21
recreational use, p. 7

subcutaneous, p. 10
sublingual, p. 11
substance abuse, p. 23
substance dependence,
  p. 23
synergism, p. 14
tolerance, p. 15
transdermal patch, p. 11

Endnotes

1. The Gallup Organization (2009). Results of Gallup Poll data. Substance Abuse and Mental Health Services Administration (2004, January 16). Availability of illicit drugs among youths. *The NSDUH Report*. Rockville, MD: Office of Applied Studies, Substance Abuse and Mental Health Administration, p. 2. Stelter, Brian (2009, September 15). A popular plant is quietly spreading across TV screens. *New York Times*, pp. C!, C4. Wax, Paul M. (2002). Just a click away: Recreational drug web sites on the Internet. *Pediatrics; 109;e96.*

2. Substance Abuse and Mental Health Services Administration (2010). *Results from the 2010 National Survey on Drug Use and Health: National findings.* Rockville, MD: Office of Applied Statistics, Substance Abuse and Mental Health Services Administration.

3. Eckholm, Erik (2009, May 28). Governments' drug-abuse costs hit $468 billion, study says. *New York Times*, p. A15. National Institute on Drug Abuse (2007). *The economic costs of drug abuse in the United States, 1992–2002.* Washington, DC: Office of National Drug Control Policy.

4. Patel, Amee B., and Fromme, Kim (2010). Explicit outcome expectancies and substance abuse: Current research and future directions. In Lawrence M. Scheier (Ed.), *Handbook of drug use etiology: Theory, methods, and empirical findings.* Washington, DC: American Psychological Association, p.153.

5. Primack, Brian; Dalton, Madeline A.; Carroll, Mary V.; Agarwal, Aaron A.; and Fine, Michael J. (2008). Content analysis of tobacco, alcohol, and other drugs in popular music. *Archives of Pediatric and Adolescent Medicine, 162,* 169–175. Ridout, Victoria, Roberts, Donald F., and Foehr, Ulla G. (2005). *Generation M: Media in the Lives of 8–18 Year-Olds.* Menlo Park, CA: Kaiser Family Foundation, Chapter 5. Snyder, Leslie B., and Nadorff, P. Gayle (2010). Youth substance use and the media. In Lawrence M. Scheier (Ed.), *Handbook of drug use etiology: Theory, methods, and empirical findings.* Washington, DC: American Psychological Association, pp. 475–491.

6. Leshner, Alan I. (1998, October). Addiction is a brain disease—and it matters. *National Institute of Justice Journal,* 2–6.

7. Jacobs, Michael R., and Fehr, Kevin O'B. (1987). *Drugs and drug abuse: A reference text.* Toronto: Addiction Research Foundation, pp. 3–5.

8. Goode, Erich (2005). *Drugs in American society* (6th ed.). New York: McGraw-Hill College, pp. 15–26.

9. Public-service message, "Frying Pan." Partners for a Drug-free America, New York, 1987.

10. Karande, Pankaj, and Mitragotri, Samir (2009). Enhancement of transdermal drug delivery via synergistic action of chemicals. *Biomembranes, 1788,* 2362–2373. Mitragotri, Samir (2005). Healing sound: The use of ultrasound in drug delivery and other therapeutic applications. *Nature Reviews: Drug Discovery, 4,* 255–260. Whitten, Lori (2009, November). Naltrexone via skin patch technology proves effectiveness of new teachnology. *NIDA Notes, 22(3),* pp. 13, 16.

11. Hawks, Richard L., and Chiang, C. Nora (1986). Examples of specific drug assays. In Richard L. Hawks and C. Nora Chiang (Eds.), *Urine testing for drugs of abuse* (NIDA Research Monograph 73). Rockville, MD: National Institute on Drug Abuse, pp. 84–112. Julien, Robert M. (2001). *A primer of drug action* (9th ed.). New York: Worth, pp. 27–31. McKim, William A. (2000). *Drugs and behavior: An introduction to behavioral pharmacology* (4th ed.). Upper Saddle River, NJ: Prentice-Hall, pp. 1–25.

12. Lankester, E. Ray (1889). Mithridatism. *Nature, 40,* 149.

13. Siegel, Shepard (1990). Drug anticipation and the treatment of dependence. In Barbara A. Ray (ed.), *Learning factors in substance abuse* (NIDA Research Monograph 84). Rockville, MD: National Institute on Drug Abuse, pp. 1–24.

14. Gerevich, Jóseph, Bácskai, Erika, Farkas, Lajos, and Danics, Zoltán (2005, July 25). A case report: Pavlovian conditioning as a risk factor of heroin "overdose" death. *Harm Reduction Journal, 2,* 11 (online publication). Siegel, Shepard (1975). Evidence from rats that morphine tolerance is a learned response. *Journal of Comparative and Physiological Psychology, 89,* 489–506. Siegel, Shepard; Hinson, Riley E.; Krank, Marvin D.; and McCully, Jane. (1982). Heroin "overdose" death: Contri-

bution of drug-associated environmental cues. *Science*, 216, 436–437.

15. Brecher, Edward M., and the editors of *Consumer Reports*. (1972). *Licit and illicit drugs.* Mount Vernon, NY: Consumers Union.

16. Siegel, Shepard (1999). Drug anticipation and drug addiction. The 1998 H. David Archibald Lecture. *Addiction, 94,* 1113–1124.

17. Frezza, Mario; DiPadova, Carlo; Pozzato, Gabrielle; Terpin, Maddalena; Baraona, Enrique; and Lieber, Charles S. (1990). High blood alcohol levels in women: The role of decreased gastric alcohol dehydrogenase activity and first-pass metabolism. *New England Journal of Medicine, 322,* 95–99.

18. Nakawatase, Tomoko V., Yamamoto, Joe, and Sasao, Toshiaki (1993). The association between fast-flushing response and alcohol use among Japanese Americans. *Journal of Studies on Alcohol, 54,* 48–53.

19. Goodman, Deborah (1992, January–February). NIMH grantee finds drug responses differ among ethnic groups. *ADAMHA News,* pp. 5, 15. Johnson, Ronald C., Nagoshi, Sylvia Y., Schwitters, Kirk S., Bowman, Frank M., et al. (1984). Further investigation of racial/ethnic differences and of familial resemblances in flushing in response to alcohol. *Behavior Genetics, 14,* 171–178.

20. Perez-Stable, Eliseo J.; Herrera, Brenda; Jacob III, Peyton; and Benowita, Neal L. (1998). Nicotine metabolism and intake in black and white smokers. *Journal of the American Medical Association, 280,* 152–156.

21. Goode, Erich (1999). *Drugs in American society* (5th ed.). New York: McGraw-Hill College, p. 9.

22. Kornetsky, Conan (1976). *Pharmacology: Drugs affecting behavior.* New York, Wiley, p. 23. Morris, David B. (1999). Placebo, pain, and belief: A biocultural model. In Anne Harrington (ed.), *The placebo effect: An interdisciplinary exploration.* Cambridge, MA: Harvard University Press, pp. 187–207. Shapiro, Arthur K., and Shapiro, Elaine (1997). *The powerful placebo: From ancient priest to modern physician.* Baltimore: Johns Hopkins University Press.

23. Beecher, H. K. (1959). *Measurement of subjective responses: Quantitative effects of drugs.* New York: Oxford University Press. Waber, Rebecca L.; Shiv, Baba; Cannon, Ziv; and Ariely, Dan (2008). Commercial features of placebo and therapeutic efficacy. *Journal of the American Medical Association, 299,* 1016–1017.

24. Benedetti, F. (2002). How the doctor's words affect the patient's brain. *Evaluation and the Health Professions, 25,* 369–386.

25. De la Fuente-Fernández, R., and Stoessl, A. J. (2002). The biochemical bases for reward: Implications for the placebo effect. *Evaluation and the Health Professions, 25,* 387–398. Flaten, Magne Arve, Simonsen, Terje, and Olsen, Harald (1999). Drug-related information generates placebo and nocebo responses that modify the drug response. *Psychosomatic Medicine, 61,* 250–255. Levinthal, Charles F. (1988). *Messengers of paradise:*

Opiates and the brain. Anchor Press/Doubleday. Talbot, Margaret (2000, January 9). The placebo prescription. *New York Times Magazine,* pp. 34–39, 44, 58–60. Wager, Tor D. (2005). The neural basis of placebo effects in pain. *Current Directions in Psychological Science, 14,* 175–179.

26. Quitkin, Frederic M. (1999). Placebos, drug effects, and study design: A clinician's guide. *American Journal of Psychiatry, 156,* 829–836.

27. Blum, Kenneth. (1991). *Alcohol and the addictive brain.* New York, Free Press, p. 17.

28. Pinel, John P. J. (2003). *Biopsychology* (5th ed.). Boston: Allyn and Bacon, p. 398.

29. Simpson, D. Dwayne, and Marsh, Kerry L. (1986). Relapse and recovery among opioid addicts 12 years after treatment. In Frank M. Tims and Carl G. Leukefeld (Eds.), *Relapse and recovery in drug abuse* (NIDA Research Monograph 72). Rockville, MD: National Institute on Drug Abuse, pp. 86–103.

30. Halikas, James A. (1997). Craving. In Joyce H. Lowinson, Pedro Ruiz, Robert B. Millman, and John G. Langrod (Eds.), *Substance abuse: A comprehensive textbook* (3rd ed.). Baltimore: Williams and Wilkins, pp. 85–90. Pickens, Roy, and Thompson, Travis (1968). Cocaine-reinforced behavior in rats: Effects of reinforcement magnitude and fixed-ratio size. *Journal of Pharmacology and Experimental Therapeutics, 161,* 122–129.

31. Hoffmeister, F. H., and Wuttke, W. (1975). Psychotropic drugs as negative reinforcers. *Pharmacological Reviews, 27,* 419–428. Yokel, R. A. (1987). Intravenous self-administration: Response rates, the effect of pharmacological challenges and drug preferences. In Michael A. Bozarth (Ed.), *Methods of assessing the reinforcing properties of abused drugs.* New York: Springer-Verlag, pp. 1–34.

32. Johanson, Chris E. (1984). Assessment of the abuse potential of cocaine in animals. In John Grabowski (Ed.), *Cocaine: Pharmacology, effects, and treatment of abuse.* Rockville, MD: National Institute on Drug Abuse, pp. 54–71.

33. Quotation from Goode, Erich. (1989). *Drugs in American society* (3rd ed.). New York: McGraw-Hill, p. 49. Data from Bozarth, Michael A., and Wise, Roy A. (1985). Toxicity associated with long-term intravenous heroin and cocaine self-administration in the rat. *Journal of the American Medical Association, 254,* 81–83.

34. Stewart, Jane, De Wit, Harriet, and Eikelboom, Roelof (1984). Role of unconditioned and conditioned drug effects in the self-administration of opiates and stimulants. *Psychological Review, 91,* 251–268.

35. American Psychiatric Association (2000). *Diagnostic and statistical manual. Text Revision* (4th ed.). Washington, DC: American Psychiatric Association, pp. 191, 197, and 199.

36. Schmalleger, Frank (2009). *Criminal justice today: An introductory text for the 21st century* (10th ed.). Upper Saddle River, NJ: Pearson Education, pp. 583–584.

chapter 2

Understanding the Drug Problem in America

After you have completed this chapter, you should have an understanding of

- The nature of drug toxicity
- The DAWN statistics as measures of acute drug toxicity
- Judging drug toxicity from drug-related deaths
- Patterns of drug use among adolescents, college students, and young adults in the United States
- Patterns of drug use among diverse populations in the United States
- Club drugs as well as the nonmedical use of prescription pain relievers, prescription stimulant medications, and nonprescription cough-and-cold medications.

I'm a park ranger assigned to a small community park in a moderate-income-to-affluent suburban town. The park has three manicured baseball fields and about four acres of woods. About a hundred yards into the woods is a hangout where the debris includes a home-made bong used to smoke drugs and lots of needles. Heroin used to be the last thing on the minds of public safety officers and unarmed park rangers like myself just a few years ago. Now we find heroin even in cars outside youth baseball games, less than twenty yards away from kids and parents; heroin overdose cases are on the increase as well. Last night, a young man was spotted sitting on a stoop in the middle of a nice neighborhood. We knew that he had been arrested with 77 pills—Vicodin, OxyContin, the usual stuff—about three weeks ago. But there he was again looking dazed and disoriented. A friend on the local police force told me about a 17-year-old guy whose car was stopped last week. Fresh needle marks were seen on the inside of both his arms; the car smelled of marijuana. When they determined that the car and driver were clean, they let him go. The information was relayed by the police to a recently formed heroin task force in the county. "We'll see him again," the police officer said. An hour later, the young man was spotted outside a fast-food restaurant known to be a popular place for drug dealers.

The problems associated with drug use and abuse, whether the drug itself is alcohol, nicotine, a prescription medication, a household product, or an illicit drug, pervade our society. As emphasized in the last chapter, drug-taking behavior is a significant concern for all of us. This chapter will examine two broadly defined aspects of the drug problem in American society. The first aspect focuses on the potential physical harm that drugs can have on our bodies. It is important to understand the potential toxicity of drugs as a major public-health issue. What are the medical consequences of specific forms of drug-taking behavior? What are the potential risks to one's physical health? The second aspect focuses on the extent to which drug-taking behavior is undertaken by specific populations in our society. Which subpopulations are most affected? To what extent do our attitudes toward drug-taking behavior influence the inclination to engage in drug use and abuse? Answers to these and other questions serve to guide us in providing effective drug-abuse prevention and treatment programs (see Chapter 16).

The Problem of Drug Toxicity

When we say that a drug is toxic, we are referring to the fact that it may be dangerous, poisonous, or may in some way interfere with a person's normal functioning. Technically, any substance, no matter how benign, has the potential for **toxicity** if the **dose**—the amount in which the substance is taken—is high enough. The question of a drug's safety, or its relative safety when compared to other drugs, centers on the possibility that it may be toxic at relatively low doses. We certainly do not want people to harm themselves accidentally when taking the drug in the course of their daily lives. When there is a possibility that the *short-term* effects of a particular drug will trigger a toxic reaction, then this drug is identified as having some level of **acute toxicity**.

To understand the principle of toxicity in general, we need to examine an S-shaped graph called the **dose-response curve** (Figure 2.1a). Let us assume that we have the results of data collected from laboratory tests of a hypothetical sleep-inducing drug. Increases in the dose level of the drug are producing the desired sleep-inducing effect in an increasingly large percentage of a test population of mice. At 10 milligrams (mg), 50 percent of the population has fallen asleep; at 50 mg, 100 percent has done so. There is always some variability in individual reactions to any drug; some mice may be internally resistant to the drug's effect, whereas others may be quite susceptible. We cannot predict *which animal* will fall asleep with 10 mg of the drug, only that the probability is 50 percent. Any one animal may fall asleep with an extremely low dose or a dose of 50 mg.

We define the **effective dose (ED)** of a drug having a specific effect on a test population in terms of probabilities, from 0 to 100 percent. For example, the ED50 of a drug refers to the effective dose for 50 percent of the population; ED99 refers to the effective dose for 99 percent of the population. In this case, the ED numbers refer to the drug's effect of producing sleep. The same drug may be producing other effects (muscular relaxation, for instance) at lower doses; these

toxicity (tox-IS-ih-tee): The physical or psychological harm that a drug might present to the user.

dose: The quantity of drug that is taken into the body, typically measured in terms of milligrams (mg) or micrograms (µg).

acute toxicity: The physical or psychological harm a drug might present to the user immediately or soon after the drug is ingested into the body.

dose-response curve: An S-shaped graph showing the increasing probability of a certain drug effect as the dose level rises.

effective dose (ED): The minimal dose of a particular drug necessary to produce the intended drug effect in a given percentage of the population.

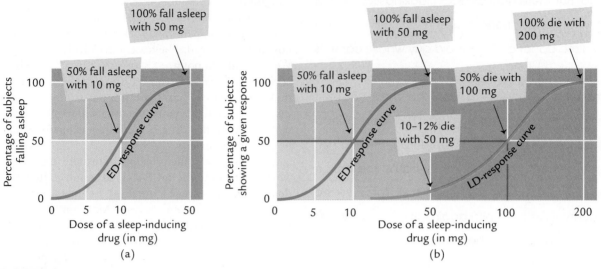

FIGURE 2.1

(a) An effective dose-response curve, and (b) an effective dose-response curve (left) alongside a lethal dose-response curve (right).

drug effects would have their own separate dose-response curves. It is a good idea to remember that we are looking at the properties of a drug *effect* here, not the properties of the drug itself.

Now we can look at Figure 2.1b, where the effective dose-response curve is represented along with another S-shaped dose-response curve, also gathered from laboratory testing, in which the "response" is death. It makes sense that the second curve should be shifted to the right because the **lethal dose (LD)** generally involves greater amounts of a drug than the amounts necessary to produce an effect.

Emphasis should be placed on the word "generally" because the lethal dose-response curve overlaps with the effective dose-response curve in this example. While a 100-mg dose has to be taken to kill 50 percent of the test

---

lethal dose (LD): The minimal dose of a particular drug capable of producing death in a given percentage of the population.

therapeutic index: A measure of a drug's relative safety for use, computed by the ratio of the lethal dose for 50 percent of the population over the effective dose for 50 percent of the population.

margin of safety: The ratio of a lethal dose for 1 percent of the population to the effective dose for 99 percent of the population.

---

population, it can be seen that a dose of as little as 50 mg (or less) is lethal for at least a few of them. The LD50 of a drug refers to the lethal dose for 50 percent of the population; LD1 refers to a relatively lower dose that is lethal for only one percent of the population.

It is useful to combine the effective and lethal doses of a drug in a ratio to arrive at some idea of that drug's toxicity. The ratio of LD50/ED50 is called the **therapeutic index**. If the LD50 for a drug is 450 mg and the ED50 is 50 mg, then the therapeutic index is 9. In other words, you would have to take nine times the dose that would be effective for half the population to incur a 50 percent chance of dying.

It can be argued, however, that a 50 percent probability of dying represents an unacceptably high risk even for a drug that has genuine benefits. To be more conservative in the direction of safety, the ratio of LD1/ED99 is often calculated. Here we are calculating the ratio between the dose that produces death in one percent of the population and the dose that would be effective in 99 percent. This second ratio, called the **margin of safety**, should be as high as possible. The higher the ratio, the safer, or less toxic, is the drug. It can be seen that the margin of safety for the hypothetical drug examined in Figure 2.1 would present serious toxicity issues.

The therapeutic index or the margin of safety is very helpful when considering the toxicity of drugs that are manufactured by recognized pharmaceutical companies and regulated by the U.S. Food and Drug Administration (FDA), keeping in mind the possibility that a person might intentionally or unintentionally take a higher-than-recommended dose of the drug. But what about the toxicity risks in consuming illicit drugs? The unfortunate reality of street drugs is that the buyer has no way of knowing what he or she has bought until the drug has been used, and then it is frequently too late.

Few, if any, illicit drug sellers make a pretense of being ethical businesspeople; their only objectives are to make money and avoid prosecution by the law. Frequently, the drugs they sell are diluted with either inert or highly dangerous ingredients. Adulterated heroin, for example, may contain a high proportion of milk sugar as an inactive filler and a dash of quinine to simulate the bitter taste of real heroin, when the actual amount of heroin that is being sold is far less than the "standard" street dosage.

At the other extreme, the content of heroin may be unexpectedly high and lead to a lethal overdose, or the adulterated product may contain animal tranquilizers, arsenic, strychnine, insecticides, or other highly toxic substances. Cocaine, LSD, marijuana, and all the other illicit drugs available to the drug abuser, as well as look-alike drugs that are unauthorized copies of popular prescription medications, present hidden and unpredictable risks of toxicity. Even if drugs are procured from a friend or from someone you know, these risks remain. Neither of you is likely to know the exact ingredients. The dangers of acute toxicity are always present.

Given the uncertainty that exists about the contents of many abused drugs, what measure or index can we use to evaluate the effects of acute toxicity on individuals in society? A natural tendency is to look first to the news headlines; think of all the well-known public figures who have died as a direct consequence of drug misuse or abuse (Drugs… in Focus). Such examples, however, can be misleading. Celebrities are not necessarily representative of the drug-using population in general, and the drugs prevalent among celebrities, because of their expense, may not represent the drugs most frequently encountered by the rest of society. To have some idea of the toxic effects of psychoactive drugs in a broader context, we have to turn to the institutions that contend with drug toxicity on a daily basis: the emergency departments of hospitals around the country.

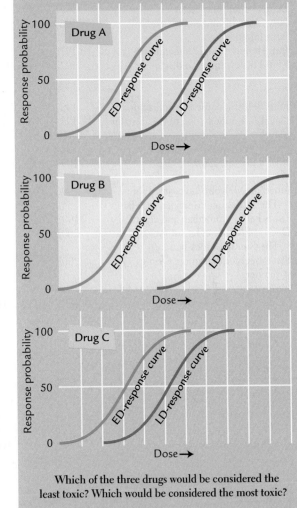

Quick Concept Check 2.1

Understanding Dose-Response Curves

Check your understanding of dose-response curves and the toxicity of drugs by answering the following questions.

The following three sets of dose-response curves show the effective and lethal responses to three drugs A, B, and C.

Which of the three drugs would be considered the least toxic? Which would be considered the most toxic?

Answer: Drug B is the least toxic drug. Drug C is the most toxic drug.

Drugs... in Focus

Acute Toxicity in the News: Drug-Related Deaths

The following famous people have died either as a direct consequence or as an indirect consequence of drug misuse or abuse.

Name	Year of Death	Age	Reasons Given for Death
Marilyn Monroe, actress	1962	36	Overdose of Nembutal (a sedative-hypnotic medication); circumstances unknown
Lenny Bruce, comedian	1966	40	Accidental overdose of morphine
Judy Garland, singer and actress	1969	47	Accidental overdose of sleeping pills
Janis Joplin, singer	1970	27	Accidental overdose of heroin and alcohol
Jimi Hendrix, singer and guitarist	1970	27	Accidental overdose of sleeping pills
Elvis Presley, singer and actor	1977	42	Cardiac arrhythmia suspected to be due to an interaction of antihistamine, codeine, and Demerol (a painkiller) as well as Valium and several other tranquilizers
John Belushi, comedian and actor	1982	33	Accidental overdose of heroin combined with cocaine
David A. Kennedy, son of U.S. senator Robert F. Kennedy	1984	28	Accidental interaction of cocaine, Demerol, and Mellaril (an antipsychotic medication)
Len Bias, college basketball player	1986	22	Cardiac-respiratory arrest from accidental overdose of cocaine
River Phoenix, actor	1993	23	Cardiac-respiratory arrest from accidental combination of heroin and cocaine
Jonathan Melvoin, keyboardist for The Smashing Pumpkins rock band	1996	34	Accidental overdose of heroin
Chris Farley, comedian and actor	1998	33	Accidental overdose of heroin and cocaine
Dee Dee Ramone, bassist for The Ramones rock band	2002	49	Accidental overdose following an injection of an undisclosed drug of abuse
Steve Bechler, Baltimore Orioles pitcher	2003	23	Multiple organ failure due to heatstroke, suspected to be related to the use of Xenadrine RFA-1, a weight-control dietary supplement containing ephedra
Bobby Hatfield, singer, The Righteous Brothers	2003	63	Heart failure following overdose of cocaine
Mitch Hedberg, comedian	2005	37	Heart failure, related to heroin and cocaine use
Anna Nicole Smith, model and actress	2007	39	Accidental overdose of the sedative-hypnotic choral hydrate, with intestinal flu and bacterial infection being contributing factors
Heath Ledger, actor	2008	28	Acute intoxication from combined use of six prescription medicines for pain, anxiety, insomnia, and nasal congestion
Michael Jackson, songwriter, entertainer	2009	50	Cardiac arrest due to an intravenous administration of the hypnotic drug propofol (brand name: Diprivan), possibly interacting with a number of antianxiety medications
Greg Giraldo, comedian	2010	44	Accidental overdose of prescription medication and alcohol

Note: Celebrities whose drug-related deaths have been attributed to the toxicity of alcohol alone or nicotine, tars, or carbon monoxide in tobacco products are not included in this listing.

Sources: Various media reports.

The DAWN Reports

The U.S. government currently gathers data concerning drug-related medical emergencies in major metropolitan hospitals through a program called the **Drug Abuse Warning Network (DAWN)**. Two basic types of information are reported. The first concerns the number of times an individual visits an emergency department (ED, not

Emergency medical service (EMS) crews frequently have to deal with drug-related cases.

First of all, statistics about ED visits *related to the use of alcohol alone* are limited in the DAWN reporting system to such use by individuals younger than twenty-one years of age. In other words, such medical emergencies are resulting, by definition, from underage drinking. DAWN statistics are not collected for ED visits involving alcohol use alone by individuals who are twenty-one years old or older. There is a very good reason for this exclusion. If all emergencies related to alcohol use alone were reported, the numbers would far exceed those related to any other drug. Considering the enormous number of alcohol-related automobile accidents and alcohol-related personal injuries that end up in emergency departments (see Chapter 13), the examination of ED visits related to other circumstances would be obscured if all alcohol-related ED visits were included.

Second, an important message in the ED-visit statistics is the considerable toxicity resulting from *alcohol-in-combination*. This term refers to the use of

Drug Abuse Warning Network (DAWN): A federal program in which metropolitan hospitals report the incidence of drug-related lethal and nonlethal emergencies.

drug-related ED visit: An occasion on which a person visits an emergency department (ED) for a purpose that is related to recent drug use.

to be confused with the ED used to indicate "effective dose") for any reason that is connected to recent drug use. These **drug-related ED visits** involve a wide range of drug-related situations: suicide attempts, malicious poisoning, overmedication, and adverse reactions to medications, as well as the use of illicit drugs, the use of dietary supplements, and the nonmedical use of prescription or over-the-counter (OTC) drugs. The second type of information concerns the number of drug-related deaths, as determined by a coroner or medical examiner.[1]

Approximately 46 percent of all ED visits in 2008 were associated with either drug abuse or drug misuse. Two-thirds of all *drug-related ED visits* involved an adverse experience with either a prescription or an OTC medication (33 percent), with illicit drugs alone (25 percent) or with a combination of medications and illicit drugs (8 percent). Figure 2.2 shows the distribution of drug-related ED visits due to seven major circumstances.[2]

The proportion of drug-related ED visits involving alcohol use (see Figure 2.2) requires some explanation.

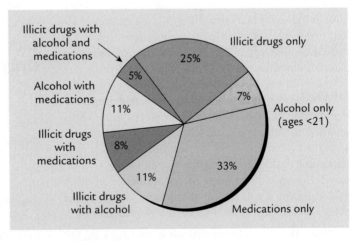

FIGURE 2.2

Drug-related ED visits in 2008, by type of drug involvement.

Source: Substance Abuse and Mental Health Services Administration (2009). *Drug Abuse Warning Network, 2008: Selected tables of national estimates of drug-related emergency department visits.* Rockville, MD: Office of Applied Studies, Substance Abuse and Mental Health Services Administration. Drug combinations.

alcohol in conjunction with another drug, regardless of one's age. About one-fourth (26 percent) of drug-related ED visits in 2008 involved some use of alcohol in combination with an illicit drug, with a prescription or OTC medication, or with an illicit drug and a medication.[3]

Emergencies Related to Illicit Drugs

What types of illicit drugs are most likely to result in an ED visit? In 2008, of the approximately 993,000 illicit-drug-related ED visits, the largest number of cases involved cocaine, followed by marijuana, heroin, stimulants (principally methamphetamine), and PCP, in that order. In general, patients in 2008 were about twice as likely to be male as female in ED visits involving illicit drugs, with the ratio increasing to about six to one in cases involving LSD.[4]

Drug-Related Deaths

Current DAWN statistics on the number of drug-related deaths in the United States are not reported on a nation-wide basis but instead in terms of selected metropolitan areas. While this information prevents us from getting an overall national picture, it does allow us to examine some differences in drug-related problems as they exist in various regions of the country. For example, a similar number of opiate drug-related deaths in 2008 (Figure 2.3) in metropolitan Washington, D.C. and metropolitan San Diego, California (261 versus 245), with respective populations in an almost two-to-one ratio (5.3 million versus 3.0 million), is indicative of a relatively greater opiate drug problem in San Diego rather than an equivalent concern in these two cities. In mathematical terms, we are using two different denominators in arriving at the prevalence rate.

In addition, a particular metropolitan area in the DAWN survey may have a somewhat different drug problem "profile." Cocaine use, for example, is prominently reported in drug-related deaths in most metropolitan areas surveyed in the DAWN report but plays a relatively minor role in drug-related deaths in San Diego, California. Yet, despite differences in the incidence of drug-related deaths across metropolitan areas in the United States, a number of generalizations can be made:

- In nearly all metropolitan areas surveyed in the DAWN report, opiate drugs (predominantly heroin but also including morphine and methadone) and cocaine are the two most frequently reported drugs. In the six representative metropolitan areas shown in Figure 2.3, opiate drugs exceed cocaine in terms of the degree of involvement in a drug-related death. Alcohol (chiefly alcohol in combination with some

other drug but also including alcohol ingested by someone younger than 21 years old) is commonly in third place and almost always in the top five.

- Typically, medications used to treat anxiety and depression are in the top five most frequently reported drugs in drug-related death cases. However, the presence of these categories of licit drugs in the "top five" listing should be interpreted carefully. The amounts ingested in these circumstances either far exceed the recommended dosage levels or have been combined with one or more other drugs.

- In general, it is far more common for drug-related deaths to be a result of multiple-drug (polydrug) use than from single-drug (monodrug) use. Nonetheless, Figure 2.3 clearly shows that a substantial number of deaths result from the single-drug use of opiates and cocaine. In the cases of alcohol, antianxiety medication, and antidepressant medication, it is extremely unusual for a death to result from the use of any of these drugs alone.

- Marijuana is far less prominent in drug-related deaths and, when there are reports of its involvement, it is almost exclusively in the context of multiple-drug rather than single-drug use.

- Methamphetamine use as a cause of a drug-related death is largely underestimated in the DAWN statistics, because of reliance on reports from large metropolitan areas rather than from smaller, rural areas in the United States, where methamphetamine is a significant public health concern (see Chapter 8).[5]

Judging Drug Toxicity from Drug-Related Deaths

The finding that the use of heroin (and other opiate drugs) or cocaine alone is frequently involved in drug-related deaths is particularly striking when you consider the fact that heroin and cocaine users constitute a relatively small proportion of the total number of illicit drug users, and certainly in terms of the general population. The fact that there are more instances of heroin use in drug-related deaths than instances of cocaine use underestimates the potential lethality of heroin, since there are far fewer heroin users than cocaine users in the United States. In contrast, the rare association of marijuana with a drug-related death actually *overestimates* its potential lethality, given its widespread use within a much larger group of people.

In short, a judgment about the relative toxicity of illicit drugs requires an understanding of how frequently a particular drug is used in the general population. All other facts being equal, if one illicit drug produces twice as many

FIGURE 2.3

Drug-related deaths in 2008: A tale of six cities.

Source: Substance Abuse and Mental Health Services Administration (2010). *Drug Abuse Warning Network, 2008: Area profiles of drug-related mortality.* Rockville, MD: Office of Applied Studies, Substance Abuse and Mental Health Services Administration, pp. 51, 63, 108, 121, 162, and 228.

Note: The population in parentheses refers to the population surveyed in the DAWN report. Opiates/opioids refers primarily to heroin.

deaths as a second drug but the number of users of the first drug is twice that of the second, then the toxicity levels of the two drugs should be considered equivalent.

Demographics and Trends

By examining DAWN statistics from 1980 to 2008, we can arrive at some idea of the changes that have taken place in the frequency of medical emergencies over almost three decades of surveys. For example, a dramatic increase in the number of cocaine-related emergencies occurred in the 1980s as a result of the rise of cocaine abuse and crack cocaine abuse. A decade later, an upturn in heroin-related emergencies took place during the 1990s, as the purity of available heroin increased and the availability of heroin use without a needle injection caused heroin-related emergency rates to rise.

Since the mid-1990s, significant concerns have emerged about the increase in ED visits arising from the use of two categories of drugs. One category consists of illicit club drugs that includes Ecstasy, GHB, ketamine, LSD, and methamphetamine. The other category includes opiate-based prescription pain relievers, also known as *narcotic analgesics* (see Chapter 7). Figure 2.4 shows the sharp rise in medical emergencies related to oxycodone (brand name: Percocet) and hydrocodone (brand name: Vicodin) from 1994 to 2002. Later in the chapter, we will review the medical emergencies related to the abuse of prescription stimulant medications and over-the-counter cough-and-cold medications.[6]

From Acute Toxicity to Chronic Toxicity

Through the DAWN surveys, we are able to appreciate the extent of acute toxicity involved in the ingestion of a particular drug, but we are unable to get an illuminating picture of the negative consequences of using a particular drug over a long period of time. Examples of **chronic toxicity** can be found in a wide range of psychoactive drugs, either legally or illegally obtained. Ironically, it is the chronic use of alcohol and tobacco, both of which are legally available in our society, that

chronic toxicity: The physical or psychological harm a drug might cause over a long period of use.

FIGURE 2.4

Trends in drug-related ED visits involving hydrocodone and oxycodone, 1994–2002.

Note: Under a new DAWN reporting system initiated in 2004, there were approximately 89,000 ED visits in 2008 due to the use of hydrocodone/combinations and 105,000 ED visits due to the use of oxycodone/combinations.

Source: Substance Abuse and Mental Health Administration (2004, July). Oxycodone, hydrocodone, and polydrug use, 2002. *DAWN Report*, p. 1. Substance Abuse and Mental Health Services Administration (2009). *Drug Abuse Warning Network*, 2008. *Selected tables of national estimates of drug-related emergency department visits*. Rockville, MD: Office of Applied Studies, Substance Abuse and Mental Health Services Administration, Table: ED visits by drug.

causes by far the greatest adverse health effects. As we will see in Chapters 13 and 14, the number of people who die each year as a result of drinking alcohol or smoking tobacco far outstrips the number of fatalities from the abuse of illicit drugs (Figure 2.5).

A number of important issues with respect to drug-taking behavior will be examined in the chapters ahead. What exactly are the problems associated with *chronic* drug use? What is the most productive way of looking at drug dependence in general? How has our society responded to the problems of drug-taking behavior over the years? How successful have we been in dealing with these problems? What new strategies are there to handle drug-related problems in a more effective way?

Patterns of Drug Use in the United States

How is it possible to obtain information that would give us a statistical picture of drug-taking behavior today? Assuming that we cannot conduct large-scale random

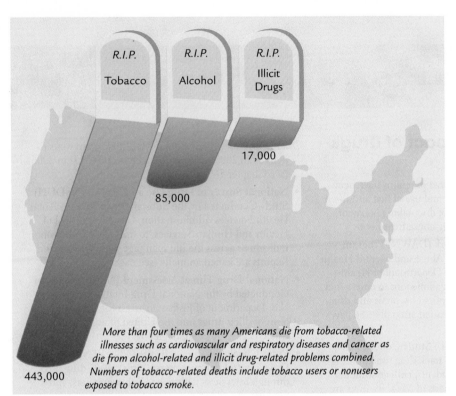

FIGURE 2.5

U.S. deaths per year from tobacco, alcohol, and illicit drug use.

Sources: Centers for Disease Control and Prevention (2008, November 14). Cigarette smoking-attributable morbidity, years of potential life lost, and productivity losses—United States, 2000-2004. *Morbidity and Mortality Weekly Report, 57,* 1226-1228. Mokdad, Ali H.; Marks, James S.; Stroup, Donna F.; and Gerberding, Julie L. (2004). Actual causes of death in the United States, 2000. *Journal of the American Medical Association, 291,* 1238-1245.

More than four times as many Americans die from tobacco-related illnesses such as cardiovascular and respiratory diseases and cancer as die from alcohol-related and illicit drug-related problems combined. Numbers of tobacco-related deaths include tobacco users or nonusers exposed to tobacco smoke.

drug testing, the only alternative we have is simply to ask people about their drug-taking behavior through self-reports. We encourage honesty and arrange the data-collection procedure so as to convince the respondents that their answers are confidential, but the fact remains that any questionnaire is inherently imperfect because there is no way to verify the truthfulness of what people say about themselves. Nevertheless, questionnaires are all we have, and the statistics on drug use are based on such survey measures (Drugs . . . in Focus).

One of the best-known surveys, referred to as the Monitoring the Future study, has been conducted every year since 1975 by the University of Michigan. Typically, nearly fifty thousand American students in the eighth, tenth, and twelfth grades participate in a nationally representative sampling each year, as well as more than seven thousand college students and young adults between the ages of nineteen and thirty-two (with the upper limit recently being extended to fifty).

The advantage of repeating the survey with a new sample year after year is that it enables us to look at trends in drug-taking behavior over time and compare the use of one drug relative to another. We can assume that the degree of overreporting and underreporting stays relatively constant over the years and does not affect the interpretation of the general trends.

Since the surveys are conducted in schools, high school dropouts are unavailable as respondents. This group represents roughly 15 percent of the potential high school graduates each year, according to U.S. Census statistics. As a result, it is conceivable that the interpretation of specific prevalence rates for various forms of drug-taking behavior may be underestimated. Recent analyses by researchers at the University of Michigan have indicated that rates would be slightly higher if dropouts were included, particularly for the most dangerous drugs such as heroin, crack cocaine, and PCP, the use of which is highly correlated with educational aspirations and attainment. However, we can assume that this bias would be relatively constant over time, so an analysis of trends in prevalence rates from year to year can still be made.[7]

Survey questions concerning drug use have been phrased in four basic ways:

- Whether an individual has ever used a certain drug in his or her lifetime
- Whether an individual has used a certain drug over the previous year
- Whether an individual has used a certain drug within the previous thirty days
- Whether an individual has used a certain drug on a *daily* basis during the previous thirty days

Drugs... in Focus

Measuring the Impact of Drugs on Our Society

A number of government-sponsored programs have been instituted to track the availability and use of licit and illicit drugs, the health consequences of drug-taking behavior, drug-trafficking patterns, and drug-abuse treatment.

- **Drug Abuse Warning Network (DAWN) Program** Conducted by the Substance Abuse and Mental Health Services Administration, U.S. Department of Health and Human Services, to track admissions to emergency departments of major metropolitan hospitals and drug-related facilities. Reports are issued annually (see pages 33–46).

- **Monitoring the Future (MTF) Study** Conducted by the University of Michigan to track drug use and drug attitudes among secondary students, college students, and young adults. Annual reports of MTF findings are released in December through a press release. More extensive statistical information is published in the following year (see pages 37–43).

- **Arrestee Drug Abuse Monitoring II (ADAM II) Program** Conducted by the National Institute of Justice, U.S. Department of Justice, to track the prevalence of ten illicit drugs (including methamphetamine, cocaine, heroin, and marijuana) through urine tests among male adult arrestees. The original ADAM program was suspended in 2003 and reintroduced as ADAM II in 2006 (see Chapter 5).

- **National Survey of Drug Use and Health (NSDUH) Study** Conducted by the Substance Abuse and Mental Health Services Administration, U.S. Department of Health and Human Services, to track drug use among individuals across the life span (age twelve or older). Reports are issued annually (see page 43).

- **National Drug Threat Assessment (NDTA) Program** Conducted by the National Drug Intelligence Center, U.S. Department of Justice, to assess the trafficking patterns of illicit drugs into the United States. Reports are issued each year (see Chapter 5).

- **Pulse Check** Conducted by the Office of National Drug Control Policy to assess "street level" drug use through interviews with police, ethnographers, and treatment providers in major metropolitan areas. Reports are issued semiannually.

- **Treatment Episode Data Set (TEDS) Program** Conducted by the Substance Abuse and Mental Health Services Administration, U.S. Department of Health and Human Services, to track demographic and substance abuse characteristics of individuals admitted to (and discharged from) substance abuse treatment facilities. Reports are issued annually (see Chapter 16).

You can see that these questions distinguish three important degrees of involvement with a given drug. The first question focuses on the extent of experimentation, including individuals who may have taken a drug only once or twice in their lives and who have stayed away from it ever since. The second and third questions focus on the extent of current but moderate drug use, while the fourth question focuses on the extent of heavy drug use. What do the numbers tell us?

Illicit Drug Use among High School Seniors

We are naturally concerned with any level of drug-taking behavior among U.S. high school seniors, but it is at least encouraging to know that 2009 statistics of drug use have declined from prevalence levels in the late 1990s and are substantially lower than they were at the end of the 1970s. Here are a few examples of where we are today and where we were at an earlier time (Figure 2.6).

- In 2009, 37 percent of high school seniors reported use of an illicit drug during the past year, less than the 54 percent reporting such use in the peak year of 1979.

- In 2009, 33 percent of seniors reported marijuana use during the past year, less than the 51 percent reporting such use in 1979.

- Cocaine use during the past year was reported by 3 percent of the seniors, less than one-fourth the number reporting such behavior in the peak year of 1985.

- Nonmedical use of inhalants has held steady at between 3 and 5 percent since 2001, about one-half the number reporting such behavior in the mid-1990s.

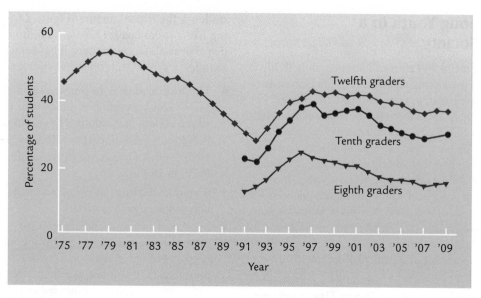

FIGURE 2.6

Trends in annual prevalence of illicit drug use among eighth, tenth, and twelfth graders.

Source: Johnston, Lloyd D.; O'Malley, Patrick M.; Bachman, Jerald G.; and Schulenberg, John E. (2009, December 14). Teen marijuana use tilts up, while some drugs decline in use. University of Michigan News Service, Ann Arbor, Figure 1.

Despite the reduction in prevalence rates, however, the absolute percentages in 2009 are still substantial. They indicate that more than one out of three high school seniors used some form of illicit drug over the last twelve months, with marijuana being by far the most frequently consumed illicit drug. About one in thirty had used cocaine, and about one in twenty-five had used inhalants on a nonmedical basis.[8]

Illicit Drug Use among Eighth Graders and Tenth Graders

Since 1991, we have collected extensive survey information about illicit drug use among students as early as the eighth grade. As Figure 2.7 shows, the upward trend in the percentages of drug use among eighth and tenth graders from 1991 to 1996 paralleled a similar trend among high school seniors. At the time, the data from these two groups reflected a level of drug involvement that was quite alarming. Drug-abuse professionals were concerned about the potentially negative effect on still younger children, as they observed the drug-taking behavior of their older brothers and sisters. Fortunately, the upward trend among the eighth graders in several categories has reversed its course substantially since 1996 (Table 2.1), as has been the case among tenth graders to a somewhat lesser degree.[9] It is

TABLE 2.1

Percentage of drug use among eighth graders, 2009

	2009	CHANGE SINCE 1996
Been drunk in past year	12.2	38% down
Marijuana in past year	11.8	36% down
Cocaine in past year	1.6	47% down
Amphetamines in the past year	4.1	45% down
Inhalants in past year	8.1	34% down
Use of cigarettes in past 30 days	6.5	69% down
Daily use of cigarettes	2.7	74% down

Source: Johnston, Lloyd D.; O'Malley, Patrick M.; Bachman, Jerald G.; and Schulenberg, John E. (2009, December 14). Teen marijuana use tilts up, while some drugs decline in use. University of Michigan News Service, Ann Arbor, Tables 2, 3, and 4.

now expected that in the years ahead, as eighth graders progress through high school, their increasing disinclination toward drug use will be reflected in declining prevalence rates among older secondary school students.

Drugs among Youth in a Diverse Society

In looking at racial and ethnic differences in both illicit and licit drug use among adolescents in the University of Michigan survey, certain consistent patterns emerge. For eight major categories of drugs (marijuana, inhalants, hallucinogens, LSD, Ecstasy, cocaine, crack cocaine, and non-injected heroin), drug use among African American seniors is lower than that among white students. In addition, levels of daily cigarette smoking and binge drinking among African American seniors are substantially below those of white students. A comparison of African American, Hispanic/Latino, and white seniors (Table 2.2) shows that Hispanic/Latino seniors have the highest annual prevalence rate of use of crack cocaine.[10]

Understanding Illicit Drug Use among Adolescents, 1975–2009

Over more than three decades of tracking the prevalence rate of illicit drug use among secondary school

TABLE 2.2

Percentages of white, African American, and Hispanic/Latino high school seniors who used a particular drug or engaged in a drug-related behavior in the past year

	WHITE	AFRICAN AMERICAN	HISPANIC/ LATINO
Marijuana	34.3	28.6.	28.8
Inhalants	4.1	1.6	3.0
Hallucinogens	6.3	1.2	3.3
LSD	2.6	0.7	1.3
Ecstasy	4.6	2.4	3.9
Cocaine	4.4	0.7	4.0
Crack cocaine	1.4	0.9	1.6
Heroin (no needle)	0.6	0.3	0.4
Binge drinking (in last two weeks)	29.0	12.0	22.6
Daily cigarettes	13.9	5.4	6.4

Source: Johnston, Lloyd D.; O'Malley, Patrick M.; Bachman, Jerald G.; and Schulenberg, John E. (2010). Data from 2008 and 2009 surveys combined. *Monitoring the Future: National survey results on drug use, 1975–2009. Volume 1: Secondary school students 2009*. Rockville, MD: National Institute on Drug Abuse, Tables 4-6 and 4.-8.

students, the overall picture (Figure 2.6) ends up looking like a roller-coaster ride (which, from the perspective of drug-abuse researchers, it has been indeed). Here are a few essential features to help put it all together:

- The historical peak in prevalence rates occurred in 1979. This was followed by a steep decline in the 1980s, ending in a historical low point in 1992.
- Prevalence rates started to climb again in the early 1990s, reaching another peak (smaller than that of 1979) in 1997.
- A gradual decline has occurred since 1997, particularly among eighth graders.
- In general, as you would expect, changes in the trend of prevalence rates among high school seniors have been preceded a few years earlier by the shifting prevalence rates among eighth graders. Rates among eighth graders can be considered as a "leading indicator" of future rates in older students.

Drug Use among College Students and Young Adults

The University of Michigan survey also offers insight into drug use among college students and young adults. Compared to high school seniors, college students report roughly equivalent annual prevalence rates in the use of illicit drugs in general (36 percent for college students versus 37 percent for high school seniors). A prominent exception is marijuana, where the prevalence rate among college students is higher. Table 2.3 shows the lifetime, past-year, and past-month prevalence rates among college students with respect to five major types of illicit drugs.[11]

When you examine the drug-taking behavior of young adults (not necessarily college students) by tracking them at two-year intervals for as long as fourteen years after graduating from high school, an interesting pattern emerges. Evidently, the new freedoms of young adulthood initially lead to an increase in substance use for some individuals. Not surprisingly, those young adults who frequently go out at night for fun and recreation are the ones who are most likely to drink heavily, smoke heavily, and use illicit drugs. As these people grow older, these relationships weaken. The link between going out and cigarette smoking, for example, virtually disappears by the time they are in their late twenties and early thirties. On average, drug use at these ages drops substantially from levels reported in high school, as young adults begin making personal commitments, marrying, and starting families.

TABLE 2.3

Percentage of illicit drug use among college students, aged 19-22

	EVER IN LIFETIME	IN PAST TWELVE MONTHS	IN PAST THIRTY DAYS
Marijuana	47.50	32.8	18.5
Hallucinogens	8.01	4.7	1.0
Cocaine	8.15	4.2	1.3
Crack cocaine	1.03	0.3	0.1
Heroin	0.85	0.2	0.1

Source: Johnston, Lloyd D.; O'Malley, Patrick M.; Bachman, Jerald, G.; and Schulenberg, John E. (2010). Monitoring the Future: National survey results on drug use, 1975–2009. Vol. II: College students and adults ages 19–50. Bethesda, MD: National Institute on Drug Abuse, Tables 2-1, 2-2, and 2-3.

Not surprisingly, non-drug-using wives have a major influence in reducing their husbands' level of drug use. Personal setbacks such as divorces, however, produce an increase in drug use, often to the same levels as when they were in high school. In other words, in hard times, an individual will revert to old patterns of drug-taking behavior.[12]

Patterns of Alcohol Use

Not surprisingly, the prevalence percentages related to the use of alcohol are much higher than for illicit drugs. While 23 percent of high school seniors in 2009 reported use of illicit drugs in the past month, almost half (44 percent) drank an alcoholic beverage, with 25 percent reporting an instance of *binge drinking*, defined as having five or more drinks in a row at least once in the past two weeks. These figures are down substantially from those found in surveys conducted in 1980, when 72 percent of high school seniors reported that they had consumed alcohol in the past month, and 41 percent reported binge drinking.

One explanation for the decline from 1980 to 2009 is the reduced accessibility to alcohol for this age group, with all U.S. states now having adopted a 21-year-or-older requirement. Despite the long-term downward trend and a suggestion of further decline in alcohol use in recent years, however, the present level of alcohol consumption among high school seniors remains a matter of great concern. Alcohol consumption on a regular basis is widespread for individuals in

this age group despite the fact that it is officially illegal for any of them to purchase alcoholic beverages (Chapter 12). Efforts to reduce underage drinking by enforcing restrictions of alcohol sales to minors, unfortunately, have met with only partial success. In 2009, 62 percent of eighth graders found it "fairly easy" or "very easy" to obtain alcohol beverages, down from 76 percent in 1992. About 92 percent of seniors reported the same, a judgment that had not changed since 1992. The drinking habits of college students, however, have shown relatively little change since the mid-1990s. In 2009, 66 percent of college students surveyed drank at least once in the past month, and 40 percent reported an instance of binge drinking at least once in the past two weeks. [13]

Patterns of Tobacco Use

Roughly 11 percent of high school seniors in 2009 had established a regular habit of nicotine intake by smoking at least one cigarette every day. In fact, nicotine remains the drug most frequently used on a daily basis by high school students, although present-day rates are substantially lower than those observed in 1977, when more than twice as many high school seniors (29 percent) smoked cigarettes. From the mid-1990s, there had been a steady decline in smoking rates in eighth and tenth graders as well as seniors, owing to the national attention directed towards cigarette smoking among young people. Nonetheless, in 2009, about 5 percent of seniors and 2 percent of tenth graders reported smoking at least a half-pack of cigarettes per day, a strikingly high level for these age groups, considering the legal obstacles they face when attempting to obtain cigarettes.[14]

Somewhat fewer college students smoke cigarettes than high school seniors. The reason is not a matter of a change in smoking behavior from high school to college, but rather reflects differences between the two populations. Non-college-bound seniors are about three times more likely than college-bound seniors to smoke at least a half-pack of cigarettes per day. Therefore, the difference in smoking rates between seniors and college students is chiefly a result of excluding the heavier smokers in the survey as students progress from secondary to postsecondary education. In 2009, about 8 percent of college students smoked cigarettes on a daily basis, with about 4 percent smoking more than half a pack per day.[15]

Perceived Risk and Drug Use

To understand the changing patterns of drug use among young people over the years and what trends might unfold in the future, it is helpful to look at their *perception of the risks involved in drug use* during the same span of time. A troubling trend reflected in the University of Michigan surveys during the 1990s was the steady decline in the percentages of high school students, college students, and young adults who regarded regular drug use as potentially dangerous. These responses contrasted with reports beginning in 1978 that had shown a steady increase in such percentages (Figure 2.7). A spokesperson for the 1996 Michigan survey offered one possible reason for this reversal:

> *This most recent crop of youngsters grew up in a period in which drug use rates were down substantially from what they had been 10 to 15 years earlier. This gave youngsters less opportunity to learn from others' mistakes and resulted in what I call "generational forgetting" of the hazards of drugs.*[16]

Also troubling during much of the 1990s were changes in the way our society dealt with the potential risks of drug use. Drug abuse prevention programs in schools were scaled back or eliminated because of a lack of federal funding, parents were communicating less with their children about drug use, anti-drug public service messages were less prominent in the media than they were in the 1980s, and media coverage in this area declined. At the same time, the cultural influences of the music and entertainment industry were, at best, ambivalent on the question of drug-taking behavior, particularly with respect to marijuana smoking (see Chapter 10). All these elements can be seen as having contributed to the upward trend in drug use during this period.

The reciprocal relationship between perceived risk of harm in regular drug use and the likelihood of drug use itself is clear in Figure 2.7, in the case of marijuana smoking trends across a span of more than thirty years. For the most part, the percentages who consider marijuana smoking as presenting a great risk form a *mirror image of*

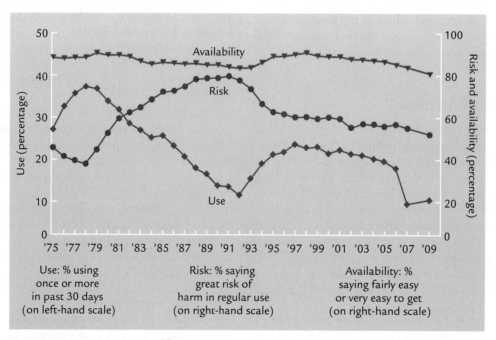

FIGURE 2.7

Trends in perceived availability of marijuana, perceived risk of marijuana use, and prevalence of marijuana use in the past month for high school seniors.

Source: Johnston, Lloyd D.; O'Malley, Patrick M.; Bachman, Jerald G.; and Schulenberg, John E. (2009, December 14). Teen marijuana use tilts up, while some drugs decline in use. University of Michigan News Service, Ann Arbor, Tables 3, 7, and 13.

TABLE 2.4

Illicit drug use during the past year among persons in the United States age twenty-six or older in 2009

	ESTIMATED NUMBERS OF USERS
Any illicit drug	21,052,000
Marijuana and hashish	14,923,000
Cocaine	2,784,000
Crack	818,000
Heroin	395,000
Hallucinogens	1,395,000
LSD	122,000
Ecstasy	935,000
Methamphetamine	779,000
Inhalants	508,000
Nonmedical use of any psychotherapeutic medication (not including over-the-counter drugs)	9,093,000
Pain relievers	6,788,000
OxyContin	695,000
Antianxiety medications	3,213,000
Sedatives	526,000
Any illicit drug other than marijuana	11,513,000

Source: Substance Abuse and Mental Health Services Administration (2010). *Results from the 2009 National Survey on Drug Use and Health: National findings. Detailed tables.* Rockville, MD: Office of Applied Studies, Substance Abuse and Mental Health Services Administration, Tables 1.7A and 1.8A.

the percentages who report smoking marijuana at least once in the past month.[17]

Patterns of Illicit Drug Use in Adults Aged Twenty-Six and Older

A comprehensive examination of the prevalence rates of illicit drug use among Americans in several age groups across the life span has been accomplished by the National Survey on Drug Use and Health (formerly the National Household Survey on Drug Abuse). Table 2.4 shows the percentages of illicit drug use among persons aged twenty-six or older in 2009. About 11 percent of this population (more than 21 million people) reported using an illicit drug over the past twelve months, about 7 percent (nearly 15 million people) used marijuana or hashish, and about 5 percent (more than 9 million people) engaged in the nonmedical (recreational) use of a prescription-type pain reliever, tranquilizer, stimulant, or sedative. As with the results of the University of Michigan survey, however, there are some limitations to the interpretation of these estimates. Patients institutionalized for either medical or psychiatric treatment as well as homeless people are not included in the collection of sample data.[18]

Looking to the Future and Learning from the Past

What does the future hold with respect to drug-taking behavior and problems associated with it? Where should we direct our concerns? Predictions are always tricky to make, but with regard to drug-taking behavior there are historical patterns that can serve as guides.

Old Drugs, New Drugs

One certainty is that specific drugs will continue to come into and fall out of favor. New drugs will appear on the scene, and others may reappear like ghosts from the past, sometimes in new forms and involving new faces in the drug underground. As one researcher has pointed out, "There is always something old and something new in the U.S. drug scene."[19]

As cocaine, for example, has declined in popularity in the United States since the 1990s, heroin has reemerged as a major drug of abuse. During this time, the distribution of injectable heroin has been supplemented by a more potent blend that could be snorted like powder cocaine or smoked like crack cocaine. On the one hand, these new forms of drug-taking behavior are safer, circumventing the traditional need for a hypodermic syringe and the associated dangers of being infected by nonsterile needles. As a result, the possibility of becoming infected with hepatitis or the virus responsible for acquired immunodeficiency syndrome (AIDS) is avoided. On the other hand, new populations of people who had been turned off by heroin because of their fear of needles have been introduced to it for the first time.[20]

LSD and other hallucinogens, once the darlings of the psychedelic generation in the 1960s, have staged a comeback during this period of time as well.

Club Drugs

A serious concern in today's drug scene has been the popularity of "club drugs," a term referring to substances typically ingested at all-night dance parties ("raves"), dance clubs, and bars. Examples of club drugs include MDMA (Ecstasy), GHB, ketamine, Rohypnol, methamphetamine, and LSD. When used in combination with alcohol, as they often are, these drugs carry considerably increased health risks, beyond their own individual toxicities. Since many club drugs are colorless, tasteless, and odorless, they can be slipped unobtrusively into drinks by individuals who want to intoxicate or sedate others. The potential danger of sexual assault, therefore, is a major problem.[21] Drugs… in Focus examines the major features of these six club drugs. A more detailed discussion will follow in Chapter 8 (methamphetamine), Chapter 9 (LSD, MDMA, and ketamine), and Chapter 11 (GHB and Rohypnol).

Drugs… in Focus

Facts about Club Drugs

MDMA (methylenedioxymethamphetamine)

- Street names: Ecstasy, XTC, X, E, Adam, Clarity, Lover's Speed, Hug Drug, Euphoria, M&M
- Variations: MDA (methylenedioxyamphetamine), MDEA (methylenedioxyethylamphetamine)
- Forms: Tablet or capsule
- Drug type: Stimulant and hallucinogen
- Behavioral effects: Appetite suppression, excitation, perceptual distortions
- Physiological effects: Increased heart rate and blood pressure, dehydration
- Length of effect: 3 to 6 hours
- Toxicity: Marked increase in body temperature; possible heart attack, stroke, or seizure (see Chapter 8)

GHB (gamma-hydroxybutyrate)

- Street names: Grievous Bodily Harm, G, Liquid X, Liquid Ecstasy, Georgia Home Boy, Goop Soup
- Variations: Gamma-butyrolactone (GBL)
- Forms: Clear liquid, tablet, capsule, or white powder

- Drug type: Depressant
- Behavioral effects: Intoxication, euphoria, sedation, anxiety reduction
- Physiological effects: Central nervous system depressant, stimulation of growth-hormone release
- Length of effect: Up to 4 hours
- Toxicity: Overdoses produce drowsiness, loss of consciousness, impaired breathing, coma, potential death. GHB greatly potentiates the sedative action of alcohol (see Chapter 11).

Ketamine

- Street names: K, Special K, Vitamin K, Ket
- Variations: None
- Forms: Liquid, white powder snorted or smoked with marijuana or tobacco, intramuscular injection
- Drug type: Hallucinogen
- Behavioral effects: Dream-like state of consciousness, hallucinations
- Physiological effects: Increased blood pressure, potential seizures, and coma
- Length of effect: 1 hour

- Toxicity: Impaired attention and memory, impaired motor coordination, disorientation (see Chapter 9)

Rohypnol (flunitrazepam)
- Street names: Roofies, Rophies, Roche, Rope, Forget-me pill
- Variations: None
- Forms: Tablet dissolvable in beverages
- Drug type: Antianxiety drug
- Behavioral effects: Sedation
- Physiological effects: Decreased blood pressure, visual disturbances, gastrointestinal disturbances
- Length of effect: 8 to 12 hours
- Toxicity: Anterograde amnesia (loss of memory for events experienced under its influence). Rohypnol effects are greatly potentiated by alcohol (see Chapter 11).

Methamphetamine
- Street names: Speed, Ice, Meth, Crystal, Crystal Meth, Crank, Fire, Glass, Ice, Rock Candy
- Variations: Amphetamines, with varying degrees of similarity
- Forms: Many forms; methamphetamine can be smoked, snorted, injected, or orally ingested.

- Drug type: Stimulant
- Behavioral effects: Increased alertness and energy
- Physiological effects: Increased heart rate and blood pressure, decreased appetite
- Length of effect: Several hours
- Toxicity: Possible heart attack or cardiovascular collapse, seizures, cerebral hemorrhage, and coma (see Chapter 8)

LSD (lysergic acid diethylamide)
- Street names: Acid, Boomers, Yellow Sunshines, Barrels, Blotters, Cubes, Domes, Lids, Wedges
- Variations: Hallucinogens, with varying degrees of similarity
- Forms: Crystalline material soluble in water
- Drug type: Hallucinogen
- Behavioral effects: Distortions of visual perceptions, distortions of time and space
- Physiological effects: Increased heart rate and blood pressure, sweating, tremors
- Length of effect: 30 to 90 minutes, though effects might last several hours
- Toxicity: Numbness, nausea (see Chapter 9)

Sources: Brands, Bruna, Sproule, Beth, and Marshman, Joan (1998). *Drugs and drug abuse: A reference text.* Toronto: Addiction Research Foundation. Ricaurte, George A., and McConn, Una D. (2005). Recognition and management of complications of new recreational drug use. *Lancet, 365,* 2137–2145.

Nonmedical Use of Prescription Pain Relievers

Although present-day prevalence rates among adolescents and young adults for several categories of illicit drugs are much lower than rates observed in the late 1990s (see Figure 2.2), the incidence of nonmedical (recreational) use of prescription pain relievers has remained at relatively high levels and has become a major social problem. In the U.S. in 2009, about four million young adults, aged 18 to 25 years, had used prescription pain relievers on a recreational basis in the past year; about 1.6 million used them on a recreational basis during the previous month.[22] Hydrocodone (brand name: Vicodin), oxycodone (brand names: Percodan, Percocet), and sustained-release oxycodone (brand name: OxyContin) have been the principal drugs involved (see Chapter 7).

A related problem concerns the "extramedical" (outside medical) use of prescription pain relievers, available until recently with ease through Internet pharmacies. Individuals obtaining Vicodin and other prescription pain relievers are not necessarily using the drugs for recreational purposes; they are essentially self-medicating, without medical supervision. Unfortunately, this practice can have dangerous consequences (Portrait).

Nonmedical Use of Prescription Stimulant Medications

For decades, individuals with attention deficit disorder (ADD) have been successfully treated with a number of prescription stimulant medications, principally methylphenidate (brand name: Ritalin) and a combination of dextroamphetamine and levoamphetamine

In 2001, Ryan Haight, a multi-sport athlete and A student from La Mesa, California, died at the age of 18 of an overdose of Vicodin he had obtained over the Internet. He had no intention of using Vicodin for recreational purposes; the purpose was to help him deal with back pain he had been suffering. He had secretly placed the order after claiming in an online questionnaire to be a 25-year-old with back pain (he would not have been able to order the drug if he had admitted to being younger than 21 years of age).

"Just the night before," his mother Francine Haight (see photo above), a registered nurse, remembers: "We had dinner together after he came home from work at a nearby retail store. He used my Jacuzzi tub because he said his back bothered him from lifting things at work... After one of his friends told us he got them [Vicodin tablets] off the Internet, we gave our computer to the DEA [Drug Enforcement Administration] to investigate."

Ryan had never seen a doctor about his back, yet he got the drug delivered to his home in a matter of days. To her amazement, his mother later found hundreds of Internet pharmacy Web sites selling controlled substances that included generic versions of OxyContin and Vicodin as well as antianxiety medications like Xanax and Valium and stimulants like Ritalin and Adderall—all without the usual requirement of a written medical prescription. She decided to create a Web site of her own, dedicated to the memory of young people like her son who have died from prescription drug overdose, and she set about persuading lawmakers of the need to curb the dangerous proliferation of Internet pharmacies.

The Ryan Haight Online Pharmacy Consumer Protection Act was signed into law in 2008 and implemented in 2009. It stipulates that a doctor must conduct a face-to-face examination of a patient before dispensing any medication for a legitimate medical condition. Internet pharmacies are not illegal, but they must post truthful information as to their physical location, the license numbers of their pharmacists, and get an additional endorsement from the DEA in order to conduct business over the Internet, even if the pharmacy already exists as a brick-and-mortar establishment. The Act also makes it a crime to use the Internet to advertise the illegal sale of a controlled substance (Chapter 1). Penalties for violations of the Ryan Haight Act of up to twenty years in prison can be imposed. It is also easier now for states' attorneys general to prosecute violations committed by online pharmacies outside their states. This is a particular problem inherent in transactions carried by Internet businesses.

Prior to the enactment of the Ryan Haight Act, the DEA found that 85 percent of all Internet prescription sales involved controlled substances, in comparison to 11 percent of prescriptions filled by regular pharmacies. It is evident that online sales were particularly suited to encourage drug misuse.

Speaking on behalf of the DEA, Acting Administrator Michele M. Leonhart has expressed her strong support for this new regulatory authority: "Cyber-criminals illegally peddling controlled substances over the Internet have invaded households and threatened America's youth for far too long by supplying pharmaceuticals with a few clicks of a mouse and a credit card number. This landmark piece of legislation will bring rogue pharmacy operators out of the shadows by establishing a clear standard for legitimate online pharmaceutical sales."

Sources: Eckholm, Erik (2008, July 9). Abuses are found in online sales of medications. *New York Times.* Quotations from McKenna, Corey (2008, October 2). Ryan Haight Act will require tighter restrictions on Internet Pharmacies. *Government Technology.* www.govtech.com/gt/419355. McKenna, Corey (2009, April 15). New rules implement Ryan Haight Act. *Government Technology.* www.govtech.com/gt/639985.

(brand name: Adderall). A growing concern, however, has centered around two principal forms of drug misuse. The first is the practice of taking these drugs at higher doses than prescribed or combining them with alcohol. The second is the practice of diverting these drugs, that is transferring the medication of one patient for whom it is prescribed to another individual for whom it is not prescribed, either by selling them or giving them away to friends. Nonmedical use of Adderall is of special interest due to its potential for dependence and abuse (see Chapter 8). Approximately one out of sixteen full-time college students (6.4 percent) in surveys conducted during 2006 and 2007 reported nonmedical use of Adderall during the past year.[23] In these cases, the drug-taking behavior has been either recreational (to achieve a state of euphoria) or instrumental (to be able to study late into the night).

Nonmedical Use of Nonprescription Cough-and-Cold Medications

Approximately 6 percent of high school seniors reported in 2009 taking OTC cough-and-cold medications, such as Coricidin HBP Cough and Cold Tablets, Robitussin products, and NyQuil, containing the cough suppressant dextromethorphan (abbreviated DXM) in the past year for the purpose of getting high, a practice commonly referred to as "robo-tripping" or "skittling." In 2006, nearly 1 million individuals between twelve and twenty-five years of age were estimated to have misused OTC dextromethorphan products in the previous year. The alcohol content (up to 10 percent) in many of these products compounds the health-related problems. The easy availability of dextromethorphan for people of all ages and the increased risk of brain damage, seizure, and death associated with high doses of dextromethorphan are matters of great concern in today's drug scene.[24]

Why Drugs?

As will be seen in the next chapter, drug-taking behavior has been around for a very long time. Given this history, it is safe to say that there will always be an attraction to the drug experience. We can make this prediction on the basis of understanding the character of psychoactive drugs themselves, namely their ability to cause an alteration in consciousness. For a time, they can make us feel euphoric, light-headed, relaxed, or powerful, and there is little doubt that all this feels good. There may be other non-pharmacological ways of arriving at these states of mind, but drugs are easy and quick. They also seem to increase awareness of the environment and give the impression of a feeling that we are seeing or hearing things in a more intense way. No matter whether we are young or old, rich or poor, drugs can allow us to retreat from an uncomfortable environment, to feel no pain.

Unfortunately, in every generation there will be young people who are alienated from their families and the community of adults around them, who will be attracted to groups of people who are going through a similar experience. They will seek some form of temporary release from an unhappy existence. There will be a younger generation seeking some form of rebellion against traditional values. And there will be adolescents who will use drugs simply to have a good time with their friends.

Despite our best efforts to prevent it from happening, there will be young people who are simply willing to try anything new, including drugs. Their curiosity to find out "what it's like" is a motivation that dates back to the earliest times in human history, when we nibbled on the plants in the field just to find out how they tasted. In the modern era, drug experimentation is neither a new nor a singular phenomenon; it can involve an alcoholic drink, an inhaled solvent from some household product, a cigarette, or an illicit drug. The next two chapters will concern the historical and theoretical perspectives on the phenomenon of drug-taking behavior.

Summary

The Problem of Drug Toxicity

- A drug's harmful effects are referred to as its toxicity. Acute toxicity can be measured in terms of either a drug's therapeutic index or its margin of safety, each of which can be computed from its effective dose-response and lethal dose-response curves.

The DAWN Reports

- Drug Abuse Warning Network (DAWN) statistics, which reflect drug-related lethal and nonlethal emergencies in major metropolitan hospitals in the United States, offer another measure of acute drug toxicity. In general, DAWN statistics show that opiate-based drugs (primarily heroin) and cocaine are both highly toxic and that many emergencies involve drugs being taken in combination with alcohol. There are also recent concerns about the increasing number of emergencies associated with club drugs and prescription pain relievers.

Patterns of Drug Use in the United States

- Surveys of illicit drug use among high school seniors in 2009 have shown that over the last twelve months, 37 percent of seniors used an illicit drug, 33 percent smoked marijuana, and 3 percent used cocaine.
- During the 1990s, marijuana use among high school seniors rose significantly, as did the use of other illicit drugs. Since 1997, however, there has been a steady decline in illicit drug use among eighth and tenth graders.

- Drug use in general and the use of individual psychoactive drugs vary greatly along racial and ethnic lines.
- The prevalence rate in 2009 for alcohol use in the past month among high school seniors was 44 percent and among college students was 66 percent. Roughly 11 percent of high school seniors and 8 percent of college students smoked at least one cigarette every day in 2009.
- Over the last thirty years or so, the prevalence trends for regular drug use and perceived risk form an almost exact mirror image to each other. As perceived risk goes up, the level of regular drug use goes down.
- In 2009, more than 21 million Americans aged twenty-six or older had used an illicit drug of some kind during the past twelve months. Nearly 15 million Americans used marijuana or hashish, and more than 9 million Americans engaged in the recreational use of a prescription pain reliever during this time period.

Looking to the Future and Learning from the Past

- Predictions regarding future drugs and drug-taking behaviors are largely founded on patterns from the past. New drugs will undoubtedly come on the scene; old drugs that are out of favor might regain popularity.
- A serious concern in recent years has been the emergence of recreational drug use involving a group of drugs referred to as club drugs. These drugs include MDMA (Ecstasy), GHB, ketamine, Rohypnol, methamphetamine, and LSD.
- Relatively high prevalence rates for recreational use of prescription drugs and over-the-counter (OTC) drugs among young people have raised serious concerns. Examples of abused drugs in this category include pain medications such as Vicodin and OxyContin, stimulant medications normally prescribed for individuals diagnosed with Attention Deficit Disorder (ADD), and dextromethorphan in popular cough-and-cold remedies.

Key Terms

acute toxicity, p. 29	dose-response curve, p. 29	drug-related ED visit, p. 33	margin of safety, p. 30
chronic toxicity, p. 36	Drug Abuse Warning	effective dose (ED), p. 29	therapeutic index, p. 30
dose, p. 29	Network (DAWN), p. 33	lethal dose (LD), p. 30	toxicity, p. 29

Endnotes

1. Substance Abuse and Mental Health Services Administration (2009)., *Drug Abuse Warning Network 2008; Selected tables of national estimates of drug-related emergency department visits* (Rockville, MD: Office of Applied Studies, Substance Abuse and Mental Health Services Administration. Substance Abuse and Mental Health Services Administration (2010). *Drug Abuse Warning Network, 2008: Area profiles of drug-related mortality.* Rockville, MD: Office of Applied Studies, Substance Abuse and Mental Health Services Administration.
2. Substance Abuse, *Drug Abuse Warning Network 2008, Selected tables*, Drug combinations.
3. Ibid.
4. Substance Abuse, *Drug Abuse Warning Network 2008, Selected tables*, Illicit drugs. Gender: Male, Gender: Female.
5. Substance Abuse, *Area profiles of drug-related mortality*, pp. 51, 63, 108, 121, 162, and 228.6.
6. Sean E. McCabe and Carol J. Boyd, "Sources of prescription drugs for illicit use," *Addictive Behaviors*, 30 (2005), pp. 1342-1350. Substance Abuse and Mental Health Administration (2004, July). Club drugs, 2002 update. *DAWN Report*, p. 3. Substance Abuse and Mental Health

Administration (2004, July). Oxycodone, hydrocodone, and polydrug use, 2002. *DAWN Report*, p. 1. Substance Abuse and Mental Health Services Administration (2007, January 10). Misuse of over-the-counter cough and cold medications among persons aged 12 to 25. *The NSDUH Report*, pp. 1–4. Substance Abuse and Mental Health Services Administration (2010). *Results from the 2009 National Survey on Drug Use and Health: National findings. Detailed tables.* Rockville, MD: Office of Applied Studies, Substance Abuse and Mental Health Services Administration, Table 1.54A.
7. Johnston, Lloyd D.; O'Malley, Patrick M.; Bachman, Jerald G.; and Schulenberg, John E. (2010a). *Monitoring the future: National survey results on drug use, 1975–2009. Vol. I: Secondary school students 2009.* Bethesda, MD: National Institute on Drug Abuse. Johnston, Lloyd D.; O'Malley, Patrick M.; Bachman, Jerald G.; and Schulenberg, John E. (2010b). *Monitoring the future: National survey results on drug use, 1975–2009. Vol. II: College students and adults ages 19–50, 2009.* Bethesda, MD: National Institute on Drug Abuse.
8. Lloyd D. Johnston, Patrick D. O'Malley, Jerald G. Bachman, and John E. Schulenberg, "Teen marijuana use tilts

up, while some drugs decline in use," *University of Michigan News Service* (December 14, 2009a), Tables 2, 3, and 4.

9. Ibid.

10. Johnston, O'Malley, Bachman, and Schulenberg (2010a), *Monitoring the Future, Vol. I*, Tables 4-6 and 4.8.

11. Johnston, O'Malley, Bachman, and Schulenberg (2010b), *Monitoring the Future, Vol. II*, Table 2-2.

12. Bachman, Jerald G.; O'Malley, Patrick M.; Schulenberg, John E.; Johnston, Lloyd D.; Bryant, Alison L.; and Merline, Alicia C. (2002). *The decline of substance use in young adulthood: Changes in social activities, roles, and beliefs.* Mahwah, NJ: Lawrence Erlbaum Associates. Bachman, Jerald G.; Wadsworth, Katherine N.; O'Malley, Patrick M.; and Johnston, Lloyd D. (1997). *Smoking, drinking, and drug use in young adulthood: The impacts of new freedoms and new responsibilities.* Mahwah, NJ: Lawrence Erlbaum Associates. Leonard, Kenneth E., and Homish, Gregory G. (2005, Spring) Changes in marijuana use over the transition into marriage. *Journal of Drug Issues*, 409–430.

13. Johnston, O'Malley, Bachman, and Schulenberg (2009a), Teen marijuana tilts up, Tables 3, 11, 12, 13, and page 4, 27. Johnston, O'Malley, Bachman, and Schulenberg (2010b), *Monitoring the Future, Vol. II*, Table 2.2, 2.3, and 9.4.

14. Johnston, Lloyd D.; O'Malley, Patrick M.; Bachman, Jerald G.; and Schulenberg, John E. (2009b, December 14). Smoking continues gradual decline among U.S. teens, smokeless tobacco threatens a comeback. University of Michigan News Service, Ann Arbor, Table 1.

15. Johnston, O'Malley, Bachman, and Schulenberg (2010b), *Monitoring the Future, Vol. II*, Table 9-4.

16. Johnston, Lloyd D. (1996, December 19). The rise in drug use among American teens continues in 1996. News release from the University of Michigan, Ann Arbor, pp. 6–7.

17. Johnston, O'Malley, Bachman, and Schulenberg (2009a), Teen marijuana tilts up, Tables 2, 7, and 13.

18. Substance Abuse and Mental Health Services Administration (2009). *Results from the 2008 National Survey on Drug Use and Health: National findings.* Rockville, MD: Office of Applied Studies, Substance Abuse and Mental Health Services Administration. Substance Abuse and Mental Health Services Administration (2010). *Results from the 2009 National Survey on Drug Use and Health: Detailed tables.* Rockville, MD: Office of Applied Studies, Substance Abuse and Mental Health Services Administration, Tables 1.7A and 1.8A.

19. Inciardi, James A. (2007). *The war on drugs III.* Boston: Allyn and Bacon, p. 69.

20. Archibald, Randal C. (2009, May 31). In heartland death, traces of heroin's spread. *New York Times*, pp. 1, 24. Hernandez, Daisy (2003, March 23). Heroin's new generation: Young, white, and middle class. *New York Times*, p. 34.

21. Substance Abuse and Mental Health Services Administration, Club drugs.

22. Substance Abuse and Mental Health Services Administration (2008, June 19). Nonmedical use of pain relievers in substate regions: 2004 to 2006. *The NSDUH Report*, Substance Abuse and Mental Health Services Administration (2010), *Results from the 2009 National Survey: Detailed tables*, Table 1.54A.

23. McCabe and Boyd, Sources of prescription drugs. McCabe, Sean E., Teter, Christian J., and Boyd, Carol J. (2004). The use, misuse, and diversion of prescription stimulants among middle and high school students. *Substance Use and Misuse*, 39, 1095-1116. Substance Abuse and Mental Health Services Administration (2009, April 7). Nonmedical use of Adderall among full-time college students. *The NSDUH Report*, pp.1–4.

24. Johnston, O'Malley, Bachman, and Schulenberg (2009a), Teen marijuana tilts up, Table 2, Substance Abuse and Mental Health Services Administration (2008, January 10). Misuse of over-the-counter cough and cold medications among persons aged 12 to 25. *The NSDUH Report*, pp. 1–4.

chapter 3

The History of Drug Use and Drug-Control Policy

If the Chinaman cannot get along without his "dope," we can get along without him.

> —American Pharmaceutical Association, 1902

Most of the attacks upon white women of the South are the direct result of the cocaine-crazed Negro brain. . . . Negro cocaine fiends are now a new Southern menace.

> —New York Times, February 8, 1914

Liquor traffic is un-American, pro-German, crime-producing, food-wasting, youth-corrupting, home-wrecking, and treasonable.

> —The Anti-Saloon League, 1918

Under marijuana, Mexicans become very violent, especially when they become angry, and will attack an officer even if a gun is drawn on him. They seem to have no fear; I have also noted that under the influence of this weed they have enormous strength and that it will take several men to handle one man, while under ordinary circumstances one man could handle him with ease.

—*A Texas police officer, 1927*

Today... little has changed in the method of operations for drug dealers and anonymous criminals. Cyber crime, hackers, dial a dope, online pharmaceuticals, drug pushers are all doing one thing: creating chaos in society. The more stress and tension that hidden chaos merchants inflict in society, the more dope that is pushed in on the populace, the greater the distractions from the truly important purposes of life.

—*A drug and alcohol rehabilitation advisor, 2008*

The use of consciousness-altering drugs has been a part of human life in almost every culture and in every age of recorded history. Psychoactive drugs have been used in the context of religious rituals, health care, celebration, and recreation. In most societies, the use of some drugs has been permitted, whereas the use of other drugs has been prohibited, often depending on the type of drug that is being used, the drug's effects, and who is using the drug. An understanding of the history of drug use and our efforts to control drug use forms the basis for an understanding of present-day drug abuse and the problems associated with it.

Over the course of our nation's history, attitudes toward certain drugs and certain forms of drug-taking behavior have fluctuated between enthusiastic acceptance and passionate rejection. Heroin, marijuana, cocaine, and numerous other drugs all have had periods of popularity and periods of disapproval. In the late 1800s, for example, America experienced an epidemic of cocaine use. This was followed by a rejection in the early 1900s and a reemergence in the second half of the 1970s, followed by another period of rejection beginning in the 1980s and extending to the present day.

American drug control policy also has had its own historical swings, with policies themselves not always being founded on rational decision-making and empirical data. Decisions to outlaw some drugs while legalizing others have sometimes been based on fear, hysteria, politics, ethnic prejudice, and racism. As we will see, legal prohibition of a particular drug has too often been associated with fear of a given drug's effect on a threatening minority group. It is important to examine the history of drugs and drug-taking behavior and the history of drug-control policy in the United States in order to arrive at the best strategies for dealing with present-day drug use and abuse.

Drugs in Early Times

Try to imagine the accidental circumstances under which a psychoactive drug might have been discovered. Thousands of years ago, perhaps hundreds of thousands of years ago, the process of discovery would have been as natural as eating, and the motivation as basic as simple curiosity. In cool climates, next to a cave dwelling may have grown a profusion of blue morning glories or brightly colored mushrooms, plants that produce hallucinations similar to LSD. In desert regions, yellow-orange fruits grew on certain cacti, the source of the hallucinogenic drug peyote. Elsewhere, poppy plants, the source of opium, covered acres of open fields. Coca leaves, from which cocaine is made, grew on shrubs along the mountain valleys throughout Central and South America. The hardy cannabis plant, the source of marijuana, grew practically everywhere.[1]

It is entirely possible that some of the curiosity of humans was inspired by observing the unusual behavior of animals as they fed on these plants. Within their own experience, somewhere along the line people made the connection between the chewing of willow bark (the source of modern-day aspirin) and the relief of a headache or the eating of the senna plant (a natural laxative) and the relief of constipation.

Of course, some of these plants made people sick, and many were sufficiently poisonous to cause death. The plants that had the strangest impact, however, were the ones that produced hallucinations. Having a sudden vision of something totally foreign to everyday experiences must have been overwhelming, like a visit to another world. Individuals with prior knowledge about such plants, as well as about plants with therapeutic powers, would eventually acquire great power over

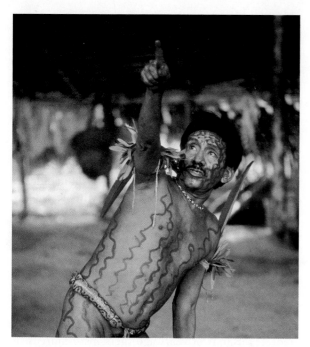

In a wide range of world cultures throughout history, hallucinogens have been regarded as having deeply spiritual powers. Under the influence of drugs, this modern-day shaman communicates with the spirit world.

others in the community. This knowledge was the beginning of **shamanism,** a practice among primitive societies dating back, by some estimates, more than 40,000 years, in which an individual called a **shaman** acts as a healer through a combination of trances and plant-based medicines, usually in the context of a local religious rite. Shamans still function today in remote areas of the world, often alongside practitioners of modern medicine, and hallucination-producing plants still play a major role in present-day shamanic healing.[2]

shamanism: The philosophy and practice of healing in which the diagnosis or treatment is based on trance-like states, either on the part of the healer (shaman) or the patient.

shaman (SHAH-men): A healer whose diagnosis or treatment of patients is based at least in part on trances. These trances are frequently induced by hallucinogenic drugs.

Ebers Papyrus: An Egyptian document, dated approximately 1500 B.C., containing more than 800 prescriptions for common ailments and diseases.

placebo (pla-CEE-bo) effect: Any change in a person's condition after taking a drug, based solely on that person's beliefs about the drug rather than on any physical effects of the drug (see Chapter 1).

With the development of centralized religions in Egyptian and Babylonian societies, the influence of shamanism would gradually decline. The power to heal through one's knowledge of drugs passed into the hands of the priesthood, which placed a greater emphasis on formal rituals and rules than on hallucinations and trances.

The most extensive testament to the development of priestly healing during this period is a 65-foot-long Egyptian scroll known as the **Ebers Papyrus,** named after the British Egyptologist who acquired it in 1872. This mammoth document, dating from 1500 B.C., contains more than eight hundred prescriptions for practically every ailment imaginable, including simple wasp stings and crocodile bites, baldness, constipation, headaches, enlarged prostate glands, sweaty feet, arthritis, inflammations of all types, heart disease, and cancer. More than a hundred of the preparations contained castor oil as a natural laxative. Some contained the "berry of the poppy," which is now recognized as referring to opium. Other ingredients were quite bizarre: lizard's blood, the teeth of swine, the oil of worms, the hoof of an ass, putrid meat with fly specks, and crocodile dung (excrement of all types being highly favored for its ability to frighten off the evil spirits of disease).[3]

How successful were these strange remedies? It is impossible to know because records were not kept on whether or not patients were cured. Although some of the ingredients, such as opium and castor oil, had true medicinal value, it may be that much of the improvement from these concoctions was psychological rather than physiological. In other words, improvement in the patient's condition resulted from the *belief* on the patient's part that he or she would be helped, a phenomenon known as the **placebo effect** (see Chapter 1).

Along with substances that had genuine healing properties, other psychoactive drugs were put to other uses. In the early Middle Ages, Viking warriors ate the mushroom *Amanita muscaria* (known as "fly agaric") and experienced increased energy, which resulted in wild behavior in battle. They were called "Berserkers" because of the bear skins they wore, and reckless, violent behavior has come to be called "berserk." Later, witches operating on the periphery of Christian society created "witch's brews," which were said to induce hallucinations and a sensation of flying. The brews were mixtures made of various plants such as mandrake, henbane, and belladonna. The toads that they included in their recipes did not hurt either: We know now that the sweat glands of toads contain a chemical related to DMT, a powerful hallucinogenic drug, as well as bufotenine, a drug that raises blood pressure and heart rate (see Chapter 9).[4]

Drugs in the Nineteenth Century

By the end of the nineteenth century, the medical profession had made significant strides with respect to medical healing. Morphine was identified as the active ingredient in opium, a drug that had been in use for at least three thousand years, and had become the physician's most reliable prescription to control the pain of disease and injury. The invention of the syringe made it possible to deliver morphine directly and speedily into the bloodstream.

Morphine quickly became a common treatment for pain during the Civil War, a time during which a surgeon's skill was often measured by how quickly he could saw off a wounded patient's limb. Unfortunately, following the war, morphine dependence among Civil War veterans was so widespread that it was called the "soldier's disease."Doctors also recommended morphine injections for women to treat the pain associated with "female troubles," and by the late 1890s, morphine dependence among women made up almost half of all cases of drug dependence in the United States (see Chapter 7).[5]

Cocaine, having been extracted from South American coca leaves, was also a drug in widespread use and taken quite casually in a variety of forms. The original formula for Coca-Cola (as the name suggests) contained cocaine until 1903, as did Dr. Agnew's Catarrh Powder, a popular remedy for chest colds. In the mid-1880s, Parke, Davis, and Company (merged with Pfizer, Inc. in 2002) was selling cocaine and its botanical source, coca, in more than a dozen forms, including coca-leaf cigarettes and cigars, cocaine inhalants, a coca cordial, and

In the latter part of the nineteenth century in the United States, cocaine was a popular ingredient in over-the-counter medications. These products were totally unregulated, and customers included children as well as adults.

an injectable cocaine solution.[6] A Viennese doctor named Sigmund Freud, who was later to gain a greater reputation for his psychoanalytical theories than for his ideas concerning psychoactive drugs, called cocaine a "magical drug." Freud would later reverse his position when a friend and colleague became dependent on cocaine (see Chapter 8).[7]

During the nineteenth century, America's public attitude toward drug use was one of **laissez-faire**, roughly translated from the French as "allow [people] to do as they please," which means that there was little regulation or control of drugs. In fact, the United States was the only major Western nation that allowed the unlimited distribution, sale, and promotion of psychoactive drugs during this period. The result was a nation of medicinal and recreational drug users that has been described as a "dope fiend's paradise." [8]

There were two major factors that explain why there were no major drug control policies during this period. First, unlike many European nations, the United States did not have any agencies regulating the medical field, and because doctors and pharmacists were unlicensed, it was not difficult to call oneself a doctor and distribute drugs. The American Medical Association (AMA) was established in 1847, but only a fraction of practicing health professionals were members during the 1800s. Doctors of this era had no choice but to rely upon untested and potentially toxic chemicals to treat both physical and psychological disorders (Drugs . . . in Focus). A second factor was the issue of states' rights. During the nineteenth century, the prevailing political philosophy was a belief in the strict separation of state and federal powers, especially in southern states. Therefore, the regulation of drugs was left to the states, most of which had few, if any, drug laws. For the federal government to pass laws limiting the use of any drug would have been seen as a serious challenge to the concept of states' rights.[9]

Drug Regulation in the Early Twentieth Century

By 1900, the promise of medical advances in the area of drugs was beginning to be matched by concerns about the dependence that some of these drugs could

laissez-faire (LAY-say FAIR) (Fr.): The philosophy of exerting as little governmental control and regulation as possible.

Drugs... in Focus

Abraham Lincoln, Depression, and Those "Little Blue Pills"

It is well known to historians that Abraham Lincoln suffered from long bouts of melancholy, a condition that would today be diagnosed as major depression. What is less known is that Lincoln had been advised by his physician to take what he called his "little blue pills" to help him elevate his mood.

A few months into his presidency, in 1861, however, Lincoln stopped taking these pills, complaining that they made him "cross." During the late 1850s, Lincoln had experienced episodes of bizarre behavior that included towering rages and mood changes that appeared out of nowhere or were responses to innocuous and sometimes trivial circumstances. It is reasonable to assume that the symptoms were, as Lincoln himself surmised, due to the "little blue pills."

It is a good thing that Lincoln made this decision. The medication he was taking was a common nineteenth-century remedy for depression, called *blue mass*. It consisted of licorice root, rosewater, honey, sugar, and rose petals. But the main ingredient in these blue-colored pills, about the size of peppercorns, was approximately 750 micrograms of mercury, a highly toxic substance. At the common dosage level of two or three pills per day, individuals ingested nearly nine thousand times the amount of mercury that is considered safe by current health standards.

If Lincoln had continued to take blue mass for his depression, he undoubtedly would have continued to experience the behavioral and neurological symptoms common to chronic mercury poisoning as he led the nation during the Civil War. Fortunately, the symptoms of mercury poisoning in Lincoln's case were reversible after he stopped taking blue mass. Lincoln would suffer from severe bouts of depression until his death in 1865, but America was spared what might have been a catastrophe of historic proportions.

Postscript: Mercury poisoning was quite common throughout the nineteenth century, as this substance's toxic properties had not yet been discovered or fully appreciated. Hat makers were particularly susceptible to mercury toxicity because they would routinely rub mercury into the felt material of hats to preserve them for commercial sale, absorbing the substance through their fingers. Symptoms of severe mood swings and eventually dementia were commonly observed among people in this profession and eventually became the basis for the expression "mad as a hatter."

Source: Hirschhorn, Norbert, Feldman, Robert G., and Greaves, Ian (2001, Summer). Abraham Lincoln's blue pills: Did the 16th President suffer from mercury poisoning? *Perspectives in Biology and Medicine,* pp. 315–322.

produce. Probably the two most important factors that fueled the movement toward drug regulation in the beginning of the twentieth century were (1) the abuse of patent medicines and (2) the association of drug use with minority groups. Between 1890 and 1906, numerous **patent medicines** were sold that included such ingredients as alcohol, opium, morphine, cocaine, and marijuana.

The term "patent medicine" can be misleading. Generally, one thinks of a patented product as one that is registered with the government, providing the producers with the exclusive right to sell that product. However, patent medicines around the turn of the twentieth century were not registered with the federal government or any other agency, and their formulas were often kept secret. Manufacturers did not have to list the ingredients of patent medicines on the bottle label or the package in which they were sold. One of the most popular methods of marketing patent medicines was the traveling medicine show, which included magicians and other performers, and culminated with a "pitch man" whose function was to convince the gathering crowd to buy his patent medicine.[10]

As the popularity of patent medicines grew, so did drug abuse. Unlike many of today's drug abusers, the typical nineteenth-century abuser was a white middle- or upper-class married woman who became dependent upon a patent medicine. In response to the growing number of drug-dependent Americans, President Theodore Roosevelt proposed a federal law that

patent medicine: A drug or combination of drugs sold through peddlers, shops, or mail-order advertisements.

would regulate misbranded and adulterated foods, drinks, and drugs. This proposal was met with strong opposition from the business sector, which was making a good profit from the patent medicine industry. Public opinion swayed in Roosevelt's direction after Upton Sinclair published *The Jungle* in 1906, a novel that exposed the unsanitary conditions of the meat packing industry in Chicago. The book depicted how diseased cattle and hogs, as well as human body parts, were sometimes included in packaged food and how much of the meat sold to the general public included undesirable parts of animals scraped from slaughterhouse floors. Congress responded by passing the 1906 Pure Food and Drug Act, which required all packaged foods and drugs to list the ingredients on the label of the product.

The new law did not prevent drugs from being sold, but it did require manufacturers to identify specific drugs that might be contained in these patent medicines. Thus cocaine, alcohol, heroin, and morphine could still be in patent preparations as long as they were listed as ingredients.[11]

Drug Regulation, 1914–1937

By the second decade of the twentieth century, calls for expanded drug regulation were spurred in large part by a growing prejudice against minority groups in America that were believed to be involved in drug use. As we will see, this social phenomenon impacted upon the eventual prohibition of opium and heroin, cocaine, and marijuana, as well as the temporary prohibition of alcohol.

The movement toward federal drug control legislation, in general, was met with resistance from southern politicians, who believed that such actions were yet another intrusion of the federal government into state affairs. It has been speculated that, in order to overcome this resistance from southerners during this time, a propaganda campaign was launched that associated African Americans with cocaine. Southern newspapers began printing stories of the cocaine-induced raping of white women and demonstrations of superhuman strength.[12] One of the more bizarre myths was that cocaine made African Americans unaffected by .32 caliber bullets, a claim that is said to have caused many southern police departments to switch to .38 caliber revolvers. The propaganda campaign was successful; Southerners

A rare photograph of life inside a Chinese opium den in San Francisco in the 1870s.

became more afraid of African Americans than of an increase in federal power and offered their support for the Pure Food and Drug Act and later the Harrison Act of 1914.[13]

Another example of how racism became interwoven with drug policy was the identification of Chinese workers with the smoking of opium. After the Civil War, the United States had imported Chinese workers to help build the rapidly expanding railroads. The Chinese brought with them the habit of smoking opium, which many Americans believed led to prostitution, gambling, and overall moral decline. When the major railroad systems were completed, Chinese workers began to migrate into western cities such as San Francisco. Working for low wages, the Chinese, some Americans feared, would take jobs from whites and the "big bosses" of business would use cheap Chinese labor as a means of preventing union organization. Hostility and violence against the Chinese became common. The first anti-drug legislation in the United States was an ordinance enacted in 1875 by the City of San Francisco prohibiting the operation of opium dens—establishments in which the smoking of opium occurred. Other states followed San Francisco's lead by prohibiting opium smoking, and in 1887, Congress prohibited the possession of smokable opium by Chinese citizens.[14]

The Harrison Act of 1914

The origins of the landmark Harrison Act of 1914 can be traced back to an issue of foreign trade. While many Americans detested the Chinese and their habit of smoking opium, at the same time, the U.S. government wanted to open up trade with China. China refused to purchase American goods, however, because of the poor treatment of Chinese people in the United States. To increase its influence in China and to improve its trade position, the United States initiated a number of international conferences to attempt to control the worldwide production and distribution of narcotics, especially opium. Recognizing the enormous population of opium abusers within their own country, Chinese leaders were eager to participate in such conferences.

At an international conference held in the Hague in 1912, the United States was accused of maintaining a double standard. According to its critics, the U.S. government was attempting to pass international agreements to regulate the drug trade while at the same time having no domestic control of drug production and distribution within its own borders. In response, Congress passed the Harrison Act, named after its sponsor, Representative Francis Burton Harrison of New York.[15]

The Harrison Act was designed to regulate drug abuse through government taxation and became the basis for narcotics regulation in the United States for more than a half-century. The act required anyone importing, manufacturing, selling, or dispensing cocaine and opiate drugs to register with the Treasury Department, pay a special tax, and keep records of all transactions. Because the act was a revenue measure, enforcement was made the responsibility of the Department of the Treasury and the commissioner of the Internal Revenue Service.

Cocaine was not defined as a narcotic under the law, but it became lumped together with opiates and often was referred to as a narcotic as well. Although application of the term to cocaine was incorrect ("narcotic" literally means "stupor-inducing," and cocaine is anything but that), the association has unfortunately stuck. Later, several restricted drugs, including marijuana and the hallucinogen peyote, also were officially classified as narcotics without regard to their pharmacological characteristics. Today, many people still think of any illegal drug as a narcotic, and for many years, the bureau at the Treasury Department charged with drug enforcement responsibilities was the Bureau of Narcotics, and its agents were known on the street as "narcs."

Technically, the Harrison Act did not make opiates and cocaine illegal. Physicians, dentists, and veterinarians could prescribe these drugs "in the course of their professional practice only." What this phrase meant was left to a good deal of interpretation. The Treasury Department viewed the maintenance of patients on these drugs, particularly opiates, as beyond medical intentions, and the Supreme Court upheld this interpretation. Between 1915 and 1938, thousands of physicians in the United States found themselves in violation of the law.

Eventually, physicians stopped issuing prescriptions for drugs now covered under the Harrison Act. As a result, a new class of criminal was created, driving individuals to seek drugs through the black market. In what would become a continuing and unfortunate theme in the history of drug law enforcement legislation, the Harrison Act failed to reduce drug-taking behavior. Instead, it created a new lucrative market for organized crime that continues to the present-day.

Alcohol and the Prohibition Era

Since the 1800s, there had been movements for the prohibition of alcohol in the United States (see Chapter 13), and although several states had passed anti-alcohol measures, prohibitionists were never quite able to gain national support for their movement. World War I, however, changed public sentiment, particularly with respect to a prominent minority group. During the war, anti-immigrant sentiment had begun to flourish, especially against German Americans, who were prominent in the business of making beer. Prohibitionists launched a campaign to convince Americans that the production of beer was part of a German plot to undermine America's willpower and deplete the cereal grains that were needed to make food for the soldiers in Europe. Prohibitionists were rural white Protestants, generally antagonistic toward Irish and Italian immigrants who were gaining political power in metropolitan areas such as Chicago and New York. To many who were behind the movement, prohibition represented a battle between America's Protestant rural towns and America's "sinful," immigrant-filled cities.[16]

In January 1919, Congress passed the Eighteenth Amendment to the U.S. Constitution, which outlawed the manufacture and sale of alcohol, except for industrial use. Nine months after the amendment was passed, it was followed by passage of the Volstead Act, authored by Representative Andrew Volstead of Minnesota. The Volstead Act provided for the federal enforcement of the Eighteenth Amendment by creating a Prohibition Bureau under control of the Treasury Department. Unfortunately, agents of the Prohibition Bureau developed a reputation as being inept and corrupt. Some viewed the bureau as a training school for bootleggers because agents frequently left law enforcement to embark upon their own criminal enterprises. One of the Prohibition Bureau's heroes, Eliot Ness, became famous for organizing a team of agents known as "The Untouchables," so-named because of their reputation for honesty and refusal to take bribes. Eliot Ness and his Untouchables were eventually able to arrest, prosecute,

PORTRAIT   Eliot Ness and the Untouchables

Shortly after graduating from the University of Chicago with a degree in business administration and political science, Eliot Ness accepted an appointment as an agent with the U.S. Treasury Department's Prohibition Bureau during a time when bootlegging was rampant throughout the nation. The Chicago branch of the Prohibition Bureau had a reputation for being corrupt, and it was difficult to find an honest law enforcement agent working in the city. Ness developed a reputation for his reliability and honesty and was given the job of assembling and leading a team to go after the liquor operations of famous gangster Al Capone. Capone was one of the most powerful and successful bootleggers in the country and operated thousands of illegal distilleries, breweries, and speakeasies in the Chicago area.

Ness was given the personnel records of the entire Prohibition Bureau, from which he was to select a small team of reliable agents. Ness selected nine men. One of Ness's first operations was to close down eighteen of Capone's operations in Chicago in one night. The raids were all scheduled to occur simultaneously at nine thirty at night so that they could make a clean sweep before the news got out to Capone. Ness's men led the raiding parties, and given the poor reputation of the average prohibition agent, Ness's men made sure that none of the men in the raiding parties had the opportunity to make a telephone call before the raid. With a sawed off shotgun in his arms, Ness and his men charged through the front door, yelling, "Everybody keep his place! This is a federal raid!" The operation was a success. Eighteen stills were shut down, and fifty-two people were arrested. Over the coming months, Ness and his team closed down numerous illegal stills and breweries worth an estimated $1 million.

Capone, feeling the pinch of Ness's operations, believed that every man had his price and made several attempts to bribe Ness and his men, but he had no success. In one instance, a man threw an envelope filled with cash into a car driven by one of Ness's men. Ness's agents caught up with the car and threw the money back into the gangster's car. Ness later called a press conference to talk about Capone's failed bribery attempt. Ness wanted Capone's organization to realize that there were still law enforcement agents who could not be bought. The press conference was carried by newspapers all over the country, one of which coined the term "The Untouchables."

Ness's war with Capone came to an end in 1931 when Al Capone was convicted of tax evasion. Capone, with his extravagant life-style, had not filed an income tax return for several years, and even though his lawyers continually warned him of his vulnerability to the Internal Revenue Service (IRS), Capone always felt that he was above the law. Some have claimed that Ness was an egomaniac who craved the spotlight and used his crusade against Capone to gain attention. Ness responded to the issue of his motivation by explaining why he took the job: "Unquestionably, it was going to be highly dangerous. Yet I felt it was quite natural to jump at the task. After all, if you don't like action and excitement, you don't go into police work. And what the hell, I figured, nobody lives forever!"

Many years later, Ness and his unit's exploits became a household word through the popular TV series *The Untouchables* (1959–1963)and the 1987 film costarring Kevin Costner and Sean Connery.

Sources: Heimel, Paul W. (1997). *Eliot Ness: The real story.* Coudersport, PA: Knox Books. Kobler, John (1971). *The life and world of Al Capone.* New York: G. P. Putnam's Sons.

---

and convict one of the most notorious crime figures of the time, Al Capone (Portrait).[17]

Prohibition failed to produce an alcohol-free society and spurred numerous social problems. Many citizens had little regard for the new law and continued to consume alcohol in underground nightclubs and bars known as **speakeasies** or "blind pigs." Alcohol itself became dangerous to consume. Before prohibition, large companies and the government controlled the manufacture of alcohol. During prohibition, criminal organizations controlled the manufacture and distribution of alcohol, sometimes adding dangerous adulterants such as kerosene that produced paralysis, blindness, and even death.

Because of Prohibition, the "Roaring Twenties" became one of the most lawless periods in American history. The court system was stretched beyond its limits. By the time **Prohibition** ended, nearly 800 gangsters in the city of Chicago alone had been killed in bootleg-related killings. Overall disregard for the law had become commonplace, and enforcement of Prohibition legislation became largely

speakeasies: Business establishments that sold liquor illegally during the Prohibition era.

Prohibition: A period between 1920 and 1933 in the United States when alcohol manufacture and sale was illegal.

ineffectual. At one point, a jury hearing a bootlegging case in California was itself put on trial after they literally drank the evidence! The jurors argued that they had simply sampled the evidence to determine whether or not it contained alcohol. Evidently, the jury had been overly enthusiastic in their inquiry. The defendant charged with bootlegging had to be acquitted because the evidence in the case had been consumed.[18] By the early 1930s, the significant social problems brought on by Prohibition were beginning to put pressure on political leaders to reconsider the concept of alcohol prohibition. In addition, there was an increasing need to restore the federal revenue dollars from taxes on alcohol, in order to help finance Depression-era programs.Before Prohibition, taxes on alcohol had been one of the primary sources of revenue for the federal government. In 1933, the Eighteenth Amendment was repealed by the Twenty-first Amendment, and Prohibition as a national policy was over.[19]

After the repeal of national Prohibition, regulatory control over alcohol was returned to the states. In 1966, the last "dry" state, Mississippi, became "wet." Later in the 1970s, thirty states lowered the legal drinking age to eighteen, but in the 1980s, concerns began to be raised over the large number of young people dying in alcohol-related traffic accidents. Congress responded by authorizing the Transportation Department to withhold federal highway funds for any state that did not raise the minimum drinking age to twenty-one. This mandate made twenty-one the uniform drinking age across the United States.

Marijuana and the Marijuana Tax Act of 1937

As with opium, cocaine, and alcohol, public concerns about marijuana did not surface until the drug was linked to a minority group—namely, migrant Mexican workers. During the 1920s, Mexican laborers emigrated to the United States to perform jobs that white workers refused to do, such as picking cotton, fruit, and vegetables on large farms in the Southwest. Some of the Mexican workers would smoke marijuana as a drug of entertainment and relaxation. When the Depression struck the United States, many white workers would take just about any job they could get, and public opinion supported sending the Mexican workers home. Many white laborers in the Southwest began to band together and form organizations such as the "Key Men of America" and the "American Coalition," whose goal was to "Keep America American." Leaders of these organizations believed that marijuana and the problems with Mexican immigration were closely connected, and many southwestern police chiefs agreed. Newspaper

stories began to circulate telling of how marijuana made users become sexually excited and violently insane.[20]

The first commissioner of the newly formed Federal Bureau of Narcotics (FBN), Harry J. Anslinger, saw the marijuana issue as a way to gain national attention and extend the power of FBN. Congressional committees heard testimony from Anslinger, who relied on sensational tales of murder, insanity, and sexual promiscuity that were brought on by marijuana, referred to as the "killer weed." Movies produced and released in the 1930s, such as *Reefer Madness* (now a cult classic on many university campuses) and *Marihuana: Weed with Roots in Hell*, supported Anslinger's propaganda campaign by depicting innocent young people committing terrible acts under the influence of marijuana. The result was the Marijuana Tax Act of 1937, which did not outlaw marijuana but required that a tax be collected on its manufacture and sale. Each time marijuana was sold, the seller had to pay a tax of as much as $100 per ounce for a transfer tax stamp. Failure to possess such a stamp was a federal offense, and not surprisingly, tax stamps were rarely issued (see Chapter 10). This effectively made marijuana illegal, and the drug was prohibited in this manner until the Controlled Substance Act of 1970.

Drugs and Society from 1945 to 1960

In the recreational drug scene of post–World War II United States, smoking was considered romantic and sexy. It was the era of the two-martini lunch, when

The television series, Mad Men, has effectively depicted the casual glamor of cigarette smoking in late 1950s and early 1960s.

social drinking was at its height of popularity and acceptance. Cocktail parties dominated the social scene. There was little or no public awareness that alcohol or nicotine consumption could be considered drug-taking behavior.

On the other hand, the general perception of certain drugs such as heroin, marijuana, and cocaine was simple and negative: They were considered bad and illegal, and "no one you knew" had anything to do with them. Illicit drugs were seen as the province of criminals, the urban poor, and nonwhites.[21] The point is that, during this period, a whole class of drugs was outside the mainstream of American life. Furthermore, an atmosphere of fear and suspicion surrounded people who took such drugs. Commissioner Anslinger in the 1950s accused the People's Republic of China of selling opium and heroin to finance the expansion of Communism. Drug abuse now became un-American, and Congress became convinced that penalties for illicit drug use were too lenient. Congress passed the Boggs Act in 1951 that increased the penalties of previously enacted marijuana and narcotics laws. Under the Boggs Act, marijuana and narcotics were lumped together under uniform penalties, which provided for a minimum sentence of two years for first-time offenders and up to ten years for repeat offenders. Later, Congress passed the Narcotics Control Act of 1956, which further increased the penalties for drug violations. The sale of heroin to individuals under the age of eighteen, for example, was made a capital offense. The Narcotics Control Act also authorized the FBN and customs agents to carry firearms and serve search warrants. The basis of these laws was the belief that strict drug laws and an increase in drug-law enforcement would curb future drug demand.

Turbulence, Trafficking, and Treatment, 1960–1980

During the 1960s, the basic premises of American life—the beliefs that working hard and living a good life would bring happiness and that society was stable and calm—were being undermined by the reality of the Vietnam War abroad and social unrest at home. The large adolescent and college-aged cohort born after World War II, often referred to as the "baby boomers" or

The famous Woodstock Festival concert drew an estimated 500,000 people to a farm in upstate New York in the summer of 1969. According to historian David Musto, "It was said that the (use of marijuana) at the gigantic Woodstock gathering kept peace—as opposed to what might have happened if alcohol had been the drug of choice."

"hippie" generation, was challenging many accepted cultural norms and the established hierarchy. Many young people were searching for new answers to old problems, and their search led to experimentation with drugs that their parents had been taught to fear. The principal symbol of this era of defiance against the established order, or indeed against anyone over thirty years old, was marijuana. No longer would marijuana be something foreign to Middle America. Marijuana, as well as new drugs such as LSD, became associated with the sons and daughters of white middle-class families. Illicit drug use, once a problem associated with minority populations, inner cities, and the poor, was now too close to our personal lives for us to ignore.

Along with the turbulence of the period came a disturbing increase in heroin abuse across the country. In the early 1970s, reports surfaced estimating that up to 15 percent of the American troops returning home from Vietnam had been heroin abusers. Organized crime groups established the **French connection,** in which opium grown in Turkey was converted into heroin in

> **French connection:** A term referring to the supply route of heroin in the 1960s from Turkey (where opium poppies were grown) to port cities in France (where heroin was manufactured) to cities in the United States (where heroin was distributed).

southern French port cities, smuggled into America, and then sold on the streets of major cities. A new form of crudely processed heroin from Mexico, known as "black tar," was beginning to be sold throughout the western United States. Heroin abuse increased in many inner cities, and heroin abuse was later connected to a rise in the crime rate, specifically a growing number of robberies and burglaries committed by heroin abusers to get money to buy drugs.[22]

For President Richard Nixon, elected in 1968, illicit drug use became a major political issue. He declared a "total war on drugs," ordering his senior staff to make the reduction of drug abuse one of their top priorities. In 1970, the Nixon administration persuaded Congress to pass the Comprehensive Drug Abuse Prevention and Control Act, popularly known as the "Controlled Substance Act." The act was passed to consolidate the large number of diverse and overlapping drug laws as well as the duplication of efforts by several different federal agencies. The act established five schedules for the classification of drugs, based upon their approved medical uses, potential for abuse, and potential for producing dependence. As a result of the 1970 Controlled Substance Act, the control of drugs has been placed under federal jurisdiction regardless of state regulations.

The 1970 act also shifted the administration of drug enforcement from the Treasury Department to the Justice Department, creating the Drug Enforcement Administration (DEA). The DEA was given the control of all drug-enforcement responsibilities, except those related to ports of entry and borders, which were given to the U.S. Customs Service. DEA agents were to conduct drug investigation, collect intelligence about general trends in drug trafficking and drug production, and coordinate efforts among federal, state, and local law enforcement agencies. The DEA's mission today remains both domestic and foreign. Agents are stationed in foreign countries, and although they do not possess arrest powers, they act as liaisons with foreign law enforcement agencies. Both the DEA and the Federal Bureau of Investigation (FBI) share responsibility for enforcement of the Controlled Substance Act of 1970, and the director of the DEA reports to the director of the FBI, who in 1982 was given responsibility for supervising all drug-law enforcement efforts and policies.

President Nixon also believed that reducing the supply of drugs from overseas sources could curb drug abuse in the United States. In the 1970s, the federal government estimated that 80 percent of the heroin reaching the United States was produced from opium poppies grown in Turkey. As mentioned earlier, the opium was shipped to southern French port cities, where it

was converted to heroin and then later smuggled into the United States. In an attempt to reduce the amount of heroin coming into the United States, the Nixon administration threatened to cut off aid to Turkey if that country did not put an end to the export of opium. Nixon also promised Turkey millions of dollars in aid to make up for the subsequent losses resulting from reduced poppy cultivation. Initially, this action did lead to a shortage of heroin on American streets in 1973. The decline in heroin production, however, did not last long. In 1974, Mexico became a primary source of opium production, and in response, the U.S. government began to finance opium eradication programs in Mexico (see Chapter 6).[23]

Another response of the Nixon administration to drug abuse, particularly with regard to the increase in heroin dependence, was to finance a number of treatment programs for drug dependent individuals. These treatment programs ranged from inpatient detoxification and therapeutic communities to newly created methadone outpatient programs. Methadone is a long-acting opiate that is taken orally in order to prevent heroin withdrawal symptoms for up to twenty-four hours (see Chapter 7). Methadone maintenance programs were designed to wean heroin abusers off of heroin by allowing them to have a better chance at employment and ending the need to commit crimes to maintain their abuse. After an initial report of the drug's success in 1966, methadone's popularity quickly spread. Methadone maintenance programs represented the first time that the federal government made a commitment to drug-abuse treatment in the community.

By 1972, some of the Nixon administration's anti-drug programs appeared to be working. There was a national network of methadone treatment centers, and successful eradication efforts. Turkey had agreed to stop growing opium, and Mexico was cooperating with U.S. law enforcement. The price of heroin was up, the purity level was down, and there was a decrease in the number of drug overdose cases. When President Gerald Ford took the White House in 1974, however, the nation's attention was diverted from drug abuse to other issues, such as unemployment, inflation, and an energy crisis. Illicit drug use was no longer an important issue. Ford's policy toward illicit drug use was based on the attitude that drug abuse was here to stay, but government actions could contain the problem. The administration also believed that some drugs were more dangerous than others and that anti-drug policies should be directed at controlling the supply and demand of those drugs which posed the greatest threat to society.

President Jimmy Carter, elected in 1976, was more tolerant toward drug use than Ford and even favored decriminalization of the possession of small amounts of marijuana. President Carter stated: "Penalties against possession of a drug should not be more damaging to an individual than the use of the drug itself, and where they are, they should be changed. Nowhere is this more clear than in the laws against the possession of marijuana in private for personal use."[24] By 1978, eleven states followed Carter's lead and decriminalized small amounts of marijuana. California and Oregon made possession of one ounce or less of marijuana a citable misdemeanor with a maximum penalty of $1,000, and there were no increased penalties for repeat offenders.[25] Relaxed attitudes toward drugs reached a peak in 1979. An astounding 53 percent of high school seniors in 1979 reported using an illicit drug over the past twelve months, compared with 37 percent of high school seniors in 2009 (see Chapter 1).[26]

Renewed Efforts at Control, 1980–2000

With the decade of the 1980s came significant changes in the mood of the country in the form of a social and political reaction to earlier decades. If the media symbol formerly had been the "hippie," now it was the "yuppie," a young, upwardly mobile professional. The political climate became more conservative in all age groups. With regard to drugs, the concern about heroin dependence was being overshadowed by a new fixation: cocaine. At first, cocaine took on an aura of glamour and (because it was so expensive) became a symbol of material success. The media spotlight shone on a steady stream of celebrities in entertainment and sports who used cocaine. Not long after, however, the harsh realities of cocaine dependence were recognized. The very same celebrities who had accepted cocaine into their lives were now experiencing the consequences; many of them were in rehabilitation programs, and some had died from cocaine overdoses. To make matters worse, in 1985, a new form of cocaine called "crack," smokeable and cheap, succeeded in extending the problems of cocaine dependence to the inner cities of the United States, to segments of American society that did not have the financial resources to afford cocaine itself. In the glare of intense media attention, crack dependence soon took on all the aspects of a national nightmare.

In the 1970s, there had been generally a lack of public interest and even some tolerance of drug use. As mentioned earlier, in several U.S. states there was even a trend toward deregulation. In the 1980s, however, the lack of public interest in drug use began to shift as grassroots groups began to demand that something be done about "America's drug problem." During the presidency of Ronald Reagan, drug abuse became a major political and social issue. President Reagan declared an all-out war on drugs, and First Lady Nancy Reagan launched her "Just Say No" campaign, which focused mostly on white middle-class children who had not yet tried drugs. Reagan's war on drugs focused on a policy of controlling the supply of drugs by increasing the budgets of drug enforcement agencies and providing foreign aid to such countries as Colombia, Peru, Bolivia, and Mexico. Demand was to be reduced by enacting laws that imposed some of the harshest penalties ever for drug-law violators.

With popular sentiment once again turned against drugs, Congress rewrote virtually all of the nation's drug laws in record time. In 1984, Congress passed the Comprehensive Crime Control Act, which increased the penalties for violations of the Controlled Substance Act and expanded asset-forfeiture law, allowing both local and federal drug enforcement agencies to keep most of the money made from the sale of seized assets (see Chapter 6). Two years later, Congress passed the Anti-Drug Abuse Act of 1986, which placed mandatory minimum sentences for federal drug convictions, eliminating a judge's discretion in pronouncing a sentence. Different mandatory minimum sentences were to be given for possession of powder and crack cocaine. The new law imposed a prison sentence of five to forty years for possession of 500 grams of powder cocaine or 5 grams of crack cocaine. This mandatory sentence could not be suspended, nor could the offender be paroled or placed on probation. The Anti-Drug Abuse Act of 1986 also created a "kingpin" statute under which the heads of drug trafficking organizations could receive mandatory life imprisonment if convicted of operating a continuing criminal enterprise.

One of the most important drug laws passed in the 1980s was the Anti-Drug Abuse Act of 1988. This legislation created a cabinet-level Director of National Drug Control Policy, often referred to in the media as the "Drug Czar," whose job was to coordinate federal activities with respect to both drug supply and demand reduction. The first director was former Education Secretary William J. Bennett, who believed that individual users of drugs should accept moral responsibility for their behavior. Bennett believed that drug laws should be strict so that drug users would understand that involvement in the illegal drug trade has clear consequences. The law created harsher penalties for the possession of drugs; penalties for selling drugs to minors were enhanced; and the act reinstated the death penalty for anyone convicted as a "drug kingpin" or anyone convicted of a drug-related killing. The act also addressed alcohol use, especially the problem of drunk driving, by providing federal money to states that instituted tough penalties for drunk drivers. Lastly, the act addressed the issues of drug use in schools and in the workplace by requiring educational institutions and businesses to establish a system to ensure that students and workers remained drug-free. This provision later established the basis for drug testing in schools and in the workplace.

Drugs... in Focus

A History of American Drug Legislation

1794   A federal tax on whiskey leads to the Whiskey Rebellion in western Pennsylvania (see Chapter 13).

1868   Pharmacy Act of 1868 requires registration of those dispensing drugs.

1875   The Anti-Opium Smoking Act is passed in San Francisco.

1906   Pure Food and Drug Act requires all packaged foods and drugs to list the ingredients on the label of the product.

1914   The Harrison Narcotic Act is designed to regulate addiction and drug abuse through government taxation.

1919   Congress passes the Eighteenth Amendment, which outlaws the manufacture and sale of alcohol, except for industrial use.

1933   Congress passes the Twenty-first Amendment, which repeals the Eighteenth Amendment.

1937   The Marijuana Tax Act places a tax on the manufacture and sale of marijuana.

1951   The Boggs Act increases the penalties for drug offenses.

1956   Selling heroin to someone under the age of eighteen can result in the death penalty.

1970   Comprehensive Drug Abuse Prevention and Control Act, popularly known as the Controlled Substance Act, establishes five schedules for the classification of drugs based upon their approved medical uses, potential for abuse, and potential for producing dependence.

1984   Congress passes the Comprehensive Crime Control Act, which enhances the penalties for violations of the Controlled Substance Act and expands asset-forfeiture law, allowing both local and federal drug enforcement agencies to keep the majority of the money made from the sale of seized assets.

1986   Congress passes the Anti-Drug Abuse Act of 1986, which places mandatory sentences for federal drug convictions, eliminating a judge's discretion in pronouncing a sentence.

1988   The Anti-Drug Abuse Act of 1988 increases penalties for drug offenses involving children and creates a cabinet-level position of Director of National Drug Control Policy, often referred to in the media as "Drug Czar."

1996   Arizona Proposition 200 and California Proposition 215 are passed, which legalize the use of marijuana for medicinal purposes within these two states (see Chapter 10).

1996   Comprehensive Methamphetamine Control Act increases the penalties for trafficking and manufacture of methamphetamine and its precursor chemicals.

2000   GHB (gamma-hydroxybutyrate) is added to the list of Schedule I controlled substances.

2003   The Illicit Drug Anti-Proliferation Act, aimed at the promoters of "raves," holds persons more accountable for knowingly renting, leasing, or maintaining any place where drugs are distributed or manufactured.

2004   Anabolic Steroid Control Act of 2004 adds several new steroids and steroid precursors to the list of controlled substances.

2005   The Combat Methamphetamine Epidemic Act establishes nationwide sales restrictions on precursor chemicals and law enforcement initiatives for the seizure of domestic methamphetamine laboratories.

2009   The Tobacco Control Act gives the FDA authority to regulate the sale and manufacture of tobacco products.

The wave of anti-drug legislation in the 1980s (Drugs . . . in Focus) profoundly changed America's criminal justice system. Law enforcement budgets increased as more officers had to be hired to enforce drug laws. The number of drug violators increased to the highest level ever, and courts became backlogged with drug case after drug case. The number of inmates in U.S. prisons and jails rose nearly 100 percent from 1985 to 1996, and the budget for prisons increased by more than 160 percent.[27] Prison building became one of the biggest public works businesses in America; hundreds of new prisons sprang up across the country. Fortunately, by the end of the 1990s, the extent of crack abuse had greatly diminished, crime rates had begun to fall, and rates of illicit drug use began to decline. It is still being debated, however, to what extent these changes were due to the "get tough" policy on drugs or how much were due to an overall aging of the U.S. population or other sociocultural factors.

The 1990s and the beginning of the twenty-first century can be characterized by a general lack of political interest in drug abuse. During his first term in office from 1992 to 1996, President Bill Clinton placed little emphasis on drug abuse and reduced the staff of the Office of National Drug Control Policy by 83 percent, a move that he ascribed to keeping his campaign promise to reduce the White House staff by 25 percent. As the 1996 election approached and a rise in marijuana use among youth became publicized, Clinton was subject to the criticism that he had neglected America's drug problem. In response, Clinton declared his own war on drugs and appointed a retired four-star military general, Barry McCaffrey, to be his "Drug Czar." Clinton urged Congress to appropriate a $100 million increase in the budget for drug interdiction and increased foreign aid to stop the supply of drugs at their source. In addition, he signed the Comprehensive Methamphetamine Control Act into law in 1996. Designed to curb the use of methamphetamine, this act increased the penalties for trafficking and manufacture of methamphetamine and its precursor chemicals.

The Globalization of Drug Regulation, 2001—Present

After the events of September 11, 2001, the war on terrorism became a more pressing matter for President George W. Bush than the war on drugs. An effort

Quick Concept Check 3.1

Understanding the History of U.S. Drug-control Legislation

Test your understanding of American drug-control legislation by matching the statement on the left with the associated drug on the right.
Note: Some of the answers may be used more than once.

1. Dependence on this drug among Civil War veterans was so common that it was called the "soldier's disease" or the "army disease."

2. This drug was associated with Chinese immigrants working on American railroads during the 1800s.

3. In order to get federal drug legislation passed, a propaganda campaign was launched that associated African Americans with this drug.

4. The opposition to this drug was intertwined with a negative reaction toward German, Italian, and Irish immigrants.

5. This drug was linked to Mexican migrant workers.

6. The Nixon administration initiated programs in the late 1960s that were designed to wean addicts off of heroin.

7. During Jimmy Carter's presidency in the late 1970s, several states voted to decriminalize this drug.

8. During Ronald Reagan's presidency in the 1980s, abuse of this drug became a major public concern.

a. marijuana
b. opium
c. cocaine
d. morphine
e. alcohol
f. heroin
g. methadone

Answers: 1. d.   2. b.   3. c.   4. e.   5. a.   6. g.
7. a.   8. c.

was made, however, to combine the two problems into one all-encompassing policy. During the Clinton presidency, aid to Colombia had risen to a previously unprecedented level of $88 million, but this money was tightly restricted to police and counterdrug efforts and not intended to support Colombia's war against insurgent groups. In 2002, Bush changed the U.S. strategy by granting the Colombian government the funding to combat drug trafficking as well as terrorism, two struggles that in the view of the Bush administration had become one. At that time, Colombia was awarded $650 million in U.S. aid to begin a unified campaign against drug trafficking and the activities of groups designated as terrorist organizations.[28]

In recent years, our global efforts to control drug trafficking have been complicated by economic and political aspects of U.S. foreign policy. Our relations with the country of Mexico, for example, have been strained by the fact that Mexico continues to be a major trafficking route not only for cocaine from South America and heroin from Mexico itself, but also a source of marijuana cultivation and a manufacturing source of methamphetamine, and illegal medications. Efforts to reduce the cultivation of opium in the rugged, mountainous areas of Afghanistan, presently the supplier of approximately 94 percent of the world's supply of heroin, have been intertwined with efforts to control the political influence of regional warlords, whether they have terrorist associations or not. The interconnected and sometimes opposing goals of America's drug-control policy and global foreign policy continue to be a major challenge in the effort to regulate drug-taking behavior both in the United States and around the world.[29]

Domestic Drug Regulation, 2001-Present

The USA PATRIOT Act of 2001, enacted as a response to the September 11th attacks, increased the ability for federal authorities to tap telephones and wireless devices, monitor Internet communications, and tighten the enforcement of money laundering activities, as well as protect U.S. borders. These powers were not only directed toward possible acts of terrorism but also other criminal acts such as drug trafficking. The reauthorization of the legislation (referred to as PATRIOT II) relaxed certain provisions that had been criticized as being restrictive of individual civil liberties and closed some loopholes in the 2001 Act with regard to terrorist financing. Significantly, PATRIOT II contained a subsection called the Combat Methamphetamine Epidemic Act that restricted access to over-the-counter cold medications that could be used to manufacture methamphetamine (see Chapter 8). Limits on the amounts purchased were established, and consumers were required to provide photo identification and sign in a store log at the time of purchase. In addition, funding was authorized for the federal Meth Hot Spots program, intended to support state and local law enforcement agencies in the enforcement and prosecution of individuals committing methamphetamine offenses.

Summary

Drugs in Early Times

- Probably the earliest experiences with psychoactive drugs came from tasting naturally growing plants. Individuals with knowledge about such plants were able to attain great power within their societies.

- Ancient Egyptians and Babylonians in particular had extensive knowledge of both psychoactive and nonpsychoactive drugs. Some of these drugs had genuine beneficial effects, while others did not.

Drugs in the Nineteenth Century

- Medical advances in the 1800s allowed isolation of the active ingredients within many psychoactive substances. For example, morphine was identified as the major active ingredient in opium.

- During the nineteenth century, there was little regulation or control of drugs, and the U.S. government imposed no limitations on their distribution, sale,

and promotion. The result was a century of widespread and uncontrolled medicinal and recreational drug use.

Drug Regulation in the Early Twentieth Century

- The effects of drug dependence began to become a social concern. The two most important factors that fueled the movement toward drug regulation in the beginning of the twentieth century were (1) the abuse of patent medicines and (2) the association of drug use with socially marginalized minority groups.

Drug Regulation, 1914-1937

- The Harrison Act of 1914 was the first of several legislative efforts to impose criminal penalties on the use of opiates and cocaine.

- Passage of the Eighteenth Amendment resulted in the national prohibition of alcohol in the United States from 1920 to 1933.

- The Marijuana Tax Act of 1937 required that a tax stamp be issued to anyone selling marijuana. Tax stamps, however, were rarely issued, making marijuana essentially illegal. The drug was prohibited in this way until the Controlled Substance Act of 1970.

Drugs and Society from 1945 to 1960

- During the 1940s and 1950s, the use of illicit drugs such as heroin, cocaine, and marijuana was outside the mainstream of American life.
- Legislation during the 1950s imposed increasingly severe penalties for drug violations.

Turbulence, Trafficking, and Treatment, 1960–1980

- In the 1960s and 1970s, the use of marijuana and hallucinogenic drugs among young people spread across the nation, along with an increase in problems related to heroin.
- President Richard Nixon declared a "total war on drugs," directing the reduction in drug abuse as one of America's top priorities. Two aspects of this initiative were the international pressure on specific foreign nations to reduce the source of illicit drugs entering the United States and the establishment of drug-abuse treatment programs.
- The Comprehensive Drug Act of 1970 established a federal drug-control system based upon a classification of drugs in five groups called schedules, I through V. Under this act, a drug is "scheduled" on the basis of its approved medical uses, potential for abuse, and potential for producing dependence.
- By the end of the 1970s, drug-control policy in the United States shifted to a position of relative tolerance with regard to drug-taking behavior. In some U.S. states, the possession of small amounts of marijuana was decriminalized.

Renewed Efforts at Control, 1980–2000

- A decline in heroin abuse in the 1980s was matched by an increase in cocaine abuse and the emergence of crack as a cheap, smokable form of cocaine.
- During the 1980s, a wave of federal drug legislation increased the penalties for the possession and trafficking of illicit drugs. As a result, the number of drug violators rose to record levels, and courts became backlogged with drug cases. The number of inmates in U.S. prisons and jails rose nearly 100 percent from 1985 to 1996.

The Globalization of Drug Regulation, 2001–Present

- The 1990s and the beginning of the twenty-first century can be characterized by a general lack of political interest in drug abuse. After the events of September 11, 2001, however, the war on drugs became intertwined with the war on international and domestic terrorism.

Domestic Drug Regulation, 2001– Present

- The USA PATRIOT Act of 2001 was enacted as a response to the September 11th attacks, increasing the ability for federal authorities to monitor communications related to possible terrorist activities, tighten money laundering enforcement, and increase the protection of U.S. borders. These powers were directed toward other criminal acts, including drug trafficking.
- The reauthorization of the legislation, known as PATRIOT II, included a program to restrict access to over-the-counter cold medications that could be used in the manufacture of methamphetamine.

Key Terms

Ebers Papyrus, p. 52
French connection, p. 59
laissez-faire, p. 53

patent medicine, p. 54
placebo effect, p. 52

Prohibition, p. 57
shaman, p. 52

shamanism, p. 52
speakeasies, p. 57

Endnotes

1. Caldwell, A. E. (1970). *Origins of psychopharmacology: From CPZ to LSD*. Springfield, IL: C. C. Thomas, p. 3. Muir, Hazel (2003, December 20; 2004, January 9). Party animals. *New Scientist*, pp. 56–59.
2. De Foe, Vincenzo (2003). Ethnomedical field study in northern Peruvian Andes with particular reference to divination practices. *Journal of Ethnopharmacology*, 85, 243–256. Del Castillo, Daniel (2002, November 22). Just what the shaman ordered. *The Chronicle of Higher Education*, p. A72. Metzner, Ralph (1998). Hallucinogenic drugs and plants in psychotherapy and shamanism. *Journal of Psychoactive Drugs*, 30, 333–341.

3. Bryan, Cyril P. (1930). *Ancient Egyptian medicine: The Papyrus Ebers.* Chicago: Ares Publishers. Inglis, Brian (1975). *The forbidden game: A social history of drugs.* New York: Scribners, pp. 11–36.

4. Grilly, David (1998). *Drugs and human behavior.* (3rd ed.). Boston: Allyn and Bacon, p. 2.

5. Sneader, Walter (1985). *Drug discovery: The evolution of modern medicines.* New York: Wiley, pp. 15–47. Stearns, Peter N. (1998). Dope fiends and degenerates: The gendering of addiction in the early twentieth century. *Journal of Social History*, 31, 809–814.

6. Bugliosi, Vincent (1991). *Drugs in America: The case for victory.* New York: Knightsbridge Publishers, p. 215.

7. Freud, Sigmund (1884). *Über coca (On ca). Centralblatt für die gesammte Therapie.* Translated by S. Pollak (1884). *St. Louis Medical and Surgical Journal*, 47.

8. Brecher, Edward M. (1972). *Licit and illicit drugs.* Boston: Little, Brown, p. 3.

9. Musto, David F. (1987). *The American disease: Origins of narcotics control.* New York: Oxford University Press.

10. Young, James Harvey. (1961). *The toadstool millionaires: A social history of patent medicines in America before regulation.* Princeton, NJ: Princeton University Press.

11. Latimer D., and Goldberg, J. (1981). *Flowers in the blood: The story of opium.* New York: Franklin Watts.

12. Helmer, John (1975). *Drugs and minority oppression.* New York: Seabury Press.

13. Cloyd, Jerald W. (1982). *Drugs and information control: The role of men and manipulation in the control of drug trafficking.* Westport, CT: Greenwood.

14. Musto, *The American disease.* Latimer and Goldberg, *Flowers in the blood.*

15. Latimer and Goldberg, *Flowers in the blood.*

16. Cashman, Sean D. (1981). *Prohibition.* New York: Free Press. Coffey, Thomas M. (1975). *The long thirst: Prohibition in America, 1920–1933.* New York: Norton, pp. 196–198. Gusfield, Joseph R. (1963). *The symbolic crusade: Status politics and the American temperance movement.* Urbana, IL: University of Illinois Press. Sinclair, Andrew. (1962). *The era of excess: A social history of the prohibition movement.* Boston: Little, Brown.

17. Woodiwiss, Michael (1988). *Crime, crusaders and corruption: Prohibition in the United States, 1900–1987.* Totawa, NJ: Barnes and Noble.

18. Behr, E. (1996). *Prohibition.* New York: Arcade. *New York Times*, January 7, 1928.

19. Sinclair, Andrew (1962). *The era of excess.*

20. Musto, *The American disease.*

21. Helmer, *Drugs and minority oppression.* Schlosser, Eric (2003). *Reefer madness: Sex, drugs, and cheap labor in the American black market.* Boston: Houghton Mifflin, p. 245.

22. Musto, *The American disease.*

23. Marshall, Elliot (1971). Cold turkey: heroin. The source supply. *New Republic*, 165, 23–25.

24. Carter, James Earl, Jr. (1979). President's message to the Congress on drug abuse. *Federal Strategy for Drug Abuse and Drug Traffic Prevention*, pp. 66–67.

25. Himmelstein, Jerome L. (1983). *The strange career of marijuana: Politics and ideology of drug control in America.* Westport, CT: Greenwood.

26. Johnston, Lloyd D.; O'Malley, Patrick M.; Bachman, JeraldG.; and Schulenberg, John E. (2009, December 14). Teen marijuana use tilts up, while some drugs decline in use. University of Michigan News Service, Ann Arbor, Table 2.

27. Bureau of Justice Statistics (1998). *U.S. Department of Justice sourcebook of criminal justice statistics.* Washington, DC: Bureau of Justice Statistics.

28. Adam, Isacson (2003). Washington's new war in Colombia: The war on drugs meets the war on terror. *NACLA Report on the Americas*, 36, pp. 5–11.

29. Lacey, Marc (2008, December 5). Hospitals now a theater in Mexico's drug war. *New York Times*, pp. A1, A18. Shanker, Thom (2008, December 23). Obstacle in bid to curb Afghan trade in narcotics. *New York Times*, p. A6.

chapter 4

Theoretical Perspectives on Drug Use and Abuse

After I got married and had kids, I wanted to quit smoking weed. I stopped smoking for two weeks and didn't have any withdrawal symptoms like the shakes or anything, but sometimes certain things would make me want to smoke again. Like if I heard an old Dead song or saw someone I used to get high with, I kind of had an urge to light up a joint. And every time I got drunk, I wanted to end the night with a bong hit. I still get high sometimes if I go out with some of my old friends, but I never tell my wife. She would kick me out of the house.

—*A twenty-seven-year-old marijuana user*

Why do people take drugs? We all take drugs, of course, for genuine therapeutic reasons, to relieve ourselves of pain or symptoms that arise from a range of physical or psychological disorders. But why do people take drugs on a purely recreational basis? Is it for sheer pleasure, to escape from a life of boredom, to suppress feelings of sorrow and depression, to fit in with a group of friends, to relieve stress? There are so many different reasons why people use and abuse drugs that arriving at a satisfactory explanation presents an enormous challenge. The fact is that no one has developed a single theory that explains why some people are more prone to drug abuse than others, and, indeed, an effort to determine a single explanation probably is doomed to failure. As sociologist Erich Goode has commented, "Hardly any researcher in the field believes that one factor, and one alone, explains the phenomenon under investigation." Instead, we must be content with a variety of explanations, some having to do with drug-taking behavior in general and others having to do with the abuse of a specific drug.[1]

The oldest theory of drug abuse, and arguably the oldest theory to explain disapproved behavior in general, has its origin in demonology. Why would someone do something bad? Answer: "Because the devil made him do it."

In the last two hundred years or so, we have moved away from believing that evil spirits invoke bad behavior, but this belief underlies the way some people still think about drug abuse. Drug abusers are sometimes considered to be individuals who are morally deficient, who, because of personal inadequacies, overindulgence, a weakness of will, or other character flaw, have "succumbed to the clutches of a fiendish dope peddler." A nonreligious version of this point of view is referred to as the **moral model** of drug abuse. According to the moral model, drug-taking behavior is simply a matter of personal choice that we have made in our lives, not a consequence of a biological defect, a psychological dysfunction, or sociological circumstances.

The implications can be profound with respect to the ways in which drug abusers are held responsible for their actions and the way the criminal justice system views drug-taking behavior in general. As drug counselors Gary Fisher and Thomas Harrison explain it

A 1988 Supreme Court decision found that crimes committed by an alcoholic were willful misconduct

---

moral model: An explanation for drug use in which drug-taking behavior is attributed to personal inadequacies, overindulgence, a weakness of will, or other serious character flaw.

---

and not the result of a disease. . . . Certainly, the manner in which states [in the United States] deal with drunk driving violations may relate to the moral model. In states where violators are not assessed for chemical dependency and where there is no diversion to treatment, the moral model guides policy. If excessive alcohol use is the result of personal choice, then violators should be punished.[2]

As we will see, present-day explanations of drug use and abuse have gone beyond the moral model. In this chapter, we will review theories of drug use and abuse from three broad perspectives: biological, psychological, and sociological.

Biological Perspectives on Drug Abuse

When we theorize about the origins of drug abuse from a biological perspective, we are referring to specific physical mechanisms in specific individuals that influence the initial experience with drugs or an engagement in drug abuse over a period of time. Biological theories have focused primarily on genetic factors, physiological factors, and neurochemical systems in the brain.

Genetic Factors

As genetic research has advanced over the years, particularly since the completion of the mapping of the human genome in 2000, a great deal of attention has focused on the contribution that certain genetic traits make toward the abuse of a range of drugs. Environmental factors are also undoubtedly important. Recent studies have shown, however, that genetic factors play an equal or greater role. Studies of different strains of mice and rats, for example, have found that some have a genetic propensity to become dependent upon cocaine, whereas other strains are more susceptible to the dependence-producing effects of opiates.[3]

Most studies concerning genetic factors in humans have focused on alcoholic individuals, and a growing research literature indicates that alcoholism has a genetic component (see Chapter 14). Family studies have shown that children of alcoholics are four times more likely than other children to become alcoholics (Figure 4.1). Identical twins (those who have identical genetic compositions) are more likely to have a similar risk for alcoholism than fraternal twins, who share only half their genetic traits with each other. In addition, children who have at least one alcoholic biological parent

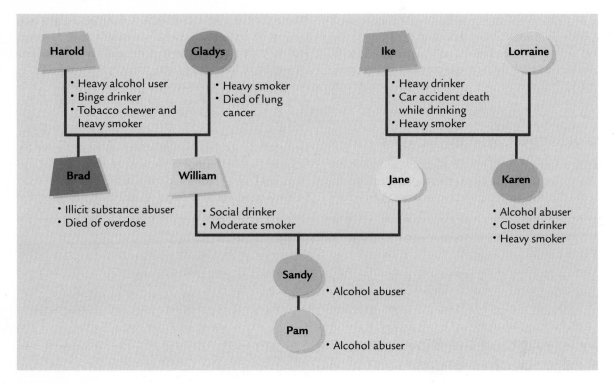

FIGURE 4.1

The genogram of two alcohol abusers, Pam and Sandy, reveals that alcohol and other substances have been abused for four generations, causing family problems and death throughout the family's history.

Source: Stevens, Patricia, and Smith, Robert L. (2005). *Substance abuse counseling: Theory and practice* (3rd ed.). Boston: Allyn and Bacon, p. 94.

and were adopted by nonalcoholic parents are three times more likely to have a problem with alcohol, even when they have been raised in a low-risk environment.[4]

We have yet to identify the single gene that may be responsible for the emergence of alcoholism, and it is believed likely that several genes play a role in determining the level of risk. Like diabetes and heart disease, alcoholism is considered to be genetically complex, distinguishing it from diseases such as cystic fibrosis, which results from the mutation of a single gene. Genes that play an important role in alcoholism may include genes associated with liver enzymes that metabolize (break down) alcohol and genes affecting specific patterns of brain chemistry.[5]

Even so, we are not speaking of genetic factors producing these effects in a *deterministic* manner. In Erich Goode's words,

> *No researcher exploring the inherited link with alcoholism asserts that genetic factors comprise the only or even the principal factor in compulsive drinking. Rather, they posit a genetic predisposition toward alcoholism. Inheritance is one factor out of several.*

Alone, it does not "make" someone a compulsive, destructive drinker. In combination with other variables, genetic factors may facilitate or make the process more likely, however.[6]

Physiological Factors

One physiological factor hypothesized to be involved in drug abuse has to do with metabolic processes in the body. In other words, people might differ in the extent to which chemicals in the body are broken down or changed in some way to allow us to function normally. For example, it has been proposed that chronic heroin abuse might be due to a metabolic defect in the bodies of heroin abusers. Just as Type 1 diabetics have an insufficient level of insulin that prevents them from processing glucose in a normal fashion, heroin abusers may have an inborn deficiency with respect to natural opiate-like chemicals produced by the brain itself, and, as a result, they feel compelled to seek out heroin and other opiate drugs from the environment to make up for that deficiency. From this perspective, heroin abusers are "normalizing" their body by engaging in the behavior of heroin abuse. A specific dysfunctional system in the body of a heroin abuser, however, has yet to be discovered. At present, the evidence for a metabolic defect is only circumstantial; heroin-dependent individuals appear to behave *as if* they have a metabolic imbalance with respect to opiates.[7]

Neurochemical Systems in the Brain

Amphetamines, cocaine, heroin, alcohol, and nicotine may be very different from a pharmacological standpoint, but the way people and animals react to them are remarkably similar. Use of these substances results in a pattern of compulsive behavior based on an intense craving for repeating the experience. The similarities among all of these drugs and across species are numerous enough to entertain the idea that there exists a common neurochemical system in the brain that links them all together (Drugs . . . in Focus).

It may not be a coincidence that there is a special area of the brain that animals will work hard to stimulate electrically. We cannot say how they are feeling at the time, but their behavior indicates that they want to "turn on" this region of their brains. Their compulsive efforts

Drugs... in Focus

Understanding the Biochemistry of Psychoactive Drugs

Neurons are specialized cells, designed to receive and transmit information. There are an estimated 100 billion neurons in the brain, making the brain arguably the most complex organ of the body. Importantly, neurons are interconnected with other neurons, providing the basis for communication of information within the nervous system.

The transfer of information from neuron to neuron is controlled by the activity of chemical molecules called neurotransmitters. Specifically, neuron A communicates with neuron B at a juncture point referred to as the synapse. Neurotransmitters are released from neuron A into the synapse and they are "delivered" to neuron B in order for communication to occur. Special receptor sites embedded in neuron B receive the neurotransmitters that have been released. When the neurotransmitter molecules have successfully locked into the receptor site (an event called *receptor binding*), the communication between neurons A and B has been accomplished.

Here is a partial list of neurotransmitters that play a role in the effects of alcohol and other drugs:

- *Acetylcholine* influences heart rate, learning, and memory.
- *Dopamine* affects motor control, mood, and feelings of euphoria. Dopamine plays a major role in producing feelings of craving that encourage a continuing pattern of compulsive drug-taking behavior.
- *Serotonin* affects sensory perception, sleep, mood, and body temperature. Alterations in serotonin have been related to hallucinatory effects of such drugs as LSD and psilocybin.

Abnormal levels of serotonin have been associated with depression and other mood disorders.

- *Endorphins* are natural pain killers produced by the brain and bear a remarkable resemblance to morphine.
- *Norpinephrine* influences sleep, blood pressure, heart rate, and memory. Along with serotonin, norpinephrine has been associated with the regulation of mood.
- *Gamma-aminobutyric acid* (GABA) influences levels of anxiety and general excitation in the brain. Antianxiety medications, often referred to as tranquilizers, stimulate GABA-releasing neurons, providing a reduction in feelings of stress and fear.
- *Glutamate* is the basis for the effects of PCP (angel dust) and ketamine. It is also involved in drug craving and the likelihood of drug-abuse relapse. Current development of new drugs that block glutamate receptors in the brain shows great promise for future drug abuse treatment.

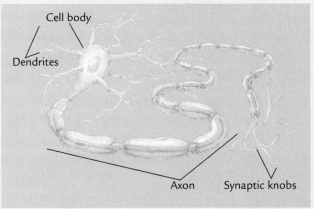

to receive this stimulation are unmistakable. Could there be a connection to the craving, the intense "rush," and compulsive drug-taking behavior associated with heroin, cocaine, amphetamines, or a host of other dependence-producing drugs?

There are two key elements in understanding the intensely rewarding effect of certain psychoactive drugs. The first of these is the existence of brain chemicals called **neurotransmitters** that allow neurons (brain cells) to communicate with each other. A specific neurotransmitter of interest with respect to drug abuse is **dopamine**. The second is the existence of a group of neurons in the brain called the **nucleus accumbens.**

When laboratory animals are administered amphetamines, heroin, cocaine, alcohol, or nicotine, for example, there is an increased level of dopamine activity in the nucleus accumbens. Administration of any substance that interferes with dopamine activity in this region eliminates the desire of animals to work for the self-administration of these abused drugs. While we cannot say, of course, that these animals no longer experience feelings of craving as a result, you will recall that self-administration behavior in animals closely parallels the pattern of human behavior that characterizes psychological dependence (see Chapter 1). Therefore, these studies can be used to understand the neural changes that occur as a consequence of drug abuse. Considering the evidence now in hand, a persuasive argument can be made that dopamine-related processes in the nucleus accumbens underlie the reinforcing effects of many abused drugs. Research also shows an involvement of the nucleus accumbens in compulsive gambling and eating disorders.[8]

Research on the influence of dopamine in drug dependence has the potential to allow us to understand why some individuals may be more susceptible than others to drug-taking behavior. In one study, for example, twenty-three drug-free men with no history of drug abuse were given doses of methylphenidate (brand name: Ritalin), a psychoactive stimulant when ingested by adults. Twelve of the men experienced a pleasant feeling, nine felt annoyed or distrustful, and two felt nothing at all. Measurements of **dopamine receptors** in the brains of these subjects showed a consistent pattern. *The men with the least concentration of dopamine receptors were the ones experiencing pleasant effects.*[9] It is reasonable to hypothesize that those individuals with the fewest dopamine receptors might be the most vulnerable to drug abuse. Their drug-taking behavior might, in part, be a compensation for an inadequate level of dopamine activity that normally would have made it possible to experience pleasurable feelings without drugs (Portrait).

Psychological Perspectives on Drug Abuse

Psychological perspectives on drug abuse typically draw on either psychoanalytic or non-psychoanalytic theories of personality or the behavioral processes of human learning.

Psychoanalytic Theories

Psychoanalytic theories of drug abuse are derived from the work of Sigmund Freud (1856–1939), the founder of psychoanalysis, and focus on internal psychological disturbances that begin in early childhood. According to Freud, one's personality consists of three basic systems: the id, the ego, and the superego. The id, present at birth, consists of instinctual animal impulses or drives, such as hunger and sex. On an unconscious level, the id continually seeks pleasure, is self-serving, and disregards others who get in the way. At the time of birth and immediately thereafter, humans are essentially "all id." The ego, however, is the part of the personality that becomes conscious and rational. The ego develops when a child begins to recognize that he or she cannot "get away with everything," that his or her actions have specific consequences, and that fundamental needs should and eventually will be satisfied in an appropriate context of socially approved behavior. The development of the superego represents the internalization of societal norms and serves as one's social conscience. As a person develops a superego, feelings of guilt and shame arise when social norms are violated.

neurotransmitter: A chemical that makes it possible for neurons (brain cells) to communicate with each other in normal brain functioning. Some examples of neurotransmitters are dopamine, serotonin, GABA, and endorphins.

dopamine (DOPE-ah-meen): A neurotransmitter in the brain whose chemical activity is related to emotionality and motor control.

nucleus accumbens (NEW-clee-us ac-CUM-buns): A region of the brain considered to be responsible for the reinforcing effects of several drugs of abuse.

dopamine receptors: Specialized areas of neurons that enable dopamine to change the neuron's functioning.

psychoanalytic theories: Theoretical explanations based upon the writings of Sigmund Freud and those influenced by him. In terms of drug use and abuse, psychoanalytic concepts include subconscious processes that develop in early childhood, a fixation on the oral stage of development, expressions of power, and self-loathing.

Nora D. Volkow—Imaging the Face of Addiction in the Brain

It is one thing to speculate about the effects of drug abuse on the brain, to assert that the transition from initially being a voluntary drug user to becoming a compulsive drug user is a matter of subtle but significant brain changes. It is quite another thing to show the physical effects themselves. But that is precisely what Nora D. Volkow and her associates at the Brookhaven National Laboratory in New York have done. Using a brain scanning technique called positron emission tomography (PET), neural activity in the human brain can be captured in graphic detail. Volkow and her colleagues have shown that chronic cocaine abuse leads to the loss of about 20 percent of the dopamine receptors in the nucleus accumbens. This effect appears to be long-lasting, enduring for up to four months after the last cocaine exposure, even though the cocaine abuser no longer has cocaine in his or her system. Volkow estimates that a comparable decline in dopamine receptors would take at least 40 years to accomplish in a drug-free brain.

It is not surprising that the nucleus accumbens, with its rich concentration of dopamine receptors, would be the site of this dramatic change. Dopamine and the nucleus accumbens have been associated with feelings of reward and pleasure in a wide range of behavioral activities, from drug use to compulsive exercising to gambling. As Volkow says, "It is through activation of these circuits that we are motivated to do the things we perceive as pleasurable. If you have a decrease in dopamine receptors that transmit pleasurable feelings, you become less responsive to the stimuli such as food or sex, that normally activate them." The irony is that it may be precisely those individuals who have fewer dopamine receptors who may be inclined to engage in drug-taking behavior in the first place; the drug exposure evidently makes the deficit worse. As one drug researcher has put it, "In the end, [these people] could be much worse off biologically than when they started."

Following Volkow's pioneering work on brain imaging, other mysteries about drug abuse are being unlocked. For example, what creates the intense craving for specific drugs once an individual has been first exposed to them? The answer lies in the research of Anna R. Childress and her associates at the University of Pennsylvania. When chronic drug abusers were shown video segments of drug-associated paraphernalia (a picture of a syringe or a mound of white powder), brain scans revealed a change in activity in an area of the limbic system. The connection between the limbic system and one's emotional behavior in times of stress makes it reasonable to hypothesize that this area of the brain, in this instance, would be involved in feelings of drug craving.

In 2003, Nora D. Volkow was appointed director of the National Institute of Drug Abuse (NIDA), the first woman to lead this federal agency in its history.

Sources: Childress, Anna Rose; Mozley, David; McElgin, William; Fitzgerald, Josh; Reivich, Martin; and O'Brian, Charles P. (1999). Limbic activation during cue-induced cocaine craving. *American Journal of Psychiatry, 156,* 11–18. National Institute on Drug Abuse (2003, January 23). Press release: Dr. Nora D. Volkow named new director of NIDA. Bethesda, MD: National Institute on Drug Abuse. Volkow, Nora D.; Wang, Gene-Jack; Fowler, Joanna S.; Logan, Jean; Gatley, Samuel J.; Hitzemann, Richard; Chen, A. D.; and Pappas, Naomi. (1997). Decrease in striatal dopaminergic responsiveness in detoxified cocaine-dependent subjects. *Nature, 386,* 830–833.

Psychoanalytic theory asserts that a strong and healthy ego is ultimately the product of a delicate psychological balancing act in which everyday decisions are maintained in such a way as to minimize excessive out-of-control pressures from the id on the one hand and excessive pressures of guilt and anxiety from the superego on the other. You might notice a connection between the psychoanalytic viewpoint and the basic tenets of the moral model, discussed earlier.

Another psychoanalytic concept that is used to explain drug abuse is the idea that most of us pass through (and advance beyond) an oral and narcissistic stage of development in infancy, a time when our basic needs of food, water, and feelings of security are satisfied orally. Drug abusers, however, are thought to be fixated on the oral stage well past infancy. Psychoanalyst Otto Fenichel theorized that individuals engage in drug abuse to satisfy an archaic oral longing, a sexual longing, a need for security, and a need for the maintenance of self-esteem. All of these needs, he argued, exist in the earliest years of life and, in drug abusers, continue to exert influence, resulting in an orally based pattern of drug-taking behavior.[10]

Some psychoanalytic theorists focus on the symbolism of "getting high," representing an expression of power in the sense that the drug abuser is striving for superiority over others and, importantly, is attempting to rise above a self-deprecating sense of self. Other theorists view drug dependence in terms of an unconscious death wish, the ultimate form of self-loathing. The self-destructive lifestyle of drug abuse is viewed as a failure of ego functioning that, under normal and healthier circumstances, should promote self-care, self-protection, and self-esteem.[11]

Behavioral Theories

In contrast to psychoanalytic theories that emphasize internal struggles of human personality or primitive impulses and drives, **behavioral theories** emphasize the role of learning through reinforcement. According to the behavioral point of view, practically all of human behavior is learned. In other words, drug-taking behavior leading to drug abuse and dependence is a consequence of having modified one's behaviors in specific ways as a result of being rewarded.

The overarching principle of behavioral theory is that any behavior that is followed by a reward (reinforcement) is more likely to be repeated in the future. Repeated rewards will result in a continuing pattern of behavior that can be weakened only when these reinforcers are removed (a process called extinction) or other behaviors are now reinforced (a process called counter-conditioning). Individuals using a drug with a high reinforcement potential typically report that they care more about obtaining and using the drug than just about anything else in their life. In this case, reinforcers related to drug-taking behavior exceed or overcome *competing* reinforcers, such as the benefits and satisfactions derived from a job, money, or friends and family.

While behavior theorists make the distinction between positive reinforcement (gained through the attainment of a pleasurable circumstance) and negative reinforcement (gained through the reduction of a painful or uncomfortable circumstance), the principle of reinforcement remains the same. The reinforcement of heroin abuse, therefore, can focus either on the re-experiencing of the euphoric feelings associated with heroin or on the relief from uncomfortable feelings associated with heroin withdrawal.

Which aspect of reinforcement is emphasized among drug abusers in general can determine the pattern of drug-taking behavior. Those guided by the positive reinforcement of the drug experience are often referred to as *euphoria seekers* and those guided by the negative reinforcement of withdrawal relief are referred to as *maintainers*. Euphoria seekers typically display a compulsive pattern of drug-taking behavior.[12]

In the case of heroin abuse, maintainers tend to consume just enough heroin to avoid the withdrawal symptoms that would occur if their pattern of heroin abuse were to cease. They try to stay within the conventionality of their social community as they "nurse" their habit along. Euphoria-seekers, however, are inclined to be so heavily into the pleasurable aspects of heroin that their lives have spiraled out of control. They have descended into a life-style dominated by the drug. Social conventionality is no longer possible. In Chapter 7, we will examine studies of heroin abusers (called chippers), who are classified as maintainers rather than euphoria-seekers. Clearly, their lives are extremely precarious—a testament to the reinforcing power of heroin.[13]

Behavioral theorists also assert that specific cues or situations have the capability of stimulating powerful drug cravings brought on by memories of past pleasurable (reinforcing) experiences. Through a process of Pavlovian conditioning, drug users will associate drug use with certain visual cues, specific friends and situations, or even a song. Cigarette smokers, for example, commonly report that it is difficult to abstain from smoking when drinking alcohol, talking on the phone, or driving a car if these circumstances have been closely associated with smoking behavior. Some marijuana users report cravings after seeing paraphernalia used in smoking marijuana, such as a bong or pipe, while heroin injectors may crave heroin after viewing a hypodermic needle. The importance of Pavlovian conditioning was discussed in the context of behavioral tolerance in Chapter 1.

behavioral theories: Theoretical explanations of behavior based upon the effect of reinforcement on learned responses to one's environment.

A visual image of white powder, resembling lines of cocaine, tends to elicit powerful feelings of craving among individuals with earlier experiences of cocaine abuse.

Conditioned cues are very difficult to break and can present major obstacles to overcome on the path to drug-abuse recovery. Drug-abuse treatment efforts are often cut short by the appearance of cues that have played an important part in previous drug-taking behavior. Counseling professionals believe that it is essential that individuals break both their pharmacological and their psychological (behavioral) dependence on drugs to return to and maintain a drug-free life.

Non-psychoanalytic Personality Theories

Psychological explanations of drug abuse can also emphasize a constellation of personality traits that distinguish drug abusers from nonabusers, without reference to psychoanalytic concepts. A general theme is that antisocial personality disorder, anxiety, and depression are more common among drug abusers. Individuals with antisocial personality disorder are typically impulsive, sensation seeking, and immature. Individuals displaying these traits may be more prone to abuse drugs because of their increased need for stimulation, excitement, and immediate gratification. Sensation-seeking people are essentially risk-takers ("edgewalkers"), and drug use epitomizes risk-taking behavior, particularly in adolescence.[14]

Interestingly, as pointed out in Chapter 1, risk-seeking does not appear to be a pervasive element in the natural world. Our attraction to the use of hallucinogens such as LSD (see Chapter 8) as a means for altering one's conscious experience, for example, is not commonly shared by animals. While animals may self-administer drugs such as cocaine and other stimulants with a level of compulsiveness that matches the human experience, a number of other drugs are not attractive at all, judging from the animals' reluctance to work for their administration. Hallucinogens, in particular, are examples of drugs that animals clearly prefer to leave alone.[15]

Drug abusers typically demonstrate poor judgment, have difficulty learning from their mistakes, are emotionally insensitive to others, and are unable to form long-lasting relationships with other people. It is believed that anxiety and depression are immediate precursors to drug abuse, in that drugs elevate one's mood and relieve feelings of stress. In effect, individuals

> **anomie (AN-eh-MEE):** In sociological terms, feelings of frustration and alienation when individuals see themselves as not being able to meet the demands of society. Anomie theory is sometimes referred to as strain theory.

suffering from anxiety and depression are engaging in a pattern of self-medication. It is well known, however, that patterns of drug abuse can actually induce anxiety and depression or make matters worse (see Chapter 14 in the case of alcohol abuse).

While psychologists have studied specific personality traits that are more frequently observed in drug abusers, they have not been able to identify a unique set of personality traits for such individuals. For example, alcohol abusers tend to be more independent, nonconformist, and impulsive, but these same traits are also found in successful athletes.[16]

Sociological Perspectives on Drug Abuse

For sociologists, environmental and societal factors play an especially important role in drug use and abuse. The focus of sociological theories is quite different from the focus of theories associated with either a biological or psychological perspective:

> [The] most crucial ... is not the characteristics of the individual, but the situations, social relations, or social structures in which the individual is, or has been, located. More specifically, it is the individual located within specific [social] structures.[17]

During the Vietnam War, for example, a large proportion of American troops used and abused heroin, which was available in Vietnam at extraordinarily high levels of purity. It is reasonable to assume that easy access to heroin in the context of being in a strange and dangerous environment encouraged them to turn to heroin for escape and relief (see Chapter 7). However, only one in eight soldiers continued to use heroin after returning home to a "normal" life. Evidently, the social context of their drug-taking behavior was a crucial factor in allowing them to make this shift .[18]

Sociological perspectives on drug use and abuse will be represented by anomie or strain theory, social control or bonding theory, differential association theory, subcultural recruitment and socialization theory, and labeling theory.

Anomie/Strain Theory

In 1893, sociologist Emile Durkheim used the term **anomie** to describe the feelings of frustration and alienation that exist among individuals who see themselves as not being able to meet the demands of society.[19] Durkheim studied the effects of anomie as they pertained to suicide, while sociologist Robert Merton in 1968 applied the concept to other forms of deviant behavior, such as drug use. Merton believed that every society includes a set of cultural goals and means to achieve them (norms). In most cases, members of society can reach these cultural goals, or at least have some hope of reaching them, by following certain socially defined means. In the United States and other economically developed nations of the world, the primary cultural goal is economic success, and individuals aspire to reach this goal through the acceptable social norm of hard work. When someone is unable to obtain economic success, the result is a feeling of frustration and anomie. This sense of anomie or strain (hence the terms, anomie theory or strain theory) is highest among disadvantaged segments of the population, who experience high rates of crime and drug use in their everyday lives.[20]

Merton classified five possible adaptations or responses to anomie when someone is unable to achieve cultural goals through acceptable means. The five adaptations of conformity, innovation, ritualism, retreatism, and rebellion will be reviewed in the context of drug use and abuse.[21]

- In the first adaptation of *conformity*, individuals accept both culturally defined goals and the prescribed means for achieving them. They may find it necessary to scale down their aspirations, work hard, and save money, while continuing to follow legitimate paths. In this sense, conformity is not deviant behavior but rather an adjustment in their lives. It is also the most common mode of response when contending with anomie. This type of adaptation would lead to a decision not to use or abuse drugs that are outside the mainstream of our culture. It would not, however, discourage the use of alcohol or nicotine if drinking and tobacco smoking were acceptable drug-taking behaviors.

- In the second adaptation of *innovation*, individuals retain the dominant cultural goal of monetary success but choose to reject legitimate avenues of goal attainment. Unlike conformity, innovation involves illegal behavior. Aspiring to be a drug dealer in order to achieve economic success is an example of innovation.

  - In the third adaptation of *ritualism*, individuals reject the goal of economic success (considering it unattainable) but continue to accept the means of working in legitimate areas of life. An example is the burnt-out factory worker who uses illicit drugs to get through the day without "making waves" and then goes home to get drunk or "stoned."

  - In the fourth adaptation of *retreatism*, individuals reject both the goal of economic success and the means of hard work. They have, in effect, given up. Members belonging to this category include individuals who have developed a dependence on alcohol or other drugs. Retreatists can be viewed as double failures. First, they have been unable to find success through conformity. Second, they have not been able to find success as an innovator through criminal activity. Ironically, drug dependent individuals retreat in this way with the expectation that they are entering a seemingly undemanding world. The harsh reality, however, is that drug dependence itself sets off a never-ending series of brutal demands, on both a physical and psychological level. Perhaps only in the case of a

INHALANTS...
(Sprays / Aerosols / Glues)

EVIL SPIRITS THAT BREAK THE BONDS BETWEEN OURSELVES AND OUR ELDERS, DISRUPT THE CIRCLE OF OUR FAMILY SYSTEM, DESTROY THE HARMONY BETWEEN US AND ALL CREATION.

FOR OUR OWN SURVIVAL, THE SURVIVAL OF OUR FAMILY, OUR TRIBE AND THE INDIAN NATION, WE MUST RESIST THESE SPIRITS OF DEATH.

This prevention message focuses on inhalant abuse among American Indian children, adolescents, and young adults, addressing feelings of anomie through the sociocultural filter of their community.

Chinese opium smoker (see Chapter 7) would a retreatist adaptation approach the fantasy of a completely undemanding existence.

■ In the fifth adaptation, *rebellion*, individuals not only reject both the goal of economic success and the means of working but also seek to overturn the social system and replace it with an alternate set of values. These individuals are the radicals and revolutionaries of society who break the law in an attempt to change it. An example is the rebellious youth of the "hippie" subculture of the 1960s. Their association with marijuana and LSD use and their involvement with a wide range of psychoactive substances were components of a political act of rebellion. The popular slogan of the time, "sex, drugs, and rock and roll," represented their rebellious response to the anomie they felt at the time.

It is conceivable that someone's personal adaptation to feelings of anomie could be a combination of the above possibilities.

A survey of more than 9,000 high school students in 1990 found that feelings of anomie or strain were important predictors of drug use. Students who have a negative response to questions such as, "When you are older, do you expect to own more possessions than your parents do now?" or to the statement, "My life is in my hands, and I am in control of it" were more likely to engage in drug-taking behavior.[22]

Anomie theory, however, does tend to oversimplify a complex problem. We know that people who have attained economic success have, at the same time, become dependent on drugs and alcohol. Rock stars and celebrities of all kinds, for example, have become dependent on drugs such as cocaine, heroin, alcohol, and prescription medication. In fact, celebrity status in our society encourages such involvement. Moreover, anomie theory fails to explain why one person chooses to be a ritualist, for instance, whereas another becomes an innovator. Finally, anomie theory disregards the potential impact of interpersonal relationships, such as peer group association, differential access to drugs, and the degree of attachment to one's community and family.

Social Control/Bonding Theory

A second major sociological perspective on drug use and abuse is **social control theory.** According to social control

social control theory: A sociological theory of drug use based on weakened social bonds between an individual and social entities such as family, religious affiliation, school, and community. Social control theory is sometimes referred to as bonding theory.

Treatment for drug-related problems is optimized when there is positive involvement from the family and the social bond of attachment is strengthened.

theorists, all human beings are, by nature, rule breakers. The bonds that people have to society and its moral code are what keep them from breaking the law and remaining socially controlled (hence the terms, social control theory or bonding theory). When an individual is strongly bonded to his or her family, religious affiliation, school, or community, that individual is less likely to engage in delinquent behavior. When these bonds become weakened, deviant behavior, such as drug use, results.

Social control theorists identify four social bonds that promote conformity: attachment, commitment, involvement, and belief.[23] *Attachment* refers to one's closeness to significant others, such as parents, peers, and teachers. Individuals will conform to social norms and refrain from drug use because they seek the approval of these significant individuals. *Commitment* refers to an individual's investment and pursuit in reaching conventional goals, such as the attainment of a good education and a satisfying job. *Involvement* refers to the extent to which one is associated with conventional activities within a school, community, or religious affiliation. *Belief* refers to how well an individual has internalized the moral values of society, such as honesty, perseverance, and respect for authority. Attention to social bonds is important in the design of effective prevention and treatment programs (see Chapter 16).

Empirical tests of predictions made by social control theory with regard to drug use are mixed. Several studies have found that variables such as parental attachment and school attachment are related to lower rates of drug use among youths, whereas other studies have found that relationships with peers act as a more important predictor of drug use than attachment to one's family or school. In fact, the primary weakness of social control theory is that it underestimates the importance of the role of delinquent friends, while overestimating the importance of involvement in conventional social activities. Studies have consistently found that patterns of adolescent alcohol and drug use are strongly related to drug abusers having friends who also engage in this behavior. Yet there is no explanatory role for peers in social control theory.[24]

Differential Association Theory

The third major sociological perspective is **differential association theory.** Originally proposed by sociologist Edwin Sutherland in 1939 as a general theory of deviance, differential association theory has served in recent years as a theoretical foundation for some of the most important research on illicit drug use. The basic premise of the theory is that deviant behavior such as drug use is learned in interactions and communications with other individuals. This learning takes place within relatively intimate groups, such as family and friends. Significant others (parents and friends) often communicate pro-drug or anti-drug messages. When one's attitudes and beliefs favoring drug use exceed one's attitudes and beliefs against drug use, the likelihood increases that drug use will occur. In other words, if an adolescent has a greater number of friends who encourage and use drugs than friends who discourage and do not use drugs, he or she is more likely to engage in that behavior.[25]

From a differential association perspective, the process of learning to use drugs also involves learning the techniques to use drugs and learning how to enjoy the experience. First-time marijuana users, for example, must learn how to roll a "joint" and how to hold the marijuana smoke in their lungs for a period of time to obtain the drug's full effects (see Chapter 10). First-time heroin users must learn how to "cook" or prepare the heroin for intravenous injections by placing the drug in a spoon with water, then heating the substance with a lighter or match to liquify the heroin. Heroin users also must learn the correct method of injecting the drug without damaging their veins (see Chapter 7). Individuals who use LSD or MDMA (Ecstasy) for the first time may be frightened. Users may experience social withdrawal, anxiety, and paranoia (Chapter 9). Peers often play an important role in calming novice users and in teaching them to focus on the positive aspects of the drug experience rather than the negative ones. These techniques are typically demonstrated in small, intimate groups. In fact, very few, if any, adolescents begin using drugs alone or with strangers present at the time.[26]

Identifying oneself as a drug user typically emerges from being immersed in a social network of friends who share a similar outlook in life. Some drug-using youths take part in a drug subculture that plays a pivotal role in teaching them about illicit drugs. A **subculture** is a subdivision within a dominant culture that has its own norms, beliefs, and values. It exists within the larger society, not apart from it. Several important American drug subcultures include the "hippie" subculture of the 1960s that promoted the use of marijuana and LSD or the rave subculture that has promoted the use of Ecstasy. Drug subcultures not only teach young users about the skills for successfully using drugs but also point out the way to obtain drugs, how to avoid getting "ripped off," and sometimes how to manufacture the drugs themselves. A strong sense of social bonding within a drug subculture, usually with its own subculture language, provides the motivation for continued drug use (Drugs . . . in Focus).

Subcultural Recruitment and Socialization Theory

The fourth major sociological perspective draws on the assumptions of differential reinforcement theory but focuses more directly on the dynamic relationships that drug abusers have with respect to each other. According to **proponents of subcultural recruitment and socialization theory,** such as Erich Goode and Bruce Johnson, a selective interaction exists in which individuals are drawn to drug users because they recognize a compatibility of social values. As Goode has expressed it,

> *Even before someone uses a drug for the first time, he or she is "prepared for" or "initiated into" its use—or, in a sense, socialized in advance—because his or her values are already somewhat consistent with those of the drug subculture.*[27]

The social bonding of individuals in the subculture increases as a direct function of drug-taking behavior becoming more and more a central focus of their social interactions.

The dominant influence of peers, however, applies primarily to adolescent drug abuse, according

---

differential association theory: A sociological theory of drug use based upon the premise that drug-taking behavior is learned in interactions and communications with other individuals.

subculture: A subdivision within a dominant culture that has its own norms, beliefs, and values. An example is a drug subculture that provides the social bonding for continued drug use and abuse.

subcultural recruitment and socialization theory: A theoretical perspective on drug abuse that focuses on specific relationships that drug abusers have with respect to each other within a cohesive subculture and the changes that occur in this subculture over time.

Drugs... in Focus

The Private Language of a Drug Subculture

A powerful bond within a subculture is a common language that makes sense only for people within it and is virtually unintelligible to people on the outside. This communication system is largely hidden from the mainstream culture of the society at large. In the case of a marijuana drug subculture in New York City, a personal language provides a socially constructed way of talking, expressing, and interacting among marijuana users and distributors.

Sociologist Bruce Johnson and his associates have examined the importance of "argot" (invented slang) on maintaining the identity of the subculture as well as establishing boundaries with subcultures defined by other types of drugs. In their words, they "constitute important verbal threads that effectively connect participants." They can be standard words with special meanings or completely new words. Here are some examples:

- *Bambu*—marijuana rolling papers
- *One and a Dutch*—a single tabacco cigarette and a blunt (marijuana in a Dutch Master cigar shell)
- *Kind*—good-quality marijuana, shortened form for *kind bud*, shortened further to *kb*

- *Baked, crunked, blazed*—under the influence of marijuana
- *Beastin'*—rushing the process of smoking; not willing to wait one's turn and thus rushing everyone around them
- *Puff-puff-pass*—promoting equality among smokers in group settings, meaning each person takes two inhalations and then passes the marijuana to the next person, until everyone has smoked or the marijuana joint is finished

A private language is a characteristic feature of any deviant subculture, whether the focus is a particular illicit drug such as heroin, cocaine, or Ecstasy or a specialized illicit activity such as computer hacking.

Sources: Holt, Thomas (2007). Subcultural evolution? Examining the influence of on- and off-line experiences on deviant subcultures. *Deviant Behavior, 28*, 171–198. Furst, R. Terry; Johnson, Bruce D.; Dunlap, Eloise; and Curtis, Richard (1999). The stigmatized image of the "crack head": A sociocultural exploration of a barrier to cocaine smoking among a cohort of youth in New York City. *Deviant Behavior, 20*, 153–181. Johnson, Bruce D.; Bardhi, Flutura; Sifraneck, Stephen J.; and Dunlap, Eloise (2006). Marijuana argot as subculture threads: Social constructions by users in New York City. *British Journal of Criminology, 46*, 46–77. Quotation on page 46.

---

to the studies of Denise Kandel. In later stages of drug abuse, when the drugs of choice change from a concentration on beer, wine, cigarettes, liquor, and marijuana to drugs such as cocaine and heroin, drug abusers tend to break away from a tightly focused subcultural group and move toward a set of less intimate relationships. At this point, there is typically a close relationship with only one drug-abusing friend, an individual who shares the same social attitudes, behaviors, and problems.[28]

Labeling Theory

The fifth major sociological perspective is **labeling theory** Labeling theorists argue that virtually everyone has experimented with drugs at some time in his or her life. This experimentation is referred to as **primary deviance**: nonconformity that is temporary, exploratory, and easily concealed. Primary deviant acts, such as drug experimentation, often go unnoticed, and individuals who commit these acts do not generally regard themselves as deviants and are not labeled as such by others. Once the drug use is discovered and made public by others, however, the situation changes. At this point, drug users are labeled as deviant, and they are often seen in a new light by others as a "stoner" or "dope head." It becomes difficult for users to shed this new status.

Eventually, users begin to internalize the newly acquired label and continue to use drugs because others expect them to do so. In other words, the individual changes his or her self-perception to fit the expectations of others. Behavior now continues as

labeling theory: A sociological theory of drug use that emphasizes the process by which a drug user internalizes a newly acquired label of deviance and continues a pattern of drug-taking behavior that is based on the expectations of others.

primary deviance: Nonconformist behavior associated with drug experimentation. It is temporary, exploratory, and easily concealed from others.

FIGURE 4.2

The biopsychosocial model asserts that there are multiple pathways to drug abuse.

Source: Modified from Margolis, Robert D., and Zweben, Joan E. (1998). *Treating patients with alcohol and other drug problems: An integrated approach.* Washington, DC: American Psychological Association, pp. 76–87.

secondary deviance, in the form of a persistent pattern of nonconformity by the individual who has been labeled as deviant. Drug users who do not wish to be labeled as deviant may choose to keep their drug use covert or, in time, may become a member of a drug subculture.

According to labeling theorists, social class distinctions play a major role in determining whether an individual might be labeled in a negative manner. A businessman who drinks three vodka martinis at lunch, for example, is much less likely to be labeled as deviant than a factory worker who drinks three beers at lunch. As discussed in Chapter 3, policy decisions regarding which drugs to outlaw and which to legitimize have often been associated with an underlying fear of a minority group whose drug use has become labeled as socially deviant.[29]

Integrating Theoretical Perspectives on Drug Abuse

Success in drug-abuse treatment rests upon the recognition that there are multiple pathways to drug abuse. For each individual, a specific combination of biological, psychological, and sociological factors plays a role in getting that person to the point at which treatment

is necessary. As mentioned in Chapter 1, this integrated, combinational approach to treatment, referred to as the **biopsychosocial model** (Figure 4.2), is important not only in understanding drug abuse but in understanding drug-taking behavior in general.[30]

Risk Factors and Protective Factors

In a direct and straightforward manner, researchers have asked high school seniors to report their personal reasons for taking drugs.[31] The most frequently occurring responses among the classes of 1983 and 1984 have included "to have a good time with my friends" (65 percent), "to experiment or see what it's like" (54 percent), "to feel good or

secondary deviance: Persistent nonconformist behavior by an individual who has been labeled as deviant and whose deviant behavior (e.g., drug use) is based upon expectations of others.

biopsychosocial model: A theoretical perspective on drug use that recognizes the biological, psychological, and sociological factors underlying drug-taking behavior and encourages an integrated approach toward drug-abuse treatment.

Quick Concept Check 4.1

Understanding Theoretical Perspectives on Drug Use and Abuse

Check your understanding of the theories of drug use and abuse by matching the statement (on the left) with appropriate theory (on the right).

1. Virtually everyone has experimented with drugs at some time in their life. However, when this drug use is discovered, users may be stigmatized and labeled as deviant by others.

2. People denied access to societal goals will suffer from strain and respond by conforming, rebelling, illegally innovating, or retreating. According to this theory, most drug users are retreatists.

3. Drug-taking behavior is strengthened through positive and negative reinforcement.

4. Deviant behavior such as drug use is learned in interaction and communication with other persons.

5. Drug abuse and drug addiction arise from internal disturbances that develop in early childhood.

6. It is the bond to society and its moral orders that keeps individuals from breaking the law.

7. Adolescent drug abuse is characterized by a tightly focused subcultural group based on intimate relationships among group members.

a. Behavioral theory
b. Psychoanalytic theory
c. Social control theory
d. Differential association theory
e. Anomie theory
f. Labeling theory
g. Social recruitment and socialization theory

Answers: 1. f 2. e 3. a 4. d 5. b 6. c 7. g

risk factors: Factors in an individual's life that increase the likelihood of involvement with drugs.

protective factors: Factors in an individual's life that decrease the likelihood of involvement with drugs and reduce the impact that any risk factor might have.

get high" (49 percent), and "to relax or relieve tension" (41 percent). These responses were similar to reasons given by the class of 1976 in earlier surveys, and there is no reason to suspect significant differences today.

These studies are interesting not only for the insights they have provided but also for the way they have been carried out. There was no theoretical perspective behind the question. In other words, the research was not theory-driven.

A large literature has accumulated that deals with the relationship between a given variable (pertaining to an individual's life-style, family makeup, environmental condition, etc.) and the likelihood that drug use will occur. Based on the information gained in such studies, we find it useful to consider that a given person has a certain degree of vulnerability with respect to drug-taking behavior.

This personal vulnerability can be shaped by two separate groups of factors in a person's life. The first are **risk factors**, which make it *more likely* that a person will be involved with drugs; the second are **protective factors**, which make it *less likely* that a person will be involved with drugs. Together, risk factors and protective factors combine to give us some idea about the likelihood that drug-taking behavior will occur. The emphasis, however, should be on the phrase "some idea." We still cannot know for certain which individuals would use drugs and which ones would not. Any predictions about drug use would be probabilistic, not deterministic.

Nonetheless, an understanding of risk factors and protective factors in general and knowledge about which factors apply to a given individual are useful pieces of information in the development of effective drug prevention programs. Identifying the population with the highest risk toward drug use is the first step toward allocating the necessary time, effort, and money to lower the chances that drug-related problems will occur.

Specific Risk Factors

Certain factors that may appear to be strong risk factors for drug-taking behavior in general (socioeconomic status, for example) turn out to have an association that is far from simple and may depend upon the particular drug under discussion. The most reliable set of risk factors consists of psychosocial characteristics that reflect a tendency toward nonconformity within society. Young people who take drugs are more inclined to attend school irregularly, have poor relationships with their parents, or get into trouble in general. As discussed earlier, sociologists refer to such individuals as members of a deviant subculture.[32]

The effects of participating in a socially deviant subculture are highlighted by the increased probability that an individual will display some level of drug-taking behavior. For example, the odds of youths aged twelve to seventeen using marijuana during the past year are more than six times (6.25 times to be precise) greater among those who had at least a few close friends who tried or used marijuana than among those who did not have such friends (the second listed risk factor in Table 4.1). To put this risk factor in perspective, the "odds ratio" is considerably lower than the twenty-seven times greater likelihood of developing lung cancer after decades of smoking more than a pack of cigarettes each day (versus never smoking at all). Therefore, we are more likely to be wrong in predicting marijuana use on the basis of one's association with close friends who use marijuana than in predicting lung cancer on the basis of years of cigarette smoking. Nonetheless, studies of risk factors are important elements in our overall understanding of the complexities of drug-taking behavior.

The leading risk factors for marijuana use include the perceived prevalence of marijuana use by friends in and out of school and the perceived prevalence of use in the community. Individual attitudes toward marijuana smoking, and, in particular, the attitude of friends toward marijuana smoking are also significant risk factors. The most significant risk factor, however, is the inclination toward delinquent (antisocial) behavior. By contrast, economic deprivation as measured by a low household income, fails to be a risk factor for marijuana use.[34]

TABLE 4.1

Major risk factors: Odds ratios for marijuana use over the past year among youths aged 12–17 as related to specific questions

RISK FACTOR	REPRESENTATIVE QUESTION	ODDS RATIO
Antisocial behavior	"How many times have you gotten into a serious fight at school or at work?"	7.10
Friends' marijuana use	"How many friends would you say use marijuana?"	6.25
Perceived prevalence of marijuana use in school	"How many of the students in your grade in school would you say use marijuana?"	4.78
Individual attitudes toward marijuana use	"How would you feel (positively) about someone your age trying marijuana?"	4.47
Friends' attitudes toward marijuana use	"How do you think your close friends would feel (positively) about your trying marijuana?"	4.37
Marijuana use in community	"How many adults who you know personally would you say used marijuana?"	4.14
Perceived risk of marijuana use	"How (little) do you think people risk harming themselves physically and in other ways when they smoke marijuana?"	3.48
Marijuana available in community	"How easy would it be to get some marijuana, if you wanted some?"	2.72
Lack of parental monitoring	"How (seldom) have your parents checked on whether you did your homework?"	2.60

Note: By definition, risk factors have odds ratios greater than 1. Behavior is more likely to occur if a risk factor is present, through a multiplier designated by the odds ratio. The higher the odds ratio, the stronger the risk factor. Risk factors related to multiple substance use/availability/attitudes tend to have higher odds ratios than risk factors related to use/availability/attitudes associated with marijuana alone.

Source: Wright, Douglas, and Pemberton, Michael (2004). *Risk and protective factors for adolescent drug use: Findings from the 1999 National Household Survey on Drug Use.* Rockville, MD: Office of Applied Studies, Substance Abuse and Mental Health Services Administration, Chapter 3 and Appendix A.

Specific Protective Factors

Protective factors provide the basis for someone to have stronger resistance against the temptations of drugs, to have a degree of resilience against engaging in a drug-taking life-style, despite the presence of risk factors in that person's life.[35] It is important that we not see these protective factors, however, as simply the inverted image, or the negation of, opposing risk factors. Rather, each group of factors operates independently of the other. One way of thinking about protective factors is to view them as a kind of insurance policy against the occurrence of some future event that you hope to avoid. For example, the third listed protective factor in Table 4.2 shows an odds ratio of 0.45, indicating that youths aged twelve to seventeen who answer "yes" to the question , "Do you like going to school?" are about one-half (.45 to be precise) as likely to have tried or

TABLE 4.2

Major protective factors: Odds ratios for marijuana use over the past year among youths aged 12–17 as related to specific questions

PROTECTIVE FACTOR	REPRESENTATIVE QUESTION	ODDS RATIO
Sanctions against substance use in school	*"How much trouble do you think a student in your grade would be in if he or she got caught using an illegal drug?"*	0.28
Parents as sources of social support	*"Would you select your mother or father as a source of social support?"*	0.40
Commitment to school	*"Do you like going to school?"*	0.45
Religiosity	*"How many times did you attend religious services?"*	0.47
Extracurricular activities	*"Have you participated in at least two extracurricular activities in or out of school?"*	0.52
Parental encouragement	*"How often did your parents let you know that you'd done a good job?"*	0.59
Exposure to prevention messages in school	*"Have you had a special class or some information in your school about drugs or alcohol?"*	0.63
Exposure to prevention messages in the media	*"Have you seen or heard any alcohol or drug prevention messages outside of school?"*	0.70

Note: By definition (see text), protective factors have odds ratios less than 1. The lower the odds ratio, the stronger the protective factor. Behavior is less likely to occur if a protective factor is present, through a multiplier designated by the odds ratio.

Source: Wright, Douglas, and Pemberton, Michael (2004). *Risk and protective factors for adolescent drug use: Findings from the 1999 National Household Survey on Drug Use.* Rockville, MD: Office of Applied Studies, Substance Abuse and Mental Health Services Administration, Chapter 3 and Appendix A.

used marijuana during the past year than youths who answer, "no."[36]

Protective factors can serve as a buffering element among even high-risk adolescents, allowing

Peer influence is a major factor in predicting the extent of drug-taking behavior during adolescence. It can represent either a risk factor or a protective factor for drug abuse.

them to have a greater degree of resilience against drug-taking behavior and a higher resistance to drug use than they would have had otherwise. In one study, protective factors were examined in one thousand high-risk male and female adolescents in the seventh and eighth grades, and information was collected on their drug use later in high school. As the number of protective factors increased, the resistance of these students to drug use increased as well. With six or more such factors in their lives, as many as 56 percent of the high-risk adolescents showed a resistance to drug use three years later. In contrast, with three or fewer factors, only 20 percent of the youths were drug-free.[37]

In research by the Search Institute in Minneapolis, as many as forty protective factors have been identified, referred to collectively as *developmental assets*.[38] These developmental assets have been found to increase resistance not only to drug-taking behavior (such as problem alcohol use and illicit drug use) but to other high-risk behaviors (such as sexual activity and violence) as well (Figure 4.3).

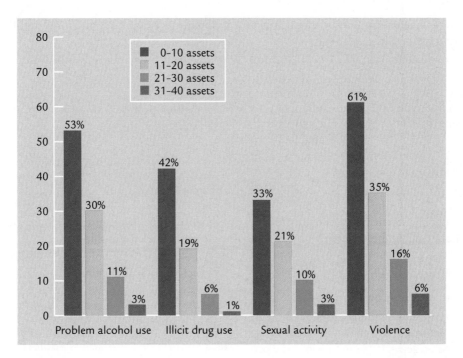

FIGURE 4.3

The percentages of four high-risk behaviors as a function of the number of developmental assets, based on responses of sixth- to twelfth-grade youth.

Source: This graph is made available with permission from DEVELOPMENTAL ASSETS: A Synethesis of the Scientific Research on Adolescent Development by Peter C. Scales and Nancy Leffert. Copyright (c) 1999 by Search Institute (R). No other use is permitted without prior permission from Search Institute, 615 First Avenue NE, Minneapolis, MN 55413. All rights reserved. To learn more about assets or view a list of 40 Developmental Assets (R), visit www.search-institute.org.

Summary

Biological Perspectives on Drug Abuse

● Biological perspectives on drug abuse refer to specific physical mechanisms in specific individuals that influence the initial experience with drugs or an engagement with drug abuse over a period of time. Theories from this perspective have focused on genetic factors, physiological factors, and neurochemical systems in the brain.

● Research on genetic factors has concentrated primarily on explanations for alcohol abuse and alcoholism. The consensus in this literature is that there is a genetic predisposition toward alcoholism.

● Physiological factors include metabolic deficiencies that set the stage for individuals to seek out drugs to "normalize" their bodies. A metabolic-defect concept has been applied to the study of heroin abuse.

● Research on the role of neurochemical systems in drug abuse has concentrated on the functioning of dopamine in the nucleus accumbens. Drug-taking behavior has been hypothesized to be a compensation for an inadequate number of dopamine receptors necessary to experience pleasurable feelings without drugs.

Psychological Perspectives on Drug Abuse

● Psychological perspectives on drug abuse draw on either theories of personality or the behavioral processes of human learning.

● Psychoanalytic theories of personality, derived from the writings of Sigmund Freud, focus on psychological disturbances that have their origin in early childhood. Concepts include the competition of id and superego processes for dominance in ego functioning, oral fixation in development, and self-destructive behavior as an expression of self-loathing.

- Behavioral theories emphasize the pivotal role of reinforcement in the learning of drug-taking behaviors. Behavioral theorists have studied the influence of positively reinforcing experiences inherent in the drug experience itself as opposed to negatively reinforcing experience of gaining relief from uncomfortable withdrawal symptoms in predicting the manner in which heroin is abused.

- Non-psychoanalytic personality theories consider the personality traits that distinguish drug abusers from nonabusers, without reference to psychoanalytic concepts. A central theme in these theories is the role of sensation-seeking among individuals as a predisposing characteristic for drug experimentation and abuse.

Sociological Perspectives on Drug Abuse

- Sociological perspectives emphasize the important role of environmental and social factors in drug use and abuse. Theories generated from a sociological perspective include anomie/strain theory, social control/bonding theory, differential association theory, subcultural recruitment and socialization theory, and labeling theory.

- Anomie/strain theorists assert that drug use and abuse result from feelings of frustration and alienation existing in individuals who see themselves as not being able to meet the demands of society. Adaptations to feelings of anomie include conformity, innovation, ritualism, retreatism, and rebellion.

- Social control/bonding theory identifies attachment, commitment, involvement, and belief as four social bonds that promote conformity and the disinclination to be a drug user.

- The basic premise of differential association theory is that drug use is learned in interactions and communications with significant others such as parents and friends.

- In subcultural recruitment and socialization theory, the focus is on the dynamic relationships among drug abusers as a cohesive group. In adolescent patterns of drug abuse, peer influence is the dominant factor in maintaining the subculture; in later stages, drug abusers tend to break away from a tightly focused subcultural group and move toward a set of less intimate relationships.

- Labeling theory emphasizes the process through which individuals continue to use drugs because others expect them to do so. Drug users who are labeled as deviant may "find comfort" in being a member of a drug subculture.

Risk Factors and Protective Factors

- Investigations of risk factors and protective factors in drug-taking behavior are not theory-driven. A relationship is sought between a given variable (an individual's lifestyle, family makeup, environmental condition, etc.) and the likelihood that drug use will occur.

- Risk factors for drug-taking behavior in adolescence include a tendency toward nonconformity within society and the influence of drug-using peers.

- Protective factors for drug-taking behavior include an intact home environment, a positive educational experience, and conventional peer relationships.

Key Terms

anomie, p. 74
behavioral theories, p. 73
biopsychosocial model, p. 79
differential association
    theory, p. 77

dopamine, p. 71
dopamine receptors, p. 71
labeling theory, p. 78
moral model, p. 68
neurotransmitters, p. 71

nucleus accumbens, p. 71
primary deviance, p. 78
protective factors, p. 80
psychoanalytic theories, p. 71
risk factors, p. 80

secondary deviance, p. 79
social control theory, p. 76
subcultural recruitment and
    socialization theory, p. 77
subculture, p. 77

Endnotes

1. Goode, Erich (2005). *Drugs in American society* (6th ed.). Boston: McGraw-Hill College. Quotation on p. 55.
2. Fisher, Gary L., and Harrison, Thomas C. (2000). *Substance abuse: Information for school counselors, social workers, therapists, and counselors.* Boston: Allyn and Bacon. Quotation on p. 57. Goode, *Drugs.* Miller, William R., and Hester, Reid K. (1995). Treatment for alcohol problems: Toward an informed eclecticism. In William R. Miller and Reid K. Hester (Eds.), *Handbook of alcoholism treatment approaches* (2nd ed.). Boston: Allyn and Bacon, pp. 1–11.
3. George, F. R., and Goldberg, S. R. (1989). Genetic approaches to the analysis of addictive processes. *Trends in Pharmacological Science, 10,* 78–83. LeGrand, Lisa N.;

Iacono, William G.; and McGue, Matt (2005, March–April). Predicting addiction. *American Scientist*, pp. 140–147.

4. Sher, Kenneth J. (1991). *Children of alcoholics: A critical appraisal of theory and research.* Chicago: University of Chicago Press.

5. Herman, Aryeh. I.; Philbeck, John W.; Vasilopoulos, Nicholas L.; and DePetrillo, Paolo B. (2003). Serotonin transport promoter polymorphism and differences in alcohol consumption behavior in a college study population. *Alcohol and Alcoholism*, 38, 446–449. National Institute on Alcohol Abuse and Alcoholism (2003). *Is there a genetic relationship between alcoholism and depression?* Rockville, MD: National Institute on Alcohol Abuse and Alcoholism. Nurnberger, John I., and Bierut, Laura Jean (2007, April). Seeking the connections: Alcoholism and our genes. *Scientific American*, 46–53.

6. Goode, *Drugs.* Quotation on p. 56.

7. Goode, *Drugs*, pp. 56–57. Myerson, David J. (1969). Methadone treatment of addicts. *New England Journal of Medicine*, 281, 380. Prendergast, Michael L., and Podus, Deborah (1999, May 10). Methadone debate reflects deep-rooted conflicts in field.*Alcoholism and Drug Abuse Weekly*, p. 5.

8. Heidbreder, Christian A., and Hagan, Jim J. (2005). Novel pharmacotherapeutic approaches to the treatment of drug addiction and craving. *Current Opinion in Pharmacology*, 5, 107–108. Nestler, Eric J., and Malenka, Robert C. (2004, March). The addicted brain. *Scientific American*, pp. 78–85. Phillips, Paul E. M.; Stuber, Garret D.; Heien, Michael L, A. V.; Wightman, R. Mark; and Carelli, Regina. M. (2003). Subsecond dopamine release promotes cocaine seeking. *Nature*, 422, 614–618. Weiss, Freidbert (2005). Neurobiology of craving, conditioned reward, and relapse. *Current Opinion in Pharmacology*, 5, 9–19.

9. Volkow, Nora D.; Wang, Gene-Jack; Fowler, Joanna S.; Logan, Jean; Gatley, Samuel J.; Gifford, Andrew; Hitzemann, Robert; Ding, Yu-Shin; and Pappas, Naomi (1999). Prediction of reinforcing responses to psychostimulants in humans by brain dopamine D_2 receptor levels. *American Journal of Psychiatry*, 156, 1440–1443.

10. Fenichel, Otto (1945). *The psychoanalytic theory of neurosis.* New York: Norton. Fields, Richard (2004). *Drugs in perspective* (5th ed.). New York: McGraw-Hill Higher Education.

11. Fields, *Drugs in perspective.* Gottheil, Edward (ed.) (1983). *Etiological aspects of alcohol/drug abuse.* Springfield, IL: Charles C. Thomas. Stanton, M. Duncan, and Todd, Thomas C. (Eds.) (1982). *The family therapy of drug abuse and addiction.* New York: Guilford Press.

12. Goode, *Drugs*, pp. 57–60.

13. Hser, Yih-Ing; Hoffman, Valerie; Grella, Christine; and Anglin, M. Douglas (2001). A 33-year follow-up of narcotics addicts. *Archives of General Psychiatry*, 58, 503–508. Zinberg, Norman E. (1984). *Drugs, set, and setting: The basis for controlled intoxicant use.* New Haven, CT: Yale University Press, pp. 46–81.

14. Cristie, Kimberly A.; Burke, Jack; Regier, Darrel A.; Rae, Donald S.; Boyd, Jeffrey H.; and Locke, Ben Z. (1988). Epidemiological evidence for early onset of mental disorders and higher risk of drug abuse in young adults. *American Journal of Psychiatry*, 145, 971–975. Fields, *Drugs in perspective*, p. 8. Lewis, C. E. (1984). Alcoholism, antisocial personality, narcotic addiction: An integrative approach. *Psychiatric Developments*, 3, 22–35. Shedler, Jonathan, and Block, Jack (1990). Adolescent drug users and psychological health: A longitudinal inquiry. *American Psychologist*, 45, 612–630.

15. Yokel, Robert A. (1987). Intravenous self-administration: Response rates, the effect of pharmacological challenges and drug preferences. In Michael A. Bozarth (Ed.), *Methods of assessing the reinforcing properties of abused drugs.* New York: Springer-Verlag, pp. 1–34.

16. Kerr, John S. (1996). Two myths of addiction: The addictive personality and the issues of free choice. *Human psychopharmacology*, 11, 39–45. Ross, Helen E.; Glaser, Frederick B.; and Germanson, Teresa (1988). The prevalence of psychiatric disorders in patients with alcohol and other drug problems. *Archives of General Psychiatry*, 45, 1023–1031.

17. Goode, *Drugs*, p. 63.

18. Robins, Lee N. (1974). *The Vietnam drug user returns.* Special Action Office for Drug Abuse Prevention Monograph Series A, No. 2, Contract HSM-42-72-75.

19. Durkheim, Emile (1951). *Suicide* (translated by John Spaulding and George Simpson). New York: Free Press.

20. Agnew, Robert (1992). Foundation for a general strain theory of crime and delinquency. *Criminology*, 30, 47–87. Merton, Robert K. (1968). *Social theory and social structure.* New York: Free Press.

21. Merton, *Social theory.*

22. Lorch, Barbara D. (1990). Social class and its relationship to youth substance use and other delinquent behaviors. *Social Work Research Abstracts*, 26, 25–34.

23. Akers, Ronald L. (1992). *Drugs, alcohol, and society: Social structure, process, and policy.* Belmont CA: Wadsworth, pp. 8–9. Hirschi, Travis (1969). *Causes of delinquency.* Los Angeles: University of California Press.

24. Burkett, Steven R., and Warren, Bruce O. (1987). Religiosity, peer associations, and adolescent marijuana use: A panel study of underlying causal structures. *Criminology*, 25, 109–131. Durkin, Keith F., Wolf, Timothy W., and Clark, Gregory (1999). Social bond theory and binge drinking among college students: A multivariate analysis. *College Student Journal*, 33, 450–462. Durkin, Keith F.; Wolfe, Timothy; and Clark, Gregory A. (2005). College students and binge drinking: An evaluation of social learning theory. *Sociological Spectrum*, 25, 255–272. Guo, Jie; Hill, Karl J.; Hawkins, David; Catalano, Richard F.; and Abbott, Robert D. (2002). A developmental analysis of sociodemographic, family, and peer

effects on adolescent illicit drug initiation. *Journal of the American Academy of Child and Adolescent Psychiatry, 41*, 838–846.

25. Sutherland, Edwin H. (1939). *Principles of criminology* (3rd ed.). Philadelphia: Lippincott.

26. Becker, Howard S. (1953). Becoming a marijuana user. *American Journal of Sociology, 59*, 235–242. Faupel, Charles E. (1991). *Shooting dope: Career contingencies of hard-core heroin users.* Hirsch, Michael L., Conforti, Randall W., and Graney, Carolyn, J. (2001). The use of marijuana for pleasure: A replication of Howard S. Becker's study of marijuana use. *Journal of Social Behavior and Personality, 5*, 497–510.

27. Goode, *Drugs*, pp. 71–74. Quotation on p. 71. Johnson, Bruce (1973). *Marijuana users and drug subcultures.* New York: Wiley-Interscience. Johnson, Bruce (1980). Toward a theory of drug subcultures. In Dan J. Lettieri et al. (Eds.), *Theories on drug abuse*, pp. 110–119.

28. Kandel, Denise B. (1973). Adolescent marijuana use: Role of parents and peers. *Science, 181*, 1067–1070. Kandel, Denise B. (1980). Developmental stages in adolescent drug involvement. In Dan J. Lettieri et al. (Eds.), *Theories on drug abuse*, pp. 120–127. Kandel, Denise B., and Mark Davies (1991). Friendship networks, intimacy, and drug use in young adulthood: A comparison of two competing theories. *Criminology, 29*, 441–467.

29. Becker, Howard S. (1963). *Outsiders: Studies in the sociology of deviance.* New York: Free Press. Erickson, K. (1962). Notes on the sociology of deviance. *Social Problems, 9*, 397–414. Lemert, Edwin M. (1951). *Social pathology.* New York: McGraw-Hill.

30. Margolin, Robert D., and Zweben, Joan E. (1998). *Treating patients with alcohol and other drug problems: An integrated approach.* Washington, DC: American Psychological Association, pp. 76–87.

31. Johnston, Lloyd D., and O'Malley, Patrick M. (1986). Why do the nation's students use drugs and alcohol? Self-reported reasons from nine national surveys. *The Journal of Drug Issues, 16*, 29–66.

32. Goode, *Drugs*, pp. 68–71.

33. Substance Abuse and Mental Health Services Administration (2001). *Risk and protective factors for adolescent drug use: Findings from the 1997 National Household Survey on Drug Abuse.* Rockville, MD: Office of Applied Studies, Substance Abuse and Mental Health Services Administration, pp. 27–42. Watts, W. David, and Wright, Loyd S. (1990). The drug use–violent delinquency link among adolescent Mexican-Americans. In Mario De la Rosa, Elizabeth Y. Lambert, and Bernard Gropper (Eds.), *Drugs and violence: Causes, correlates, and consequences* (NIDA Research Monograph 103). Rockville, MD: National Institute on Drug Abuse.

34. Wright, Douglas, and Pemberton, Michael (2004). *Risk and protective factors for adolescent drug use: Findings from the 1999 National Household Survey on Drug Abuse.* Rockville, MD: Office of Applied Studies, Substance Abuse and Mental Health Services Administration, Chapter 3 and Appendix A

35. Scheier, Lawrence M., Botvin, Gilbert J., and Baker, Eli (1997). Risk and protective factors as predictors of adolescent alcohol involvement and transitions in alcohol use: A prospective analysis. *Journal of Studies in Alcohol, 58*, 652–667. Scheier, Lawrence M., Newcomb, Michael D., and Skager, Rodney (1994). Risk, protection, and vulnerability to adolescent drug use: Latent-variable models of three age groups. *Journal of Drug Education, 24*, 49–82.

36. Wright and Pemberton, *Risk and protective factors*, Chapters 3 and Appendix A.

37. Smith, Carolyn; Lizotte, Alan J.; Thornberry, Terence P.; and Krohn, Marvin D. (1995). Resilient youth: Identifying factors that prevent high-risk youth from engaging in delinquency and drug use. In J. Hagan (Ed.), *Delinquency and disrepute in the life course.* Greenwich, CT: JAI Press, pp. 217–247.

38. Scales, Peter C., and Leffert, Nancy (1999). *Developmental assets: A synthesis of the scientific research on adolescent development.* Minneapolis: Search Institute. Search Institute (2001, February). *Profiles of student life: Attitudes and behavior.* Minneapolis: Search Institute.

chapter 5

Drugs and Crime

After you have completed this chapter, you should have an understanding of

- The relationship between drug use and crime
- The structure of the illicit drug trade
- Production and trafficking of heroin
- Production and trafficking of cocaine
- Production and trafficking of marijuana
- Production and trafficking of methamphetamine
- Production and trafficking of hallucinogens
- Drug-related crime and gangs
- Common methods of money laundering

In the last couple of years we have found a large number of marijuana plots in the Chattahoochee National Forest. Growers are planting their marijuana in this area to escape forfeiture laws. So I came up with this idea that I never thought would work but I figured was worth a try. I typed a letter and left it at one of the larger plots we found in the national forest. The letter said, "You have been caught by the Lumpkin County Sheriff's Office. We have had you under constant surveillance. If you do not turn yourself in by calling the following number, your penalties for growing marijuana will be doubled."

I couldn't believe it, but it actually worked. I had one grower call me and turn himself in. He claimed that he was only growing marijuana for personal use. I didn't even have to pick him up. He drove to the sheriff's office and turned himself in. Incredible but true!

—*A sheriff's deputy from Lumpkin County, Georgia*

For law-enforcement officers and other criminal justice professionals who contend with drugs and crime on a daily basis, the drug–crime connection is all too real and an inarguable fact of contemporary society. As stated in a training manual sponsored by the International Association of Chiefs of Police, "If there is a reduction in the number of people who abuse drugs in your community, there will be a reduction in the commission of certain types of crime in your community." For the general public, the news headlines reporting acts of social violence linked to the world of illicit drugs are relentless. Wherever we look, illicit drugs and crime are seen as being bound together in a web of greed and callous disregard for human life.

Currently, research on drugs and crime is supported primarily by two federal agencies, the National Institute of Justice (NIJ) and the National Institute on Drug Abuse (NIDA). There is an increasingly close collaboration between NIJ and NIDA as they tackle the complex issues surrounding a major social problem in the United States today. This chapter will concern itself with the facts as well as the still-unanswered questions about drugs and crime in our society.[1]

Defining Drug-related Crime

Crimes that involve *illicit* drugs can be divided into two general categories: (1) drug-defined offenses and (2) drug-related offenses. **Drug-defined offenses** are violations of laws prohibiting the possession, use, distribution, or manufacture of illegal drugs. The possession of cocaine, the cultivation of marijuana, and the sale of methamphetamine are all examples of drug-defined offenses. Today, more than 50 percent of all federal prison inmates are serving time for drug-defined offenses, more than for any other type of criminal offense. While rates of illicit drug use in the United States have declined by roughly 50 percent since 1979 (see Chapter 2), the number of adult drug arrests has tripled. In 2009, the number of arrests for drug-abuse violations exceeded 1.6 million. It is reasonable to conclude, therefore, that the increase in incarceration rates of drug

drug-defined offense: Violation of laws that prohibit the possession, use, distribution, and manufacture of illegal drugs.

drug-related offense: Offense in which a drug contributes to the commission of a crime, either by virtue of the drug's pharmacological effects or the economic need to secure the drug itself.

offenders reflects an intensified effort to step up drug-law enforcement rather than an increase in drug use. Since the mid-1980s, state and federal legislatures have enacted a wide range of criminal laws with respect to the selling and possession of illicit drugs, and judges have imposed longer prison sentences for drug offenders. The average time currently served by someone convicted of a drug offense is 42 months, slightly less than the length of sentence for those convicted of arson and possession of explosives or weapons.[2]

Drug-related offenses are offenses that do not involve a violation of a drug law *per se*, but rather a violation of a law of some other type. The crime a drug user commits might be caused by the acute effects of the drug itself or the need on the part of the drug user to gain money to purchase drugs. While these crimes most often come to mind as those associated with drug use, it is important to recognize that a drug-related crime can also relate to violent behaviors that are associated with a drug-dealing life. Violence can result from disputes over territory between rival gangs involved in drug dealing, punishment for defrauding a buyer, retaliation toward police informants, or acts committed simply to enforce discipline. Drug use, the drug business, and the violence connected with both are all aspects of a lifestyle that increases one's risk of becoming a victim or perpetrator of drug-related crime. As we will see, it is the character of the drug-use lifestyle that is primarily responsible for the complex relationship between drugs and crime.

Understanding Drug Use and Crime

Drug use and the commission of criminal acts are strongly correlated. It is virtually impossible to find an empirical study that has failed to find a relationship between these two behaviors. Not surprisingly, individuals who drink alcohol and/or use drugs are significantly more likely to commit crimes than are individuals who neither drink nor use drugs.

Historically, the process by which drug use and crime is linked has been explored through three major perspectives. The first perspective is called the *enslavement model*, also referred to as the "medical model." It asserts that individuals become forced into a life of crime and drug abuse, either from social situations such as poverty or from a personal condition such as a physical disorder. In other words, criminal activity and drug use or abuse arise together from a common adverse circumstance in one's life. The *predisposition* model, also referred to as the "criminal model," asserts that drug abusers are far from law-abiding citizens in the first place and that they have already been involved in criminal activity prior to initial drug use. A predisposition toward criminal activity is increased by the fact that criminals exist in social subcultures in which drug use is readily accepted and encouraged. The *intensification model*, essentially a combination of the previous perspectives, asserts that drug use tends to perpetuate a life of crime. In the words of one prominent researcher, "Drug use freezes its devotees into patterns of criminality that are more acute, dynamic, unremitting, and enduring than those of other [non-drug-using] offenders." In short, criminal careers have already begun, but they are intensified by one's involvement with drug use. The intensification model is able to account for two basic facts in the drug–crime research literature: (1) criminal careers typically begin prior to drug use and (2) criminal activity declines substantially during times of drug abstinence.[3]

Collecting the Statistics on Drugs and Crime

Figure 5.1 shows information gained from a recently revised version of the Arrestee Drug Abuse Monitoring (ADAM) Program, known as ADAM II, conducted on an annual basis since 2006 by the U.S. Department of Justice. In ADAM II, a sampling of individuals who have been apprehended for a serious offense in ten selected U.S. metropolitan sites are tested through urinalysis for a number of illicit drugs within 48 hours of arrest.

ADAM II statistics indicate that drug use among an arrestee population is much higher than in the general U.S. population. In 2009, the majority of arrestees tested positive for at least one illicit drug, with the percentage varying from 56 percent in Charlotte, North Carolina to 82 percent in Chicago. From 12 percent to 28 percent of arrestees (depending upon the region of the country) tested positive for more than one substance. In general, the most common substances identified during testing were, in descending order: marijuana, cocaine, heroin, and methamphetamine.

ADAM II statistics confirm our suspicions about the correlation between drug use and criminal behavior.[4] But do they indicate a causative relationship? Can we conclude from the ADAM II statistics that drug use *caused* crime to occur because drugs were in an arrestee's bloodstream? That prison inmates are more likely than not to have been drug users prior to their sentencing may suggest that drug users are more likely than nonusers to commit crimes, but does this imply that

	Percentage Testing Positive for Any of Ten Drugs	Percentage Testing Positive				
	0 20 40 60 80 100	Marijuana	Cocaine	Heroin	Methamphetamine	Multiple Drugs
Atlanta, GA	65	37	37	3	<1	14
Charlotte, NC	56	36	25	2	<1	12
Chicago, IL	82	49	33	18	1	28
Denver, CO	70	45	29	5	4	19
Indianapolis, IN	62	44	22	7	1	17
Minneapolis, MN	63	47	19	6	4	18
New York, NY	69	41	32	9	0	25
Portland, OR	65	40	16	10	13	20
Sacramento, CA	68	46	11	6	31	27
Washington, DC	74	47	29	15	<1	23

FIGURE 5.1

Urine test results for illicit drug use among male adult arrestees in ten U.S. cities in 2009. The most common substances identified during testing were, in descending order: marijuana, cocaine, heroin, and methamphetamine, though distinct regional differences can be noted. Methamphetamine use was identified with arrestees primarily in the western regions of the U.S.

Source: Office of National Drug Control Policy (2010, June). ADAM II. 2009 Annual report. Arrestee Drug Abuse Monitoring Program II. Washington, DC: Office of National Drug Control Policy, Executive Office of the President, Tables 3.3, 3.4, and 3.5.

drug use was responsible for the criminal offense for which these individuals were incarcerated?

In order to untangle the sometimes confusing body of research concerning the possible *causal* relationship between drugs and crime, it is useful to break down the question into three specific theoretical positions: (1) drug use causes crime, (2) crime causes drug use, and (3) both drug use and crime share common causes.

Hypothesis I: Drug Use Causes Crime

Throughout the history of the United States, it has been commonly believed that there exists a causative relationship between *drug use and crime*. The establishment of laws restricting access to certain drugs has been based on the premise that *drug use causes crime* and that these laws serve to reduce the criminal behavior that drug-taking behavior produces.

Unfortunately, as discussed in Chapter 3, racial and ethnic prejudices have often played a role in the creation of legislation of this type. The legal prohibition of a particular drug has been associated, at times, with society's fear of a given drug's effect on a threatening minority group. Some of these fears have included the belief that opium would facilitate sexual contact between Chinese and white Americans (see Chapter 7), that cocaine would cause southern blacks to rape white women (see Chapter 8), or that marijuana would incite violence among Mexicans (see Chapter 10). In order to evaluate the supposition that drug causes crime, research studies have focused on the possibility that a causal relationship might be either pharmacologically or economically driven.

Pharmacological violence refers to the effect of a drug having a direct physiological influence on an offender committing an act of violence. The implication is that a specific drug caused violent behavior as a result of the drug being present in the individual's system. Although the ADAM II statistics show that a large proportion of people have some drug in their system at the time of arrest (or the time of testing, up to 48 hours afterward), it is difficult to say whether the offense was committed as a result of the influence of that drug. The main criticism of pharmacological explanations stems from the fact that the length of time for which

pharmacological violence: Violent acts committed while the perpetrator is under the influence of a particular psychoactive substance, with the implication that the drug itself caused the violence to occur by altering one's mental state.

traces of drug use can be detected in a standard urinanalysis drug test can range from a matter of days to two months in the case of marijuana (see Table 12.3). Therefore, testing positive for a drug indicates only that the individual *might* have become violent while under the influence of the drug, if indeed that drug has the potential for creating an acute episode of violence in the first place.

In some instances, the physiological nature of the drug itself makes the possibility of a pharmacological explanation for interpersonal violence quite unlikely. Marijuana, for example, makes the user more lethargic than active, in effect quite mellow in circumstances in which there may be some interpersonal conflict. Heroin produces a passive state of mind (hence the expression, "being on the nod"), thus reducing the inclination toward violent behavior. In fact, as rates of heroin abuse rise, the incidence of crimes against individuals (as opposed to crimes against property) declines.[5]

On the other hand, psychoactive stimulants such as methamphetamine and cocaine or the hallucinogen PCP (known as "angel dust") produce an on-edge frame of mind and a social paranoia that can potentially lead to violent behavior (see Chapters 8 and 9). Yet, even in these cases, we need to be careful in interpreting studies linking violence with the abuse of these drugs.[6] For example, in a study conducted at an Atlanta medical center, more than half of all patients being treated for acute cocaine intoxication were reported to be aggressive, agitated, and paranoid just prior to and at the time of hospital admission. It is impossible to determine whether these patients were mentally unstable prior to their taking cocaine. People who have long-standing psychological problems may be overrepresented in any population of cocaine abusers.[7] Crack cocaine has the reputation of making the crack smoker irritable, paranoid, and inclined to lash out at another person at the slightest provocation, but whether these effects are due to being under the influence of the drug is unclear. The same mood states and tendencies toward violence are observed during time of *crack withdrawal* as well as crack intoxication.

Of all the psychoactive drugs that we could consider, the one with the most definitive and widely reported links to violent behavior toward individuals is alcohol. Of course, millions of people drink alcohol and never become violent, but the chances that violence will occur are increased when people are drinking. In such cases, the violence is clearly pharmacological because the effects of being drunk from the ingestion of alcohol are apparent almost immediately. On a domestic level, males involved in violent spousal abuse commonly report having been drinking or having been drunk during the times that abuse has occurred. Moreover, violent crime outside the home is strongly related to alcohol intoxication. The more violent the crime, the greater is the probability that the perpetrator of the crime was drunk while committing it. Studies show that a majority of all homicides and almost a majority of all sexually aggressive acts (rapes and attempted rapes) are committed while the offender is drunk. From the victim's perspective, alcohol intoxication on the part of the offender accounts for about 20 percent of occasions in which *a violent act of any kind* has been committed.[8] The linkage between alcohol and violence will be explored in more detail in Chapter 13.

Economic explanations of the drug–crime link refer to the possibility that drug use will cause users to commit a crime for the specific purpose of obtaining money to buy drugs. A drug-related crime committed under these circumstances is referred to as an **economically compulsive crime**.

The extent to which economically compulsive criminal behavior occurs can be quite extreme. A 1990 study of crack cocaine users, for example, showed that 59 percent participated in 6,669 robberies over a twelve-month period, averaging thirty-one robberies per individual. While most of these robberies were carried out to obtain drugs, they were not always break-ins and holdups. Sometimes the crime involved the theft of drugs from drug dealers or other users.[9] Nonetheless, a large proportion of the crimes committed to obtain drug money involved violent acts directed against individuals within the community. Particular targets included storekeepers, children, and the elderly.

When considering property crime as a means for financing drug abuse, we can ask the question: To what extent is this particular crime related to "market conditions" (that is, the price of the drug at the time)? In the early 1970s, when heroin abuse was particularly problematic, it was the case that elevations in heroin prices (caused by reducing its availability) coincided with a higher level of property crime; when heroin prices were low, the crime level decreased. The implication was that heroin abusers committed property crimes in order to maintain a stable consumption of heroin. Therefore, the deliberate elevation of heroin prices tended to increase the incidence of property crime among heroin users. On the other hand, price increases for heroin had no impact on the incidence of other forms of criminal behavior nor did it reduce the number of heroin users.[10]

Does the heroin price/property crime relationship as noted in the 1970s hold for other historical periods and other drugs of abuse? In the case of methamphetamine abuse during the 1990s, the picture appears to have been somewhat different. The passage of federal legislation in 1995 and 1997 greatly restricted public access to ingredients used in the manufacture of methamphetamine (see Chapter 8) and resulted in dramatically higher methamphetamine prices. Higher prices led to a general *reduction* in methamphetamine-related property crimes and a decline in methamphetamine use, particularly among light users. Since methamphetamine abuse was a relatively new phenomenon at the time, the preponderance of methamphetamine users were in a "light user" category. Evidently, fewer property crimes were committed because there were fewer light methamphetamine users to commit them. Heavy methamphetamine users showed less of a change in their drug usage or criminal behavior.[11]

The way in which property crime rates respond to higher drug prices, therefore, may depend on *the character of the drug user population*. Property crimes may be more likely to be reduced as drug prices increase when the population in question is comprised of significant numbers of newly initiated drug users. For these individuals, the level of drug usage would be relatively low, and they would be the ones who would be inclined to give up the drug (perhaps switching to other forms of drug use) when the costs rise. The population of heroin users in the 1970s was comprised of fewer individuals of this type. Long-standing heroin users, less inclined to relinquish their drug of choice, would engage in greater levels of property crime as costs rise; they would need more money.

Whether or not criminal behavior increases or decreases as a result of drug prices, the specific economically compulsive crime a drug user commits can be differentiated on the basis of the drug user's gender. Males are more likely to commit crimes against persons (muggings), property (burglary and car theft), or drug laws (distribution and trafficking), whereas females are more likely to commit crimes against the public order, such as prostitution. One study, for example, found that 64 percent of female crack users exchanged sex for money to buy drugs and that 24 percent reported trading sex for drugs. In "crack houses,"

economically compulsive crime: Criminal act committed by a drug abuser in order to obtain money to buy drugs.

women and young girls often bartered sex for crack cocaine. Many of these women remained in the crack houses for extended periods of time, providing sexual favors to multiple customers in order to acquire a continuous supply of the drug.[12]

Hypothesis II: Crime Causes Drug Use

The drug–crime connection also can be addressed from the supposition that *crime causes drug use*. In this view, persons who are predisposed to commit crimes also use drugs. Drugs may be used before a criminal offense to bolster courage or afterward to celebrate success. Thieves and rapists, for example, may consume alcohol and stimulants to give them energy and increase their confidence. Prostitutes may turn to alcohol and drugs as a method of coping with the stresses of their way of life. It is also common for successful criminals or "gangsters" to keep large stores of illicit drugs to show off their wealth and success. In these cases, drug use is part of an overall criminal lifestyle within a deviant subculture. You might recognize this viewpoint as relating to the subcultural recruitment and socialization theory of drug-taking behavior, discussed in Chapter 4.

The theoretical position that crime causes drug use is supported by the fact that longitudinal studies (studies conducted over a period of time) have found that initial involvement in criminal activity begins *prior* to experimentation with drugs for many users. Several studies of drug users in Miami, conducted during the 1970s and 1990s, found that the only drug use that preceded the first crime they committed was the use of alcohol and marijuana. Use of more expensive drugs, such as heroin and cocaine, usually did not begin until two to four years after their first crime.[13] A survey of inmates in Michigan, California, and Texas prisons found that only 20 percent of those who used drugs reported that their drug use began prior to their first crime, and more than 52 percent reported that they began using drugs and committing crimes at about the same time.[14] The National Youth Survey Family Study conducted by the University of Colorado, which followed 1,700 youths over a ten-year period, also supported the idea that initial involvement in criminal activity often preceded drug use. Their first criminal offense preceded their first alcohol use in 63 percent of cases, and their first criminal offense preceded their first marijuana use in 93 percent of cases.[15]

Hypothesis III: Drug Use and Crime Share Common Causes

A third explanation of the relationship between drug use and crime is based on the supposition that *drug use and crime share a common cause*. According to this perspective, drug use and crime do not cause one or the other but are both aspects of an overall deviant lifestyle or culture. In other words, social risk factors lead to deviant behavior, and deviant behavior includes both drug abuse and criminal activity.

Frequently, for example, individuals with a greater chance of abusing drugs have a number of socioeconomic disadvantages, such as a low level of education, a broken family, little or no social supervision, and low social status, that also produce a greater chance of criminal behavior.[16] In this case, there may not be a direct relationship between drug use and crime but rather an indirect relationship that has been called by the U.S. Department of Justice **interactional circumstances**.[17] While the effects of marijuana may not directly motivate a user to commit crime, both marijuana use and crime may be common characteristics of an overall deviant lifestyle. In short, the type of person who is a heavy drug user also could be the type of person who is likely to have short-term goals supported by illegal activities and is more likely to be exposed to situations and persons that encourage criminal behavior.[18]

A study of 559 males in Philadelphia, for example, found that 96 percent of those who used marijuana said that they "never" or "almost never" felt an urge to hurt someone while under the influence of the drug. An overwhelming majority of the respondents said that marijuana made them feel more peaceful and passive than before its use.[19] On the other hand, the Philadelphia study did find that individuals who used marijuana were significantly more likely than nonusers to have committed multiple criminal offenses. The results of this study show that marijuana use on its own may not have caused crime *per se*, but may have been part of a lifestyle of people who commit crime. The relationship may be due to the fact that the same types of people who are most likely to commit crime—young males of lower socioeconomic status—are also the same types of people who are most likely to use drugs.[20]

> **interactional circumstances:** The idea that there may not be a direct relationship between drug use and crime but rather an indirect relationship.

A substantial number of drug users become involved in drug distribution as their drug-using careers progress and hence become part of a criminal subculture that uses violence to maintain control over its "business." Researchers refer to the term **systemic violence** as violence that arises from the activities of drug dealing. Systemic violence can result from such situations as territorial disputes, the consequences of selling inferior grades of illicit drugs, and fraudulent handling of funds from drug sales (Figure 5.2).

The prominence of systemic violence in crack cocaine abuse during the 1980s was particularly striking in the lives of young adult males involved in this form of drug-taking behavior. Studies show that as the involvement of a youth in crack distribution increased, the more likely it was that the person would become involved in criminal violence. The enormous value of the drug itself relative to its quantity (the contents of a plastic sandwich bag often being worth thousands of dollars) added to the intensity of interpersonal contacts. Transactions were conducted under great uncertainty as to whether the other party might be a law-enforcement officer or informant. In addition, the most violent drug users often were the most respected role models for young people. Many adolescents living in communities dominated by the crack cocaine market felt the need to prove that they could be brutal in order to avoid being harassed by their peers. It is likely that the pressure to be an accepted member of such a community was more responsible for a drug abuser's committing frequent violent acts than the effects of the drugs themselves or the need for money to buy drugs.

Not surprisingly, when street sales of crack cocaine declined in the 1990s, there was an accompanying decline in homicide rates and violent crime in areas where crack sales had been dominant. Community policing procedures focused on breaking up drug gangs and large street-level drug markets, thereby changing the pattern of drug buying and selling.[21] A criminal justice researcher put it this way:

> The reconfiguration of drug markets in the mid-1990s appreciably reduced the level of neighborhood violence. As distribution retired indoors, turf battles were eliminated, and because organizers of the drug business hired a few trusted friends rather than easily replaceable workers, there was less conflict between them. Distributors were robbed by users less frequently because they were more protected selling indoors to known customers.[22]

We can conclude from studies of the nature of the drug–crime relationship that it is not possible to explain drug use and crime in terms of a simple overall cause-and-effect relationship. A heroin addict from a low socioeconomic neighborhood preparing to commit a robbery against a rival dealer may ingest alcohol or stimulants to provide the courage to commit the crime. In the case of a prostitute, there are circumstances under which drug use precedes prostitution, circumstances under which prostitution precedes drug use, and circumstances under which initiation into both drug use and prostitution occurs at about the same time (Drugs . . . in Focus).[23]

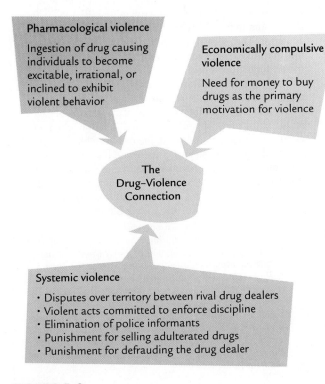

Pharmacological violence

Ingestion of drug causing individuals to become excitable, irrational, or inclined to exhibit violent behavior

Economically compulsive violence

Need for money to buy drugs as the primary motivation for violence

The Drug–Violence Connection

Systemic violence

- Disputes over territory between rival drug dealers
- Violent acts committed to enforce discipline
- Elimination of police informants
- Punishment for selling adulterated drugs
- Punishment for defrauding the drug dealer

FIGURE 5.2

The Goldstein tripartite model of drugs and violence, showing the importance of distinguishing three major types of drug-related violence.

Source: Goldstein, Paul (1985, Fall). The drug-violence nexus: A tripartite framework. *Journal of Drug Issues,* 493–506.

systemic violence: Violent acts that arise from the traditionally aggressive patterns of behavior that exist within a network of illicit drug trafficking and distribution.

Drugs... in Focus

From HeroinGen and CrackGen to BluntGen—The Rise and Fall of Drugs and Violence

From a sociological point of view, the impact of drug use on violent crime over the last forty years or so can be examined in terms of the dominant drug of abuse at a particular time. Sociologists Bruce D. Johnson, Andrew Golub, and Eloise Dunlap have divided the drug scene in inner-city New York City into three distinct eras, each defined by a specific drug subculture and set of shared social norms. Each subculture has been guided by a set of expected behaviors that have dictated what subculture participants must do, what they must refrain from doing, and what the consequences are for noncompliance. An agreed-upon set of norms defining their conduct allows participants to function as if on "automatic pilot."

The HeroinGen

According to their analysis, the period 1960–1973 was the era of heroin injection and a subculture of heroin-abusing participants (the heroin-injection generation, or HeroinGen for short). In the peak year of 1968, the HeroinGen members were between fifteen and twenty-five years old. Quite often, they had grown up in a subculture of alcohol abuse, with their parents being heavy alcohol consumers. In mid-adolescence, HeroinGen members were turned on to marijuana, but by 1964–1965, heroin had hit the New York streets in a major way. The promise was that heroin would give them a better high than marijuana or alcohol, and a process of introduction into heroin use began. A dominant feature of the subculture was the act of robbery. The conduct norms for HeroinGen members were clear:

> Locate ordinary citizens who are apt to carry a lot of cash. Try to identify persons leaving banks on paydays. Target working-class and pink-collar workers who typically cash their payroll checks. Hold up businesses with other robbers. . . . Don't attempt to rob someone when stoned on alcohol or heroin.

Handguns were rarely carried or used; instead, knives and blunt instruments were the weapons of choice.

The CrackGen

Crack cocaine became available around 1984 in New York City and other metropolitan communities. Subculture members, born between 1955 and 1969, came of age during the height of the cocaine/crack era (1985–1989). For these individuals, called the Crack Generation or CrackGen, conduct norms were quite different from those of the HeroinGen. Crack use was carried out in intensive binges. Hyperactivity, rapid cycling between euphoria and dysphoria, and paranoia dominated their behavior.

Sales of crack became so profitable that the entire illicit drug industry revolved around it. Vicious competition between crack dealers ensued. The key factor was "keeping the money and product straight." At this point, handguns became commonplace. There were 218 recorded drug-related homicides in New York in 1988 alone, as well as other forms of systemic violence.

> Other violent acts, such as assaulting a subordinate or shooting him in the kneecap, were mostly unrecorded in official statistics. However, the number of crippled young men wheeling themselves around the inner-city provides ample testament to this brutality.

The BluntGen

By the 1990s, remaining members of the CrackGen were in their thirties and increasingly isolated as they continued their compulsive drug-taking behavior. In their place were members of the Marijuana/Blunt subculture (BluntGen, for short). Born in the 1970s, the BluntGen smoked marijuana as a cigar. They would combine funds in a peer group to buy marijuana, occasionally committing a crime to get money for their purchases. They saw no need for handguns.

Evidence shows that members of the BluntGen viewed the ravages of the lives of HeroinGen and CrackGen members as a reason to limit their pursuit of drug-taking behavior to the use of marijuana and alcohol. The subculture of assault and disregard for human life had been transformed into a subculture of "stay safe, stay alive." Rates of violence and non-drug-related criminality, relative to that of an earlier era, declined sharply. Conduct norms of the BluntGen even impacted on alcohol abuse in a positive way. Here is a description of current drug use among BluntGen members:

> A typical blunt-using episode will involve two or three peers in their twenties sharing a half ounce of marijuana and two or three quarts of malt beer over two to five hours. While passing the marijuana blunt around, each person will also sip beer or malt liquor so that everyone enjoys a modest high while talking and listening to rap music. The conduct norms discourage rapid ingestion of alcohol and displays of drunken comportment. . . . If one consistently and rapidly consumes large quantities of alcohol, acts drunk, or is violent toward others, that person will be sanctioned and, if necessary, excluded from the blunt-sharing group at future times.

Source: Johnson, Bruce D., Golub, Andrew, and Dunlap, Eloise (2006). The rise and decline of hard drugs, drug markets, and violence in inner-city New York. In Alfred Blumstein and Joel Wallman (Eds.), *The crime drop in America*. New York: Cambridge University Press, pp. 164–206. Quotations on pages 173, 178, 180, and 186.

The Social Structure of Illicit Drug Dealing

As with other businesses, the illicit drug business can be divided into various "stages" of production and distribution that include (1) cultivation and manufacturing, (2) importation, (3) wholesale distribution, and (4) retail distribution. For drugs such as cocaine and heroin, peasant farmers living in remote locations in the world carry out the actual cultivation and initial processing. Growers then sell the drugs to importers or drug traffickers who smuggle large quantities into the United States and other worldwide markets. Once inside the United States, the drugs are sold to wholesalers who later sell smaller quantities to lower-level retail sellers or street dealers, often in adulterated forms.

In general, drug dealers at the retail ("street") level follow two types of drug distribution models: (1) the freelance model and (2) the business model.[24] As we will see, the first model can evolve into the second, as the character of drug dealing matures from an informal style of interaction to a more formal one.

Independent individuals working together without a previously established relationship characterize the **freelance model** of retail drug distribution. These dealers and buyers are not part of any large-scale drug organization. It is a "cash only" business, in that the buyer must pay for the drugs at the time of purchase. Both wholesalers and retailers usually do not "front" the drugs, and the price of a drug is negotiated at the time of the buy. Dealers may have many different buyers, some of whom they never see again after a given transaction is completed. If transactions occur successfully, dealers and buyers may negotiate similar arrangements on a more regular basis, but there is no expectation that they will cooperate in the future.

The freelance model typically is associated with the street sale of marijuana and hallucinogens such as LSD and MDMA (Ecstasy). Marijuana sellers are more likely to operate independently than as part of an organized operation, and marijuana often is sold through acquaintance or referral networks. LSD and MDMA are sold principally at concerts, nightclubs, and raves, where sellers and buyers do not know each other, providing a level of anonymity combined with a sense of being part of a common subculture.

In the early years of crack cocaine abuse, from 1984 to 1987, the freelance model dominated as the means by which crack was sold and distributed. The principal drug dealer was a "juggler" who would buy a supply of ten to twenty vials of crack and sell them at a standard retail price, approximately twice the initial cost. When the supply was sold, the juggler would "re-up" by obtaining a new supply that would then be sold. Through several cycles, a freelance seller could make up to fifty deals a day. Since most of these freelancers used their product themselves, however, the quantity of sales did not produce substantial incomes. Less than ten percent of dealers during this period had lengthy drug-dealing careers.[25]

> **freelance model:** A model of retail drug distribution in which dealers and buyers transact their business with relative anonymity, outside of the structure of a large-scale drug organization.

In contrast, the **business model** of street dealing is organized as a "business" in a hierarchical fashion with numerous individuals occupying a range of roles. At the center of the business model is the crew boss who receives a supply of drugs from the wholesaler. Drugs are "fronted" at each level of the organization. The wholesaler fronts the drugs to the crew boss, who then divides the drugs and fronts them to street dealers, often called "runners." Runners most often are young (aged fourteen to twenty-three) males recruited from inner-city neighborhoods. Each crew boss may have as many as 20 runners working under his direction. Runners are assigned to work at a particular street location, sell only at a given price, and then hand over all of the money to the crew boss. As the drugs are sold, the money flows up the chain, from runners, to crew boss, and back to the wholesaler. Prices are agreed upon before the drugs are fronted. At the end of the day, each runner is paid in money or drugs for his or her work. To avoid rip-offs and robberies, each crew is guarded by an armed lieutenant who supervises several street sellers.

Crack cocaine (crack, for short) dealing organizations, located in urban neighborhoods, best exemplify the business model of street dealing. In contrast to the freelance dealer, business-model dealers and crew bosses who managed to limit their personal use of crack would soon make more than one thousand dollars per day. Competition among crack dealers would necessitate "protectors," whose worth was often measured by their violent inclinations and ability to instill fear in others. Thus, the subculture of crack abuse would become enmeshed in an environment of systemic violence.[26]

Patterns of Illicit Drug Trafficking: Past and Present

The global trade in illicit drugs is an immense and diverse enterprise. Estimates as to its total worth have ranged from $28 billion to $280 billion or upwards to $400 billion.[27] Obviously, as this enormous range of estimates indicates, the task of ascertaining the exact figure or anything close to it is extremely difficult. The key element to its "success," despite all of our efforts to make it fail, has been its ability to get the product from its production stage to the buyer on the street. Essentially, this means that a highly effective system of drug trafficking is in place. In the next sections, we will examine the trafficking of five major illicit drugs: Heroin, cocaine, marijuana, methamphetamine, and hallucinogens. More detailed information on the trafficking patterns of these drugs will be provided in Chapters 7, 8, 9, and 10.

The economic power of illicit drug trafficking, however, is only one aspect of the overall problem. In addition to the systemic violence inherent in the domestic distribution of illicit drugs, there is the enormous societal chaos in nations that harbor drug trafficking organizations. Widespread political assassinations and wanton reprisals carried out on drug enforcement officers, informants, and innocent civilians caught in the crossfire of drug trafficking have been a fact of life in Colombia and, more recently, Mexico (Drugs . . . in Focus).

The Trafficking of Heroin

The origin of heroin is opium, produced from the opium poppy, a plant that is native to the Mediterranean region of the world but grows well in any warm and moist climate. Heroin is produced from morphine, the active ingredient in raw opium (see Chapter 7). Historically, there have been four major sources of heroin: (1) the Golden Triangle, (2) the Golden Crescent, (3) Mexico, and (4) South America (Figure 5.3).

During the 1960s and 1970s, the dominant source of heroin for the U.S. market was the so-called **Golden Triangle** of Southeast Asia, comprising the countries of Thailand, Burma (Myanmar), Laos, and Vietnam. Heroin from the Golden Triangle was usually sold as a white or off-white powder, and, considering its place of origin, it was called **China White** on the street. Southeast Asian heroin was smuggled into the United States primarily via containerized maritime cargo from such locations as Taiwan and Hong Kong and often was concealed among legitimate commodities. The cargo shipments traveled to major ports of entry along the West Coast of the United States and western Canada, where they were transported eastward to cities such as Chicago and Detroit. Since the 1980s, however, the role of this region as a source of heroin in the U.S. has greatly diminished. Today, Southeast Asian heroin markets are primarily in Asia and Australia.[28]

> **business model:** A model of retail drug distribution in which drug transactions are conducted within a hierarchically structured organization.
>
> **Golden Triangle:** A once-dominant opium-producing region of Southeast Asia, now eclipsed by opium-producing nations of the Golden Crescent.
>
> **China White:** A street name for heroin from the Golden Triangle or, alternatively, a name for the synthetic opiate, fentanyl.

Drugs... in Focus

A Wave of Narcoterrorism in Mexico

In December 2009, only hours after the funeral of 30-year-old Ensign Melquisedet Angulo, hailed by the Mexican government as a naval hero for his part in a special forces operation that killed Arturo Bertrán Leyva, a high-profile drug trafficker, more than a dozen hit men with assault rifles burst into the home of Angulo's family, killing his mother, aunt, a sister and a brother. Mexican President Felipe Calderón and the military had praised the sailor as an example to all Mexicans for his courage. Normally the identities of soldiers and sailors participating in antidrug operations have been kept secret for fear of reprisals. It is not known why an exception was made in this case.

Unfortunately, the rise of terrorism associated with illicit drug trafficking (sometimes referred to as narcoterrorism) has gripped Mexico in recent years. In 2008, assailants believed to be associated with a particularly violent cartel threw grenades into a crowded plaza, killing eight and injuring dozens. Gruesome reprisals against drug-trafficking rivals, leaving decapitated heads and mutilated corpses, have become common, but the new escalation of violence has shifted to civilian populations uninvolved with the drug trade. An estimated 15,000 people have died in drug-related violence since Mr. Calderón, a champion of Mexico's antidrug efforts, was elected in 2003.

While some political leaders ask for calm and pledge redoubled efforts to fight drug trafficking in Mexico, others worry that the Angulo family murders have signaled a new and dangerous phase in the ongoing drug war in their country, resulting in an escalation to more widespread violence. They also worry that, in the foreseeable future, it will be more difficult to find new recruits in their crime-fighting operations or that the armed forces could be tempted to participate in extrajudicial killings on their own as a new paramilitary organization.

Sources: Luhnow, David and De Córdoba, José (2009, December 23). Hit men kill Mexican hero's family. *Wall Street Journal*, p. A1. Malkin, Elisabeth (2009, December 23). Vengeful fury in drug war chills Mexico. *New York Times*, pp. A1, A12.

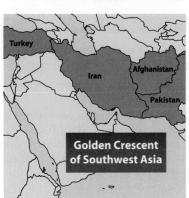

FIGURE 5.3

Primary sources of heroin in the world.

Source: National Drug Intelligence Center (2004). *National drug threat assessment 2005.* Washington, DC: U.S. Department of Justice.

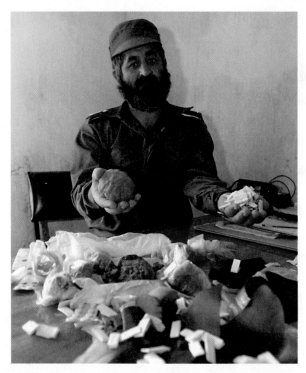

An Afghan district police chief shows confiscated hashish (in his right hand) and heroin folded into pieces of paper (in his left hand), after a routine drug bust in the southern province of Kandahar, Afghanistan.

Currently, the single largest source of heroin is the **Golden Crescent** of Pakistan, Afghanistan, Turkey, and Iran. Afghanistan alone is responsible for approximately 94 percent of the world's supply of heroin, though relatively little of this heroin is destined for the United States.

Golden Crescent: A major opium-producing region of Southwest Asia, comprising Pakistan, Afghanistan, Turkey, Iran, and former regions of the Soviet Union.

TABLE 5.1

Afghanistan heroin production (metric tons)

	1999	2000	2001	2002	2003	2004	2005	2006
Heroin Production	218	365	7	150	337	582	526	664

Note: There is an approximate 10 to 1 yield of grown opium to manufactured heroin. Opium production levels in metric tons can be estimated by multiplying by ten.

Sources: National Drug Intelligence Center (2007). *National drug threat assessment 2008.* Washington, DC: U.S. Department of Justice, Table 4. Tandy, Karen P. (2004, February 26). *DEA congressional testimony: Afghanistan: Law enforcement interdiction efforts in transshipment countries to stem the flow of heroin.* Washington, DC: Drug Enforcement Administration.

Heroin from Afghanistan allegedly helped to finance Taliban terrorist activities during the 1990s. Interestingly, in 2001, the Taliban announced a comprehensive ban on the cultivation of the opium poppy for religious reasons. Opium production plummeted from 3,676 metric tons the previous year to 74 metric tons by the end of 2001. U.S. officials believe that the ban was most likely an attempt by the Taliban to raise the price of opium, which had fallen significantly owing to the abundant supply produced in 2000. After the fall of the Taliban in 2002, opium cultivation resumed. In 2010, an estimated 3,600 metric tons were produced, down 48 percent from 2009.

Table 5.1 shows the impact of these changes in opium cultivation on the production of Afghan heroin. Although the Karzai government in Afghanistan also has banned the cultivation of opium poppies, decades of war and political unrest have left the criminal justice system in disarray, and apparently it has been difficult for the Afghan government to enforce the ban. A number of European criminal organizations, including Russian and Sicilian mafia groups, distribute Afghan heroin to markets in Europe and Asia.[29]

A third major source of heroin is Mexico. For many years, Mexican heroin was crudely processed with many impurities, typically black or brown in color, hence its name *black tar* or "Tootsie Roll" on the street. In recent years, however, there has been a dramatic increase in the level of purity, equivalent according to DEA sources to be nearly equal to traditionally higher-grade heroin from Colombia (see below). Although Mexico cultivates only 2 percent of the world's opium, Mexico's opium production is significant because virtually all the Mexican opium that is converted into heroin is destined for the United States.

Most of the opium in Mexico is grown by small, independent farmers known as *campesinos*. Individual traffickers or trafficking organizations pay a prearranged price for the opium crop, the equipment used in harvesting, and food for the farmer's family. A middleman or opium broker then collects the opium and transports it to a clandestine laboratory to be processed into heroin. One of the most powerful of the Mexican heroin trafficking organizations is the Herrera family, which has been involved in drug trafficking since the mid-1950s. The organization is comprised of multiple families, all of which are related to the Herrera family through either blood or marriage. Although the patriarch of the Herrera family, Jaime Herrera-Nevarez, was arrested in Guadalajara, Mexico, in 1987, members of the Herrera family continue to be active in the Mexican heroin trade.[30]

Mexican heroin is smuggled into the United States primarily overland across the Mexico–U.S. border via private and commercial vehicles that have been equipped with hidden compartments. Smaller quantities of Mexican heroin often are carried across the border by illegal aliens or migrant workers who hide the drugs in backpacks, in the soles of their shoes, or on their bodies. Typically, Mexican heroin is transported in private vehicles to distribution points in the Southwest and West Central regions of the United States. Over the last few years, the distribution patterns of Mexican heroin have expanded beyond the southwestern and western states to other major U.S. cities.[31]

South America is the fourth major producer of opium and heroin. By global standards, Colombia produces relatively little heroin (less than 5 percent of the world's total estimated production). However, most of the heroin used in the United States is produced in Colombia. During the 1980s and 1990s, Southeast and Southwest Asian heroin dominated the U.S. market. As the demand for cocaine in the United States began to decline in the 1990s, Colombians began cultivating opium poppies high in the Andes Mountains.[32]

South American heroin has been typically transported from Colombia to the United States by couriers aboard commercial flights from one of the Colombian airports to international airports in Miami, Atlanta, or New York. Couriers (known as "drug mules") have often swallowed small pellets of heroin that have been placed in condoms or balloons or wrapped in latex from surgical gloves. Couriers also have concealed heroin in body cavities, taped it to their bodies, or concealed it in their clothing or shoes. Larger quantities of heroin into the United States are smuggled by transporting the drug in suitcases containing heroin sewn into the seams of clothing. Alternatively, Colombian heroin traffickers have recruited Mexican couriers to transport South American heroin into the United States through Mexico. South American heroin is frequently smuggled across the Mexico–U.S. border via Mexican couriers using overland routes and via private or commercial vehicles crossing at border checkpoints.

Within the United States, ethnic Dominican criminal groups currently play a significant role in retail-level distribution of South American heroin. Colombian wholesalers of heroin usually deal directly with Dominican trafficking groups that dominate heroin markets in northeastern cities such as New York, Boston, and Philadelphia. Traditionally, heroin abusers themselves have been responsible for selling heroin at the retail level. Seven grams of heroin may be bought, for example, from a wholesaler, three grams kept for personal use, and four grams then sold at a profit on the street. Street gangs and ethnic criminal groups that once dealt only in South American cocaine are engaging in a practice that has come to be called **double-breasted dealing**, in which both cocaine and heroin are distributed together. As the number of cocaine abusers continues to decline (see Chapter 8), street gangs and other criminal groups are evidently attempting to maintain a substantial share of the drug market by selling heroin.[33]

At the street level in New York City, heroin is sold in deflated balloons or wrapped in tin foil as a "twenty bag" ($10 to $20) or by the gram ($55 to $100). Heroin often is cut or diluted with such substances as caffeine, various sugars such as lactose, and depressants such as methaqualone or phenobarbital.

The Trafficking of Cocaine

Cocaine is derived from the leaves of the coca shrub, grown in the high-altitude rain forests and fields that run along the slopes of the Andes in South America (see Chapter 8). At one time, virtually all the world's coca was cultivated in Bolivia and Peru, but crop eradication campaigns have resulted in a decline in coca production in these countries. While Bolivia and Peru remain significant players in the global cocaine market, most of the world's coca cultivation and cocaine production today takes place in Colombia (Table 5.2), a country situated in the northwestern part of South America, with coasts on both the Pacific Ocean and the Caribbean. This location has enabled traffickers to smuggle cocaine to the United States by a variety of air and sea routes. Shipments of cocaine typically move from Colombia to Mexico, Puerto Rico, the Bahamas, and the Dominican

> **double-breasted dealing:** A practice of distributing cocaine and heroin within the same drug organization.

TABLE 5.2

Andean region cocaine production (metric tons)

	PERU	BOLIVIA	COLOMBIA
2001	160	60	700
2002	175	60	585
2003	245	100	445
2004	230	115	415
2005	250	115	525
2006	265	115	550
2007	210	120	535

Note: Increases in cocaine production in Peru and decreases in Colombia in 2009, relative to 2008, have resulted in the possibility of Peru overtaking Colombia as the world's largest producer of coca in the near future.

Sources: National Drug Intelligence Center (2008). *National Drug Threat Assessment 2009.* Washington, DC: U.S. Department of Justice, Table 1. National Drug Intelligence Center (2006). *National Drug Threat Assessment 2007.* Washington, DC: U.S. Department of Justice, Table 1. Romero, Simon (2010, June 23). Peru report shows gains in coca. *New York Times*, p. A6.

Republic, where it is repackaged for shipment to south Florida, south Texas, and California.

Smuggling techniques used for transferring cocaine to U.S. markets include small commercial fishing vessels that "hug" or keep close to the coasts of eastern Caribbean islands, allowing them to blend in with other vessel traffic and minimizing the opportunity for detection. Waterproof bundles of cocaine are air-dropped to waiting boat crews, who then deliver the cocaine to shore in speedboats. Multi-ton shipments of cocaine also are smuggled through the port of Miami by being concealed in the compartments of large commercial cargo vessels.[34]

Until the early 1970s, Cuban-organized crime groups controlled the importation of cocaine from Colombia into the United States. By the mid-1970s, control of the cocaine industry shifted from Cubans to Colombians themselves.[35]

Medellin and Cali drug cartels: Two major Colombian drug cartels that controlled much of the illicit drug distribution in South America from the mid-1970s to the mid-1990s.

For the next two decades, two of the most powerful criminal organizations in history controlled the production and distribution of cocaine: the **Medellin and Cali drug cartels** (named after cities in Colombia that were their home bases). In the mid-1970s, most of the cocaine that was brought into the United States was smuggled in hidden suitcases. As the demand for cocaine in the United States exceeded supplies, several criminal entrepreneurs, one of whom was Pablo Escobar (see Portrait), formed an alliance called the Medellin Cartel. They soon realized that they could fly small airplanes loaded with cocaine into the United States, thereby avoiding the need for countless suitcase trips.

The huge profits gained from their cocaine trafficking operations were later reinvested into more sophisticated cocaine labs, better airplanes, and even an island in the Bahamas where their planes could refuel.

The Medellin Cartel became the prototype for an organizational structure that can be characterized as an onion-like layering of power and responsibility. Kingpins at the center directed operations, and groups of self-contained cells were managed by a small number of cartel managers. Each cell specialized in a different aspect of the drug business, such as production, distribution, smuggling, or money laundering. If police arrested members of one cell, a second or third cell would step up operations to fill the vacuum. Members of each cell rarely were connected directly with any of the leaders of the cartel.

During his ascendency to power, Pablo Escobar and the other leaders of the cartel set out to crush any opposition from law enforcement or the Colombian government by a campaign of terror and brutality. They were considered to be responsible for the murder of hundreds of government officials, police, prosecutors, judges, journalists, and innocent bystanders. The flamboyant lifestyle of the Medellin Cartel's leaders and their extreme use of violence, however, soon made them a primary target for both Colombian and U.S. law enforcement. By the early 1990s, the leaders of the cartel either had been gunned down by police or had turned themselves over to authorities in exchange for lenient prison sentences.

While law-enforcement anti-drug efforts focused on the high-profile Medellin Cartel for several years, the less-flashy Cali Cartel managed to operate without the same degree of law-enforcement interference. The members of the Cali Cartel were more subtle in their operations than their Medellin counterparts, relying on

PORTRAIT

Pablo Escobar—Formerly Known as the Colombian King of Cocaine

Pablo Escobar was one of the most powerful, profitable, and violent organized crime bosses in history. Escobar began his career as a small-time criminal in the slums and back roads outside Medellin, Colombia. At age twenty-six, Escobar was arrested for possession of thirty-nine pounds of cocaine, his first and only drug bust. Escobar was never tried for the crime. The arresting officer was mysteriously murdered, and nine judges refused to hear the case because of death threats. The Medellin Cartel, created by Escobar, became the first modern-day cocaine trafficking alliance. Organized along the lines of a large corporation, the cartel was vertically integrated and controlled virtually all aspects of the cocaine business from manufacturing and smuggling to wholesale distribution of cocaine in the United States. In an attempt to give himself a more legitimate image, Escobar became involved in politics, getting elected to the Colombian Congress in 1982. Not coincidentally, his governmental position gave him immunity from arrest. Escobar's career in politics, however, lasted only a short time, and he soon realized that he could gain more power in Colombia through violence and bribes than politics.

By 1984, Escobar controlled over 80 percent of the Colombian drug trade. It was estimated that Escobar was making over $2.75 billion a year, earning him a place on the *Forbes* magazine list of the wealthiest people in the world. Projecting himself as "a man of the people," Escobar built housing for the poor, schools, hospitals, and even a soccer stadium, all of which earned him favorable media coverage.

Behind the image of a "Robin Hood" figure, however, was a wave of violence and assassination specifically designed to keep Escobar's cocaine flowing. Colombia soon resembled an armed camp, where police officers, judges, public officials, and journalists were in constant fear of being assassinated. Public bombings and drive-by shootings were common, and Escobar was believed to be behind the murder of three presidential candidates, a Colombian attorney general, more than 200 judges, 100 police officers, and dozens of journalists. Pablo Escobar also was believed to be responsible for the bombing of a Colombian jetliner, causing the deaths of 107 persons. In 1990, Escobar offered a bounty of $4,000 for each police officer killed in Colombia. In the following month, 42 city police officers were murdered.

In response to the reign of terror waged by the Medellin Cartel, the Colombian government offered drug traffickers immunity from extradition to the United States if they turned themselves in. In turn, the traffickers would server shorter prison terms in Colombia. In 1991, at the age of forty-one, Pablo Escobar surrendered to authorities with the agreement that he would be placed in a specially built prison that evidently was not secure enough to hold Escobar imprisoned for long. Escobar escaped from prison, and in one the most famous manhunts in history, Escobar managed to elude a search team comprised of an elite Colombian police commando squad, members of the U.S. Central Intelligence Agency (CIA), and agents of the Drug Enforcement Administration (DEA) for over a year. Escobar moved secretly among his friends and supporters, sometimes disguising himself as a woman and hiding in secret rooms carved out between walls and under stairs. His closeness to his family, however, proved to be Escobar's weakness. After he telephoned his family in December 1993 to tell them that he was fine, his call was traced by agents of the DEA. When law-enforcement agents arrived at the house in Medellin where he was staying, Escobar attempted a last-ditch escape to the rooftop. A barrage of bullets ended his life.

Within months of Escobar's death, the Cali Cartel, a long-standing rival to the Medellin Cartel, had taken over the cocaine business in Colombia. But its newfound dominance of the cartel was soon to end. Cali Cartel leaders were arrested in Colombia in 1997 and later extradited to the United States. In 2006, a plea agreement included a judgment of forfeiture in the amount of $2.1 billion to be levied against Cali Cartel narcotic-related assets as well as businesses around the world. Today, cocaine trafficking is controlled by more than 300 "mini-cartels" in the Andean region and the FARC quasi-political organization in Colombia itself.

Sources: Brooke, James. (1990, June 7). In the capital of cocaine, savagery is the habit. *New York Times*, p. 4. Drug Enforcement Administration (2006, September 26). Cali cartel leaders plead guilty to drug and money laundering conspiracy charges. News release. Washington, DC: U.S. Department of Justice. Fedarko, Kevin (1993, December 13). Escobar's dead end. *Time*, p. 46. Lyman, Michael D., and Potter, Gary W. (2000). *Organized crime.* Upper Saddle River, NJ: Prentice Hall. Watson, Russel, and Katel, Peter. (1993, December 13). Death on the spot: The end of a drug king. *Newsweek*, pp. 18–21.

bribes over violence, conducting their business in a discreet and business-like manner, and reinvesting much of their profits from the illicit drug trade into legitimate businesses. The Cali Cartel relied heavily on political bribes for protection. Former President of Colombia, Ernesto Samper, and hundreds of Colombian congressmen and senators were accused of accepting campaign financing from the cartel.

During the 1980s, while the Medellin Cartel controlled the drug market in south Florida, the Cali Cartel controlled the distribution of cocaine in New York, later expanding its market to Europe and Asia and forming alliances with other organized-crime groups such as the Japanese Yakuza. Cali smuggling techniques also differed greatly from those of the Medellin Cartel. Members of the Medellin Cartel relied on small airplanes and speedboats, whereas the Cali Cartel smuggled most of its shipments in large cargo ships, hiding the drugs in all types of legitimate cargo, from cement blocks to bars of chocolate. The Cali Cartel outlasted the Medellin Cartel until 1995, when its leaders eventually were tracked down and arrested.[36]

The arrest of the top leaders of the Medellin and Cali drug cartels in the 1990s led to a decentralization of the cocaine trade in which the control of production and trafficking was taken over by smaller independent Bolivian, Peruvian, and Mexican organizations. These new traffickers set upon forming smaller, more controllable groups, having realized that large organizations had become too vulnerable to U.S. prosecution. Within Colombia itself, cocaine trafficking became intertwined with political insurgency, with emergence of quasi-political guerrilla organizations. Currently, the dominant organization of this type, in Colombia, the Revolutionary Armed Forces of Colombia (FARC), presently operates from a stronghold region of Colombia exceeding 42,000 square kilometers (the approximate size of Kentucky), from which kidnappings and executions are planned and coca plantations are supervised. In the late 1990s, several producers of cocaine shifted their crops to this area, experimenting with coca plants to produce a stronger coca leaf with a higher cocaine yield. Meanwhile, FARC took control of coca crops, eventually making it the richest insurgent group in history. Without any large drug cartels to contend with, guerilla groups such as FARC became no longer mere passive profiteers of the cocaine trade; they were now active participants in the processing and distribution of cocaine.[37]

In recent years, there has been some success in international drug trafficking control, with the arrest and extradition of major FARC leaders on charges of cocaine importation conspiracy. Whether or not these positive developments end up having a long-lasting effect on reducing cocaine trafficking in Colombia remains uncertain.

During the 1980s and early 1990s, the United States began to place immense pressure on drug trafficking organizations operating in the Caribbean and south Florida. As a response, traffickers in Colombia formed alliances with Mexican trafficking groups in order to transport cocaine across the southwestern border of the United States. With the disruption of the Cali and Medellin drug cartels, Mexican groups such as the Amado Carrillo-Fuentes Organization and the Arellano-Felix Organization began to consolidate their power and dominated drug trafficking along the Mexico-U.S. border and in many American cities. By the late 1990s and early 2000s, after the loss of their leaders through natural death or criminal arrest, the power and influence of these organizations declined significantly, only to be replaced by other trafficking groups.

Current intelligence reports from the Drug Enforcement Administration (DEA) indicate that approximately 72 percent of the cocaine available in the United States is smuggled across the U.S border with Mexico. Typically, cocaine shipments from South America are moved overland or by air to staging sites in northern Mexico. Large loads of cocaine generally are smuggled across the border in land vehicles, such as semi trucks, where it is often concealed in shipments of fruits and vegetables. Cocaine is also carried in small, concealed kilogram quantities across the border by "mules," persons who enter the United States either legally through ports of entry or illegally through undesignated points along the border. Once the loads of cocaine arrive in the United States, they are taken to established "safe houses" where workers watch over the cocaine and prepare it for distribution across the United States (Figure 5.4)[38]

On the street level in New York City, cocaine typically is distributed as a white crystalline powder or as an off-white chunky material that is sold by the gram. The price of a gram of cocaine ranges from $26 to $50 depending on demand, availability, and purity. The street purity of cocaine is usually less than 70 percent because it is commonly "cut" or diluted with a variety of substances. Crack cocaine is sold either in small pieces or rocks, packaged in small vials or film canisters ($5 to $10) or by the gram ($30 to $100).

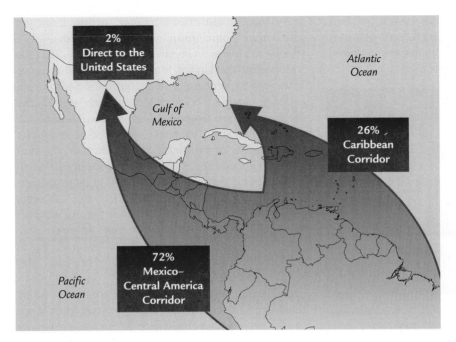

Atlantic
Ocean

Gulf of
Mexico

26%
Caribbean
Corridor

Pacific
Ocean

72%
Mexico–
Central America
Corridor

FIGURE 5.4

The flow of cocaine into the United States. Several Central American countries function as the "trans-shipment corridor" from Colombia to Mexico.

Sources: Office of Drug Control Policy (2002, March). *Annual assessment of cocaine movement.* Washington, DC: Office of National Drug Control Policy. Bureau of International Narcotics and Law Enforcement Affairs (2007, March). *2007 International narcotics control strategy report. Volume 1: Drug and chemical control.* Washington, DC: U.S. Department of State, pp. 147–149, 154–166, 173–179.

A Mexican federal agent crawls through a hidden U.S.–Mexico border tunnel, presumably used to transport drugs from Mexico to the United States.

The Trafficking of Marijuana

Mexico is currently the major foreign source for marijuana smuggled into the United States. Most of the marijuana, whether grown in Mexico or transported through Mexico from other locations such as Colombia, is smuggled across the Southwest border.

Over the past decade, the U.S. government has increased the detection and monitoring of air traffic at the Mexican border. As a result, most of the marijuana that enters the United States through this route is smuggled by land. Drug trafficking organizations operating from Mexico employ a wide variety of methods for smuggling marijuana, such as concealing the drug in false vehicle compartments located in doors, fuel tanks, seats, or tires. Marijuana often is hidden in tractor-trailer trucks among shipments of legitimate agriculture products, such as fruits and vegetables. Smaller quantities of marijuana can be smuggled across the border by horse, raft, and backpack. Once the marijuana is smuggled successfully across the border, traffickers consolidate the shipments at "safe houses" in cities such as Tucson and Houston. From these distribution sites, marijuana is transported to cities throughout the United States.[39]

Recently, there has been an enormous growth in Canadian marijuana trafficking. Canadian growers in British Columbia have begun to use sophisticated hydroponic cultivation techniques to produce a potent form of marijuana that has come to be known as **BC Bud** or "skunk weed." Hydroponic cultivation refers to a technique in which marijuana plants are grown in nutrient-rich water rather than soil. In soil, young plants spread their roots wide and have access to water and nutrients. In hydroponic cultivation, the water and nutrients are readily supplied to the plant so that the plant will grow just enough roots to keep its stem immobile and be able to absorb the supplied food and water. Plants therefore

BC Bud: British Columbia–grown marijuana, produced under hydroponic (water-based) cultivation methods.

can grow faster and grow larger leaves, flowers, and buds. BC Bud has been found to have a THC content ranging from 15 to 25 percent, more potent than commonly available hashish (see Chapter 10).

Lamps cast a yellowish glow over hydroponic cannabis plants in a recently seized marijuana cultivation laboratory.

There has also been a dramatic increase in the production of "home grown" marijuana cultivated within the United States. Domestic marijuana cultivation exists throughout the United States and ranges from a few plants grown for personal use to thousands of plants cultivated by organized criminal groups. Large-scale domestic growers most frequently plant marijuana in remote areas, often camouflaging it in surrounding vegetation. Mountainous terrain offers the opportunity to grow marijuana in hollows and other secluded areas in relative isolation from public view. Major outdoor cannabis cultivation takes place in such states as California, Hawaii, Washington, Oregon, and the Appalachian region of Kentucky and Tennessee. Approximately 80 percent of all outdoor cultivated plants eradicated by law enforcement in 2008 originated in California, Oregon, and Washington (Figure 5.5).[40]

In response to the increase in domestically grown marijuana, law-enforcement agencies have come to rely on the use of military helicopters to carry out clandestine

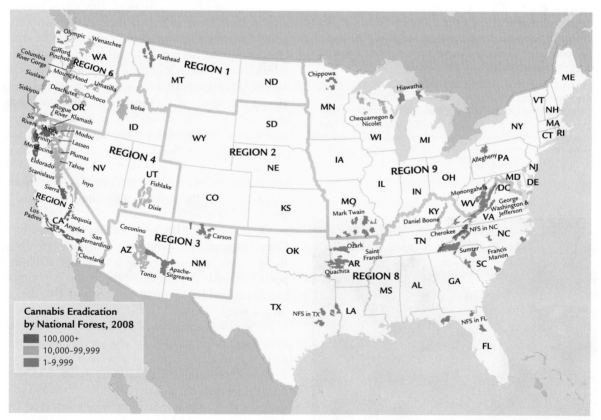

FIGURE 5.5

About half of more than 7.5 million outdoor marijuana plants seized within the United States by the Drug Enforcement Administration in 2008 were cultivated on public land. The map shows the distribution of seizures in U.S. national forests.

Source: National Drug Intelligence Center (2009). *Domestic cannabis cultivation assessment 2009.* Washington DC: U.S. Department of Justice, Figure 13.

monitoring of marijuana plots from the air. Growers have countered by covering the plots with camouflage netting or by tying the stems and branches of marijuana plants to small stakes on the ground. This type of cultivation technique produces what has become known as **spider marijuana** because the plant branches out along the ground like the legs of a spider. Out of fear of civil forfeiture, growers also have begun cultivating plants on governmental lands, such as national forests and national parks.

Like their Canadian counterparts, many domestic marijuana traffickers have taken to hydroponic cultivation indoors. Law enforcement has responded by equipping helicopters with heat-detecting devices to identify unusual sources of light or by checking for unusually high power bills of suspected growers. Growers have, in turn, countered by setting up hydroponic plots in chicken houses, which often rely on intense light and heat sources.

While Mexican drug trafficking organizations control the wholesale distribution of most of the foreign-produced marijuana in the United States, their influence becomes "diluted" at lower levels, where street-level dealers of marijuana typically reflect the demographic makeup of the local area in which it is sold. Marijuana is usually packaged for street sale by being placed in a clear plastic sandwich bag, which is then rolled up and taped. Marijuana is often sold on the street as a "dime bag" (sold for $5 to $30) or by the ounce (sold for $30 to $100).[41]

The Trafficking of Methamphetamine

During the early 1990s, methamphetamine reemerged as a popular recreational drug in the United States after a previous period of popularity in the 1960s and 1970s. Methamphetamine's chemical structure is similar to that of amphetamine, but it has a more pronounced effect on the central nervous system (see Chapter 8). It is a white, odorless, bitter-tasting crystalline powder and is commonly referred to as "speed," "meth," and "crank." The drug is usually snorted or injected intravenously and typically is sold for $100 to $150 a gram. The primary precursor chemicals for the manufacture of methamphetamine, ephedrine and pseudoephedrine, are obtained by purchasing inexpensive over-the-counter cough-and-cold medications. Throughout the 1970s and 1980s, the production and trafficking of methamphetamine were controlled by motorcycle gangs such as the Hell's Angels and other groups. It has been estimated that between 1979 and 1981, money obtained from selling methamphetamine accounted for 91 percent of the Hell's Angels

finances. Today, methamphetamine is still often referred to as "crank" because motorcyclists would hide the drug in the crankshafts of their motorcycles.

In the mid-1990s, drug trafficking organizations based in Mexico and California began to take control of the production and distribution of methamphetamine, setting up large-scale "superlabs" capable of producing as much as ten pounds of methamphetamine in a twenty-four-hour period. The entry of these organizations into the methamphetamine trade has resulted in a significant increase in the supply of high-purity, low-cost methamphetamine.

Supplies of methamphetamine have been also provided by smaller independent "mom and pop" laboratories, obtaining the ingredients necessary for manufacture from retail and convenience stores. The mountainous regions of Georgia, North Carolina, and Kentucky are

spider marijuana: A type of marijuana grown in such a way that the cannabis plant branches out along the ground like the legs of a spider.

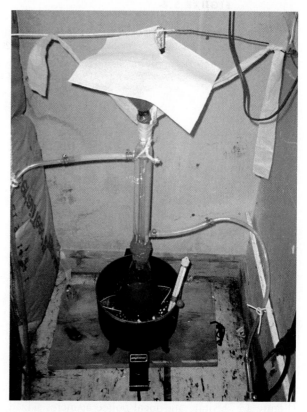

In a makeshift but sophisticated "meth factory," a combination of ephedrine, hydrochloric acid, and red phosphorus (shown as red liquid in the picture) is heated in a flask placed in an electric pot. Rubber tubes attached to each side of the glass condenser circulate cold water to reduce the escape of toxic fumes.

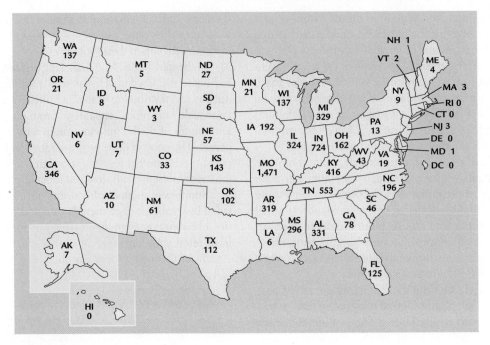

FIGURE 5.6

Geographic distribution of all methamphetamine clandestine laboratory incidents (including labs, dumpsites, chemicals/glass/equipment), 2008.

Source: National Clandestine Laboratory Database, 2008. Information courtesy of the Drug Enforcement Administration, U.S. Department of Justice, Washington, DC.

particularly suited for small-time methamphetamine (meth) cookers who often set up their operations in trailers or mobile homes located in secluded heavily forested areas. Cooks typically dispose of highly toxic wastes from the production process by dumping the material into a nearby lake, pond, or stream. The proliferation of laboratories has been fueled by the expansion of Internet sites providing access to methamphetamine "recipes." In the meantime, law-enforcement officers have referred to methamphetamine laboratories as "chemical time bombs" because of the presence of highly flammable and toxic chemicals used in methamphetamine production. Explosions and fires are common occurrences (see Chapter 8).

The number of domestic clandestine methamphetamine laboratories seized by the DEA increased from 263 in 1994 to 1,815 in 2000, a 590 percent increase (Figure 13.7). State and local police agencies seized almost 8,000 clandestine laboratories in the United States during 2001 alone.[42] The peak year for methamphetamine laboratory seizures was in 2003 and 2004, when approximately 10,000 seizures were made in each of those years (Figure 5.6). Since 2004, however, retail sales of ephedrine and pseudoephedrine products have been restricted by law, and the prevalence of small methamphetamine laboratories has decreased substantially. The federal Combat Methamphetamine Epidemic Act, passed in 2005, was successful in reducing the number of laboratory seizures within the United States. Today, methamphetamine comes largely from production facilities in Mexico.[43]

The Trafficking of Hallucinogens

Lysergic acid diethylamide (LSD) is a clear or white, odorless crystalline material that is soluble in water (see Chapter 9). The drug is usually dissolved in a solvent for application onto paper, commonly referred to as blotter paper or blotter acid. Blotter acid consists of sheets of paper soaked or sprayed with LSD and decorated with a variety of colorful designs and symbols. A sheet of paper LSD blotter may contain hundreds of small, perforated, one-quarter-inch squares, with each square representing one individual dose. The price of a single "hit" of LSD ranges from $2 to $10 depending on demand and the potency of the drug. LSD also may be found in tablet form (microdots), in thin squares of gelatin ("window panes"), or in a dissolved liquid form, which is often kept in an eye drop container or glass vial. Eyedroppers allow users to disperse hundreds of doses of LSD at large parties or concerts by dropping the drug on users' tongues.

LSD is commonly produced from lysergic acid, which, in turn, is chemically derived from the ergot fungus. Since ergot is not readily available in the United States and is regulated under the Chemical Diversion and Trafficking Act, most of the production of LSD is believed to come from sources located abroad, such as Europe and Mexico. Since the 1960s, nearly all the LSD that is produced in the United States has originated from a small number of laboratories operating in northern California.

After production, LSD usually is distributed to traffickers and users in two ways. The primary method of transportation is by mail, using overnight delivery services. LSD is frequently concealed in greeting cards, cassette tapes, plastic film containers, or articles of clothing that are mailed to a post office box established by the recipient. The post office box is usually listed under a fictitious name or business, and no return address is typically provided on the package or envelope. Rock concerts also have been a traditional means of distributing LSD. Throughout the 1970s and 1980s, traffickers used concerts of the rock band The Grateful Dead as a network to distribute and sell both large and small quantities of LSD.[44]

Phencyclidine (PCP) is a synthetic drug first used as an anesthetic, now commonly classified as a hallucinogen (see Chapter 9). Today, all the PCP encountered for sale on the street in the United States has been produced in clandestine laboratories. While chemicals needed to manufacture PCP are readily available and inexpensive, and the drug is not particularly difficult to make, it does require many complicated steps and some of those steps can be quite dangerous. Occasionally, individuals making PCP in their bathroom, kitchen, or basement are killed from the inhalation of poisonous fumes produced when the drug is being manufactured. Most of the production and distribution of PCP in the United States are controlled primarily by African American criminal groups and street gangs in California.

PCP typically is produced in a liquid form that is sprayed or sprinkled onto leafy material such as tobacco, marijuana, mint, oregano, or parsley and rolled into a cigarette or joint. One PCP joint purchased on the street usually costs from $15 to $25. Mexican drug trafficking organizations operating in the United States also produce PCP and distribute wholesale quantities to Hispanic/ Latino street gangs. Mexican organizations typically produce PCP in powder or crystal form, whereas the liquid typically is produced by African American organizations. PCP has a variety of street names including angel dust, rocket fuel, killer weed, embalming fluid, ozone, or Sherman (because the drug supposedly "hits you like a Sherman tank").[45]

Ketamine (referred to as Special K or K) is a drug that is chemically similar to PCP but produces less confusion, irrationality, and violence. Since ketamine is currently marketed as a general anesthetic for veterinary use, most of the ketamine sold on the street is stolen from supplies kept in veterinary facilities. In veterinary clinics, ketamine is found in a liquid form for injection, but ketamine sellers prefer to market the drug in a powdered or crystallized form. Ketamine powder can be snorted, smoked (sprinkled on tobacco or marijuana), or ingested by being dropped into a drink, with an effect similar to that of PCP.

Small quantities of powdered ketamine (approximately 0.2 gram) are often called "bumps" and cost about $20 each.[46]

The Gang Factor in Drug Trafficking

The association between drug trafficking activity, gang membership, and violent crime is well documented. Gang members who sell drugs are significantly more violent than gang members who do not sell drugs and are more violent than drug sellers who do not belong to gangs. In order to understand the details of this association, we need to distinguish between two fundamentally different types of gang organizations: (1) outlaw motorcycle gangs primarily in Western U.S. states, notably the Hell's Angels, the Outlaws, the Bandidos, and the Pagans, and (2) street gangs in urban communities, such as the Crips and the Bloods in Los Angeles. Since the late 1980s, law enforcement authorities as well as researchers have recognized both organizations as having become the "new faces of organized crime" in America.[47]

Motorcycle clubs can be divided into either conventional or deviant categories. By far the greatest proportion of clubs are of the conventional type, comprised of men and women who join together based on a common interest in motorcycles, riding together for pleasure and companionship, behaving in accordance with the norms of society. A very small percentage of clubs are of the deviant type, comprised of individuals who engage

Quick Concept Check 5.2

Understanding Drug Trafficking

Check your understanding of drug trafficking by matching the statement on the left with the correct answer on the right.

Note: Some of the answers may be used more than once.

1. Source country of most of the foreign-produced marijuana in the United States.
2. Most of the heroin consumed in the United States comes from this country.
3. Most of the cocaine consumed in the United States comes from this country.
4. One of the countries within the Golden Crescent.
5. One of the countries in the Golden Triangle.
6. Most of the foreign-produced methamphetamine in the United States comes from this country.
7. Most of the LSD used in the United States is produced in this country.
8. This country is a frequent transport route for Colombian heroin entering the United States.
9. Primary source region for PCP.
10. Primary source for BC Bud marijuana.

a. Afghanistan
b. Thailand
c. The Netherlands
d. United States
e. Mexico
f. Colombia
g. Canada

Answers: 1. e 2. f 3. f 4. a 5. b 6. e 7. d 8. e 9. d 10. g

in unconventional, often criminal, behavior. In essence, these "clubs" function as outlaw gangs and their behavior is characteristic of a deviant subculture (see Chapter 4). In contrast to the popular image of mythic figures

money laundering: The process where illegal sources of income are concealed or disguised to make the sources appear legitimate.

rebelling against the norms of society or misunderstood social misfits, members of outlaw motorcycle gangs typically have a history of violent behavior and criminal records that include offenses such as drug trafficking, racketeering, brawling, weapons possession, and homicide. As mentioned before, outlaw motorcycle gangs have been principal dealers and traffickers of methamphetamine, and their association with this drug continues today. Their present-day drug involvement has been documented as extending to trafficking in marijuana, cocaine, and PCP as well.[48]

The association between street gangs and drug selling became particularly striking in the 1980s during the height of crack cocaine abuse in inner-city neighborhoods. In contrast to outlaw motorcycle gangs, the largest proportion of street gangs involved in drug sales during this time were comprised of individuals between 15 and 16 years of age. The prevalence of gang members aged 18 years or older increased when drug sales reached higher levels. White and Hispanic/Latino gang members tended to be more prevalent in neighborhoods where drug involvement was relatively low, and African American gang members tended to be more prevalent in neighborhoods where drug involvement was high. The extreme levels of systemic violence during this period were attributed in large part to the drug distribution activities of street gang members and their leaders.[49]

Money Laundering

Because practically every transaction in the illicit drug business is conducted in cash, a conspicuously large number of small bills can render drug traffickers vulnerable to law enforcement interdiction. Drug traffickers cannot simply deposit their profits into a local bank. The Bank Secrecy Act of 1970 requires that financial institutions in the United States report cash transactions of $10,000 or more to the Internal Revenue Service (IRS), and these institutions must identify the depositors and the sources of the money. Drug traffickers, therefore, must rely on a variety of money-laundering methods to convert bulk amounts of drug profits into legitimate revenue. **Money laundering** refers to the process where illegal sources of income are disguised to make them appear legitimate. Money laundering conceals the illegal sources of money and gives the money a legitimate history.

One of the simplest methods of money laundering is called "smurfing," by which a number of persons, or "smurfs," deposit random amounts of less than $10,000 into variously named accounts at many different banks. Using twenty smurfs, for example, each depositing $9,000 in cash, a trafficker could launder as much as $180,000 in less than an hour and circumvent the regulations of the Bank Secrecy Act. After the money is deposited, it can be withdrawn by the trafficker to purchase money orders in U.S. funds, which are sent out of the country to purchase more drugs or for safekeeping. The technique can be quite successful, except for the fact that traffickers have to give each of their smurfs a cut of their profits. Therefore, smurfing is not the most profitable method of money laundering.

A second technique of money laundering is for traffickers to ship the money abroad and deposit it in banks located in countries that have few, if any, money laundering regulations. Commonly called "offshore banks," unregulated banks in the Caribbean nations that were formerly British colonies, such as the Cayman Islands, have become favorite laundering havens. With the seventh largest deposit base in the world, the Cayman Islands have more than 550 banks, only seventeen of which have a physical presence. All of them operate without any requirement to report transactions. Typically, these offshore banking havens have very strict policies with regard to nondisclosure, effectively shielding foreign investors from investigations and prosecutions from their home countries.[50]

One of the oldest methods of money laundering is for drug traffickers to operate a cash-based retail service business such as laundromats, car washes, vending-machine routes, video rentals, or bars and restaurants, mixing the illegal and legal cash and reporting the total as the earnings of the cover business. In fact, the term "money laundering" is said to originate from Mafia ownership of laundromats in the United States during Prohibition. Bootleggers needed to show a legitimate source for their monies, and laundromats were chosen because they were cash-transaction businesses. Later, in the 1970s, the Mafia used pizza parlors to launder money made from the sale of heroin. Acquiring a legitimate business to launder money serves to provide drug traffickers with a reportable income for tax purposes.

Alternative methods of money laundering include bribing employees of financial institutions, acquiring financial institutions, arranging business loans, using real estate transactions, and disguising the money as casino winnings. The globalization of financial markets through the growth of international trade and the expansion of international corporations has provided a range of opportunities for the conversion of illegal proceeds into what appear to be legitimate funds. It is important to note that the financial success of a drug trafficking organization is based not only on its ability to produce, distribute, and sell drugs but also on its ability to launder the money made from the illicit drug business.[51]

Summary

Understanding Drug Use and Crime

- Empirical studies on the relationship between alcohol and drug use and the commission of crime are unanimous in their findings: Crime and drug use are strongly correlated. Individuals who drink alcohol and/or use drugs are significantly more likely to commit crimes than are individuals who neither drink nor use illegal drugs. Jail and prison inmates in the United States have much higher rates of drug use relative to the general population. The principal question is whether drug use and criminal behavior have a cause-and-effect relationship.

- Pharmacological explanations suggest that the effects of a drug contribute to an offender committing a crime; that is, the drug in question causes violent or criminal behavior while the drug is actually present in the individual's system. Economic explanations of the drug–crime link suggest that drug use may cause users to commit crimes to obtain money to buy drugs to support drug-taking behavior financially. Criminal activity of this type is referred to as economically compulsive crime. Several studies show that economically compulsive crime is a major component of the link between drugs and crime. Whether drug prices coincide with increases or decreases in crimes of this type appears to depend upon the historical period examined and the specific drug of abuse.

- The drug–crime connection also can be explained from the standpoint that crime causes drug use. In this view, persons who are predisposed to commit crime also take drugs. Drugs may be used before committing an offense to bolster courage or afterward to celebrate success. The viewpoint that crime causes drug use is further supported by longitudinal studies

(studies conducted over a period of time) finding that initial involvement in criminal activity occurs prior to the experimentation with drugs for most users.

- A third way of explaining the relationship between drug use and crime is the view that both drug use and crime share a common cause. According to this perspective, drug use and crime do not cause one or the other but are both aspects of a deviant lifestyle or culture. The same types of individuals who are most likely to commit crime are also the same types who are most likely to use drugs.

The Social Structure of the Illicit Drug Dealing

- The illicit drug business can be divided into various "stages" of production and distribution that include (1) cultivation and manufacturing, (2) importation, (3) wholesale distribution, and (4) retail distribution. In this sense, the illicit drug business is no different from that of a foreign or domestic commodity on the legitimate market.

- At the retail level, drug dealers follow either the free-lance model in which dealers and buyers transact their business with relative anonymity or the business model in which drug transactions are conducted within a hierarchically structured organization.

The Trafficking of Heroin

- There are currently four major sources of heroin: (1) the Golden Triangle, (2) the Golden Crescent, (3) Mexico, and (4) South America.

- The Golden Triangle of Southeast Asia was once the world's largest source of heroin. It included such countries as Thailand, Burma (Myanmar), Laos, and Vietnam. Very little of the heroin from this region is directed to markets in the United States.

- Currently, the largest source for the world's supply of heroin is the Golden Crescent of Pakistan, Afghanistan, Turkey, and Iran. Heroin from Afghanistan helped finance Osama bin Laden and the Taliban's terrorist activities prior to 2002. Afghanistan alone is currently producing approximately 94 percent of the world's supply of heroin.

- A third major source of heroin is Mexico. Historically, Mexican heroin has been crudely processed with many impurities, black or brown in color and referred to as "black tar" or "Tootsie Roll" on the street. In recent years, the purity of Mexican heroin has increased. While Mexico cultivates only 2 percent of the world's opium, the opium crop is significant because virtually all the Mexican opium that is converted into heroin is destined for the United States.

- Most of the heroin supply in the United States originates in Colombia, transported across the Mexico-U.S. border.

The Trafficking of Cocaine

- Today, most of the world's coca cultivation and cocaine production take place in Colombia, South America. Currently, the Revolutionary Armed Forces of Colombia (FARC), an antigovernment group with political and economic power in the nation, is a principal player in the cocaine trade.

- Mexican criminal organizations are currently responsible for smuggling the majority of cocaine that is imported into the United States.

The Trafficking of Marijuana

- Mexico is currently the major foreign source for marijuana imported into the United States. Most of the marijuana, whether grown in Mexico or transported through Mexico from other locations such as Colombia, is smuggled across the Southwest border.

- In recent years, there has been a significant growth in the Canadian marijuana trade. Canadian growers in British Columbia have used sophisticated hydroponic cultivation techniques to produce a potent form of marijuana that has come to be commonly known as "BC Bud" or "skunk weed."

- Production of domestically cultivated or "home grown" marijuana has increased within the United States in the last several years. Major outdoor cannabis cultivation takes place in such states as California, Hawaii, Washington, Oregon, and the Appalachian region of Kentucky and Tennessee. Approximately 80 percent of all outdoor cultivated plants recently eradicated by law enforcement have originated in California, Oregon, and Washington alone.

The Trafficking of Methamphetamine

- Since the mid-1990s, ethnic Mexican drug trafficking organizations based in Mexico and California have begun to take control of the production and distribution of methamphetamine. These Mexican organizations operate large-scale "superlabs" capable of producing in excess of ten pounds of methamphetamine in a twenty-four-hour period.

- Smaller independent "mom and pop" laboratories have also supplied methamphetamine to users in the United States through independent clandestine laboratory operations. Prior to the imposition of restrictions on the purchase of methamphetamine precursor chemicals from retail drugstores and convenience outlets, operators of these laboratories found it easy to obtain the ingredients for making methamphetamine. In recent years, the production of methamphetamine has shifted from domestic laboratories to production facilities in Mexico.

The Trafficking of Hallucinogens

- Nearly all the LSD available in the United States is being manufactured by a small number of laboratories that have been operating in Northern California since the 1960s.

- Most of the production and distribution of PCP in the United States is controlled by African American criminal groups and street gangs in California. These groups produce PCP in a liquid form that is sprayed or sprinkled onto leafy material such as tobacco, marijuana, mint, oregano, or parsley and rolled into a cigarette or joint.

- Ketamine is chemically similar to PCP but produces less confusion, irrationality, and violence. Most of the ketamine sold on the street is stolen from stores kept in veterinary facilities, since ketamine is available legitimately as an animal anesthetic.

The Gang Factor in Drug Trafficking

- The association between drug trafficking activity, gang membership, and violent crime is well documented. Gang members who sell drugs are significantly more violent than gang members who do not sell drugs and

are more violent than drug sellers who do not belong to gangs. An understanding of the details of this association, however, depends upon the type of gang involved.

- Two fundamentally different types of gang organizations are involved in drug trafficking and distribution: (1) outlaw motorcycle gangs primarily in Western U.S. states, notably the Hell's Angels, the Outlaws, the Bandidos, and the Pagans, and (2) street gangs in urban communities, such as the Crips and the Bloods in Los Angeles. Since the late 1980s, law enforcement authorities as well as researchers have recognized both organizations as having become the "new faces of organized crime" in America.

Money Laundering

- To escape the attention of law enforcement agencies, the enormous amount of income gained from "cash only" drug distribution and sales must be converted into legitimate revenue in a process called money laundering.

- One method of money laundering, called "smurfing," is to enlist a number of individuals to deposit random amounts of less than $10,000 into accounts at many different banks. A second method is to ship the money abroad and deposit it into banks located in countries with few, if any, banking regulations. A third method is to operate cash-based retail service businesses that serve as "fronts" for illegal drug distribution activities.

Key Terms

BC Bud, p. 103
business model, p. 96
China White, p. 96
double-breasted dealing, p. 99
drug-defined offense, p. 88

drug-related offense, p. 88
economically compulsive
  crime, p. 91
freelance model, p. 95
Golden Crescent, p. 98

Golden Triangle, p. 96
interactional
  circumstances, p. 92
Medellin and Cali drug
  cartels, p. 100

money laundering, p. 108
pharmacological
  violence, p. 90
spider marijuana, p. 105
systemic violence, p. 93

Endnotes

1. International Association of Chiefs of Police (2001, December 28). Violent crime in America: Summit recommendations. Alexandria, VA: International Association of Chiefs of Police. International Association of Chiefs of Police (1989). *Reducing crime by reducing drug abuse: A manual of police chiefs and sheriffs.* Gaithersburg, MD: International Association of Chiefs of Police. Quotation on p. 5. Office of Justice Programs (2003). *Toward a drugs and crime research agenda for the 21st century.* Washington, DC: National Institute of Justice, U.S. Department of Justice.

2. Goode, Erich (2008). *Drugs in American society* (7th ed.). New York: McGraw-Hill, pp. 386–389. U.S. Department of Justice (2010, September). *Crime in the United States 2009.* Washington, DC: Federal Bureau of Investigation, U.S. Department of Justice, Table 29.

3. Goode, *Drugs in American Society*, pp. 335–337. Inciardi, James A. (1992). *The war on drugs II: The continuing epic of heroin, cocaine, crack, AIDS, and public policy.* Mountain View, CA: Mayfield. Quotation on p. 158.

4. Office of National Drug Control Policy (2010, June) ADAM II. 2009 Annual report. Arrestee Drug Abuse

Monitoring Program II. Washington, DC: Office of National Drug Control Policy, Executive Office of the President, Tables 3.3, 3.4, and 3.5.

5. De La Rosa, Mario, Lambert, Elizabeth Y., and Gropper, Bernard (1990). Introduction: Exploring the substance abuse-violence connection. In *Drugs and violence: Causes, correlates, and consequences* (NIDA Research Monograph 103). Rockville, MD: National Institute on Drug Abuse, pp. 1–7.

6. Roth, Jeffrey A. (1994, February). *Psychoactive substances and violence: Research brief.* Washington, DC: National Institute of Justice. Tyner, Elizabeth A., and Fremouw, William J. (2008). The relation of methamphetamine use and violence: A critical review. *Aggression and Violent Behavior, 13*, 285–297.

7. Gold, Mark S. (1991). *The good news about drugs and alcohol: Curing, treating and preventing substance abuse in the new age of biopsychiatry.* New York: Villard Books.

8. Bureau of Justice Statistics (2009, September). *Criminal victimization in the United States, 2008, statistical tables.* Washington, DC: U.S. Department of Justice, Table 32. Bushman, Brad J. (1993, October). Human aggression while under the influence of alcohol and other drugs: An integrative research review. *Current Directions in Psychological Science.* pp. 148–152. Collins, James J., and Messerschmidt, Pamela M. (1993). Epidemiology of alcohol-related violence. *Alcohol Health and Research World, 17*, 93–100. Foran, Heather M., and O'Leary, K. Daniel (2008). Alcohol and intimate partner violence: A meta-analytic review. *Clinical Psychology Review, 28*, 1222–1234. Goode, Erich (2008), *Drugs in American society* , pp. 343–346. Kuhns, Joseph B., and Clodfelter, Tammatha A. (2009). Illicit drug-related psychopharmacological violence: The current understanding within a causal context. *Aggression and Violent Behavior, 14*, 69–78.

9. Inciardi, James A. (1990). The crack–violence connection within a population of hard-core adolescent offenders. In Marion De La Rosa, Elizabeth Y. Lambert, and Bernard Gropper (Eds.), *Drugs and violence: Causes, correlates, and consequences* (NIDA Research Monograph 103). Rockville, MD: National Institute on Drug Abuse, pp. 92–111.

10. Silverman, Lester P., and Spruill, Nancy L. (1977). Urban crime and the price of heroin. *Journal of Urban Economics, 4*, 80–103.

11. Rafert, Greg (2007, October 23). Illicit drug policy in the United States: Will increased drug prices reduce use and drug-related crime? Presentation at the Crime and Population Dynamics 2007 Summer Workshop, Berkeley, CA. Rhodes, William; Johnston, Patrick, Han, Song; McMullen, Quentin, and Hozik, Lynne (2002, January), Illicit drugs: Price elasticity of demand and supply. Report to the National Institute of Justice, U.S. Department of Justice, Washington, DC.

12. Inciardi, J. A. (1995). Crack, crack house sex, and HIV risk. *Archives of Sexual Behavior, 24*, 249–269. McCoy, Virginia H.; Inciardi, James A.; Metsch, Lisa R.; Pottieger, Anne.; and Saum, Christine A. (1995). Women, crack and crime: Gender comparisons of criminal activity among crack cocaine users. *Contemporary Drug Problems. 22* (3), 435–452.

13. Inciardi, James A. (1979). Heroin use and street crime. *Crime and Delinquency, 25*, pp. 335–346. Inciardi, James A., and McBride, David C. (1976). Considerations in the definitions of criminality for the assessment of the relationship between drug use and crime. In Research Triangle Institute (Ed.). *Crime and drugs*, pp. 123–137. Springfield, VA: National Technical Information Service. Inciardi, James A., and Pottieger, Anne E. (1994). Crack-cocaine and street crime. *Journal of Drug Issues, 24*, pp. 273–292. Inciardi, James A., Horowitz, Robert, and Pottieger, Anne E. (1993). *Street kids, street drugs, street crime.* Belmont, CA: Wadsworth.

14. Chaiken, Jan, and Chaiken, Marcia R. (1982), *Varieties of criminal behavior.* Santa Monica, CA: Rand.

15. Elliot, Delbert S., Huizinga, David, and Menard, Scott (1989). *Multiple problem youth: Delinquency, substance use and mental health problems.* New York: Springer-Verlag.

16. Bean, Philip (2004), *Drugs and crime* (2nd ed.). Portland, OR: Willan Publishing, pp. 51–58. Harris, Jonathan (1991). *Drugged America.* New York: Four Winds Press, p. 112.

17. Bureau of Justice Statistics (1992). *Drugs, crime, and the justice system: A national report from the Bureau of justice statistics.* Washington, DC: U.S. Department of Justice.

18. White, Jason (1991). *Drug dependence.* Englewood Cliffs, NJ: Prentice Hall, p. 200.

19. Goode, Erich (1972). Excerpts from marijuana use and crime. In National Commission of Marijuana and Drug Abuse, *Marijuana: A signal of misunderstanding*, Appendix, Vol. 1. Washington, DC: U.S. Government Printing Office, pp. 447–453.

20. Goode, Erich. (2005). *Drugs in American society* (6th ed.). New York: McGraw-Hill, pp. 329–350.

21. Berger, Gilda (1989). *Violence and drugs.* New York: Franklin Watts, p. 16. Blumstein, Alfred, and Rosenfeld, Richard (1998, October). Assessing the recent ups and downs in U.S. homicide rates. *National Institute of Justice Journal*, pp. 9–11. Curtis, Richard (1998, October). The improbable transformation of inner-city neighborhoods: Crime, violence, drugs, and youths in the 1990s. *National Institute of Justice Journal*, pp. 16–17. Reuter, Peter (2009). Systemic violence in drug markets. *Crime, Law, and Social Change, 52*, 275–284.

22. Harris, *Drugged America*, p. 117.

23. Goldstein, Paul J. (1979). *Prostitution and drugs.* Lexington, MA: Lexington Books. Goldstein, Paul J. (1985, Fall). The drugs/violence nexus: A tripartite conceptual framework. *Journal of Drug Issues*, 493–506.

24. Alder, P. (1985). *Wheeling and dealing.* New York: Colombia University Press. Hamid, Ansely. (1990). The political economy of crack-related violence.

Contemporary Drug Problems 17(1), 31–78. Johnson, Bruce D., Hamid, Ansely, and Sanabria, Harry (1992). Emerging models of crack distribution. In Thomas Mieczkowski (Ed.). *Drugs, crime and social policy: Research, issues, and concerns.* Boston: Allyn and Bacon. Preble, E., and Casey, J. (1969). Taking care of business: The heroin user's life on the streets. *International Journal of Addictions, 4*, 1–24.

25. Johnson, Bruce D., Golub, Andrew, and Dunlap, Eloise (2006). The rise and decline of hard drugs, drug markets, and violence in inner-city New York. In Alfred Blumstein and Joel Wallman (Eds.), *The crime drop in America.* New York: Cambridge University Press, pp. 164–206. Office of National Drug Control Policy (2004, January). *Pulse check: Trends in drug abuse, drug markets and chronic users in 25 of America's largest cities.* Washington, DC: Office of National Drug Control Policy.

26. Drug Enforcement Administration (2001, September). *Drug trafficking in the United States.* Washington, DC: Department of Justice. Johnson, Golub, and Dunlap (2006). The rise and decline of hard drugs, pp. 164–206. Office of National Drug Control Policy (2002, April). *Pulse check: Trends in drug abuse.* Office of National Drug Control Policy (2004, January). *Pulse check: Trends in drug abuse.* Vannostrand, Lise-Marie, and Tewksbury, Richard (1999). The motives and mechanics of operating an illegal drug enterprise. *Deviant Behavior, 20*, 57–83.

27. Zagaris, Bruce, and Ehlers, Scott (2001, May). Drug trafficking and money laundering. *Foreign Policy in Focus*, p. 1. Thoumi, Francisco E. (2005, Winter). The Numbers Game: Let's All Guess the Size of the Illegal Drug Industry! *Journal of Drug Issues, 35*, 185–200.

28. Drug Enforcement Administration Press Release (2003, May 16). *Massive heroin-smuggling organization dismantled.* Washington, DC: Drug Enforcement Administration Office of Public Affairs. Drug Enforcement Administration (2002, August). *Drug intelligence brief: Anatomy of a Southeast Asian heroin conspiracy.* Washington, DC: Drug Enforcement Administration. National Drug Intelligence Center (2008). *National Drug Threat Assessment 2009.* Washington DC: U.S. Department of Justice, pp. 25–32.

29. Filkins, Dexter (2010, June 22). U.S. money financing Afghan warlords for convoy protection, report says. *New York Times*, p. A4. Moreau, Roy, and Yousafzai, Sami (2006, January 9). A harvest of treachery. *Newsweek*, pp. 32–35. Mulrine, Anna (2007, July 9). The drug trade's collateral damage. *Newsweek*, p. 33. National Drug Intelligence Center, *National Drug Threat Assessment 2009.* National Drug Intelligence Center (2006). *National Drug Threat Assessment 2007.* Washington DC: U.S. Department of Justice, pp. 14–17. Rohde, David (2007, August 26). Taliban push poppy production to a record again. *New York Times*, p. 3. Rubin, Alissa J. (2010, October 1). U.N. reports mixed resultsl on Afghan poppy crops. *New York Times*, p. A10.

30. Drug Enforcement Administration (2001). *Intelligence report: The Mexican heroin trade.* Washington, DC: Drug Enforcement Administration. National Drug Intelligence Center, *National Drug Threat Assessment 2009.* Noriega, Roger F. (2007, August 16). It's our drug war, too. How America and Mexico can defeat the cartels. *Washington Post*, p. A15.

31. National Drug Intelligence Center, *National Drug Threat Assessment 2009.* National Drug Intelligence Center. 2004. *National drug threat assessment 2005.* Washington, DC: U.S. Department of Justice.

32. Drug Enforcement Administration (2002, December). *Drug intelligence brief: Increase in Mexican couriers transporting Colombian heroin to Mexico.* Washington, DC: Drug Enforcement Administration. Guevara, Rogelio (2002, December 12). *DEA congressional testimony: Colombian heroin trafficking.* Washington DC: Drug Enforcement Administration.

33. Jacobs, Bruce A. (1999). Crack to heroin? Drug markets in transition. *British Journal of Criminology, 39*(4), 555–574. Office of National Drug Control Policy (1998, summer). *Pulse check: Trends in drug abuse.* Washington, DC: Office of National Drug Control Policy.

34. Drug Enforcement Administration (2003). *Drug trafficking in the United States.* Washington, DC: U.S. Department of Justice.

35. Abadinsky, Howard (1993). *Drug abuse* (2nd ed.). Chicago: Nelson-Hall Publisher, p. 268.

36. Constantine, Thomas A. (1998). *DEA congressional testimony: International organized crime syndicates and their impact on the United States.* Washington, DC: Drug Enforcement Administration.

37. Marshall, Donnie R. (2001). *DEA congressional testimony: Plan Colombia.* Washington, DC: Drug Enforcement Administration. Pardo, Rafael (2000). Colombia's two-front war. *Foreign Affairs, 79*, 4–15.

38. Drug Enforcement Administration (2003). *Drug trafficking in the United States.* National Drug Intelligence Center, *National Drug Threat Assessment 2009*, pp. 1–8.

39. Drug Enforcement Administration (2001). *Drug trafficking in the United States.* Washington, DC: Department of Justice. Office of National Drug Control Policy (2002). *Pulse check: Trends in drug abuse, marijuana section.* Washington, DC: Office of National Drug Control Policy.

40. Drug Enforcement Administration (2000, December). *Intelligence brief: BC bud.* Washington, DC: U.S. Department of Justice. Hafley, Sandra R., and Tewksbury, Richard (1996). Reefer madness in bluegrass country: Community structure and roles in the rural Kentucky marijuana industry. *Journal of Crime and Justice, 19*(1), 75–92. National Drug Intelligence Center, *National drug threat assessment 2009.* National Drug Intelligence Center. (2004). *National drug threat assessment 2005.* Washington, DC: U.S. Department of Justice.

41. National Institute on Drug Abuse (2001, October). *Infofacts: Marijuana.* Washington, DC: National Institute on Drug Abuse.

42. Hargraves, Guy (2000, April), Clandestine drug labs: Chemical time bombs. *FBI Law Enforcement Bulletin, 69.* Jonsson, Patrick (2003, March 21). Modern-day moonshine: Appalachia's new cottage industry: Meth. *Christian Science Monitor,* pp. 80–83.

43. McDermott, Edward J. (2006, Winter). Motorcycle gangs: The new face of organized crime. *Journal of Gang Research, 13,* 27-36. National Drug Intelligence Center, *National Drug Threat Assessment 2009.* National Drug Intelligence Center (2010). *National Drug Threat Assessment 2010.* Washington, DC: U.S. Department of Justice, pp. 32–35.

44. National Institute on Drug Abuse (2003, January). *Infofacts: LSD.* Washington, DC: National Institute on Drug Abuse.

45. Drug Enforcement Administration. (2003, May). *Drug intelligence brief: PCP: The threat remains.* Washington, DC: U.S. Department of Justice.

46. National Drug Intelligence Center, *National drug threat assessment 2005.* Drug Enforcement Administration, *Club drugs: An update.* Washington, DC: U.S. Department of Justice.

47. Barker, Thomas, and Human, Kelly M. (2009). Crimes of the Big Four motorcycle gangs. *Journal of Criminal Justice, 37,* 174–179. Bellair, Paul E., and McNulty, Thomas L. (2009). Gang membership, drug selling, and violence in neighborhood context. *Justice Quarterly, 26,* 644–669. Howell, James C., and Decker, Scott H. (1999, January).

The youth gangs, drugs, and violence connection. *OJJDP Juvenile Justice Bulletin.* Washington, DC: Office of Juvenile Justice and Delinquency Prevention, U.S. Department of Justice. McDermott, Edward J. (2006, Winter). Motorcycle gangs: The new face of organized crime. *Journal of Gang Research, 13,* 27-36.

48. McDermott, *Motorcycle gangs.*

49. Bellair and McNulty, Gang membership. Howell, James C., and Gleason, Debra K. (1999, December). Youth gang drug trafficking. *OJJDP Juvenile Justice Bulletin.* Washington, DC: Office of Juvenile Justice and Delinquency Prevention, U.S. Department of Justice. Decker, Scott, Katz, Charles M., and Webb, Vincent J. (2008). Understanding the black box of gang organization: Implications for involvement in violent crime, drug sales, and violent victimization. *Crime and Delinquency, 54,* 153–172.

50. Mark, Clayton. (1995, September). Where the world's crooks go to do their dirty laundry. *Christian Science Monitor,* p. 1.

51. Motivans, Mark. (2003, July). *Money laundering offenders, 1994–2001.* Washington, DC: U.S. Department of Justice. Office of National Drug Control Policy (2002, January). *ONCP fact sheet: International money laundering and asset forfeiture.* Washington, DC: Office of National Drug Control Policy. Wankel, Harold D. (1996, February 28). *DEA congressional testimony: Money laundering by drug trafficking organizations.* Washington, DC: U.S. Department of Justice.

chapter **6**

Drugs and the Criminal Justice System

If I pull someone over for a traffic offense and they are acting really nervous, I usually ask if I can search their vehicle. Even though they may have drugs in their vehicle, most people still consent to the search. If they refuse to consent, then I usually call for a drug dog. When it arrives, the dog smells around the outside of the vehicle. If the dog hits on drugs, we have probable cause to conduct a search of the entire vehicle. You would not believe all the places I have found drugs. People have hidden drugs in their tires and inside hidden compartments in their dashboard, and one guy even hid cocaine in a false leg that he was wearing.

—*A sheriff's deputy from Gwinnett County, Georgia*

After you have completed this chapter, you should have an understanding of

- Attempts to control the production and/or cultivation of illicit drugs in foreign countries
- The role of law enforcement in illicit drug interdiction
- Different types of street-level drug operations
- Asset forfeiture and the federal RICO statute
- Federal and state penalties for drug trafficking
- Mandatory minimum sentencing
- Drug courts for nonviolent drug offenders

The criminal justice system in the United States plays a major role in our society's response to drug abuse. Essentially, it attempts to reduce the availability of illicit drugs to the general public and penalize the producers, distributors, and users of illicit drugs. This chapter will examine the principal strategies devised to accomplish these goals, including programs aimed at crop eradication, the control of precursor chemicals, efforts at interdiction of illicit drugs at our borders, the use of undercover operations, the use of asset forfeiture, punishments for those possessing or trafficking in illicit drugs, and the establishment of drug courts.

Law enforcement has always been, and remains, the predominant method of waging the "war on drugs" at the federal, state, and local levels. Of the billions of dollars spent, most of the money is spent on drug-law enforcement (Figure 6.1). A key goal of drug-law enforcement is to control the supply of illicit drugs by interrupting the source, transit, distribution, and eventual purchase of drugs. Therefore, it is useful to examine drug-law enforcement in terms of four major activities: (1) source control, (2) interdiction, (3) street-level enforcement, and (4) the correctional system. Chapter 16 will concern itself with efforts toward reducing the demand for illicit as well as licit drugs through prevention and treatment.

source control: Law enforcement actions that reduce or eliminate the cultivation and production of illicit drugs in foreign countries.

Source Control

Source control requires activities aimed at limiting the cultivation and production of illicit drugs in foreign countries. These activities include crop eradication, control of precursor chemicals, and the U.S. certification process.

The source-control problem in the 1970s with respect to heroin was considerably easier than it is today. At that time, 80 percent of the heroin used in the United States originated from opium poppies grown in Turkey. The opium was shipped to southern French port cities, where it was converted to heroin and then later smuggled into the United States—the "French connection." In an attempt to reduce the amount of heroin coming into the United States, the United States and France offered Turkey $35 million to ban opium production and to help Turkish farmers develop new cash crops. Initially, this action did lead to a shortage of heroin on American streets in 1973. The success of the Turkish initiative led to the official adoption of a more comprehensive crop-eradication strategy as a means for reducing illicit drug supplies in the U.S.[1]

The nature of the illicit drug trade today, however, is quite different from what it was in the 1970s. In recent years, we have been challenged by the geographical diversity in the sources of cultivation and production of illicit drugs and the fact that the sources themselves can change so rapidly. The Drug Enforcement Administration (DEA) Heroin Signature Program, for example, is designed to provide indications of the geographic origins of heroin at the wholesale level. Heroin samples are drawn from port-of-entry seizures as well as seizures and purchases

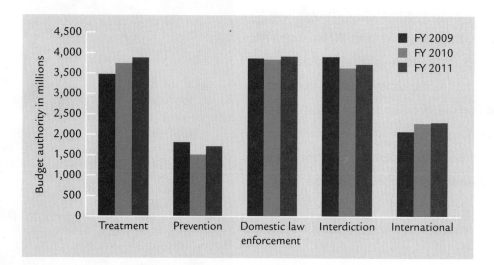

FIGURE 6.1

U.S. federal drug control budget (in millions) for fiscal years 2008, 2009, and 2010

Source: Office of National Drug Control Policy (2009, May). National drug control strategy FY 2010 budget summary. Washington, DC: Office of National Drug Control Policy, p. 1.

submitted to DEA laboratories. Purity and, if possible, geographic sources of the heroin are evaluated. Exact purity levels are relatively easy to ascertain, but an exact determination of where the drugs have originated is much more difficult.

Crop Eradication

Crop eradication programs have focused on the reduction of crop yields with respect to opium poppies, coca plants, and marijuana plants in their countries of origin. Eradication programs are driven by the premise that decreasing marijuana cultivation and opium and coca cultivation for the production of heroin and cocaine respectively makes these drugs more expensive, and potentially reduces the level of drug use (see Drugs . . . in Focus, Chapter 5). Crops are eradicated both manually and with herbicides. Herbicides (chemicals that kill plants) are either sprayed or dropped from the air as pellets that melt into the soil when it rains.

Coca plants are destroyed in a crop eradication program in Colombia. These efforts have been financed, in large part, by the U.S. Department of State through the Andean Counterdrug Initiative.

The counter-moves of source nations for illicit drugs illustrate the difficulty of reducing drug supplies by means of crop eradication. For example, from 1998 to 2002, intensive coca eradication programs in Colombia were implemented.[2] By 2006, these programs had succeeded in reducing Colombian coca cultivation in traditional growing areas, but growers simply moved out of these locations to clear the land and establish coca fields in more inaccessible areas, less known for large-scale cultivation. Growers have taken to adopting radical pruning (drastic cutting back the coca bush, often down to the ground, to protect the plants from aerial spraying) and vigorous replanting of sprayed coca. These procedures have promoted rapid regeneration or replacement of sprayed coca fields.[3] Clearly, eradication efforts have produced, at best, only short term, localized benefits.

Whether or not the adverse environmental impact of crop eradication programs outweighs the benefits in illicit drug control has been hotly debated. Proponents of crop eradication claim that coca production can be considered more harmful to the environment than crop eradication. Multiple harvests of coca on steep mountain slopes accelerate soil erosion, and improper use of dangerous chemical fertilizers causes water contamination. In addition, the processing of coca leaves into cocaine paste involves a series of toxic chemicals that causes further environmental pollution. On the other hand, it can be argued that the herbicide chemicals used in crop eradication have produced irreversible contamination of local water supplies, and the relocation of coca fields to previously uncultivated land has produced extensive deforestation that have reduced valuable rain forest resources.[4]

Unfortunately, in many impoverished regions of the world, crop eradication results in a disruption of an already-fragile local economy. The cultivation of marijuana, coca, or opium poppies for many poor families represents their only source of significant income. On occasion, tensions between peasant farmers and governmental agencies have risen to levels of confrontation. In 1996, for example, more than 50,000 peasants from several remote areas in southern Colombia converged on larger towns to protest the fumigation of their fields of coca and poppies. The demonstrators burned vehicles and tried to block local airstrips to disrupt the local economy. Two peasants were killed and several others

crop eradication: Programs in which opium poppies, coca plants, and marijuana plants are destroyed in their countries of origin, prior to transport overseas.

were injured. To put a halt to the revolt, the Colombian army resorted to blowing up the few roads leading to the main towns to obstruct the way of the demonstrators.[5]

To avoid a similar revolt, the Peruvian government in 2002 launched a financial plan, backed by the United States, to provide money for peasant farmers who voluntarily got rid of their coca crops. In this instance, no soldiers or police were assigned to take part in the eradication effort. Their absence was intended to avoid conflict between the government and the approximately 400,000 families that subsisted directly or indirectly through coca production. Families received $150 in Peruvian currency for every hectare (2.47 acres) of destroyed coca. The Peruvian government also attempted to promote alternative crops for the farmers, such as corn, banana trees, and rubber. The peasants who received money, however, found it difficult to stop growing coca because the alternatives were far less lucrative.[6]

It is, therefore, questionable whether crop eradication can be a successful strategy for reducing illicit drug supplies in the world. While worldwide cocaine production declined by approximately eight percent between 2006 and in 2007, primarily as a result of coca eradication programs, empirical studies of both crop eradication and crop substitution programs have found that these programs have had little impact on the production of either cocaine or opium.[7] The available evidence has shown that, on a global level, there rarely has been more than a 10 percent decrease of any one type of illicit crop in any given year. Even when there is a reduction in the cultivation of a particular crop, such as coca or opium poppies, in one part of the world, there is typically an increase in the cultivation in another part of the world. Over the years, crop eradication programs in Peru and Bolivia, for example, have led to an increase in coca production in Colombia, and vice versa. This is often called the "push down, pop up phenomenon" or the "balloon effect." Nonetheless, the U.S. government continues to endorse aerial spraying of coca and poppies as a strategy for disrupting the production of cocaine and heroin.[8]

precursor chemicals: Substances required for the production of illicit drugs. Examples are acetic anhydride and pseudoephedrine for the production of methamphetamine.

certification: The process by which the United States has the option of withholding foreign aid to a country if that country is judged to be noncompliant with U.S. counter-drug efforts, by virtue of its participation in major illicit drug production and/or trafficking.

Monitoring Precursor Chemicals

The monitoring and control of **precursor chemicals** and other substances used in the manufacture of illicit drugs is also a significant method of attacking illicit drug production before the drugs themselves enter the market. With the exception of cannabis (the botanical plant from which marijuana is obtained, see Chapter 10), every illicit drug requires an alteration of the natural product by specific chemicals before it reaches its final consumable form. While these chemicals are produced by legitimate companies, their involvement in illicit drug trade is accomplished by being diverted by illegitimate chemical companies or by criminal organizations.

DEA agents regularly monitor and track large shipments of precursor chemicals entering the United States. In one program called "Operation Purple," implemented to reduce the illicit manufacture of cocaine in South America, the DEA monitors and tracks shipments of potassium permanganate, the chemical oxidizer of choice for cocaine production.[9] The DEA also monitors shipments of acetic anhydride, the most commonly used chemical agent in heroin processing, and pseudoephedrine, the primary precursor chemical used in the production of methamphetamine. There is also an attempt to assist other countries in their monitoring and control of precursor chemicals, but many nations either lack the capacity to determine whether the import or export of precursor chemicals is related to illicit drug production or else fail to meet goals for precursor-chemical reduction due to internal political pressures. The problem is complicated by the fact that precursor chemicals are often transshipped through third-party countries in an attempt to disguise their purpose or destination.

Certification

A third method by which the United States attempts to control the production of illicit drugs in foreign countries is through a certification process. Enacted by Congress in 1986, **certification** is a process in which the U.S. government evaluates the cooperation of foreign countries in counter-drug efforts. Each year, the president is required to compile a list of countries that have been determined to be major illicit producing and/or drug transit countries. Countries on this list are then divided into three categories: (1) those that are fully compliant with U.S. counter-drug efforts ("certified"), (2) those not compliant with U.S. efforts ("decertified"), and (3) those that are noncompliant but certified based on vital U.S. national interests. If a country is decertified, U.S. law requires that all foreign aid be withheld until the president determines whether the country should be certified. In addition, U.S. representatives to multinational banks such as the World Bank and the International Monetary Fund are required to vote against any loans or grants to a decertified country.[10]

Interdiction

With respect to the attempt of the United States to prevent drugs from being smuggled across our borders by denying drug smugglers the use of air, land, and maritime routes, a strategy known as **interdiction**, the challenges are enormous. Consider the difficulty of monitoring the entirety of an international border with Mexico and Canada stretching nearly 7,000 miles. Each year, according to the U.S. Customs and Border Protection Agency, 60 million people enter the United States on more than 675,000 commercial and private flights, while another six million arrive by sea and 370 million by land. More than 116 million land vehicles cross borders with Canada and Mexico. More than 90,000 merchant and passenger ships dock at U.S. ports, off-loading in excess of nine million shipping containers and 400 million tons of cargo. More than 150,000 pleasure boats and other vessels visit U.S. coastal towns on a regular basis. Any one of these planes, land vehicles, or marine vessels could carry contraband cargo.[11]

An additional challenge comes from the continual ingenuity of the drug smuggler in attempts to circumvent standard interdiction controls. Over the years, law-enforcement agents have witnessed shipments of cocaine fashioned into plastic statues of the Virgin Mary, packed in hollow plaster shells shaped and painted to resemble yams, implanted in a man's thigh, and hidden beneath a shipment of iced fish fillets. A shipment of boa constrictors from Colombia was once confiscated with their intestines stuffed with condoms full of cocaine.[12] In 1994, federal agents at Kennedy Airport in New York noticed an emaciated and ailing sheepdog on a flight from Bogota, Colombia. X-rays and surgery revealed that five pounds of cocaine in ten rubber balloons had been surgically implanted in the dog's abdomen. New York Police Department detectives later arrested a twenty-two-year-old man from New Jersey when he came to claim the animal. The dog survived the surgery to remove the condoms and was taken to the Canine Enforcement Training Center in Virginia, where its handlers named it, appropriately enough, "Cokie."[13]

With tightened security after September 11, 2001, it has become difficult for drug traffickers to use air cargo as a method of smuggling drugs into the United States. In an

A police officer collects heroin capsules after displaying them during a news conference in Panama in 2004. A police operation uncovered some fifteen kilograms of heroin, one of the largest confiscations in Panama, from a group of five Colombians.

extreme tactical response, traffickers have resorted to using women from Colombia and other Andean nations as well as other regions of the Caribbean to act as drug "mules." The female mules sometimes swallow as many as fifty condoms filled with cocaine or heroin and then board a flight on a commercial airline. They are often given a topical anesthetic to deaden the throat before ingesting the condoms and then are told to use laxatives to help them "retrieve" the condoms after reaching their destination. Unfortunately, these condoms sometimes break and leak into the stomach, causing a drug overdose and death. Most of these "mules" are desperate for money and enter the business willingly. There are, however, an increasing number of women who are forced into the drug trade. The traffickers have been known to kidnap a woman's

interdiction: Efforts to prevent illicit drugs from being transported across the U.S. border.

TABLE 6.1

Drug Seizures by the Drug Enforcement Administration, 2006–2009

DRUG	2006	2007	2008	2009
Cocaine (in kilograms)	69,826	96,713	49,823	49,339
Heroin (in kilograms)	805	625	599	642
Marijuana (in kilograms)	322,438	356,472	660,969	666,120
Methamphetamine (in kilograms)	1,711	1,086	1,540	1,703
Hallucinogens (in dosage units)	4,606,277	5,636.305	9,199,693	2,954,251

Note: One kilogram equals 2.2 pounds. Drug amounts refer to amounts seized in DEA operations in a given year. They do not necessarily reflect the quantities on a year-to-year basis that are available on the illicit drug market.

Source: Drug Enforcement Administration (2010). The System to Retrieve Information on Drug Evidence (STRIDE) Program. Washington, DC: Drug Enforcement Administration, U.S. Department of Justice.

children or other family members and threaten to kill the hostages unless the woman successfully smuggles drugs into the United States.[14] Table 6.1 lists recent DEA drug seizures for cocaine, heroin, marijuana, methamphetamine, and hallucinogens.

Changes in airport security also have caused traffickers to scale back their smuggling of drugs through airports and redirect their drug shipments over the nation's highways. Most of this smuggling occurs at the U.S.–Mexican border, where drug traffickers use various types of vehicles to conceal their contraband, ranging from cars, commercial trucks, and tractor trailers to minivans. These vehicles are fitted with hidden compartments, known as "traps," where the drugs are concealed. In some cases, complex sequences of dashboard buttons and switches are required to provide access to concealed compartments in and/or under seats, in both the center and overhead consoles, or behind air-conditioning vents. In 2002, U.S. Customs agents discovered at the southwest border in Arizona more than fourteen pounds of marijuana in a hidden compartment located in the dash of a minivan. The packages of marijuana were wrapped in cotton and placed in a sealed rectangular mold made of a honey and wax mixture. The marijuana escaped detection by drug-detecting dogs.[15]

Federal Agencies Involved in Interdiction

The primary federal agencies involved in drug interdiction include the DEA, the U.S. Customs and Border Protection Agency, the U.S. Coast Guard, and the U.S. military. Of these agencies, only the DEA has drug-law enforcement as its only responsibility. Employing more than 4,000 officers with the authority to make arrests and carry firearms, the DEA investigates major drug-law violators, enforces regulations governing the manufacture and dispensing of controlled substances, and performs various other functions to prevent and control drug trafficking. DEA agents also work overseas, where they engage in undercover operations in foreign countries, work in cooperation with foreign governments to apprehend major drug traffickers, help to train foreign law enforcement officials, and collect intelligence about general trends in drug trafficking, drug production

An X-ray view of a truck stopped at the Mexico-U.S. border with immigrants concealed in the cargo area.

(illicit farming operations and laboratories), and criminal organizations operating in the illicit drug trade.

The U.S. Customs and Border Protection Agency, operating under the Department of Homeland Security, is responsible for curtailing the flow of illicit drugs across America's borders. More than 17,000 border patrol officers screen incoming travelers, conveyances, and cargo at more than 300 ports of entry across the United States, often working with drug-detection dogs. The Customs and Border Protection Agency also employs a number of special agents who are responsible for conducting investigations into drug smuggling and money laundering schemes. The agency maintains several specialized branches as well. The Marine Branch, for example, is responsible for interdicting drugs in near-shore waters by stopping and searching incoming vessels that behave suspiciously, especially small boats with large engines commonly referred to as "go-fast boats." The Air Branch is responsible for interdicting suspicious aircraft, such as small low-flying aircraft operating at night. Once a suspicious aircraft has been detected, it is normally tracked and forced down by high-speed chase planes and then searched. Customs inspectors are not hampered by constitutional protections that typically limit the power of other law enforcement agencies; they can search a person, vehicle, or container at ports of entry or near to a U.S. shoreline without probable cause.

The U.S. Coast Guard is the lead federal agency for maritime drug interdiction and shares responsibility for air interdiction with the U.S. Customs and Border Protection Agency. The Coast Guard is a key player in combating the flow of illegal drugs to the United States by denying smugglers the use of maritime routes in the "transit zone," a six-million-square-mile area including the Caribbean, the Gulf of Mexico, and the Eastern Pacific. Coast Guard ships can stop and board any maritime vessel operating within a twelve-mile radius of U.S. shoreline. Like Customs inspectors, Coast Guard personnel do not have to establish probable cause before boarding and searching a vessel at sea.[16]

In recent years, Coast Guard agents have had to contend with drug traffickers using semi-immersible submarine-like boats as the means for transport. These semi-subs are either self-propelled vessels or towed by other vessels, and they are capable of carrying up to 12 metric tons of cargo. As a response to the Coast Guard's tactic of using snipers in helicopters to shoot out engines on drug traffickers' speedboats (see Chapter 5), these new vessels are especially designed with engines beneath water level. In 2008, a major Coast Guard interdiction operation succeeded in the capture of one of these semi-subs off the coast of Guatemala, and seized approximately seven metric tons of Colombian cocaine.[17]

Members of the U.S. Coast Guard law enforcement team gather in Miami around more than 5,000 pounds of cocaine seized from a Honduran fishing boat off the coast of Colombia. The drugs were discovered hidden in compartments within the fuel tank, and eight Colombians were arrested. The 110-foot boat was later towed to Miami and confiscated.

A Colombian soldier stands next to a number of 33-foot-long semi-submersible vessels captured off the coast of Colombia in 2007. Because they leave very small wakes, the crude subs are difficult to detect visually from the air or by radar.

Drugs... in Focus

A Forty-Year Chronology of Drug Interdiction

Since the late 1960s, when the "war on drugs" was officially declared, a number of significant events have occurred in the area of illicit drug seizures and interceptions in the United States. Here are some of the highlights:

- 1969: In September, Operational Intercept forces the essential closure of the U.S.–Mexico border. Customs Department personnel examine every vehicle crossing the border from Mexico in a three-minute inspection. The two-week operation brings economic havoc on both sides of the border. As a result, Mexico agrees to fight the marijuana trade more aggressively, but there is little long-term impact on the smuggling of marijuana into the United States.

- 1972: The French connection is severed. A joint U.S.–French initiate carries out successful busts of Marseilles-based heroin organization, controlled by Corsican and U.S. criminal groups.

- 1979: Carlos Lehder, a key member of the Medellin Cartel, initiates a new method of cocaine smuggling, when he purchases Norman's Cay in the Bahamas as a refueling stopover for small planes transporting cocaine from Colombia to the United States. A Bahamian crackdown on Lehder's operation in 1982 causes Lehder to flee the island, though operations continue for another year.

- 1984: DEA and Colombian police discover Transquilandia, a cocaine-processing laboratory controlled by the Medellin Cartel, located deep in the Colombian jungle. In a coordinated bust operation, fourteen laboratory complexes are destroyed, as well as seven airplanes and 13.8 metric tons of cocaine. Conservative estimates of the assets seized or destroyed are set at $1.2 billion.

- 1984: DEA and Mexican officials raid a large marijuana cultivation and processing complex in the Chihuahua desert, in what is termed the "Bust of the Century." Seven thousand workers are arrested, and 5,000 to 10,000 tons of high-grade marijuana worth $2.5 billion are found and destroyed.

- 1998: Operation Casablanca leads to the indictment of three Mexican and four Venezuelan banks, as well as the arrest of 167 individuals in the largest money-laundering probe in U.S. history.

- 2002: Two commandants of the Autodefensas Unidas de Colombia (AUC) are arrested in an elaborate cocaine-for-arms deal. Paramilitary weapons worth $25 million were to be purchased by the group. Colombian officials claim that the AUC is responsible for 804 assassinations, 203 kidnappings, and 75 massacres with 507 victims, as well as their involvement with cocaine trafficking and distribution.

- 2005: Operation Cali Exchange results in twenty-four indictments, eighteen arrests, and the seizure of more than $7 million, more than 2,000 kilograms of cocaine, and more than 500 pounds of marijuana in a raid on a major drug-trafficking and money-laundering organization operating in the United States, as well as Panama, Colombia, the Dominican Republic, Brazil, and the Bahamas.

- 2007: DEA and Coast Guard seize approximately 19 metric tons of cocaine being smuggled aboard a Panamanian motorboat. The lost revenue to drug traffickers as a result of this raid is estimated to be approximately $300 million.

- 2008: Major drug-trafficker Eduardo Arellano-Felix is apprehended in Tijuana, Mexico.

- 2009: Project Coronado results in the arrest of 303 individuals in 19 states, all involved in the La Familia cocaine and methamphetamine cartel with headquarters in the state of Michoacan, Mexico.

Sources: Frontline—Public Broadcasting Service (2000). Thirty years of America's drug war: A chronology. In Huggins, Laura E. (Ed.), *Drug war deadlock: The policy battle continues.* Stanford, CA: Hoover Institute Press, Stanford University. Information courtesy of the Drug Enforcement Administration, U.S. Department of Justice, Washington, DC.

The U.S. military supports the drug interdiction efforts of many federal and state drug enforcement agencies by providing air and ground observation and reconnaissance, environmental assessments, intelligence analysts and linguists, and transportation and engineering support. Military training teams also teach civilian law enforcement officers such skills as combat lifesaving, surveillance techniques, and advanced and tactical military operations that can be used in counter-drug operations. Military personnel can support counter-drug efforts, but they cannot search or arrest drug traffickers. Law enforcement agencies and the military both benefit from this relationship. Police are able to use military resources, and service members are able to practice their military skills in real-world situations.

The U.S. military is also active in drug interdiction by working with foreign militaries and law enforcement agencies in many drug-producing countries. It provides intelligence, strategic planning, and training for anti-drug operations in several Latin American countries, such as Colombia, Mexico, Peru, and Bolivia. A key element of the military's anti-drug program in Latin America is its Tactical Analysis Teams (TATs), made up of a small number of U.S. Special Forces and military intelligence personnel. These teams gather intelligence and plan operations that are carried out by host nations and DEA agents.

Critics have claimed that there are a number of problems inherent in the use of TATs. First, TATs are aiding and training troops of foreign militaries that have documented records of human rights violations without insisting on fundamental reforms in those countries. A second problem with the use of TATs is that, in some cases, U.S. military personnel actually may be training future drug traffickers. In several Latin American countries, such as Bolivia, most of the American-trained army personnel are required to serve only one year in the military. Upon release from the service, some of these soldiers work for the drug traffickers, who pay substantial salaries, or become drug traffickers themselves, after having learned skills useful in avoiding drug interdiction by legitimate authorities.[18]

Technically speaking, the Posse Comitatus Act of 1878 forbids the military to be used as a law enforcement agency within the borders of the United States. The law was designed originally to bar federal troops from policing southern states after the Civil War and to protect Americans against abuses by their own military by dictating that federal troops could not enter private land or dwellings and could not detain or search civilians. In 1988, Congress expanded the National Guard's role in drug interdiction and allowed the guard to be actively involved in drug-law enforcement. In 2010, President Obama ordered up to 1,200 additional National Guard troops to be stationed in the Southwest, joining a few hundred Guard members previously assigned to help local law enforcement officials in reducing drug smuggling along the U.S.-Mexico border.

How does the National Guard circumvent the Posse Comitatus Act? The key to National Guard involvement in drug operations is the word "federal" in the language of the Posse Comitatus Act. Since 1912, the National Guard has had a two-tier mission to serve both the state and federal governments. Guard units involved in anti-drug operations typically work for the state government under the supervision of a state governor. Therefore, while the soldiers' salary and other benefits are paid by the federal government, it is argued that they are not bound by the Posse Comitatus Act. Critics claim, however, that the National Guard is a federal agency and that when the guard is involved in drug-law enforcement operations, it is violating federal law.[19]

Profiling and Drug-Law Enforcement

Over the years, drug-law enforcement agents have often developed "drug courier profiles" to help them identify potential drug smugglers. In *United States v. Sokolow* (1989), the U.S. Supreme Court ruled that drug courier profiles at airports could be used as a legitimate law-enforcement tool, the Fourth Amendment to the U.S. Constitution notwithstanding. In this case, Andrew Sokolow, a young African American male dressed in a black jumpsuit with gold jewelry, purchased two airline tickets with $1,200 in cash. Sokolow flew from Honolulu to Miami, planning to return to Hawaii forty-eight hours later. He also was traveling under a false name, did not check any luggage, and appeared very nervous. Drug agents him at the Honolulu airport and used a drug-sniffing dog, which led them to 1,063 grams of cocaine in his carry-on luggage. Chief Justice William H. Rehnquist stated, "While a trip from Honolulu to Miami, standing alone, is not a cause for any sort of suspicion, here there was more: Surely few residents of Honolulu travel from that city for twenty hours to spend forty-eight hours in Miami during the month of July." In a seven-to-two decision, the Court ruled that the drug courier profile could provide a "reasonable basis" for officials to suspect that a person is transporting drugs (Drugs ... in Focus).

The most significant criticism of drug-courier profiling is that some law enforcement officers have created their own profiles based solely on race, ethnicity, or national origin rather than on the behavior of an individual, a practice that has become known as **racial profiling**. In the late 1990s, racial profiling became a major topic of controversy. National and local media reports often proclaimed that racial profiling was a significant social

racial profiling: A practice of arresting or detaining an individual for possible drug violations, based on race, ethnicity, or national origin rather than on the individual's behavior.

Drugs... in Focus

Drug Smuggler Profiles

Profile for Commercial Airline Smuggling

1. Arriving from an identified source country
2. Traveling alone
3. Traveling by an unusual itinerary, such as a rapid turn-around time
4. Carrying little luggage or a large-quantity suitcase
5. Purchasing airline tickets with cash
6. Displaying unusual nervousness
7. Passenger tries to avoid questioning
8. Passenger makes contradictory statements during questioning

Profile for Automobile Smuggling

1. Unusually wide tires
2. Rear of vehicle visibly weighted down
3. Welding marks along edges of vehicle
4. Accumulation of trash inside vehicle that suggests long stretches without stopping
5. Lack of vehicle registration
6. Spare tire in back seat
7. Driver displaying unusual nervousness
8. Signs of drug use
9. Conflicting or inconsistent stories concerning destination among the driver and passengers

Profile for Maritime Smuggling

1. No fishing gear or nets visible on fishing vessel
2. Crew does not wave back to passing law-enforcement vessel or aircraft
3. Erratic course change when sighted by law-enforcement vessel or aircraft
4. Not sailing in usual shipping lanes or fishing grounds
5. Hatches padlocked and extra fuel drums on deck
6. Vessel does not use running lights at night
7. Vessel does not respond to radio contact or claims radio trouble
8. Vessel does not fly nationality flag

Profile for Small Aircraft Smuggling

1. Aircraft landing or flying after dark
2. Propellers, undersurface, and lower sides of aircraft pitted or scratched with grass stains or dirt from landing on grass fields or dirt roads
3. Aircraft parked far from airport offices or in a remote part of the airfield
4. Van, truck, or motor home camper parked near aircraft
5. Factory-installed long-range fuel tanks
6. Aircraft windows covered by curtains, tape, or other material
7. Pilots or passengers reluctant to leave aircraft unattended when refueling or ground servicing
8. Pilots or passengers showing large amounts of cash when paying for fuel or parts
9. Pilots or passengers reluctant to discuss points of origin or point of destination
10. Removal of passenger seats inside the aircraft

Profile for Postal Package Smuggling

1. Heavily taped packages
2. Packages that smell of masking agents such as coffee or perfume
3. False return addresses or zip codes
4. Packages originating from a source country
5. Packages sent from person to person
6. Packages with handwritten labels

Sources: Langan, Mark T. (1996). Profiling postal packages, *FBI Law Enforcement Bulletin*, 65 (2.3), pp. 17–21. Macdonald, John M., and Kennedy, Jerry (1983). *Criminal investigation of drug offenses: The narc's manual.* Springfield, IL: Charles C. Thomas. *United States v. Sokolow,* 490 U.S. 1 (1989).

---

problem, and national surveys confirmed that most Americans agreed. In a 1999 Gallup Poll, more than half the Americans polled believed that police actively engaged in the practice of racial profiling, and 81 percent said that they disapproved of the practice. When responses to survey questions were broken down by race, 56 percent of whites and 77 percent of African Americans believed that racial profiling was a pervasive problem.[20]

One of the most common complaints about racial profiling was the claim that police were stopping vehicles simply because the race of the driver did not appear to "match" the type of automobile he or she was driving. In a widely publicized case, Dr. Elmo Randolph, a forty-two-year-old African American dentist, was stopped more than fifty times over an eight-year span while driving a BMW car to his office near Newark. New Jersey state troopers, believing that Dr. Randolph was "driving the wrong car," would pull Dr. Randolph over, check his license, and ask him if he had any drugs or weapons in his car. Randolph claims that he did not drive at excessive speeds and that he had never been issued a ticket.[21]

The experience of Dr. Randolph and other minority drivers in New Jersey led the New Jersey State Police in 1999 to conduct a study on the race and ethnicity of persons stopped by state troopers. They found that New Jersey state troopers had indeed engaged in racial profiling along the New Jersey Turnpike. Although individuals of color comprised 13.5 percent of the New Jersey Turnpike population, they represented 41 percent of those stopped on the turnpike and 77 percent of those searched. Studies in other U.S. states also have found that police regularly engage in racial profiling.[22]

Police officers who defend racial profiling often believe that African Americans, Latinos, Asians, and other minorities are more likely to carry drugs than their white counterparts. Several studies, however, suggest that African Americans and Latinos are no more likely than whites to be in the possession of illicit drugs. One study of motorists on an interstate highway in Maryland found that 28 percent of African American drivers and passengers who were searched were found with contraband, compared with 29 percent of white drivers.[23] In New York in 1988 and 1989, 13 percent of whites were arrested for possessing illicit drugs compared with 11 percent of African Americans and 11 percent of Latinos.[24] A study of drug interdiction at major U.S. airports found that African Americans (6 percent) and Latinos (3 percent) were *less* likely to possess illicit contraband than whites (7 percent). In 2003, under a Justice Department directive, racial and ethnic profiling was officially banned at all federal agencies with law-enforcement powers. The only exception applies to investigations involving terrorism and national security.[25]

Street-Level Drug-Law Enforcement

As the third aspect of drug-law enforcement, street-level drug-law enforcement is the responsibility of federal agencies, state agencies, or local sheriffs' and police departments. Increasingly, these different agencies are joining forces and working together to form multijurisdictional drug task forces. Most of these task forces are coalitions of five or more local and state agencies that work closely with federal law enforcement agencies. Multijurisdictional task forces allow agencies at different levels of government to share funds, personnel, and intelligence and allow drug agents to track drug traffickers across many different jurisdictions. Nationwide, an estimated 21 percent of local police departments and 40 percent of sheriffs' offices have had one or more officers assigned full time to a drug task force.[26] Four major drug-law enforcement operations currently used by police departments to apprehend drug offenders are (1) the reverse sting, (2) the controlled buy, (3) the undercover buy, and (4) the "knock and talk."

The **reverse sting** is a drug-law enforcement operation in which undercover agents pose as drug dealers and sell a controlled substance or imitation version of a controlled substance to buyers. Community policing programs have made reverse stings popular because such operations can be used as a method of "cleaning up" a neighborhood. The reverse sting operation also makes money for law enforcement because asset forfeiture laws allow agencies to keep at least part of the proceeds made in these operations. The reverse sting has been criticized on the grounds that such operations attack only the demand side of the drug problem. Drug abusers are arrested, but the drug dealers or drug traffickers are not.

Undercover operations frequently involve the use of an informant. In the **controlled buy** operation, an undercover informant buys the drug under the supervision of the police. The informant may be a paid informant or a person who has been convinced by agents to "roll over" on other traffickers because they themselves have been charged with the possession or trafficking of an illicit drug. In the latter case, criminal charges against the informant may be either reduced or dropped for their participation in the operation. After agents have gained confidence in the informant, the informant is allowed to set up a controlled buy. Before the informant enters the dwelling in which the buy is to take place, he or she is usually searched to ensure that

reverse sting: A law-enforcement operation in which an undercover agent posing as a drug dealer sells a controlled substance, or an imitation of it, to a buyer.

controlled buy: A law-enforcement operation in which an undercover informant buys an illicit drug under the supervision of the police.

there are no drugs on his or her person before conducting the buy. After the buy has been made, the informant is again searched and asked to turn over the drugs bought in the transaction. To protect the identity of the informant, arrests are usually not made at the time of the buy. Warrants are obtained and later executed within ten days.

There are two types of **undercover buy** operations: (1) the buy-bust and (2) the buy-walk. During a buy-bust operation, an undercover agent makes a buy, and immediately thereafter, the seller is arrested for the drug sale. During a buy-bust, an undercover agent sets up a drug deal for a specified time and location. A cover team monitors the transaction via surveillance equipment, which is either hidden on the agent or in the room. After a "bust signal" is given by the undercover agent, a cover team rapidly moves in to make the arrest. Generally, the undercover agent is also "arrested" to protect his or her identity.

In a buy-walk operation, an undercover agent buys drugs but does not arrest the dealer at the time of the deal. The drug deal is used to obtain a warrant for the dealer that is served at a later time. The advantage of this operation is that it protects the identity of the undercover agent while at the same time ensuring his or her immediate safety during the time of the operation. Buy-walk operations are often used when a drug deal takes place at the residence of a drug dealer and officer safety is a concern.

The **knock and talk** is an operation that is used when officials receive information that an individual is dealing drugs but do not have probable cause to seek a search warrant. In this case, agents arrive at a suspect's residence, knock on the door, identify themselves as police officers, and ask permission to enter the residence. Once inside, agents ask the suspect if any one in the residence is producing or dealing drugs. After the suspect responds to the allegations, agents ask for permission to search the residence for illicit drugs.

The element of surprise obviously is an important factor in the success of the knock and talk. If there has been no prior warning, suspects do not expect law-enforcement officers to knock on their door and confront them with an allegation. To "confuse" suspects, agents often make misleading allegations. To find evidence against a marijuana dealer, agents may state that they believe the suspect is producing methamphetamine at his residence. Knowing that such charges are ridiculous, even though they are dealing in marijuana, suspects usually allow a **consent search**. Agents state that approximately 75 to 85 percent of drug dealers waive their constitutional right to privacy and consent to a search. When later asked why they consent to such a search, dealers often state, "I thought I would have been in worse trouble if I didn't let you search" or "I didn't know I had the right to refuse." Once evidence of illicit drug trafficking is found, agents typically make an arrest or return with a **search warrant**.[27]

Asset Forfeiture and the RICO Statute

Asset forfeiture refers to the seizure by the government of cash, cars, homes, and other property that the government claims are the result of criminal activity. Authorization for this strategy in law enforcement was created as part of the Organized Crime Control Act of 1970. A section of this legislation, known as the **Racketeer Influenced and Corrupt Organization (RICO) statute** (or simply, RICO), pertained to the prevention of criminal infiltration of legitimate businesses. It was a response to the practice of funneling ("laundering") profits from criminal activity, whether drug-related or not, into financial dealings of an unrelated commercial enterprise. This had been for many years a popular strategy of criminal organizations to circumvent detection by law enforcement (Chapter 5).

undercover buy: A law-enforcement operation in which an undercover law-enforcement agent buys an illicit drug in order to arrest the drug seller. The two types are the buy-bust and the buy-walk.

knock and talk: A law-enforcement operation in which agents ask for permission to search a residence for illicit drugs after asking the suspect whether anyone in the residence has been engaged in drug production or dealing.

consent search: A procedure in which law-enforcement agents ask and receive permission from a suspect to inspect a residence or vehicle for illicit drugs.

search warrant: A court-ordered document providing law-enforcement agents the right to search a residence or vehicle for illicit drugs.

asset forfeiture: A process used in drug-law enforcement in which cash, automobiles, homes, and other property are seized if these items have been acquired or used as a result of criminal activity.

RICO statute: The Racketeer Influenced and Corrupt Organization (RICO) statute, pertaining to the prevention of criminal infiltration of legitimate businesses. It was enacted as a section of the Organized Crime Control Act of 1970.

The principle of asset forfeiture, known as the **relation-back doctrine**, is that "because the government's right to illicit proceeds relates back to the time they are generated, anything acquired through the expenditure of those proceeds also belongs to the government."[28] In 1978, asset forfeiture was authorized to be used in the federal prosecution of controlled-substance trafficking cases. Since then, many states have passed legislation authorizing their own asset forfeiture procedures when dealing with the violation of state drug laws.

TABLE 6.2

DEA asset seizures in 2009

TYPE OF ASSET	NUMBER OF SEIZURES	VALUE
Cash	10,027	$768,310,882
Weapons	1,169	949,381
Real property	603	647,348,701
Vehicles	6,565	135,839,293
Vessels	141	9,883,134
Aircraft	33	20,111,143
Other	141	229,456,370
Total	18,679	1,811,898,904

Note: Total assets seized in 2005 and 2006 have values of $496,000,000 and $507,000,000, respectively.

Source: Information courtesy of the Drug Enforcement Administration, U.S. Department of Justice.

Forfeiture is particularly useful in drug-law enforcement because it reduces the financial incentive to reap the often enormous profits that are involved in drug trafficking and disrupts a drug-trafficking organization by seizing any vehicles, boats, planes, or property used to transport or produce illicit drugs. As shown in Table 6.2, the DEA made more than 18,000 domestic seizures of nondrug property, valued at approximately $1.8 million in 2009 as a result of drug investigations. Currently, the U.S. Marshalls Service is assigned to the management and care of more than $1.7 billion worth of property seized through the federal asset forfeiture program.[29]

There are two types of forfeitures: criminal (*in personam*) forfeitures and civil (*in rem*) forfeitures. The distinction between criminal and civil forfeitures is based upon whether the penalty pertains to a person or a thing. Criminal forfeitures are primarily against a specific person and result after a conviction for a crime to which the forfeited property is related. This can occur upon showing during the course of sentencing or plea-bargaining that the property is contraband (illegally obtained through the profit of a crime). Such criminal forfeitures are subject to all the constitutional and statutory procedural safeguards available under criminal law, and the forfeiture case and the criminal case are both tried together. Forfeiture must be included in the

relation-back doctrine: The principle behind the authority for asset forfeiture, in which the government asserts that it has the right to illicit proceeds relating back to the time they were generated.

indictment of the defendant, which means that the grand jury must find a basis for the forfeiture as well as punishment for the criminal offense itself.

Civil forfeitures, on the other hand, are *in rem* actions based upon the unlawful use of property, irrespective of its owner's culpability. Traditionally, civil forfeiture has operated on the premise that the property itself is the guilty party, and the fact that the forfeiture of the property affects an individual's property rights is not considered. With civil forfeiture, the offender does not need to be convicted or even charged with a crime because it is contended that the property "itself" is guilty. The property owner's guilt or innocence is therefore irrelevant, and civil forfeiture proceedings can be pursued independently or in lieu of a criminal trial.

Forfeitures have existed for thousands of years and are traceable to biblical and pre-Judeo-Christian times. Early English law recognized a kind of forfeiture known as "deodand," which required forfeiture of the instrument of a person's death. The principle was based on the legal fiction that the instrument causing death was deemed "guilty property" capable of doing further harm. For example, if a domesticated animal killed a person, it would be forfeited, usually to the King, whether or not its owner was responsible. The original purpose for creating this legal fiction was to satisfy the superstition that a dead person would not lie in tranquility unless the "evil property" was confiscated and viewed by the deceased's family as the object of their retribution. The King often used forfeiture to enhance royal revenues, and this corrupt practice led to the statutory abolishment of deodand in England in 1846.[30]

The Confiscation Act of 1862, passed during the Civil War, authorized the use of *in rem* civil procedures against southern rebels and their sympathizers who possessed property in the North. The law stated that the properties seized were to be used for supporting the Union cause in waging its war. The federal government at the time was responding to a Confederate law that confiscated the southern properties belonging to supporters of the Union. It was not until the late twentieth century, however, that civil forfeiture was "rediscovered" to address a pressing social concern: the war on drugs. The justification for extending forfeiture into the realm of illicit drug control was one of deterrence. Legislators believed that imprisonment of drug traffickers often was treated by criminal organizations as a mere cost of business, and therefore, forfeiture could be used to attempt to reduce their profits, in effect striking where it would really hurt.

The 1970 Comprehensive Drug Abuse Prevention and Control Act provided, in part, for the forfeiture of property used in connection with controlled substances.

In 1978, the law was expanded to include all profits from drug trafficking and all assets purchased with drug profits as items subject to forfeiture. The scope of the statute was further amended in 1984 to include all property that was used, or intended to be used, in a drug offense, and every drug offense, from simple possession to mass distribution, could trigger forfeiture. In recent years, civil asset forfeiture has become the weapon of choice in combating illicit drug trafficking and distribution in America. In the 1990s, a series of U.S. Supreme Court decisions established guidelines for its implementation. Law-enforcement officers argue that civil forfeiture allows them to combat drug crime by attacking the economic viability of drug-trafficking organizations while at the same time raising money for future law enforcement operations. Critics argue that forfeiture laws distort law-enforcement priorities. In many states, local, state, and federal agencies have pooled personnel and resources to form multiagency drug task forces. Many of these task forces finance themselves, at least in part, through asset forfeiture. By allowing such agencies to rely on asset forfeiture as a source of revenue, critics claim, the law enforcement priorities are shifted from efforts toward crime control to "funding raids" (see Portrait).

While it is claimed that forfeiture promotes the accomplishment of law-enforcement goals, it turns out that 80 percent of seizures are unaccompanied by any criminal prosecution.[31] This may stem from the fact that, for many law enforcement agencies, civil forfeiture creates a temptation to depart from legitimate law-enforcement goals in order to maximize funding. Some police departments now prefer to arrest drug buyers rather than drug sellers by employing a "reverse sting," the chief attraction being the confiscation of a buyer's cash rather than a seller's drugs.

Supporters of asset forfeiture claim that the lack of criminal prosecutions in such a large number of forfeiture cases is attributed to the need for police and prosecuting attorneys to offer a substantial bargaining chip in plea-bargaining negotiations. Defendants may be given the choice of not fighting the civil forfeiture procedure in exchange for avoiding criminal prosecution. This type of arrangement would benefit both the prosecutor and the prosecuted. The government would be able to "punish" defendants in legally weak cases that involve inadmissible or insufficient evidence, and the defendant would escape the monetary and social costs of a criminal conviction. Advocates of forfeiture also argue that forfeiture is an effective tool because it deters criminal activity, saves taxpayers' money by allowing law enforcement to self-fund many of their operations, and increases police officer morale.[32]

On October 2, 1992, a task force composed of Los Angeles County sheriff's deputies, DEA agents, and U.S. Park Service officers executed a search warrant on California millionaire Donald Scott's 250-acre estate. The search warrant was based on information from an informant that marijuana was being grown on Scott's land.

The task force arrived at Scott's house around 9:00 a.m. and broke down the door. Scott's wife claimed that the deputies pushed her from the kitchen into the living room, and then she screamed, "Don't shoot me. Don't kill me." The noise awakened Donald Scott from his sleep, and he came down the stairs holding a .38 caliber snub-nosed revolver over his head. When he pointed it in the direction of the deputies, they shot and killed him. When Scott's wife ran to the body, drug agents "hustled her out of the house." Recorded phone conversations also show that while Scott lay dead or dying in a pool of blood, police used his phone to make calls and answered a call from one of Scott's neighbors, telling the neighbor that Scott was "busy." A search of Scott's ranch did not find one trace of marijuana or any other illicit drug.

The Ventura County District Attorney's Office concluded that the Sheriff's Department was motivated, at least in part, by a desire to seize and forfeit Scott's land for the government. Deputies and DEA agents knew that Scott's estate was an extremely valuable piece of real estate, and most of the proceeds from the sale of the property would go to the Sheriff's Department. In fact, sheriff's deputies had several documents on their desks that estimated the amount of money the department could get for the sale of Scott's land.

The investigation also showed that the search warrant that was used in the drug raid was not supported by probable cause. The District Attorney's office recommended that, in the future, when preparing search warrant affidavits, law-enforcement officers should not compromise their objectivity based upon forfeiture concerns. Regardless of whether a given search warrant may result in the forfeiture of valuable property, officers should ensure that there is adequate probable cause.

Not surprisingly, Scott's death generated several lawsuits. Scott's widow and four of his children filed a $100 million wrongful death suit against the county and the federal government. After eight years, attorneys for Los Angeles County and the federal government finally agreed to award the family $5 million in return for dropping the wrongful death lawsuit.

The Sheriff's Department still maintains that its deputies did nothing wrong and the sheriff himself sued Ventura County's District Attorney for slander and defamation. A state appeals court declared that the district attorney was within his First Amendment rights when he criticized the Sheriff's Department. The court ordered the sheriff to pay the district attorney $50,000 in legal fees. The sheriff declared bankruptcy, and no payments were ever made.

Sources: Bradbury, Michael D. (1993). Report on the death of Donald Scott. Office of the District Attorney, Ventura, CA, March 30, 1993. Ciotti, Paul (2000). Ranch-coveting officials settle for killing owner, WorldNetDaily.com, January 23, 2000.

Drugs and the Correctional System

Most inmates in U.S. prisons and jails are serving time for drug-law violations (Table 6.3). Drug offenders serving time in federal prisons have more than tripled from 16 percent of the total prisoner population in 1970 to 51 percent in 2009, an increase generated by an intensified effort to step up drug-law enforcement as well as the prosecution and punishment of drug offenders (see Chapter 2). In 2009, approximately 1.7 million arrests were made in this category, accounting for about one in eight of the total number. It is estimated that in 2009, a drug arrest was made every 19 seconds. More than 82 percent had been for drug possession.[33]

Federal and State Penalties for Drug Trafficking

Current federal law under the Controlled Substance Act of 1970 and subsequently revised in 1986, 1988, and 2010 (Chapters 1 and 3) defines **drug trafficking** as the unauthorized manufacture, distribution by sale or gift, or possession with intent to distribute of any controlled substance. The severity of the penalties has varied according to the schedule of the controlled substance involved, with Schedule I violations being the most

drug trafficking: The unauthorized manufacture of any controlled substance, its distribution by sale or gift, or possession of such a substance with intent to distribute it.

TABLE 6.3

Inmates serving time in federal prison by type of offense

Offense	Number	Percent
Drug offense	100,627	51.3%
Weapons, explosives, arson	29,740	15.2%
Immigration violation	22,327	11.4%
Robbery	8,631	4.4%
Extortion, fraud, bribery	9,997	5.1%
Burglary, larceny, property offense	6,868	3.5%
Homicide, aggravated assault, kidnapping	5,450	2.8%
Sex offense	8,430	4.3%
Banking and insurance, counterfeiting, embezzlement	840	0.4%
Violations related to courts and corrections	661	0.3%
Continuing criminal enterprise	532	0.3%
National security violation	94	<.01%
Miscellaneous	1,970	1.0%

Note: Percentages reflect the number of inmates arrested for a type of offense within the total federal inmate population of 211,014.

Source: Federal Bureau of Prisons (2010, July). *Quick facts about the Bureau of Prisons.* Washington, DC: Federal Bureau of Prisons, U.S. Department of Justice.

severely punished and Schedule V violations being the least (Table 6.4). As a result of the Anti-Drug-Abuse Acts of 1986 and 1988, a number of special circumstances also are considered in arriving at the penalty imposed:

- Penalties are doubled for first-offense trafficking of Schedule I or II controlled substances if death or bodily injury results from the use of such substances.

- Penalties for the sale of drugs by a person over twenty-one years of age to someone under the age of

---

simple possession: Having on one's person any illicit or nonprescribed controlled substance for one's own use.

drug paraphernalia: Products that are considered to be used to administer, prepare, package, or store illicit drugs.

mandatory minimum sentencing: A policy that requires a judge to impose a fixed minimal term in prison for individuals convicted of certain crimes, regardless of the individual's role in the crime or other mitigating circumstances.

---

eighteen are increased to up to double those imposed for sale to an adult.

- Penalties for the sale of drugs within 1,000 feet of an elementary or secondary school are increased to up to double those imposed when the sale is made elsewhere.

- Fines for companies or business associations are generally 2.5 times greater than for individuals. In either case, penalties include the forfeiture of cars, boats, or planes that have been used in the illegal conveyance of controlled substances.

- If a family is living in public housing, the entire family can be evicted if a family member is convicted of criminal activity, including drug trafficking, on or near the public-housing premises.

Federal penalties for **simple possession**, defined as having on one's person any illegal or nonprescribed controlled substance in *any* of the five schedules for one's own use, are much simpler. First-offense violators face a maximum of one-year imprisonment and a fine of between $1,000 and $5,000. Second-offense violators face a minimum of fifteen days up to a maximum of two years and a fine of up to $10,000.[34]

Federal penalties set the standard for the punishment of drug offenses in the United States, but most drug-related offenses are prosecuted at the state rather than the federal level, and state regulations for simple possession and drug trafficking can vary widely. In cases of simple possession of small amounts of marijuana, some U.S. states might be more lenient (see Chapter 10), whereas in cases of heroin possession some states might be more stringent (see Chapter 7). Certain aspects of drug-taking behavior, such as the day-to-day regulation of alcohol sales and distribution, are regulated primarily by state and local municipalities, unless interstate commerce is involved. States and local municipalities have also taken on regulatory authority with regard to **drug paraphernalia**, products whose predominant use is to administer, prepare, package, or store illicit drugs. Nearly all U.S. states have statutes making it unlawful to sell these items to minors, unless they are accompanied by a parent or legal guardian. In addition, the importation, exportation, and advertising of drug paraphernalia are prohibited.[35]

Mandatory Minimum Sentencing

For more than thirty years, mandatory minimum sentencing for drug offenders was a fact of life. Arguably, no other legislative policy had contributed more to the increase in the number of drug offenders in U.S. prisons than the policy of mandatory minimum sentencing. Essentially, **mandatory minimum sentencing** required

TABLE 6.4

Federal Trafficking Penalties—Controlled Substances Other than Marijuana

DRUG/SCHEDULE	QUANTITY	PENALTIES	QUANTITY	PENALTIES
Powder Cocaine (Schedule II)	500–4999 gms mixture*	**First Offense:** Not less than 5 yrs, and not more than 40 yrs. If death or serious injury, not less than 20 yrs. or more than life. Fine of not more than $2 million if an individual, $5 million if not an individual**	5 kgs or more mixture	**First Offense:** Not less than 10 yrs, and not more than life. If death or serious injury, not less than 20 yrs. or more than life. Fine of not more than $4 million if an individual, $10 million if not an individual.
Crack Cocaine (Schedule II)	28–279 gms mixture*		50 gms or more mixture	
Fentanyl (Schedule II)	40–399 gms mixture		400 gms or more mixture	
Fentanyl Analogue (Schedule I)	10–99 gms mixture		100 gms or more mixture	
Heroin (Schedule I)	100–999 gms mixture	**Second Offense:** Not less than 10 yrs, and not more than life. If death or serious injury, life imprisonment. Fine of not more than $4 million if an individual, $10 million if not an individual	1 kg or more mixture	**Second Offense** Not less than 20 yrs, and not more than life. If death or serious injury, life imprisonment. Fine of not more than $8 million if an individual, $20 Million if not an individual.
LSD (Schedule I)	1–9 gms mixture		10 gms or more mixture	
Methamphetamine (Schedule II)	5–49 gms pure or 50–499 gms mixture		50 gms or more pure or 500 gms or more mixture	
PCP (Schedule II)	10–19 gms pure or 100–999 gms mixture		100 gm or more pure or 1 kg or more mixture	**2 or More Prior Offenses:** Life imprisonment

		PENALTIES
Other Schedule I & II drugs (and any drug product containing Gamma Hydroxybutyric Acid)	Any amount	**First Offense:** Not more than 20 yrs. If death or serious injury, not less than 20 yrs, or more than life. Fine of $1 million if an individual, $5 million if not an individual. **Second Offense:** Not more than 30 yrs. If death or serious injury, not less than life. Fine of $2 million if an individual, $10 million if not an individual
Flunitrazepam (Schedule IV)	1 gm or more	
Other Schedule III drugs	Any amount	**First Offense:** Not more than 5 yrs. Fine of not more than $250,000 if an individual, $1 million if not an individual.
Flunitrazepam (Schedule IV)	30 to 999 mgs	**Second Offense:** Not more than 10 yrs. Fine of not more than $500,000 if an individual, $2 million if not an individual
All other Schedule IV drugs	Any amount	**First Offense:** Not more than 3 yrs. Fine of not more than $250,000 if an individual, $1 million if not an individual.
Flunitrazepam (Schedule)	Less than 30 mgs	**Second Offense:** Not more than of 6 yrs. Fine of not more than $500,000 if an individual, $2 million if not an individual.
All Schedule V drugs	Any amount	**First Offense:** Not more than 1 yr. Fine of not more than $100,000 if an individual, $250,000 if not an individual. **Second Offense:** Not more than of 2 yrs. Fine of not more than $200,000 if an individual, $500,000 if not an individual.

*Under the Fair Sentencing Act of 2010, equivalent penalties for possessing quantities of powder cocaine or crack cocaine have been changed from a 100-to-1 ratio to a 18-to-1 ratio. In addition, the five-yr. mandatory sentence for simple possession of crack cocaine has been eliminated.

**Five-year mandatory sentence for simple possession of crack cocaine has been eliminated.

Note: Trafficking penalties distinguish between Schedule I drugs excluding marijuana and marijuana itself (Tables 6.4 and 6.5).

Sources: Associated Press (2010, August 4). Obama signs new cocaine bill. Drug Enforcement Administration, U.S. Department of Justice.

TABLE 6.5

Federal Trafficking Penalties—Marijuana

DRUG	QUANTITY	1ST OFFENSE	2ND OFFENSE
Marijuana	1,000 kg or more mixture; or 1,000 or more plants	• Not less than 10 yrs, not more than life • If death or serious injury, not less than 20 yrs, not more than life • Fine of not more than $4 million if an individual, $10 million if other than an individual	• Not less than 20 yrs, not more than life • If death or serious injury, mandatory life • Fine of not more than $8 million if an individual, $20 million if other than an individual
Marijuana	100 kg to 999 kg mixture; or 100 to 999 plants	• Not less than 5 yrs, not more than 40 yrs • If death or serious injury, not less than 20 yrs, not more than life • Fine of not more than $2 million if an individual, $5 million if other than an individual	• Not less than 10 yrs, not more than life • If death or serious injury, mandatory life • Fine of not more than $4 million if an individual, $10 million if other than an individual
Marijuana	more than 10 kgs hashish; 50 to 99 kg mixture more than 1 kg of hashish oil; 50 to 99 plants	• Not more than 20 yrs • If death or serious injury, not less than 20 yrs, not more than life • Fine of $1 million if an individual, $5 million if other than an individual	• Not more than 30 yrs • If death or serious injury, mandatory life • Fine of $2 million if an individual, $10 million if other than individual
Marijuana	1 to 49 plants; less than 50 kg mixture	• Not more than 5 yrs • Fine of not more than $250,000, $1 million if other than individual	• Not more than 10 yrs • Fine of $500,000 if an individual, $2 million if other than individual
Hashish	10 kg or less		
Hashish Oil	1 kg or less		

a judge to impose a fixed minimal term in prison for individuals convicted of certain crimes, regardless of the individual's role in the crime or other mitigating circumstances. Guidelines for sentences were based on the type of drug, the weight of a drug, and the number of prior convictions, and offenders were required to serve their entire sentence (or in some states a minimum of 85 percent) without parole. Under federal law, for example, anyone convicted of selling 500 grams of powder cocaine received a minimum prison sentence of five years. A judge could issue a sentence shorter than the mandatory minimum only if the defendant provided "substantial assistance" or cooperation in the prosecution of another offender. This means that if the defendant had implicated someone else in a crime (rightly or wrongly), he or she could possibly escape a mandatory sentence. Even then, however, the prosecutor, not the judge, had the power to decide whether this "assistance" was valuable enough to warrant a reduction in sentence.

Proponents of mandatory sentencing have believed that the policy is an effective deterrent to drug use and drug trafficking because it enhances awareness of the consequences of breaking the law and keeps drug offenders off the streets. Supporters of tough sentences for drug crimes have claimed that the "drug epidemic" has had a devastating effect on many communities, and the law is needed to protect these vulnerable communities by keeping drug offenders in prison. Mandatory sentences also have made the task of judges easier by allowing each offender to be sentenced equally under the law. Judges no longer have had to weigh conflicting evidence in the course of deciding how much time a convicted offender would spend in jail or prison. In addition, mandatory sentences have aided prosecutors and police because such lengthy sentences tended to persuade lower-level drug dealers to testify against upper-level ones (Drugs . . . in Focus).

Critics of mandatory sentencing, however, have maintained that such sentences are one of the principal reasons that the U.S. prison population has grown so rapidly since the 1980s. Mandatory minimum sentencing has, according to critics, filled our prisons with minor players, such as drug abusers, rather than major drug traffickers. They argue that as federal and state governments

Drugs... in Focus

Penalties for Crack versus Penalties for Cocaine in 2010: Correcting an Injustice

Under the 1986 Anti-Drug Abuse Act, the penalties for possession of crack (the smokable form of cocaine) were much more severe than those for possession of cocaine itself (the powder form). A mandatory minimum prison sentence of five years was imposed upon conviction of possessing more than 500 grams of powder forms of cocaine, whereas the possession of as little as 5 grams of crack can result in the same penalty. This became known as the 100-to-1 penalty ratio. In 1988, the federal penalty for possession of more than 5 grams of cocaine powder was set at a minimum of one-year imprisonment; the penalty for possessing an equivalent amount of crack was set at a minimum of five years.

This disparity, according to critics of this policy, had resulted in far more African Americans in prison for five years or more than white drug offenders. Why? Statistics showed that whites were more likely to snort or inject cocaine, whereas African Americans were more likely to smoke cocaine in its cheaper crack form. The differential effects of drug-law enforcement for the two forms of cocaine were reflected in a drug offense inmate population that was currently divided along racial lines. On the one hand, 90 percent of crack cocaine convictions involved African Americans; on the other, nearly two-thirds of powder cocaine abusers in the United States were white. Moreover, it was more common for offenses relating to the possession of powder cocaine to be prosecuted under state regulations, under which mandatory minimum sentences frequently did not apply.

In 2007, the United States Sentencing Commission, the agency that establishes guidelines for federal prison sentences, unanimously voted to lighten punishments retroactively for some crimes related to crack cocaine possession. As a result, the stark disparity that had existed for more than twenty years in penalties for powder cocaine and crack cocaine was narrowed, and more than 19,000 prisoners became eligible for early release. As many as 17,000 others incarcerated for a crack-related offense, however, could not benefit from the change. These prisoners had been given the absolute minimum term in the first place or were arrested with huge amounts of crack cocaine.

In 2010, the Fair Sentencing Act was signed into law, narrowing the gap between penalties involving crack cocaine and powder cocaine. Under the new regulations, the amount of crack cocaine subject to the five year minimum sentence was increased from 5 grams to 28. The former 100-to-1 rule now would be the 28-to-1 rule. In addition, the Sentencing Commission has been directed to review and amend its guidelines to increase penalties for persons convicted of using violence while trafficking in illicit drugs.

Sources: Hatsukami, Dorothy K., and Fischman, Marian W. (1996). Crack cocaine and cocaine hydrochloride: Are the differences myth or reality? *Journal of the American Medical Association, 276,* 1580–1588. Stout, David (2007, December 12). Retroactively, panel reduces drug sentences. *New York Times,* pp. A1, A31. Weinreb, Arthur (2010, August 4). Obama signs fair sentencing act into law. *http://news.suite101.com.* Wren, Christopher S. (1997, July 22). Reno and top drug official urge smaller gap in cocaine sentences. *The New York Times,* pp. A1, A12.

---

continued to spend billions of dollars on prisons, they neglected other social needs, such as drug-abuse prevention and education. It has not been uncommon for several U.S. states to have faster-growing prison budgets than drug-abuse education budgets, a particularly disturbing trend given that spending more money on treatment, education, and other social programs actually could reduce the number of persons who abuse drugs (see Chapter 17).[36]

In the last several years, laws regarding mandatory sentencing have been modified or rescinded, largely through the lobbying of such organizations as the Families Against Mandatory Minimums (FAMM), the U.S. Sentencing Commission, the American Psychological Association, the National Association of Criminal Defense Lawyers, and the American Bar Association. All have endorsed and promoted the end of mandatory sentencing. Since 1993, at least six U.S. states have repealed or reformed their mandatory sentencing laws. In Michigan, possession with intent to deliver more than 650 grams of heroin or cocaine once carried a mandatory life sentence with no chance of parole. This law now has been changed to twenty years to life, with the possibility of parole after fifteen years. In Mississippi, sentencing laws passed in 1995 required drug offenders, even those convicted of simple possession of a controlled substance, to serve 85 percent of their sentence, no matter the circumstances of their incarceration; now the maximum sentence has been reduced to less than 25 percent. As of 2009, judges in New York who had previously had no discretion in sentencing now have leeway in deciding whether a drug offender should be sent to a substance-abuse treatment center instead of prison. Thousands of inmates convicted of nonviolent drug offenses in New York can now apply to have their sentences reduced or set aside. At the federal level, a major U.S. Supreme Court decision in 2007 ruled that federal district judges had broad discretion to impose what would be, in their judgment, reasonable sentences in criminal proceedings, even if federal guidelines were more stringent.[37]

Other U.S. states are beginning a policy shift from punishment in any form to the option of treatment for drug offenders. California state law now permits judges to impose a sentence of treatment rather than imprisonment for many first-time drug possession offenses. A drug conviction is then removed from the offender's record if he or she completes a treatment program. Arizona has established a similar program where individuals convicted of drug possession are placed on probation and assigned to drug treatment rather than prison.[38]

Drug Courts

Drug courts are specialized courts designed to handle adult, nonviolent offenders with substance abuse problems, incorporating an intensely supervised drug treatment program as an alternative to standard sentencing. Several of the characteristics of drug courts include early identification and placement of eligible participants, drug treatment with clearly defined rules and goals, a nonadversarial approach, a monitoring of abstinence, judicial involvement and interaction with the participants, and a team approach in which judges, defense attorneys, prosecutors, probation officers, and treatment counselors coordinate their efforts. Those offenders who complete the program successfully may have their charges dropped or sentences revoked, whereas unsuccessful participants are returned to the regular court system and face possible imprisonment. Since the first drug

drug courts: Specialized court systems that handle adult, nonviolent offenders of drug laws, incorporating a supervised drug treatment program as an alternative to standard criminal sentencing.

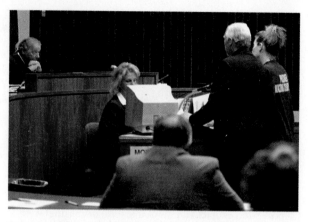

The court system in the United States is greatly burdened with the large number of cases that involve drug-law violations. The establishment of drug courts is an effort to help ease this burden.

court began operation in Florida in 1989, more than 2,000 drug courts have come into operation across the United States.[39]

The first step in a drug court program begins with defense attorneys, probation officers, or prosecutors referring a potential candidate to the drug court itself. A probation officer then screens candidates for eligibility. Candidates must be judged (using a screening instrument) to be serious drug abusers, cannot be on parole, and cannot have a prior serious or violent felony conviction. When he or she agrees to enter the program, the candidate waives his or her right to a jury and agrees to enter a treatment program for a year, during which he or she is subject to random drug tests. Participants are supervised by a probation officer to ensure that they adhere to program rules.

Numerous studies have shown that drug court programs are successful. First of all, they decrease the rate of criminal recidivism (repeated arrests). In a sample of 17,000 drug-court graduates nationwide within one year of graduating from the program, only 16 percent had been rearrested and charged with a felony offense, which was approximately one-third the level observed in drug offenders not participating in a drug court. Second, they are cost effective. Approximately $250 million in incarceration costs have been saved each year in New York State alone by diverting 18,000 nonviolent drug offenders into treatment. Third, drug courts increase the length of time an individual remains in treatment. The coercive power of the criminal justice system with respect to getting into treatment and staying in treatment is dramatic. Ordinarily, between 40 percent and 80 percent of drug abusers drop out of treatment within ninety days, and between 80 percent and 90 percent drop out within twelve months. In sharp contrast, more than two-thirds of drug-court participants complete a treatment program lasting a year or more. The benefits of drug court programs have been demonstrated in nonurban as well as urban communities.[40]

Clearly, the drug-court movement represents a shift away from a criminal justice policy oriented toward punishing drug users to a policy that focuses on treatment and recovery. Several U.S. states have begun to develop driving-under-intoxication (DUI) courts, whereas other U.S. states are expanding the drug treatment programs within their correctional facilities.

According to experts in the field of drug-abuse treatment, the mandated treatment approach in drug-court programs is more likely to result in a successful outcome than in circumstances in which the decision to go into treatment is made on a voluntary basis. One man in a Boston drug court expressed his feelings in this way:

> Drug court at first was just getting in the way of my using. But I think without drug court, I probably would never have went to Gaven House, got me a program, got me in line for getting sober. I didn't want to be here, but at the same time now that it's almost over, I'm kind of grateful for it, because I probably would not have stopped or even wanted to. You know? So I'm grateful for drug court.[41]

Since the early 1990s, a number of special problem-solving court programs have been created to foster treatment for other psychosocial difficulties. Mental-health courts, for example, provide a means for mentally ill defendants who have committed nonviolent criminal offenses to receive psychiatric evaluation and treatment. Other programs address problems of domestic violence (Drugs . . . in Focus).[42]

Drugs... in Focus

A Simulated Debate: Should We Legalize Drugs?

The following discussion of viewpoints represents the opinions of people on both sides of the controversial issue of the legalization of drugs. Read them with an open mind. Don't think you have to come up with the final answer, nor should you necessarily agree with the argument you heard last. Many of the ideas in this discussion come from the sources listed.

Point

Legalization would get the problem under some degree of control. The "war on drugs" does nothing but increase the price of illicit drugs to what the market will bear, and it subsidizes the drug dealers and drug kingpins around the world. If we legalize drugs, we can take the profit out of the drug business because legalization would bring the price down dramatically. We could regulate drug sales, as we do now with nicotine and alcohol, by setting up centers that would be licensed to sell cocaine and heroin, as well as sterile syringes, while any drug sales to minors would remain a criminal offense. Regulations would also ensure that drugs maintained standards of purity; the health risks of drug contamination would be drastically reduced.

Counterpoint

Legalization is fundamentally immoral. How can we allow people to run to the nearest store and destroy their lives? Don't we as a society have a responsibility for the health and welfare of people in general? If the drugs (pure or impure) were available, the only effect would be to increase the number of drug abusers. When Britain allowed physicians to prescribe heroin to "registered" addicts, the number of heroin addicts rose five-fold (or more according to some informal estimates), and there were then cases of medical abuse as well as drug abuse. A few unscrupulous doctors were prescribing heroin in enormous amounts, and a new drug culture was created.

Point

How moral is the situation now? We have whole communities living at the mercy of drug dealers. Any increase in drug users would be more than compensated for by the gains of freedom from such people. Even if the sale of crack were kept illegal, conceding that this drug is highly dangerous to society, we would have an 80 percent reduction in the black market for drugs, a substantial gain for the welfare of society. We can't guarantee that our inner cities would no longer be places of hopelessness and despair, but at least we would not have the systemic violence associated with the drug world. Besides, with all the money saved from programs set up to prevent people from getting hold of illicit drugs, we could increase the funding for drug treatment programs for all the drug abusers who want them and for research into ways of understanding the nature of drug dependence.

Counterpoint

No doubt, many drug abusers seek out treatment and want to break their drug dependence. Perhaps there may be some individuals who seek treatment under legalization because there would no longer be a social stigma associated with drug abuse, but many drug abusers have little or no long-term commitment toward drug treatment. In the present situation, the illegality of their behavior allows us to compel them to seek and stay in treatment, as well as monitor their abstinence by periodic drug testing. How could we do this when the drug was legal? Besides, how would we approach the education of young people if drugs were legal? We could not tell them that cocaine would give them cancer or emphysema, as we warn them of the dangers of nicotine, only that it would prevent them from being a productive member of society and would have long-term effects on their brains. If the adults around them were allowed to use cocaine, what would be the message to the young? Simply wait until you're twenty-one?

Point

We already have educational programs about alcohol abuse; the message for heroin and cocaine abuse would be similar. The loss of productivity due to any increased availability of drugs would not be as significant as the present loss of productivity we have with alcohol and cigarettes. With the tax revenues obtained from selling drugs legally, we could have money for more extensive anti-drug advertising. We could send a comprehensive message to our youth that there are alternatives to their lives that do not include psychoactive substances. In the meantime, we would be removing the "forbidden fruit" factor in drug-taking behavior. Drugs wouldn't be a big deal.

Counterpoint

Arguing that people take drugs because drugs are forbidden or hard to get ignores their basic psychological allure. If you lowered the price of a very expensive sports car, would you have fewer people wanting to buy one? Of course not. People would want a fast car because they like fast cars, just as people will still want to get high on drugs. Legalizing present drugs would only encourage the development of more dangerous drugs in the future. Look at what happened with crack. Cocaine was bad enough, but when crack appeared on the scene, it made the situation far worse.

Point

It can be argued that crack was marketed because standard cocaine powder was too expensive for people in the inner cities. If cocaine had been legally available, crack might not ever have been created because the market would not have been there. Even with crack remaining illegal under a legalization plan, there is at least the possibility that the appeal of crack would decline. The trend has been lately that illegal drugs are getting stronger, while legal drugs (alcoholic beverages and cigarettes) are getting weaker as people become more health-conscious. Legalization might make presently illicit drugs weaker in strength, as public opinion turns against them. The main problem we face is that spending 60 percent of a multi-billion-dollar drug-law-enforcement program on the "supply" side of the question, and only 40 percent on reducing the demand for drugs is not working. If one source of drugs is controlled, another source takes its place. The link between drugs and crime is a direct result of the illegality of drugs. It's not the individuals with drug dependence that are destroying the country; it's the drug dealers. Right now, the criminals are in charge. We have to change that. Only legalization would take away their profits and refocus our law-enforcement efforts on other crimes that continue to undermine our society.

Counterpoint

The frustration is understandable, but let's not jump into something merely because we're frustrated. We can allocate more funds for treatment without making drugs legal. We can increase funds for scientific research without making drugs legal. We need a more balanced program, not an entirely new one. Polls do not indicate general support for drug legalization. Between 60 percent and 80 percent of the U.S. public supports continued prohibition of drugs. Most citizens appear to recognize that legalization would make a bad situation worse, not better.

Critical Thinking Questions for Further Debate

1. Is it valid in this debate to make a distinction between "hard drugs" such as heroin and cocaine and "soft drugs" such as marijuana and hallucinogens?

2. What is your prediction of what would happen if all our drug-abuse-prevention efforts were focused exclusively on the Harm Reduction approach?

Sources: Dennis, Richard J. (1990, November). The economics of legalizing drugs. *The Atlantic*, 126–132. Goldstein, Avram (2001). *Addiction: From biology to drug policy* (2nd ed.). New York: Oxford University Press. Goode, Erich (1997). *Between politics and reason: The drug legalization debate*. New York: St. Martin's Press. Gray, James P. (2001). *Why our drug laws have failed and what we can do about it*. Philadelphia: Temple University Press. Kleiman, Mark A. R. (2001, May/June). Science and drug abuse control policy. *Society*, 7–12. Levinthal, Charles F. (2003). *Point/counterpoint: Opposing perspectives on issues of drug policy*. Boston: Allyn and Bacon, Chapter 1. U.S. Department of Justice, Drug Enforcement Administration. *Speaking out against drug legalization*. http://www.usj.gov. Wilson, James Q. (1990, February). Against the legalization of drugs. *Commentary*, 21–28.

Summary

- Of the billions of federal dollars spent annually on the "war on drugs," the greatest proportion of the money is spent on drug-law enforcement.
- There are four general levels of present-day drug-law enforcement: (1) source control, (2) interdiction, (3) street-level enforcement, and (4) the correctional system.

Source Control

- Source control involves actions focusing on reducing the cultivation and production of illicit drugs in foreign countries.
- Crop eradication programs involve the destruction of opium poppies, coca plants, and marijuana plants in their countries of origin. Crops are eradicated both manually and with herbicides. Critics point out that these programs have been responsible for causing environmental damage and disrupting the local economy of many rural regions in Latin America.
- Agents of the U.S. Drug Enforcement Administration (DEA) regularly monitor and track large shipments of precursor chemicals to prevent them from reaching the producers of illicit drugs.
- "Certification" is a process by which the U.S. government evaluates the cooperation of foreign countries in counter-drug efforts.

Interdiction

- Interdiction efforts attempt to prevent drugs from being smuggled across the U.S. border by denying drug smugglers the use of air, land, and maritime routes. The primary agencies involved in drug interdiction include the DEA, the U.S. Customs and Border Protection Agency, the U.S. Coast Guard, and the United States military. The DEA is the only federal agency that has drug-law enforcement as its only responsibility.
- Over the years, drug-law enforcement agents have developed "drug-courier profiles" to help in the identification of potential drug smugglers. Police officers have been criticized for developing profiles based solely on race, a practice known as racial profiling.

Street-Level Drug-Law Enforcement

- The reverse sting is a drug-law enforcement operation in which undercover agents pose as drug dealers and sell a controlled substance or imitation version of a controlled substance to buyers.
- The controlled buy is an operation in which an undercover informant makes a drug buy under the supervision of the police.
- Undercover buy operations involve an undercover agent making a drug buy. The seller may be arrested immediately after the deal, or the drug deal may be used to obtain a search warrant to be served at a later time. The "knock and talk" occurs when agents arrive at a suspect's residence and ask permission to conduct a consent search of the residence.
- Asset forfeiture is the process by which the government seizes cash, cars, homes, and other property that it claims have been involved in or associated with criminal activity.

Asset Forfeiture and the RICO Statute

- Criminal forfeitures result after a conviction for a crime to which the forfeited property is related. Civil forfeitures are based upon the unlawful use of property, irrespective of its owner's culpability. With civil forfeiture, the offender does not need to be convicted or even charged with a crime, since the contention is that the property "itself" is guilty.
- Authority for asset forfeiture in law enforcement was created as part of the Organized Crime Control Act of 1970. A section of this legislation, known as the Racketeer Influenced and Corrupt Organization (RICO) statute, pertained to the prevention of criminal infiltration of legitimate businesses.
- Critics argue that forfeiture laws distort law enforcement priorities from crime control to "funding raids."

Drugs and the Correctional System

- Inmates serving time for drug-law violations currently dominate prison populations in the United States. Federal guidelines for drug-law violations make the distinction between drug trafficking and simple possession of controlled substances.
- Mandatory minimum sentencing has required a judge to impose a fixed minimal length of imprisonment for individuals convicted of certain crimes, regardless of a person's role in the crime or other

mitigating factors. In recent years, there has been a significant shift toward providing judges with a greater degree of discretion in their sentencing of drug offenders.

- Drug courts are specialized courts designed to handle adult, nonviolent offenders with substance abuse problems. They involve an intensely supervised drug treatment program as an alternative to standard sentencing.

Key Terms

asset forfeiture, p. 126
certification, p. 118
consent search, p. 126
controlled buy, p. 125
crop eradication, p. 117
drug courts, p. 134

drug paraphernalia, p. 130
drug trafficking, p. 129
interdiction, p. 119
knock and talk, p. 126
mandatory minimum
    sentencing, p. 130

precursor chemicals, p. 118
racial profiling, p. 123
relation-back doctrine,
    p. 127
reverse sting, p. 125

RICO statute, p. 126
search warrant, p. 126
simple possession, p. 130
source control, p. 116
undercover buy, p. 126

Endnotes

1. Marshall, Elliot (1971, July 27). Cold turkey: Heroin: The source supply. *New Republic, 165*(4), 23–25. National Drug Intelligence Center (2008). *National drug threat assessment 2009.* Washington, DC: U.S. Department of Justice, National Narcotics Intelligence Consumers Committee (1996). *The supply of illicit drugs to the United States.* Washington, DC: National Narcotics Intelligence Consumers Committee.
2. Office of National Drug Control Policy (2003, February). *National drug control strategy update 2003.* Washington, DC: Office of National Drug Control Policy.
3. National Drug Intelligence Center (2007). *National drug threat assessment 2008.* Washington, DC: U.S. Department of Justice, pp. 1–2.
4. Vargas, Ricardo (2002). The anti-drug policy, aerial spraying of illicit crops and their social, environmental and political impacts on Colombia. *Journal of Drug Issues, 32,* 11–61.
5. Matheson, Mary (1996, August 12). Colombian leader tries to please U.S. on drugs, but ignites peasant revolt. *Christian Science Monitor, 88,* 7–8.
6. Lama-Tierramrica, Abraham (2002, November 18). Peru: Cash for farmers who destroy their coca crops. *Global Information Network,* p. 1.
7. National Drug Intelligence Center, *National drug threat assessment 2009,* p. 2. Office of National Drug Control Policy. *National drug control strategy update 2003.*
8. Farrell, Graham (1998). A global empirical review of drug crop eradication and United Nations crop substitution and alternative development strategies. *Journal of Drug Issues, 28,* 395–437.
9. Office of National Drug Control Policy (1999). *ONCP fact sheet: Efforts to control precursor chemicals.* Washington, DC: Office of National Drug Control Policy.
10. U.S. Department of State (2003, January 31). *The certification process: Fact sheet released by the Bureau of International Narcotics and Law Enforcement Affairs.* Washington, DC: U.S. Department of State.
11. Drug Enforcement Administration, U.S. Department of Justice, 2004.
12. Miller, D. W. (1994, December 19). Canine carrier. *U.S. News and World Report, 117,* 14.
13. Ibid.
14. McCleland, Susan (2003, July 28). Drug mules. *Maclean's, 116,* 25–31. Philbert, James (2009, November 9). Don't be drug mules . . . Top cop advises women. *The Trinidad Guardian.* http://guardian.co.tt.
15. Drug Enforcement Administration (2003). *Drug intelligence brief: Common vehicle concealment methods.* Washington, DC: Drug Enforcement Administration.
16. Office of National Drug Control Policy (2003, March). *Drug data summary fact sheet.* Washington, DC: Office of National Drug Control Policy. Office of National Drug Control Policy (2002, September 5). *ONDCP fact sheet: Interdiction operations.* Washington, DC: Office of National Drug Control Policy. Information Courtesy of U.S. Coast Guard.
17. http://www.news.navy.mil, the official web site for the U.S. Navy.
18. Peters, Katherine M. (2003, April). Troops on the beat. *Government Executive, 35,* 56. Shanker, Thom (2008, December 23). Obstacle seen in bid to curb Afghan trade in narcotics. *New York Times,* p. A6. Zirnite, Peter (1998, April). The militarization of the drug war. *Current History, 97,* 166–186.
19. Archibold, Randal C. (2010, May 26). National Guard will be deployed to aid at border. *New York Times,* p. A1, A3. Vaughn, Ed (1992, December). National Guard involvement in the drug war. *Justicia, the Newsletter of the Judicial Process Commission,* p. 1.
20. *United States v. Sokolow* (1989). 490 U.S. 1. Gallup Poll Organization (1999, December 9). *Gallup poll*

organization poll release: Racial profiling is seen as widespread, particularly among young black men. Princeton, NJ: Gallup Poll Organization.

21. Hosenball, Mark (1999, May 17). It is not the act of a few bad apples: Lawsuit shines the spotlight on allegations of racial profiling by New Jersey state troopers. *Newsweek,* pp. 34–35.

22. Verniero, Peter, and Zoubek, Paul (1999, April 20). *New Jersey Attorney General's interim report of the state police review team regarding allegations of racial profiling.* Trenton, NJ: Office of the New Jersey Attorney General.

23. Lamberth, John (1999, April 16). Driving while black: A statistician proves that prejudice still rules the road. *Washington Post,* p. C1.

24. New York Attorney General (1999, December 1). *New York City Police, "stop and frisk" practices: A report to the people of New York from the Office of the Attorney General.* New York: New York Office of the Attorney General.

25. U.S. Customs Service (1998). *Personal searches of air passengers results: Positive and negative.* Washington, DC: U.S. Customs Service.

26. Bureau of Justice Statistics (2003, January). *Sheriff's offices 2000.* Washington, DC: Bureau of Justice Statistics, U.S. Department of Justice.

27. Paterline, Brent (2003). *Drug Identification and Investigation for Law Enforcement.* Temecula, CA: Staggs Publishing.

28. Schmalleger, Frank (2009). *Criminal justice today: An introductory text for the 21st century.* Upper Saddle River, NJ: Pearson Prentice Hall, p. 604.

29. Drug Enforcement Administration (2005). *DOJ computerized asset program.* Washington, DC: Drug Enforcement Administration, U.S. Department of Justice. United States Marshals Service (2009, February 9). U.S. Marshals Fact Sheet: Asset Forfeiture Program.

30. Finkelstein J. (1973). The goring ox: Some historical perspectives on deodands, forfeitures, wrongful death and the Western notion of sovereignty. *Temple Law Quarterly, 46,* 169–290.

31. Maguire, Kathleen, and Pastore, Anne L. (Eds.) (1995). *Sourcebook of criminal justice statistics 1994.* Washington, DC: Bureau of Justice Statistics, U.S. Department of Justice.

32. Hawkins, C. W., Jr., and Payne, T. E. (1999). Civil forfeiture in law enforcement: An effective tool or cash register justice? In J. D. Sewall (Ed.), *Controversial issues in policing.* Boston: Allyn and Bacon, pp. 23–34.

33. Bureau of Prisons (2010, September 25). Quick facts about the Bureau of Prisons. Washington, DC: U.S. Department of Justice. Federal Bureau of Investigation (2009). *Arrests: Crime in the United States 2009.* Washington, DC: U.S. Department of Justice, Table 29.

34. Drug Enforcement Administration, U.S. Department of Justice. Statutes of the Controlled Substances Act of 1970, as amended and revised in 1986 and 1988.

35. Healey, Kerry (1988). *State and local experience with drug paraphernalia laws.* Washington, DC: U.S. Government Printing Office, pp. 69–73.

36. Donohue, John J., III, and Siegelman, Peter (1998). Allocating resources among prisons and social programs in the battle against crime. *Journal of Legal Studies, 27,* 30–43. Horowitz, Heather, Sung, Hung-En, and Foster, Susan E. (2006, January–February). The role of substance abuse in U.S. juvenile justice systems and populations. *Corrections Compendium,* pp. 1–4, 24–26.

37. Associated Press (2009, December 20). Prison population to have first drop since 1972. Greenhouse, Linda (2007, December 11). Justices restore judges' control over sentencing. *New York Times,* pp. A1, A28. Peters, Jeremy W. (2009, March 11). Legislation to overhaul Rockefeller drug laws advances swiftly. *New York Times,* p. 20. Stout, David (2007, December 12). Retroactively, panel reduces drug sentences. *New York Times,* pp. A1, A31.

38. Harrison, Blake (2001, July/August). Rethinking drug policy. *State Legislatures, 27,* 53–61.

39. General Accounting Office (2002). *Drug courts: Better DOJ data collection and evaluation efforts needed to measure impact of drug court programs.* Washington, DC: General Accounting Office. Office of National Drug Control Policy (2005, February). The President's National Drug Control Strategy. Washington, DC: Office of National Drug Control Policy.

40. Gottfredson, D.C., Najaka, S. S., and Kearley, B. (2003). Effectiveness of drug treatment courts: Evidence from a randomized trial. *Criminology and Public Policy, 2,* 401–426. Huddleston, C. West, Freeman-Wilson, Karen, and Boone, Donna L. (2004, May). *Painting the current picture: A national report card on drug courts and other problem-solving court programs in the United States.* Alexandria, VA: National Drug Court Institute. National Institute of Justice (2006, June). *Drug courts: The second decade.* Washington, DC: National Institute of Justice, U.S. Department of Justice.

41. Galloway, Alyson L., and Drapela, Laurie A. (2006). Are effective drug courts an urban phenomenon? Considering their impact on recidivism among a nonmetropolitan adult sample in Washington State. *International Journal of Offender Therapy and Comparative Criminology, 50,* 280–293. Goldkamp, John S. (2001). Do drug courts work? Getting inside the drug court black box. *Journal of Drug Issues, 31,* 27–73. Huddleston, C. West; Freeman-Wilson, Karen; Marlowe, Douglas B.; and Russell, Aaron (2005, May). *Painting the current picture: A national report card on drug courts and other problem-solving court programs in the United States.* Alexandria, VA: National Drug Court Institute. Meyer, William G., and Ritter, William A. (2001). Drug courts work. *Federal Sentencing Reporter, 14,* 179–186. Quotation from Home Box Office (2007, March). Mandated Treatment. www.hbo.com/addiction.

42. Huddleston et al. (2005), *Painting the current picture.*

chapter **7**

Narcotics: Opium, Heroin, and Synthetic Opiates

After you have completed this chapter, you should have an understanding of

- The history of opium and opium-derived drugs
- The effects of narcotic drugs on the mind and body
- The neurochemical basis for opiate effects
- Patterns of heroin abuse
- The potential lethality of heroin abuse
- The issue of controlled heroin intake
- Treatment strategies for heroin dependence
- Medical uses of opiates and opiate-like drugs
- Current use and abuse of OxyContin and other narcotic analgesic medications

Mary, age sixteen, is a self-described "garbage head"—she will ingest anything she thinks will give her a high. Recently, her drug of choice has been OxyContin. She downs a few pills with a shot of vodka, calling the combination "the sorority girl's diet cocktail" because it allows for a stronger state of intoxication and has fewer calories than alcohol alone.

After Mary had a tonsillectomy, her surgeon wrote a prescription for eighty tablets of OxyContin for postoperative pain. Mary took sixty of them over the next two weeks, averaging five a day.

Presently, Mary is in substance abuse treatment, focusing on the problem of prescription medication abuse. When asked whether he had read Mary's medical chart detailing her history of substance abuse before prescribing OxyContin, instead of alternatives such as acetaminophen, Mary's surgeon replied, sheepishly, "Well, I guess I wasn't thinking."[1]

There is no escaping the love-hate relationship we have with opium and the opiates that are derived from it. Here is a family of drugs that has the astonishing power to banish pain from our lives and at the same time the power to enslave our minds.

This chapter will concern itself with the medical uses and recreational abuses of opiate-derived and opiate-related drugs. Together, these drugs are referred to as **narcotics** (from the Greek word for "stupor"), in that they produce a dreamlike effect on the user and at higher doses induce a state of sleep. The most important characteristic of narcotic drugs, however, is that they have powerful analgesic properties; they greatly reduce feelings of pain.

As noted in Chapter 3, the term "narcotic" often has been used inappropriately to mean *any* illicit psychoactive drug or at least any drug that causes some degree of dependence, including such unlikely examples as cocaine and amphetamine, which are anything but sleep-inducing. Even today, the term can be misleading, because other drugs (barbiturates, for example) having no relationship to opium are far more effective in inducing sleep (see Chapter 11). Nonetheless, we are stuck with this inexact terminology; it is not likely to disappear anytime soon.

Narcotic drugs, in general, are divided into three major categories. The first includes **opium** and three natural components that can be extracted from it: morphine, codeine, and thebaine (Figure 7.1). The second category includes opium derivatives that are created by making slight changes in the chemical composition of morphine. The best example of this type is heroin. Although technically an opiate derivative, heroin is commonly included with morphine, codeine, and thebaine, and collectively all four chemicals, along with opium itself, are referred to simply as **opiates.** The third category includes synthetic drugs that are not chemically related to morphine or any of its derivatives but nonetheless produce opiate-like effects that are behaviorally indistinguishable from the effects of opiates

narcotics: A general term technically referring to opiate-related or opiate-derived drugs. It is often mistakenly used to include several other illicit drug categories as well.

opium: An analgesic and euphoriant drug acquired from the dried juice of the opium poppy.

opiates: Any ingredients of opium or chemical derivatives of these ingredients. The term generally refers to opium, morphine, codeine, thebaine, and heroin.

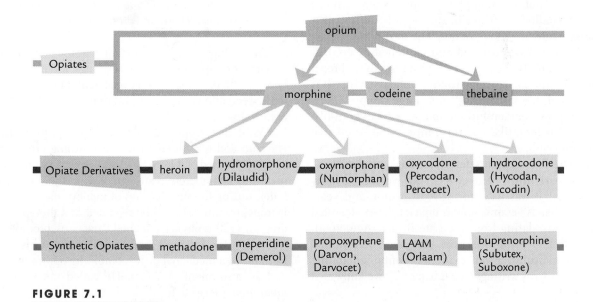

FIGURE 7.1

Major opiates, opiate derivatives, and synthetic opiates. (Note: Brand names are shown in parentheses.)

Sources: Physicians' desk reference (64th ed.) (2010). Montvale, NJ: Medical Economics Data. Raj, P. Prithvi (1996). *Pain medicine: A comprehensive review.* St. Louis: Mosby.

themselves. Drugs of this type are commonly referred to as **synthetic opiates** or *synthetic opiate-like drugs.* This last category is a result of a continuing effort to discover drugs that achieve the same degree of analgesia as opiates but lack the potential for abuse.

Opium in History

Like cocaine, the origins of heroin and other opiates go back to the fields of faraway times and places. This particular story begins with the harvesting of raw opium in remote villages of Myanmar (formerly Burma), Laos, Thailand, Afghanistan, Kazakhstan, Mexico, Colombia, Peru, and other countries where the weather is hot and labor is cheap. The source is the opium poppy, known by its botanical name as *Papaver somniferum* (literally "the poppy that brings sleep"), an annual plant growing three to four feet high. Its large flowers are typically about four or five inches in diameter and can be white, pink, red, or purple. This variety is the only type of poppy that produces opium; common garden plants such as the red Oriental poppy and the yellow California poppy look similar but do not produce psychoactive effects.

The present-day method of opium harvesting has not changed much in more than three thousand years. When the petals of the opium poppy have fallen but the seed capsule of the plant underneath the petals is not yet completely ripe, laborers make small, shallow incisions in the capsules, allowing a milky white juice to ooze out. The next day, this substance will have oxidized and hardened by contact with the air. At this point, the opium is reddish brown in color and has the consistency of heavy syrup. It is collected, plant by plant, onto large poppy leaves. Later, it will darken further and form small gum-like balls that look like tar, taste bitter, and smell like new-mown hay.[2]

The first written references to opium date back to the early third century B.C., but we can be fairly sure that it was used for at least a thousand years before that. A ceramic opium pipe has been excavated in Cyprus, dating from the Late Bronze Age, about 1200 B.C. Cypriot vases from that era depict incised poppy capsules. From evidence contained in the Ebers Papyrus writings (see Chapter 2), we know that

Oxidized/hardened syrup collected (handwritten)

use for thmd use. (handwritten)

An Afghan villager harvests his opium crop in a field of opium poppies.

Egyptians were knowledgeable about the medicinal value of opium.[3]

In the second century A.D., Claudius Galen, a famous Greek physician and surgeon to Roman gladiators, recommended opium for practically everything. He wrote that it:

> . . . resists poison and venomous bites, cures chronic headache, vertigo, deafness, apoplexy, dimness of sight, loss of voice, asthma, coughs of all kinds, spitting of blood, tightness of breath, colic, . . . jaundice, hardness of the spleen, . . . urinary complaints, fever, . . . leprosies, the troubles to which women are subject, melancholy, and all pestilences.[4]

Galen's enthusiasm for the instrumental use of opium is an early example of "over-prescribing." Interestingly, however, there are no records in ancient times that refer to the recreational use of opium or to any problems of opium dependence.[5]

Western Europe was introduced to opium in the eleventh and twelfth centuries by returning crusaders who had learned of it from the Arabs. At first, opium was used only by sorcerers as an ingredient in their potions. Later, during the first stirrings of modern medicine in Europe, opium began to be regarded as a therapeutic drug. In 1520, a physician named Paracelsus, promoting himself as the foremost medical authority of his day, introduced a medicinal drink combining opium, wine, and an assortment of spices. He called the mixture *laudanum* (derived from the Latin phrase meaning "something to be praised"), and before long the formula of Paracelsus was being called the stone of immortality. Even though Paracelsus himself denounced many of the doctrines of earlier physicians in history, he continued the time-honored tradition of recommending opium for practically every known disease.

In 1680, the English physician Thomas Sydenham, considered the father of clinical medicine, introduced a highly popular version of opium drink similar to that of Paracelsus, called Sydenham's Laudanum. For the next two hundred years or so, the acceptable means of taking opium among Europeans and later Americans would be in the form of a drink, either Sydenham's recipe or a host of variations.

Sydenham's enthusiasm for the drug was no less than that of his predecessors. "Among the remedies," he wrote, "which it has pleased Almighty God to give man to relieve his sufferings, none is so universal and so efficacious as opium."[6] The popularity of opium drinking eventually would lead to the emergence of opium as a recreational drug in Europe and the United States.

The Opium War

Sometime in the eighteenth century, China invented a novel form of opium use, opium smoking, which eventually became synonymous in the Western mind with China itself. However, for at least eight hundred years before that, the Chinese used opium only in a very limited way. They took it almost exclusively on a medicinal basis, consuming it orally in its raw state as a highly effective painkiller and treatment for diarrhea (see Table 7.1).

The picture changed dramatically in the eighteenth century, strangely enough, when the British people discovered and fell in love with Chinese tea. British merchants in China wanted to buy tea and send it home, but what could they sell to the Chinese in exchange? The problem was that there were few, if any, commodities that China really wanted from the outside. In their eyes, the rest of the world was populated by "barbarians" with an inferior culture, offering little or nothing the Chinese people needed.

The answer was opium. In 1773, British forces had conquered Bengal Province in India and suddenly had a monopoly on raw opium. Here was an opportunity to introduce Indian-grown opium to China as a major item of trade. Not surprisingly, the Chinese government was opposed to an influx of this drug into China. Nonetheless, opium soon flooded into the country, smuggled in by local British and Portuguese merchants, which enabled the British government and its official trade representative, the East India Company, to maintain a public image of not being directly involved in the opium trade. Huge quantities of opium found a ready market in southern port cities such as Canton. Opium smoking and opium dependence soon became a major social problem. Despite repeated edicts by the Chinese emperor to reduce the use of opium within China or cut the supply line from India, the monster flourished.[7]

In 1839, tensions had reached a peak. In a historic act of defiance against the European powers, including Britain, an imperial commissioner appointed by the Chinese emperor to deal with the opium problem once and for all confiscated a shipment of opium and burned it publicly in Canton. Events escalated shortly thereafter, until open fighting between Chinese and British soldiers broke out. The Opium War had begun.

By 1842, British artillery and warships had overwhelmed a nation unprepared to deal with European firepower. In a humiliating treaty, China was forced to sign over to Britain the island of Hong Kong and its harbor (until the distant year of 1997), grant to British merchants exclusive trading rights in major Chinese ports, and pay a large amount of money to reimburse Britain for losses during the war. Despite these agreements, fighting broke out again between 1858 and 1860, with French and American forces joining the British. In a treaty signed in 1860, China was required to legalize opium within its borders. The Opium War succeeded in opening up the gates of China, much against its will, to the rest of the world.[8]

Opium in Britain

opium dens vs. parlors for the british

To the average Briton in the mid-1800s, the Opium War in China was purely a trade issue, a faraway conflict with little or no direct impact on his or her daily life. Nonetheless, opium itself was everywhere. The important difference between China and Britain with respect to opium was not in the *extent* of its consumption but in the *way* it was consumed. The acceptable form of opium use in Victorian England was opium drinking in the form of laudanum, whereas the Asian practice of opium smoking was linked to a perceived lifestyle of vice and degradation and associated with the very lowest fringes of society. The contrast was strikingly ironic. Opium dens, with all the evil connotations that the phrase has carried into modern times, were the places where opium was *smoked*; the respectable parlors of middle-class British families were the places where opium was *drunk*.

In a sense, opium was the aspirin of its day. Supplies of British opium were unlimited and cheaper than gin or beer. Medical opinion was at most divided on the question of any potential harm; there was no negative public opinion and seldom any trouble with the police. As long as there were no signs of opium smoking, a chronic opium abuser was considered no worse than a drunkard. Nearly all infants and young children in

Britain during this period were given opium, often from the day they were born. Dozens of laudanum-based patent medicines (with appealing names like Godfrey's Cordial, A Pennysworth of Peace, and Mrs. Winslow's Soothing Syrup) were used to dull teething pain or colic, or merely to keep the children quiet. The administration of opium to babies was particularly attractive in the new, industrial-age lifestyle of female workers, who had to leave their infants in the care of elderly women or young children when they went off to work in the factories.[9]

Out of this climate of acceptance sprang a new cultural phenomenon: the opium-addict writer. Just as LSD and other hallucinogens were to be promoted in the 1960s as an avenue toward a greatly expanded level of creativity and imagination (see Chapter 9), a similar belief was spreading among intellectuals during this period with respect to opium. The leader of the movement was Thomas DeQuincey, and his book *Confessions of an English Opium Eater*, published in 1821, became the movement's bible. It is impossible to say how many people started to use opium recreationally as a direct result of reading DeQuincey's ecstatic revelations about "opium eating" (by which he meant opium drinking in the form of laudanum), but there is no doubt that the book made the practice fashionable. English authors enamored with laudanum included Elizabeth Barrett Browning and Samuel Taylor Coleridge (whose poem, *Kubla Khan*, was undoubtedly inspired by an opium high).

Opium in the United States

In many ways, opium consumption in the United States paralleled its widespread use in Britain. In one survey of

A nineteenth-century advertising card for Mrs. Winslow's Soothing Syrup, a popular opium remedy, was directed toward young mothers and their children.

thirty-five Boston drugstores in 1888, 78 percent of the prescriptions that had been refilled three or more times contained opium. Opium poppies were cultivated in Vermont and New Hampshire, in Florida and Louisiana, and later in California and Arizona. It was not until 1942 that the growing of opium poppies was outlawed in the United States.

Women outnumbered men in opium use during the nineteenth century by as much as three to one. The principal reason for this gender difference lay in the social attitudes toward women at the time. Men could engage in the recreational use of alcohol in the time-honored macho tradition, but such use among women was not considered respectable. Only opium use, in the form of laudanum and similar products, was open to American women. As one historian succinctly put it, ". . . husbands drank alcohol in the saloon; wives took opium at home."[10]

Throughout the 1800s, opium coexisted alongside alcohol, nicotine (in tobacco products), and cocaine as the dominant recreational drugs of the day. As late as 1897, the Sears, Roebuck mail-order catalog was advertising laudanum for sale at about six cents an ounce, while other opium products were addressed specifically to the alcoholic. In a clever marketing move directed to alcoholic men, Sears's "White Star Secret Liquor Cure" was advertised as designed to be added to the gentleman's after-dinner coffee so that he would be less inclined to join his friends at the local saloon. In effect, he would probably fall asleep at the table, since the "cure" was opium. If customers became dependent on opium, perhaps as a result of taking the "liquor cure," then fortunately they could order "A Cure for the Opium Habit," promoted on another page of the same catalog. If you guessed that the ingredients in this one included a heavy dose of alcohol, you would be right.[11] Opium dependence was frequently replaced by cocaine habits (see Chapter 8) and vice versa.

Given the openness of opium drinking in the nineteenth-century United States, we can only surmise that the fanatical reaction against the practice of opium smoking was based on anti-Chinese prejudice. It is clear that intense hostility existed toward the thousands of Chinese men and boys brought to the West in the 1850s and 1860s to build the railroads. Since most of the Chinese workers were recruited from the Canton area, where opium trafficking was particularly intense, the practice of opium smoking was well known to them, and it served as a safety valve for an obviously oppressed society of men. In 1875 San

This late-nineteenth-century illustration of young working girls in a New York City opium den was part of a widespread media campaign at the time to outlaw the smoking of opium.

active ingredient. He called it morphium, later changed to **morphine,** in honor of Morpheus, the Greek god of dreams. For the first time, more than three-fourths of the total weight of opium (containing inactive resins, oils, and sugars) could be separated out and discarded. Morphine represented roughly 10 percent of the total weight of opium, but it was found to be roughly ten times stronger than raw opium. All the twenty-five or so opiate products that were eventually isolated from opium were found to be weaker than morphine and formed a far smaller proportion of opium. Besides morphine, other major opiate products were **codeine** (0.5 percent of raw opium) and **thebaine** (0.2 percent of raw opium), both of which were found to have a considerably weaker opiate effect.

In the scientific community, Sertürner's discovery was recognized as a major achievement of its time. It was not until 1856, however, with the invention of the hypodermic syringe, that morphine became a widely accepted medical drug. With the syringe it could be injected into the bloodstream rather than administered orally, bypassing the gastrointestinal tract and speeding the delivery of effects. The new potential of a morphine injection coincided with the traumas of the Civil War in the United States (1861–1865) and later of the Franco-Prussian War in Europe (1870–1871).

Information about the syringe came too late for morphine injections to be widespread during the American conflict, but millions of opium pills and oral doses of morphine were distributed to soldiers injured in battle. It is not surprising that large numbers of soldiers became dependent on opiates and maintained the condition in the years that followed. After the Civil War, opiate dependence in general was so widespread among returning veterans that the condition was often called the "soldier's disease."[14]

Against the backdrop of increasing worry about opiate dependence, a new painkilling morphine derivative called **heroin** was introduced into the market in 1898 by the Bayer Company in Germany, the same company that had been highly successful in developing acetylsalicylic acid as an analgesic drug and marketing it as

Francisco outlawed opium smoking for fear, to quote a newspaper of the time, that "many women and young girls, as well as young men of respectable family, were being induced to visit the dens, where they were ruined morally and otherwise."[12] No mention was ever made of any moral ruin resulting from drinking opium at home. The anti-Chinese prejudice with respect to opium paralleled racial prejudice in America with respect to cocaine (see Chapter 3).

A federal law forbidding opium smoking soon followed, whereas the regulation of opium use by any other means failed to receive legislative attention at that time. By the beginning of the twentieth century, however, the desire for social control of opium dens became overshadowed by the emergence of opium-derived drugs that presented a substantially greater threat to society than smoked opium.[13]

Morphine and the Advent of Heroin

In 1803, a German drug clerk named Friedrich Wilhelm Adam Sertürner first isolated a yellowish white substance in raw opium that turned out to be its primary

morphine: The major active ingredient in opium.

codeine (COH-deen): One of the three active ingredients in opium, used primarily to treat coughing.

thebaine (THEE-bayn): One of three active ingredients in opium.

heroin: A chemical derivative of morphine. It is approximately three times as potent as morphine and a major drug of abuse.

"Bayer's Aspirin." About three times stronger than morphine, and, strangely enough, believed initially to be free of morphine's dependence-producing properties, heroin (from the German *heroisch*, meaning "powerful") was hailed as an entirely safe cough suppressant (preferable to codeine) and as a medication to relieve the chest discomfort associated with pneumonia and tuberculosis. In retrospect, it is incredible that from 1895 to 1905, no fewer than forty medical studies concerning injections of heroin failed to pick up on its potential for dependence! The abuse potential of heroin, which we now know exceeds that of morphine, was not fully recognized until as late as 1910.[15]

Why is heroin more potent than morphine? The answer lies in its chemical composition. Heroin consists of two acetyl groups joined to a basic morphine molecule. These attachments make heroin more fat-soluble and hence more rapidly absorbed into the brain. Once inside the brain, the two acetyl groups break off, making the effects of heroin chemically identical to that of morphine. One way of understanding the relationship between the two drugs is to imagine morphine as the contents inside a plain cardboard box and the heroin as the box with gift wrapping. The contents remain the same, but the wrapping increases the chances that the box will be opened.

Opiates and Heroin in American Society

The end of the nineteenth century marked a turning point in the history of opium and its derivatives. Opiate dependence would never again be treated casually. By 1900, there were, by one conservative estimate, 250,000 opiate-dependent people in the United States, and the actual number could have been closer to 750,000 or more. If we rely on the upper estimate, then we are speaking of roughly one out of every hundred Americans, young or old, living at that time. Compare this figure with the 2009 estimate of 195,000 Americans (aged twelve or older) who have used heroin within the past month out of a current population roughly four times the population in 1900, and you can appreciate the impact that opiate abuse was having on American society in the early twentieth century.[16]

The size of the opiate-abusing population alone at that time probably would have been sufficient grounds for social reformers to seek some way of controlling these drugs, but there was also the growing fear that the problems of opiate abuse were becoming closely associated with criminal elements. There was

a gnawing anxiety that opiates were creating a significant disruption in American society. A movement began to build toward instituting some system of governmental regulation.

Opiate Use and Abuse after 1914

The Harrison Act of 1914 (see Chapter 2) radically changed the face of opiate use and abuse in the United States. It ushered in an era in which the abuser was

> ... no longer seen as a victim of drugs, an unfortunate with no place to turn and deserving of society's sympathy and help. He became instead a base, vile degenerate who was weak and self-indulgent, who contaminated all he came in contact with and who deserved nothing short of condemnation and society's moral outrage and legal sanction.[17]

The situation, however, did not change overnight. Most importantly, the 1914 legislation did not actually ban opiate use. It simply required that doctors register with the Internal Revenue Service the opiate drugs (as well as cocaine and other coca products) that they were prescribing to their patients and pay a small fee for the right to prescribe such drugs. The real impact of the new law came later, in the early 1920s, as a result of several landmark decisions sent down from the U.S. Supreme Court. In effect, the decisions interpreted the Harrison Act more broadly. Under the Court's interpretation of the Harrison Act, no physician was permitted to prescribe opiate drugs for "nonmedical" use. In other words, it was now illegal for addicted individuals to obtain drugs merely to maintain their habit, even from a physician.

Without a legal source for their drugs, opiate abusers were forced to abandon opiates altogether or to turn to illegal means, and the drug dealer suddenly provided the only place where opiate drugs could be obtained. In 1924 a new law outlawed the importation of opium into the United States if the opium was to be made into heroin. Since there was ordinarily no way of telling what the destination of imported opium might be, the presumption was always that its purpose was illegal. As a result, legitimate opium sources were cut off, and the importation of opium or any opium-related drug was now in the hands of the smuggler.

Heroin became the perfect black market drug. It was easier and more profitable to refine it from raw opium overseas and ship it into the country in small bags of odorless heroin powder than it was to transport raw opium with its characteristic odor. In addition, because it had to be obtained illegally, heroin's price tag skyrocketed to thirty to fifty times what it had cost when it was available from legitimate sources.[18]

With the emergence of restrictive legislation, the demographic picture changed dramatically. No longer were the typical takers of narcotic drugs characterized as female, predominantly white, middle-aged, and middle-class, as likely to be living on a Nebraskan farm as in a Chicago townhouse. In their place were young, predominantly white, urban adult males, whose opiate drug of choice was intravenous heroin and whose drug supply was controlled by increasingly sophisticated crime organizations. In the minds of most Americans, heroin could be comfortably relegated to the social fringes of America.[19]

Heroin Abuse in the 1960s and 1970s

Three major social developments in the 1960s brought the heroin story back into the mainstream of the United States. The first began in late 1961, when a crackdown on heroin smuggling resulted in a significant shortage of heroin on the street. The price of heroin suddenly increased, and heroin dosages became more adulterated than ever before. Predictably, the high costs of maintaining heroin dependence encouraged new levels of criminal behavior, particularly in urban ghettos. Heroin abuse soon imposed a cultural stranglehold on many African American and Latino communities in major U.S. cities.

A second development, beginning in the 1960s, affected the white majority more directly. Fanned by extensive media attention, a youthful counterculture of hippies, flower children, and the sexually liberated swept the country.

It was a time of unconventional fashions and anti-establishment attitudes. In unprecedented numbers, middle- and upper-class people experimented with illegal drugs to get high. They smoked marijuana; tried the new synthetic properties of amphetamines and barbiturates; rediscovered the almost forgotten product of the coca plant, cocaine; and, for the first time, people from the mainstream of American life began to experiment with derivatives of the opium poppy. Thus, heroin addiction made its insidious way back to the forefront of national concern.[20]

Finally, disturbing news about heroin abuse began to appear that focused not only on Americans at home but also on American armed forces personnel stationed in Vietnam. Reports beginning in the late 1960s indicated an increasingly widespread recreational abuse of heroin, along with alcohol, marijuana, and other drugs, among U.S. soldiers. One returning Vietnam veteran related the atmosphere of polydrug abuse at the time:

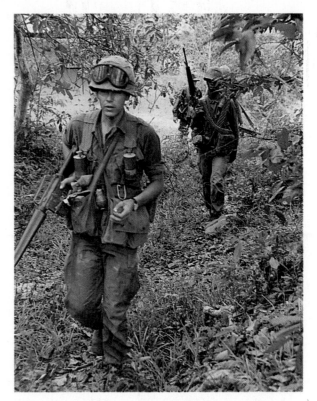

Military involvement in Vietnam brought U.S. soldiers in contact with unusually potent doses of heroin and other psychoactive drugs.

The last few months over there were unbelievable. My first tour there in '67, a few of our guys smoked grass, you know. Now the guys walk right in the hootch with a jar of heroin or cocaine. Almost pure stuff. Getting smack [heroin] is like getting a bottle of beer. Everybody sells it. Half my company is on the stuff.[21]

With respect to heroin, the problem was exacerbated by the fact that Vietnamese heroin was 90 to 98 percent pure, compared to 2 to 10 percent pure in the United States at the time, and incredibly cheap to buy. A 250-mg dose of heroin, for example, could be purchased for $10, whereas the standard intravenous dose on the streets of a major U.S. city would amount to only 10 mg. A comparable 250 mg of highly diluted U.S. heroin would have cost about $500. With the purity of heroin supplies so high, most U.S. soldiers smoked or sniffed it to get an effect; some drank it mixed with alcohol, even though most of the drug was lost as it was filtered through the liver en route to the bloodstream.[22]

Beyond the concern about the soldiers overseas, there was also the worry that at least one in ten Vietnam veterans would be returning home hopelessly dependent on heroin. It was estimated from survey data that about 11 percent of Army returnees in 1971 were regular users of heroin and about 22 percent had tried it at least once. Urine tests (appropriately named Operation Golden Flow), conducted near the end of a soldier's tour of duty, revealed a percentage of about one-half of that level, but there were strong indications that users in uniform had voluntarily given up heroin prior to their being shipped home.

Fortunately, a comprehensive investigation in 1974 showed that only 1 to 2 percent of Vietnam veterans were regular heroin abusers one year following their return from overseas, approximately the same percentage as those entering the military from the general population.

Even if the original numbers of heroin abusers in Vietnam had been exaggerated in the first place (and evidence now suggests that the story was hyped out of proportion by the media at the time), the low number among returnees presents an interesting question. What happened to the heroin abusers after they returned? It has been proposed that heroin use was situationally specific to involvement in Vietnam. Once returning soldiers were home in the states, the environmental cues and motivational factors for drug abuse were no longer present.[23] Does that mean it is possible to abuse heroin without becoming dependent on it? This question will be addressed later in the chapter.

Heroin and Synthetic Opiates since the 1980s

At one time, the major source of white powder heroin smuggled into the United States was Turkey, where the opium was grown, and the center of heroin manufacture and distribution was Marseilles in southern France (the infamous French connection, as popularized in the 1970 movie of the same name). International control over the growing of Turkish opium in 1973 closed this route of heroin distribution, but it succeeded only in encouraging other parts of the world to fill the vacuum. The "Golden Triangle" region of Laos, Myanmar (formerly Burma), and Thailand became the principal players in providing the United States with heroin. Joining

---

black tar: A potent form of heroin, generally brownish in color, originating in Mexico.

fentanyl (FEN-teh-nil): A chemical derivative of thebaine, used as a prescription painkiller. The street name for fentanyl and related compounds is China White.

---

southeast Asian heroin suppliers were southwest Asian nations such as Afghanistan, Pakistan, and Iran (in the "Golden Crescent"), as well as the central Asian nations of Kazakhstan, Kyrgystan, Tajikistan, Turkmenistan, and Uzbekistan that had been, until 1991, regions of the Soviet Union. As a consequence of these new sources, the purity of imported heroin increased at this time from around 5 percent to over 18 percent.[24]

Although the growth of crack cocaine abuse in the 1980s pushed the issue of heroin abuse temporarily off the front page, heroin abuse itself continued in new forms and variations. One significant development was the appearance around 1985 of a relatively pure and inexpensive form of Mexican heroin called **black tar.** In addition, new synthetic forms of heroin were appearing on the street, created in illegal drug laboratories within the United States. One such synthetic drug was derived from **fentanyl,** a prescription narcotic drug. Chemical modifications of fentanyl, anywhere from ten to a thousand times stronger than heroin, were sold under the common name "China White." The risks of overdose death increased dramatically.

From a technical point of view, fentanyl derivatives and other similar "designer drugs" were legal, owing to a loophole in the drug laws; because they were not chemically identical to heroin, no specific law applied to them. In 1986 the Controlled Substance Analogue Act closed this unfortunate loophole. The laws now state that any drug with a chemical structure or pharmacological effect similar to that of a controlled substance is as illegal as the genuine article. The mid-1990s witnessed still another shift in the pattern of heroin trafficking. The dominant supply of white powder heroin in the United States, judged from the analysis of drug seizures, no longer originated in Asia but rather South America, principally Colombia (see Chapter 5).

Street heroin from South American sources was now both cheaper and purer. Heroin purities exceeded 60 percent, at least ten times more powerful than the typical street heroin in the 1970s. In 1994, a 90-percent-pure brand of heroin circulating in New York City took heroin abusers by surprise; several overdose deaths occurred within a period of five days. Street prices for a milligram of heroin in New York fell from $1.81 in 1988 to as little as 37 cents in 1994. By government estimates, heroin consumption nationwide in 1996 had doubled from a decade earlier. As one writer put it, "If the U.S. auto industry cut the price of its sedans by half and redesigned them to go 180 mph, no one would wonder why sales hit the roof."[25]

In the mid-1990s, there was also a shift in the perception of heroin abuse itself. As the popularity of cocaine abuse declined and the incidence of crack abuse began to ebb, the spotlight once more turned toward the allure of heroin. For a brief time, popular movies (*Pulp Fiction* in 1994, *Trainspotting* in 1995) and fashion photography (Calvin Klein fragrance advertisements in 1996) provided provocative images that glamorized heroin abuse, a phenomenon the media dubbed "heroin chic."

The increased potency of present-day heroin has produced a significant effect on the way heroin is abused. Due to the availability of increasingly pure heroin, the drug no longer needs to be injected. Instead, it can be snorted (inhaled through the nose) or smoked. New heroin abusers are frequently smoking mixtures of heroin and crack cocaine or heating heroin and inhaling its vapors. These methods of heroin abuse may avoid potential HIV infections or hepatitis through contaminated needles, but they do not prevent the dependence that heroin can produce or the risk of heroin overdose.

Unfortunately, heroin snorting or smoking has opened the door to new populations of potential heroin abusers who had previously stayed away from the drug because of their aversion to hypodermic needles. University of Michigan surveys from 1997 to 2009 indicate that 1 to 2 percent of all high school seniors report heroin use at some time in their lives, with a majority of them smoking heroin rather than injecting it. However the prevalence rate among young people is generally higher than the national average and is currently rising in suburban communities, particularly in the Northeast.[26]

Quick Concept Check 7.1

Understanding the History of Opiates

Check your understanding of the history of opiates by answering the following questions. Imagine yourself to be living as a male adult in the year 1900. Check yes or no to indicate whether the following psychoactive drugs would be available to you.

1. heroin	☐ yes	☐ no
2. opium	☐ yes	☐ no
3. fentanyl	☐ yes	☐ no
4. oxycodone	☐ yes	☐ no
5. morphine	☐ yes	☐ no

Answers: 1. yes   2. yes   3. no   4. no   5. yes

Effects on the Mind and the Body

Recreational opiate use in the United States involves a range of drugs other than heroin itself, but we will concentrate on the acute effects from the perspective of the heroin abuser. We have to be careful, however, to recognize that the specific effects are quite variable. The intensity of a response to heroin changes as a function of (1) the quantity and purity of the heroin taken, (2) the route through which heroin is administered, (3) the interval since the previous dose of heroin, and (4) the degree of tolerance of the user to heroin itself. In addition, there are psychological factors related to the setting, circumstances, and expectations of the user that make an important difference in what an individual feels after taking heroin.[27] Nonetheless, there are several major effects that occur often enough to qualify as typical of the experience.

If heroin is injected intravenously, there is an almost immediate tingling sensation and sudden feeling of warmth in the lower abdomen, resembling a sexual orgasm, for the first minute or two. There is a feeling of intense euphoria, variously described as a "rush" or a "flash," followed later by a state of tranquil drowsiness that heroin abusers often call being "on the nod." During this period, which lasts from three to four hours, any interest in sex is greatly diminished. In the case of male heroin abusers, the decline in sexual desire is due, at least in part, to the fact that opiates reduce the levels of testosterone, the male sex hormone.[28]

An individual's first-time experience with heroin may be considerably unpleasant. Opiates in general cause nausea and vomiting, as the reflex centers in the brain are suddenly stimulated. Some first-time abusers find the vomiting so aversive that they never try the drug again; others consider the discomfort largely irrelevant because the euphoria is so powerful.

There are a number of additional physiological changes in the body. A sudden release of histamine in the bloodstream produces an often intense itching over the entire body and a reddening of the eyes. Heroin also causes pupillary constriction, resulting in the characteristic "pinpoint pupils" that are used as an important diagnostic sign for narcotic abuse in general. Like sedative-hypnotic drugs (see Chapter 11), heroin reduces the sensitivity of respiratory centers in the medulla to levels of carbon dioxide, resulting in a depression in breathing. At high doses, respiratory depression is a major risk factor that can result in death. Blood pressure is also depressed from heroin intake. Finally, a distressing, though nonlethal, effect of heroin is the slowing down of the gastrointestinal tract, causing a labored defecation and intense constipation.[29]

How Opiates Work in the Brain

It is useful to view the neurochemical basis for a number of psychoactive drugs in terms of their influence on specific neurotransmitters in the brain. For example, the stimulant effects of cocaine and amphetamine are related to changes in dopamine and norepinephrine (see Chapter 8). In the case of opiate drugs, however, as a result of major discoveries in the 1970s, it is clear that we are dealing with a more direct effect: the activation of receptors in the brain that are specifically sensitive to morphine.

During the 1960s, suspicions grew that a morphine-sensitive receptor, or a family of them, exists in the brain. One major clue came from the discovery that small chemical alterations in the morphine molecule would result in a group of new drugs with strange and intriguing properties. Not only would these drugs produce little or no *agonistic* effects—that is, they would not act like morphine—but they would instead act as *opiate antagonists*—that is, they would reverse or block the effects of morphine (Figure 7.2).

The most complete opiate antagonist to be identified, **naloxone** (brand name: Narcan), has turned out to have enormous therapeutic benefits in the emergency treatment of narcotic-overdose patients. In such cases, intramuscular or intravenous injections of naloxone reverse the depressed breathing and blood pressure in a matter of a minute or so, an effect so fast that emergency department specialists view the reaction as "miraculous." The effect lasts for one to four hours. Higher doses of naloxone bring on symptoms that are similar to those observed following an abrupt withdrawal of narcotic drugs. Interestingly, in normal undrugged people, naloxone produces only negligible changes, either on a physiological or a psychological level. Only if morphine or other narcotic drugs are already in the body does naloxone have an effect.[30]

Beyond its practical application, the discovery of naloxone had theoretical implications as well. The argument went as follows: If such small molecular changes could so dramatically transform an agonist into an antagonist, then the drugs must be acting on some receptor in the brain that can be easily excited or inhibited.

> **naloxone (nah-LOX-ohn):** A pure antagonist for morphine and other opiate drugs. Brand name is Narcan.
>
> **endogenous opioid peptides (en-DODGE-eh-nus OH-pee-oid PEP-tides)** also known as *endorphins:* A class of chemicals produced inside the body that mimic the effects of opiate drugs.

Morphine

Naloxone

FIGURE 7.2

Only minor differences exist between a morphine molecule and a naloxone molecule. Yet, naloxone is a complete antagonist to morphine.

The concept of a special morphine-sensitive receptor fulfilled these requirements.

The actual receptors themselves were discovered in 1973, precisely where you would have expected them to be: in the spinal cord and brain, where pain signals are known to be processed, and in the limbic system of the brain, where emotional behaviors are coordinated. In other words, it was clear that the analgesic and euphoric properties of morphine were due to stimulation of these receptors.

Why would these receptors exist in the first place? No one seriously considers the possibility that receptors in the brain have been patiently waiting during millions of years of evolutionary history for the day that the juice of the opium poppy could finally slip inside them! The only logical answer is that we must be producing our own morphine-like chemicals that activate these receptors.

As a result of a series of important discoveries from 1975 to the early 1980s, three groups of natural morphine-like molecules have been identified: enkephalins, beta-endorphins, and dynorphins. Together, they are known as **endogenous opioid peptides,** inasmuch as they are all (1) peptide molecules (amino acids strung together like a necklace), (2) opiate-like in function (hence the word, opioid), and (3) produced within the nervous system. Unfortunately, this is such an unwieldy name that more frequently they are simply referred to as *endorphins*.

What can we then conclude about the effect of opiates on the brain? The answer, as we now understand it, is that the brain has the ability to produce its own "opiate-like" substances, called endorphins, and contains a special set of receptor sites to receive them. By an amazing quirk of fate, the opium poppy yields a similarly shaped chemical that fits into these receptor sites, thus producing equivalent psychological and physiological effects. Naloxone acts as an opiate antagonist because its structural features enable it to fit into these receptor sites, replacing the opiate molecules that have gotten in. The receptors themselves, however, are *inactivated* by naloxone. This is why naloxone can "undo" the acute effects of an opiate drug like heroin (Drugs . . . in Focus).

Drugs... in Focus

Endorphins in Our Lives: A Psychosocial Perspective

From the discovery of endorphins in the 1970s, there emerged a new understanding not only of how pain is controlled in the brain but also of the role that opiate-like chemicals play in our daily lives. Here is a sampling of research findings that consider the psychosocial aspects of brain endorphins:

- *Pain and Stress.* Under stressful circumstances, people can become temporarily analgesic (relatively insensitive to pain) without the use of any external drugs. There are well-documented cases of soldiers who have ignored their injuries during the heat of battle, athletes who are unaware of their pain until the game is over, and individuals in primitive societies who endure painful religious rituals without complaint. Increased levels of endorphins may be a contributing factor in making these phenomena possible.

- *Acupuncture.* The Chinese technique of acupuncture, the inserting of needles into the skin at precisely defined points in the body, is completely reversible by naloxone. It is reasonable, therefore, to conclude that acupuncture produces increased levels of endorphins.

- *Labor and Childbirth Pain.* Endorphin levels measured in the placental bloodstream of pregnant women near to the time of childbirth are greatly elevated from levels normally present in nonpregnant women, reaching a peak during labor itself. It is believed that, as a result, women in labor are enduring less pain than they would have if endorphin levels were unchanged. Endorphins may protect them against an even greater amount of discomfort.

- *The "Runner's High."* Some studies have shown increased levels of endorphins among compulsive runners and other athletes. This increase could explain the euphoria, and in some instances analgesia, felt during strenuous physical exercise. Nonetheless, there also are increased levels of adrenalin at the same time, which cannot be ruled out as contributing to this effect.

- *Anorexia.* Emaciated anorexic women have been found to have higher endorphin levels than control patients without anorexic symptoms. When body weight returns to normal, endorphin levels decline. Anorexic women often report feeling euphoric, particularly while engaging in physical exercise.

- *Chocolate Cravings.* Laboratory rats like chocolate, seemingly as much as humans do. In tasks in which they are trained to work for chocolate rewards, injections of naloxone make them less eager to perform the tasks. It is possible that at least a portion of the pleasure of eating chocolate is linked to the release of endorphins.

- *Separation Anxiety.* When morphine is administered to young animals, they become less inclined to cry when they are separated from their mothers. Naloxone, on the other hand, increases the incidence of separation cries. After low doses of morphine, pairs of rats are more inclined to engage in chasing, jostling, and "pinning" behaviors that constitute the rodent version of social play. Naloxone causes these behaviors to decrease. It is likely that endorphins serve to reinforce social attachment and other behaviors essential to the development of normal social interactions. Conversely, abnormal endorphin responses could contribute to the development of dysfunctional social behaviors.

Sources: Dum, J., and Herz, A. (1984). Endorphinergic modulation of neural reward systems indicated by behavioral changes. *Pharmacology, Biochemistry, and Behavior, 21,* 259–266. Panksepp, Jaak (2006). Emotional endorphenotypes in evolutionary psychiatry. *Progress in Neuropsychopharmacology and Psychiatry, 30,* 774–784. Levinthal, Charles F. (1988). *Messengers of Paradise: Opiates and the Brain. The struggle over pain, rage, uncertainty, and addiction.* New York: Anchor Press/Doubleday.

A long-acting form of naloxone, **naltrexone** (brand name: ReVia, previously marketed as Trexan), administered orally three times per week, has since been found to be a useful medication in the treatment of heroin abuse, mainly for patients who are highly motivated to stop their drug-taking behavior. A high level of motivation is required for success because naltrexone counteracts the powerful rewarding effects of heroin but does not help reduce the craving for it or the lingering effects of withdrawal. Highly motivated patients may include doctors, nurses, and other health professionals who must end a pattern of heroin abuse to retain their licenses and former heroin abusers on parole who are at risk of returning to prison if they suffer a relapse. Injectable slow-release formulations that extend the effects of naltrexone over thirty days or more are presently being investigated in order to free patients from having to rely on a more frequent oral administration schedule. In the meantime, a once-per-month slow-release form of naltrexone (brand name: Vivitrol) has been available for the treatment of alcohol dependence since 2006 (see Chapter 13). In 2009, a combined naltrexone and extended-release morphine capsule (brand name: Embeda) was introduced to provide a morphine-induced analgesia while reducing the possibility of

abuse. The combination makes it impossible to crush and snort the capsules, because crushing releases the naltrexone and counteracts the morphine effect (see page 161 on the problems of OxyContin abuse).[31]

Patterns of Heroin Abuse

The dominant route of administration in heroin abuse is intravenous injection, usually referred to as either *mainlining* or *shooting*. Heroin also can be administered by a variety of other routes. Heroin smoking is popular in Middle Eastern countries and in Asia, but until very recently it has seldom been observed in the United States. Newcomers to heroin may begin their abuse either by snorting the drug through the nose or injecting it subcutaneously (*skin-popping*). Experienced heroin abusers may snort heroin to avoid using a needle or choose the subcutaneous route when they can no longer find veins in good enough condition to handle an intravenous injection. As mentioned earlier, an oral administration of heroin is usually worthless because absorption is extremely poor. American soldiers in Vietnam who were abusing heroin often took the drug orally, but because of the extremely high purity of the heroin being consumed their effective dose levels equaled or slightly exceeded levels found on American streets at the time (Drug Trafficking Update).

naltrexone (nal-TREX-ohn): A long-lasting form of naloxone. Brand name prior to 1994 was Trexan, brand name has since been changed to ReVia.

Drug Trafficking Update
Heroin

- **Origins:** South American heroin remains dominant among heroin abusers in the United States, though Mexican heroin has increased in recent years, particularly for markets in the eastern United States. In 2008, the wholesale purity of Mexican heroin rose to 40 percent, the highest level since 2005. In contrast, South American heroin purity is approximately 57 percent. The capacity of Mexican drug trafficking organizations (DTOs) to occupy a greater share of the heroin market in cities historically dominated by South American heroin may be a factor in future years.

- **Points of Entry:** South American heroin typically is transported into the United States in relatively small quantities by couriers on commercial air carriers to international airports in New York and Miami. Mexican drug-trafficking organizations also transport this heroin overland across the U.S.–Mexico border.

- **Traffickers:** Colombian and Dominican drug-trafficking organizations are the primary wholesale distributors of white-powder heroin in markets in the eastern United States, particularly New York, Philadelphia, Newark, and the New England area. Most retail heroin distributors at the local level consist of street gangs that often obtain heroin from multiple sources. There have been significant increases in heroin overdoses in many U.S. markets, including relatively small communities.

Source: Gall, Carlotta (2006, September 3). Opium harvest at record level in Afghanistan. *New York Times,* pp. 1, 12. National Drug Intelligence Center (2010). *National Drug Threat Assessment 2010.* Washington, DC: National Drug Intelligence Center, U.S. Department of Justice, pp. 30–32.

Tolerance and Withdrawal Symptoms

A prime feature of chronic heroin abuse is the tolerance that develops, but the tolerance effects themselves do not occur in every bodily system. Gastrointestinal effects of constipation and spasms do not show much tolerance at all, whereas the distinctive pupillary responses (the pinpoint feature of the eyes) eventually subside with chronic use. The greatest signs of tolerance are seen in the degree of analgesia, euphoria, and respiratory depression. The intense thrill of the intravenous injection will be noticeably lessened. The overall decline in heroin reactions, however, is dose-dependent. If the continuing dose level is high, then tolerance effects will be more dramatic than if the dose level is low.

The first sign of heroin withdrawal, a marked craving for another fix, generally begins about four to six hours after the previous dose and intensifies gradually to a peak over the next thirty-six to seventy-two hours, with other symptoms beginning a few hours later (Table 7.1).

TABLE 7.1

Symptoms of administering heroin and of withdrawing heroin

ADMINISTERING	WITHDRAWING
Lowered body temperature	Elevated body temperature
Decreased blood pressure	Increased blood pressure
Skin flushed and warm	Piloerection (gooseflesh)
Pupillary constriction	Tearing, runny nose
Constipation	Diarrhea
Respiratory depression	Yawning, panting, sneezing
Decreased sex drive	Spontaneous ejaculations and orgasms
Muscular relaxation	Restlessness, involuntary twitching and kicking movements*
Nodding, stupor	Insomnia
Analgesia	Pain and irritability
Euphoria and calm	Depression and anxiety

Note: *Probably the source of the expression "kicking the habit."

Source: Adapted from Grilly, David M. (2006). *Drugs and human behavior* (5th ed.). Boston: Allyn and Bacon, p. 229.

The abuser is essentially over the withdrawal period in five to ten days, though mild physiological disturbances-chiefly elevations in blood pressure and heart rate- are observed as long as six months later. Generally, these long-term effects are associated with a gradual withdrawal from heroin rather than an abrupt one.

The overall severity of heroin-withdrawal symptoms is a function of the dosage levels of heroin that have been sustained. When dosage levels are in the "single digits" (less than 10 percent), the withdrawal symptoms are comparable to a moderate to intense case of the flu. In more severe cases, the withdrawal process can result in a significant loss of weight and body fluids. With recent increases in the purities of street heroin in the 1990s, the symptoms of withdrawal are greater. Only rarely, however, is the process of heroin withdrawal life threatening, unlike the withdrawal from barbiturate drugs (see Chapter 11).

It should not be surprising that withdrawal symptoms are essentially the mirror image of symptoms observed when a person is under the influence of heroin. If we are dealing with a group of endorphin-sensitive receptors that are, in the case of the heroin abuser, being stimulated by the opiates coming in from the outside, then it is reasonable to assume that, over time, the production of endorphins would decline. Why produce stuff on your own when you are getting it from an external source? By that argument, withdrawal from heroin would then be a matter of cutting off those receptors from that external source, resulting in a reaction opposite to the one that would have occurred had the receptors been satisfied in the first place. Over a period of time, coinciding with the withdrawal period for a heroin abuser, we would expect that the normal production of endorphins would reestablish itself and there would be little or no need for the external supply of heroin.

The receptor explanation for heroin dependence sounds reasonable and does account for the presence of withdrawal symptoms, but unfortunately, it is an oversimplification for heroin abuse in general. We would expect that once the endorphin-sensitive receptors regain their natural supply of endorphins, heroin abuse should end, but we know that it does not.

In the case of heroin abusers, their tendency to continue taking heroin is propelled by a number of factors. There is, first of all, the combination of fear and distress associated with the prospect of experiencing withdrawal symptoms, along with a genuine craving for the effects themselves, reflecting the physical and psychological dependence that heroin inflicts.

In addition, as discussed in Chapter 1, long-term heroin abuse frequently produces such a powerful conditioned-learning effect that the social setting in which the drug-taking behavior has occurred takes on reinforcing properties of its own. Even the act of inserting a needle can become pleasurable. Some heroin abusers (called *needle freaks*) continue to insert needles into their skin and experience heroin-like effects even when there is no heroin in the syringe. In effect, the heroin abuser is responding to a placebo. Any long-term treatment for heroin abuse, as will be discussed in a later section, must address a range of physical, psychological, and social factors to be successful.

The Lethality of Heroin Abuse

Considering the number of hospital emergencies and deaths associated with heroin abuse (see Chapter 2), you might be surprised that one would question the toxicity of heroin itself. To understand the toxicity of heroin, we first need to separate the effects of chronic heroin abuse from the drug's acute effects. From a long-term perspective with regard to one's physical health, heroin is considered relatively nontoxic, particularly when compared to several other drugs of abuse. As one expert has put it:

> Unlike alcohol, the amphetamines, and the barbiturates, which are toxic to the body over the long run with relatively heavy use, the narcotics are relatively safe. The organs are not damaged, destroyed, or even threatened by even a lifetime of narcotic addiction. There are no major malformations of the body, no tissue damage, no physical deterioration directly traceable to the use of any narcotic, including heroin.[32]

A notable exception, however, is found in the case of heroin administered through inhalation. Smoked heroin has been linked to leukoencephalopathy, an incurable neurological disease in which a progressive loss of muscle coordination can lead to paralysis and death, as well as kidney degeneration.[33]

On the other hand, it is abundantly clear that the practice of heroin abuse is highly dangerous and potentially lethal. The reasons have to do with situations resulting from the acute effects of the drug.

- Heroin has a relatively small ratio of LD (lethal dose) to ED (effective dose). Increase a dose that produces a high in a heroin abuser by ten or fifteen times and you will be in the dosage range that is potentially fatal. As a result, death by overdose is an ever-present risk. If we take into account the virtually unknown potency of street heroin in any given fix, we can

Quick Concept Check 7.2

Understanding the Effects of Administering and Withdrawing Heroin

Without peeking at Table 5.1, check your understanding of the effects of heroin, relative to withdrawal symptoms, by noting whether the following symptoms are associated with administering heroin or withdrawing it.

SYMPTOM	ADMINISTERING	WITHDRAWING
1. coughing and sneezing		
2. skin flushed and warm		
3. decreased sex drive		
4. yawning and panting		
5. pain and irritability		
6. pupillary constriction		
7. increased blood pressure		
8. diarrhea		
9. analgesia		

Answers: 1. withdrawing   2. administering
3. administering   4. withdrawing   5. withdrawing
6. administering   7. withdrawing   8. withdrawing
9. administering

appreciate the hazards of a drug overdose. The "bag" sold to a heroin abuser may look like the same amount each time, but the actual heroin content could be anywhere from none at all to 90 percent. Therefore, it is easy to underestimate the amount of heroin being taken in.

- The user risks possible adverse effects from any toxic substance that has been "cut" with the heroin. Adding to the complexity, deaths from heroin overdose are frequently consequences of synergistic combinations of heroin with other abused drugs such as stimulants like cocaine or depressants like alcohol, Valium, or barbiturates. In some cases, individuals have smoked crack as their primary drug of abuse and snorted heroin to ease the agitation associated with crack. In other cases, lines of cocaine and heroin are alternately inhaled in a single session, a practice referred to as "criss-crossing." A list of street names for heroin and heroin combinations appears in Table 7.2.

- It is also possible that some heroin abusers develop unstable levels of tolerance that are tied to the environmental setting in which the heroin is administered. As a result of conditioned tolerance, a heroin dose experienced in an environment that has not been previously associated with drug taking may have a significantly greater effect on the abuser than the same dose taken in more familiar surroundings.

TABLE 7.2

Street names for opiate drugs

TYPE OF OPIATE	STREET NAME
morphine	Big M, Miss Emma, white stuff, M, dope, hocus, unkle, stuff, morpho
white heroin	junk, smack, horse, scag, H, stuff, hard stuff, dope, boy, boot, blow, jolt, spike, slam
Mexican heroin	black tar, tootsie roll, chapapote (Spanish for "tar"), Mexican mud, peanut butter, poison, gummy balls, black jack
heroin combined with amphetamines	bombitas
heroin combined with cocaine	dynamite, speedball, whizbang, goofball
heroin combined with marijuana	atom bomb, A-bomb
heroin combined with cocaine and marijuana	Frisco special, Frisco speedball
heroin combined with cocaine and morphine	cotton brothers
codeine combined with Doriden (a nonbarbiturate sedative-hypnotic)	loads, four doors, hits

Sources: U.S. Department of Justice, Drug Enforcement Administration. (1986). *Special report: Black tar heroin in the United States*, p. 4. U.S. Department of Justice, Bureau of Justice Statistics Clearinghouse. (1992). *Drugs, crime, and the justice system*, pp. 24–25.

Consequently, the specific effect on the abuser is highly unpredictable (see Chapter 1).

- Although the overriding danger of excessive amounts of heroin is the potentially lethal effects of respiratory depression, abusers can die from other physiological reactions. In some instances, death can come so quickly that the victims are found with a needle still in their veins; such deaths are usually due to a massive release of histamine or to an allergic reaction to some filler in the heroin to which the abuser was hypersensitive. Intravenous injections of heroin increase the risks of hepatitis or HIV infections, and unsterile water used in the mixing of heroin for these injections can be contaminated with bacteria.

- An extra risk began to appear during the mid-1980s. In some forms of synthetic heroin illicitly produced in clandestine laboratories in the United States, manufacturers failed to remove an impurity called MPTP that destroys dopamine-sensitive neurons in the substantia nigra of the midbrain. As a result, young people exposed to this type of heroin acquired full-blown symptoms of Parkinson's disease that are virtually identical to the symptoms observed in elderly patients suffering from a progressive loss of dopamine-sensitive neurons in their brains.

Heroin Abuse and Society

Over the years, society has had to deal with the reality of drug abuse in many forms, many people still look upon heroin abuse as the ultimate drug addiction and view the heroin abuser as the ultimate "dope addict." It is true that many heroin abusers fit this image: people driven to stay high on a four- to eight-hour schedule, committing a continuing series of predatory crimes.

Yet the actual picture of the present-day heroin abuser is more complex. A major study has shown that although robbery, burglary, and shoplifting accounted for 44 percent of an abuser's income and for nearly two-thirds of that abuser's criminal income, a substantial amount of income came from either victimless crimes (such as pimping or prostitution) or noncriminal activity. Often a heroin abuser would work in some capacity in the underground drug industry and be paid in heroin instead of dollars (see Chapter 5).[34]

A related question with regard to our image of the heroin abuser is whether controlled heroin abuse is possible. Is heroin abuse a situation that is, by definition, out of control? For most heroin abusers, the answer is yes. Yet for some individuals, heroin may not be a compulsion.

The practice of controlled or paced heroin intake is referred to as **chipping,** and the occasional heroin abuser is known as a *chipper.*

An important study conducted by Norman E. Zinberg in 1984 analyzed a group of people who had been using heroin on a controlled basis for more than four years.[35] Over the course of one year, 23 percent reported taking heroin less than once a month, 36 percent reported taking it one to three times a month, and 41 percent reported taking it twice a week. Four years of exposure to heroin would seem to have been sufficient time to develop a compulsive dependence, but that did not happen. The observation that most compulsive heroin-dependent individuals never had any period of controlled use implies that controlled heroin abuse might not be merely an early transitional stage that will eventually turn into uncontrolled heroin dependence.

The chipper and the classic heroin abuser seem to belong to two separate populations. What factors differentiate them? Zinberg's study showed that, unlike compulsive heroin abusers, occasional abusers tend to avoid heroin use in the presence of known addicts, rarely use heroin on a binge basis, and most often know the heroin dealer personally. Their motivations are different as well. Occasional abusers tend to use heroin for relaxation and recreation rather than to escape from difficulties in their lives or to reduce depression and anxiety. From a behavioral standpoint, the chipper appears to be avoiding the environmental influences (the social setting) that reinforce drug dependence.

While the Zinberg findings have provided support for the possibility of long-term heroin abuse on a controlled basis, newer evidence from studies of heroin abusers over more than three decades—a period of time much longer than that studied by Zinberg—indicates a somewhat darker scenario. during the 1970s, 1980s, and 1990s, a series of follow-up investigations were carried out on nearly six hundred male heroin abusers who had been admitted to a compulsory drug-treatment program for heroin-dependent criminal offenders from 1962 to 1964. By 1996–1997, only 42 percent of individuals in

the original sample (on average, about fifty-eight years old at the time) were available for interview. About 9 percent were of unknown status, and 49 percent had died. The most common cause of death (22 percent) was accidental poisoning from heroin adulterants or heroin overdose. Homicide, suicide, or accident accounted for 20 percent of the deaths, with the remainder being related to liver disease, cardiovascular disease, or cancer. Regarding the drug-taking behavior of the survivors, the researchers concluded that heroin dependence had been very difficult for them to avoid. As the principal investigator of the study has expressed it:

> *Although many of the survivors reported that they had been able to stop using heroin for extensive periods, fewer than half reported abstinence for periods of more than five years. Abstinence for five years significantly reduced the likelihood of relapse, but even among those who achieved fifteen years of abstinence, a quarter still relapsed.*[36]

Moreover, large proportions of these men were engaged in alcohol, cocaine, or amphetamine abuse as well. The bottom line is this: Dabbling in a drug as potentially dependence-inducing as heroin is an extremely risky business. To paraphrase the words of a nationally prominent drug abuse counselor, it is equivalent to playing a pharmacological form of Russian roulette.

Treatment for Heroin Abuse

For the heroin abuser seeking treatment for heroin dependence, the two primary difficulties are the short-term effects of heroin withdrawal and the long-term effects of heroin craving. Any successful treatment, therefore, must combine a short-term and long-term solution.

Opiate Detoxification

Traditionally, it has been possible to make the process of withdrawal from heroin, called **detoxification** ("detox"), less distressing to the abuser by reducing the level of heroin in a gradual fashion under medical supervision rather than withdrawing from heroin "cold turkey" (a term inspired by the gooseflesh appearance of the abuser's skin during abrupt withdrawal). In medical settings, a synthetic opiate such as **propoxyphene** (brand name: Darvon) or **methadone** has been administered to replace the heroin initially; then doses of these so-called transitional drugs are decreased over a period of two weeks or so.[37]

chipping: The taking of heroin on an occasional basis.

detoxification: The process of drug withdrawal in which the body is allowed to rid itself of the chemical effects of the drug in the bloodstream.

propoxyphene (pro-POX-ee-feen): A synthetic opiate useful in treating heroin abuse. Brand name is Darvon.

methadone: A synthetic opiate useful in treating heroin abuse.

Methadone Maintenance

For the heroin abuser seeking out medical treatment for heroin dependence, the most immediate problem is getting the drug out of the abuser's system during detoxification with a minimum of discomfort and distress. In some procedures, the administration of naloxone has been used to speed up withdrawal and reduce the severity of physiological symptoms.

After detoxification, however, the long-term problem of drug dependence remains. The craving for heroin persists, and the abuser most often has little choice but to return to a drug-oriented environment where the temptations to satisfy the craving still exist. Since the mid-1960s, one strategy has been to have a detoxified heroin abuser participate in a program in which oral administrations of the synthetic opiate methadone are essentially substituted for the injected heroin. This treatment approach, called **methadone maintenance,** was initiated in New York City through the joint efforts of Vincent Dole, a specialist in metabolic disorders, and Marie Nyswander, a psychiatrist whose interest had focused on narcotic dependence. Their idea was that if a legally and carefully controlled narcotic drug was available to heroin abusers on a regular basis, the craving for heroin would be eliminated, their drug-taking life-style would no longer be needed, and they could turn to more appropriate social behaviors such as steady employment and a more stable family life. The general philosophy behind their program was that heroin abuse was essentially a chronic metabolic disorder requiring a long-term maintenance drug for the body to "normalize" the drug abuser, in the same way as a diabetic patient would need a maintenance supply of insulin to normalize the level of blood glucose.

There are several advantages of the methadone maintenance approach in heroin abuse treatment. Since it is a legal, inexpensive narcotic drug (when dispensed through authorized drug-treatment centers), criminal activity involved in the purchase of heroin on the street can be avoided. Methadone is slower acting and more slowly metabolized so that, unlike heroin, its effects last approximately twenty-four hours and can be easily absorbed through an oral administration. Because it is an opiate drug, methadone binds to the endorphin-sensitive receptors in the brain and prevents feelings of heroin craving, yet the rush of a heroin high is avoided, thanks to its slow absorption by brain tissue.

Typically, clients in the program come to the treatment center daily for an oral dose of methadone, dispensed in orange juice, and the dose is gradually increased to a maintenance level over a period of four to six weeks. The chances of an abuser turning away from illicit drug use are increased if the higher doses of methadone are made conditional on a "clean" (drug-free) urinanalysis.[38]

As a social experiment, methadone-maintenance programs have met with a mixture of success and failure. On the one hand, evaluations of this program have found that 71 percent of former heroin abusers who have stayed in methadone maintenance for a year or more have stopped intravenous drug taking, thus reducing the risk of AIDS. In a major study, drug-associated problems declined from about 80 percent to between 17 and 28 percent, criminal behavior dropped from more than 20 percent to less than 10 percent, and there was a slight increase in permanent employment.[39] Although it attracts only a fraction of the heroin-dependent community, methadone maintenance does attract those who perceive themselves as having a negligible chance of becoming abstinent on their own.[40]

On the other hand, maintenance programs are not without problems. The first has to do with the moral question of opiate maintenance itself. Some critics have seen these treatments as a "cop-out" that perpetuates rather than discourages the sense of low self-esteem among heroin abusers, as a system that serves the needs of society over the needs of the individual. Methadone programs, they argue, simply substitute one type of dependence for another, and the goal should eventually be abstinence from all drugs.[41]

Although maintenance programs do help many heroin abusers, particularly those who stay in the program over an extended period of time, there are strong indications that the programs do not help the overall vulnerability toward drug abuse in general. In other words, methadone blocks the yearning for heroin, but it is less effective in blocking the simple craving to get high. Alcohol abuse among methadone-maintenance clients, for example, ranges from 10 to 40 percent, suggesting that alcohol may be substituting for opiates during the course of treatment, and one study found that as many as 43 percent of those who had successfully given up heroin had become dependent on alcohol. Cocaine and methamphetamine abuse can be problems as well. Unfortunately, urinanalysis tests may be scheduled too infrequently to allow identification of other patterns of drug abuse among the clients in these programs.[42] Furthermore, methadone is sometimes diverted away from the clinics

methadone maintenance: A treatment program for heroin abusers in which heroin is replaced by the long-term intake of methadone.

and onto the streets for illicit use. The availability of street methadone remains a matter of great concern.[43]

Alternative Maintenance Programs

Two alternative orally administered maintenance drugs for heroin abusers have been recently developed that may avoid the problems associated with the daily dosage approach of methadone programs. The first is the synthetic opiate **LAAM** (levo-alpha-acetylmethadol), marketed under the brand name Orlaam. The advantage of LAAM is its substantially longer duration, relative to methadone, so that treatment clients need to receive the drug only three times a week instead of every day.[44]

The second drug is the synthetic opiate **buprenorphine** (brand name: Subutex), also available as a three-times-a-week medication. Both medications have been shown to be useful in treating heroin-abuse. To reduce the potential for buprenorphine tablets to be made into an injectable form and abused, buprenorphine is also available in combination with naloxone (brand name: Suboxone). If the tablets are crushed and dissolved into an injectable solution, the combined formulation triggers undesirable withdrawal symptoms.

The advantage of buprenorphine as a heroin-abuse treatment is that it can be prescribed by office-based physicians rather than having to be dispensed through maintenance centers, as is the case with methadone or LAAM. When it is combined with naloxone, the abuse potential of buprenorphine is minimized and, while long-term blockage of opiate receptors occurs, there is less of an opiate "high."

LAAM: The synthetic narcotic drug levo-alpha-acetylmethadol used in the treatment of heroin abuse. Brand name is Orlaam.

buprenorphine (BYOO-preh-NOR-feen): A synthetic opiate used in the treatment of heroin abuse. Brand names are Subutex and (in combination with naloxone) Suboxone.

Help Line
Sustained-Release Buprenorphine: A New Era in Heroin Abuse Treatment

When buprenorphine (brand name: Subutex) and its combination with naloxone (brand name: Subuxone) were FDA-approved in 2002, a new era of heroin abuse treatment began. Since buprenorphine is only a partial activator of opiate-sensitive receptors in the brain, as opposed to full activators such as heroin and methadone, clients in treatment are more likely to discontinue their heroin intake without experiencing withdrawal symptoms, and the symptoms that do occur are considerably milder. At the same time, buprenorphine administration avoids the typical heroin effects of euphoria and respiratory depression. There is also no evidence of significant reduction of cognitive or motor performance in the course of long-term buprenorphine maintenance.

Typical buprenorphine therapy begins with an induction phase, in which buprenorphine is administered in a medically monitored setting following heroin abstention for 12–24 hours, while the individual is in the early stages of heroin withdrawal. In the stabilization and maintenance phases of treatment, buprenorphine dosage levels are adjusted on an individualized basis.

Two significant developments have, in recent years, expanded the social benefits of buprenorphine as a heroin-abuse treatment. First, a sustained-release version of buprenorphine, administered by injection at a treatment facility on a once-per-month basis, is now available. As a result, heroin abusers in treatment need to visit the physician's office only on a monthly basis. Second, new federal legislation enacted in 2007 allows certified physicians to treat up to 100 patients at any one time. Previous regulations had limited caseloads to no more than 30 patients.

Where to go for assistance:

www.buprenorphine.samhsa.gov/about.html

This web site, sponsored by the Substance Abuse and Mental Health Services Administration of the U.S. Department of Health and Human Services, provides extensive information on treatment options and a listing of available buprenorphine treatment locations. More than 800 physicians are certified for buprenorphine treatment in New York State alone.

Sources: Martin, Kimberly R. (2004, September). Once-a-month medication for heroin addiction? *NIDA Notes,* p. 9. Mitka, Mike (2003). Office-based primary care physicians called on to treat the "new" addict. *Journal of the American Medical Association, 290,* 735–738. Opioid detox study shows buprenorphine improves retention rate for teens (2005, October 10). *Alcoholism and Drug Abuse Weekly,* pp. 1–2. Substance Abuse and Mental Health Services Administration (2007, January/February). Buprenorphine: Patient limits increase. *SAMHSA Report,* p. 7.

Buprenorphine treatment substantially reduces the cost to public health clinics because it can be administered more widely in less-secured medical locations, such as primary care clinics and physicians' offices. It also reduces the inconvenience and stigmatization faced by treatment clients, particularly for teenage heroin abusers who would be disinclined to seek treatment at facilities that are associated with older people (Help Line).[45]

Behavioral and Social-Community Programs

To help deal with the tremendous social stresses that reinforce a continuation of heroin abuse, programs called **therapeutic communities (TCs)** have been developed (examples include Daytop Village, Samaritan Village, and Phoenix House). These "mini-communities" are drug-free residential settings based on the idea that stages of treatment and recovery should reflect increased levels of personal and social responsibility on the part of the abuser. Peer influence, mediated through a variety of group processes is used to help individuals learn and assimilate social norms and develop more effective social skills. Typically, counselors are former heroin abusers or former abusers of other drugs who have successfully given up drugs.[46]

Other approaches have been developed that combine detoxification, treatment with naltrexone, psychotherapy, and vocational rehabilitation under one comprehensive plan of action. These programs, called **multimodality programs,** are designed to focus simultaneously on the multitude of needs facing the heroin abuser, the goal being a successful reintegration into society. As a continuing effort to help the recovering heroin abuser, there are also twelve-step group support programs such as Narcotics Anonymous, modeled after similar programs for those recovering from alcohol or cocaine dependence.

Medical Uses of Opiate and Opiate-Related Drugs

We have focused on the acute effects of opiate and opiate-related drugs in the context of heroin abuse, but it is also important to look at the beneficial effects that these drugs can have in a medical setting (Table 7.3).

Beneficial Effects

Excluding heroin, which is a Schedule I controlled substance in the United States and therefore unavailable even for medical use, opiate and opiate-related drugs are administered with three primary therapeutic goals in mind: the relief of pain, the treatment of acute diarrhea, and the suppression of coughing.

The first and foremost medical use of narcotic drugs today is for the treatment of pain. For a patient suffering severe pain following surgical procedures or from burns or cancer, the traditional drug of choice has been morphine. Recently, pain treatment with fentanyl through a transdermal patch administration has been found to be more effective as an analgesic than morphine in an oral time-release administration. It is preferred by patients with chronic pain because the pain relief is achieved with less constipation and an enhanced quality of life.[47]

The second application capitalizes on the effect of opiates in slowing down peristaltic contractions in the intestines that occur as part of the digestive process. As noted earlier, one problem associated with the chronic abuse of heroin, as well as of other opiates, is constipation. However, for individuals with dysentery, a bacterial infection of the lower intestinal tract causing pain and severe diarrhea, this negative side effect becomes desirable. The control of diarrhea by an opiate is literally life saving, since acute dehydration (loss of water) from diarrhea frequently can be fatal. Fortunately, the opioid medication loperamide (brand name: Imodium), which is available on an over-the-counter basis, effectively controls diarrhea symptoms by its action on the gastrointestinal system. Because it cannot cross the blood-brain barrier, loperamide does not produce any psychoactive effects.

The third application focuses on the capacity of these drugs to suppress the cough reflex center in the brain. In cases in which an **antitussive** (cough-suppressing) drug is necessary, codeine is frequently prescribed, either by itself or combined with other medications such as aspirin or acetaminophen (brand names: Tylenol, among others). As an alternative treatment for coughing, a nonaddictive, nonopiate drug, **dextromethorphan,** is

therapeutic communities: Living environment for individuals in treatment for heroin and other drug abuse, where they learn social and psychological skills needed to lead a drug-free life.

multimodality programs: Treatment programs in which a combination of detoxification, psychotherapy, and group support is implemented.

antitussive: Having an effect that controls coughing.

dextromethorphan (DEX-troh-meh-THOR-fan): A popular non-narcotic ingredient used in over-the-counter cough remedies.

TABLE 7.3

Major opiate-related drugs in medical use

GENERIC NAME	BRAND NAME*	RECOMMENDED DOSE FOR ADULTS	GENERIC NAME	BRAND NAME*	RECOMMENDED DOSE FOR ADULTS
morphine	Avinza	30–120 mg (oral, combined immediate release, and time release)		Percocet	5 mg (oral) with acetaminophen
				Percodan	4.5 mg (oral) with aspirin
	Duramorph	5–10 mg (i.v.)	hydrocodone	Hycodan	5 mg (oral)
	Kadian	20–100 mg (oral, time release)		Vicodin	5 mg (oral) with acetaminophen
	MS Contin	15–200 mg (oral, time release)	methadone	Dolorphine	5–10 mg (oral, i.v., or s.c.)
			meperidine	Demerol	50–100 mg (oral, i.m., i.v.)
	Oromorph	15–100 mg (oral)	propoxyphene	Darvocet-N	50 mg (oral) with acetaminophen
	Oromorph SR	15–100 mg (oral, time release)	fentanyl	Darvon	65 mg (oral)
	Embeda	20–100 mg morphine/ 0.8–4 mg naltrexone (oral, sustained-release)		Duragesic	12.5–100 mcg/hour (extended-release transdermal patch)
	Roxanol	10–30 mg (oral)	pentazocine	Talwin	12.5 mg (oral) with aspirin
codeine		30–60 mg (oral, i.m., or s.c.)	fentanyl	Duragesic	2.5–10 mg (time release by transdermal patch)
hydromorphone	Dilaudid	1–8 mg (oral, i.m., i.v., or s.c.)			
	Palladone	12–32 mg (oral, time release)		Actiq	"lollipop" form
			tramadol	Ultram	50–100 mg (oral)
oxymorphone	Numorphan	1–1.5 mg (i.m. or s.c.)		Ultracet	50–100 mg (oral) with acetaminophen
oxycodone	OxyContin	10–160 mg (oral, time release)			

*Only a portion of the brands are listed here. Some opiate-related drugs are available only under their generic names, and some are available under either their generic or their brand names.

Note: i.v. = intravenous; i.m. = intramuscular; s.c. = subcutaneous.

Source: Physicians' desk reference (64th ed.) (2010). Montvale, NJ: Medical Economics Data.

available in over-the-counter syrups and lozenges as well as in combination with antihistamines. The "DM" designation in these cough-control preparations refers to dextromethorphan. Unfortunately, the abuse of dextromethorphan among young people, who are consuming it on a recreational basis, has become a new public health concern (see Chapter 2).

Potential Adverse Effects

Given the many simultaneous effects of opiates on the body, it is natural that some concerns should be attached to their medical use, even though the overall effect is beneficial. For example, respiration will be depressed for four to five hours following even a therapeutic dose of morphine, so caution is advised when the patient suffers from asthma, emphysema, or pulmonary heart disease. Nausea and vomiting also can be a problem for patients receiving morphine, especially if they walk around immediately afterward. As a result, patients are advised to remain still, either sitting or lying down, for a short period following their medication. In addition, opiate medications decrease the secretion of hydrochloric acid in the stomach and reduce the pushing of food through the intestines, a condition that can lead to intestinal spasms. Finally, although opiates have a sleep-inducing effect in high doses, it is not recommended that they be used as a general sedative-hypnotic treatment, unless sleep is being prevented by pain or coughing.[48]

Misuse or Abuse of Prescription Pain Medications

Since the late 1990s, there has been a dramatic increase in cases in which prescription pain medications—synthetic opiates developed with the intention to be used for the relief of pain—have been subject to abuse. Three medications of this type have been particularly problematic and are an increasingly significant public health concern: the continuous-release form of oxycodone (brand name: **OxyContin**), hydrocodone with acetaminophen (brand name: Vicodin), and oxycodone with acetaminophen (brand name: Percocet). All of these medications are classified in the United States as Schedule II controlled substances, according to the Controlled Substances Act of 1970.

Introduced in 1995, OxyContin was promoted initially as being relatively safe from potential abuse and as more acceptable to the general public because it lacked the social stigma associated with morphine. Its FDA-approved formulation permits OxyContin to be taken orally and absorbed slowly over a period of twelve hours, killing the pain without inducing a sudden feeling of euphoria. However, when OxyContin tablets are crushed and then either swallowed or inhaled as a powder, or are injected after diluting the powder into a solution, the effect can be similar to that of heroin. Even with the prescribed formulation, some patients have suffered severe withdrawal symptoms, similar to those experienced during heroin withdrawal, when they abruptly stopped taking high-dosage levels of the medication.[49]

OxyContin abusers vary widely across in socioeconomic status, geographic location, and gender. Particularly striking have been the outbreaks in the United States of OxyContin abuse and the criminal activity that

is associated with obtaining it (when legitimate prescription access fails) in rural towns and small cities, places where traditional opiate-related abuse cases have been relatively rare (Portrait).

Recent efforts have been made to reduce OxyContin abuse in a number of ways. An FDA-mandated warning label now states that the drug is as potentially addictive as morphine and that chewing, snorting, or injecting it could be lethal. In 2010, a new formulation of OxyContin was introduced, with an added chemical called Remoxy that changes the tablet into a gummy, less easily abusable substance when crushed or dissolved.[50]

Vicodin and Percocet are based on synthetic opiates (hydrocodone and oxycodone, respectively) that have been available for a longer period of time, and they unfortunately have a longer record of abuse and dependence. The problem lies not only in misuse on the part of the individual for whom these medications have been prescribed but also in the diversion of these medications to others for whom no prescription had been made.

In general, the nonmedical use of prescription pain relievers is extensive, particularly among young adults. It has been estimated that in 2009, more than 8 million young adults aged eighteen to twenty-five (about 24 percent of individuals in this age group) had used a prescription pain reliever for nonmedical reasons in their lifetime. Approximately 2.1 million (6.2 percent) had used OxyContin, 6.1 million (18 percent) had used Vicodin, and 3.2 million (10 percent) had used Percocet for nonmedical reasons in their lifetime. In 2008, the number of ED visits related to prescription pain relievers exceeded the number of ED visits related to illicit drugs.

Diversion is the primary mechanism by which these medications are obtained. More than half of total cases (55 percent) reported that the prescription pain reliever had been obtained free from a friend or relative, and in three out of four cases that friend or relative had obtained the drug through a legitimate medical prescription.[51]

Nonmedical use of prescription pain relievers is widespread in high schools as well. According to the University of Michigan survey, 10 percent of high school seniors in 2009 reported nonmedical use of Vicodin during the previous year, and 5 percent reported nonmedical use of OxyContin.[52]

OxyContin: A time-release form of oxycodone, used in the treatment of chronic pain.

By 2000, Barry Tuttle's pain had become so excruciating that he was on the verge of suicide. A former salesman of plumbing supplies in North Plainfield, New Jersey, Tuttle (above left photo) had endured pulsating back pain for six years. Seven surgeries, endless doctor's appointments, thousands of pills, acupuncture, and other alternative treatments had all proved unsuccessful. When Tuttle began taking OxyContin, however, a relatively normal life-style returned. His perceived pain level (on a scale of 1 to 10, with 10 being the most horrible pain imaginable) was an acceptable 2 or 3—a dramatic improvement from his continual ratings of 8 or 9 before the advent of OxyContin. The drug had literally saved his life.

For every Barry Tuttle, however, there is a Russell Fitch (above right photo). Prescribed OxyContin following hip-replacement surgery, Fitch found that the drug was difficult to give up even after his recovery was complete. In 1999, this resident of rural Maine was convicted of selling guns to finance the purchase of a steady supply of OxyContin. In May 2001, while on parole for the firearms theft

conviction, Fitch was charged with walking into a pharmacy with a gun and pushing a note across the counter that read: "Give me all your OxyContin or I will shoot you."

Fitch is not alone in his descent into criminal activity as a result of compulsive OxyContin abuse. Arrests have been made in all parts of the United States (the drug has been called the "rural heroin") for crimes ranging from simple theft to murder and drug trafficking, all related to the illicit abuse of this drug. At the same time, demands to remove OxyContin from the market until an abuse-reducing formulation is developed would return people like Barry Tuttle to a life of abject misery. From Tuttle's perspective, some individuals simply cannot handle any form of a powerful drug. Perhaps, in the absence of OxyContin, Fitch would have become dependent on something else. In Tuttle's words, "Drugs don't addict people. People addict people."

The problem is that it is difficult to predict which path a patient will follow. As a neurologist and pain-management specialist has expressed it, "A practicing

physician has to be mindful that someone, even if they don't come with 'addict' written all over them, may be one. The physician has to establish a relationship with the patient they're taking care of on a long-term basis."

Note: In May 2007, three top executives of Purdue Pharma, the company that makes OxyContin, pleaded guilty to criminal charges that, from 1995 to 2001, they had misled federal regulators, physicians, and patients about the potential for OxyContin to be an abused drug. The company agreed to $600 million in fines and other payments; the executives themselves were fined $34 million for their wrongdoing.

Sources: Adler, Jerry (2003, October 20). In the grip of a deeper pain. *Newsweek*, pp. 48–49. Meier, Barry (2003). *Pain killer: A "wonder" drug's trail of addiction and death.* New York: Rodale Press. Meier, Barry (2007, May 11). Narcotic maker guilty of deceit over marketing. *New York Times*, pp. A1, C4. Susman, Tina (2001, July 29). Good drug, bad drug: OxyContin eases pain, lures addicts. *Newsday*, pp. A6, A36. Quotations on p. A36.

Summary

Opium in History

- A drug with a very long history, opium has been used for medicinal and recreational purposes for approximately 5,000 years.

- During the nineteenth century, opium even figured in global politics as the instigating factor for the Opium War fought between China and Britain. At the time, opium use was widespread in Britain and the United States at all levels of society.

Morphine and the Advent of Heroin

- The discovery of morphine in 1803 as the principal active ingredient in opium revolutionized medical treatment of pain and chronic diseases.

- At the end of the nineteenth century, heroin was introduced by the Bayer Company in Germany. Initially, it was believed that heroin lacked the dependence-producing properties of morphine.

Opiates and Heroin in American Society

- The abuse potential of morphine and especiallyof heroin was not fully realized until the beginning of the twentieth century. Social and political developments in the United States after the passage of the Harrison Act in 1914 drove heroin underground, where it acquired a growing association with criminal life.

- Heroin abuse became associated with African American and other minority communities in urban ghettos after World War II; later, the drug revolution and the military involvement in Vietnam during the 1960s and 1970s brought the issues of heroin abuse to a wider population.

Effects on the Mind and the Body
- The effects of narcotic drugs such as heroin include euphoria, analgesia, gastrointestinal slowing, and respiratory depression.
- Respiratory depression is the major risk factor for heroin intake.

How Opiates Work in the Brain
- Since the 1970s, we have known that the effects of morphine and similar drugs are the result of the activation of morphine-sensitive receptors in the brain.
- Three families of chemical substances produced by the brain bind to these receptors. These chemicals are collectively known as endorphins.

Patterns of Heroin Abuse
- Chronic heroin abuse is subject to tolerance effects over time. Withdrawal effects include intense craving for heroin and physical symptoms such as diarrhea and dehydration.
- One of the major problems surrounding heroin abuse is the unpredictability in the content of a heroin dose.

Treatment for Heroin Abuse
- Treatment for heroin abuse includes short-term detoxification and long-term interventions that address the continuing craving for the drug and physical dependence factors in the body.
- Methadone-maintenance programs focus primarily on the physiological needs of the heroin abuser, whereas therapeutic communities and support groups focus on his or her long-term reintegration into society.

Opiate Use, Misuse and Abuse
- In medical settings, narcotic drugs have been extremely helpful in the treatment of pain, in the treatment of dysentery, and in the suppression of coughing.
- Side effects of opiate-based medications include respiratory depression, intestinal spasms, and sedation.
- There has been great concern since the late 1990s that prescription pain relievers have been diverted to nonmedical purposes and are subject to abuse. The three medications of this type are OxyContin, Vicodin, and Percocet. More than half of young adults who have used a prescription pain reliever for nonmedical reasons report that the drug was obtained free from a friend or relative.

Key Terms

antitussive, p. 159
black tar, p. 148
buprenorphine, p. 158
chipping, p. 156
codeine, p. 145
detoxification, p. 156
dextromethorphan, p. 159
endogenous opioid
   peptides, p. 150

fentanyl, p. 148
heroin, p. 145
LAAM, p. 158
methadone, p. 156
methadone maintenance,
   p. 157
morphine, p. 145
multimodality
   programs, p. 159

naloxone, p. 150
naltrexone, p. 152
narcotics, p. 141
opiates, p. 141
opium, p. 141
OxyContin, p. 161
propoxyphene, p. 156
synthetic opiates, p. 142

thebaine, p. 145
therapeutic communities,
   p. 159

Endnotes

1. Modified from Markel, Howard (2005, December 27). When teenagers abuse prescription drugs, the fault may be the doctor's. *New York Times*, p. F5.
2. Levinthal, Charles F. (1988). *Messengers of paradise: Opiates and the brain.* New York: Anchor Press/Doubleday, p. 4.
3. Courtwright, David T. (2001). *Forces of habit: Drugs and the making of the modern world.* Cambridge, MA: Harvard University Press, pp. 31–39. Merlin, M. D. (1984). *On the trail of the ancient opium poppy.* Cranbury, NJ: Associated University Press.
4. Scott, James M. (1969). *The white poppy: A history of opium.* New York: Funk and Wagnalls, p. 111.
5. Nencini, Paolo (1997). The rules of drug-taking: Wine and poppy derivatives in the ancient world. VIII. Lack of evidence of opium addiction. *Substance Use and Misuse,* 32, 1581–1586.
6. Levinthal, *Messengers of paradise,* pp. 3–25. Snyder, Solomon H. (1977). Opiate receptors and internal opiates. *Scientific American,* 236 (3), 44.
7. Beeching, Jack (1975). *The Chinese opium wars.* New York: Harcourt Brace Jovanovich, p. 23. Hanes, W.

Travis III, and Sanello, Frank (2002). *The opium wars.* Napierville, IL: Sourcebooks.

8. Owen, David E. (1934). *British opium policy in China and India.* New Haven, CT: Yale University Press. Waley, Arthur (1958). *The opium war through Chinese eyes.* London: Allen and Unwin.

9. Fay, Peter W. (1975). *The opium war 1840–1842.* Chapel Hill: University of North Carolina Press, p. 11.

10. Brecher, Edward M., and the editors of *Consumer Reports* (1972). *Licit and illicit drugs.* Boston: Little, Brown, p. 17.

11. Kaplan, Eugene H., and Wieder, Herbert. (1974). *Drugs don't take people; people take drugs.* Secaucus, NJ: Lyle Stuart.

12. Brecher, *Licit and illicit drugs,* pp. 42–43.

13. Levinthal, *Messengers of paradise,* pp. 16–17.

14. Courtwright, David T. (1982). *Dark paradise: Opiate addiction in America before 1940.* Cambridge, MA: Harvard University Press, p. 47.

15. Inciardi, James A. (2002). *The war on drugs III.* Boston: Allyn and Bacon, p. 24. Terry, Charles E., and Pellens, Mildred. (1928/1970). *The opium problem.* Montclair, NJ: Patterson Smith.

16. Substance Abuse and Mental Health *Services Administration* (2010). *Results from the 2009 National Survey on Drug Use and Health: Detailed tables.* Rockville, MD: Office of Applied Studies, Substance Abuse and Mental Health Services Administration, Table 1.1A.

17. Smith, Roger (1966). Status politics and the image of the addict. *Issues in Criminology,* 2 (2), 172–173.

18. Zackon, Fred (1986). *Heroin: The street narcotic.* New York: Chelsea House Publishers, p. 44.

19. McCoy, Alfred W., with Read, Cathleen B., and Adams, Leonard P. (1972). *The politics of heroin in southeast Asia.* New York: Harper and Row, pp. 5–6.

20. Zackon, *Heroin,* p. 45.

21. Bentel, David J., Crim, D., and Smith, David E. (1972). Drug abuse in combat: The crisis of drugs and addiction among American troops in Vietnam. In David E. Smith and George R. Gay (Eds.), *It's so good, don't even try it once: Heroin in perspective.* Englewood Cliffs, NJ: Prentice Hall, p. 58.

22. Karch, Steven B. (1996). *The pathology of drug abuse* (2nd ed.). Boca Raton, FL: CRC Press, p. 288. McCoy, *The politics of heroin,* pp. 220–221.

23. Kuzmarov, Jeremy (2010). *The myth of the addicted army: Vietnam and the modern war on drugs.* Amherst, MA: University of Massachusetts Press. Robins, Lee N., David, Darlene H., and Goodwin, Donald W. (1974). Drug use by U.S. Army enlisted men in Vietnam: A follow-up on their return home. *American Journal of Epidemiology,* 99 (4), 235–249.

24. Greenhouse, Steven (1995, February 12). Heroin from Burmese surges as U.S. debates strategy. *New York Times,* p. 3.

25. Holloway, Lynette (1994, August 31). 13 heroin deaths spark wide police investigation. *New York Times,* pp. A1, B2.

Leland, John (1996, August 26). The fear of heroin is shooting up. *Newsweek,* pp. 55–56. Quotation on p. 56.

26. Herbert, Keith (2010, January 3). Deadly drug's toll in black and white. *Newsday,* pp. A5-A6. Hernandez, Daisy (2003, May 23). Heroin's new generation: Young, white, and middle class. *New York Times,* p. 34. Johnston, Lloyd D.; O'Malley, Patrick M.; Bachman, Jerald G.; and Schulenberg, John E. (2009, December 14). Teen marijuana use tilts up, while some drugs decline in use. University of Michigan News Service, Ann Arbor, Table 1. Jones, Richard G. (2008, January 13). Heroin's hold on the young. *New York Times,* Long Island section, pp. 1, 8. National Drug Intelligence Center (2006). *National Drug Threat Assessment 2007.* Washington, DC: U.S. Department of Justice, pp. 14-17.Richey, Warren (1996, October 26). Boycott groups: Klein ads carry scent of "heroin chic." *Christian Science Monitor,* p. 3. Thomson, Stephanie (2005, September 26). Heroin chic OK, cocaine use not. *Advertising Age,* pp. 3–4.

27. Winger, Gail, Hofmann, Frederick G., and Woods, James H. (1992). *A handbook on drug and alcohol abuse: The biomedical aspects.* New York: Oxford University Press, 1992, pp. 44–46.

28. Abel, Ernest L. (1985). *Psychoactive drugs and sex.* New York: Plenum Press, pp. 175–204.

29. Winger, Hofmann, and Woods, *Handbook on drug and alcohol abuse,* pp. 46–50.

30. Jaffe, Jerome H., and Martin, William M. (1985). Opioid analgesics and antagonists. In Alfred C. Gilman, Louis S. Goodman, Theodore W. Rall, and Ferid Murad (Eds.), *The pharmacological basis of therapeutics* (7th ed.). New York: Macmillan, pp. 491–531. Julien, Robert M. (2005), *A primer of drug action* (10th ed.). New York: Worth, pp. 490–492.

31. Levinthal, *Messengers of paradise.* Mathias, Robert (2003, March). New approaches seek to expand naltrexone use in heroin treatment. *NIDA Notes,* 17 (6), p. 8. Self, David W. (1998). Neural substrates of drug craving and relapse in drug addiction. *Annals of Medicine,* 30, 379–389.

32. Goode, Erich (1999). *Drugs in American society* (5th ed.). New York: McGraw-Hill, p. 328. Strang, J., Griffiths, P., and Gossop, M. (1997). Heroin smoking by "chasing the dragon": Origins and history. *Addiction,* 92, 673–684.

33. Karch, Steven B. (2002). *Pathology of drug abuse* (3rd ed.). Boca Raton, FL: CRC Press, p. 323.

34. Johnson, Bruce D.; Goldstein, Paul J.; Preble, Edward; Schmeidler, James; Lipton, Douglas S.; Spunt, Barry; and Miller, Thomas (1985). *Taking care of business: The economics of crime by heroin abusers.* Lexington, MA: Lexington Books.

35. Zinberg, Norman E. (1984). *Drug, set, and setting: The basis for controlled intoxicant use.* New Haven, CT: Yale University Press, pp. 46–81.

36. Hser, Yih-Ing; Hoffman, Valerie; Grella, Christine; and Anglin, M. Douglas (2001). A 33-year follow-up of nar-

cotics addicts. *Archives of General Psychiatry, 58,* 503–508. Goode, Erica (2001, May 22). For users of heroin, decades of despair. *New York Times,* p. F5. National Institute on Drug Abuse (2001). 33-year study finds lifelong, lethal consequences of heroin addiction. *NIDA Notes, 16* (4), 1, 5, 7. Quotation on p. 5. Treaster, Joseph B. (1992, July 22). Executive's secret struggle with heroin's powerful grip. *New York Times,* pp. A1, B4.

37. Schuckit, Marc A. (1995). *Drug and alcohol abuse: A clinical guide to diagnosis and treatment* (4th ed.). New York: Plenum Press, pp. 155–162.

38. Stitzer, Maxine L.; Bickel, Warren K.; Bigelow, George E.; and Liebson, Ira A. (1986). Effect of methadone dose contingencies on urinalysis test results of polydrug-abusing methadone-maintenance patients. *Drug and Alcohol Dependence, 18,* 341–348.

39. Maddux, James F., and Desmond, David P. (1997). Outcomes of methadone maintenance 1 year after admission. *Journal of Drug Issues, 27,* 225–238. Sees, Karen L.; Delucchi, Kevin L.; Masson, Carmen; Rosen, Amy; Clark, H. Westley; et al. (2000). Methadone maintenance vs 180-day psychosocially enriched detoxification for treatment of opioid dependence. *Journal of the American Medical Association, 283,* 1303–1310.

40. Office of National Drug Control Policy (2000, April). Methadone. *ONDCP Drug Policy Information Clearinghouse Fact Sheet.* Washington, DC: Office of National Drug Control Policy.

41. Prendergast, Michael L., and Podus, Deborah (1999, May 10). Methadone debate reflects deep-rooted conflicts in field. *Alcoholism and Drug Abuse Weekly,* p. 5.

42. Wasserman, David A.; Korcha, Rachel; Havassy, Barbara E.; and Hall, Sharon M. (1999). Detection of illicit opioid and cocaine use in methadone maintenance treatment. *American Journal of Drug and Alcohol Abuse, 25,* 561–571.

43. Faupel, Charles E. (1991). *Shooting dope: Career patterns of hard-core heroin users.* Gainesville: University of Florida Press, pp. 170–173. Gollnisch, Gernot (1997). Multiple predictors of illicit drug use in methadone maintenance clients. *Addictive Behaviors, 22,* 353–366. Substance Abuse and Mental Health Services Administration (2003, January). Narcotic analgesics. *The DAWN report.* Rockville, MD: Office of Applied Studies, Substance Abuse and Mental Health Services Administration, Figure 2.

44. Eissenberg, Thomas; Bigelow, George F.; Strain, Eric C.; Walsh, Sharon L.; Brooner, Robert K.; Stitzer, Maxine L.; and Johnson, Rolley E. (1997). Dose-related efficacy of levomethadryl acetate for treatment of opioid dependence: A randomized clinical trial. *Journal of the American Medical Association, 277,* 1945–1951.

45. Martin, Kimberly R. (2004, September). Once-a-month medication for heroin addiction? *NIDA Notes, 19* (3), p. 9. Mitka, Mike (2003). Office-based primary care physicians called on to treat the "new" addict. *Journal of the American Medical Association, 290,* 735–736. O'Connor, Amahad (2004, August 4). New ways to loosen addiction's grip. *New York Times,* pp. F1, F6.

46. National Institute on Drug Abuse (2002). Therapeutic community. *National Institute on Drug Abuse Research Report.* Rockville, MD: National Institute on Drug Abuse.

47. Allan, Laurie; Hays, Helen; Jensen, Niels-Henrik; Le Polain de Waroux, Bernard; Bolt, Michiel; Royden, Donald; and Kalso, Eija (2001). Randomised crossover trial of transdermal fentanyl and sustained release oral morphine for treating chronic non-cancer pain. *British Medical Journal, 322,* 1154–1158.

48. Jaffe and Martin, Opioid analgesics and antagonists.

49. Kalb, Claudia (2001, April 9). Playing with pain killers. *Newsweek,* pp. 45–48. Meier, Barry, and Petersen, Melody (2001, March 5). Sales of painkiller grew rapidly but success brought a high cost. *New York Times,* pp. A1, A15. Rosenberg, Debra (2001, April 9). How one town got hooked. *Newsweek,* pp. 49–50. Tough, Paul (2001, July 29). The alchemy of OxyContin. *New York Times Magazine,* pp. 31–37, 52, 62–64.

50. Ammann, Melinda (2003, April). The agony and the ecstasy. *Reason,* pp. 28–34. Meier, Barry (2003, November 23). The delicate balance between pain and addiction. *New York Times,* pp. F1, F6. Basbaum, Allan I., and Julius, David (2006, June). Toward better pain control. *Scientific American,* pp. 60–67. FDA approves new formulation of OxyContin (2010, April 5). News release from the U.S. Food and Drug Administration, Washington, DC.

51. Centers for Disease Control and Prevention (2010, June 18). Emergency department visits involving nonmedical use of selected prescription drugs—United States, 2004–2008. *Morbidity and Mortality Weekly Report, 59,* 705–709. Substance Abuse and Mental Health Services Administration (2009). *National Survey of Drug Use and Health: Detailed tables.* Rockville, MD: Substance Abuse and Mental Health Services Administration, Tables 1.56A, 1.56B, 1.89A, 1.89B, 6.47B, and 6.48B.

52. Johnston, O'Malley, Bachman, and Schulenberg (2009). Teen marijuana use tilts up, Table 2.

chapter **8**

The Major Stimulants: Cocaine and Amphetamines

S. F. is a brilliant, young physician attending a case conference at a metropolitan medical center where he is a resident. He has been on call for thirty-six hours and cannot concentrate on the presentation. S. F. is lonely, depressed, and overworked. All he can think about is his fiancée, Martha, who is several hundred miles away. He knows that her father will not permit her to marry until he is able to support her, and with his loans and meager salary, that could take years. He excuses himself from the conference, takes a needle syringe from the nurses' station, and locks himself in a bathroom stall. He fills the syringe with cocaine and plunges the needle into his arm. Within seconds, the young doctor feels a rush of euphoria. His tears dry up; he regains his composure and quickly rejoins the conference.

—The date is 1884, the place is Vienna,
and the physician is Sigmund Freud

After you have completed this chapter, you should have an understanding of

- The history of cocaine
- How cocaine works in the brain
- Patterns of cocaine abuse
- Treatment programs for cocaine abuse
- The history of amphetamines
- How amphetamines work in the brain
- Patterns of methamphetamine abuse
- Stimulant treatment for attention deficit/hyperactivity syndrome (ADHD)

The time, place, and identity of S. F. in this fictionalized clinical vignette, based upon the facts of Freud's life, may have surprised you, but unfortunately the overall picture of cocaine abuse is all too familiar.[1] The year could have been 1984 (or any other year since then) instead of 1884, and the individual involved could have been anyone twenty-eight years old, as Freud was at the time, or some other age. Freud was extremely lucky; he never became dependent upon cocaine, although a close friend did and countless numbers of people have succumbed to cocaine dependence since Freud's time.

The story of cocaine is both ancient and modern. While its origins stretch back more than four thousand years, cocaine abuse continues to represent a major portion of the present-day drug scene. For this reason, it is important to understand its history, the properties of the drug itself, and the ways it has the ability to control and ultimately, in many cases, destroy a person's life.

This chapter will focus not only on cocaine but also on a group of stimulant drugs, referred to collectively as amphetamines. Although cocaine and amphetamines are distinct in terms of their pharmacology (their characteristics as biochemical substances), there are enough similarities in their behavioral and physiological effects to warrant their being discussed together.

In general, cocaine and amphetamines represent the two major classes of psychoactive stimulants, drugs that energize the body and create intense feelings of euphoria.

The Social History of Cocaine

Cocaine is derived from small leaves of the coca shrub (*Erythroxylon coca*), grown in the high-altitude rain forests and fields that run along the slopes of the Peruvian and Bolivian Andes in South America. Like many other psychoactive drugs, cocaine use has a long history. We can trace the practice of chewing coca leaves, which contain about 2 percent cocaine, back to the Inca civilization, which flourished from the thirteenth century until its conquest by the Spaniards in 1532, as well as to other Andean cultures dating back five thousand years. Coca was considered a gift from the god Inti to the Incas, allowing them to endure a harsh and physically demanding life in the Andes.[2]

To this day, coca chewing is part of the culture of this region. It is estimated that about 2 million Peruvian men who live in the Andean highlands, representing 90 percent of the male population in that area, chew coca leaves.[3] These people, called *acullicadores*, mix their own blend of coca, chalk, lime, and ash to achieve the desired effects, whether their goal is to fight fatigue or socialize with friends.[4]

This form of cocaine use among these people produces few instances of toxicity or abuse. The reason lies in the very low doses of cocaine that chewed coca leaves provide; in this form, absorption from the digestive system is slow, and relatively little cocaine enters the bloodstream and is distributed to the brain (see Chapter 1). A much more serious problem has been the introduction of a coca paste containing a much higher percentage of cocaine mixed with tobacco. It is called a *bazuco* and smoked as a cigarette. Making matters worse, dangerously high levels of kerosene, gasoline, and ether are involved in the coca-refining process and end up as adulterants in the cigarettes themselves.[5]

Cocaine in Nineteenth-Century Life

Coca leaves were brought back to Europe from the Spanish colonies soon after the conquest of the Incas, but their potency was nearly gone after the long sea voyage. Perhaps, it was said at the time, the legendary effects of coca were merely exaggerations after all. Coca leaves were ignored for nearly three hundred years. By the late 1850s, however, the active ingredient of the coca plant had been chemically isolated. In 1859, the German chemist Alfred Niemann observed its anesthetic effect on his tongue and its bitter taste and named it "cocaine." Interest in the drug was renewed, and by the 1860s the patent medicine industry in the United States and Europe (see Chapter 3) had lost no time in taking advantage of cocaine's appeal.

Commercial Uses of Cocaine

By far the most successful commercial use of cocaine in the nineteenth century was a mixture of coca and wine invented in 1863 by a Corsican chemist and businessman, Angelo Mariani. We know now that the combination of alcohol and cocaine produces a metabolite with an elimination half-life several times longer than cocaine alone, so the mixture tends to be quite intoxicating (see Help Line).

cocaine: An extremely potent and dependence-producing stimulant drug, derived from the coca leaf.

No wonder "Vin Mariani" became an instant sensation.

In a stroke of marketing genius, Mariani also invented the concept of the "celebrity endorsement." Over the next few decades, advertisements for Vin Mariani carried testimonials from satisfied customers such as U.S. President William McKinley, Thomas Edison, the surgeon general of the U.S. Army, General Ulysses S. Grant, Sarah Bernhardt, Jules Verne, the Prince of Wales, the czar of Russia, and Popes Pius X and Leo XII. In a letter to Mariani, Frederic Bartholdi, sculptor of the Statue of Liberty, wrote that if he had been drinking Vin Mariani while designing the statue, it would have been more than three times taller.[6] We can only assume that his remark was intended to be complimentary.

Meanwhile in the United States, Atlanta pharmacist John Pemberton promoted an imitation form of Vin Mariani that he called French Wine Cola. In 1885, however, as a concession to the American temperance movement, he took out the alcohol (see Chapter 13), added carbonated water, and reformulated the basic mixture to combine the coca with the syrup of the African kola nut containing about 2 percent caffeine. Coca-Cola was born.

On the strength of the beverage containing both coca and caffeine, early advertisements for Coca-Cola

In the late nineteenth century, the Coca-Cola Company advertised its beverage in medicinal terms. A company letterhead of this period spoke of Coca-Cola as containing "the tonic properties of the wonderful coca plant."

emphasized the drink as a stimulating brain tonic that made you feel more productive and as a remedy for such assorted nervous ailments as sick headaches and melancholia (a word used at the time to mean depression).[7] The medicinal slant to the early promotion of Coca-Cola is probably the reason why soda fountains first appeared and continued for years to be located in drugstores.[8]

A number of competing brands with similar formulations sprang up with names such as Care-Cola, Dope Cola, Kola Ade, and Wiseola.[9] Eventually, public pressure brought about official restrictions on the patent medicine industry, which, by the beginning of the twentieth century, was marketing more than fifty thousand unregulated products.[10] The Pure Food and Drug Act of 1906 specified that all active ingredients had to be listed on patent medicine labels. In Canada, the Proprietary and Patent Medicine Act of 1908 banned cocaine from patent medicines entirely, but in the United States no further restrictions on cocaine sales or use were imposed until the Harrison Act of 1914 (see Chapter 3).

The Coca-Cola Company, aware of the growing tide of public sentiment against cocaine, changed the formula in 1903 from regular coca leaves to decocainized coca leaves, which eliminated the cocaine but retained the coca flavoring that remains to this day (Drugs . . . in Focus). The "pause that refreshed" America would henceforth be due only to the presence of sugar and caffeine.

The use of cocaine also was becoming a major factor in the practice of medicine. In the United States, William Halstead, one of the most distinguished surgeons of the time and one of the founders of the Johns Hopkins School of Medicine, studied the effect of cocaine in anesthetizing nerves and whole limbs. In the process, he acquired a cocaine habit of his own (which was replaced several years later by dependence on morphine). It was in Europe, however, that the psychological implications of cocaine were explored most extensively, ironically through the triumphs and tribulations of Sigmund Freud.

Drugs... in Focus

What Happened to the Coca in Coca-Cola?

Every day, in a drab factory building in the New Jersey suburb of Maywood, a select team of employees of the Stepan Company carries out a chemical procedure that has been one of the primary responsibilities of the company since 1903. They remove cocaine from high-grade coca leaves. The remainder, technically called "decocainized flavor essence" is then sent to the Coca-Cola Company as part of the secret recipe for the world's favorite soft drink.

Each year, the Stepan Company is legally sanctioned by the U.S. government (and carefully monitored by the DEA) to receive shipments of about 175,000 kilograms of coca leaves from Peruvian coca farms, separate the cocaine chemically, and produce about 1,750 kilograms of high-quality cocaine. Its annual output is equivalent to approximately 20 million hits of crack, worth about $200 million if it were to make it to the illicit drug market. Fortunately, the Stepan Company has an impeccable security record.

In case you are wondering what happens to the cocaine after it is removed from the coca leaves, it turns out that Stepan finds a legitimate market in the world of medicine. Tincture of cocaine is used regularly as a local anesthetic to numb the skin prior to minor surgical procedures such as stitching up a wound. Surgeons frequently use cocaine as a topical ointment when working on the nose or throat.

As a result, the Stepan Company essentially has it both ways. It is the exclusive U.S. supplier of cocaine for use in medical settings as well as decocainized coca for your next can of Coke. As the *Wall Street Journal* put it, "The two markets end up sending Stepan's products into virtually every bloodstream in America."

Sources: Inciardi, James A. (2002). *The war on drugs III.* Boston: Allyn and Bacon, p. 21. Miller, Michael W. (1994, October 17). Quality stuff: Firm is peddling cocaine, and deals are legit. *Wall Street Journal*, pp. A1, A14.

Freud and Cocaine

In 1884 Freud was a struggling young physician, given to bouts of depression and self-doubt but nonetheless determined to make his mark in the medical world. He had read a report by a German army physician that supplies of pure cocaine helped soldiers endure fatigue and feel better in general. Freud secured some cocaine for himself and found the experience exhilarating; his depression lifted, and he felt a new sense of boundless energy. His friend and colleague Dr. Ernst von Fleischl-Marxow, taking morphine and enduring a painful illness, borrowed some cocaine from Freud and found favorable results as well.

Before long, Freud was distributing cocaine to his friends and his sisters and even sent a supply to his fiancée Martha Bernays. In the words of Freud's biographer Ernest Jones, "From the vantage point of our present knowledge, he was rapidly becoming a public menace."[11] We can gain some perspective on the effect cocaine was having on Freud's behavior at this time through an excerpt from a personal letter to Martha:

> Woe to you, my Princess, when I come. I will kiss you quite red and feed you till you are plump. And if you are forward you shall see who is the stronger, a gentle little girl who doesn't eat enough or a big wild man who has cocaine in his body [underlined in the original]. In my last severe depression I took coca again and a small dose lifted me to the heights in a wonderful fashion. I am just now busy collecting the literature for a song of praise to this magical substance.[12]

Within four months, his "song of praise" essay, "Über Coca" (Concerning Coca), was written and published.

Unfortunately, fame that the essay brought Freud was short-lived, and the sweetness of his romance with cocaine soon turned sour. Freud himself escaped becoming dependent upon cocaine, though later in his life he clearly became dependent on nicotine (see Chapter 14). His friend, Fleischl, however, was not so lucky. Within a year, Fleischl had increased his cocaine dose to twenty times the amount Freud had taken and had developed a severe cocaine-induced psychosis in which he experienced hallucinations that snakes were crawling over his skin (a phenomenon now referred to as **formication**). Fleischl suffered six years of painful agony and anguish until his death.

formication: Hallucinatory behavior produced by chronic cocaine or amphetamine abuse, in which the individual feels insects or snakes crawling either over or under the skin.

The story of Freud's infatuation with cocaine and his later disillusionment with it is essentially a miniature version of the modern history of cocaine itself.[13] Between 1880 and 1910, the public reaction to cocaine went from wild enthusiasm to widespread disapproval. As this chapter will later describe, a similar cycle of attitudes swept the United States and the world between 1970 and 1985.

Acute Effects of Cocaine

While the effects of cocaine on the user vary in degree with the route of administration, the purity of the dose, and the user's expectations about the experience, certain features remain the same. The most prominent reaction is a powerful burst of energy. If the cocaine is injected intravenously or smoked, the extremely intense effect (often referred to as a "rush" or "high") is felt within a matter of seconds, and lasts only five or ten minutes. If the drug is snorted through the nose, the effect is less intense than when injected or smoked but lasts somewhat longer, approximately 15 to 30 minutes.

Users also experience a general sense of well-being, although in some instances cocaine may precipitate a panic attack.[14] As levels of cocaine diminish, the mood changes dramatically. The user becomes irritable, despondent, and depressed (Figure 8.1). These aftereffects are uncomfortable enough to produce a powerful craving for another dose.

The depression induced in the aftermath of a cocaine high can lead to thoughts of suicide. In 1985, during one of the peak years of cocaine abuse in the

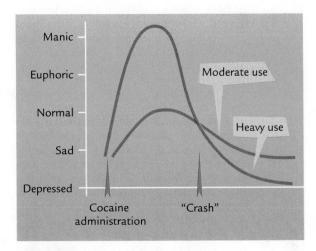

FIGURE 8.1

Ups and downs of a typical dose of cocaine.

Understanding the Social History of Cocaine

Check your understanding of the history of cocaine by matching the names on the left with the identifications on the right. Be careful; some identifications may not match up with any of the names.

1. Angelo Mariani
2. John Pemberton
3. William Halstead
4. Sigmund Freud
5. Ernst von Fleischl-Marxow

a. Friend of Sigmund Freud; first documented case of cocaine psychosis

b. Developer of Coca-Cola, originally containing cocaine

c. Early advocate of restricting cocaine use in the United States

d. Cofounder of Johns Hopkins Medical School; early developer of cocaine to anesthetize nerves and whole limbs

e. A popular figure in present-day Peru

f. Early advocate of cocaine use; originator of psychoanalysis

g. Promoter of a popular coca-laced wine

Answers: 1. g 2. b 3. d 4. f 5. a

United States, as many as one out of five suicide victims in New York City showed evidence of cocaine in their blood at autopsy. The prevalence of cocaine use was greatest among victims who were in their twenties and thirties, and for African Americans and Latinos.[15] In a 1989 survey of teenage callers to the 1-800-COCAINE hotline, one out of seven reported a previous suicide attempt.[16] On the basis of these studies, cocaine use has become recognized as a significant risk factor for suicide attempts.

Cocaine's effect on sexual arousal is often cited as having been the basis for calling it "the aphrodisiac of the 1980s." On the one hand, interviews of cocaine users frequently include reports of spontaneous and prolonged erections in males and multiple orgasms in females during initial doses of the drug. On the other hand, cocaine's reputation for increasing sexual performance (recall Freud's reference in his letter to Martha) may bias users toward a strong expectation that there will be a sexually stimulating reaction, when in reality the effect is a much weaker one. As one cocaine abuser expressed it, "Everybody says that it's an aphrodisiac. Again, I think some people say it because it's supposed to be. I think that it's just peer group identification. . . . I never felt that way. I was more content to sit there and enjoy it."[17] The fact is that chronic cocaine use results in decreased sexual performance and a loss of sexual desire, as the drug essentially takes the place of sex.

Cocaine produces a sudden elevation in the sympathetic branch of the autonomic nervous system. Heart rate and respiration are increased, while appetite is diminished. Blood vessels constrict, pupils in the eyes dilate, and blood pressure rises. The cocaine user may start to sweat and appear suddenly pale. The powerful sympathetic changes can lead to a cerebral hemorrhage or congestive heart failure. Cardiac arrhythmia results from cocaine's tendency to bind to heart tissue itself. As you may recall from Chapter 2, cocaine is the drug most often involved in drug-related hospital emergency department visits and one of the drugs most frequently involved in drug-related deaths.[18]

Given the extreme excitatory effects of cocaine on bodily organs, it is not surprising that behavioral skills would be adversely affected. In a study of drivers showing reckless behavior on the road, those found to have been under the influence of cocaine were wildly overconfident in their abilities, taking turns too fast or weaving through traffic. One highway patrol officer called this behavior "diagonal driving. They were just as involved in changing lanes as in going forward." Yet they passed the standard sobriety tests (such as walking a straight line) that are designed to detect alcohol intoxication.[19]

Chronic Effects of Cocaine

Repeated and continued use of cocaine produces undesirable mood changes that can be alleviated only when the person is under the acute effects of the drug. Chronic cocaine abusers are often irritable, depressed, and paranoid. As was true in Fleischl's experience with cocaine, long-term abuse can produce the disturbing hallucinatory experience of formication. The sensation of "cocaine bugs" crawling on or under the skin can become so severe that abusers may scratch the skin into open sores or even pierce themselves with a knife to cut out the imaginary creatures. These hallucinations, together with feelings of anxiety and paranoia, make up a serious mental disorder referred to as **cocaine psychosis**.

When snorted, cocaine causes bronchial muscles to relax and nasal blood vessels to constrict; the opposite effects occur when the drug wears off. As the bronchial muscles contract and nasal blood vessels relax, chronic abusers endure continuously stuffy or runny noses and bleeding of nasal membranes. In advanced cases of this problem, the septum of the nose can develop lesions or become perforated with small holes, both of which present serious problems for breathing.

Medical Uses of Cocaine

When applied topically on the skin, cocaine has the ability to block the transmission of nerve impulses, deadening all sensations from the area. The use of cocaine as an anesthetic for nasal, lacrimal duct (tear duct), and throat surgery remains its only legitimate medical application.[20]

While cocaine is available for use in these situations, other topical anesthetics are typically preferred since they present fewer problems in their use. One disadvantage of cocaine is that it might be inadvertently absorbed into the bloodstream, leading to an acute cocaine response that is unrelated to the anesthetic effect. Another problem is that cocaine produces intense vasoconstriction (constriction of blood vessels). This can be helpful in reducing bleeding during a surgical procedure, but the intensity of the vasoconstriction may have undesirable side-effects. Finally, the local anesthetic effects are brief because cocaine breaks down so rapidly and would require reapplications to be effective. Other local anesthetics, such as lidocaine (brand name: Xylocaine), have the advantage of being active over a longer period of time and not causing the problems associated with cocaine.

---

cocaine psychosis: A set of symptoms, including hallucinations, paranoia, and disordered thinking, produced from chronic use of cocaine.

kindling effect: A phenomenon in the brain that produces a heightened sensitivity to repeated adminstrations of some drugs, such as cocaine. This heightened sensitivity is the opposite of the phenomenon of tolerance.

How Cocaine Works in the Brain

Cocaine greatly enhances the activity of dopamine, and, to a lesser extent, norepinephrine in the brain. In the case of both neurotransmitters, the actual effect is to stimulate receptors longer and to a greater degree. Unlike the amphetamines (discussed later in this chapter), the structure of cocaine does not appear to resemble the structure of either norepinephrine or dopamine, so why cocaine should block their reuptake so effectively is not at all clear. Nonetheless, what has been determined is that the acute effect of euphoria experienced through cocaine is directly related to an increase in dopamine in the region of the brain that controls pleasure and reinforcement in general: the nucleus accumbens (see Chapter 4, page 71). The current scientific thinking is that this alteration in brain chemistry has a profound effect on an individual's decision-making skills and an individual's potential for developing a dependence on cocaine (or some other drug of abuse).

Chronic cocaine abuse, however, leads to the loss of about 20 percent of the dopamine receptors in this region of the brain over time. The depletion of dopamine receptors among long-term cocaine abusers has been observed up to four months after the last cocaine exposure, even though the cocaine abuser no longer has cocaine in his or her system. As a result, there is a tendency toward a decline in the experience of pleasure from any source. In fact, cocaine abusers frequently report that their craving for cocaine no longer stems from the pleasure they felt when taking it initially. Their lives may be in a shambles and the acute effects of euphoria from cocaine may no longer be strong, but they still crave the drug more than ever. In other words, there is now a disconnection between "liking" and "wanting."[21]

One feature of cocaine is quite unlike that of other psychoactive drugs. While cocaine abusers over repeated cocaine exposures develop a pattern of drug tolerance to its euphoric effect, they develop a pattern of sensitization (a heightened responsiveness) with respect to motor behavior and brain excitation. This phenomenon, referred to as the **kindling effect**, makes cocaine particularly dangerous because cocaine has the potential for setting off brain seizures. Repeated exposure to cocaine can lower the threshold for seizures, through a sensitization of neurons in the brain over time. As a result of the kindling effect, deaths from cocaine overdose may occur from relatively low dose levels.[22]

Present-Day Cocaine Abuse

The difficult problems of cocaine abuse in the United States and around the world mushroomed during the early 1970s and continue to the present day, although the incidence of abuse is down from peak levels reached around 1986. In ways that resembled the brief period of enthusiasm for cocaine in 1884, attitudes during the early period of this "second epidemic" were incredibly naive. Fueled by media reports of use among the rich and famous, touted as the "champagne of drugs," cocaine became synonymous with the glamorous life.

The medical profession at this time was equally nonchalant about cocaine. The widely respected *Comprehensive Textbook of Psychiatry* (1980) stated the following: "If it is used no more than two or three times a week, cocaine creates no serious problem . . . At present chronic cocaine use does not usually present a medical problem."[23]

These attitudes began to change as the 1980s unfolded. The death of actor-comedian John Belushi in 1982, followed by the drug-related deaths of other entertainers and sport figures (see Drugs . . . in Focus, page 32) produced a reversal of opinion about the safety and desirability of cocaine. The most influential development, however, was the emergence of crack cocaine on the drug scene in the mid-1980s, which will be examined in the next sections.

From Coca to Cocaine

To understand the full picture of present-day cocaine abuse, it is necessary to examine the various forms that cocaine can take, beginning with the extraction of cocaine from the coca plant itself (Figure 8.2). During the initial extraction process, coca leaves are soaked in various chemical solvents so that cocaine can be drawn out of the plant material itself. Leaves are then crushed, and alcohol is percolated through them to remove extraneous matter. After sequential washings and a treatment with kerosene, the yield is cocaine that is approximately 60 percent pure. This is the coca paste that is, as mentioned earlier, is combined with tobacco and smoked in many South American countries.

Cocaine in this form, however, is not water-soluble and therefore cannot be injected into the bloodstream. An additional step of treatment with oxidizing agents and acids is required to produce a water-soluble drug. The result is a white crystalline powder called **cocaine hydrochloride**, about 99 percent pure cocaine and classified chemically as a salt.

FIGURE 8.2

Steps in producing various forms of cocaine from raw coca.

When in the form of cocaine hydrochloride, the drug can be injected intravenously or snorted. The amount injected at one time is about 16 mg. Intravenous cocaine also can be combined with heroin in a highly dangerous mixture called a *speedball*.

If cocaine is snorted, the user generally has the option of two methods. In one method, a tiny spoonful of cocaine is carried to one nostril while the other nostril is shut, and the drug is taken with a rapid inhalation. In the other method, cocaine is spread out on a highly polished surface (often a mirror) and arranged with a razor blade in several lines, each containing from 20 to 30 mg. The cocaine is then inhaled into one nostril by means of a straw or rolled piece of paper. During the early 1980s, a $100 bill was a fashionable choice, drawing attention to the level of income necessary to be using cocaine in the first place.[24]

---

cocaine hydrochloride: The form of cocaine that is inhaled (snorted) or injected into the bloodstream.

From Cocaine to Crack

Options for using cocaine widened with the development of **free-base cocaine** during the 1970s and **crack cocaine** (or simply **crack**) during the mid-1980s. In free-base cocaine, the hydrochloride is removed from the salt form of cocaine, thus liberating it as a "free base." The aim is to obtain a smokable form of cocaine, which, by entering the brain more quickly, produces a more intense effect. The technique for producing free-base cocaine, however, is extremely hazardous, since it is necessary to treat cocaine powder with highly flammable agents such as ether. If the free base still contains some ether residue, igniting the drug will cause it to explode into flames.

Crack cocaine is the result of a cheaper and safer chemical method, but the objective is essentially the same: a smokable form of cocaine. Treatment with baking soda yields small rocks, which can then be smoked in a small pipe.[25] When they are smoked, a cracking noise accompanies the burning, hence the origin of the name "crack."

There is no question that the effect of cocaine when smoked exceeds the effect of cocaine when snorted; for some users, it even exceeds the effect of cocaine when injected. Inhaling high-potency cocaine (the purity of cocaine in crack averages about 75 percent) into the lungs, and almost immediately into the brain, sets the stage for a pattern of psychological dependence. And at a price of $5 to $10 per dose, cocaine is no longer out of financial reach (Table 8.1). These factors make crack cocaine abuse particularly problematic.

Beyond its effect on the user, however, is the effect on the society where crack is prevalent. Women who are crack abusers find that their drug cravings overwhelm their maternal instincts, resulting in their neglecting basic needs of their children, either in postnatal or prenatal stages of life. In New York, for example, the number of reported cases of child abuse and neglect increased from 36,000 in 1985 to 59,000 in 1989, a change largely attributed to the introduction of crack. Inner-city crime and violence skyrocketed (Figure 8.3).[26] As the hugely profitable crack-cocaine trade took root, systemic violence became a fact of life for people living in the inner cities of America (see Chapter 5).

TABLE 8.1	
Street names for cocaine	
TYPE OF COCAINE	**STREET NAME**
Cocaine hydrochloride (powder)	blow, C, coke, big C, lady, nose candy, snowbirds, snow, stardust, toot, white girl, happydust, cola, flake, pearl, Peruvian lady, freeze, geeze, doing the line
Free-base cocaine	freebase, base
Crack cocaine	crack, rock, kibbles and bits, crell
Crack cocaine combined with PCP (see Chapter 9)	beam me up Scottie, space cadet, tragic magic
Cocaine combined with heroin	speedball, snowball
Cocaine combined with heroin and LSD	Frisco special, Frisco speedball

Sources: Drug Enforcement Administration and the Office of National Drug Control Policy, Washington, DC.

Although crack abuse remains a problem today, the number of new crack abusers has declined substantially, particularly in urban communities. In 1998, whereas 36 percent of all males over thirty-six years old who were arrested in New York in 1998 had used crack, little more than 4 percent of those fifteen to twenty years old had done so. A principal reason for this change in prevalence rates has been the present-day stigmatized image of the "crack head," considered by one's peers to be a social loser in his or her community.[27]

Workers restore the famous "Crack is Wack" mural in Harlem River Park, New York City, originally painted in 1986 at the height of the crack cocaine abuse epidemic.

free-base cocaine: A smokable form of cocaine.

crack cocaine or crack: A smokable form of cocaine.

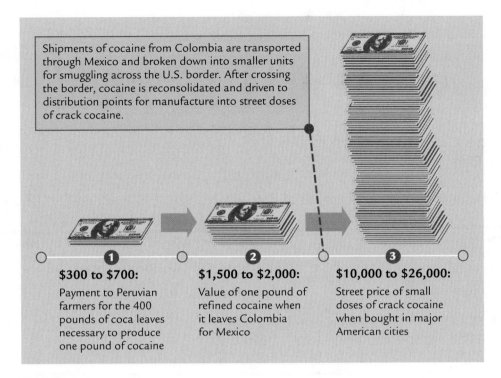

Shipments of cocaine from Colombia are transported through Mexico and broken down into smaller units for smuggling across the U.S. border. After crossing the border, cocaine is reconsolidated and driven to distribution points for manufacture into street doses of crack cocaine.

❶ $300 to $700:
Payment to Peruvian farmers for the 400 pounds of coca leaves necessary to produce one pound of cocaine

❷ $1,500 to $2,000:
Value of one pound of refined cocaine when it leaves Colombia for Mexico

❸ $10,000 to $26,000:
Street price of small doses of crack cocaine when bought in major American cities

FIGURE 8.3

From coca farm prices in Peru to street prices as crack cocaine. The value increases by approximately 8600 percent, from as little as $300 to as much as $26,000 for the 400 pounds of coca required to produce the one pound of cocaine and eventually the equivalent amount of crack.

Patterns of Cocaine Abuse

In 2009, the National Survey on Drug Use and Health estimated that approximately 37 million Americans aged 12 or older had used cocaine at some time in their lives, 4.8 million had used it during the past year, and 1.6 million had used it during the past month. Approximately 8.4 million Americans had used crack at some time in their lives, 1 million had used it during the past year, and 492,000 had used it during the past month. The past month prevalence rate for crack in 2009 had declined by 43 percent, relative to 2006.[28]

Although the present-day incidence of cocaine abuse in the United States is lower than it was during the 1980s, medical emergencies associated with cocaine use, as measured through the DAWN statistics, have increased dramatically. In 2008, there were approximately 482,000 cocaine-related ED visits reported by metropolitan hospitals. It is evident that emergency departments have borne a great burden in the

acute care of cocaine abusers, just as law-enforcement agencies have borne the burden of reducing the availabity of cocaine and cocaine-derivatives (Drugs . . . in Focus).[29]

Treatment Programs for Cocaine Abuse

One way of grasping the magnitude of the cocaine-abuse problem is to look at the number of people who have wanted to get help. In 1983, a nationwide toll-free hotline, 1-800-COCAINE, was established as a twenty-four-hour service for emergency and treatment information. From 1983 to 1990, more than 3 million callers responded, averaging more than 1,000 per day.[30]

The statistics gathered from the hotline during the 1980s also revealed the changed face of cocaine abuse over that span of time. In 1983, the typical cocaine abuser was college educated (50 percent),

Drugs... in Focus

Cocaine Contamination in U.S. Paper Currency

In recent years, a strange but reliable phenomenon has come to light with respect to the paper currency that Americans handle every day: the contamination of this currency with detectable levels of cocaine. In 2001, analyses were made of fifty randomly sampled one-dollar bills from five cities in the United States and Puerto Rico (Baltimore, Chicago, Denver, Honolulu, and San Juan). Detectable amounts of cocaine were found in an astounding 92 percent of these bills.

The explanation for this finding is based on the pattern of cocaine abuse and the present-day system of currency processing and distribution. Contamination is believed to begin with the handling of currency during cocaine trafficking (see Chapter 5) and with the rolling up of bills for cocaine snorting. The contaminated money is then transferred from bill to bill during automated counting in banks and other financial institutions. The extremely high incidence of cocaine-contaminated money is attributed to cross-contamination after the act of drug-taking behavior, rather than to the behavior itself. The lower incidence of contamination with respect to other illicit drugs such as methamphetamine or heroin is due largely to the relatively lower prevalence rates of abuse in general and the fact that currency is not as likely to be directly involved in their consumption.

Source: Jenkins, Amanda J. (2001). Drug contamination of U.S. paper currency. *Forensic Science International, 3,* 189–193.

---

employed (83 percent), earning more than $25,000 per year (52 percent), and taking cocaine powder intranasally (61 percent). By 1988, however, the typical cocaine abuser had not gone to college (83 percent) and was earning less than $25,000 per year (80 percent). From 1983 to 1988, the percentage of individuals reporting an abuse of a free-base form of cocaine had more than doubled to 56 percent. In 1986 alone, one year after the introduction of crack, half of all calls to the hotline referred to problems of crack abuse.[31]

Treating cocaine abuse presents difficulties that are peculiar to the power of cocaine itself. This is the way one treatment expert has put it:

> Coming off cocaine is one of the most anguished, depressing experiences. I've watched people talk about coming off freebase and one of the things I noticed was the nonverbal maneuvers they use to describe it. It looks like they're describing a heart attack. They have fists clenched to the chest. You can see that it hurts. They can recreate that hurt for you because it's a devastating event. They'll do almost anything to keep from crashing on cocaine. And on top of that they'll do just about anything to keep their supply coming. Postcocaine anguish is a strong inducement to use again—to keep the pain away.[32]

The varieties of treatment for cocaine abuse all have certain features in common. The initial phase is detoxification and total abstinence: The cocaine abuser aims to achieve total withdrawal with the least possibility of physical injury and minimal psychological discomfort. During the first twenty-four to forty-eight hours, the chances are high that there will be profound depression, severe headaches, irritability, and disturbances in sleep.[33]

In severe cases involving a pattern of compulsive use, the cocaine abuser needs to be admitted for inpatient treatment in a hospital facility. The most intensive interventions, medical supervision with psychological counseling, can be made in this kind of environment. The early stages of withdrawal are clearly the most difficult, and the recovering abuser can benefit from the around-the-clock attention that only a hospital staff can give.

The alternative approach is an outpatient program, under which the individual remains at home but travels regularly to a facility for treatment. An outpatient program is clearly a less expensive route to take, but it works only for those who recognize the destructive impact of cocaine dependence on their lives and enter treatment with a sincere desire to do whatever is needed to stop.[34]

For cocaine abusers who have failed in previous attempts in outpatient treatment or for those who are in denial of their cocaine dependence, an inpatient approach may be the only answer. For most abusers, it is important to stay away from an environment where cocaine and other drugs are prevalent and peer pressure to resume drug-taking behavior is intense. This factor is particularly crucial among adolescents:

Peer acceptance is of utmost importance to adolescents. In order to interrupt the addiction cycle, youth are cautioned to avoid drug-using friends. Since many addicted adolescents are alienated from the mainstream and what few friends they have are users, this challenge can appear overwhelming. Recovering adolescents often comment that they can't find friends who don't at least drink.[35]

A third alternative is a combined approach in which a shortened inpatient program, seven to fourteen days in length, is followed by an intensive outpatient program that continues for several months (Portrait).

Whether on an inpatient or an outpatient basis, there are several approaches for treatment. One alternative is

PORTRAIT

Robert Downey, Jr.—Cleaning Up His Life after Cocaine

The parade of celebrities who have struggled against cocaine abuse is seemingly endless. Over the years, we have witnessed their personal triumphs and failures and have seen some lives lost (see Chapter 2), some careers lost, and occasionally careers regained. In 1986, the nation was galvanized by the untimely deaths of college basketball player Len Bias and professional football player Dan Rogers within months of each other; the death of comedian and actor John Belushi had occurred just four years earlier. The deaths of River Phoenix in 1993, Chris Farley in 1998, and Mitch Hedberg in 2005, all of them due to a lethal combination of cocaine and heroin, have underscored the ever-present dangers of drug-taking behavior.

Fortunately, the story of Robert Downey, Jr., an Academy Award nominee for his performance in the title role of the movie *Chaplin* in 1992, has all the marks of a Hollywood comeback screenplay—the story of a life and career derailed for several years by the abuse of cocaine and other drugs but somehow managing to come out right in the end. For a time, his fans held their breath as events unfolded. By January 2003, Downey, at the age of thirty-seven, could remark, "I'm a little older. I'm mildly wiser. My frequent appearances on Court TV have brought me to another

level than just always 'the acting guy.' . . . I think I've become very, I don't want to say real, but I'm very tangible to people." He made these comments while at the premiere of a new film, his first since he had completed a year-long court-ordered drug rehabilitation program in 2002. At the time, he was about one year into a three-year probation period, after pleading no-contest to cocaine possession and being under the influence during a November 2000 arrest in a Palm Springs hotel (see photo on left).

In 1999, Downey had spent a year in prison after being convicted on charges of cocaine possession. Upon his release, he was featured on the successful *Aly McBeal* TV show, only to be fired in 2000. His drug-abuse problems had first begun making headlines in 1996 when he was found with cocaine, heroin, and a pistol in his car.

In earlier editions of the text, this Portrait feature portrayed the story of Robert Downey, Jr. in considerably less positive terms. However, today there is reason for optimism. His self-destructive life-style appears to be over. As he has said, "I think part of my destiny has to be realizing that I'm not the poster boy for drug abuse."

In 2008, Downey achieved a major comeback in his starring role in the

successful blockbuster movie *Iron Man* (see photo on right). He has followed with starring roles in *Sherlock Holmes* in 2009 and *Iron Man 2* in 2010. His personal life seems to have regained a stability that bodes well for the future. Nonetheless, like any recovering substance abuser, Downey acknowledges the fragility of his life:

If I see somebody who is throwing their life away with both hands and is raging around and destroying their family, I can't understand that person. I'm not in that sphere of activity anymore, and I don't understand it any more than I understood 10 or 20 years ago that somehow everything was going to turn out O.K. from this lousy, exotic, and dark triple chapter of my life . . . I don't think I will ever go that fast again, but that is based on my behavior moment to moment, whether I'm able to maintain this nice groove I'm on or whether it will all go away in a second for something that I could justify or rationalize was none of my own doing."

Sources: Carr, David (2008, April 20). Been up, been down. Now? Super. *New York Times*, pp. 1, 13. Third quotation, p. 13. Robert Downey Jr. cleans up (2005, October 26). CNN.com. Second quotation. Downey's back, older and "mildly wiser" (2003, January 21). First quotation. *Newsday*, p. A12. Lemonick, Michael D. (2000, December 11). Downey's downfall. *Time*, p. 97.

the self-help support group Cocaine Anonymous, modeled after the famous twelve-step Alcoholics Anonymous program (see Chapter 14). In this program, recovering cocaine abusers meet in group sessions, learn from the life experiences of other members, and gain a sense of accomplishment from remaining drug-free in an atmosphere of fellowship and mutual support. In another drug-treatment option, cocaine abusers meet with cognitive-behavioral therapists, who teach them new ways of acting and thinking in response to their environment. During the course of cognitive-behavioral therapy, cocaine abusers are urged to avoid situations that lead to drug use, recognize and change irrational thoughts, manage negative moods, and practice drug-refusal skills. While the success rates of both approaches are approximately the same for patients in cocaine-abuse treatment overall, some evidence suggests that a cocaine abuser's personal characteristics may affect the kind of treatment that will work best (Figure 8.4). Whatever the approach taken, however, it is clear that an intensive relearning process has to go on because cocaine abusers often cannot remember a life without cocaine.[36]

Currently, pharmacological approaches in cocaine-abuse treatment, as well as the combination of pharmacological and behavioral approaches, are being vigorously pursued. A promising example of a purely pharmacological strategy is the development of the compound gamma-vinyl-GABA (GVG), currently available as an antiepileptic drug called Vigabatrin. Essentially, it has been established that GVG "short-circuits" the reinforcing effect of cocaine by preventing the sudden surge of dopamine in the brain when cocaine is administered. Animals that have become cocaine-dependent no longer self-administer the drug after taking GVG and are no longer attracted to locations that have been associated with cocaine in the past. In other words, GVG allows animals to resist the conditioned cues for chronic cocaine use. Preliminary evidence indicates that GVG is effective in a similar way in humans, and large-scale randomized double-blind clinical trials (see Chapter 1) are currently underway.[37]

The potential for relapse is particularly challenging among recovering cocaine abusers, primarily as a result of powerful conditioned cues that have been associated with the drug. A specialist in cocaine abuse rehabilitation tells this story: "A woman was doing well in treatment. Then one day she was changing her baby's diaper. She used baby powder and the sight of the white powder induced a tremendous craving for cocaine."[38] The development of any drug that reduces craving would be a great advance in the treatment of cocaine dependence and in the prevention of problems associated with cocaine dependence.

The continuing investigation of treatment and prevention approaches to cocaine abuse reflects a general orientation toward reducing the negative impact of drug-taking behavior on the individual and society (the "demand" side), as opposed to reducing the availability of the drugs themselves (the "supply" side). The Drug Trafficking Update focuses on information regarding governmental efforts to disrupt the supply line of cocaine into the United States.

FIGURE 8.4

Percentage of patients achieving four consecutive weeks of cocaine abstinence, comparing two types of treatment.

Source: Adapted from Shine, Barbara (2000, March). Some cocaine abusers fare better with cognitive-behavioral therapy, others with 12-step programs. *NIDA Notes, 15* (1), 9.

Amphetamines

One of humanity's fondest dreams is to have the power of unlimited endurance, to be able to banish fatigue from our lives, to be fueled by endless energy as though we had discovered some internal perpetual-motion machine. We all have wanted, at some time in our lives, to be a super-hero. Cocaine, as we know, gives us that illusion. The remainder of this chapter will examine another powerful drug source for these feelings of invincibility: amphetamines. As we will see, the attractions and problems of abuse associated with cocaine and amphetamines are very similar.

The Social History of Amphetamines

The origin of modern amphetamines dates back almost five thousand years to a Chinese medicinal herb called *ma huang (Ephedra vulgaris)* that was used to clear bronchial passageways during bouts of asthma and other forms of respiratory distress. According to Chinese legend, this herb was first identified by the Emperor Shen Nung, who also is credited with the discovery of tea and marijuana.

German chemists isolated the active ingredient of *ma huang* in 1887, naming it ephedrine. It was soon obvious

that ephedrine stimulated the sympathetic nervous system in general. In 1932, the pharmaceutical company Smith, Kline and French Laboratories marketed a synthetic form of ephedrine called **amphetamine** under the brand name Benzedrine as a nonprescription CNS stimulant appetite suppressant and bronchial dilator.

During World War II, both U.S. and German troops were being given amphetamine to keep them awake and alert. Japanese kamikaze pilots were on amphetamine during their suicide missions. The advantages over cocaine, the other stimulant drug available at the time, were two-fold: Amphetamine was easily absorbed into the nervous system from the gastrointestinal tract, so it could be taken orally, and its effects were much longer lasting.

After the war, amphetamine use was adapted for peacetime purposes. Amphetamine, often referred to as "bennies," was a way for college students to stay awake to study for exams and for long-distance truck drivers to fight fatigue on the road. Truckers would take a "St. Louis" if they had to go from New York to Missouri and back or a "Pacific turnabout" if they needed to travel completely across country and back, without stopping to sleep.[39]

> **amphetamine (am-FEH-ta-meen):** A family of ephedrine-based stimulant drugs.

In the meantime, the word got around that amphetamine produced euphoria as well, and soon amphetamine began to be sought for recreational purposes. People found ways of opening up the nonprescription amphetamine inhalers, withdrawing the contents, and getting high by drinking it or injecting it intravenously. Since each inhaler contained 250 mg of amphetamine, there was enough for several powerful doses. During the early 1960s, injectable amphetamines could be bought with forged prescriptions or even by telephoning a pharmacy and posing as a physician. By 1965, amendments to federal drug laws tightened the supply of prescription amphetamines, requiring manufacturers, wholesalers, and pharmacies to keep careful records of amphetamine transactions, but amphetamines soon became available from illegal laboratories.[40]

Amphetamine abuse in the United States reached a peak around 1967, declining slowly over the 1970s as other stimulant drugs , notably cocaine, grew in popularity. By 1970, 10 percent of the U.S. population over fourteen years of age had used amphetamine, and more than 8 percent of all drug prescriptions were for amphetamine in some form.[41] For about two decades afterward, amphetamine abuse steadily faded from prominence in the drug scene. Cocaine and later crack cocaine became the dominant illicit stimulant of abuse. Only since the mid-1990s has amphetamine abuse resurfaced as a significant social concern.

The Different Forms of Amphetamine

To understand amphetamine abuse, both past and present, it is necessary to know something about the molecular structure of amphetamines themselves and their relationship to important neurotransmitters in the brain. As you can see at the top of Figure 8.5, amphetamine can be represented chiefly as carbon (C), hydrogen (H), and nitrogen (N) atoms, in a prescribed arrangement. What you are seeing, however, is only one version of amphetamine, the "right-handed" form, since amphetamine contains a "left-handed" version as

FIGURE 8.5

The molecular structure of dextroamphetamine, methamphetamine, dopamine, and norepinephrine.

well (imagine a mirror image of Figure 8.5). The more potent version is the right-handed form, called dextroamphetamine or **d-amphetamine** (brand name: Dexedrine). It is stronger than the left-handed form, called levoamphetamine or l-amphetamine, which is not commonly available. A modified form of d-amphetamine, formulated by substituting CH_3 (called a methyl group) instead of H at one end, is called **methamphetamine**. This slight change in the formula allows for a quicker passage across the blood-brain barrier and therefore a more powerful effect on the brain. It is methamphetamine (*meth, speed,* or *crank*) that has been the primary form of amphetamine abuse in recent years.

How Amphetamines Work in the Brain

We can get a good idea of how amphetamines work in the brain by looking carefully at the molecular structures of dopamine and norepinephrine alongside d-amphetamine and methamphetamine in Figure 8.5. Notice how similar they all are, with only slight differences among them. Because of the close resemblance to dopamine and norepinephrine, it is not hard to

d-amphetamine: Shortened name for dextroamphetamine, a potent form of amphetamine, marketed under the brand name Dexedrine.

methamphetamine: A type of amphetamine, once marketed under the brand name Methedrine. Methamphetamine abusers refer to it as meth, speed, or crank.

imagine amphetamines increasing the activity level of these two neurotransmitters.

Acute Effects of Amphetamines

The acute effects of amphetamine, in either d-amphetamine or methamphetamine form, closely resemble those of cocaine. However, amphetamine effects extend over a longer period of time. For intervals of eight to twenty-four hours, there are signs of increased sympathetic autonomic activity such as faster breathing and heart rate as well as hyperthermia (increased body temperature) and elevated blood pressure. Users experience feelings of euphoria and invincibility, decreased appetite, and an extraordinary boost in alertness and energy. Adverse and potentially lethal bodily changes include convulsions, chest pains, and stroke. In 2008, approximately 66,000 of all drug-related ED visits in the United States were attributable specifically to methamphetamine abuse, accounting for about two-thirds of visits related to stimulant abuse in general.[42]

Chronic Effects of Amphetamines

The chronic effects of amphetamine abuse are both bizarre and unpleasant, particularly in the case of methamphetamine. Heavy methamphetamine abusers may experience formication hallucinations similar to those endured by cocaine abusers. They may become obsessed with the delusion that parasites or insects have lodged in their skin and so attempt to scratch, cut, or burn their skin in an effort to remove them. It is also likely that they will engage in compulsive or repetitive behaviors that are fixated upon ordinarily trivial aspects of life; an entire night might be spent, for example, counting the corn flakes in a cereal box. Compulsive jaw movements and teeth grinding can cause significant dental damage over time.[43]

The most serious societal consequence of methamphetamine abuse is the appearance of paranoia, wildly bizarre delusions, hallucinations, tendencies toward violence, and intense mood swings. In the words of one health professional, "It's about the ugliest drug there is."[44] Because the symptoms have been observed with the chronic abuse of amphetamines of any type, they are referred to collectively as **amphetamine psychosis.**

These "psychotic" effects, often persisting for weeks or even months after the drug has been withdrawn (called "tweaking" by the drug-abuse community), so closely resemble the symptoms of paranoid schizophrenia that it has been speculated that the two conditions have the same underlying chemical basis in the brain: an over-stimulation of dopamine-releasing neurons in those regions that control emotional reactivity.[45] A study of heavy methamphetamine users has shown changes in chemical metabolites in those regions of the brain that are associated with Parkinson's disease, suggesting that this group may be predisposed to acquiring Parkinson symptoms later in life, due to their methamphetamine exposure. Fortunately, however, recent evidence indicates that chemical changes in the brain in chronic methamphetamine users can be at least partially reversed by abstaining from the drug for a year or more.[46]

Methamphetamine Abuse

In the United States, the emergence of widespread methamphetamine abuse was intermingled with the marijuana and LSD scene during San Francisco's "Summer of Love and Peace" in 1967. Almost from the beginning, however, speed freaks—as methamphetamine abusers were called—whose behaviors were anything but loving or peaceful, became the outcasts of that society:

> These wild-eyed, manic burnout cases would blither on endlessly, rip off anything not welded in place, then go into fits of erratic and violent behavior . . . . They were shunned by other sorts of drug users, and ended up congregating with the only segment of the population who could stomach their company—other speed freaks.[47]

In the meantime, prescription amphetamines, widely administered during the 1960s for weight control and as a way to combat drowsiness, resulted in large numbers of abusers from practically every segment of society. Even though d-amphetamine was classified as a Schedule II drug in 1970 and the number of d-amphetamine prescriptions decreased by 90 percent from 1971 and 1986, the pills were still out there, and people found ways to continue an abusive pattern of drug-taking behavior.

---

amphetamine psychosis: A set of symptoms, including hallucinations, paranoia, and disordered thinking, resulting from high doses of amphetamines.

Present-Day Patterns of Methamphetamine Abuse

As crack cocaine became increasingly associated with the urban poor and powder cocaine with upscale affluence in the 1980s, amphetamine abuse declined dramatically. In the 1990s, however, as crack cocaine and powder cocaine abuse began to diminish, methamphetamine abuse reemerged on the drug scene. Once identified with the countercultural 1960s, methamphetamine became a major stimulant of abuse in the United States, with its popularity now concentrated among working-class people rather than among the poor or the affluent (Table 8.2).

TABLE 8.2

Street names for amphetamines

TYPE OF AMPHETAMINE	STREET NAME
Amphetamine in general	bennies, uppers, ups, A, pep pills, white crowns, whites
Dextroamphetamine	dexies, cadillacs, black beauties
Methamphetamine*	meth, speed, Tina, crank, little whites, white crosstops, crystal meth, quill, yellow bam, zip, go fast, chalk, shabu, spoosh, get go
Smokable methamphetamine*	ice, crystal, crystal meth, L.A., L.A. glass, quartz, cristy, hanyak, Christina, Tina
Methcathinone (a synthetic analog of methamphetamine)	khat, cat, goob

*Slang terms often confuse smokable and nonsmokable forms of methamphetamine, so some street names may overlap the two categories.

Sources: Drug Enforcement Administration and the Office of National Drug Control Policy, Washington, DC.

---

ice: A smokable form of methamphetamine hydrochloride. It is often referred to as crystal meth, due to its quartz-like appearance.

Methamphetamine . . . made inroads among many blue-collar people because it did not carry the stigma of being a hard drug . . . It's what people used to get them through a shift at the factory or keep up on a construction site.[48]

Methamphetamine became one of the few drugs reported as equally or more prevalent than other illicit drugs in areas outside America's inner cities.

In the early 1990s, distribution of methamphetamine was dominated by organized groups operating out of southern California and Mexico, with trafficking routes extending through several U.S. states, including Arizona, Colorado, Iowa, Missouri, Nebraska, North Dakota, and Texas. Soon after, however, thousands of "homegrown" methamphetamine laboratories began to proliferate in small towns and rural areas throughout the nation, typically situated in mobile homes, campers, vans, and easily hidden farm sheds, making their detection by law enforcement agencies extremely difficult. As of 2006, retail outlets have been required by federal law to limit the sales of numerous cold remedies that contain pseudoepinephrine—an essential ingredient in the making of methamphetamine. In effect, products that have formerly been "over-the-counter" are now "behind-the-counter." Customers cannot make a legitimate purchase of more than the equivalent of approximately seventy 60 mg tablets per day and must provide photo identification upon purchase and sign a logbook recording the transaction. Because liquid anhydrous ammonia, commonly used as a farm fertilizer, is another ingredient in the making of methamphetamine, fertilizer dealers have resorted to the installation of security systems to protect their supplies from theft.

While output of these small domestic laboratories is relatively small, the adverse impact on a local level is considerable. Toxic residue from methamphetamine manufacture, approximately five pounds of waste for every one pound of methamphetamine produced, has seeped into the soil and contaminated rivers and streams. Children have suffered from the inhalation of toxic fumes emitted during the process of methamphetamine manufacture, from fire and explosions that result from the volatile ingredients, and from abuse and neglect by methamphetamine-dependent parents (Drugs . . . in Focus).[49]

Methamphetamine has become a major club drug in New York, Los Angeles, and other cities (see Chapter 2). A smokable form of methamphetamine hydrochloride called **ice** (also referred to as *crystal meth*)

Drugs... in Focus

Methamphetamine Abuse in the Heartland of America

The methamphetamine abuse epidemic in Watauga County, North Carolina, had gotten so bad that it has nicknamed itself "the county that never sleeps." Dozens of methamphetamine laboratories in the region were raided. Every fire emergency was treated as if it were a "meth-lab fire."

Watauga County was not alone. A survey of more than 500 county sheriffs in the United States, conducted by the National Association of Counties in 2005, documented the alarming proportions of meth abuse across the country since 2000. Fifty-eight percent of sheriffs in the survey regarded methamphetamine abuse as the biggest drug problem they faced, ahead of concerns about heroin, cocaine, or marijuana.

The law enforcement and criminal justice challenges have been immense. In half of the counties surveyed, one in five current prison inmates had been incarcerated due to methamphetamine-related crimes. In 17 percent of the counties, more than half of the inmate population had been incarcerated for such crimes. A majority of sheriffs reported that methamphetamine use was the major contributing factor for increases in robberies or burglaries, domestic violence, and simple assaults. At the same time, only one in six counties reported that they had the financial resources to support a methamphetamine rehabilitation center or program.

The adverse impact on children has been of particular concern. There have been significant increases in cases in which children need to be placed out of the home as a result of neglect and abuse by parents who are methamphetamine abusers or a child's proximity to the hazards of methamphetamine labs. Nearly three-fourths of county child welfare officials in California and Colorado, for example, have reported increases in such cases since 2000. More than 69 percent of counties in Minnesota reported an increase in methamphetamine-related child placements between 2004 and 2005.

Two exacerbating factors have made it particularly difficult for these children. First, methamphetamine abuse has been concentrated in mostly rural areas, where social service networks are ill prepared to handle the increased numbers of foster children. Second, the chances of reunifying families torn apart by methamphetamine abuse has been considerably lower than in cases involving other forms of drug abuse, due to the relatively high rate of relapse in treatment.

As is the case with any pattern of substance abuse, the picture of methamphetamine abuse in America is constantly in a state of flux. As a response, for example, to the federal law in 2006 setting restrictions on acquiring basic ingredients for methamphetamine production, California-based traffickers have resorted to a form of "smurfing" (see Chapter 5), by soliciting homeless individuals to travel from store to store to purchase legal or below-legal amounts of pseudoephedrine from drugstores. Meanwhile, the number of "superlabs" in Mexico has increased dramatically, with ingredients obtained from sources in South America.

Sources: Combat Meth Act added to 2006 spending bill (2005, October 15). *Alcoholism and Drug Abuse Weekly,* p. 7. Doyle, Rodger (2006, August). The crystal crisis: Meth abuse moves eastward. *Scientific American,* p. 28. National Association of Counties (2005, July 5). The meth epidemic in America. Two surveys of U.S. counties: The criminal effect of meth on communities and the impact of meth on children. Washington, DC: National Association of Counties. Reports suggest gain in fight on meth labs (2006, June 20). *New York Times,* p. A15. National Drug Intelligence Center (2009, June). Situation Report: Pseudoephedrine smurfing fuels surge in large-scale methamphetamine production in California. Washington, DC: National Drug Intelligence Center, U.S. Department of Justice. National Drug Intelligence Center (2008). *National Methamphetamine Threat Assessement 2009.* Washington, DC: National Drug Intelligence Cewnter, U.S. Department of Justice. Substance Abuse and Mental Health Services Administration (2007, January 26). Methamphetamine use. *The NSDUH Report.* Washington, DC: Office of Applied Studies, Substance Abuse and Mental Health Services Administration. Zernike, Kate (2005, July 11). A drug scourge creates its own form of orphan. *New York Times,* pp. A1, A15.

is particularly dangerous. Its name originates from its quartz-like, chunky crystallized appearance. Ice appeared on the drug scene in Hawaii in the late 1980s, but its abuse did not expand to the mainland to a significant degree until the latter 1990s. The combination of a purity of 98 to 100 percent and a highly efficient delivery route through the lungs produces a high level of potential for dependence. The association of its use with high-risk sexual behavior is a major public-health concern.[50]

Methamphetamine abuse produces an enormous increase in alertness and energy, but frightening hallucinations and compulsive behaviors also can occur.

Methamphetamine Abuse Treatment

Even though methamphetamine and cocaine are similar in their stimulant effects and both trigger a major release of dopamine in the brain, the pattern of drug-taking behavior for each type of drug has its own distinctive character. Methamphetamine abusers typically use the drug throughout their waking day, at two- to four-hour intervals, in a pattern that resembles taking medication. Cocaine abusers typically use the drug in the evening and nighttime rather than during the day, taking it in a continuous (binge-like) fashion until all the cocaine on hand has been exhausted. This latter pattern of drug-taking behavior fits the typical picture of the recreational user.

The duration of response to the two drugs helps to explain the differences in usage. Methamphetamine effects generally last longer than cocaine effects.

Therefore, cocaine abusers need relatively more frequent administrations to maintain their "high." On tests that evaluate different forms of cognitive functioning, methamphetamine and cocaine abusers show significant differences in the type of cognitive impairment that is produced. Methamphetamine abusers are generally impaired on tests of perceptual speed or manipulation of information, effects observed to a lesser extent among cocaine abusers. The greatest difference between the two groups is observed when tests require both speed and the manipulation of information.[51]

On the other hand, the course of methamphetamine withdrawal—and of amphetamine withdrawal in general—is very similar to the course of events described earlier for cocaine. First, there is the "crash" when the abuser feels intense depression, hunger, agitation, and anxiety within one to four

My friends.
My future.

I lost everything to meth.

800 662 HELP
methresources.gov

An anti-meth abuse advertisement, part of a national campaign launched in 2010, is aimed at curbing meth abuse among young American Indians.

hours after the drug-taking behavior has stopped. Withdrawal from amphetamines, during total abstinence from the drug, takes between six and eighteen weeks, during which the intense craving for amphetamine slowly subsides.

As in cocaine-abuse treatment, there are inpatient and outpatient programs for methamphetamine abuse, depending on the circumstances and motivation of the abuser. Self-help groups such as Cocaine Anonymous can be useful as well, since the symptoms of amphetamine withdrawal and cocaine withdrawal are nearly identical. Methamphetamine abusers represent approximately one in twelve individuals in treatment for substance abuse, but relatively few methamphetamine abusers attempt treatment, much less succeed in recovery. The reason is that they perceive themselves as remaining in control over their drug use, despite evidence to the contrary. As a major government report has expressed it:

> *This perception is particularly dangerous because the crossover from initial use to loss of control is rapid for meth users, and generally they have lost control long before they can acknowledge it . . . This attitude of denial makes it difficult to convince meth abusers to enter and stay in treatment.*[52]

Overall, methamphetamine abusers find it extremely difficult to become drug-free, and their relapse rate is one of the highest for any category of illicit or licit drug abuse (Drug Trafficking Update).

Drug Trafficking Update
Methamphetamine

- **Origins:** Domestic small-scale production of methamphetamine, under intense law enforcement pressure and domestic sale restrictions for precursor chemicals, has declined substantially since 2005. In addition, importation of pseudoephedrine from Canada into the United States has been curtailed. Filling the void are methamphetamine laboratories in rural locations in California, operated by Mexican criminal groups.

- **Points of Entry:** Methamphetamine is primarily produced domestically. Importation of precursor chemicals for methamphetamtine from Mexico has been reduced, due to increased governmental restrictions, though significant drug seizures continue at the U.S.–Mexico border.

- **Traffickers:** Distribution of methamphetamine is now dominated by Mexican criminal groups.

Source: National Drug Intelligence Center (2010). *National Drug Threat Assessment 2010.* Washington, DC: National Drug Intelligence Center, U.S. Department of Justice, pp. 32-35. National Drug Intelligence Center (2006). National Drug Intelligence Center (2008). *National Drug Threat Assessment 2009.* Washington, DC: National Drug Intelligence Center, U.S. Department of Justice, pp. 9–15. National Drug Intelligence Center (2007). *National Drug Treatment Assessment 2008.* Washington, DC: Natinal Drug Intelligence Center, U.S. Department of Justice, pp. 19–23.

Medical Uses for Amphetamines and Similar Stimulant Drugs

Although amphetamines in general continue to present potential problems of abuse, there are approved medical applications for amphetamines and amphetamine-like stimulant drugs in specific circumstances. Stimulant drugs are prescribed primarily for elementary-school-age children diagnosed as unable to maintain sufficient attention levels and impulse control in school or as behaviorally hyperactive. These symptoms are collectively referred to as **attention deficit/hyperactivity disorder (ADHD)**. When there is no evidence of hyperactivity, the designation is shortened to *attention deficit disorder (ADD)*.

ADHD is the most common psychological disorder among children. It is estimated that 3 to 7 percent of all school-age children meet the criteria for ADHD. The prevalence rate is three times greater and the symptoms are generally more severe for boys than for girls. These children have average to above-average intelligence but typically underperform academically. As many as two-thirds of school-age children with ADHD have at least one other psychiatric disorder, including anxiety and depression.[53]

Despite the public image of ADHD as an exclusively childhood phenomenon, longitudinal studies have shown that ADHD symptoms persist from childhood into adolescence in about 75 percent of the cases and into adulthood in about 50 percent of the cases.[54]

Stimulant Medications for ADHD

Commonly prescribed stimulant medications for the treatment of ADHD include oral administrations of an amphetamine-like drug, methylphenidate (brand name: Ritalin), a combination of dextroamphetamine and amphetamine (brand name: Adderall), and a combination of dextroamphetamine and the amino acid lysine, lisdexfamine (brand name: Vyvanse).

For decades, Ritalin dominated the market in prescriptions written for ADHD. While a growing number of alternative medications are now available for this purpose, Ritalin remains the most recognizable "brand" with respect to ADHD treatment. In this

attention deficit/hyperactivity disorder (ADHD):
A behavioral disorder characterized by increased motor activity and reduced attention span.

drug's original formulation, the rapid onset and short duration of Ritalin requires two administrations during a school day: one at breakfast and another at lunchtime, supervised by a school nurse. In the evening, blood levels of Ritalin decline to levels that permit normal sleep. Adderall has a longer duration of action, making it possible to administer a single dose and avoiding school involvement in treatment. In comparative studies, Ritalin and Adderall have been found to be equivalent in effectiveness.[55]

New drug treatments for ADHD have become available that are essentially variations of the traditional methylphenidate medication. They include a sustained-release formulation (brand name: Concerta), a formulation that produces an initial rapid dose of methylphenidate followed by a second sustained-release phase (brand name: Metadate), and a chemical variation of methylphenidate that allows for a longer duration of action (brand names: Attenade, Focalin). A methylphenidate patch (brand name: Daytrana), designed to release the drug through the skin slowly over a period of nine hours, was approved in 2006.

About 70 percent of the approximately 1 million children in the United States who take stimulants for ADHD each year respond successfully to the treatment. In 1999, a major study examining the effects of medication over a fourteen-month period found that medication was more effective in reducing ADHD symptoms than behavioral treatment and nearly as effective as a combined approach of medication and behavioral treatment.

One side effect of stimulant medications is a suppression of height and weight gains during these formative years, reducing growth to about 80 to 90 percent normal levels. Fortunately, growth spurts during the summer, when children are typically no longer taking medication (referred to as "drug holidays"), usually compensate for this problem. Discontinuance of medication, however, has to be carefully monitored. Symptoms such as lethargy, lack of motivation, and, in some cases, depression can occur during this time.

A more serious concern is the increased risk of cardiovascular disease due to the effects of stimulant drugs. In 2006, the FDA recommended a "black box" warning on ADHD medications as a guide for patients and physicians. Recent studies indicate that stimulant treatment for ADHD in childhood does not increase the risk for substance abuse later in life. In fact, the risks for future problems with alcohol and other drugs appear to be reduced.[56]

Until recently, the phenomenon of *reducing* hyperactivity with methylphenidate and related stimulant drugs, rather than increasing it, had been quite puzzling to professionals in this field. It is now known that orally administered methylphenidate and related stimulant drugs produce a relatively slow but steady increase in dopamine activity in the brain (see Chapter 4). This change in brain chemistry is hypothesized to have two effects that are beneficial to an individual with ADHD. First, increased dopamine may amplify the effects of environmental stimulation, while reducing the background firing rates of neurons. Thus, there would be a greater "signal-to-noise" ratio in the brain, analogous to having now a stronger radio signal received by a radio that no longer emits a large amount of background static. The behavioral effect would be an improvement in attention and decreased distractibility. Symptoms of ADHD may be a result of not having a sufficient "signal-to-noise" ratio in the processing of information for tasks that require concentration and focus. Second, increased dopamine may heighten one's motivation with regard to a particular task, enhancing the salience and interest in that task and improving performance. An individual might perform better on a task simply because he or she likes doing it. The slow rate of absorption achieved through oral administration (Chapter 1) and the relatively slow action of dopamine release in the brain avoids the emotional high that is experienced when stimulants are smoked, snorted, or injected.[57]

The theory that increased activity in dopamine alone accounts for the reduction in ADHD symptoms, however, may be incomplete. In 2003, a new medication, atomoxetine (brand name: Strattera), was approved by the FDA for the treatment of ADHD in both children and adults. Since Strattera produces an increase in norepinephrine activity in the brain, it is possible that lowered norepinephrine levels may play a role in ADHD as well. Strattera has been marketed as a once-a-day non-stimulant medication that reduces ADHD symptoms by increasing norepinephrine levels—not dopamine levels—in the brain. The full story may be either that both norepinephrine and dopamine are jointly involved in ADHD or that ADHD itself may be two separable disorders, one related to dopamine activity and the other related to norepinephrine activity. According to this hypothesis, the symptoms may overlap to such a degree that it is difficult to distinguish the two disorders on a strictly behavioral basis.

Ritalin and Adderall Abuse

In 1996, the Swiss pharmaceutical company Ciba-Geigy sent letters to hundreds of thousands of pharmacies and physicians in the United States, warning them to exert greater control over Ritalin tablets and prescriptions to obtain them. The alert came in response to reports that Ritalin was becoming a drug of abuse among young people, who were crushing the tablets and snorting the powder as a new way of getting a stimulant high. Diversion of prescription medications was beginning to be a concern.

Since then, the problem of stimulant medication abuse, primarily the nonmedical use of Adderall, has become a major issue. Approximately 6 percent of full-time college students aged 18 to 22 have reported using Adderall nonmedically in the past year. While it is not known whether they are using Adderall to get a stimulant high or to enhance school performance by being able to study late into the night, there are indications that it is the first reason rather than the second. Nearly 90 percent report that they also have been binge drinkers in the past month and more than half are heavy alcohol users. Approximately 80 percent have used marijuana in the past year and 45 percent have been nonmedical users of prescription pain relievers. Nonetheless, a growing number of cases appear to be motivated by the potential for cognitive enhancement (Drugs . . . in Focus).[58]

Other Medical Applications

Narcolepsy (an unpredictable and uncontrollable urge to fall asleep during the day) is another condition for which stimulant drugs have been applied in treatment. In 1999, modafinil (brand name: Provigil) was approved for treating narcolepsy. The advantage of Provigil over traditional stimulant treatments such as dextroamphetamine is that it does not present problems of abuse and produces fewer adverse side effects. Alternative medications for narcolepsy that do not work by stimulating the CNS are presently under development.[59]

There are also several amphetamine-like drugs available to the public, some of them on a nonprescription basis, for use as nasal decongestants. In most cases, their effectiveness stems from their primary action on the peripheral nervous system rather than on the CNS. Even so, the potential for misuse exists: Some users continue to take these drugs over a long period of time because stopping their use may result in unpleasant rebound effects such as nasal stuffiness. This reaction, by the way, is similar to the stuffy nose that is experienced in the chronic administration of cocaine.[60]

Drugs... in Focus

Stimulant Medications as "Smart Pills"

When twenty-four-year-old Jeff Ewing was first prescribed Adderall to help him maintain his focus after a major automobile accident cost him a year at a midwestern university, he was surprised to find so many healthy students who were taking the same drug to help them study. Some of them were concentrating all of their study time into two nights, when ordinarily it would have required a week.

Approximately 9 percent of students in a New England liberal arts college reported in 2006 taking stimulants for nonmedical purposes, essentially as a cognitive enhancement. In a surprising (and controversial) survey published in 2008 in *Nature*, one of the world's leading scientific journals, 62 percent of respondents said that they took Ritalin to enhance their mental performance. Fourteen hundred presumably healthy people in sixty different countries participated in the survey.

The report has sparked a number of interesting ethical questions. Would we need, for example, an asterisk next to someone's future Nobel or Pulitzer Prize if it was determined that cognitive performance-enhancing drugs were used? Such a move has been considered for sports records achieved by athletes who were taking anabolic steroids and other performance-enhancing drugs when they set these records (see Chapter 12). Why not in the case of cognitive performance-enhancing drugs? Conversely, would a disclaimer (perhaps a negative urinalysis) be required on a professor's tenure candidacy file to indicate that the record of productivity was achieved without the aid of cognitive performance-enhancing drugs?

This particular pattern of drug-taking behavior has not received much notice from law enforcement agencies or the FDA as of yet. As Richard Restak of the American Neuropsychiatric Association has put it, these drugs users are "an entirely different population of people—from the unmotivated to the supermotivated . . . [They] may be at the top of the class, instead of the ones hanging around the corners."

Sources: Carroll, Bronwen C., McLaughlin, Thomas J., and Blake, Diane R. (2006). Patterns and knowledge of nonmedical use of stimulants among college students. *Archives of Pediatric and Adolescent Medicine, 160,* 481–485. Students tapping pills for academic boost (2006, June 20). *Newsday,* p. B13, quotation. Greely, Henry; Sahakian, Barbara; Harris, John; Kessler, Ronald C.; Gazzaniga, Michael; et al. (2008). Toward responsible use of cognitive-enhancing drugs by the healthy. *Nature, 456* 702–705. Harris, John, and Quigley, Mulreann (2008). Commentary on "Professor's little helper": Humans have always tried to improve their condition. *Nature, 451,* 521. Stix, Gary (2009, October). Turbocharging the brain. *Scientific American,* 46–55.

Summary

The Social History of Cocaine

- Cocaine, one of the two major psychoactive stimulants, is derived from coca leaves grown in the mountainous regions of South America. Coca chewing is still prevalent among certain groups of South American Indians.

- During the last half of the nineteenth century, several patent medicines and beverages were sold that contained cocaine, including the original (pre-1903) formulation for Coca-Cola.

- Sigmund Freud was an early enthusiast of cocaine as an important medicinal drug, promoting cocaine as a cure for morphine dependence and depression. Soon afterward, Freud realized the strong dependence that cocaine can bring about.

Acute Effects of Cocaine

- Cocaine produces a powerful burst of energy and sense of well-being. In general, cocaine causes an elevation in the sympathetic autonomic nervous system.

Chronic Effects of Cocaine

- Long-term cocaine use can produce hallucinations and deep depression, as well as physical deterioration of the nasal membranes if cocaine is administered intranasally.

Medical Uses of Cocaine

- The only accepted medical application for cocaine is its use as a local anesthetic.

How Cocaine Works in the Brain

- Within the CNS, cocaine blocks the reuptake of dopamine and norepinephrine. As a result, the activity level of these two neurotransmitters in the brain is enhanced.

Present-Day Cocaine Abuse

- Compared with the permissive attitude toward cocaine use seen during the 1970s and early 1980s, attitudes toward cocaine use since the second half of the 1980s have changed dramatically.

- The emergence in the mid-1980s of relatively inexpensive, smokable crack cocaine expanded the cocaine-abuse problem to new segments of the U.S. population and made cocaine abuse one of the major social issues of our time.

Treatment Programs for Cocaine Abuse

- Cocaine abusers can receive treatment through inpatient programs, outpatient programs, or a combination of the two. Relapse is a continual concern for recovering cocaine abusers.

Amphetamines

- Amphetamines, the second of the two major psychoactive stimulants, have their origin in a Chinese medicinal herb, used for thousands of years as a bronchial dilator; its active ingredient, ephedrine, was isolated in 1887.

- The drug amphetamine (brand name: Benzedrine) was developed in 1927 as a synthetic form of ephedrine. By the 1930s, various forms of amphetamines, specifically d-amphetamine and methamphetamine, became available around the world.

Acute and Chronic Effects of Amphetamines

- Amphetamine is effective as a general arousing agent, as an antidepressant, and as an appetite suppressant, in addition to its ability to keep people awake for long periods of time.

- The acute effects of amphetamines resemble those of cocaine, but amphetamines (when taken in large doses) have the particular feature of producing symptoms of paranoia, delusions, hallucinations, and violent behaviors, referred to as amphetamine psychosis. The bizarre behaviors of the "speed freak" illustrate the dangers of chronic amphetamine abuse.

Present-Day Patterns of Methamphetamine Abuse and Treatment

- With the emphasis on cocaine abuse during the 1980s, amphetamine abuse was less prominent in the public mind. Recently, however, there has been a resurgence of amphetamine-abuse cases involving methamphetamine, particularly in nonurban regions of the United States.

- Treatment for methamphetamine abuse generally follows along the same lines as treatment for cocaine abuse.

Medical Uses for Amphetamines and Similar Stimulant Drugs

- Amphetamine-like stimulant drugs have been developed for approved medical purposes.

- Methylphenidate (brand name: Ritalin), atomoxetine (brand name: Strattera), and dextroamphetamine (brand name: Adderall) are three examples of drugs prescribed for children diagnosed with attention deficit/hyperactivity disorder (ADHD). Recently, there has been growing concern about the nonmedical use of these medications, either for recreational purposes or to stay alert for longer periods of time.

- Other medical applications for amphetamine-like drugs include their use as a treatment for narcolepsy and as a means for the temporary relief of nasal congestion.

Key Terms

amphetamine, p. 179
amphetamine psychosis, p. 181
attention deficit/hyperactivity disorder (ADHD), p. 186

cocaine, p. 167
cocaine hydrochloride, p. 173
cocaine psychosis, p. 172
crack cocaine or crack, p. 174

d-amphetamine, p. 180
formication, p. 170
free-base cocaine, p. 174

ice, p. 182
kindling effect, p. 172
methamphetamine, p. 180

1. Rosencan, Jeffrey S., and Spitz, Henry I. (1987). Cocaine reconceptualized: Historical overview. In Henry I. Spitz and Jeffrey S. Rosencan (Eds.), *Cocaine abuse: New directions in treatment and research*. New York: Brunner/Mazel, p. 5.

2. Inciardi, James A. (2002). *The war on drugs III*. Boston: Allyn and Bacon, p. 129. Inglis, Brian (1975). *The forbidden game: A social history of drugs*. New York: Scribner's, pp. 49–50. Montoya, Ivan D., and Chilcoat, Howard D. (1996). Epidemiology of coca derivatives use in the Andean region: A tale of five countries. *Substance Use and Misuse, 31*, 1227–1240.

3. Jaffe, Jerome (1985). Drug addiction and drug abuse. In Louis S. Goodman and Alfred Gilman (Eds.), *The pharmacological basis of therapeutics* (7th ed.). New York: Macmillan, p. 552.

4. Nahas, Gabriel G. (1989). *Cocaine: The great white plague*. Middlebury, VT: Paul S. Eriksson, pp. 154–162.

5. Kusinitz, Marc (1988). *Drug use around the world*. New York: Chelsea House Publishers, pp. 91–95.

6. Karch, Steven B. (1996). *The pathology of drug abuse* (2nd ed.). Boca Raton, FL: CRC Press, pp. 2–3. Nuckols, Caldwell C. (1989). *Cocaine: From dependency to recovery* (2nd ed.). Blue Ridge Summit, PA: Tab Books, p. x.

7. Brecher, Edward M., and the editors of *Consumer Reports* (1972). *Licit and illicit drugs*. Boston: Little, Brown, p. 270. Weiss, Roger D., and Mirin, Steven M. (1987). *Cocaine*. Washington, DC: American Psychiatric Press, p. 6.

8. McKim, William A. (2007). *Drugs and behavior* (6th ed.). Upper Saddle River, NJ: Prentice Hall, p. 243.

9. Erickson, Patricia G.; Adlaf, Edward M.; Murray, Glenn F.; and Smart, Reginald G. (1987). *The steel drug: Cocaine in perspective*. Lexington, MA: D. C. Heath, p. 9.

10. Musto, David (1973). *The American disease: Origins of narcotic control*. New Haven, CT: Yale University Press.

11. Jones, Ernest (1953). *The life and work of Sigmund Freud*. Vol. 1. New York: Basic Books, p. 81.

12. Ibid., p. 84.

13. Brecher, *Licit and illicit drugs*, pp. 272–280.

14. Aronson, T. A., and Craig, T. J. (1986). Cocaine precipitation of panic disorder. *American Journal of Psychiatry, 143*, 643–645. National Institute on Drug Abuse (2010, March). *NIDA InfoFacts: Cocaine*. Rockville, MD: National Institute on Drug Abuse.

15. Marsuk, Peter M.; Tardiff, Kenneth; Leon, Andrew C.; Stajic, Marina; Morgan, Edward B.; and Mann, J. John (1992). Prevalence of cocaine use among residents of New York City who commited suicide during a one-year period. *American Journal of Psychiatry, 149*, 371–375.

16. Office of Substance Abuse Prevention (1989). *What you can do about drug use in America* (DHHS publication No. ADM 88–1572). Rockville, MD: National Clearinghouse for Alcohol and Drug Information.

17. Philips, J. L., and Wynne, R. D. (1974). *A cocaine bibliography—nonannotated*. Rockville MD: National Institute on Drug Abuse, 1974. Cited in Ernest L. Abel. (1985). *Psychoactive drugs and sex*. New York: Plenum Press, p. 100.

18. Kaufman, Marc J.; Levin, Jonathan M.; Ross, Marjorie H.; Lange, Nicholas; Rose, Stephanie L.; Kukes, Thellea J.; Mendelson, Jack H.; Lukas, Scott E.; Cohen, Bruce M.; and Renshaw, Perry F. (1998). Cocaine-induced cerebral vasoconstriction detected in humans with magnetic resonance angiography. *Journal of the American Medical Association, 279*, 376–380.

19. Experiment in Memphis suggests many drive after using drugs (1994, August 28). *New York Times*, p. 30.

20. Courtesy of the American Academy of Otolaryngology-Head and Neck Surgery, March 1998.

21. Whitten, Lori (2009, April). Low dopamine receptor availability may promote cocaine addiction. *NIDA Notes, 22 (3)*, 15, 18. Robinson, Terry E., and Berridge, Kent C. (2000). The psychology and neurobiology of addiction: An incentive-sensitization view. *Addiction, 95* (supplement), S91–S117. Volkow, Nora D.; Wang, Gene-Jack; Fowler, Joanna S.; Logan, Jean; Gatley, Samuel J.; Hitzemann, Richard; Chen, A. D.; and Pappas, Naomi. (1997). Decrease in striatal dopaminergic responsiveness in detoxified cocaine-dependent subjects. *Nature, 386*, 830–833.

22. Robinson, Terry E. (1993). Persistent sensitizing effects of drugs on brain dopamine systems and behavior: Implications for addiction and relapse. In Stanley G. Korenman and Jack D. Barchas (Eds.), *The biological basis of substance abuse*. New York: Oxford University Press, pp. 373–402. Weiss and Mirin, *Cocaine*, pp. 48–49.

23. Kaplan, Harold I., Freedman, Arnold M., and Sadock, Benjamin J. (1980). *Comprehensive textbook of psychiatry*. Vol. 3. Baltimore, MD: Williams and Wilkins, p. 1621.

24. Flynn, John C. (1991). *Cocaine: An in-depth look at the facts, science, history, and future of the world's most addictive drug*. New York: Birch Lane/Carol Publishing, pp. 38–46.

25. Ibid., p. 44.

26. Humphries, Drew (1998). Crack mothers at 6: Prime-time news, crack/cocaine, and women. *Violence against Women, 4*, 45–61. Massing, Michael (1998). *The fix*. New York: Simon and Schuster, p. 41. Singer, Lynn T.; Minnes, Sonia; Short, Elizabeth; Arendt, Robert; Farkas, Kathleen; Lewis, Barbara; Klein, Nancy; Russ, Sandra; Min, Meeyoung O.; and Kirchner, H. Lester (2004). Cognitive outcomes of preschool children with prenatal cocaine exposure. *Journal of the American Medical Association, 291*, 2448–2456.

27. Egan, Timothy (1999, September 19). A drug ran its course, then hid with its users. *New York Times,* pp. 1, 46. Furst, R. Terry; Johnson, Bruce D.; Dunlap, Eloise; and Curtis, Richard (1999). The stigmatized image of the "crack head": A sociocultural exploration of a barrier to cocaine smoking among a cohort of youth in New York City. *Deviant Behavior, 20,* 153–181.

28. Substance Abuse and Mental Health Services Administration (2010). *Results from the 2009 National Survey on Drug Use and Health: Detailed tables.* Rockville, MD: Office of Applied Studies, Substance Abuse and Mental Health Services Administration, Table 1.1A.

29. Barrionuevo, Alexei (2008, February 23). Cheap cocaine floods a slum in Argentina, devouring lives. *New York Times,* pp. A1, A6. Hearn, Kathy (2006, April 5). Abuse of the highly addictive cocaine by-product "paco" is causing officials to revamp drug laws. *Christian Science Monitor,* p. 4. Ryzik, Melena (2007, June 10). Cocaine: Hidden in plain sight. *New York Times,* Section 9, ppp. 1, 9. Quotation on pp. 1 and 9. Substance Abuse and Mental Health Services Administration (2009). *Drug Abuse Warning Network,* 2008. *Selected tables of national estimates of drug-related emergency department visits.* Rockville, MD: Office of Applied Studies, Substance Abuse and Mental Health Services Administration, ED visits by drug.

30. Gold, Mark S. (1990). *800–COCAINE.* New York: Bantam Books.

31. Nuckols, *Cocaine,* pp. 144–146. Lee, Felicia R. (1994, September 10). A drug dealer's rapid rise and ugly fall. *New York Times,* pp. 1, 22.

32. Nuckols, *Cocaine,* p. 42.

33. Ibid., pp. 71–72.

34. Weiss and Mirin, *Cocaine,* p. 125.

35. Fox, C. Lynn, and Forbing, Shirley E. (1992). *Creating drug-free schools and communities: A comprehensive approach.* New York: HarperCollins, p. 165.

36. Shine, Barbara (2000, March). Some cocaine abusers fare better with cognitive-behavioral therapy, others with 12-step programs. *NIDA Notes, 15* (1), 9–11.

37. Brodie, Jonathan D.; Figueroa, Emilia; Laska, Eugene M., and Dewey, Stephen L. (2005). Safety and efficacy of gamma-vinyl GABA (GVG) for the treatment of methamphetamine and/or cocaine addiction. *Synapse, 55,* 122–125. Schiffer, Wynne K., Marsteller, Douglas, and Dewey, Stephen L. (2003). Sub-chronic low dose gamma-vinyl GABA (vigabatrin) inhibits cocaine-induced increases in nucleus accumbens dopamine. *Psychopharmacology, 168,* 339–343. Information from ClinicalTrials.gov, a service of the U.S. National Institutes of Health, June 2009.

38. Barnes, Deborah M. (1988). Breaking the cycle of addiction. *Science, 241,* p. 1029. Whitten, Lori (2005, August). Cocaine-related environmental cues elicit physiological stress responses. *NIDA Notes, 20* (1), pp. 1, 6–7.

39. McKim, William A. (2000). *Drugs and behavior* (4th ed.). Upper Saddle River, NJ: Prentice Hall, p. 205.

40. Brecher, *Licit and illicit drugs,* pp. 282–283.

41. Greaves, George B. (1980). Psychosocial aspects of amphetamine and related substance abuse. In John Caldwell (Ed.), *Amphetamines and related stimulants: Chemical, biological, clinical, and sociological aspects.* Boca Raton, FL: CRC Press, pp. 175–192. Peluso, Emanuel, and Peluso, Lucy S. (1988). *Women and drugs.* Minneapolis: CompCare Publishing.

42. Substance Abuse and Mental Health Services Administration (2009). *Drug Abuse Warning Network,* 2008, ED visits by drug.

43. Goode, Erich (2005). *Drugs in American society* (6th ed.). New York: McGraw-Hill College, p. 276.

44. Bai, Matt (1997, March 31). White storm warning: In Fargo and the prairie states, speed kills. *Newsweek,* pp. 66–67. Quotation by Mark A. R. Kleiman, p. 67.

45. McKim (2007), *Drugs and behavior,* p. 249.

46. Ernst, Thomas; Chang, Linda; Leonido-Yee, Maria; and Speck, Oliver (2000). Evidence for long-term neurotoxicity associated with methamphetamine abuse: A 1H MRS study. *Neurology, 54,* 1344–1349. London, E. D.; Simon, S. L.; Berman, S. M.; Mandelhern, M. A. et al. (2004). Mood disturbances and regional cerebral metabolic abnormalities in recently abstinent methamphetamine abusers. *Archives of General Psychiatry, 61,* 73–84. Sheff, David (2008). *Beautiful boy: A father's journey through his son's addiction.* New York: Houghton Mifflin. Sheff, Nic (2008), pp. 113–115. *Tweak: Growing up with methamphetamine.* New York: Ginee See Books/Atheneum Books for Young Readers.

47. Young, Stanley (1989, July). Zing! Speed: The choice of a new generation. *Spin magazine,* pp. 83, 124–125. Reprinted in Erich Goode (Ed.) (1992), *Drugs, society, and behavior 92/93.* Guilford, CT: Dushkin Publishing, p. 116.

48. Johnson, Dirk (2004, January 4). Across rural America, drug casts a grim shadow. New York Times, pp. A1, A19. Quotation on p. A19.

49. Butterfield, Fox (2004, January 4). Across rural America, drug casts a grim shadow. *New York Times,* p. 10. Harris, Gardiner (2005, December 15). Fighting methamphetamine, lawmakers reach accord to curb sales of cold medicines. *New York Times,* p. A33. Jefferson, David J. (2005, August 5). America's most dangerous drug. *Newsweek,* p. 41–48. Johnson, Dirk (2004, March 8). Policing a rural plague: Meth is ravaging the Midwest. *Newsweek,* p. 41. National Association of Counties (2006, January). *The meth epidemic in America.* Washington, DC: National Association of Counties. Zernicke, Kate (2006, February 26). With scenes of blood and pain, ads battle methamphetamine in Montana. *New York Times,* p. 18. National Drug Intelligence Center (2008, December). *National Methamphetamine Threat Assessment 2009.* Washington, DC: National Drug Intelligence Center, U.S. Department of Justice, p. 5.

50. Jacobs, Andrew J. (2004, January 12). The beast in the bathhouse: Crystal meth use by gay men threatens to

reignite an epidemic. *New York Times*, pp. B1, B5. Shernoff, Michael (2005, July-August). Crystal's sexual persuasion. *The Gay & Lesbian Review*, pp. 24–26.

51. Zickler, Patrick (2001). Methamphetamine, cocaine abusers have different patterns of drug use, suffer different cognitive impairments. *NIDA Notes*, 16 (5), 11–12.

52. National Institute of Justice (1999, May). *Meth matters: Report on methamphetamine users in five western cities.* Washington, DC: National Institute of Justice, U.S. Department of Justice. Quotation on p. xii. Substance Abuse and Mental Health Services Administration (2009). Highlights for 2007 Treatment Episode Data Set (TEDS). Rockville, MD: Substance Abuse and Mental Health Administration, Table 1b.

53. Findling, Robert L. (2008). Evolution of the treatment of attention-deficit/hyperactivity disorder in children. *Clinical Therapeutics*, 30, 942–957. Julien, Robert M. (2001). *A primer of drug action* (9th ed.). New York: Worth, pp. 207–213.

54. Julien, *A primer of drug action*, p. 208. Wilens, Timothy E. (2003). Drug therapy for adults with attention-deficit hyperactivity disorder. *Drugs*, 63, 2385–2411. Wilens, Timothy E.; Biederman, Joseph; Spencer, Thomas J.; and Prince, Jefferson (1995). Pharmacotherapy of adult attention deficit/hyperactivity disorder: A review. *Journal of Clinical Psychopharmacology*, 15, 270–279. Wilens, Timothy E., and Fusillo, Steven (2007). When ADHD and substance use disorders intersect: Relationship and treatment implications. *Current Psychiatry Reports*, 9, 408–414.

55. Julien, *A primer of drug action*, pp. 211–212.

56. Nissen, Steven E. (2006, April 6). ADHD drugs and cardiovascular risks. *New England Journal of Medicine*, pp. 1445–1448. The MTA Cooperative Group (1999). A 14-month randomized clinical trial of treatment strategies for attention-deficit/hyperactivity disorder. *Archives of General Psychiatry*, 56, 1073–1086. Upadhyaya, Himanshu P. (2008). Substance use disorders in children and adolescents with attention-deficit/hyperactivity disorder: Implications for treatment and the role of the primary care physician. *Journal of Clinical* Psychiatry, 10, 211–221. Wilens, Timothy E.; Faraone, Stephen V.; Biederman, Joseph; and Gunawardene, Samantha (2003). Does stimulant therapy of attention deficit/hyperactivity

disorder beget later substance abuse? A meta-analytic review of the literature. *Pediatrics, 111*, 179–185.

57. Julien, *A primer of drug action*, p. 211. Volkow, Nora D.; Wang, Gene.-Jack; Fowler, Joanna S.; Logan, Jean; Gerasimov, Madina; Maynard, Laurence; Ding, Yu-Shin; Gatley, Samuel J.; Gifford, Andrew; and Franceschi, Dinko (2001). Therapeutic doses of oral methylphenidate significantly increase extracellular dopamine in the human being. *Journal of Neuroscience, 21* (121RC), 1–5. Volkow, Nora D.; Wang, Gene-Jack; Kollins, Scott H.; Wigal, Tim L.; Newcorn, Jeffrey H.; et al. (2009). Evaluating dopamine reward pathway in ADHD: Clinical implications. *Journal of the American Medical Association*, 302, 1084–1091.

58. Arria, Amelia M., Caldeira, Kimberly M., O'Grady, Kevin E.; Vincent, Kathryn B.; et al. (2008). Nonmedical use of prescription stimulants among college students: Associations with attention-deficit-hyperactivity disorder and polydrug use. *Pharmacotherapy*, 28, 156–169. Marks, Alexandria (2000, October 31). Schoolyard hustler's new drug: Ritalin. *Christian Science Monitor*, p. 1. Substance Abuse and Mental Health Services Administration (2009, April 7). Nonmedical use of Adderall among full-time college students. *The NSDUH Report*, pp. 1–4. Thomas, Karen (2000, November 27). Stealing, dealing and Ritalin: Adults and students are involved in abuse of drug. *USA Today*, p. D1. Wilens, Timothy E.; Adler, Lenard A.; Adams, Jill; Sgambati, Stephanie; Rotrosen, John; et al. (2008). Misuse and diversion of stimulants prescribed for ADHD: A systematic review of the literature. *Journal of the American Academy of Child and Adolescent Psychiatry*, 47, 21–31.

59. Green, P. M. and Stillman, M. J. (1998). Narcolepsy. Signs, symptoms, differential diagnosis, and management. *Archives of Family Medicine*, 7, 472–478. Johnston, Lloyd D.; O'Malley, Patrick M.; Bachman, Jerald G.; and Schulenberg, John E. (2009, December 14). Teen marijuana use tilts up, while some drugs decline in use. University of Michigan News Service, Ann Arbor, Table 1. Tuller, David (2002, January 8). A quiet revolution for those prone to nodding off. *New York Times*, p. F7.

60. Julien, Robert M. (1998). *A primer of drug action* (8th ed.). New York: Freeman, pp. 141–143.

chapter 9

LSD and Other Hallucinogens

I was forced to interrupt my work in the laboratory in the middle of the afternoon and proceed home, being affected by a remarkable restlessness combined with a slight dizziness. At home I lay down and sank into a not unpleasant intoxicated-like condition, characterized by an extremely stimulated imagination. In a dreamlike state with eyes closed . . . I perceived an uninterrupted stream of fantastic pictures, extraordinary shapes with intense, kaleidoscopic play of colors.

—Albert Hofmann, reflecting on his
first encounter with LSD
LSD: My Problem Child *(1980)*

After you have completed this chapter, you should have an understanding of

- The classification of hallucinogenic drugs
- The history of LSD
- Facts and fictions about LSD effects
- Prominent hallucinogens other than LSD
- The special dangers of MDMA (Ecstasy), phencyclidine (PCP), and ketamine
- Current issues concerning *Salvia divinorum* (Salvia) abuse

On an April afternoon in 1943, Albert Hofmann, a research chemist at Sandoz Pharmaceuticals in Basel, Switzerland, went home early from work, unaware that his fingertips had made contact with an extremely minute trace of a new synthetic chemical he had been testing that day. The chemical was **lysergic acid diethylamide (LSD),** and as the opening passage indicates, Hofmann unknowingly experienced history's first "acid trip." Three days later, having pieced together the origin of his strange experience, he decided to try a more deliberate experiment. He chose a dose of 0.25 mg, a concentration that could not, so he thought, possibly be effective. His plan was to start with this dose and gradually increase it to see what would happen.

The dose Hofmann had considered inadequate was actually about five times greater than an average dose for LSD. As he later recalled his experience,

> My condition began to assume threatening forms. Everything in my field of vision wavered and was distorted as if seen in a curved mirror. I also had the sensation of being unable to move from the spot.[1]

A little while later, his experience worsened:

> The dizziness and sensation of fainting became so strong at times that I could no longer hold myself erect, and had to lie down on a sofa. My surroundings had now transformed themselves in more terrifying ways. Everything in the room spun around, and the familiar objects and pieces of furniture assumed grotesque, threatening forms . . . I was seized by the dreadful fear of going insane. I was taken to another place, another time.[2]

His experience then became pleasant:

> Kaleidoscopic, fantastic images surged in on me, alternating, variegated, opening and then closing themselves in circles and spirals . . . It was particularly remarkable how every acoustic perception, such as the sound of a door handle or a passing automobile, became transformed into optical perceptions. Every sound generated a vividly changing image, with its own consistent form and color.[3]

Hofmann's vivid remembrances are presented here at length because they succinctly convey some of the

major facets of a hallucinogenic drug experience: the distortions of visual images and body sense, the frightening reaction that often occurs when everyday reality is so dramatically changed, and the strange intermingling of visual and auditory sensations. These effects will be considered later in more detail as this chapter explores the bizarre world of hallucinogenic drugs.

Like many of the drugs that have been examined in the preceding chapters, hallucinogenic drugs such as LSD and several others have a story that belongs both in our contemporary culture and in the distant past. Hofmann worked in the modern facilities of an international pharmaceutical company, but the basic material on his laboratory bench was a fungus that has been around for millions of years. It has been estimated that as many as six thousand plant species around the world have some psychoactive properties.[4] This chapter will focus on a collection of special chemicals called *hallucinogenic drugs* or simply **hallucinogens,** often pharmacologically dissimilar to one another but with the common ability to distort perceptions and alter the user's sense of reality.

A Matter of Definition

Definitions are frequently reflections of one's attitude toward the thing that is being defined, and the terminology used to describe hallucinogens is no exception. For those viewing these drugs with a "positive spin," particularly for those who took LSD in the 1960s, hallucinogens have been described as *psychedelic,* meaning "mind-expanding" or "making the mind manifest." In cases where a spiritual experience has been reported, such as with the ingestion of *ayahuasca,* hallucinogens have been *entheogenic,* meaning "generating the divine within." On the other hand, for others viewing these drugs with more alarm than acceptance, the popular descriptive adjectives have been *psychotomimetic,* meaning "having the appearance of a psychosis," *psychodysleptic,* meaning "mind-disrupting," or even worse, *psycholytic,* meaning "mind-dissolving." You can see that the description one chooses to use conveys a strong attitude, pro or con, with regard to these psychoactive substances.

As a result of all this emotional baggage, describing these drugs as hallucinogenic, meaning "hallucination-producing," is probably the most even-handed way of defining their effects; that is the way they will be referred to in this chapter. Some problems, however, still need to be considered. Technically, a hallucination is the reported perception of something that does not physically exist. For example, a schizophrenic patient might hear voices that no one else hears, and therefore we must conclude (at least the nonschizophrenic world must conclude) that such voices are not real. In the case of hallucinogens, the effect is more complicated because we are dealing with a perceived alteration in the existing physical environment. Some researchers have suggested using the term *illusionogenic*, as a more accurate way of describing drugs that produce these kinds of experiences.

We also should be aware of another qualification when we use the term "hallucinogen." Many drugs that produce distinctive effects when taken at low to moderate dose levels turn out to produce hallucinations when either the dose levels are extremely high or drug use is extended over a period of time. Examples of this possibility appeared in Chapter 8 with cocaine and amphetamines and will appear in Chapter 11 with inhalants. Here the category of hallucinogens will be limited to only those drugs that produce marked changes in

perceived reality at relatively low dosages and in acute circumstances only.

Classifying Hallucinogens

It is relatively easy to define what hallucinogens are by virtue of their effects on the users, but classifying them can be complicated. In general, most hallucinogens can be classified in terms of the particular neurotransmitter in the brain (see Chapter 4) that bears a close resemblance to the molecular features of the drug. Basically, we are speaking of three possible neurotransmitters: serotonin, norepinephrine, and acetylcholine. A relatively small remainder of hallucinogens, however, bears no resemblance to any neurotransmitter at all.

Table 9.1 shows the overall four-group classification scheme. The first three categories are (1) hallucinogens

TABLE 9.1

Major categories of hallucinogens

CATEGORY	SOURCE
Hallucinogens related to serotonin	
lysergic acid diethylamide (LSD)	a synthetic derivative of lysergic acid, which is, in turn, a component of ergot
psilocybin	various species of North American mushrooms
lysergic acid amide or morning glory seeds	morning glory seeds
dimethyltryptamine (DMT)	the bark resin of several varieties of trees and some nuts native to Central and South America
harmine	the bark of a South American vine
Hallucinogens related to norepinephrine	
mescaline	the peyote cactus in Mexico and the U.S. Southwest
2,5-dimethoxy-4-methylamphetamine (DOM or more commonly STP)	a synthetic mescaline-like hallucinogen
MDMA (Ecstasy) and MDA	two synthetic hallucinogens
Hallucinogens related to acetylcholine	
atropine	*Atropa belladonna* plant, known as deadly nightshade, and the datura plant
scopolamine (hyoscine)	roots of the mandrake plant, henbane herb, and the datura plant
hyoscyamine	roots of the mandrake plant, henbane herb, and the datura plant
ibotenic acid	*Amanita muscaria* mushrooms
Miscellaneous hallucinogens	
phencyclidine (PCP)	a synthetic preparation, developed in 1963, referred to as angel dust
ketamine	a PCP-like hallucinogen
Salvia divinorum	a hallucinogenic Mexican herb, in the mint family

Source: Schultes, Richard E., and Hofmann, Albert (1979). *Plants of the gods: Origins of hallucinogenic use.* New York: McGraw-Hill.

FIGURE 9.1

Botanical sources for four hallucinogenic drugs: (a) *Claviceps tulasne* (ergot), (b) *Amanita muscaria* (ibotenic acid), (c) *Atropa belladonna* (atropine), (d) *Datura stramonium*, called jimsonweed (atropine, scopolamine, and hyoscyamine). They are shown the same size, when in actuality they are not.

that are chemically similar to serotonin (LSD, psilocybin, morning glory seeds, DMT, and harmine), (2) hallucinogens that are chemically similar to norepinephrine (mescaline, DOM, MDMA, and MDA), and (3) hallucinogens that are chemically similar to acetylcholine (atropine, scopolamine, hyoscyamine, and ibotenic acid). The fourth category comprises three hallucinogens (PCP, ketamine, and *salvia divinorum*) that are chemically unlike any known neurotransmitter; these drugs will be called miscellaneous hallucinogens. Most of these drugs have natural botanical origins (see four examples in Figure 9.1).

Lysergic Acid Diethylamide (LSD)

The most widely known hallucinogen is LSD, which does not exist in nature but is synthetically derived from ergot, a fungus present in moldy rye and other grains.

---

ergot (ER-got): A fungus infecting rye and other grains.

ergotism: A physical and/or psychological disorder acquired by ingesting ergot-infected grains. One form of ergotism involves gangrene and eventual loss of limbs; the other form is associated with convulsions, disordered thinking, and hallucinations.

One of the compounds in ergot, lysergic acid, is highly toxic, inducing a condition called **ergotism**. Historians have surmised that widespread epidemics of ergotism (called St. Anthony's fire) occurred periodically in Europe during the Middle Ages, when extreme famine forced people to bake bread from infected grain (Drugs . . . in Focus).

In one particularly deadly episode in 944, an outbreak of ergotism claimed as many as forty thousand lives. The features of this calamity were two-fold. One form of ergotism produced a reduction in blood flow toward the extremities, leading to gangrene, burning pain, and the eventual loss of limbs. The other form produced a tingling sensation on the skin, convulsions, disordered thinking, and hallucinations.[5]

Even though the link between this strange affliction and ergot in moldy grain has been known since the 1700s, outbreaks of ergotism have continued to occur in recent times. A major outbreak took place in a small French community in 1951. Hundreds of townspeople went totally mad on a single night:

Many of the most highly regarded citizens leaped from windows or jumped into the Rhône, screaming that their heads were made of copper, their bodies wrapped in snakes, their limbs swollen to gigantic size or shrunken to tiny appendages . . . Animals went berserk. Dogs ripped bark from trees until their teeth fell out.[6]

Drugs... in Focus

Strange Days in Salem: Witchcraft or Hallucinogens?

In the early months of 1692, in Salem, Massachusetts, eight young girls suddenly developed a combination of bizarre symptoms: disordered speech, odd body postures, and convulsive fits. They also began to accuse various townspeople of witchcraft. During the summer, in a series of trials, more than 150 people were convicted of being witches and 20 were executed. Accusations were also made in neighboring villages in the county and in Connecticut. Nothing approaching the magnitude of the Salem witch trials has since occurred in American history.

Over the years, a number of theories have attempted to account for these strange events: a case of adolescent pranks, general hysteria, or some kind of political scapegoating. An interesting and controversial speculation has been advanced that these girls were showing the hallucinogenic and convulsive symptoms of ergotism, acquired from fungus-infected rye grain. Arguments that support this theory include the following:

- Rye grain, once harvested, was stored in barns for months, and the unusually moist weather in the area that year could have promoted the growth of ergot fungus during storage. Of twenty-two Salem households with some afflicted member, sixteen were located close to riverbanks or swamps.

- Children and teenagers would have been particularly vulnerable to ergotism because they ingest more food, and hence more poison, per pound of body weight than do adults.

- The Salem girls as well as the accused "witches" frequently displayed hallucinatory behavior and physical symptoms common to convulsive ergotism.

The role of ergotism in the Salem witch trials of 1692 has been vigorously debated by both historians and pharmacologists. The readings listed below provide more information on this intriguing possibility.

Sources: In favor: Caporael, Linnda R. (1976). Ergotism: The Satan loosed in Salem? *Science, 192,* 21–26. Matossian, Mary K. (1982). Ergot and the Salem witchcraft affair. *American Scientist, 70,* 355–357. Matossian, Mary K. (1989). *Poisons of the past: Molds, epidemics, and history.* New Haven, CT: Yale University Press, pp. 113–122. Against: Spanos, Nicholas P., and Gottlieb, Jack (1976). Ergotism and the Salem village witch trials. *Science, 194,* 1390–1394.

Albert Hofmann's professional interest in lysergic acid centered on its ability to reduce bleeding and increase contractions in smooth muscle, particularly the uterus. He was trying to find a nontoxic chemical version that would be useful in treating problems associated with childbirth. The LSD molecule was number twenty-five in a series of variations that Hofmann studied in 1938, and his creation was officially named LSD-25 for that reason. He thought at the time that the compound had possibilities for medical use but then went on to other pursuits. He returned to these investigations five years later in 1943, the year of his famous LSD experience.

The Beginning of the Psychedelic Era

Sandoz Pharmaceuticals applied for Food and Drug Administration (FDA) approval of LSD in 1953, and as was a common practice at the time, the company sent out samples of LSD to laboratories around the world for scientific study. The idea was that LSD might be helpful in the treatment of schizophrenia by allowing psychiatrists to gain insight into subconscious processes, which this drug supposedly unlocked. One of the researchers intrigued by the potential psychotherapeutic applications of LSD was the psychiatrist Humphrey Osmond of the University of Saskatchewan in Canada, who coined the word "psychedelic" to describe its effects and whose interest also extended to other hallucinogens such as mescaline.

In 1953, Osmond introduced the British writer Aldous Huxley to mescaline, and Huxley later reported his experiences, under Osmond's supervision, in his essay *The Doors of Experience.* Prior to 1960, LSD was being administered to humans under fairly limited circumstances, chiefly as part of research studies in psychiatric hospitals and psychotherapy sessions on the West Coast. As would be revealed later in court testimony in the 1970s, there were also top-secret experiments conducted by the Central Intelligence Agency (CIA), which was interested in LSD for possible application in espionage work. Word of its extraordinary effects, however, gradually spread to regions outside laboratories or hospitals. One of those who picked up on these events was a young clinical psychologist and lecturer at Harvard University named Timothy Leary.

Leary's first hallucinatory experience (in fact his first psychoactive drug experience of any kind, other than alcoholic intoxication) was in Mexico in 1960, when he ate some mushrooms containing the hallucinogen psilocybin. This is his recollection of his response:

During the next five hours, I was whirled through an experience which could be described in many extravagant metaphors but which was above all and without question the deepest religious experience of my life.[7]

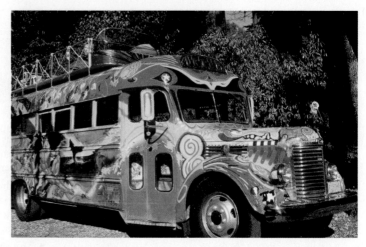

The multicolored images, inspired by the LSD experience, epitomized the psychedelic era of the 1960s.

Back at Harvard, his revelations sparked the interest of a colleague, Richard Alpert (later to be known as Baba Ram Dass). The two men were soon holding psilocybin sessions with university students and whoever else was interested, on and off campus. At first these studies retained some semblance of scientific control. For example, a physician was on hand, and objective observers of behavior reported the reactions of the subjects. Later, these procedures were altered. Physicians were no longer invited to the sessions, and Leary himself began taking the drug at the same time. His argument was that he could communicate better with the subject during the drug experience, but his participation seriously undermined the scientific nature of the studies.

In 1961, Leary, Alpert, and other associates turned to LSD as the focus of their investigations, in their homes and other locations off the Harvard campus. Though these experiments were technically separate from the university itself, public relations concerns on the part of the Harvard administration were mounting. Leary further aggravated the situation through his increasingly incendiary writings. In a 1962 article published in the *Bulletin of the Atomic Scientists*, he suggested that the Soviets could conceivably dump LSD into the water supply and, to prepare for such an attack, Americans should dump LSD into their own water supply so that citizens would then know what to expect. Needless to say, the U.S. government was not amused.

In 1963, after a Harvard investigation, Leary and Alpert were dismissed from their academic positions, making it the first time in the twentieth century that a Harvard faculty member had been fired. As you can imagine, such events brought enormous media exposure.

Leary was now "Mr. LSD" (see Portrait), and suddenly the public became acquainted with a class of drugs that had been previously unknown to them.[8]

For the rest of the 1960s, LSD became not only a drug but also one of the symbols for the cultural revolt of a generation of youth against the perceived inadequacies of the established, older generation. Leary himself told his followers that they were "the wisest and holiest generation that the human race has ever seen" and advised them to "turn on to the scene, tune in to what's happening; and drop out—of high school, college, grade school . . . and follow me, the hard way."[9] The era has been described in this way:

There were psychedelic churches, ashrams, rock festivals, light shows, posters, comic books and newspapers, psychedelic jargon and slang. Every middle-sized city had its enclaves, and there was a drug culture touring circuit . . . Everyone had his own idea of what was meant by turning on, tuning in, and dropping out— his own set and setting—and the drug culture provided almost as many variations in doctrine, attitude, and way of life, from rational and sedate to lewd and violent, as the rest of society.[10]

To borrow the words of songwriter and singer Bob Dylan, "the times were a-changin'," but not always for the better. LSD became a battleground unto itself. In congressional hearings on LSD use by the nation's youth, scientists, health officials, and law-enforcement experts testified to a growing panic over the drug. Newspaper stories emphasized the dangers with alarmist headlines: "A monster in our midst—a drug called LSD" and "Thrill drug warps mind, kills," among them. Sandoz quietly allowed its LSD patent to lapse in 1966 and did everything it could to distance itself from the controversy. Hofmann himself called LSD his "problem child."

In 1966, LSD was made illegal, later becoming a Schedule I drug, with possession originally set as a misdemeanor and later upgraded to a felony. By the 1970s, LSD had become entrenched as a street drug, and taking LSD had become a component of the already dangerous world of illicit drugs. The story of LSD will be updated in a later section, but first it is important to understand the range of effects that LSD typically produces.

Acute Effects of LSD

LSD is considered one of the most, if not *the* most, powerful psychoactive drugs known. Its potency is so great that effective dose levels have to be expressed in terms of micrograms, one-millionths of a gram, often called *mikes*. The typical street dose ranges from 50 to 150 micrograms, though sellers often claim that their product contains more. The effective dose can be as small as 10 micrograms, with only one-hundredth of a percent being absorbed into the brain. You can appreciate the enormous potency of LSD by comparing these figures to the fact that a single regular-strength aspirin tablet contains 325,000 micrograms of aspirin.[11]

Taken orally, LSD is rapidly absorbed into the bloodstream and the brain, and its effects begin to be felt within thirty to sixty minutes. Once its concentration has peaked (in about ninety minutes), the elimination half-life, or the time it takes for 50 percent of the drug to diminish in the bloodstream (see Chapter 1), is approximately three hours. Within five to twelve hours, LSD effects are over.[12]

Surprisingly, given its extreme potency, the toxicity of LSD is relatively low. Generalizing from studies of animals given varying doses of LSD, we can estimate that a lethal dose of LSD for humans would have to be roughly three hundred to six hundred times the effective dose, a fairly comfortable margin of safety. In 2008, the DAWN statistics showed that less than 0.1 percent of all drug-related ED visits were associated with the ingestion of LSD. To this day, there has been only one definitive case in which a death has been attributed solely to an LSD overdose.[13]

Street forms of LSD may contain color additives or adulterants with specific flavors, but the drug itself is odorless, tasteless, and colorless. LSD is sold on the street in single-dose "hits." It is typically swallowed in the form of powder pellets (microdots) or gelatin chips (window-panes) or else licked off small squares of absorbent paper that have been soaked in liquid LSD (blotters). In the past, blotters soaked with LSD have been decorated with pictures of mystical symbols and signs, rocket ships, or representations of Mickey Mouse, Snoopy, Bart Simpson, or other popular cartoon characters.

LSD initially produces an excitation of the sympathetic autonomic activity: increased heart rate, elevated blood pressure, dilated pupils, and a slightly raised body temperature. There is an accompanying feeling of restlessness, euphoria, and a sensation that inner tension has been released. There may be laughing or crying, depending on one's expectations and the setting.[14]

LSD blotters with Bart Simpson images. Notice the perforations allowing for single-dose "window panes."

synesthesia: A subjective sensation in a modality other than the one being stimulated. An example is a visual experience when a sound is heard.

Between thirty minutes and two hours later, a "psychedelic trip" begins, characterized by four distinctive features. The best way to describe these effects is in the words of individuals who have experienced them:[15]

- Images seen with the eyes closed.

  Closing my eyes, I saw millions of color droplets, like rain, like a shower of stars, all different colors.

- An intermingling of senses called **synesthesia**, which usually involves sounds being perceived as hallucinatory visions.

  I clapped my hands and saw sound waves passing before my eyes.

- Perception of a multilevel reality.

  I was sitting on a chair and I could see the molecules. I could see right through things to the molecules.

- Strange and exaggerated configurations of common objects or experiences.

  A towel falling off the edge of my tub looked like a giant lizard crawling down.

  When my girlfriend was peeling an orange for me, it was like she was ripping a small animal apart.

During the third and final phase, approximately three to five hours after first taking LSD, the following features begin to appear:

- Great swings in emotions or feelings of panic.

  It started off beautifully. I looked into a garden . . . and suddenly, it got terrible . . . and I started to cry . . . And then, my attention wandered, and something else was happening, beautiful music was turned on . . . Then suddenly I felt happy.

- A feeling of timelessness.

  Has an hour gone by since I last looked at the clock? Maybe it was a lifetime. Maybe it was no time at all.

- A feeling of ego disintegration, or a separation of one's mind from one's body.

  Boundaries between self and nonself evaporate, giving rise to a serene sense of being at one with the universe. I recall muttering to myself again and again, "All is one, all is one."

Whether these strong reactions result in a "good trip" or a "bad trip" depends heavily on the set of expectations for the drug, the setting or environment in which the LSD is experienced, and the overall psychological health of the individual.

Effects of LSD on the Brain

LSD closely resembles the molecular structure of serotonin. Therefore, it is not surprising that LSD should have effects on receptors in the brain that are sensitive to serotonin (see Chapter 4). As a result of research in the 1980s, it turns out that the critical factor behind LSD's hallucinogenic effects lies in its ability to stimulate a special subtype of serotonin-sensitive receptors called serotonin-2A receptors. In fact, all hallucinogens, even those drugs whose structures do not resemble serotonin, are linked together by a common ability to excite these receptor sites. Drugs that specifically block serotonin-2A receptors, leaving all other subtypes unchanged, will block the behavioral effects of hallucinogens. In addition, the ability of a particular drug to produce hallucinogenic effects is directly proportional to its ability to bind to serotonin-2A receptors.[16]

Patterns of LSD Use

The enormous publicity surrounding Timothy Leary and his followers in the 1960s made LSD a household word. As many as fifty popular articles about LSD were published in major U.S. newspapers and magazines between March 1966 and February 1967 alone. By 1970, however, the media had lost interest, and hardly anything was appearing about LSD. Even so, while media attention was diminishing, the incidence of LSD abuse was steadily rising. In four Gallup Poll surveys conducted between 1967 and 1971, the percentage of college students reported to have taken LSD at least once in their lives rose dramatically from 1 to 18 percent.[17]

From the middle 1970s to the early 1990s, the numbers showed a steady decline. By 1986, the University of Michigan survey indicated that the lifetime incidence of LSD taking among high school seniors was 7 percent, down from 11 percent in 1975. By the end of the 1990s, prevalence rates were once again on the rise, reaching and later exceeding the levels of a quarter-century earlier. Since 1997, however, LSD use has declined substantially. Three percent of high school seniors in 2009 reported taking LSD at some time in their lives. A parallel trend has been observed in college students.

It should be noted that today's LSD users are different from those of a previous generation in a number of ways. Typical LSD users now take the drug less frequently and, because the dosage of street LSD is presently about one-fourth the level common to the 1960s and 1970s, they remain high for a briefer period of time. Their motivation behind using LSD is also not the same. They report using LSD simply to get high, rather than to explore alternative states of consciousness or gain a greater insight into life. For current users, LSD no longer has the symbolic or countercultural significance that it had in an earlier time.[18]

Facts and Fictions about LSD

Given the history of LSD use and the publicity about it, it is all the more important to look carefully at the facts about LSD and to unmask the myths. It is useful to examine six basic questions that are frequently asked about the acute and chronic effects of this drug.

Will LSD Produce Substance Dependence?

There are three major reasons why LSD is not likely to result in drug dependence, despite the fact that the experience at times is quite pleasant.[19] First, LSD and other hallucinogens cause the body to build up a tolerance to their effects faster than any other drug category. As a result, one cannot remain on an LSD-induced high day after day, for an extended period of time. Second, LSD is not the drug for someone seeking an easy way to get high. As one drug expert has put it,

> The LSD experience requires a monumental effort. To go through eight hours of an LSD high—sensory bombardment, psychic turmoil, emotional insecurity, alternations of despair and bliss, one exploding insight upon the heels of another, images hurtling through the mind as fast as the spinning fruit of a slot machine—is draining and exhausting in the extreme.[20]

Third, the LSD experience seems to control the user rather than the other way around. It is virtually impossible to "come down" from LSD at will. Besides, the unpredictability of the LSD experience is an unpopular feature for those who would want a specific and reliable drug effect every time the drug is taken.

Will LSD Produce a Panic Attack or Psychotic Behavior?

One of the most notorious features of LSD is the possibility of a bad trip. Personal accounts abound of sweet, dreamlike states rapidly turning into nightmares. Perhaps the greatest risks are taken when a person is slipped a dose of LSD and begins to experience its effect without knowing that he or she has taken a drug. But panic reactions may also occur even when a person is fully aware of having taken LSD. Although the probability of having a bad trip is difficult to estimate, there are very few regular

Help Line

Emergency Guidelines for a Bad Trip on LSD

- Stay calm with the individual. Do not move around quickly, shout, cry, or become hysterical. Any sense of panic on your part will make an LSD panic worse. Speak in a relaxed, controlled manner.

- Reassure the individual that the situation is temporary and that you will not leave until he or she returns to a normal state. Encourage the individual to breathe deeply and calmly. Advise him or her to view the trip as though watching a movie or TV program.

- Reduce any loud noises or bright lights but do not let the individual be in the dark. Darkness tends to encourage hallucinations in a person under LSD.

- Allow the individual to move around without undue restrictions. He or she can sit, stand, walk, or lie down if this helps the situation. You can divert attention from the panic by encouraging the individual to beat time to music or by dancing.

- If your assistance does not produce a reduction in the panic, seek out medical attention immediately.

Where to go for assistance:

http://drugabuse.gov/infofacts/hallucinogens.html

The National Institute on Drug Abuse (NIDA) sponsors an extensive series of web sites related to drug use and abuse.

Sources: Palfai, Tibor, and Jankiewicz, Henry (1991). *Drugs and human behavior.* Dubuque, IA: W. C. Brown, p. 445. Robbins, Paul R. (1996). *Hallucinogens.* Springfield, NJ: Enslow Publishers, pp. 83–85. Trulson, Michael E. (1985). *LSD: Visions or nightmares.* New York: Chelsea House, p. 101.

LSD abusers who have not experienced a bad trip or had a disturbing experience as part of an LSD trip. The best treatment for adverse effects is the companionship and reassurance of others throughout the period when LSD is active. Help Line includes some specific procedures for dealing with LSD panic episodes.

Despite the possibility of an LSD panic, there is no strong evidence that the panic will lead to a permanent psychiatric breakdown. Long-term psychiatric problems are relatively uncommon; one study conducted in 1960 showed that there was no greater probability of a person's attempting suicide or developing a psychosis after taking LSD than when undergoing ordinary forms of psychotherapy.[21] The incidents that do occur typically involve people who were unaware that they were taking LSD, showed unstable personality characteristics prior to taking LSD, or were experiencing LSD under hostile or threatening circumstances.

The possible link between the character of LSD effects and certain symptoms of schizophrenia also has been examined closely. It is true that on a superficial level, the two behaviors show some similarities, but there are important differences. LSD hallucinations are primarily visual, are best seen in the dark, and, as we noted earlier, are more accurately characterized as illusions or pseudo-hallucinations; schizophrenic hallucinations are primarily auditory, are seen with open eyes, and qualify as true hallucinations. Individuals taking LSD are highly susceptible to suggestion and usually try to communicate the experience to others, whereas the schizophrenic individual is typically resistant to suggestion and withdrawn from his or her surroundings. Therefore, it is unlikely that LSD is mimicking the experience of schizophrenia.

Will LSD Increase Your Creativity?

The unusual visual effects of an LSD experience may lead you to assume that your creativity is enhanced, but the evidence indicates otherwise. Professional artists and musicians creating new works of art or songs while under the influence of LSD typically think that their creations are better than anything they have yet produced, but when the LSD has worn off, they are far less impressed. Controlled studies generally show that individuals under LSD *feel* that they are creative, but objective ratings do not show a significant difference from levels prior to the LSD.[22]

Will LSD Damage Your Chromosomes?

In March 1967, a study published in the prestigious scientific journal *Science* described a marked increase in chromosomal abnormalities in human white blood cells that had been treated with LSD in vitro (that is, the cells were outside the body at the time).[23] Shortly after, three other studies were reported in which chromosomal abnormalities in the white blood cells of LSD abusers were higher than those of people who did not use drugs, whereas three additional studies reported no chromosomal effect at all.

By the end of that year, a second study was published by the people whose report had started the controversy in the first place. They wrote that eighteen LSD abusers had two to four times the number of chromosomal abnormalities in their white blood cells, when compared with fourteen control subjects. Interestingly, the subjects in this study were not exactly model citizens. Every one of them had taken either one or more of amphetamines, barbiturates, cocaine, hallucinogens, opiates, or antipsychotic medication, and some had abused more than one of these substances.

The picture was confused, to say the least. Not only were many of these studies never replicated, but many were methodologically flawed in the first place. Most important, when studies actually looked at the chromosomes of *reproductive cells themselves* for signs of breakage from exposure to LSD, the results were either ambiguous or entirely negative. By 1971, after nearly a hundred studies had been carried out, the conclusion was that LSD did not cause chromosomal damage in human beings at normal doses, and that there was no evidence of a high rate of birth defects in the children of LSD users.[24] Yet, in the highly politicized climate of the late 1960s, the media tended to emphasize the negative findings without subjecting their validity or relevance to any scrutiny. The public image of LSD causing genetic (mutation-generating) damage still persists, despite the lack of scientific evidence. This is not to say, however, that there is no basis for exercising some degree of caution. Women should avoid LSD, as well as other psychoactive and many nonpsychoactive drugs, during pregnancy, especially in the first three months.[25]

Will LSD Have Residual (Flashback) Effects?

One of the most disturbing aspects of taking LSD is the possibility of reexperiencing the effects of the drug long after the drug has worn off, sometimes as long as several years later. These experiences are referred to as *hallucinogen persisting perception disorder*, or simply "flashbacks." The likelihood of LSD flashbacks is not precisely known. Some studies estimate its rate of incidence as only 5 percent, whereas others estimate it as high as 33 percent. It is reasonable to assume that the range of estimates is related to differences in the dosage levels ingested.

Flashback effects sometimes can be frightening and at other times can be quite pleasant; they can occur among LSD novices or "once-only" drug takers as well as among experienced LSD abusers. They can appear without warning, but there is a higher probability that they will occur when the individual is beginning to go to sleep or has just entered a dark environment.[26]

Because they are not common to any other psychoactive drug, the reason why LSD flashbacks might occur is not well understood. It is possible that LSD has a peculiar ability to produce some biochemical changes that remain dormant for a period of time and then suddenly reappear or that some remnant of the drug has the ability to persist over extended periods of time. It is also possible that individuals who ingest LSD are highly suggestible to social reminders about the original exposure to LSD.

Whether LSD produces major long-term deficits in the behavior of the user remains largely unknown. Memory problems and visuospatial impairments have been reported in some studies but not confirmed in others. Unfortunately, several problems persist in research studies examining long-term effects of LSD. Often, they have included either individuals with a history of psychiatric disorders prior to LSD ingestion or regular users of other illicit drugs and alcohol. As a result, it has been impossible in these studies to tease apart the long-term effects of LSD alone from other factors.[27]

Will LSD Increase Criminal or Violent Behavior?

As noted in Chapter 5, it is very difficult to establish a clear cause-and-effect relationship between a drug and criminal or violent behavior. In the highly charged era of the 1960s, stories related to this question were publicized and conclusions were drawn without any careful examination of the actual facts. Take, for example, the 1964 case of a woman undergoing LSD therapy treatment who murdered her lover three days after her last LSD session.[28] The details of the case, overlooked by most subsequent media reports, reveal that the woman had been physically abused by the man, he had caused her to have an abortion, and the woman already had a serious mental disorder before going into treatment. The fact that the homicide took place well after the LSD had left her body indicates that the murder was not pharmacologically based (see Chapter 5). Other cases in which violent behavior appeared to be associated with an LSD experience turned out to be associated with the use of other hallucinogenic drugs instead.

It is possible, however, that an individual can "freak out" on LSD. The effects of a euphoriant drug such as LSD can lead to a feeling of invulnerability. This feeling, in turn, can lead to dangerous and possibly life-threatening behavior. We cannot reliably estimate the likelihood of these effects or pinpoint the circumstances under which they might occur; we should recognize that psychological reactions to LSD are inherently unpredictable, and caution is advised.

Psilocybin and Other Hallucinogens Related to Serotonin

The source of the drug **psilocybin** is a family of mushrooms native to southern Mexico and Central America. Spanish chroniclers in the sixteenth century wrote of "sacred mushrooms" revered by the Aztecs as *teonanacatl* (roughly translated as "God's flesh") and capable of providing extraordinary visions when eaten. Their psychoactive properties had been known for a long time, judging from stone-carved representations of these mushrooms discovered in El Salvador and dating back to as early as 500 B.C. Today, shamans in remote villages in Mexico and Central America (see Chapter 3) continue the use of psilocybin mushrooms, among other hallucinogenic plants, to provide healing on both physical and spiritual levels.[29]

In 1955, a group of Western observers documented the hallucinogenic effects of the *Psilocybe mexicana* in a native community living in a remote mountainous region of southern Mexico. Three years later, samples worked their way to Switzerland, where Albert Hofmann, already known for his work on LSD, identified the active ingredient and named it psilocybin. As was his habit, Hofmann sampled some of the mushrooms himself and wrote later of his reactions:

> *Thirty minutes after my taking the mushrooms, the exterior world began to undergo a Mexican*

Psilocybe mexicana mushrooms, the source of psilocybin.

psilocybin (SIL-oh-SIGH-bin): A serotonin-related hallucinogenic drug originating from a species of mushrooms.

psilocin (SIL-oh-sin): A brain chemical related to serotonin, resulting from the ingestion of psilocybin.

lysergic acid amide (LAA) (lye-SER-jik ASS-id A-mide): A hallucinogenic drug found in morning glory seeds, producing effects similar to those of LSD.

character . . . I saw only Mexican motifs and colors. When the doctor supervising the experiment bent over me to check my blood pressure, he was transformed into an Aztec priest.[30]

An interesting question is whether the Aztec character of these hallucinogenic effects was simply a result of suggestion, given the social context in which drug-taking behavior was occurring, or, alternatively, Aztec designs may have been inspired over the centuries by the effects of psilocybin.

Once ingested, psilocybin loses a portion of its molecule, making it more fat-soluble and more easily absorbed into the brain. This new version, called **psilocin**, is the actual agent that works on the brain. Because LSD and psilocin are chemically similar, the biochemical effects are also similar. Cross-tolerance will occur (see Chapter 1). If you develop a tolerance to LSD, you have become tolerant to psilocybin effects, and vice versa.[31]

Far less potent than LSD, psilocybin is effective at dose levels measured in the more traditional units of milligrams rather than in micrograms. At doses of 4 to 5 mg, psilocybin causes a pleasant, relaxing feeling; at doses of 15 mg and more, hallucinations, time distortions, and changes in body perception appear. A psilocybin trip generally lasts from two to five hours, considerably shorter than an LSD trip.

Individuals who have experienced both kinds of hallucinogens report that, compared to LSD, psilocybin produces effects that are more strongly visual, less emotionally intense, and more euphoric, with fewer panic reactions and less chance of paranoia. On the other hand, experimental studies of volunteers taking high doses of psilocybin have established that the drug produces drastic-enough changes in mood, sensory perception, and thought processes to qualify as a psychotic experience.

Like LSD, psilocybin (often called simply "shrooms") has become relatively easy to obtain as a drug of abuse. In 2009, about 41 percent of high school seniors reported that non-LSD hallucinogens (including "shrooms") were "fairly easy" or "very easy" to get, whereas about 26 percent felt the same way about LSD itself.[32]

Lysergic Acid Amide (LAA)

In addition to their reverence for psilocybin mushrooms, the Aztecs ingested locally grown morning glory seeds, calling them *ololuiqui*, and used their hallucinogenic effects in religious rites and healing. Like many Native American practices, the recreational use of morning glory seeds has survived in remote areas of southern Mexico. In 1961, Albert Hofmann (once again) identified the active ingredient in these seeds as **lysergic acid amide (LAA)**, after having sampled its hallucinogenic properties. As the chemical name suggests, this drug is a close relative to LSD.

The LAA experience, judging from Hofmann's report, is similar to that of LSD, though LAA is only one-tenth to one-thirtieth as potent and the hallucinations tend to be dominated by auditory rather than visual images. Commercial varieties of morning glory seeds are available to the public, but to minimize their abuse, suppliers have taken the precaution of coating them with an additive that causes nausea and vomiting, if they are eaten.[33]

Dimethyltryptamine (DMT)

The drug **dimethyltryptamine (DMT)** is obtained chiefly from the resin of the bark of trees and nuts native to the West Indies as well as to Central and South America, where it is generally inhaled as a snuff. An oral administration does not produce psychoactive effects. The similarity of this drug's effects to those of LSD and its very short duration gave DMT the reputation during the psychedelic years of the 1960s of being "the businessman's LSD." Presumably, someone could take a DMT trip during lunch and be back at the office in time for work in the afternoon.

An inhaled 30 mg dose of DMT produces physiological changes within ten seconds, with hallucinogenic effects peaking around ten to fifteen minutes later. Paranoia, anxiety, and panic also can result at this time, but most symptoms are over in about an hour.[34] A chemical found in *Bufo* toads is similar to DMT (see Drugs . . . in Focus).

dimethyltryptamine (DMT) (dye-METH-il-TRIP-ta-meen): A short-acting hallucinogenic drug.

bufotenine (byoo-FOT-eh-neen): A serotonin-related drug obtained either from a bean plant in Central and South America or from the skin of a particular type of toad.

cyanosis (SIGH-ah-NOH-sis): A tendency for the skin to turn bluish purple. It can be a side effect of the drug bufotenine.

Drugs... in Focus

Bufotenine and the *Bufo* Toad

Bufotenine is a drug with a strange past. Found in a family of beans native to Central and South America, bufotenine is better known as a chemical that can be isolated from the skin and glands of the *Bufo* toad, from which it gets its name. As noted in Chapter 2, *Bufo* toads figured prominently in the magical potions of European witches. Evidence also exists that *Bufo* toads were incorporated into the ceremonial rituals of ancient Aztec and Mayan cultures. Largely as a result of these historical references, it has been widely assumed that bufotenine was the primary contributor to the psychoactive effects of these concoctions and that bufotenine itself is a powerful hallucinogen.

It turns out that these conclusions are wrong. The few studies in which human volunteers were administered bufotenine indicate that the substance induces strong excitatory effects on blood pressure and heart rate but no hallucinatory experiences. Some subjects report distorted images with high dosages of the drug, but this might well occur as oxygen is cut off from parts of the body, particularly the optic nerve carrying visual information to the brain. It is likely that whatever hallucinogenic effects *Bufo* toads may produce are brought on by another chemical also found in these toads that functions similarly to the hallucinogen DMT.

Despite the confusion as to which substance is responsible for its psychoactive properties, *Bufo* toads continue to fascinate the public. Wildly exaggerated and frequently unsubstantiated accounts of "toad licking" and "toad smoking" periodically circulate in the media. Reportedly, a small group calling themselves Amphibians Anonymous was formed in the late 1980s; the group's motto was "Never has it been so easy to just say no."

The bottom line, however, is that the dangers of consuming toad tissue are substantial. Besides the extreme cardiovascular reactions, toxic effects include a skin condition called **cyanosis** (literally, "turning blue"). Actually, the description may be an understatement. Skin color has been observed to be closer to an eggplant purple.

Sources: Horgan, J. (1990, August). Bufo abuse. *Scientific American*, pp. 26–27. Iniardi, James A. (2002). *The war on drugs III.* Boston: Allyn and Bacon, pp. 4–5. Lyttle, Thomas, Goldstein, David, and Gartz Jochen (1996). Bufo toads and bufotenine: Fact and fiction surrounding an alleged psychedelic. *Journal of Psychoactive Drugs, 28,* 267–290.

Harmine

Among native tribes in the western Amazon region of South America, the bark of the *Banisteriopsis* vine yields the powerful drug **harmine**. A drink containing harmine, called *ayahuasca*, is frequently used by local shamans for healing rites. It is chemically similar to serotonin, like LSD and the other hallucinogens examined so far. Its psychological effects, however, are somewhat different. Unlike LSD, harmine makes the individual withdraw into a trance, and the hallucinatory images (often visions of animals and supernatural beings) are experienced within the context of a dreamlike state. Reports among shamans refer to a sense of suspension in space or flying, falling into one's body, or experiencing one's own death.[35]

Hallucinogens Related to Norepinephrine

Several types of hallucinogens have a chemical composition similar to that of norepinephrine. As you may recall from Chapter 8, amphetamines are also chemically similar to norepinephrine. Consequently, some of the norepinephrine-related hallucinogens are capable of producing amphetamine-like stimulant effects. This is the case with MDMA (Ecstasy) but not with mescaline or DOM.

Mescaline

The hallucinogen **mescaline** is derived from the **peyote** plant, a spineless cactus with a small, greenish crown that grows above ground and a long carrot-like root. This cactus is found over a wide area, from the southwestern United States to northern regions of South America, and many communities in these regions have discovered its psychoactive properties. Given the large distances between these groups, it is remarkable that they prepare and ingest mescaline in a highly similar manner. The crowns of the cactus are cut off, sliced in small disks called buttons, dried in the sun, and then consumed. An effective dose of mescaline from peyote is 200 mg, equivalent to about five buttons. Peak response to the drug takes place thirty minutes to two hours after consumption. Mescaline is still used today as part of religious worship among many American Indians in the United States and Canada (Drugs . . . in Focus).

The psychological and physiological effects of mescaline are highly similar to those of LSD, though some have reported that mescaline hallucinations are more sensual, with fewer changes in mood and the sense of self. Nonetheless, double-blind studies comparing the reactions to LSD and mescaline show that subjects cannot distinguish between the two when dose levels are equivalent. Although the reactions may be the same, the mescaline trip comes at a greater price, as far as physiological reactions are concerned. Peyote buttons taste extremely bitter and can cause vomiting, headaches, and, unless the stomach is empty, distressing levels of nausea.[36]

Today, mescaline can be synthesized as well as obtained from the peyote cactus. The mescaline molecule resembles the chemical structure of norepinephrine but stimulates the same S_{2A} receptors as LSD and other hallucinogens that resemble serotonin. As a result, mescaline and LSD share a common brain mechanism.[37]

DOM

A group of synthetic hallucinogens have been developed that share mescaline's resemblance to amphetamine but do not produce the strong stimulant effects of amphetamine. One example of these synthetic drugs, **DOM (short for 2,5-dimethoxy-4-methylamphetamine)**, appeared in the 1960s and 1970s, when it was frequently combined with LSD and carried the street name of STP. To some, the nickname was a reference to the well-known engine oil additive; to others the letters stood for "serenity, tranquility, and peace" or alternatively "super terrific psychedelic." It is roughly eighty times more potent than mescaline, though still far weaker than LSD. At low doses of about 3 to 5 mg, DOM produces euphoria; with higher doses of 10 mg or more, severe hallucinations result, often lasting from sixteen to twenty-five hours. Though similar to LSD in many respects, DOM has the reputation of producing a far greater incidence of panic attacks, psychotic episodes, and other symptoms of a very bad trip. Cases have been reported of STP being added as an adulterant to marijuana.[38]

harmine (HAR-meen): A serotonin-related hallucinogenic drug frequently used by South American shamans in healing rituals.

mescaline (MES-kul-leen): A norepinephrine-related hallucinogenic drug. Its source is the peyote cactus.

peyote (pay-YO-tay): A species of cactus that is the source for the hallucinogenic drug mescaline.

DOM: A synthetic norepinephrine-related hallucinogenic drug, derived from amphetamine. DOM or a combination of DOM and LSD is often referred to by the street name STP.

Drugs... in Focus

Present-Day Peyotism and the Native American Church

Among American Indians within the United States, the ritual use of peyote buttons, called *peyotism*, can be traced to the eighteenth century when the Mescalero Apaches (from whom the word *mescaline* was derived) adopted the custom from Mexican Indians who had been using peyote for more than three thousand years. By the late 1800s, peyotism had become widely popular among tribes from Wisconsin and Minnesota to the West Coast. It was not until the early twentieth century, however, that peyote use became incorporated into an official religious organization, the Native American Church of North America, chartered in 1918.

The beliefs of the Native American Church membership, estimated to include anywhere from 50,000 to 250,000 American Indians in the United States and Canada, combine traditional tribal customs and practices with Christian morality. To them, life is a choice between two roads that meet at a junction. The Profane Road is paved and wide, surrounded by worldly passions and temptations. The Peyote Road is a narrow and winding path, surrounded by natural, unspoiled beauty; it is also a path of sobriety (since alcohol poisons the goodness of the body), hard work, caring for one's family, and brotherly love. Only the Peyote Road leads to salvation. In their weekly ceremonies, lasting from Saturday night until Sunday afternoon, church members swallow small peyote buttons as a sacrament, similar to the ritual of taking Holy Communion, or drink peyote tea. It is considered sacrilegious to take peyote outside the ceremonies in the church.

While peyote remains classified as a Schedule I drug and therefore banned, federal law and the laws of twenty-three U.S. states have exempted the sacramental use of peyote from criminal penalties. The Religious Freedom Restoration Act of 1993 established an exemption from federal and state controlled substance laws when peyote is used for religious purposes in traditional American Indian ceremonies. In 2005, a study found that peyote use among church members does not result in impairments on tests of memory, attention, and other aspects of cognitive functioning.

Today, a handful of people are licensed by state and federal authorities to harvest peyote for religious purposes in south Texas near Laredo. This locale is the only place in the United States where peyote grows in the wild. As one of the harvesters has put it, "This is sacred ground to a lot of American Indian tribes. To some, the land here is very holy because it is the home to the sacred peyote."

Sources: Calabrese, Joseph D. (1997). Spiritual healing and human development in the Native American Church: Toward a cultural psychiatry of peyote. *Psychoanalytic Review, 84,* 237–255. Halpern, John H.; Sherwod, Andrea, R.; Hudson, James I.; Yurgelum-Tod, Deborah; and Pope, Harrison G., Jr. (2005). Psychological and cognitive effects of long-term peyote use among Native Americans. *Biological Psychiatry, 58,* 624–631. Indian religion must say no (1990, October 6). *The Economist,* pp. 25–26. Milloy, Ross E. (2002, May 7). A forbidding landscape that's Eden for peyote. *New York Times,* p. A20. Quotation on p. A20. Morgan, George (1983). Recollections of the peyote road. In Lester Grinspoon and James B. Bakalar (Eds.), *Psychedelic reflections.* New York: Human Sciences Press, pp. 91–99.

The peyote cactus, source of mescaline.

MDMA (Ecstasy)

Another synthetic amphetamine-related hallucinogen, abbreviated **MDMA**, first appeared on the scene in the 1980s. Although subject to abuse as a new designer

MDMA (Ecstasy): A synthetic norepinephrine-related hallucinogenic drug. Once considered useful for psychotherapeutic purposes, this drug is now known to produce significant adverse side effects, including neuronal hyperthermia, dehydration, and neurochemical changes.

drug, it also became known to a number of psychiatrists who used the drug as part of their therapy, believing that MDMA had a special ability to enhance empathy among their patients. In fact, some therapists at the time suggested the name *empathogens* (meaning "generating a state of empathy") to describe MDMA and related drugs. Eventually, after several years of hesitations and reversals, the Drug Enforcement Administration put MDMA permanently on the Schedule I list of controlled substances, indicating that there is no accepted medical application for the drug.[39]

Since the early 1990s, MDMA has become prominent among the new club drugs (see Chapter 1), especially popular at dance clubs and all-night "rave" parties. Widely available under names such as Ecstasy (not to be confused with the stimulant Herbal Ecstasy), E, XTC, X, Essence, Clarity, and Adam, MDMA has the reputation of having the stimulant qualities of amphetamines and the hallucinogenic qualities of mescaline.

The physical health concerns with respect to Ecstasy center on its short-term and long-term toxicity. The principal acute effect is severe hyperthermia (and heatstroke), which can be lethal when Ecstasy is ingested while engaged in the physical exertion of dancing in an already overheated club environment. The dehydration associated with hyperthermia causes an elevation in blood pressure and heart rate and places a strain on kidney functioning. These problems are compounded by the highly risky practice of "Ecstasy stacking," in which multiple Ecstasy tablets are taken at once or Ecstasy is combined with LSD, alcohol, marijuana, or other drugs. Ecstasy use also has been linked to long-term cognitive impairments and emotional difficulties. Heavy and prolonged Ecstasy use can produce confusion, anxiety, sleep problems, reductions in impulse control, and declines in memory and attention. In general, women show greater behavioral effects from chronic Ecstasy use than do men.[40] The Help Line feature summarizes the major areas of MDMA toxicity.

In 2009, according to the University of Michigan survey, about 7 percent of high school seniors and about 2 percent of eighth graders reported having taken Ecstasy at some point in their lives. After a sharp rise in prevalence rates observed between 1998 and 2001 in these

Help Line

MDMA Toxicity: The Other Side of Ecstasy

- **Possible Physical Effects**
  Hyperthermia and heatstroke
  Dehydration and electrolyte depletion
  Irregular heartbeat or increased heart rate
  Kidney and liver failure
  Jaw-clenching and other forms of muscle spasms
  Long-term neurochemical changes
- **Possible Psychological Effects**
  Agitation and confusion
  Depression and anxiety
  Long-term impairments in memory recall

Note: As with other illicit drugs, adulterated versions raise significant concerns. In the case of MDMA, adulterants include dextromethorphan (a common cough suppressant) at approximately thirteen times the dose found in over-the-counter cough medications. At this dosage, dextromethorphan itself functions as a hallucinogen and inhibits sweating, increasing the risk of hyperthermia and heatstroke. More powerful hallucinogens and hyperthermic drugs have also been identified as adulterants in MDMA batches.

In 2003, the federal RAVE (Reducing Americans' Vulnerability to Ecstasy) Act was signed into law, making it unlawful to "knowingly open, lease, rent, use, or maintain any place, whether permanently or temporarily for the purpose of manufacturing, distributing, or using any controlled substance." Supporters of the law view it as helping to reduce illicit drug use in dance clubs; opponents view it more as reflection of prejudice against youth culture.

Where to go for assistance:

www.nida.nih.gov/infofacts/ecstasy.html

This web site is sponsored by the National Institute on Drug Abuse, with an extensive treatment on the hazards of Ecstasy (MDMA).

Sources: Boils, Karen I. (1999). Memory impairment in abstinent MDMA ("Ecstasy") users. *Journal of the American Medical Association, 281,* 494. Chonin, Neva (2003, April 27). Congress acts out against club culture. *San Francisco Chronicle,* p. 35. Leshner, Alan I. (2002). Ecstasy abuse and control: Hearing before the Senate Subcommittee on Governmental Affairs—July 30, 2001. Statement for the record. *Journal of Psychoactive Drugs, 34,* 133–135. Schwartz, Richard H., and Miller, Norman S. (1997). MDMA (Ecstasy) and the rave: A review. *Pediatrics, 100,* 705–708. Stryker, Jeff (2001, September 25). For partygoers who can't say no, experts try to reduce the risks. *New York Times,* p. F5.

groups (peaking in 2001 at 12 percent and 5 percent, respectively), Ecstasy use has been on the decline, probably due to publicity about its adverse health effects. However, a worrisome trend began in 2005, with a *decreasing* number of high school seniors and eighth graders judging Ecstasy use to represent a great risk of harm. This trend will be watched carefully in coming years to see if a resurgence in Ecstasy as a recreational drug may be on the horizon.[41]

Drug Enforcement Administration (DEA) officials have theorized that the popularity of narcotic analgesics (prescription painkillers) such as OxyContin and Vicodin (see Chapters 1 and 7) has outstripped that of Ecstasy in recent years, in part because of their greater availability and lower expense.[42]

Hallucinogens Related to Acetylcholine

Of the acetylcholine-related hallucinogens, some enhance the neurotransmitter and some inhibit it. Examples include *Amanita muscaria* mushrooms, atropine, scopolamine, and hyoscyamine.

Amanita muscaria

The **Amanita muscaria** mushroom, also called the fly agaric mushroom because of its ability to lure and sedate flies and other insects, grows in the upper latitudes of the Northern Hemisphere, usually among the roots of birch trees. The mushroom has a bright red cap speckled with white dots; the dancing mushrooms in Walt Disney's film *Fantasia* were inspired by the appearance (if not the hallucinogenic effects) of this fungus (see Figure 9.1b).

Amanita mushrooms are one of the world's oldest intoxicants. Many historians hypothesize that this mushroom was the basis for the mysterious and divine substance called soma that is celebrated in the *Rig-Veda*, one of Hinduism's oldest holy books, dating from 1000 B.C. It is strongly suspected that amanita mushrooms were used in Greek mystery cults and were he basis for the legendary "nectar of the Gods" on Mount Olympus.[43]

The effects of amanita mushrooms can be lethal if dose levels are not watched very carefully. They produce muscular twitching and spasms, vivid hallucinations, dizziness, and heightened aggressive behavior. It was briefly mentioned in Chapter 2 that Viking warriors were reputed to have ingested amanita mushrooms before sailing off to battle. The drug-induced strength and savagery of these "berserk" invaders were so widely feared that a medieval prayer was written especially for protection from their attacks: "From the intolerable fury of the Norseman, O Lord, deliver us."[44]

The Hexing Drugs and Witchcraft

A number of natural plants contain chemicals that share a common feature: the ability to block the parasympathetic effects of acetylcholine in the body. The drugs with this ability, called *anticholinergic drugs*, produce specific physiological effects. The production of mucus in the nose and throat, and in the mouth, is reduced. Body temperature is elevated, sometimes to very high fever levels. Heart rate and blood pressure go up, and the pupils dilate considerably. Psychological effects include a feeling of delirium, confusion, and a loss of memory for events occurring during the drugged state.[45] The amnesic property is one of the primary reasons for the minimal street appeal of these drugs.

The principal anticholinergic drugs are **atropine**, **scopolamine** (also called hyoscine), and **hyoscyamine**. They are found in various combinations and relative amounts in a large number of psychoactive plants. Four of the better known ones are examined here.

- Atropine is principally derived from the *Atropa belladonna* plant, also called deadly nightshade. Its lethal reputation is quite justified, since it is estimated that ingesting only a dozen or so berries is sufficient for death to occur. Many recipes for poisons through history have been based on this plant. At lower, more benign dose levels, plant extracts can be applied to the eyes, causing the pupils to dilate. Egyptian and Roman women used this technique to enhance their beauty or at least improve their appearance. The term "belladonna" ("beautiful lady") originates from this

***Amanita muscaria* (a-ma-NEE-ta mus-CAR-ee-ah):** A species of mushroom containing the hallucinogenic drug ibotenic acid.

atropine (AT-tro-peen): An anticholinergic hallucinogenic drug derived from the *Atropa belladonna* plant.

scopolamine (scoh-POL-ah-meen): An anticholinergic hallucinogenic drug. Also called hyoscine.

hyoscyamine (HEYE-oh-SEYE-eh-meen): An anticholinergic hallucinogenic drug found in mandrake, henbane, and various species of the datura plant.

***Atropa belladonna* (a-TROH-pah BEL-ah-DON-ah):** A plant species, also called deadly nightshade, whose berries can be highly toxic. It is the principal source of atropine.

application. The psychological effects of atropine are generally associated with the anticholinergic effects of heart-rate acceleration and general arousal.

- The **mandrake** plant is an oddly shaped potato-like plant with a long forked root that has traditionally been imagined to resemble a human body. In ancient times, mandrake was considered to have aphrodisiac properties. According to medieval folklore, mandrake plants supposedly shrieked when they were uprooted, understandably driving people mad. Mandrake contains a combination of atropine, scopolamine, and hyoscyamine. Because low doses act as a depressant, mandrake has been used as a sedative-hypnotic drug to relieve anxiety and induce sleep. At higher doses, it produces bizarre hallucinations and muscular paralysis.

- **Henbane** is a strong-smelling herb, native to widespread areas of the Northern Hemisphere, with purple-veined, yellowish flowers and hairy leaves. Its English name, meaning "harmful to hens," originates from the observation that henbane seeds were toxic to chickens and other birds. The lethal possibilities for henbane potions have been described by writers since the days of the Roman Empire. Hamlet's father in Shakespeare's play was supposedly murdered with henbane poison. Lower doses of henbane, however, have been used in a more benign way, as an anesthetic and painkiller. We now know that the predominant drugs in henbane are scopolamine and hyoscyamine.

- Various species of the datura plant, containing a combination of atropine, scopolamine, and hyoscyamine, grow wild in locations throughout the world. In the United States, one particular species, ***Datura stramonium***, is called "jimsonweed," a contraction of "Jamestown weed" (the name given to it by early American colonists). Consumption of the seeds or berries of jimsonweed produces hypnotic and hallucinogenic effects, together with disorientation, confusion, and amnesia. At high doses, jimsonweed is quite toxic. In recent years, there have been occasional reports of hospitalizations and even deaths among

teenagers who have eaten jimsonweed seeds as an inexpensive way to get high.[46]

During medieval times, mixtures of deadly nightshade, mandrake, and henbane were responsible for the psychoactive effects of witches' potions, producing a disastrous combination of physiological and psychological effects. Satanic celebrations of the Black Mass centered on the ingestion of such brews. The atropine, in particular, produced a substantial elevation in arousal, probably leading to the feeling that the person was flying (or at least capable of it), while the hallucinogenic effects enabled the person to imagine "communing with the Devil."[47] Witches were reputed to have prepared these mixtures as ointments and rubbed them on their bodies and on broomsticks, which they straddled. The chemicals would have been easily absorbed through the skin and the membranes of the vagina. The Halloween image of a witch flying on a broomstick has been with us ever since.

Quick Concept Check 9.1

Understanding the Diversity of Hallucinogens

Check your understanding of the psychological differences among major hallucinogens by matching each hallucinatory experience (in the left column) with the hallucinogenic drug most apt to produce such effects (in the right column).

PSYCHOLOGICAL EXPERIENCE	HALLUCINOGEN
1. "The images I saw were Mexican designs as if they were created by an Aztec artist."	DMT
	LSD
2. "As I heard the bells, I also saw the vibrations move through the air."	*Atropa belladonna*
	psilocybin
3. "The hallucinations were gone sixty minutes after they had started."	mescaline
	Amanita
4. "As I ate the red-topped mushrooms, I felt my muscles twitch. I could see vivid hallucinations."	*muscaria*
5. "I felt as if I were flying through the air."	

Answers: 1. psilocybin 2. LSD, principally 3. DMT 4. *Amanita muscaria* 5. *Atropa belladonna*

---

mandrake: A potato-like plant containing anticholinergic hallucinogenic drugs.

henbane: An herb containing anticholinergic hallucinogenic drugs.

***Datura stramonium* (duh-TOOR-ah strah-MOH-nee-um):** A species of the datura family of plants with hallucinogenic properties. In the United States, the plant is called jimsonweed.

Miscellaneous Hallucinogens

Three hallucinogens are referred to as miscellaneous hallucinogens because they do not have any chemical resemblance to either serotonin, norepinephrine, or acetylcholine. They are phencyclidine, ketamine, and *Salvia divinorum*.

Phencyclidine (PCP)

Perhaps the most notorious of all the hallucinogens is **phencyclidine (PCP)**, commonly known as *angel dust*. Technically PCP is a synthetic depressant, and it was originally introduced in 1963 as a depressant drug by the Parke-Davis pharmaceutical company, under the brand name of Sernyl. It was marketed as a promising new surgical anesthetic that had the advantage of not depressing respiration or blood pressure or causing heartbeat irregularities as some other anesthetics do. In addition, PCP had a higher therapeutic ratio than many other anesthetics available at that time. By 1965, however, it was withdrawn from human applications after reports that nearly half of all patients receiving PCP showed signs of delirium, disorientation, hallucinations, intense anxiety, or agitation. In 1979, PCP was classified as a Schedule II controlled substance and is still used as an anesthetic for animal surgery.

The weird combination of stimulant, depressant, and hallucinogenic effects makes PCP difficult to classify. Some textbooks treat the discussion of PCP in a chapter on hallucinogens, as is done here, whereas others include it in a chapter on stimulants because some features of PCP intoxication resemble the effect of cocaine. A growing consensus of opinion has it that PCP should be described as a *dissociative anesthetic hallucinogen* because it produces a feeling of being dissociated or cut off from one's environment.

PCP can be administered orally, intravenously, or by inhalation, but commonly it is smoked either alone or in combination with other drugs. Whatever its mode of administration, the results are extremely dangerous, with an unpredictability that far exceeds that of LSD or other hallucinogens. The symptoms may include manic excitement, depression, severe anxiety, sudden mood changes, disordered and confused thought, paranoid thoughts, and unpredictable aggression. Because PCP has analgesic properties as well, individuals taking the drug often feel invulnerable to threats against them and may be willing and able to withstand considerable pain. The mechanism behind PCP effects appears to be the blocking of a specific subtype of glutamate receptors in the brain (see Chapter 4).

Hallucinations also occur, but they are quite different from the hallucinations experienced under the influence of LSD. There are no colorful images, no intermingling of sight and sound, no mystical sense of being "one with the world." Instead, a prominent feature of PCP-induced hallucinations is the change in one's body image. As one PCP abuser has expressed it:

> The most frequent hallucination is that parts of your body are extremely large or extremely small. You can imagine yourself small enough to walk through a key hole, or you can be lying there and all of a sudden you just hallucinate that your arm is twice the length of your body.[48]

Individuals under the influence of PCP also may stagger, speak in a slurred way, and feel depersonalized or detached from people around them. A prominent feature is a prolonged visual stare, often called "doll's eyes."

The effects of PCP last from as little as a few hours to as long as two weeks, and they are followed by partial or total amnesia and dissociation from the entire experience. Considering these bizarre reactions, it is not surprising that PCP deaths occur more frequently from the behavioral consequences of the PCP experience than from its physiological effects. Suicides, accidental or intentional mutilations, drownings (sometimes in very

Quick Concept Check 9.2

Understanding PCP

Check your understanding of the effects of PCP by listing three major features of PCP intoxication that are significantly different from the effects of other hallucinogens.

Answer: Correct responses can include any of the following: analgesia, amnesia, prolonged stare, absence of synesthesia, absence of mysticism, unpredictable aggression, extreme disorientation, feelings of being cut off from oneself or the environment.

phencyclidine (PCP) (fen-SIGH-klih-deen): A dissociative anesthetic hallucinogen that produces disorientation, agitation, aggressive behavior, analgesia, and amnesia. It has various street names, including angel dust.

small amounts of water), falls, and threatening behavior leading to the individual's being shot are only some of the possible consequences.[49]

Patterns of PCP Abuse

It is strange that a drug with so many adverse effects would be subject to deliberate abuse, but such is the case with PCP. Reports of PCP abuse began surfacing in 1967 among the hippie community in San Francisco, where it became known as the PeaCe Pill. Word quickly spread that PCP did not live up to its name. Inexperienced PCP abusers were suffering the same bizarre effects as had the clinical patients earlier in the decade. By 1969, PCP had been written off as a garbage drug, and it dropped out of sight as a drug of abuse.

In the early 1970s, PCP returned under new street names and in new forms (Table 9.2). No longer a pill to be taken orally, PCP was now in powdered or liquid form. Powdered PCP could be added to parsley, mint, oregano, tobacco, or marijuana, rolled as a cigarette, and smoked. Liquid PCP could be used to soak leaf mixtures of all types, including manufactured cigarettes, which could then be dried and smoked. Many new users have turned to PCP as a way to boost the effects of marijuana.

TABLE 9.2	
Street names for phencyclidine (PCP) and PCP-like drugs	
PCP	jet fuel
angel dust	sherms (derived from the reaction that it hits you like a Sherman tank)
monkey dust	
peep	superkools
supergrass	cyclones
killer weed	zombie dust
ozone	ketamine
embalming fluid	special K
rocket fuel	

Note: In the illicit drug market, PCP and ketamine are frequently misrepresented and sold as mescaline, LSD, marijuana, amphetamine, or cocaine.

Source: Milburn, H. Thomas (1991). Diagnosis and management of phencyclidine intoxication. *American Family Physician, 43,* 1293.

ketamine (KET-ah-meen): A dissociative anesthetic hallucinogen related to phencyclidine (PCP).

Making matters worse, as many as 120 different designer-drug variations of PCP have been developed in illicit laboratories around the country and the world. The dangers of PCP abuse, therefore, are complicated by the difficulty in knowing whether a street drug has been adulterated with PCP and what version of PCP may be present. Unfortunately, the common practice of mixing PCP with alcohol or marijuana adds to the unpredictability of the final result.[50]

Ketamine

Ketamine, a drug chemically similar to PCP, is also classified as a dissociative anesthetic hallucinogen. Like PCP, ketamine has a mixture of stimulant and depressive properties, though its depressive effect is more extreme and does not last as long as that of PCP. Ketamine (brand name: Ketalar) was used as an emergency surgical anesthetic on the battlefield in Vietnam as well as in standard hospital-based operations in which gaseous anesthetics could not be employed. It has also been used occasionally in short surgical procedures involving the head and neck or in the treatment of facial burns where it is not possible to use an anesthetic mask. Adverse side effects, however, have limited its therapeutic use. These problems include unpredictable and sometimes violent jerking and twitching of the body, as well as vivid and unpleasant dreams during and after surgery. During recovery, patients may experience hallucinations and feelings of disorientation. Delayed effects of ketamine, such as nightmares, have been reported to occur for weeks or longer after surgery.[51]

Ketamine abuse began to be reported in the 1980s. More recently, under the names "Special K" and "Vitamin K," it has been included among current club drugs on the scene (see Chapter 1). Its popularity has increased among college students and patrons of dance clubs and all-night "rave" parties. Like PCP, ketamine produces a dream-like intoxication, accompanied by an inability to move or feel pain. There are also experiences of dizziness, confusion, and slurred speech. As is the case with dissociative hallucinogens, ketamine produces amnesia, in that abusers frequently cannot later remember what has happened while under its influence. The primary hazard of acute ketamine ingestion is the depression of breathing. Little is known, however, of the chronic effects of extended ketamine abuse over time, except that experiences of "flashbacks" have been reported. As with PCP, the effects of ketamine are associated with the blocking of specific glutamate receptors.

As with other club drugs that produce depressive effects on the central nervous system, there is the dangerous potential for ketamine to be abused as a "date-rape" drug. Women who may unwittingly take the drug can be rendered incapacitated, without the ability to recall the experience. In 1999, ketamine became classified as a Schedule III controlled substance (Drug Trafficking Update).[52]

Salvia divinorum

The Mexican herb, *Salvia divinorum* (commonly referred to as Salvia), has a long tradition as a shamanic treatment for diarrhea, headache, rheumatism, and abdominal discomfort. When smoked, chewed, or brewed as a tea, Salvia produces intense visual hallucinations (resembling the effect of psilocybin-containing mushrooms), laughter, and an "out of body" dissociative experience. Its potency approaches that of LSD, but the effects are very short-lived. In one recent study of Salvia users, 85 percent reported Salvia effects lasting less than 15 minutes.

Considerable media attention has been directed toward recreational use of Salvia. At present, it has not been classified as a controlled substance under the federal Controlled Substance Act. The DEA is currently pursuing the possibility of classification as a Schedule I drug, but until that occurs Salvia remains legally available

through numerous Internet web sites. In a growing number of U.S. states and countries around the world, Salvia has been officially classified as an illicit drug, along with other hallucinogens.

According to the 2009 University of Michigan survey, 6 percent of high school seniors reported using Salvia in the past year. In a smaller sample of college students reporting in 2006, 23 percent of students had heard of Salvia. About seven percent had used it at some time in their life, but the prevalence rate plummeted to less than one percent when asked whether they had used it in the last month. The "snapshots" that surveys of this kind reveal are twofold. First of all, it is virtually certain that extensive media attention will have, by now, dramatically increased the level of awareness about Salvia and its legal availability through Internet sources, so that most adolescents and young adults will have heard about it. Second, it is likely that Salvia may be attractive to those experimenting with a hallucinogen but not particularly attractive to chronic drug users. The particularly intense and unpredictable character of the Salvia experience as well as its very short duration will be unpleasant to many. A majority of the first-time Salvia users in the college sample said that they would not want to use it again.[53]

Salvia divinorum (SAL-via di-vi-NOR-um) or **Salvia:** A Mexican leafy herb with short-duration hallucinogenic effects.

Summary

A Matter of Definition

- Hallucinogens are, by definition, drugs that produce distortions of perception and of one's sense of reality. These drugs have also been called psychedelic ("mind-expanding") drugs. In some cases, users of hallucinogens feel that they have been transported to a new reality.

- Other classes of drugs may produce hallucinations at high dose levels, but hallucinogens produce these effects at low or moderate dose levels.

Classifying Hallucinogens

- Hallucinogens can be classified in four basic groups. The first three relate to the chemical similarity between the particular drug and one of three major neurotransmitters: serotonin, norepinephrine, or acetylcholine.

- The fourth, miscellaneous group includes synthetic hallucinogens, such as phencyclidine (PCP) and ketamine, which bear little resemblance to any known neurotransmitter.

Lysergic Acid Diethylamide (LSD)

- Lysergic acid diethylamide (LSD), the best-known hallucinogenic drug, belongs to the serotonin group. It is synthetically derived from ergot, a toxic rye fungus that has been documented as being responsible for thousands of deaths over the centuries.

- Albert Hofmann synthesized LSD in 1943, and Timothy Leary led the psychedelic movement that popularized LSD use in the 1960s.

- Although the LSD experience is often unpredictable, certain features are commonly observed: colorful hallucinations, synesthesia in which sounds often appear as visions, a distortion of perceptual reality, emotional swings, a feeling of timelessness, and an illusory separation of mind from body.

- It is now known that LSD affects a subtype of brain receptors sensitive to serotonin, referred to as serotonin-2A receptors.

- In the early 1990s, there was a resurgence in LSD abuse, particularly among young individuals, a trend that began to reverse in 1997.

Facts and Fictions about LSD

- LSD does not produce psychological or physical dependence and has only a slight chance of inducing a panic or psychotic state (providing that there is a supportive setting for the taking of LSD).

- LSD does not elevate one's level of creativity. It does not damage chromosomes (though there remains a chance of birth defects if a woman ingests LSD when she is pregnant), and a relationship between LSD abuse and violent behavior has not been established. Flashback experiences, however, are potential hazards.

Psilocybin and Other Hallucinogens Related to Serotonin

- Other hallucinogens related to serotonin are psilocybin, lysergic acid amide (LAA), dimethyltryptamine (DMT), and harmine.

Hallucinogens Related to Norepinephrine

- Mescaline is chemically related to norepinephrine, even though S_2 receptors are responsible for its hallucinogenic effects.

- Two synthetic hallucinogens, DOM and MDMA, are variations of the amphetamine molecule. MDMA (Ecstasy) is currently a popular club drug, but research studies indicate that it poses serious health risks to the user.

Hallucinogens Related to Acetylcholine

- A number of anticholinergic hallucinogens, so named because they diminish the effects of acetylcholine in the parasympathetic nervous system, have been involved in sorcery and witchcraft since the Middle Ages.

- These so-called hexing drugs contain a combination of atropine, scopolamine, and/or hyoscyamine. Sources for such drugs include the deadly nightshade plant, mandrake roots, henbane seeds, and the datura plant family.

Miscellaneous Hallucinogens: Phencyclidine (PCP), Ketamine, and *Salvia divinorum*

- A dangerous form of hallucinogen abuse involves phencyclidine (PCP). Originally a psychedelic street drug in the 1960s, PCP quickly developed a reputation for producing a number of adverse reactions.

- PCP reappeared in the early 1970s, in smokable forms either alone or in combination with marijuana. Extremely aggressive tendencies, as well as behaviors resembling acute schizophrenia, have been associated with PCP intoxication.

- Ketamine is popular as a club drug that produces a dream-like intoxication, accompanied by an inability to move or feel pain. Like PCP, ketamine also produces amnesia and potentially a depression in breathing.

- *Salvia divinorum* (or simply Salvia) is a Mexican leafy herb, with short-duration hallucinogenic effects when smoked, chewed, or brewed as a tea. It is regarded by the DEA as a "drug of concern," considering its growing popularity as a recreational drug, though it is not presently classified as a Schedule I drug under the Controlled Substances Act.

Key Terms

Amanita muscaria, p. 209
Atropa belladonna, p. 209
atropine, p. 209
bufotenine, p. 205
cyanosis, p. 205
Datura stramonium, p. 210
dimethyltryptamine (DMT), p. 205

DOM, p. 206
ergot, p. 196
ergotism, p. 196
hallucinogens, p. 194
harmine, p. 206
henbane, p. 210
hyoscyamine, p. 209
ketamine, p. 212

lysergic acid amide (LAA), p. 204
lysergic acid diethylamide (LSD), p. 194
mandrake, p. 210
MDMA (Ecstasy), p. 207
mescaline, p. 206

peyote, p. 206
phencyclidine (PCP), p. 211
psilocin, p. 204
psilocybin, p. 204
Salvia divinorum, p. 213
scopolamine, p. 209
synesthesia, p. 200

Endnotes

1. Hofmann, Albert (1980). *LSD: My problem child.* New York: McGraw-Hill, p. 17.
2. Ibid., pp. 17–18.
3. Ibid., p. 19.
4. Brophy, James J. (1985). Psychiatric disorders. In Marcus A. Krupp, Milton J. Chatton, and David Werdegar (Eds.), *Current medical diagnosis and treatment.* Los Altos, CA: Lange Medical Publication, p. 674.
5. Mann, John (1992). *Murder, magic, and medicine.* New York: Oxford University Press, pp. 41–51.
6. Fuller, John G. (1968). *The day of St. Anthony's fire.* New York: Macmillan, preface.
7. Leary, Timothy (1973). The religious experience: Its production and interpretation. In Gunther Weil, Ralph Metzner, and Timothy Leary (Eds.), *The psychedelic reader.* Secaucus, NJ: Citadel Press, p. 191.
8. Lattin, Don (2010). *The Harvard psychedelic club.* New York: HarperCollins. Lee, Martin A., and Shlain, Bruce (1985). *Acid dreams: The complete social history of LSD.* New York: Grove Weidenfeld, pp. 71–118.
9. Greenfield, Robert (2006). *Timothy Leary: A biography.* New York: H. Silberman Book/Harcourt. Leary, Timothy (1968). *High priest.* New York: New American Library, p. 46. Manchester, William R. (1974). *The glory and the dream: A narrative history of America, 1932–1972.* Boston: Little, Brown, p. 1362.
10. Grinspoon, Lester, and Bakalar, James B. (1979). *Psychedelic drugs reconsidered.* New York: Basic Books, p. 68.
11. Brown, F. Christine (1972). *Hallucinogenic drugs.* Springfield, IL: Charles C Thomas, pp. 46–49. Goode, Erich (2008). *Drugs and American society* (7th ed.). New York: McGraw-Hill College, p. 260.
12. Schuckit, Marc A. (1995). *Drug and alcohol abuse: A clinical guide to diagnosis and treatment* (4th ed.). New York: Plenum, pp. 189–190.
13. Jacobs, Michael R., and Fehr, Kevin O'B. (1987). *Drugs and drug abuse: A reference text* (2nd ed.). Toronto: Addiction Research Foundation, p. 345. Substance Abuse and Mental Health Services Administration (2009). Drug Abuse Warning Network, 2008: Selected tables of national estimates of drug-related emergency department visits. Rockville, MD: Office of Applied Studies, Substance Abuse and Mental Health Services Administration.
14. Brophy, Psychiatric disorders. Jacobs and Fehr, *Drugs and drug abuse,* pp. 337–347.
15. Goode, *Drugs and American society,* pp. 261–263. Snyder, Solomon H. (1986). *Drugs and the brain.* New York: Freeman, pp. 180–181.
16. Aghajanian, G. K., and Marek, G. J. (1999). Serotonin and hallucinogens. *Neuropsychopharmacology, 21 (Suppl. 2),* 16S–23S. Gresch, Paul J.; Smith, Randy, L.; Barrett, Robert J.; and Sanders-Bush, Elaine (2005). Behavioral tolerance to lysergic acid diethylamide is associated with reduced serotonin-2A receptor signaling in rat cortex. *Neuropsychopharmacology, 30,* 1693–1702. Julien, Robert M. (2005). *A primer of drug action* (10th ed.). New York: Worth, p. 602.
17. Goode, *Drugs and American society,* p. 259.
18. Brands, Bruna, Sproule, Beth, and Marshman, Joan (1998). *Drugs and drug abuse: A reference text.* Toronto, Canada: Addiction Research Foundation, p. 328.

Henderson, Leigh A., and Glass, William J. (Eds.) (1994). *LSD: Still with us after all these years.* New York: Lexington Books. Johnston, Lloyd D.; O'Malley, Patrick M.; Bachman, Jerald G.; and Schulenberg, John E. (2009, December 14). Teen marijuana use tilts up, while some drugs decline in use. University of Michigan News Service, Ann Arbor, Table 1. Johnston, Lloyd D.; O'Malley, Patrick M.; Bachman, Jerald G.; and Schulenberg, John E. (2010). *Monitoring the future: National survey results on drug use, 1975–2009. Vol. II: College students and adults ages 19–50.* Bethesda, MD: National Institute on Drug Abuse, Table 2-1. Karch, Steven B. (1996). *The pathology of drug abuse* (2nd ed.). Boca Raton, FL: CRC Press, p. 269.

19. Goode, *Drugs and American society*, pp. 265–266.

20. Ibid., p. 266.

21. Cohen, Sidney (1960). Lysergic acid diethylamide: Side effects and complications. *Journal of Nervous and Mental Diseases, 130,* 30–40. Levine, Jerome, and Ludwig, Arnold M. (1964). The LSD controversy. *Comprehensive Psychiatry, 5* (5), 314–321.

22. Wells, Brian (1974). *Psychedelic drugs: Psychological, medical, and social issues.* New York: Jason Aronson, pp. 170–188.

23. Cohen, M. M., and Marmillo, M. J. (1967). Chromosomal damage in human leukocytes induced by lysergic acid diethylamide. *Science, 155,* 1417–1419.

24. Dishotsky, Norman I.; Loughman, William D.; Mogar, Robert E.; and Lipscomb, Wendell R. (1971). LSD and genetic damage. *Science, 172,* 431–440. Grinspoon and Bakalar, *Psychedelic drugs reconsidered,* pp. 188–191.

25. Brown, *Hallucinogenic drugs,* pp. 61–64. Wells, *Psychedelic drugs,* pp. 104–109.

26. Abraham, Henry D. (1983). Visual phenomenology of the LSD flashback. *Archives of General Psychiatry, 40,* 884–889. Schlaadt, Richard G., and Shannon, Peter T. (1994). *Drugs: Use, misuse, and abuse.* Englewood Cliffs, NJ: Prentice-Hall, p. 273.

27. Halpern, John H., and Pope, Harrison G. (1999). Do hallucinogens cause residual neuropsychological toxicity? *Drugs and Alcohol Dependence, 53,* 247–256.

28. Knudsen, Knud (1964). Homicide after treatment with lysergic acid diethylamide. *Acta Psychiatrica Scandinavica, 40* (Supplement 180), 389–395.

29. Metzner, Ralph (1998). Hallucinogenic drugs and plants in psychotherapy and shamanism. *Journal of Psychoactive Drugs, 30,* 333–341.

30. Hofmann, *LSD,* p. 112.

31. Brown, *Hallucinogenic drugs,* pp. 81–88.

32. Johnston, O'Malley, Bachman, and Schulenberg (2009a), Teen marijuana use tilts up, Table 13. Vollenweider, Franz X.; Vollenweider-Scherpenhuyzen, Margaret F. I.; Babler, Andreas; Vogel, Helen; and Hell, Daniel (1998). Psilocybin induces schizophrenia-like psychosis in humans via a serotonin-2 agonist action. *Neuroreport, 9,* 3897–3902.

33. Hofmann, *LSD,* pp. 119–127. Schultes, Richard E., and Hofmann, Albert (1979). *Plants of the gods: Origins of hallucinogenic use.* New York: McGraw-Hill, pp. 158–163.

34. Brands, Sproule, and Marshman, *Drugs and drug abuse,* pp. 512–513.

35. Frecska, Ede, White, Keith, D., and Luna, Luis E. (2003). Effects of Amazonian psychoactive beverage *ayuhuasca* on binocular rivalry: Interhemispheric switching or interhemispheric fusion? *Journal of Psychoactive Drugs, 35,* 367–374. Grinspoon and Bakalar, *Psychedelic drugs reconsidered,* pp. 14–15. Trichter, Stephen, Klimo, Jon, and Krippner, Stanley (2009). Changes in spirituality among ayahuasca ceremony novice participants. *Journal of Psychoactive Drugs, 41,* 121–134.

36. Ibid., pp. 20–21. Hollister, Leo E., and Sjoberg, Bernard M. (1964). Clinical syndromes and biochemical alterations following mescaline, lysergic acid diethylamide, psilocybin, and a combination of the three psychotomimetic drugs. *Comprehensive Psychiatry, 5,* 170–178.

37. Jacobs, Barry L. (1987). How hallucinogenic drugs work. *American Scientist, 75,* 386–392.

38. Brecher, Edward, and the editors of *Consumer Reports* (1972). *Licit and illicit drugs.* Boston: Little, Brown, pp. 376–377.

39. Metzner, Hallucinogenic drugs and plants. Schmidt, C. J. (1987). Psychedelic amphetamine, methylenedioxymethamphetamine. *Journal of Pharmacology and Experimental Therapeutics, 240,* 1–7.

40. Boils, Karen I. (1999). Memory impairment in abstinent MDMA ("Ecstasy") users. *Journal of the American Medical Association, 281,* 494. Leshner, Alan I. (2002). Ecstasy abuse and control: Hearing before the Senate Subcommittee on Governmental Affairs—July 30, 2001. Statement for the record. *Journal of Psychoactive Drugs, 34,* 133–135. Vollenweider, Franz X.; Liechti, Matthias E.; Gamma, Alex; Greer, George; and Geyer, Mark (2002). Acute psychological and neurophysiological effects of MDMA in humans. *Journal of Psychoactive Drugs, 34,* 171–184.

41. Cloud, John (2000, June 5). The lure of ecstasy. *Time,* pp. 62–68. Feuer, Alan (2000, August 6). Distilling the truth in the ecstasy buzz. *New York Times,* pp. 25, 28. Johnston, O'Malley, Bachman, and Schulenberg (2009a), Teen marijuana use tilts up, Tables 1, 5, and 7. Martins, Silvia, S., Mazzotti, Guido, and Chilcoat, Howard D. (2005). Trends in ecstasy use in the United States from 1995 to 2001: Comparison with marijuana users and association with other drug use. *Experimental and Clinical Psychopharmacology, 13,* 244–252.

42. Johnston, Lloyd D.; O'Malley, Patrick M.; Bachman, Jerald G.; and Schulenberg, John E. (2007, December 11). Overall, illicit drug use by American teens continues gradual decline in 2007. University of Michigan News Service, Ann Arbor. Quotation on p. 4.

43. Wasson, R. Gordon (1968). *Soma: Divine mushroom of immortality*. New York: Harcourt, Brace and World.

44. Cohen, Sidney (1964). *The beyond within: The LSD story*. New York: Atheneum, p. 17.

45. Ramachandran, Vilayanur S., and Hubbard, Edward M. (2003, May). Hearing colors, tasting shapes. *Scientific American*, pp. 52–59.

46. Clark, Jason D. (2005). The roadside high: Jimson weed toxicity. *Air Medical Journal*, 24, 234-237. Schultes and Hofmann, *Plants of the gods*, pp. 106–111.

47. Schultes and Hofmann, *Plants of the gods*, pp. 86–91.

48. James, Jennifer, and Andresen, Elena (1979). Sea-Tac and PCP. In Harvey V. Feldman, Michael H. Agar, and George M. Beschner (Eds.), *Angel dust: An ethnographic study of PCP users*. Lexington, MA: Lexington Books, p. 133.

49. Grinspoon and Bakalar, *Psychedelic drugs reconsidered*, pp. 32–33. Petersen, Robert C., and Stillman, Richard C. (1978). Phencyclidine: An overview. In Robert C. Petersen and Richard C. Stillman (Eds.), *Phencyclidine (PCP) abuse: An appraisal* (NIDA Research Monograph 21). Rockville, MD: National Institute on Drug Abuse, pp. 1–17. Robbins, *Hallucinogens*, pp. 12–14. Seeman, P., Ko, F., and Tallerico, T. (2005). Dopamine receptor contribution to the action of PCP, LSD and ketamine psychotomimetics. *Molecular Psychiatry*, 10, 877–883.

50. Trends in PCP-related emergency department visits (2004, January). *The DAWN Report*, pp. 1–4.

51. Brands, Sproule, and Marshman, *Drugs and drug abuse*, pp. 523–525.

52. Ibid. Feds classify ketamine as controlled substance (1999, August 2). *Alcoholism and Drug Abuse Weekly*, p. 7.

53. Braiker, Brian (2008, May 19). Old herb, new controversy. *Newsweek*, pp. 40-41. González, Débora, Riba, Jordi, Bouso, José Carlos, Gómez-Jarabo, Gregorio, et al. (2006). Pattern of use and subjective effects of *Salvia divinorum* among recreational users. *Drug and Alcohol Dependence*, 85, 157–162. Johnston, O'Malley, Bachman, and Schulenberg (2009a), Marijuana use tilts up, Table 2. Julien, *A primer of drug action*, p. 619. Khey, David N., Miller, Bryan Lee, and Griffin, O. Hayden (2008). *Salvia divinorum* use among a college student sample. *Journal of Drug Education*, 38, 297–306.

chapter 10

Marijuana

Hunters and fishermen have snared the most ferocious creatures, from the tiger to the shark, in its Herculean weave . . . Hangmen have snapped the necks of thieves and murderers with its fiber. Obstetricians have eased the pain of childbirth with its leaves. Farmers have crushed its seeds and used the oil within to light their lamps. Mourners have thrown its seeds into blazing fires and have had their sorrows transformed into blissful ecstasy by the fumes that filled the air . . .

It is as vigorous as a weed. It is ubiquitous. It flourishes under nearly every possible climatic condition. It sprouts from the earth not meekly, not cautiously in suspense of where it is and what it may find, but defiantly, arrogantly, confident that whatever the conditions it has the stamina to survive.

—*Ernest L. Abel, referring to the cannabis plant
(source of hemp and marijuana)*
Marihuana, the First Twelve Thousand Years *(1980)*

It might be fair to characterize *Cannabis sativa*, the botanical source of marijuana, as a scrawny weed with an attitude. Whether it is hot or cold, wet or dry, cannabis will grow abundantly from seeds that are unbelievably hardy and prolific. A handful of cannabis seeds, tossed on the ground and pressed in with one's foot, will usually anchor and become plants. Its roots devour whatever nutrients there are in the soil, as Ernest Abel (see above) has expressed it, "like a vampire sucking the life blood from the earth."[1]

As a result, marijuana has managed to grow in some unorthodox places. It can be found in median strips of interstate highways and in ditches alongside country roads. The top prize for most unusual location, if the story is true and not simply an urban legend, has to go to a variety known as Manhattan Silver. Reportedly, it originated from cannabis seeds flushed down a New York sewer during a sudden police raid in the 1960s. Once the seeds hit the sewer, they produced a plant that, in the absence of light, grew silverish white leaves instead of green—hence its name.[2]

Considering its botanical origin, it is fitting that the pharmacological effects of marijuana should show something of an independent nature as well. It is not easy to place marijuana within a classification of psychoactive drugs. When we consider a category for marijuana, we are faced with an odd assortment of unconnected properties. Marijuana produces some excitatory effects, but it is not generally regarded as a stimulant. It produces some sedative effects, but a user faces no risk of slipping into a coma or dying. It produces mild analgesic effects, but it is not related chemically to opiates or opiate-like drugs. It produces hallucinations at high doses, but its structure does not resemble that of LSD or any other drug formally categorized as a hallucinogen. Marijuana is clearly a unique drug, in a league of its own.

Few other drugs have been so politicized in recent history as marijuana. It is frequently praised by one side or condemned by the other, on the basis of emotionally charged issues rather than an objective view of research data. The pro-marijuana faction tends to dismiss or downplay reports of potential dangers and emphasize the benefits; the antimarijuana faction tends to do the opposite, pointing out that marijuana continues to be classified as a Schedule I controlled substance, along with heroin and LSD. Over the last forty years or so, marijuana often has been regarded not only as a drug with psychoactive properties but also as a symbol of an individual's attitude toward the establishment. This makes it even more critical that we look at the effects of marijuana as dispassionately as possible.

A Matter of Terminology

Marijuana (sometimes spelled *marihuana*) is frequently referred to as a synonym for cannabis, but technically the two terms need to be differentiated. Cannabis is the botanical term for the hemp plant ***Cannabis sativa.*** With a potential height of about eighteen feet, cannabis has sturdy stalks, four-cornered in cross-section, that have been commercially valuable for thousands of years in the manufacture of rope, twine, shoes, sailcloth, and containers of all kinds. Pots made of hemp fiber discovered at archaeological sites in China date the origins of cannabis cultivation as far back as the Stone Age. It is arguably the oldest cultivated plant not used for food.[3]

Spaniards brought cannabis to the New World in 1545, and English settlers brought it to Jamestown, Virginia, in 1611, where it became a major commercial crop, along with tobacco. Like other eighteenth-century farmers in the region, George Washington grew cannabis in the fields of his estate at Mount Vernon. Entries in his diary indicate that he maintained a keen interest in cultivating better strains of cannabis, but there is no reason to believe he was interested in anything more than producing a better-quality rope.

Marijuana is obtained not from the stalks of the cannabis plant but from its serrated leaves. The key psychoactive factor is contained in a sticky substance, or resin, that accumulates on these leaves. Depending on the growing conditions, cannabis will produce either a greater amount of resin or a greater amount of fiber. In a hot, dry climate—such as North Africa, for example—the fiber content is weak, but so much resin is produced that the plant looks as if it is covered with dew. In a cooler, more humid climate, such as North America, less resin is produced, but the fiber is stronger and more durable.[4]

As many as eighty separate chemical compounds, called **cannabinoids**, have been identified from cannabis resin. Among these, the chief psychoactive compound and the active ingredient that produces the intoxicating effects is **delta-9-tetrahydrocannabinol (THC)**. The

---

***Cannabis sativa* (CAN-uh-bus sah-TEE-vah):** A plant species, commonly called hemp, from which marijuana and hashish are obtained.

cannabinoids (can-NAB-ih-noids): Any of several dozen active substances in marijuana and other cannabis products.

delta-9-tetrahydrocannabinol (THC) (DEL-tah-9-TEH-trah-HIGH-dro-CAN-a-bih-nol): The active psychoactive ingredient in marijuana and hashish.

A *Cannabis* farmer carefully tends to his marijuana crop prior to final harvesting.

isolation and identification of THC in 1964 was a major step toward understanding the effects on the brain of marijuana and similar preparations obtained from *Cannabis sativa*.

Knowing these facts, we are now in a position to categorize various forms of cannabis products in terms of the origin within the cannabis plant and the relative THC concentration. The first and best known of these products, **marijuana**, consists of leaves and occasionally flowers of the cannabis plant that are first dried and then shredded. During the 1960s and 1970s, the typical

---

marijuana: The most commonly available psychoactive drug originating from the cannabis plant. The THC concentration ranges from approximately 1 to 6 percent. Also spelled marihuana.

sinsemilla (SIN-sih-MEE-yah): A form of marijuana obtained from the unpollinated or seedless portion of the cannabis plant. It has a higher THC concentration than regular marijuana, as high as 15 percent.

hashish (hah-SHEESH): A drug containing the resin of cannabis flowers. The THC concentration ranges from approximately 8 to 14 percent.

hashish oil: A drug produced by boiling hashish, leaving a potent psychoactive residue. The THC concentration ranges from approximately 15 to 60 percent.

hashish oil crystals: A solid form of hashish oil.

bhang: A liquid form of marijuana popular in India.

THC concentration of street marijuana imported from Mexico was about 1 to 2 percent. Since the early 1990s, however, THC concentrations have steadily risen to about 10 percent, primarily because of advanced outdoor and indoor cultivation methods. Marijuana, smoked as a cigarette, is the form of cannabis most familiar to North Americans.

A more potent form of marijuana, originating in California and Hawaii, is obtained by cultivating only the unpollinated, or seedless, portion of the cannabis plant. Without pollination, the cannabis plant grows bushier, the resin content is increased, and a greater THC concentration, up to 15 percent, is achieved. This form is called **sinsemilla**, from the Spanish meaning "without seed."

Another cannabis product, **hashish**, is achieved when the resin itself is scraped from cannabis leaves and then dried. Either smoked by itself or in combination with tobacco, it can have a THC concentration as high as 24 percent. The most potent forms of cannabis are **hashish oil** and **hashish oil crystals**, produced by boiling hashish in alcohol or some other solvent and filtering out the alcohol, which leaves a residue with a THC concentration ranging from 15 to 60 percent.[5]

The History of Marijuana and Hashish

The first direct reference to a cannabis product as a psychoactive agent dates from 2737 B.C., in the writings of the mythical Chinese emperor Shen Nung. The focus was on its powers as a medication for rheumatism, gout, malaria, and, strangely enough, absent-mindedness. Mention was made of its intoxicating properties, but the medicinal possibilities evidently were considered more important. In India, however, its use was clearly recreational. The most popular form, in ancient times as well as in the present day, can be found in a syrupy liquid made from cannabis leaves called **bhang**, with a THC potency usually equal to that of a marijuana cigarette in the United States.[6]

The Muslim world also grew to appreciate the psychoactive potential of cannabis, encouraged by the fact that, in contrast to its stern prohibition of alcohol consumption, the Koran did not specifically ban its use. It was here in a hot, dry climate conducive to maximizing the resin content of cannabis that hashish was born, and its popularity spread quickly during the twelfth century from Persia (Iran) in the east to North Africa in the west.

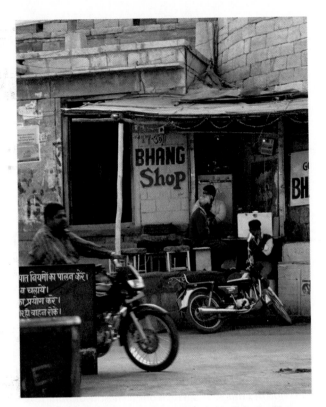

A merchant sits outside his bhang shop in North India. Bhang ki thandai is a popular cold drink prepared with bhang combined with almonds, spices, milk, and sugar. Bhang lassi, a mixture of bhang and iced yogurt, is another popular drink. It is traditional for many Hindus to drink bhang during religious festivals, particularly in Bengal during the Kali Puja (Festival of Kali, the Mother Goddess).

Hashish in the Nineteenth Century

In Western Europe knowledge about hashish or any other cannabis product was limited until the beginning of the nineteenth century. Judging from the decree issued by Pope Innocent VIII in 1484 condemning witchcraft and the use of hemp in the Black Mass, we can assume that the psychoactive properties of cannabis were known by at least some portions of the population. Nonetheless, there is no evidence of widespread use.

By about 1800, however, cannabis had become more widely known and was the subject of a popular craze. One reason was that French soldiers who had served in Napoleon's military campaigns in Egypt brought hashish back with them to their homes in France. Another reason was a wave of romanticism that swept Europe, including an increased interest in exotic stories of the East, notably the *Arabian Nights* and the tales of Marco Polo, which contained references to hashish.

In Paris during the 1840s, a small group of prominent French artists, writers, and intellectuals formed the Club des Hachichins ("Club of the Hashish-Eaters"), where they would gather, in the words of their leader, "to talk of literature, art, and love" while consuming large quantities of hashish. The recipe consisted of concentrated cannabis paste, mixed with butter, sweeteners, and flavorings such as vanilla and cinnamon. Members included Victor Hugo, Alexandre Dumas, Charles Baudelaire, and Honoré de Balzac.

Marijuana and Hashish in the Twentieth Century

Chances are that anyone living in the United States at the beginning of the twentieth century would not have heard of marijuana, much less hashish. By 1890, cotton had replaced hemp as a major cash crop in southern states, although cannabis plants continued to grow wild along roadsides and in the fields. Some patent medicines during this era contained marijuana, but it was a small percentage compared with the number containing opium or cocaine.[7]

It was not until the 1920s that marijuana smoking began to be a phenomenon of any social significance. Some historians have related the appearance of marijuana as a recreational drug to social changes brought on by Prohibition (see Chapter 13), when it was suddenly difficult to obtain good-quality liquor at affordable prices. Its recreational use was largely restricted to jazz musicians and people in show business. "Reefer songs" became the rage of the jazz world; even the mainstream clarinetist and bandleader Benny Goodman had his popular hit "Sweet Marihuana Brown." Marijuana clubs, called *tea pads*, sprang up in the major cities; more than five hundred were estimated in Harlem alone, outnumbering the speakeasies where illegal alcohol was dispensed. These marijuana establishments were largely tolerated by the authorities because at that time marijuana was not illegal and patrons showed no evidence of making a nuisance of themselves or disturbing the community. Marijuana was not considered a societal threat at all.[8]

The Antimarijuana Crusade

This picture started to change by the end of the 1920s and early 1930s. Even though millions of people had never heard of the plant, much less smoked it, marijuana suddenly became widely publicized as a "killer weed." An intense antimarijuana media campaign, orchestrated by the Federal Bureau of Narcotics (FBN), had succeeded in convincing the American public that marijuana was a pestilence singlehandedly destroying a generation of American youth (see Chapter 3).

How did this transformation occur? To understand the way in which marijuana smoking went from a localized and innocent form of behavior to a national social issue, we have to look at some important changes in American society that were taking place at the time.

The practice of smoking marijuana and the cultivation of cannabis plants for that purpose had been filtering slowly into the United States since 1900 as a result of the migration of Mexican immigrants. They entered the country through towns along the Mexican border and along the Gulf Coast. In Mexican communities, marijuana was, in the words of one historian, "a casual adjunct to life . . . a relaxant, a folk remedy for headaches, a mild euphoriant cheaply obtained for two cigarettes for the dollar."[9]

These immigrant communities were met with considerable hostility and prejudice, and the smoking of an alien and foreign-sounding substance did not smooth their reception. In effect, it was a social rerun of the Chinese-opium panic of the 1870s (see Chapter 7) but with the Mexicans on the receiving end. Rumors about the violent behavioral consequences of marijuana smoking among Mexicans spread quickly with no one bothering to check if there was any basis in fact. In addition, social upheavals during the Depression made it particularly convenient for people to vent their frustrations on an immigrant group perceived to be competing for a dwindling number of American jobs and straining an already weak economy. Antimarijuana-themed movies with provocative titles such as *Reefer Madness* and *Marihuana: Weed with Roots in Hell* were produced and distributed during the late 1930s and early 1940s with the encouragement of the FBN.

Considering the mounting hysteria against marijuana smoking and cannabis use in general during this period, it is not surprising that the Marijuana Tax Act of 1937 had little difficulty gaining support in Congress. As with the Harrison Act of 1914, the regulation of marijuana was accomplished indirectly. The act did not ban marijuana; it merely required everyone connected with marijuana, from growers to buyers, to pay a tax. It was a deceptively simple procedure that, in effect, made it virtually impossible to comply with the law. In the absence of compliance, a person was in violation of the act and therefore subject to arrest. It was the state's responsibility to make possession of marijuana or any other product of *Cannabis sativa* illegal. Shortly after the tax act of 1937

Marijuana tax stamps were issued and valid between 1937 and 1969 when the law was overturned by the U.S. Supreme Court. They became commercially available to stamp collectors in 2005.

was imposed, all of the states adopted a uniform law that did just that.

The official stance of the federal government continued to be that marijuana smoking was tied to antisocial behavior. Harry Anslinger, FBN director, wrote in 1953:

> *Those who are accustomed to habitual use of the drug are said eventually to develop a delirious rage after its administration during which they are temporarily, at least, irresponsible and prone to commit violent crimes. . . . Much of the most irrational juvenile violence and killing that has written a new chapter of shame and tragedy is traceable directly to this hemp intoxication.*[10]

Over time, the "pharmacological violence" theory (see Chapter 5) would fade into oblivion, in the absence of any evidence to support it. In its place, however, a new concept related to marijuana smoking would be introduced by the FBN: the gateway theory. According to this idea, marijuana was dangerous because its abuse would lead to the abuse of heroin, cocaine, or other illicit drugs. This gateway hypothesis will be closely examined later in the chapter.

The severity of criminal penalties for involvement with marijuana steadily increased. State judges frequently had the option of sentencing a marijuana seller or user to life imprisonment. In Georgia, a second offense of selling marijuana to a minor could be punishable by death.

Ironically, in 1969, more than three decades after its passage, the U.S. Supreme Court ruled the 1937 Marijuana Tax Act unconstitutional *precisely because marijuana possession was illegal*. The argument was made that requiring a person to pay a tax (and that was all that the 1937 act concerned) in order to possess an illegal substance amounted to a form of self-incrimination, which would be a specific violation of the Fifth Amendment to the Constitution. It turns out that the

This advertising poster for the 1942 film *Devil's Harvest* depicted the supposed evils of smoking marijuana.

case in question here was brought to the high court by none other than Timothy Leary (see the Portrait in Chapter 9), and the court's decision succeeded in overturning a marijuana conviction judged against him.[11]

Challenging Old Ideas about Marijuana

Prior to 1960, arrests and seizures for possession of marijuana were relatively rare and attracted little or no public attention. The social consensus was that marijuana was a drug that could be comfortably associated with, and isolated to, ethnic and racial minorities. It was relatively easy for most Americans to avoid the drug entirely. In any event, involvement with marijuana during the 1950s was a deviant act in an era when there was little tolerance for personal deviance.

By the mid-1960s, this consensus began to dissolve. Marijuana smoking suddenly was an attraction on the campuses of U.S. colleges and universities, affecting a wide cross-section of the nation. Strangely enough, the bizarre effects depicted in the antimarijuana movies failed to occur! At the same time, the experimental use of drugs, particularly marijuana, by young people set the stage for a wholesale questioning of what it meant to respect authority, on an individual as well as a governmental level. We will turn to the more recent issues of medical marijuana and marijuana decriminalization later in the chapter.

Acute Effects of Marijuana

In the United States, THC is usually ingested by smoking a hand-rolled marijuana cigarette referred to as a **reefer** or, more commonly, a **joint**. Exactly how much THC is administered depends on the specific THC concentration level in the marijuana (often referred to as its quality), how deeply the smoke is inhaled into the lungs, and how long it is held in the lungs before being exhaled. In general, an experienced smoker will ingest more THC than a novice smoker by virtue of being able to inhale more deeply and hold the marijuana smoke in his or her lungs longer, for twenty-five seconds or more, thus maximizing THC absorption into the bloodstream.

The inhalation of any drug into the lungs produces extremely rapid absorption, as noted in earlier chapters, and marijuana is no exception. In the case of THC, effects are felt within seconds. Peak levels are reached in the blood within ten minutes and start to decline shortly afterward. Behavioral and psychological effects generally last from two to three hours. At this point, low levels of THC linger for several days because they are absorbed into fatty tissue and excretion from fatty tissue is notoriously slow.[12]

One implication arising from a slow elimination rate is that the residual THC, left over from a previous administration, can intensify the effect of marijuana on a subsequent occasion. In this way, regular marijuana smokers often report a quicker and more easily obtained high, achieved with a smaller quantity of drug, than more intermittent smokers.[13]

It is also important to see the implication of slow marijuana elimination with regard to drug testing. Urine tests for possible marijuana abuse typically measure levels of THC metabolites (broken-down remnants of THC); because of the slow biotransformation of

reefer: A marijuana cigarette.
joint: A marijuana cigarette.

marijuana, these metabolites are detectable in the urine even when the smoker no longer feels high or shows any behavioral effects. Metabolites can remain in the body for several days after the smoking of a single joint and for several weeks later if there has been chronic marijuana smoking. Some tests are so sensitive that a positive level for marijuana can result from passive inhalation of marijuana smoke-filled air in a closed environment, even though the THC levels in these cases are substantially below levels that result from active smoking. The bottom line is that marijuana testing procedures generally are unable to indicate *when* marijuana has been smoked (if it has been smoked at all), only that exposure to marijuana has occurred (see Chapter 12).[14]

Acute Physiological Effects

Immediate physiological effects after smoking marijuana are relatively minor. It has been estimated that a human would need to ingest a dose of marijuana that was from twenty thousand to forty thousand times the effective dose before death would occur.[15] Nonetheless, there is a dose-related increase in heart rate during early stages of marijuana ingestion, up to 160 beats per minute when dose levels are high. Blood pressure either increases, remains the same, or decreases, depending primarily on whether the individual is standing, sitting, or lying down.[16] A dilation of blood vessels on the cornea resulting in bloodshot eyes peaks in about an hour after smoking a joint. Frequently there is a drying of the mouth and an urge to drink.

Other physiological reactions are inconsistent, and at least part of the inconsistency can be attributed to cultural and interpersonal influences. For example, the observation that marijuana smoking makes you feel extremely hungry and crave especially sweet things to eat (often referred to as "having the munchies") generally holds true in studies of North Americans but not for Jamaicans, who consider marijuana an appetite suppressant.

Likewise, North Americans often report enhanced sexual responses following marijuana use, whereas in India marijuana is considered a sexual depressant. These reactions, being subjective in nature, can very well be slanted in one direction or the other by the mind-set (expectations) of the marijuana smoker going into the experience. A good example is the effect on sexual responses. If you believe that marijuana turns you on sexually, the chances are that it will.

Although expectations undoubtedly play a prominent role here, we should be aware of the possibility that varying effects also may be due to differences in the THC concentration of the marijuana being smoked. In the case of sexual reactivity, studies of male marijuana smokers have shown that low-dose marijuana tends to enhance sexual desire, whereas high-dose marijuana tends to depress it, even to the point of impotence. It is quite possible that the enhancement results from a brief rise in the male sex hormone, testosterone, and that the depression results from a rebound effect that lowers testosterone below normal levels. Typically, the THC concentration in India is higher than that in North America. As a result, we would expect different effects on sexual reactivity. The same argument could be made with respect to the differences in marijuana's effect on appetite.[17]

In 2008, approximately 374,000 drug-related emergency department (ED) visits in the DAWN statistics (see Chapter 2) involved marijuana, making it the second-highest category behind cocaine. In about one-fourth of these cases, marijuana was the sole drug present in the patient's system at the time. In general, marijuana-related emergency department incidents have risen substantially in recent years, with an increase of 33 percent from 2004 to 2008. It is likely that a higher THC concentration has contributed to this increase.[18]

Acute Psychological and Behavioral Effects

Chapter 7 noted that a first-time heroin abuser frequently finds the experience more aversive than pleasurable. With marijuana, it is likely that a first-time smoker will feel no discernible effects at all. It takes some practice to be able to inhale deeply and keep the smoke in the lungs long enough (up to forty seconds) for a minimal level of THC, particularly in low-quality marijuana, to take effect. Novices often have to be instructed to focus on some aspect of the intoxicated state to start to feel intoxicated, but the psychological reactions, once they do occur, are fairly predictable.

The marijuana high, as the name implies, is a feeling of euphoria and well-being. Marijuana smokers typically report an increased awareness of their surroundings, as well as a sharpened sense of sight and sound. They often feel that everything is suddenly very funny, and even the most innocent comments or events can set off uproarious laughter. Usually mundane ideas can seem filled with profound implications, and the individual may feel that his or her creativity has been increased. As with LSD, however, no objective evidence shows that creativity is enhanced by marijuana. Commonly, time seems to pass more slowly while a person is under the influence of marijuana, and events appear to be elongated in duration. Finally, marijuana smokers frequently report that they feel sleepy and sometimes dreamy. Relatively low THC concentrations in a marijuana joint are not sufficient to be particularly sleep-inducing, though stronger cannabis preparations with higher THC can have strong sleep-inducing effects, particularly when combined with alcohol.[19]

At the same time, marijuana produces significant deficits in behavior. The major deficit is a decline in the ability to carry out tasks that involve attention and memory. Speech becomes increasingly fragmented and disjointed; individuals often forget what they, or others, have just said. The problem is that marijuana typically causes such a rush of distracting ideas to come to mind that it is difficult to concentrate on new information coming in. By virtue of a diminished focus of concentration, the performance of both short-term and long-term memory tasks is impaired. In general, these difficulties increase in magnitude as a direct function of the level of THC in the marijuana.[20]

Not surprisingly, complex motor tasks, such as driving a car, are also more poorly performed while a person is under the influence of marijuana. It is not necessarily a matter of reaction time; studies of marijuana smokers in automobile simulators indicate that they are as quick to respond as control subjects. The problem arises from a difficulty in attending to peripheral information and making an appropriate response while driving.[21] One researcher has put it this way:

> Marijuana-intoxicated drivers might be able to stop a car as fast as they normally could, but they may not be as quick to notice things that they should stop for. This is probably because they are attending to internal events rather than what is happening on the road.[22]

Given these observations in the laboratory and on the road, marijuana use is a significant risk factor for an automobile accident. Surveys that have examined accident rates among drivers testing positive for THC in their bloodstreams have shown them to be about three to seven times more likely to be involved in an accident than drivers testing negative for THC or alcohol.[23]

An additional problem is quite serious. The decline in sensorimotor performance will persist well after the point at which the marijuana smoker no longer feels high, when there has been chronic heavy marijuana use. Significant impairments in attention and memory tasks have been demonstrated among heavy marijuana users (daily smokers) twenty-four hours after they last used the drug. Therefore, we have to recognize the possibility that some important aspects of behavior can be impaired following marijuana smoking, even when an individual is not aware of it. This effect is likely due to the very slow rate at which marijuana is eliminated from the body.[24]

Acute emotional problems as a result of smoking marijuana are rare among Americans, who typically are exposed to relatively low THC concentrations, though some distortion of body image, paranoia, and anxiety may occur. It is possible that marijuana smoking among individuals predisposed toward or recovering from a psychosis may trigger psychotic behavior. Nonetheless, there is little or no support for the idea that low doses of marijuana provoke such reactions in otherwise normal individuals.

A substantially higher incidence of psychiatric problems arising from THC exposure has been reported in India and North Africa. In such cases, the THC concentrations being ingested, the frequency with which THC is ingested, and the duration of THC exposure over a lifetime are all greater than would be encountered in the United States.

It should be noted that, in general, acute marijuana-smoking effects will be directly related to the amount of THC that is ingested. Of course, this is true of research

Quick Concept Check 10.1

Understanding the Effects of Marijuana

Check your understanding of the effects of marijuana by checking off the response (on the right) that you think is appropriate to the circumstances related to marijuana or other cannabis products (on the left).

CIRCUMSTANCE	INCREASES THE EFFECT	DECREASES THE EFFECT
1. The resin content in the cannabis is low.	_____	_____
2. You have decided to inhale more deeply.	_____	_____
3. You are smoking hashish instead of marijuana.	_____	_____
4. This is the first time you have ever smoked marijuana.	_____	_____
5. The THC concentration level is relatively high	_____	_____

Answers: 1. decreases the effect   2. increases the effect
3. increases the effect   4. decreases the effect.
5. increases the effect

involving any form of drug-taking behavior. However, in the case of marijuana, the conclusions drawn from research studies concerning physiological and behavioral responses have to be examined with special care. As we noted earlier in the chapter, THC concentrations in typical marijuana joints hovered around 1 to 3 percent during the 1960s and 1970s, and most of the research was carried out during this period of time. By the mid-1990s, concentration levels were in the 4 to 4.5 percent range, and they have risen significantly since then to as high as 10 percent in currently available marijuana. Therefore, marijuana effects, as we understand them from the research literature, may be underestimates. Until a substantial amount of research is conducted on marijuana with currently available THC concentrations, it will be difficult to ascertain the precise nature of either its acute or its chronic effects as they are encountered today.[25]

Effects of Marijuana on the Brain

Ever since THC was isolated in 1964 as the primary agent for the intoxicating properties of marijuana, the next step has been to find out specifically how THC affects the brain to produce these effects. In 1990, the mechanism was discovered. Just as with morphine, special receptors in the brain are stimulated specifically by THC. They are concentrated in areas of the brain that are important for short-term memory and motor control. Unlike morphine-sensitive receptors, however, THC-sensitive receptors are not found in the lower portions of the brain that control breathing. As a result, no matter how high the THC concentration in the brain, there is no danger of accidental death by asphyxiation.

Once we have identified a specific receptor for a drug, the question inevitably becomes, "Why is it there?" As noted in Chapter 7, when the morphine-sensitive receptor was discovered, it made sense to speculate about a natural morphine-like substance that would fit into that receptor. The same speculation surrounded the discovery of the THC-sensitive receptor until 1992, when researchers isolated a natural substance, dubbed **anandamide**, that activates this receptor and appears to produce the same effects as THC in the brain.

---

anandamide (a-NAN-duh-mide): A naturally occurring chemical in the brain that fits into THC-sensitive receptor sites, producing many of the same effects as marijuana.

The functions of anandamide and THC-sensitive receptors remain largely a mystery. One study has found that THC stimulates neurons in the nucleus accumbens in rats, the same area that is affected by a host of other psychoactive drugs, including heroin, cocaine, and nicotine. The effect, however, is much weaker than with drugs that produce strong signs of dependence. Animals will self-administer marijuana in laboratory studies and, in fact, are able to discriminate high-potency from low-potency marijuana, but their behavior is not as compulsive as that observed with heroin, cocaine, or nicotine.[26]

Chronic Effects of Marijuana

Is chronic marijuana smoking harmful over a period of time? What is the extent of tolerance and dependence? Are there long-term consequences for organ systems in the body? Does marijuana lessen one's potential as a productive human being in society? Does marijuana abuse lead to the abuse of other drugs? These are questions to be considered next.

Tolerance

It is frequently reported that experienced marijuana smokers tend to become intoxicated more quickly and to a greater extent than inexperienced smokers, when exposed to marijuana joints with equivalent THC concentrations. For many years, this observation suggested that repeated administrations of marijuana produced sensitization, or reverse tolerance (a greater sensitivity), rather than tolerance (a lesser sensitivity). If this were true, then we would have been faced with the troubling conclusion that marijuana operates in a way totally opposite way to that of any other psychoactive drug considered so far. As it turns out, when animals or humans are studied in the laboratory, marijuana smoking shows tolerance effects that are consistent and clear-cut.

Why, then, is the experience of humans outside the laboratory different from that of animals? One important factor is the way we measure the quantity of THC consumed. Reaching an effective high from marijuana requires some degree of practice. For example, novice marijuana smokers may not have mastered the breathing technique necessary to allow the minimal level of THC to enter the lungs. They may have to smoke a relatively large number of marijuana joints initially before they achieve a high. Later, when they have acquired the technique, they may need fewer joints to accomplish the same effect. In these circumstances, a calculation of the number of joints consumed does not reflect the amount of THC ingested. If you were to control the THC content entering the body, as is done in laboratory studies, you would find the predictable results of tolerance over repeated administrations.

Another factor that complicates tolerance studies is the slow elimination rate of marijuana. Regular marijuana smokers are likely to have a residual amount of THC still in the system. This buildup of THC would elevate the total quantity of THC consumed with every joint and induce a quicker high. Once again, the impression of sensitization is false; the enhanced effects result from an accumulation of THC in the body. When dosage levels are controlled, the results indicate a consistent pattern of tolerance rather than sensitization. In general, tolerance effects following repeated administrations of THC are greater as the dosage level of THC increases.[27]

Withdrawal and Dependence

Withdrawal symptoms after discontinuance of marijuana smoking (that is, evidence of physical dependence) are observed in both short-term and long-term marijuana users, even when relatively low levels of THC are ingested. In one study, abstinence from smoking marijuana cigarettes with approximately 2 to 3 percent THC levels or equivalent oral doses of THC, administered four times a day over a four-day period, resulted in feelings of irritability, stomach pain, anxiety, and loss of appetite. These symptoms began within forty-eight hours and lasted at least two days.[28] Chronic marijuana users who have ingested higher levels of THC show negative physical symptoms after discontinuance that are more severe and long-lasting, resembling the withdrawal symptoms associated with the chronic use of tobacco. These symptoms, however, are substantially milder than those associated with the chronic use of heroin (Chapter 7) or alcohol (Chapter 14).[29]

There is also evidence of marijuana craving, indicating a degree of psychological dependence in some marijuana smokers, but it is difficult to measure the extent of these feelings or to determine whether these effects are due to circumstances in which marijuana is used in conjunction with other drugs. As was pointed out earlier, any definitive judgment about the possibility of psychological dependence or about the extent to which psychological dependence may occur in the average marijuana smoker must be made on the basis of research studies involving THC concentrations that are typical of currently available marijuana.[30]

Cardiovascular Effects

THC produces significant increases in heart rate, but there is no conclusive evidence of adverse effects in the cardiovascular functioning in young, healthy people. The reason why the emphasis is on a specific age group is that most of the studies looking at possible long-term cardiovascular effects have involved marijuana smokers under the age of thirty-five; little or no information has been compiled about older populations. For those people with preexisting disorders such as heart disease, high blood pressure, or arteriosclerosis (hardening of the arteries), it is known that the acute effects of marijuana on heart rate and blood pressure can worsen their condition.

Respiratory Effects and the Risk of Cancer

The technique of marijuana smoking involves the deep and maintained inhalation into the lungs of unfiltered smoke on a repetitive basis, probably the worst possible scenario for incurring chronic pulmonary problems. In addition, a marijuana joint (when compared with a tobacco cigarette) typically contains about the same levels of tars, 50 percent more hydrocarbons, and an unknown amount of possible contaminants (Table 10.1).

TABLE 10.1

A comparison of the components of marijuana and tobacco smoke

COMPONENT	MARIJUANA	TOBACCO
Carbon monoxide (mg)	17.6	20.2
Carbon dioxide (mg)	57.3	65.0
Ammonia (micrograms)	228.0	178.0
Acetaldehyde (micrograms)	1,200.0	980.0
Acetone (micrograms)*	443.0	578.0
Benzene (micrograms)*	76.0	67.0
Toluene (micrograms)*	112.0	108.0
THC (tetrahydrocannabinol) (micrograms)	820.0	—
Nicotine (micrograms)	—	2,850.0
Napthalene (nanograms)	3,000.0	1,200.0

*See Chapter 11 for information about the health risks of inhaling some of these chemicals.

Source: Julien, Robert M. (2001). *A primer of drug action* (9th ed.). New York: Worth, p. 317.

Joints are often smoked more completely because the smoker tries to waste as little marijuana as possible.

Given all these factors, marijuana smoking presents several risks. One of the immediate consequences affects the process of breathing. When marijuana is inhaled initially, the passageways for air entering and leaving the lungs widen, but after chronic exposure, an opposite reaction occurs. As a result, symptoms of asthma and other breathing difficulties are increased. Overall, even though the effects of a single inhalation of marijuana smoke present greater problems than a single inhalation of tobacco smoke, we need to remember that the patterns of consumption are far from comparable. All things considered, one joint is roughly equivalent to five cigarettes in terms of the amount of carbon monoxide intake and four cigarettes in terms of tar intake. The use of a water pipe reduces the harm somewhat, but the risks are still present.

In the respiratory tracts of heavy marijuana smokers, molecular abnormalities have been identified that resemble the changes in the respiratory tracts of cigarette smokers. A recent study has shown that long-term marijuana smoking causes an obstruction of air flow in the lungs, resulting in asthma and bronchitis. The effect of a single marijuana joint is equivalent to that of up to five tobacco cigarettes in this regard. However, marijuana smoking does not increase the risk of developing emphysema, a chronic lung disease that is associated with tobacco smoking (see Chapter 15).

Given these risks, does smoking marijuana produce a higher incidence of cancer? There is no definitive evidence of increases in lung cancer rates among marijuana smokers, after controlling for tobacco use. But it may be too soon to decisively answer the question of increased risk of cancer in general. Marijuana smokers who were twenty years old in the late 1960s have only recently reached the peak ages when cancers appear, and they smoked marijuana containing relatively low THC concentrations at the time. Those individuals more recently exposed to higher-potency marijuana, such as those whose marijuana experience began in the late 1990s, are substantially younger and it will be decades before they reach an age at which the incidence of cancer becomes a significant concern. Fortunately, there is the possibility, as is the case with cigarette smoking (see Chapter 15), that the risk of cancer declines after a person stops smoking marijuana.[31]

Effects on the Immune System

It has been demonstrated that THC has a suppressant effect on the immune system, resulting in a reduction in the body's defense reactions to infection and disease. Whether or not this effect results in an increased risk among chronic marijuana smokers of acquiring infectious diseases or other disorders related to a deficient immune system, however, remains unclear. Long-term epidemiological studies, in which marijuana-exposed and control populations are compared with regard to the frequency of various diseases, have not been conducted on a large-scale basis.[32]

Effects on Sexual Functioning and Reproduction

The reproductive systems of both men and women are adversely affected by marijuana smoking. In men, marijuana reduces the level of testosterone, reduces sperm count in the semen, and increases the percentage of abnormally formed sperm. In women, marijuana use results in a reduction in the level of luteinizing hormone (LH), a hormone necessary for the fertilized egg to be implanted in the uterus. As little as one marijuana joint smoked immediately following ovulation is evidently sufficient for this LH suppression to occur. Despite these hormonal changes in both males and females, however, little or no effect on fertility has been observed.[33]

The research is sparse on the question, but smoking marijuana during pregnancy does not appear to increase the incidence of birth defects. Studies indicate, however, a lower birth weight and shorter length among newborns, as well as a reduction in the mother's milk. It may be unfair to associate these effects specifically with marijuana smoking because other drugs, including alcohol and nicotine, are often consumed during the same period. Even so, the best advice remains that women should avoid marijuana during pregnancy.[34]

Long-Term Cognitive Effects and the Amotivational Syndrome

Though chronic exposure to marijuana frequently has been suspected of producing some form of brain damage or long-term impairment in neural functioning, there is little or no evidence in support of this idea.[35] It also has been suspected that marijuana may produce more subtle neurological changes that would affect one's personality, motivation to succeed, or outlook on life. In 1968, William McGlothin, a psychologist, and Louis West, a psychiatrist, proposed that chronic marijuana smoking among young people was responsible for a generalized sense of apathy in their lives and an indifference to any long-term plans or conventional goals. These changes were called the **amotivational syndrome**. In their words,

> *Regular marijuana use may contribute to the development of more passive, inward-turning personality characteristics. For numerous middle-class students, the subtly progressive change from conforming, achievement-oriented behavior to a state of relaxed and careless drifting has followed their use of significant amounts of marijuana . . . Such individuals exhibit greater introversion, become totally involved with the present at the expense of future goals, and demonstrate a strong tendency toward regressive, childlike magical thinking.*[36]

Essentially, McGothlin and West, and probably a sizable proportion of the American public in the late 1960s, were saying, "These people don't seem to care any more about things *that we think are important*, and marijuana's to blame for it!"

The issue of the amotivational syndrome revolves around two basic questions that need to be examined separately. The first question deals with whether such a syndrome exists in the first place, and the second deals with whether chronic abuse of marijuana is a causal factor. As to the existence of the syndrome, the evidence does suggest that students who smoke marijuana are at a disadvantage academically. Studies of high school students indicate that those who smoke marijuana on a regular basis (weekly or more frequently) earn lower grades in school (Figure 10.1), are less likely to continue on to college, are more likely to drop out, and miss more classes than those who do not smoke it.[37] In a survey of high school students graduating in the early 1980s, those who smoked marijuana on a daily basis reported several problems in their lives that are related to motivation: a loss of energy (43 percent), negative effects on relationships (39 percent), interference with work and the ability to think clearly (37 percent), less interest in other activities (37 percent), and inferior performance in school or on the job (34 percent).[38] It is likely that these percentages would be roughly the same today.

These changes are genuine, but we cannot easily establish a direct causal link between marijuana and such global problems, other than to acknowledge that the presence of THC in a student's system during school hours would be reflected later in a decline in overall academic performance. More broadly speaking, we cannot exclude the possibility that marijuana smoking may be, in the words of one expert in the field, "just one behavior in a constellation of related problem behaviors and personality and familial factors" that hamper an adolescent's ability to do well in school and in life.[39] We also cannot exclude the possibility that an involvement with marijuana may closely correlate with involvement in a deviant subculture, a group of friends and associates who feel alienated from traditional values such as school achievement and a promising future (see Chapter 4). Either of these factors, in combination with the regular ingestion of marijuana, can account for the motivational changes that are observed. The point is that we cannot conclude that such life-style changes are purely pharmacological.

It is clear that acute marijuana intoxication produces significant cognitive deficits, as evidenced by reduced scores on tasks of attentiveness and memory, but the question remains whether these problems are increased or perhaps may even become irreversible as a result of long-term marijuana use. Large and well-controlled studies have shown that cognitive deficits in heavy marijuana smokers, relative to nonusers, are observed after twelve to seventy-two hours of abstinence. In other words, the specific signs of cognitive impairment among long-term marijuana smokers may linger for as long as three days after active marijuana smoking. In one study, however, testing after twenty-eight days of abstinence revealed equivalent performance scores between nonusers and users of marijuana, even though the latter group had smoked a median of about fifteen thousand times over a period ranging

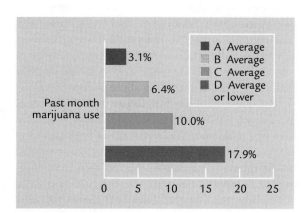

FIGURE 10.1

Percentages of past month marijuana and blunt use among students aged 12 to 17 and semester grade average.

Note: Blunts are hollowed-out cigars refilled with marijuana.

Source: Substance Abuse and Mental Health Services Administration (2007). Use of marijuana and blunts among adolescents: 2005. *The NSDUH Report*, p. 3.

amotivational syndrome: A state of listlessness and personality change involving a generalized apathy and indifference to long-range plans.

from ten to thirty-three years. No correlation was seen between the test scores after twenty-eight days of abstinence and the number of episodes of marijuana use over an individual's lifetime. Therefore, it appears that problems related to attention and memory among heavy marijuana smokers can be reversed by stopping marijuana use. It is a hopeful sign in the context of drug-abuse treatment (Chapter 16). On the other hand, recent studies indicate that specific brain abnormalities associated with long-term heavy marijuana use have a negative impact on successful information-processing abilities. These neuroanatomical changes may not be reversible.[40]

The Gateway Hypothesis

A widely publicized theory about marijuana smoking concerns the possibility of a relationship between marijuana use and the subsequent abuse of illicit drugs such as amphetamines, cocaine, or heroin. The contention that marijuana leads to a greater incidence of drug abuse in general is referred to as the **gateway hypothesis**. Just as in the consideration of the amotivational syndrome, the evidence for this hypothesis must be studied very carefully.

With respect to the gateway hypothesis, we should address three separate issues: (1) whether a fixed sequential relationship exists between the initiation of marijuana use and other forms of drug-taking behavior, (2) whether marijuana use represents a significant risk factor for future drug-taking behavior, specifically increasing the likelihood of using other illicit drugs, and (3) whether marijuana actually causes the use of other illicit drugs.

The Sequencing Question

One of the best-replicated findings in the long-term study of drug use is a developmental sequence of involvement (stages of progression) in drug-taking behavior. In the United States as well as other Western societies, use of alcohol and cigarettes precedes marijuana use, and marijuana use precedes use of other illicit drugs. As public health researcher Denise Kandel has expressed it:

> Very few individuals who have tried cocaine and heroin have not already used marijuana; the majority have previously used alcohol or tobacco.[41]

Nonetheless, it is important to point out that an overwhelming proportion of young marijuana smokers do not go on to use other illicit drugs. As expressed in a 1999 newspaper editorial on this point, "millions of baby boomers . . . once did, indeed, inhale. They later went into business, not cocaine or heroin."[42]

The Association Question

From a statistical perspective, the association between marijuana use and subsequent use of other illicit drugs is not controversial. Generally speaking, marijuana smokers are several times more likely to consume illicit drugs such as cocaine and heroin during their lifetimes than are people who never smoked marijuana. The greater the frequency of marijuana smoking and the earlier an individual first engages in marijuana smoking, the greater the likelihood of his or her becoming involved with other illicit drugs in the future.

A precise determination of the magnitude of risk involved in marijuana use requires studies that take into account a range of genetic and environmental variables that might act as risk or protective factors for drug-taking behavior (see Chapter 4). A 2003 study set out to control for these variables by investigating a specific subpopulation of twins; one member of each twin pair reported marijuana use by the age of seventeen and the other reported no marijuana use at all. Examining twins enabled the researchers to calculate the increased risk of future drug-taking behavior when environmental factors (in the case of fraternal twins) and both environmental and genetic factors (in the case of identical twins) were controlled. Results showed that early marijuana users were about two and one-half times more likely to use heroin later in life, four times more likely to use cocaine or other stimulants, and five times more likely to use hallucinogens. In general, they were twice as likely to become alcoholic and twice as likely to develop any form of illicit drug abuse or dependence.

The question of whether future twin studies using this approach will find the increased risk from marijuana use to be *higher than the increased risk from alcohol or tobacco use* remains unanswered. In any case, the fact that marijuana use is one of the risk factors for illicit drug use in other forms reinforces the need to develop intervention programs for marijuana users that might discourage subsequent drug use, as well as prevention programs for youths to reduce the incidence of marijuana use in the first place.[43]

In the final analysis, however, the statistical relationship between marijuana smoking and other forms of drug-taking behavior may simply reflect the sequential pattern of drug use among multiple-drug (polydrug) users. Essentially, drug users initiate the use of high-prevalence

gateway hypothesis: The idea that the abuse of a specific drug will inherently lead to the abuse of other, more harmful drugs.

drugs (such as alcohol, tobacco, marijuana) earlier than they initiate the use of low-prevalence drugs (such as cocaine, heroin). This effect is not due to the drugs themselves but rather to the relative differences in prevalence rates. Numerous statistical relationships exist between other types of common and uncommon behaviors:

> For example, most people who ride a motorcycle (a fairly rare activity) have ridden a bicycle (a fairly common activity). Indeed, the prevalence of motorcycle riding among people who have never ridden a bicycle is probably extremely low. Bicycle riding, however, does not cause motorcycle riding, and increases in the former will not lead automatically to increases in the latter.[44]

The Causation Question

The strongest form of the gateway hypothesis relates to the possibility of a causal link between marijuana smoking and the use of other illicit drugs. With respect to the causation issue, Erich Goode, a sociologist and drug-abuse researcher, has distinguished between two schools of thought, which he calls the intrinsic argument and the sociocultural argument. The *intrinsic argument* asserts that some inherent property of marijuana exposure itself leads to physical or psychological dependence on other illicit drugs. According to this viewpoint, the pleasurable sensations induced by marijuana create a biological urge to consume more potent substances, through a combination of drug tolerance and drug dependence. In contrast, the *sociocultural argument* holds that the relationship exists not because of the pharmacological effects of marijuana but because of the activities, friends, and acquaintances that are associated with marijuana smoking. In other words, the sociocultural explanation asserts that those who smoke marijuana tend to have friends who not only smoke marijuana themselves but also abuse other drugs. These friends are likely to have positive attitudes toward substance abuse in general and to provide opportunities for drug experimentation.

Professionals in the drug-abuse field have concluded that if any such causal link exists, the result is socioculturally based rather than related to the pharmacological properties of marijuana itself. The consensus is that any early exposure to psychoactive substances in general, and illicit drugs such as marijuana in particular, represents a "deviance-prone pattern of behavior" that will be reflected in a higher incidence of exposure to psychoactive drugs of many types later in life. It is interesting to note that early adolescent marijuana use among males also increases the risk in late adolescence of delinquency, having multiple sexual partners, not always using condoms during sex, perceiving drugs as not harmful,

and having problems with cigarettes and alcohol. Generally speaking, marijuana smokers show a greater inclination toward risk-taking behavior and are more unconventional with regard to social norms.[45]

Patterns of Marijuana Smoking

From as early as their days in elementary school, most young Americans have had to come to terms with marijuana as a pervasive element in their lives. Just as nearly all adolescents have had to decide whether to drink and whether to smoke cigarettes, they also have had to decide whether or not to smoke marijuana.

Marijuana is undoubtedly the dominant illicit drug in U.S. society today, used by 77 percent of current illicit drug users (Figure 10.2). For more than half of illicit drug users, marijuana is the *only* illicit drug being used. From the National Survey on Drug Use and Health conducted in 2009, it is estimated that an astounding 104 million Americans, about 42 percent of the U.S. population over the age of twelve, have smoked marijuana at least once during their lives. More than 16 million Americans are estimated to have smoked marijuana within the past thirty days.[46]

Among high school seniors surveyed in 2009, approximately 33 percent reported having smoked marijuana in the past year, 21 percent reported having done so in the past month, and 5 percent smoked on a daily basis. Among eighth graders, 12 percent reported smoking marijuana in the past year and 7 percent in the past month. The current status of prevention programs, understandably under considerable pressure to reduce rates of marijuana smoking as well as involvement in other drugs among young people, will be examined in Chapter 16.[47]

Current Trends as Causes for Concern

Current prevalence rates, in general, are substantially lower than those in the 1970s. Nonetheless, there is some concern that marijuana smoking rates are inching upward. In other words, the "roller-coaster ride" of marijuana use monitored over the decades (see Figure 2.1) may be entering a new upward phase. In 2009, Lloyd Johnston of the University of Michigan survey cautioned that "a key belief about the degree of risk associated with marijuana use has been in decline among young people . . . and the degree to which teens disapprove of use of the drug has recently begun to decline."[48] In 2009, high school seniors were evenly split in terms of judging "regular marijuana smoking" as representing "great risk," while seniors in 1992 had judged it as representing "great risk" by a three to one margin.[49]

A second concern with regard to present-day marijuana use has to do with an increased potency in the cannabis products that are available. As noted earlier, a typical marijuana joint in the psychedelic era three decades ago contained approximately 1 to 2 percent THC; the average concentration has now risen above 6 percent to as high as 10 percent and, in the case of recent strains of sinsemilla, as high as 15 percent. It is reasonable to assume that the adverse effects of chronic marijuana smoking will be more intense than the relatively mild symptoms associated with marijuana use in the past (Drugs . . . in Focus).

A third concern applies to any illicit street drug: the possibility for adulteration. As emphasized in earlier

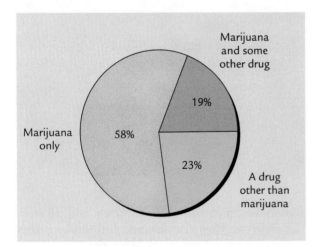

FIGURE 10.2

Types of drugs used by illicit drug users aged 12 or older in the past month in 2008.

Source: Substance Abuse and Mental Health Services Administration (2010). *Results from the 2009 National Survey on Drug Use and Health: National findings.* Rockville, MD: Office of Applied Studies, Substance Abuse and Mental Health Services Administration, p. 13.

Pie chart labels: Marijuana and some other drug 19%; Marijuana only 58%; A drug other than marijuana 23%.

The image of *Cannabis sativa* today.

Drugs... in Focus

Street Language for Marijuana

In the 1960s, when marijuana smoking first became widely popular, the street language was fairly simple. Marijuana was either "grass" or "pot," and a marijuana cigarette was a "joint." Here is an updated sampling of the street language, though the names (and prices) are constantly changing.

- marijuana: grass, weed, 420, skunk, boom, doobie, bud, herb, BC bud (Over the years, more than 600 slang names have been given to marijuana.)
- marijuana and alcohol: Herb and Al
- getting high on marijuana: getting lifted, booted, red, smoked out or choked out, hit the hay, poke, toke up, blast a stick, burn one, fly Mexican Airlines, mow the grass, boot the gong
- $3 bag of marijuana: a tray
- $5 "nickel" bag: a nick (usually just enough for one joint)
- $40 bag: a sandwich bag
- kinds of marijuana: chronic, chocolate tide, indigo, Hawaiian, Tropicana, Acapulco gold, Panama red

- water pipe similar to a bong: a shotgun
- joints: "blunts" (after the Phillies Blunt cigars that marijuana smokers cut open, hollow out, and fill with marijuana; other brands used: White Owls and Dutch Masters)
- hydro: hydroponic marijuana, grown in water

According to the National Survey on Drug Use and Health, more than 50 percent of marijuana users in 2005 between the ages of 12 and 17 used blunts in marijuana smoking. The popularity of blunts increased with age. Males reported more often than females to have smoked marijuana in a blunt during the past month.

Sources: Bureau of Justice Statistics Clearinghouse (1992). *Drugs, crime, and the justice system,* Washington, DC: Department of Justice, pp. 24–25. Henneberger, Melinda (1994, February 6). "Pot" surges back, but it's, like, a whole new world. *New York Times,* Sect. 4, p. 18. Inciardi, James A. (2002). *The war on drugs III.* Boston, Allyn and Bacon, pp. 56–57. Use of marijuana and blunts among adolescents: 2005 (2007, March 9). *The NSDUH Report,* p. 1.

---

chapters, what you buy is not always what you get. Each year brings with it a new group of ingredients, some of them newly introduced drugs and others merely inventive creations from already available materials, ready to

be combined with marijuana either to weaken its effects (and increase the profits of the seller) or to change the overall psychoactive result by some synergistic or other interactive effect (Drug Trafficking Update).

Drug Trafficking Update
Marijuana

- **Origins:** Domestic low-grade marijuana production at indoor sites throughout the United States has expanded greatly. In addition, an increasing percentage of high-grade marijuana is derived from indoor cannabis cultivation in Canada and central California. Mexican cultivation of marijuana within the United States has been expanding, though operations have been hindered in some areas by intensified eradication efforts.
- **Points of Entry:** Increasingly, foreign-based marijuana is smuggled across the U.S.–Canada border.
- **Traffickers:** High-grade marijuana distribution into the United States is controlled primarily by Canada-based

Asian criminal groups. Asian groups have also been able to establish large-scale operations within the United States, in order to avoid seizure of shipments at the Canadian border.

Source: National Drug Intelligence Center (2010). *National Drug Threat Assessment 2010.* Washington, DC: National Drug Intelligence Center, U.S. Department of Justice, pp. 36–39. National Drug Intelligence Center (2006). *National Drug Threat Assessment 2007.* Washington, DC: National Drug Intelligence Center, U.S. Department of Justice, pp. 10–13.

Medical Marijuana

Even though the medicinal benefits of marijuana have been noted for thousands of years, strong antimarijuana sentiment in the United States made it difficult until the 1970s to conduct an objective appraisal of its clinical applications. Early research in the effectiveness of marijuana to reduce intraocular (within the eye) pressure and dilate bronchioles in the lungs suggested uses as a possible therapy for glaucoma and asthma, respectively. However, new prescription medications have been shown to be as effective as marijuana in the treatment of these disorders. Today the focus has turned toward the treatment of nausea and weight loss, conditions for which medications have been unsuccessful in offering significant relief.

Nausea and Weight Loss

Chemotherapy in the course of cancer treatment produces an extreme and debilitating nausea, lack of appetite, and loss of body weight, symptoms that are clearly counterproductive in helping an individual contend with

PORTRAIT

Angel McClary, Medical Marijuana and the *Raich v. Ashcroft* Decision

In the 2005 U.S. Supreme Court case *Raich v. Ashcroft*, the legal status of medical marijuana within the state of California was overturned in favor of arguments that federal regulations prohibiting marijuana use under any circumstances were paramount. It was a landmark decision, and the consequences with respect to marijuana as a medical treatment remain uncertain. But who was behind *Raich v. Ashcroft* in this case? Who was Raich?

Angel McClary Raich was permanently disabled in 1995. Her medical condition included an inoperable brain tumor, life-threatening wasting syndrome, chronic pain disorders, seizure disorder, nausea, and scoliosis (a painful back condition). Her physician recommended cannabis use as a medication for her symptoms. In a legal deposition submitted at the time, she described her life:

I suffer greatly from severe chronic pain every single day. The prolonged pain and suffering from my medical condition significantly interferes with my quality of life. My treatment is complicated by the fact that I am violently allergic and have severe multiple sensitivities to almost all pharmaceutical medicines . . . This makes it extremely difficult for doctors to effectively help me combat my diseases. Without cannabis my life would be a death sentence.[a]

Raich's primary care physician, Dr. Frank Lucido, was the one who made the recommendation of medical marijuana. He recognized that Raich was at significant risk of malnutrition and starvation as well as suffering intolerable pain. He wrote,

Angel has no reasonable legal alternative to cannabis for the effective treatment or alleviation of her medical conditions or symptoms associated with medical conditions because she has tried essentially all other legal alternatives to cannabis and the alternatives have been ineffective or result from intolerable side effects. Angel will suffer imminent harm without access to cannabis . . . It would be malpractice to subject the patient to further unnecessary harm . . . Cannabis works well for Angel in a way that no other medicine has or can be expected to in order to alleviate Angel's medical conditions or symptoms associated with them.[b]

Raich became one of the fourteen "medical necessity" patients at the Oakland Cannabis Buyers' Cooperative who were represented in the court cases that led up to the Supreme Court. In 1996, California voters passed the Compassionate Use Act, legalizing marijuana for medical use within the state. After the Drug Enforcement Administration (DEA) seized doctor-prescribed marijuana from the home of a patient, advocates of medical marijuana sued the DEA and then–U.S. Attorney General John Ashcroft in federal district court and won. Their case was upheld until the Supreme Court decision in 2005.

In November 2005, Raich filed legal papers in a federal appeals court, arguing that federal efforts and the Supreme Court decision to restrict medical marijuana violated her constitutionally guaranteed rights to take the only medication allowing her to avoid intolerable pain and death. The brief marks a new legal strategy, claiming that the concern for federal control of interstate commerce (see text) does not apply to her use of locally grown marijuana. As Raich puts it, "I just want the opportunity to be a mother to my children without having to live in constant fear that the federal government will raid my home and throw me in jail."[c]

Sources: [a]Who Is Angel McClary Raich? Angel Wings Patient Outreach, Inc. web site, *angeljustice.org*. [b]Declaration of Frank Henry Lucido, M.D., in support of the plaintiff Angel McClary Raich, October 20, 2002, U.S. District Court for the Northern District of California. [c]Ashley, Guy (2005, November 24). Woman pursues new legal strategy in medical marijuana fight. Knight Ridder/Tribune News Service.

an ongoing fight against cancer. AIDS patients suffer from similar symptoms, as do those diagnosed with the gastrointestinal ailment Crohn's disease. Under these circumstances, standard antiemetic (antivomiting) drugs are frequently ineffective. The beneficial effect of marijuana, specifically THC, as an antiemetic drug is an important application of marijuana as a medical treatment.[50] This chapter's Portrait examines the present-day dilemma of turning to an illegal drug for medicinal purposes.

At the same time, the use of marijuana *per se* as a therapeutic agent has distinct disadvantages. First, the typical administration through smoking presents, as described earlier, a significant health risk to the lungs. Second, because marijuana is insoluble in water, suspensions in an injectable form cannot be prepared. Since 1985, however, two legal prescription drugs containing THC or a variation of it have been made available in capsule form. **Dronabinol** (brand name: Marinol) is essentially THC in a sesame oil suspension; **nabilone (brand name: Cesamet)** is a synthetic variation of THC. Both drugs have been shown to be clinically effective against nausea treatments, though the personal reactions of patients taking these drugs vary considerably.[51]

The Medical Marijuana Controversy

Even though Marinol and Cesamet are presently in use, U.S. federal authorities have resisted the reclassification of marijuana itself or of any other cannabis product from the Schedule I category of controlled substances (drugs that have no medical application) to the Schedule II category (which includes morphine and cocaine). Only a handful of "compassionate use" applications have been approved, and the entire program for reviewing new applications was curtailed in 1992.

Despite opposition from federal authorities, advocacy for the medical application of marijuana has grown considerably. Unfortunately, the facts about medical marijuana sometimes have been lost in a thicket of politics and opposing ideologies. A case in point is the interpretation of a major report on the possibility of using marijuana as a medical treatment, issued by the Institute of Medicine, a branch of the National Academy of Sciences, in 1999. In its preface, the report began by acknowledging the problems involved:

> Although marijuana smoke delivers THC and other cannabinoids to the body, it also delivers harmful substances, including most of those found in tobacco smoke. In addition, plants contain a variable mixture of biologically-active compounds and cannot be

expected to provide a precisely defined drug effect. For these reasons, this report concludes that the future of cannabinoid drugs lies not in smoked marijuana, but in chemically-defined drugs that act on the cannabinoid systems that are a natural component of human physiology.[52]

In focusing on the report's preface, the federal Office of National Drug Control Strategy has emphasized the potential health risks of marijuana smoking and the imprecision of its administration as a justification for the continued prohibition of marijuana for medical purposes. Largely ignored has been one of the report's main statements:

> Until a nonsmoked, rapid-onset cannabinoid drug delivery system becomes available, we acknowledge that there is no clear alternative for people suffering from chronic conditions that might be relieved by smoking marijuana, such as pain or AIDS wasting.[53]

In effect, the report concluded that, although smoked marijuana could not be recommend for long-term use, short-term use appeared to be suitable for treating specific conditions, when patients failed to respond well to traditional medications.

By mid-2010, fourteen U.S. States (Alaska, California, Colorado, Hawaii, Maine, Michigan, Montana, Nevada, New Jersey, New Mexico, Oregon, Rhode Island, Vermont, and Washington) had authorized marijuana smoking for the relief of pain and discomfort or the control of nausea and weight loss, when prescribed by a physician. In New Jersey, tight restrictions on medical marijuana were established: Patients must suffer from specific diseases such as cancer and glaucoma and must demonstrate severe or chronic pain, nauseas, seizures, muscle spasms, or wasting syndrome (loss of weight or body mass).[54]

In 2009, in a significant reversal of federal policy on medical marijuana, the U.S. Department of Justice announced that "It will not be a priority to use federal resources to prosecute patients with serious illnesses or their caregivers who are complying with state laws on medical marijuana, but we will not tolerate drug traffickers who hide behind claims of compliance with state law to mask activities that are clearly illegal."[55]

dronabinol (droh-NAB-ih-nol): A prescription drug containing delta-9-tetrahydrocannabinol (THC). Brand name is Marinol.

nabilone (NAB-ih-lone): A prescription drug containing a synthetic variation of delta-9-tetrahydrocannabinol (THC). Brand name is Cesamet.

Walt could spend his final days in prison instead of a hospital.

Please join the effort to protect patients who need medical marijuana for serious illnesses.

Over 400 legislators, medical professionals, religious leaders, celebrities, and organizations on the local, state, and national levels have signed a letter to President Bush asking him to allow people with AIDS, cancer, and other serious illnesses to use medical marijuana if they have the approval of their physicians ...

Dear President Bush:

Like most Americans, we believe that seriously ill people should not be subject to arrest and imprisonment for using medical marijuana with their doctors' approval.

Indeed, on March 17, 1999, the National Academy of Sciences' Institute of Medicine released its landmark report on marijuana, concluding that "there are some limited circumstances in which we recommend smoking marijuana for medical uses."[1] The IOM report urged the federal government to give seriously ill people immediate legal access to medical marijuana on a case-by-case basis.[2]

Currently, federal law confers a one-year prison sentence for possessing a small amount of marijuana for any reason — and no exception is made for medical use.

Countless seriously ill people are already using marijuana because they and their doctors believe that it is the best medicine for them. These patients should not be treated like criminals.

Consequently, we encourage you to allow people suffering from serious illnesses like AIDS, cancer, and multiple sclerosis to apply to the federal government for special permission to use marijuana to treat their symptoms.

Thank you.

As of 2009, fourteen states have legalized medical marijuana. Their ranking with respect to their leniency toward medical marijuana use is depicted here.

In effect, the Department of Justice has returned the question of medical marijuana to the jurisdiction of the states without altering its official stance on a federal level that marijuana is a controlled substance without medical use. At the same time, it has signaled the requirement that the states set up regulations that limit marijuana use to legitimate medical circumstances. The regulations set up in New Jersey are likely to be a model for state-approved medical marijuana legislation in the future.

In a national AP-CNBC poll conducted in 2010, 60 percent of American adults favored legalizing the possession of small amounts of marijuana for medical purposes, and 74 percent believed that marijuana would have a real medical benefit for some people. There were no significant differences in these poll results due to the region of the country surveyed, nor were there differences due to the type of region (urban, suburban, or rural).[56]

Canada has officially approved the medicinal use of marijuana since 2001. It is legal for Canadian patients to grow and smoke marijuana if their symptoms have been certified by a physician as warranting this treatment. It is also permitted, under these circumstances, to request marijuana, free of charge, from government-operated cannabis farms in Manitoba. In 2005, the FDA-equivalent agency in Canada approved the pre-scription use of Sativex, a liquid spray derived from the cannabis plant. More recently, the FDA has approved clinical testing of Sativex for potential sale in the United States. By providing a nonsmoking means of administration, this formulation circumvents arguments that medical marijuana smoking presents increased risks of smoking-related diseases (see Chapter 15).[57]

The Issues of Decriminalization and Legalization

What, then, should public policy be toward marijuana smoking in the United States today? To deal with this question, we need first to review how public policy with respect to marijuana regulation has evolved since the 1970s. As described earlier, the dramatic emergence during the 1960s of marijuana as a major psychoactive drug initiated a slow but steady reassessment of myths that had been attached to it for decades. By 1972, the American Medical Association, the American Bar Association, and a number of conservative-leaning commentators and public figures had proposed a liberalization of laws regarding the possession of marijuana. In 1972, the National Commission on Marijuana and Drug Abuse, authorized by the Comprehensive Drug Abuse Prevention and Control Act of 1970, encouraged state legislators around the country to consider changes in their particular regulatory statutes related to marijuana.[58] Since that time, several states, including California, New York, Colorado, Minnesota, and North Carolina, have adopted some form of decriminalization laws with respect to the possession of marijuana in small amounts (usually less than an ounce or so). Essentially, **decriminalization** has meant that possession under these circumstances is considered a civil (non-criminal) offense, punishable by a small fine, rather than imprisonment.

The era of strenuous law enforcement against marijuana smoking at low levels of usage is essentially over. As the sociologist Erich Goode has expressed it:

> *For all practical purposes, the possession of [small amounts of] marijuana has become decriminalized in the United States. Since present trends are moving toward de facto legal acceptance of small-quantity marijuana possession, it will not make a great deal of difference whether this attitude is recognized by law or not. Consequently, the debate over marijuana criminalization borders on being obsolete.*[59]

Nonetheless, as discussed in Chapter 6, the Drug Enforcement Administration continues an aggressive program to confiscate and destroy large crops of cannabis grown within the United States and to encourage foreign countries (specifically Mexico) to do the same.

You may find it surprising or not surprising (depending on your personal views) that official decriminalization has not been demonstrated to result in an upturn in the incidence of marijuana smoking. Statistics drawn from states that either have or have not decriminalized show little or no difference. In addition, attitude surveys conducted in California before and after the enactment of such statutes indicate that the acceptance of marijuana among college students actually declined following decriminalization.[60]

A soldier stands guard over the destruction of a cannabis crop. Presumably, the people living downwind of this operation have been evacuated.

Marijuana legalization is different from decriminalization in that it allows anyone over the age of 21 to purchase marijuana for his or her own use. In recent years, a number of initiatives for legalization have been pursued at the state or federal level. In November, 2010, a California state referendum to legalize marijuana possession was defeated by a 54-to-46 percent vote.

On the basis of public opinion, support for such a policy appears to be growing. A 2009 Gallup Poll on the question of whether use of marijuana should be made legal, 44 percent of Americans were in favor. From the late 1970s to the mid-1990s, acceptance of marijuana legalization had hovered around the 25 percent range. In the 2010 AP-CNBC poll cited earlier, this figure has risen to 33 percent of Americans in favor of legalizing marijuana. And even though approximately two-thirds of respondents remain opposed or uncertain, few Americans seem to believe that the legalization of marijuana would worsen crime.[61]

decriminalization: The policy of making the possession of small amounts of a drug subject to a small fine but not criminal prosecution.

Summary

A Matter of Terminology

- Marijuana is one of several products of *Cannabis sativa*, or the common hemp plant, grown abundantly throughout the world.

- Various cannabis products are distinguished in terms of the content of cannabis resin and, in turn, the concentration of THC, the active psychoactive agent.

The History of Marijuana and Hashish

- The earliest records of marijuana come from Chinese writings nearly five thousand years ago; the use of hashish originated in North Africa and Persia in the ninth or tenth centuries A.D.

- In the United States, marijuana was available in patent medicines during the late 1800s, but its popularity did not become extensive until the 1920s.

- Federal and state regulation of marijuana began in the 1930s; penalties for possessing and selling marijuana escalated during the 1940s and 1950s.

- The emergence of marijuana on American college campuses and among American youth in general during the late 1960s, however, forced a reexamination of public policy regarding this drug, leading to a more lenient approach in the 1970s.

Acute Effects of Marijuana

- Because marijuana is almost always consumed through smoking, the acute effects are rapid, but because it is absorbed into fatty tissue, its elimination is slow. It may require days or weeks in the case of extensive exposure to marijuana for THC to leave the body completely.

- Acute physiological effects include cardiac acceleration and a reddening of the eyes. Acute psychological effects, with typical dosages, include euphoria, giddiness, a perception of time elongation, and increased hunger. There are impairments in attention and memory, which interfere with complex visual–motor skills such as driving an automobile.

- The acute effects of marijuana are now known to be due to the binding of THC at special receptors in the brain.

Chronic Effects of Marijuana

- Chronic marijuana use produces tolerance effects; there is no physical dependence when doses are moderate and only a mild psychological dependence.

- Carcinogenic effects are suspected because marijuana smoke contains many of the same harmful components that tobacco smoke does, and in the case of marijuana smoking inhalation is deeper and more prolonged.

The Gateway Hypothesis

- The idea that as a result of the pharmacological effects of chronic marijuana use there exists an amotivational syndrome, characterized by general apathy and an indifference to long-range planning, has been

largely discredited. An alternative explanation for the behavioral changes is that chronic marijuana users are involved in a deviant subculture that tends to undermine traditional values of school achievement and long-term aspirations.

- Another idea that has been related to chronic marijuana use is the gateway hypothesis, which asserts that marijuana inherently sets the stage for future patterns of drug abuse. Research studies have indicated that the use of alcohol and cigarettes precedes marijuana use, and marijuana use precedes the use of other illicit drugs. In addition, marijuana use and the subsequent use of other illicit drugs are statistically correlated. However, there is little evidence that some inherent property of marijuana exposure itself leads to physical or psychological dependence on other drugs.

Patterns of Marijuana Smoking

- The current prevalence rate of marijuana smoking among adolescents and young adults is lower than in the late 1970s. However, in 2009, 33 percent of high school seniors reported smoking marijuana in the past year.

- Other areas of concern are the considerably greater potency of marijuana that is now available and the continuing potential risk of marijuana adulteration.

Medical Marijuana and Marijuana Decriminalization

- Marijuana has been useful in the treatment of glaucoma and asthma, but its most effective application to date has been in the treatment of symptoms of nausea and weight loss. By mid-2010, fourteen U.S. states had approved medical marijuana. In 2009, a significant reversal of federal policy on medical marijuana occurred when the U.S. Department of Justice announced that it would not be a national priority to use federal resources to prosecute patients with serious illnesses or their caregivers who are complying with state laws on medical marijuana. However, the federal government is still officially on record as classifying marijuana as a controlled substance without medical use.

- Present public policy in the United States toward marijuana smoking has evolved to the point of essentially decriminalizing the possession of marijuana in small amounts. Legalization is still highly controversial, although public support has gradually increased in recent years.

Key Terms

amotivational syndrome, p. 229

anandamide, p. 226

bhang, p. 220

cannabinoids, p. 219

Cannabis sativa, p. 219

decriminalization, p. 237

delta-9-tetrahydrocannabinol (THC), p. 219

dronabinol (Marinol), p. 235

gateway hypothesis, p. 230

hashish, p. 220

hashish oil, p. 220

hashish oil crystals, p. 220

joint, p. 223

marijuana, p. 220

nabilone (Cesamet), p. 235

reefer, p. 223

sinsemilla, p. 220

Endnotes

1. Abel, Ernest L. (1980). *Marihuana, the first twelve thousand years.* New York: Plenum Press, p. ix.

2. Bloomquist, Edward R. (1968). *Marijuana.* Beverly Hills, CA: Glencoe Press, pp. 4–5.

3. Abel, *Marihuana*, p. 4. Palfai, Tibor, and Jankiewicz, Henry (1991). *Drugs and human behavior.* Dubuque, IA: W. C. Brown, p. 452.

4. Abel, *Marihuana*, pp. x–xi.

5. Goode, Erich (2008). *Drugs in American society* (7th ed.). New York: McGraw-Hill Higher Education, p. 239. National Drug Intelligence Center (2009). *Domestic cannabis cultivation assessment 2009.* Washington, DC: U.S. Department of Justice, p. 4. National Drug Intelligence Center (2008). *National drug threat assessment: 2009.* Washington, DC: U.S. Department of Justice, p. 18. *Pulse check: Marijuana report.* Washington, DC: White House Office of Drug Control Policy.

6. Abel, *Marihuana*, p. 12.

7. Bonnie, Richard J., and Whitebread, Charles H. (1974). *The marihuana conviction: A history of marihuana prohibition in the United States.* Charlottesville, VA: University Press of Virginia, p. 3.

8. Abel, *Marihuana*, pp. 218–222.

9. Bonnie and Whitebread, *The marihuana conviction*, p. 33.

10. Anslinger, Harry J., and Tompkins, William F. (1953). *The traffic in narcotics.* New York: Funk & Wagnalls, pp. 37–38. Cited in Inciardi, James A. (2002). *The war on drugs III.* Boston: Allyn and Bacon, p. 46.

11. Lee, Martin A., and Shlain, Bruce (1985). *Acid dreams: The complete social history of LSD.* New York: Grove Weidenfeld.

12. Julien, Robert M. (2005). *A primer of drug action* (10th ed.). New York: Worth pp. 565–567.

13. Ibid., p. 566.

14. *Allen and Hanbury's athletic drug reference* (1992). Research Triangle Park, NC: Clean Data, p. 33. Wadler, Gary I., and Hainline, Brian (1989). *Drugs and the athlete.* Philadelphia: F. A. Davis, pp. 208–209.

15. Grinspoon, Lester, and Bakalar, James B. (1997). Marihuana. In Joyce H. Lowinson, Pedro Ruiz, Robert B. Millman, and John G. Langrod (Eds.), *Substance abuse: A comprehensive texbook* (3rd ed.). Baltimore, MD: Williams and Wilkins, pp. 199–206.

16. Jones, Reese T. (1980). Human effects: An overview. In Robert C. Petersen (Ed.), *Marijuana research findings: 1980* (NIDA Research Monograph 31). Rockville, MD: National Institute on Drug Abuse, p. 65.

17. Grilly, David M. (2006). *Drugs and human behavior* (5th ed.). Boston: Allyn and Bacon, p. 268.

18. Substance Abuse and Mental Health Services Administration (2009). *Drug Abuse Warning Network, 2008: Selected tables of national estimates of drug-related emergency department visits.* Rockville, MD: Office of Applied Studies, Substance Abuse and Mental Health Services Administration.

19. Winger, Gail; Hofmann, Frederick G.; and Woods, James H. (1992). *A handbook on drug and alcohol abuse* (3rd ed.). New York: Oxford University Press, pp. 123–125.

20. Hooker, William D., and Jones, Reese T. (1987). Increased susceptibility to memory intrusions and the Stroop interference effect during acute marijuana intoxication. *Psychopharmacology, 91*, 20–24. Ilan, Aaron B.; Gevins, A.; Coleman, M.; ElSohly, M. A.; and de Wit, H. (2005). Neurophysiological and subjective profile of marijuana with varying concentrations of cannabinoids. *Behavioural Pharmacology, 16*, 487–496.

21. Delong, Fonya L., and Levy, Bernard I. (1974). A model of attention describing the cognitive effects of marijuana. In Loren L. Miller (Ed.), *Marijuana: Effects on human behavior.* New York: Academic Press, pp. 103–117. Gieringer, Dale H. (1988). Marijuana, driving, and accident safety. *Journal of Psychoactive Drugs, 20*, 93–101.

22. McKim, William A. (2007). *Drugs and behavior* (6th ed.). Englewood Cliffs, NJ: Prentice-Hall, pp. 322–325.

23. Ramaekers, J. G.; Berghaus, G.; van Laar, M.; and Drummer, O. H. (2004). Dose related risk of motor vehicle crashes after cannabis use. *Drugs and Alcohol Dependence, 73*, 109–119.

24. Block, Robert I. (1997). Editorial: Does heavy marijuana use impair human cognition and brain function? *Journal of the American Medical Association, 275*, 560–561. Pope, Harrison G., Jr., and Yurgelun-Todd, Deborah (1996). The residual cognitive effects of heavy marijuana use in college students. *Journal of the American Medical Association, 275*, 521–527.

25. McKim, *Drugs and behavior*, pp. 313-335. Raes, Elke, Pil, Kristol, and Verstrete, Alain G. (2009). The modern trends in alcohol, drugs, and driving research. *Proceedings of the 17th International Meeting on Forensic Medicine*, 11–14. Winger, Hofmann, and Woods, *A handbook on drug and alcohol abuse*, pp. 118, 127–129.

26. Ameri, Angela (1999). The effects of cannabinoids on the brain. *Progress in Neurobiology*, 58, 315–348. Chait, L. D., and Burke, K. A. (1994). Preference for high- versus low-potency marijuana. *Pharmacology, Biochemistry, and Behavior*, 49, 643–647. Tanda, Gianluigi, Pontieri, Francesco E., and Di Chiara, Gaetano (1997). Cannabinoid and heroin activation of mesolimbic dopamine transmission by a common μ_1 opioid receptor mechanism. *Science*, 276; 2048–2049. Wickelgren, Ingrid (1997). Research news: Marijuana: Harder than thought? *Science*, 276, 1967–1968.

27. Abood, M., and Martin, B. (1992). Neurobiology of marijuana abuse. *Trends in Pharmacological Sciences*, 13, 201–206.

28. Haney, Margaret; Ward, Amie S.; Comer, Sandra D.; Foltin, Richard W; and Fischman, Marian W. (1999a). Abstinence symptoms following oral THC administration in humans. *Psychopharmacology*, 141, 385–394. Haney, Margaret; Ward, Amie S.; Comer, Sandra D.; Foltin, Richard W; and Fischman, Marian W. (1999b). Abstinence symptoms following smoked marijuana in humans. *Psychopharmacology*, 141, 395–404.

29. Budney, Alan J.; Hughes, John R.; Moore, Brent A.; and Vandrey, Ryan (2004). Review of the validity and significance of cannabis withdrawal syndrome. *American Journal of Psychiatry*, 161, 1967–1977.

30. Duffy, Anne, and Milin, Robert (1996). Case study: Withdrawal syndrome in adolescent chronic cannabis users. *Journal of the American Academy of Child and Adolescent Psychiatry*, 35, 1618–1621. Julien, Robert M. (2001). *A primer of drug action* (9th ed.). New York: Worth, pp. 320–322.

31. Mehra, Reena; Moore, Brent A.; Crothers, Kristina; Tetrault, Jeanette; and Fiellin, David A. (2006). The association between marijuana smoking and lung cancer: A systematic review. *Archives of Internal Medicine*, 166, 1359–1367.

32. Committee on Substance Abuse, American Academy of Pediatrics (1999). Marijuana: A continuing concern for pediatricians. *Pediatrics*, 104, 982–985. Friedman, Herman, Newton Catherine, and Klein, Thomas W. (2003). Microbial infections, immunomodulation, and drugs of abuse. *Clinical Biochemistry Reviews*, 16, 209–219. Hollister, Leo E. (1988). Marijuana and immunity. *Journal of Psychoactive Drugs*, 20, 3–7.

33. Brands, Bruna, Sproule, Beth, and Marshman, Joan (Eds.) (1998). *Drugs and drug abuse: A reference text* (3rd ed.). Toronto: Addiction Research Foundation. Committee on Substance Abuse, Marijuana. Grinspoon and Bakalar, Marihuana, pp. 203–204. Male infertility: Sperm from marijuana smokers move too fast, too early (2003, November 3). *Health and Medicine Week*, pp. 459–460.

34. Grinspoon and Bakalar, Marihuana, p. 203.

35. McGothlin, William H., and West, Louis J. (1968). The marijuana problem: An overview. *American Journal of Psychiatry*, 125, 372.

36. Goode, Erich (1999). *Drugs in American Society* (5th ed.). New York: McGraw-Hill College, pp. 232–233.

37. Brook, J.S., Adamas, R.E., Balka, E.B., and Johnson, E. (2002). Early adolescent marijuana use: Risks for the transition to young adulthood. *Psychological Medicine*, 32, 79–91. Fox, C. Lynn, and Forbing, Shirley E. (1992). *Creating drug-free schools and communities: A comprehensive approach*. New York: HarperCollins, p. 60. Roebuck, M. Christopher, French, Michael T., and Dennis, Michael L. (2004). Adolescent marijuana use and school attendance. *Economics of Education Review*, 23, 133–141.

38. Goode (1999), *Drugs in American society*, p. 233.

39. Fried, P. A., Wilkinson, B., and Gray, R. (2005). Neurocognitive consequences of marihuana—A comparison with pre-drug performance. *Neurotoxicology and Teratology*, 27, 231–239. Hollister, Leo E. (1986). Health aspects of cannabis. *Pharmacological Reviews*, 38, 1–20. Pope, Harrison (2002). Cannabis, cognition, and residual confounding. *Journal of the American Medical Association*, 287, 1172–1174. Solowij, Nadia; Stephens, Robert S.; Roffman, Roger A.; Babor, Thomas; Kadden, Ronald; et al. (2002). Cognitive functioning of long-term heavy cannabis users seeking treatment. *Journal of the AmericanMedical Association*, 287, 1123–1131.

40. Yücel, Murat; Solowij, Nadia; Respondek, Colleen; Whittle, Sarah; Fornito, Alex; et al. (2008, June). Regional brain abnormalities associated with long-term heavy cannabis use. *Archives of General Psychiatry*, 65, 694–701.

41. Kandel, Denise B. (2003). Does marijuana use cause the use of other drugs? *Journal of the American Medical Association*, 289, 482–483. Quotation on p. 482. Kandel, Denise B. (Ed.) (2002). *Stages and pathways of drug involvement: Examining the gateway hypothesis*. Cambridge: Cambridge University Press.

42. Cited in Medical marijuana: Editorials debate "gateway" effect (1999, April 12). *American Health Line*, URL: http://www.ahl.com.

43. Kandel, Does marijuana use cause the use of other drugs? Lynskey, Michael T.; Hath, Andrew C.; Bucholz, Kathleen K.; Slutske, Wendy S.; Madden, Pamela A. F.; et al. (2003). The escalation of drug use in early-onset cannabis users vs co-twin controls. *Journal of the American Medical Association*, 289, 427–433. Martin, Kimberly R. (2001). Adolescent treatment programs reduce drug abuse, produce other improvements. *NIDA Notes*, 16 (1), 11–12. Martin, Kimberly R. (2001). Television public service announcements decrease marijuana use in targeted teens. *NIDA Notes*, 16 (1), 14.

44. Zimmer, Lynn, and Morgan, John P. (1997). *Marijuana myths, marijuana facts: A review of the scientific evidence.* New York: Lindesmith Center, p. 37.

45. Goode (2008), *Drugs in American society,* pp. 250–251.

46. Substance Abuse and Mental Health Services Administration (2010). *Results from the 2009 National Survey on Drug Use and Health: Detailed tables.* Rockville, MD: Office of Applied Studies, Substance Abuse and Mental Health Services Administration, Tables 1.1A and 1.1B.

47. Johnston, Lloyd D.; O'Malley, Patrick M.; Bachman, Jerald G.; and Schulenberg, John E. (2009, December 14). Teen marijuana use tilts up, while some drugs decline in use. University of Michigan News Service, Ann Arbor, Tables 2, 3, and 4.

48. Johnston, O'Malley, Bachman, and Schulenberg, p. 1.

49. Johnston, O'Malley, Bachman, and Schulenberg , Table 7.

50. Cohen, Sidney (1980). Therapeutic aspects. In Robert C. Petersen (Ed.), *Marijuana research findings: 1980* (NIDA Research Monograph 31). Rockville, MD: National Institute on Drug Abuse, pp. 199–221. Julien, *pp. 577–579.* Vestag, Brian (2003). Medical marijuana center opens its doors. *Journal of the American Medical Association, 290,* 877–879.

51. Plasse, Terry F.; Gorter, Robert W.; Krasnow, Steven H.; Lane, Montague; Shepard, Kirk V.; et al. (1991). Recent clinical experience with dronabinol. International conference on cannabis and cannabinoids, Chania, Greece. *Pharmacology, Biochemistry, and Behavior, 40,* 695–700.

52. Institute of Medicine (1999). *Marijuana as medicine: Assessing the science base.* Washington, DC: National Academy Press, p. vii.

53. Inciardi, *The war on drugs III,* pp. 300–301. Institute of Medicine, *Marijuana as medicine,* p. 8.

54. Kocieniewski, David (2010, January 12). New Jersey vote backs marijuana for severely ill. *New York Times,* pp. A1, A18.

55. Johnson, Kirk (2009, October 26). States pressed into new role on marijuana. *New York Times,* pp. A1, A16. Stout, David and Moore, Solomon (2009, October 20). U.S. won't prosecute in states that allow medical marijuana. *New York Times,* pp. A1, A21. Quotation of U.S. Attorney General, Eric H. Holder, Jr.

56. AP-CNBC marijuana poll—Complete results and analysis. CNBC.com, accessed April 20, 2010. Responses to question 3.

57. Rock announces medical marijuana regulation and progress report on research and domestic supply (2001, July 4). Health Canada news release.

58. National Commission on Marihuana and Drug Abuse (1972). *Marihuana: A signal of misunderstanding.* Washington, DC: Government Printing Office, pp. 151–167.

59. Goode (1999), *Drugs in American society,* p. 401.

60. Johnston, Lloyd D. (1980, January 16). Marijuana use and the effects of marijuana decriminalization. Unpublished testimony delivered at the hearings on the effects of marijuana held by the Subcommittee on Criminal Justice, Judiciary Committee, U.S. Senate, Washington, DC, p. 5. Melamede, Robert J. (2005). Harm reduction—The cannabis paradox. *Harm Reduction Journal, 2,* 17. Sommer, Robert (1988). Two decades of marijuana attitudes: The more it changes, the more it is the same. *Journal of Psychoactive Drugs, 20,* 67–70.

61. AP-CNBC marijuana poll, responses to questions 1 and 10a. Gallup Poll (2009, October 19). U.S. support for legalizing marijuana reaches new high.

chapter 11

Depressants and Inhalants

"I remember," Julio says, taking quick, nervous puffs from his cigarette, "when I was a little kid, maybe eight or nine, and I used to take the garbage out for my mother, I'd always see tubes from airplane glue under the stairwell in our apartment house and in the alley out back. At first, glue just meant building models to me. But I'd see people sniffing it, under the stairwell. I was curious, and one day I tried it. It made me feel like I was in a trance. It wasn't really exciting, but I did it again and again until we moved, and in the new neighborhood people weren't into glue and I didn't see the empty tubes to remind me anymore."[1]

—A teenager relating his early experience with inhalant abuse

After you have completed this chapter, you should have an understanding of

- The acute and chronic effects of barbiturates as sedative-hypnotic drugs
- The search for the perfect nonbarbiturate sedative-hypnotic drug
- The development of benzodiazepines as antianxiety medications
- Newly developed sedative-hypnotics and antianxiety medications
- Present-day concerns about gamma-hydroxybutyrate (GHB)
- The history of psychoactive inhalants
- The acute effects and dangers of glue, solvent, or aerosol spray inhalation
- Patterns of inhalant abuse and its chronic effects
- Society's response to concerns about inhalant abuse
- The abuse of amyl nitrite and butyl nitrite

Just as cocaine, amphetamines, and other stimulants bring us up, depressants bring us down. Just as people desire to be stronger, faster, and more attuned to the world, they also desire to move apart from that world, reduce the stress and anxiety of their lives, and fall asleep more easily. We learned in Chapter 7 that the powerful effects of opiates not only relieve pain but also tempt people to retreat from the world around them. In Chapter 13, we will examine the age-old allure of alcohol to relax our mind and body.

In the first part of this chapter, we will focus on a group of nonopiate, nonalcoholic depressant drugs called **sedative-hypnotics,** so named because they calm us down (from the Latin verb, *sedare,* meaning "to calm or be quiet") and produce sleep (from the Greek noun, *hypnos,* meaning "sleep"). Several types of sedative-hypnotic drugs exist, ranging from drugs that were introduced more than two hundred years ago to others that have become available only recently.

A separate but related category consists of prescription drugs that provide specific relief from stress and anxiety without sedating us. These drugs have often been referred to as *tranquilizers* because of their ability to make us feel peaceful or tranquil, but we will call them by their more currently accepted name, **antianxiety drugs.** Unfortunately, sedative-hypnotics and antianxiety drugs have been subject not only to legitimate medical use but to misuse and abuse as well. Many of them can be obtained through illicit sources as street drugs and are consumed for recreational purposes. The psychological problems and physical dangers associated with the misuse and abuse of these depressants are of particular concern.

This chapter also looks at a category of depressant drugs known as **inhalants,** a group of chemicals that emit breathable vapors and produce intoxicating effects. These chemicals do not need to be acquired in a pharmacy, a convenience store, a liquor store, or even on the street. They can be found under the sink, in kitchen or bathroom cabinets, in the basement, or in the garage. Ordinary household products frequently have the potential for intoxication if they are sniffed or inhaled. When you consider that these substances are readily available to anyone in a family, including its youngest members, the consequences of their abuse become especially troubling. Glues, solvents, and other inhalant products will be examined as dangerous recreational drugs in our society today.

Barbiturates

In 1864, the German chemist Adolf von Baeyer combined a waste product in urine called *urea* and an apple extract called *malonic acid* to form a new chemical compound called *barbituric acid.* There are two often-told stories about how this compound got its name. One story has it that Von Baeyer had gone to a local tavern to celebrate his discovery and encountered a number of artillery officers celebrating the feast day of St. Barbara, the patron saint of explosives handlers. Inspired by their celebration, the name "barbituric acid" came to mind. The other story attributes the name to a relationship with a certain barmaid (perhaps at the same tavern) whose name was Barbara.[2]

Whichever story is true (if either is), Von Baeyer's discovery of barbituric acid set the stage for the development of a class of drugs called **barbiturates**. Barbituric acid itself has no behavioral effects, but if additional molecular groups combine with the acid, depressant effects are observed. In 1903, the first true barbiturate, diethyl-barbituric acid, was created and marketed under the name Veronal. Over the next thirty years, several major barbiturate drugs were introduced: **phenobarbital** (marketed in generic form), **amobarbital** (brand name: Amytal), **pentobarbital** (brand name: Nembutal), and **secobarbital** (brand name: Seconal).

Categories of Barbiturates

Barbiturates all share a number of common features. They are relatively tasteless and odorless, and at sufficient dosages, they reliably induce sleep, although the quality of sleep is a matter that will be discussed later. Because they slow down the activity of the central nervous system (CNS), the principal therapeutic application of barbiturates has been in the treatment of seizure disorders (epilepsy).

The main difference among them lies in how long the depressant effects will last; a rough classification of

sedative-hypnotics: A category of depressant drugs that provide a sense of calm and sleep.

antianxiety drugs: Medications that make the user feel more peaceful or tranquil; also called tranquilizers.

inhalants: Chemicals that produce breathable vapors. They produce euphoriant and depressant effects when sniffed or inhaled.

barbiturate (bar-BIT-chur-rit): A drug within a family of depressants derived from barbituric acid and used as a sedative-hypnotic and antiepileptic medication.

phenobarbital (FEEN-oh-BAR-bih-tall): A long-acting barbiturate drug, usually marketed in generic form.

amobarbital (AY-moh-BAR-bih-tall): An intermediate-acting barbiturate drug. Brand name is Amytal.

pentobarbital (PEN-toh-BAR-bih-tall): A short-acting barbiturate drug. Brand name is Nembutal.

secobarbital (SEC-oh-BAR-bih-tall): A short-acting barbiturate drug. Brand name is Seconal.

barbiturates is based upon this factor. Barbiturates are categorized as *long acting* (six or more hours), *intermediate acting* (four to six hours), or *short acting* (less than four hours).

Bear in mind, however, that these groups are relative only to one another. All other factors being equal, injectable forms of barbiturates are shorter acting than orally administered forms of the same drug, since it takes longer for the drug to be absorbed when taken by mouth and longer for it to be eliminated from the body (Chapter 1). Naturally, a higher dose of any drug lasts longer than a lower dose because it takes longer for all of the drug to be eliminated from the body (Table 11.1).

The barbiturates used in surgical anesthesia, such as thiopental (brand name: Pentothal), take effect extremely rapidly (within seconds) and last only a few minutes. For this reason, they are referred to as *ultra-short-acting barbiturates*. Because these features have little appeal to a person seeking a recreational drug, ultra-short-acting barbiturates are not commonly abused.

Acute Effects of Barbiturates

You can visualize the effects of barbiturates on the body and the mind in terms of points along a scale ranging from mild relaxation on one end to coma and death on the other (Figure 11.1). In this sense, barbiturate effects are the same

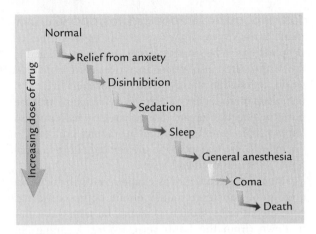

FIGURE 11.1

The downward continuum of arousal levels, as induced by depressants.

Source: Julien, Robert M. (1998). *A primer of drug action* (8th ed). Copyright © 1998 by W. H. Freeman and Company.

as the effects of depressants in general. The particular point that is achieved depends on the dose level that is taken.

At very low doses, the primary result of oral administrations of a barbiturate is relaxation and, paradoxically, a sense of euphoria. These effects derive chiefly from a disinhibition of the cerebral cortex, in which normal inhibitory influences from the cortex are reduced. These symptoms are similar to the inebriating or intoxicating effects that result from low to moderate doses of alcohol (Drugs . . . in Focus).

As the dose level increases, lower regions of the brain concerned with general arousal become affected. At therapeutic doses (one 100-mg capsule of secobarbital, for example), barbiturates make you feel sedated and drowsy. For this reason, patients are typically warned that barbiturates can impair the performance of driving a car or operating machinery. At higher doses, a hypnotic (sleep-inducing) effect is achieved.

Historically, the primary use of barbiturates has been in the treatment of insomnia, and they were widely recommended for this purpose from

TABLE 11.1			
Major barbiturates			
GENERIC NAME	**BRAND NAME**	**DURATION OF ACTION**	**RELATIVE POTENTIAL FOR ABUSE**
phenobarbital	generic*	long	low
mephobarbital	Mebaral	long	low
butalbarbital	Pheniline Forte†	intermediate	moderate
amobarbital	Amytal	intermediate	high
secobarbital and amobarbital	Tuinal	short, intermediate	high
pentobarbital	Nembutal	short	high
secobarbital	Seconal	short	high

Note: Short-acting barbiturates begin to take effect in about fifteen minutes, intermediate-acting barbiturates in thirty minutes, and long-acting barbiturates in one hour.

*Phenobarbital is also available in combination with hyoscyamine, atropine, and scopolamine under the brand name Donnatal.

†Several brands combine butalbarbital with acetaminophen.

Sources: Henningfield, Jack E., and Ator, Nancy A. (1986). *Barbiturates: Sleeping potion or intoxicant?* New York: Chelsea House, p. 24. *Physicians' desk reference* (64th ed.) (2010). Montvale, NJ: Medical Economics Company.

Drugs... in Focus

Is There Any Truth in "Truth Serum"?

The idea that a sedative-hypnotic drug such as amobarbital (Amytal, or "sodium amytal") may function as a "truth serum" is not at all new. It has been known for centuries that depressants can produce remarkable candor and freedom from inhibition. The oldest example is simple alcohol, whose effect on loosening the tongue has led to the Latin proverb *in vino veritas* ("in wine, there is truth").

Whether we are guaranteed truthfulness under any of these circumstances, however, is another matter entirely. Courts have ruled that expert opinion in criminal cases based *solely* on drug-assisted testimony cannot be admitted as evidence. Controlled laboratory studies have shown that individuals under the influence of Amytal, when pressed by questioners, are as likely to give convincing renditions of fabrications (outright lies) or fantasies as they are to tell the truth. So, perhaps, Amytal might be better described as a "tell anything serum."

Recently, the question of whether Amytal or other depressant drugs should be used to gain information has come up with regard to the interrogation of captured al Qaeda prisoners following the September 11, 2001, attacks. The United States has determined that such individuals are unlawful combatants, a designation that excludes them from protection under the Geneva Convention guidelines prohibiting such practices for prisoners of war. Officially, U.S. officials deny that depressant drugs are being used to gain information from captives under American jurisdiction. It is possible that this practice is in effect in other countries to which captives have been transferred.

The lack of evidence that truthful information may be gained through the use of depressant drugs has not changed, however. Nonetheless, military and intelligence experts point to the potential for gaining some relevant information that might be buried in drug-induced ramblings.

Sources: CBS News (2003, April 23). Truth serum: A possible weapon. www.cbsnews.com. Lillienfeld, Scott O., and Landfield, Kristin (2008). Science and pseudoscience in law enforcement. *Criminal Justice and Behavior, 35,* 1215–1230. Michaelis, James I. (1966). Quaere, whether 'in vino veritas': An analysis of the truth serum cases. *Issues in Criminology, 2* (2), 245–267.

1903, when they were first introduced, until the development of safer alternatives in the 1960s. One of the reasons why barbiturates fell from favor was that the sleep induced by these drugs turned out to be far from normal. Barbiturates tend to suppress rapid eye movement (REM) sleep, which represents about 20 percent of everyone's sleep time each night. REM sleep is associated with dreaming and general relaxation of the body. If barbiturates are consumed over many evenings and then stopped, the CNS will attempt to catch up for the lost REM sleep by producing longer REM periods on subsequent nights. This **REM-sleep rebound** effect produces vivid and upsetting nightmares, along with a barbiturate hangover the next day, during which the user feels groggy and out of sorts. In other words, barbiturates may induce sleep, but a refreshing sleep it definitely is not.[3]

The most serious acute risks of barbiturate use involve the possibility of a lethal overdose either from taking too high a dose level of the drug alone or from taking the drug in combination with alcohol, such as when a barbiturate is taken after an evening of drinking. In these instances, the sleeper can all too easily slip into coma and death, since an excessive dose produces an inhibition of the respiratory control centers in the brain. The mixture of barbiturates with alcohol produces a synergistic effect (see Chapter 1) in which the combined result is greater than the sum of the effects of each drug alone.

> *Half of the lethal dose of secobarbital combined with ¼ the lethal dose of alcohol can kill in a synergistic double whammy. In another typical case of accidental overdose, a person takes a sleeping pill and awakens drugged and confused a few minutes later, annoyed at being aroused. The person then forgetfully takes another pill, or several, from the nightstand, and goes to sleep forever. This is called "drug automatism," a good reason not to keep medications within reach of the bed.*[4]

REM-sleep rebound: A phenomenon associated with the withdrawal of barbiturate drugs in which the quantity of rapid eye movement (REM) sleep increases, resulting in disturbed sleep and nightmares.

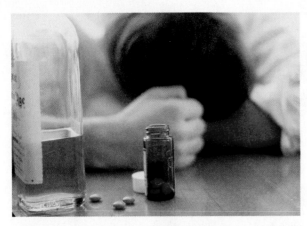

Barbiturates and alcohol have frequently been combined in attempts to commit suicide.

During the period between 1973 and 1976, barbiturates were implicated in more than half of all drug-related deaths labeled as suicide by medical examiners. In fact, the suicide potential of barbiturates is the primary reason for their decline as a prescription sedative.[5]

Chronic Effects of Barbiturates

The use of barbiturates as sleep medications often initiates a cycle of behavior that can lead to dependence. Even after brief use of barbiturates, anxiety may be temporarily increased during the day, and there may be an even greater degree of insomnia than before. In addition, because a barbiturate-induced sleep typically leaves a person feeling groggy the next morning, it is tempting to take a stimulant drug during the day to feel completely alert. At bedtime, the person still feels the stimulant effects and is inclined to continue taking a barbiturate to achieve any sleep at all. To make matters worse, the brain builds up a pharmacological tolerance to barbiturates quite quickly, requiring increasingly higher doses for an equivalent effect.

The withdrawal symptoms observed when barbiturates are discontinued indicate a strong physical dependence on the drug. A person may experience a combination of tremors ("the shakes"), nausea and vomiting, intense perspiring, general confusion, convulsions, hallucinations, high fever, and increased heart rate. Not surprisingly, considering the parallels mentioned so far with alcohol, the barbiturate withdrawal syndrome closely resembles that of withdrawal after chronic alcohol abuse.

Professionals in the treatment of drug dependence often view the effects of barbiturate withdrawal as the most distressing as well as the most dangerous type of drug withdrawal. From a medical perspective, the withdrawal process is life-threatening unless it is carried out in gradual fashion in a hospital setting. Without medical supervision, abrupt withdrawal from barbiturates carries approximately a 5 percent chance of death.[6]

Current Medical Uses of Barbiturates

Considering the problems of barbiturate use in the treatment of insomnia, it should not be surprising that the clinical use of barbiturates for this problem is essentially "obsolete."[7] Nonetheless, barbiturates continue to play an important role in the treatment of epileptic seizures. Phenobarbital and mephobarbital (two long-acting barbiturates) are prescribed to prevent convulsions. Dose levels need to be monitored carefully because the concentration must be high enough to control the development of seizures (despite the tendency for tolerance effects to occur over time) without being so high as to produce drowsiness.

Patterns of Barbiturate Abuse

There are clear indications that taking barbiturate drugs is positively reinforcing. Laboratory animals will eagerly press a lever to deliver intravenous injections of barbiturates, particularly for the short-acting types, at rates that are equal to those for cocaine.[8] When given the choice between pentobarbital and a nonbarbiturate depressant and given no knowledge as to the identity of the drugs, human drug abusers reliably select an oral dose of pentobarbital.[9]

Barbiturate abuse reached its peak in the 1950s and 1960s, later to be overshadowed by abuses of heroin, hallucinogens, nonbarbiturate depressants, amphetamines, and more recently, abuses of cocaine, crack, and various stimulants and hallucinogens (Table 11.2). The principal reason for their decline in popularity was that barbiturates became less widely available as prescription drugs. Stricter controls were placed on obtaining excessive amounts of barbiturates from pharmacies, whereas physicians, concerned with the potential of barbiturates as ways of committing suicide, became reluctant to prescribe them on a routine basis.

Despite their decline as major drugs of abuse, however, barbiturates are still being abused. The 2009 University of Michigan survey of high school seniors found that 8 percent of them had used some form of barbiturates during their lifetime, down from 17 percent in 1975, and 5 percent had taken them within the past year, down from 11 percent in 1975.[10]

TABLE 11.2

Street names for various barbiturates

TYPE OF BARBITURATE	STREET NAME
pentobarbital (Nembutal)	abbotts, blockbusters, nebbies, nembies, nemmies, yellow bullets, yellow dolls, yellow jackets, yellows
amobarbital (Amytal)	blue angels, bluebirds, blue bullets, blue devils, blue dolls, blue heavens, blues
secobarbital (Seconal)	F-40s, Mexican reds, R.D.s, redbirds, red bullets, red devils, red dolls, reds, seccies, seggies, pinks
secobarbital and amobarbital (Tuinal)	Christmas trees, double trouble, gorilla pills, rainbows, tootsies, trees, tuies
barbiturates in general	downers, down, goofballs, G.B.s, goofers, idiot pills, King Kong pills, peanuts, pink ladies, sleepers, softballs, stumblers

Note: Like any other street drug, illicit barbiturate capsules often contain an unknown array of other substances, including strychnine, arsenic, laxatives, and milk sugars. Any yellow capsule is likely to be "marketed" as Nembutal, any blue capsule as Amytal, and any red capsule as Seconal.

Source: Updated from Henningfield, Jack E., and Ator, Nancy A. (1986). *Barbiturates: Sleeping potion or intoxicant?* New York: Chelsea House, p. 82.

Nonbarbiturate Sedative-Hypnotics

As the hazards of barbiturate use became increasingly evident, the search was on for sedative-hypnotic drugs that were not derivatives of barbituric acid and, it was hoped, had fewer undesirable side effects. Unfortunately, these objectives were not realized.

One such drug, **chloral hydrate**, had been synthesized as early as 1832. As a depressant for the treatment of insomnia, it has the advantage of not producing the REM-sleep rebound effect or bringing on the typical barbiturate hangover. A major disadvantage, however, is that it can severely irritate the stomach. Like other depressants, it is also highly reactive when combined with alcohol. In the nineteenth century, a few drops of chloral hydrate in a glass of whiskey became the infamous "Mickey Finn," a concoction that left many an unsuspecting sailor unconscious and eventually "shanghaied" onto a boat for China. You might say that chloral

hydrate was an early precursor to a modern-day "date-rape" drug (see pages 253–254).

The development of **methaqualone** (brand names: Quaalude, Sopor), first introduced in the United States in 1965, was a further attempt toward achieving the perfect sleeping pill. In 1972, methaqualone had become the sixth-best-selling drug for the treatment of insomnia. During the early 1970s, recreational use of methaqualone (popularly known as "ludes" or "sopors") was rapidly spreading across the country, aided by its unfounded reputation of having aphrodisiac properties.

The problem with methaqualone was compounded by the extensive number of prescriptions written by physicians who mistakenly saw the drug as a desirable alternative to barbiturates. On the street, quantities of methaqualone were obtained from medical prescriptions or stolen from pharmacies. Methaqualone-associated deaths started to be prominently mentioned in the DAWN reports of the period (see Chapter 2). In 1984, this drug's legal status changed to that of a Schedule I drug, the most restricted classification, which indicates a high potential for abuse and no medical benefits.[11] Although it is no longer manufactured by any pharmaceutical company, methaqualone is still available as an illicit drug. It is either manufactured in domestic underground laboratories or smuggled into the country from underground laboratories abroad.

The Development of Antianxiety Drugs

If social historians consider the 1950s "the age of anxiety," then it is appropriate that this period also would be marked by the development of drugs specifically intended to combat that anxiety. These drugs were originally called *minor tranquilizers*, to distinguish them from other drugs regarded as *major tranquilizers* and developed at about the same time to relieve symptoms of schizophrenia. This terminology is no longer used today, for we now know that the pharmacological differences between the two drug categories are more than simply a matter of degree. Anxious people (and even people who are not bothered by anxiety) are not affected by drugs

chloral hydrate: A depressant drug once used for the treatment of insomnia. It is highly reactive with alcohol and can severely irritate the stomach.

methaqualone (MEH-tha-QUAY-lone): A nonbarbiturate depressant drug once used as a sedative. Brand name is Quaalude.

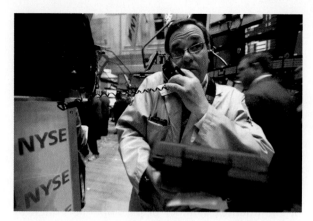

A person's job and other aspects of living are often sources of enormous stress and anxiety.

designed to treat schizophrenia. The current, and more logical, practice is to refer to drugs in terms of a specific action and purpose. The minor tranquilizers are now called *antianxiety drugs*.

The first antianxiety drug to be developed was **meprobamate** (brand name: Miltown), named in 1955 for a New Jersey town near the headquarters of the pharmaceutical company that first introduced it. Miltown became an immediate hit among prescription drugs, making its name a household word and essentially a synonym for tranquilizers in general. It was the first psychoactive drug in history to be marketed specifically as an antianxiety medication.

Meprobamate had advantages and disadvantages. On the positive side, the toxic dose was relatively high, making the possibility of suicide more remote than with alcohol, barbiturates, and other depressants. In addition, judging from the reduction in autonomic responses to stressors, there were genuine signs that people on this medication were actually less anxious[12]. On the negative side, motor reflexes were diminished, making driving more hazardous. People often complained of drowsiness,

---

meprobamate (MEH-pro-BAYM-ate): A nonbarbiturate antianxiety drug and sedative. Brand name is Miltown.

benzodiazepines (BEN-zoh-dye-AZ-eh-pins): A family of antianxiety drugs. Examples are diazepam (Valium), chlordiazepoxide (Librium), and triazolam (Halcion).

chlordiazepoxide (CHLOR-dye-az-eh-POX-ide): A major benzodiazepine drug for the treatment of anxiety. Brand name is Librium.

diazepam (dye-AZ-eh-pam): A major benzodiazepine drug for the treatment of anxiety. Brand name is Valium.

---

even at dose levels that should have only been calming them down. Meprobamate also produced both physical and psychological dependence, at slightly more than twice the normal recommended daily dose.[13] This was not a very wide margin for possible abuse, and as a result, meprobamate was classified as a Schedule IV controlled substance, requiring limits on the number of prescription refills (see Chapter 6). Because of these negative features, the clinical use of meprobamate as an antianxiety drug eventually ended. By 1960, it had been eclipsed by a different class of antianxiety drugs called *benzodiazepines*.

Benzodiazepines

The introduction of a new group of drugs, called **benzodiazepines**, was a dramatic departure from all earlier attempts to treat anxiety. On the one hand, for the first time, there now were drugs that had a *selective* effect on anxiety itself, instead of producing a generalized reduction in the body's overall level of functioning. It was their "tranquilizing" effects, rather than their sedative effects, that made benzodiazepines so appealing to mental health professionals. On the other hand, it is important to distinguish between the well-publicized virtues of benzodiazepines when they were first introduced in the 1960s and the data that accumulated during the 1970s as millions of people experienced these new drugs. Although they are certainly very useful in the treatment of anxiety and other stress-related problems, long-acting benzodiazepines are no longer recognized as the miracle drugs they were promoted to be when they first entered the market.

Medical Uses of Benzodiazepines

The first marketed benzodiazepine, **chlordiazepoxide** (brand name: Librium), was introduced in 1960, followed by **diazepam** (brand name: Valium) in 1963. Table 11.3 lists twelve of the major benzodiazepine drugs currently on the market. They are all chemically related, but their potencies and time courses vary considerably. Valium, for example, is five to ten times stronger than Librium and takes effect about an hour sooner. The relatively quicker response from Valium is a principal factor in making it more popular than Librium.

The variations in benzodiazepine effects have led to different recommendations for their medical use. Oral administrations of the relatively long-acting benzodiazepines, in general, are recommended for relief from anxiety, with the effects beginning thirty minutes to four hours after ingestion. Besides Librium and Valium,

TABLE 11.3

The leading benzodiazepines on the market

TRADE NAME	GENERIC NAME	ELIMINATION HALF-LIFE (in hours)
Long-acting benzodiazepines		
Valium	diazepam	20–100
Librium	chlordiazepoxide	8–100
Limbitrol	chlordiazepoxide and amitriptyline (an antidepressant)	8–100
Dalmane	flurazepam	70–160
Tranxene	clorazepate	50–100
Intermediate-acting benzodiazepines		
Ativan	lorazepam	10–24
Klonopin	clonazepam	18–50
Restoril	temazepam	8–35
ProSom	estazolam	13–35
Short-acting benzodiazepines		
Versed	midazolam	2–5
Halcion	triazolam	2–5
Xanax	alprazolam	11–18

Note: Klonopin is available in orally disintegrating wafers for panic-attack patients who need the medication in an easily administered form.

Source: Julien, Robert M. (1998). *A primer of drug action* (8th ed.). New York: Freeman, p. 99. *Physicians' desk reference* (64th ed.) (2010). Montvale, NJ: Medical Economics Company.

other examples of this type include flurazepam (brand name: Dalmane) and clorazepate (brand name: Tranxene).

When a very quick effect is desired, an injectable form of diazepam is used either to reduce the symptoms of agitation that follow alcohol withdrawal (delirium tremens, or the DTs), as an anticonvulsant for epileptic patients, or as a pre-anesthetic drug to relax the patient just prior to surgery. In contrast, shorter-acting oral benzodiazepines are recommended for sleeping problems because their effects begin more quickly and wear off well before morning. Examples of this type include alprazolam (brand name: Xanax), and temazepam (brand name: Restoril).

How effective are benzodiazepines for the treatment of anxiety? The best way to answer this question is to conduct a double-blind study (see Chapter 1) and compare a representative benzodiazepine such as Valium to a placebo control that looks like Valium but produces no physiological effects. In studies of this type, Valium

is observed to be helpful for about 70 to 80 percent of people with an anxiety disorder. Approximately 25 to 30 percent of them, however, are helped by the placebo alone, so it is clear that psychological factors play a significant role in the final outcome.[14]

Interestingly, benzodiazepines work best when the physician prescribing the medication is perceived as being warm, has a positive attitude toward use of antianxiety drugs, and believes that the patient will improve (Table 11.4).[15] The positive impact of such factors upon the outcome of treatment underscores the importance of the physician–patient relationship, along with the genuine pharmacological effects of the drugs themselves.

Acute Effects of Benzodiazepines

In general, benzodiazepines are absorbed relatively slowly into the bloodstream, so their relaxant effects develop more gradually and last longer than those of barbiturates. This is because benzodiazepines are absorbed from the small intestine rather than the stomach, as is the case

TABLE 11.4

Factors that predict successful treatment with benzodiazepines

Physician attributes

Warmth

Liking the patient

Feeling comfortable with the patient

Believing the patient has good prospects for improvement

Patient attributes

High verbal intelligence

Compliance with the physician

Realistic treatment goals

Low verbal hostility

High level of education

High occupational status

Marital stability

Orientation and expectations prior to treatment

Realization that problems are emotional rather than physical

Expectation that drugs will be part of the treatment

Source: Rickels, Karl (1981). Benzodiazepines: Clinical use patterns. In Stephen I. Szara and Jacqueline P. Ludford (eds.), *Benzodiazepines: A review of research results 1980* (NIDA Research Monograph 33). Rockville, MD: National Institute on Drug Abuse, p. 46.

with barbiturates. The relatively greater water solubility and, by implication, the relatively lower fat solubility of benzodiazepines also are factors.

The major advantage that benzodiazepines have over barbiturates and other drugs previously used to control anxiety is their higher level of safety. Respiratory centers in the brain are not affected by benzodiazepines, so it is rare for a person to die of respiratory failure from an accidental or intentional overdose. Even after taking fifty or sixty times the therapeutic dose, the person will still not stop breathing. It is almost always possible to arouse a person from the stupor that such a drug quantity would produce. In contrast, doses of barbiturates or nonbarbiturate sedatives that are ten to twenty times the therapeutic dose are lethal. Yet we must remember that this higher level of safety assumes that *no alcohol or other depressant drugs are being taken at the same time*.[16]

Despite the relative safety of Valium and other benzodiazepines, this drug family poses a number of medical risks for special populations. For elderly patients, for example, the rate of elimination of these drugs is slowed down significantly, resulting in the risk of a dangerously high buildup of benzodiazepines after several doses. In the case of a long-acting benzodiazepine such as Valium or Librium, the elimination half-life is as long as ten days. An elderly patient with this rate of elimination would not be essentially drug-free until two months had passed since he or she took the drug.

The continued accumulation of benzodiazepines in the elderly can produce a form of drug-induced dementia in which the patient suffers from confusion and loss of memory. Without understanding the patient's medication history, one could easily mistake these symptoms for the onset of Alzheimer's disease. An additional problem with benzodiazepines is the increased risk of falls and bone fractures. It is for these reasons that long-acting benzodiazepines are no longer recommended for this age group, and those who are currently taking these drugs are being encouraged to switch to shorter-acting forms or alternative antianxiety therapies.[17]

Chronic Effects of Benzodiazepines

The benzodiazepines were viewed originally as having few, if any, problems related to a tolerance effect or an acquired dependence. We now know that the *anxiety-relieving* aspects of benzodiazepines show little or no tolerance effects when the drugs are taken at prescribed dosages, but there is a tolerance to the *sedative* effects. In other words, when the drugs are taken for the purpose of relieving anxiety, there is no problem with tolerance, but when they are taken for insomnia, more of the drug may be required in later administrations to induce sleep.[18]

We also now know that physiological symptoms appear when benzodiazepines are withdrawn, an indication of benzodiazepine dependence. In the case of Valium and other long-acting benzodiazepines, the slow rate of elimination delays the appearance of withdrawal symptoms until between the third day and the sixth day following drug withdrawal. The first signs include an anxiety level that may be worse than the level for which the drug was originally prescribed. Later, there are symptoms of insomnia, restlessness, and agitation. In general, however, withdrawal symptoms are less severe than those observed after barbiturate withdrawal, occur only after long-term use, and are gone in one to four weeks.[19]

How Benzodiazepines Work in the Brain

The key factor in the action of benzodiazepines is the neurotransmitter gamma-aminobutyric acid (GABA), which normally exerts an inhibitory effect on the nervous system (see Chapter 4). When benzodiazepines are in the vicinity of GABA receptors, the actions of GABA are increased. The antianxiety drugs attach themselves to their own receptors on the membrane of neurons and in doing so heighten the effect of GABA. The facilitation of GABA produces a greater inhibition and a decreased activity level in the neurons involved.[20]

The receptor described here is a large protein molecule that has multiple binding locations, arranged like docking sites for different kinds of boats. As shown in Figure 11.2, the receptor consists of three

FIGURE 11.2

A simplified view of the benzodiazepine receptor.

binding sites: one for sedative-hypnotics (including the barbiturates), one for benzodiazepines (and alcohol), and one for GABA. When GABA attaches to its binding site, there is greater inhibition if the benzodiazepine sites are also occupied at the time by a benzodiazepine drug than if they are not so occupied.[21] The successful binding of a chemical at one site facilitates the binding at the others.

It is not difficult to imagine how cross-tolerance among various depressant drugs would occur. If two depressant drugs were to bind to the same receptor, the receptor would not be able to "tell the difference" between them. As far as the receptor is concerned, the effect would be the same. Evidently, sedative-hypnotics and benzodiazepines share this ability to lock into a common receptor with multiple binding locations.[22]

Patterns of Benzodiazepine Misuse and Abuse

Benzodiazepines do not present the same potential for abuse that cocaine, alcohol, or the barbiturates do, for two primary reasons. First, benzodiazepines are only weak reinforcers of behavior. When trained to press a lever for an injection of Valium, for example, laboratory animals self-administer the drug but at far less robust levels than they self-administer pentobarbital or methaqualone. Studies with normal college student volunteers show that when subjects are given the choice between a placebo and Valium and the true identity of neither choice is known, they actually prefer the placebo. For these individuals, who presumably are not drug abusers and are relatively anxiety-free, the results show no indication of a positive Valium reaction.[23] Second, the slow onset of a benzodiazepine effect prevents the sudden "rush" feeling that is characteristic of many abused drugs such as cocaine, heroin, and amphetamines.

This is *not* to say, however, that benzodiazepines fail to be abused. It is simply that their abuse exists in the context of abusing other drugs as well, a practice often referred to as *multiple substance abuse* or *polydrug abuse*. Alcoholics, for example, sometimes take benzodiazepines at work, in an attempt to relax and to avoid having the smell of alcohol on their breath. Heroin abusers may take benzodiazepines to augment their euphoria and reduce their anxiety when the opiate levels in their blood begin to fall. Cocaine abusers may take the drugs to soften the crashing feeling that is experienced as the cocaine starts to wear off.[24]

Therefore, the principal social problems surrounding the taking of benzodiazepine drugs, since their introduction in the 1960s, have arisen more from their *misuse* than from their *abuse* (see Chapter 1). The greatest concern during the 1970s was the enormous quantity of benzodiazepine prescriptions that were being written. In 1972, Valium ranked first (and Librium third) among the most frequently prescribed drugs of any type. *At the height of their popularity in 1975, more than 100 million prescriptions for benzodiazepines were processed around the world, 85 million in the United States.* It is estimated that in Western Europe and North America, 10 to 20 percent of adults were taking benzodiazepines on a fairly regular basis.[25]

Benzodiazepine use and misuse have since declined substantially in psychiatric practice as newer approaches to anxiety disorders have been pursued. Nonetheless, benzodiazepines remain widely prescribed drugs throughout the world, particularly for people over the age of sixty-five years, to treat problems of insomnia and anxiety. Although they are useful for short-term applications, unfortunate adverse side effects can arise when benzodiazepines are taken over a long period of time. The potential for cognitive impairment among elderly people and adverse effects when combined with alcohol were discussed earlier in this chapter. These possibilities have been a particular problem in European countries where wine is consumed on a regular basis.[26]

In recent years, considerable publicity has focused on the social and personal concerns surrounding the abuse of a specific benzodiazepine, flunitrazepam (brand name: Rohypnol); it is not legally available in the United States but is accessible as a "club drug" through illicit channels (Help Line).

This commercially available bar coaster is used to test for the presence of GHB in an alcoholic beverage.

Help Line

The Dangers of Rohypnol as a Date-Rape Drug

Flunitrazepam (brand name: Rohypnol) is a long-acting benzodiazepine, not unlike diazepam (Valium), except that it is approximately ten times stronger. Because of its extreme potency and the fact that it is highly synergistic with alcohol, Rohypnol is not legally available in the United States. It is, however, approved for medical use in Europe and South America, where it is marketed by Hoffmann–La Roche Pharmaceuticals as a treatment for sleep disorders and as a surgical anesthetic. The U.S. supply of Rohypnol is smuggled into the country from Mexico and South America and sold for recreational use, frequently in its original bubble packaging.

The abuse potential of Rohypnol surfaced in the mid-1990s, when the number of pills seized by the U.S. Customs Service increased by 400 percent from 1994 to 1995 alone. Increased efforts by U.S. Customs and the Drug Enforcement Administration (DEA) have drastically reduced the availability of Rohypnol in the United States, although the drug remains a matter of great concern.

Under such street names as "roofies," "rope," "wolfies," "roches," "R2," and "Mexican Valium," this drug has been promoted as an alcohol enhancer and as a strategy for getting drunk without having a blood-alcohol concentration level that would be defined as legal intoxication. Rohypnol also has been involved in numerous date-rape cases in which victims had been unknowingly slipped the drug, causing them to pass out—the ultimate vulnerable situation. The disinhibition of behavior and the subsequent loss of all memory of the experience are similar to an alcohol-induced blackout (see Chapter 13).

At one time, Rohypnol was odorless, colorless, and tasteless, so it could be easily combined with an alcoholic beverage without detection. Recently, in response to instances of abuse, Hoffmann–La Roche has taken steps to reformulate the drug so that it turns blue when dissolved in a clear liquid. This helps to make Rohypnol somewhat more noticeable to an unsuspecting drinker, but it is difficult to notice changes in beverage color under the dim illumination of a typical bar. Besides, in blue tropical drinks and punches, blue dye produces no color change at all.

Since 1996, U.S. federal law has provided for a twenty-year sentence for the use of Rohypnol in connection with rape or other violent crime. Unfortunately, Rohypnol is an increasingly accessible illicit drug. According to one law-enforcement official in Miami, "It may be easier for teenagers to obtain flunitrazepam (Rohypnol) than alcohol." A recent study has found that a variety of benzodiazepines, all marketed by Hoffmann–La Roche, are being abused and linked to sexual assaults. Because these drugs all bear the same Roche imprint on the tablets, they are collectively known as "roches."

Rohypnol is an example of a group of present-day "club drugs" that have a dangerous potential for abuse as date-rape drugs. Other examples include MDMA or Ecstasy (see Chapter 9) and GHB (to be discussed later in this chapter).

Where to go for assistance:

www.drugs.com/rohypnol.html

This web site provides free, accurate, and independent advice on more than 24,000 prescription drugs, over-the-counter drugs, and natural products.

Source: Community Epidemiology Work Group (1996). *Epidemiologic trends in drug abuse*, Volume 1: *Highlights and executive summary.* Rockville, MD: National Institute on Drug Abuse, pp. 8, 64. Quotation on p. 64. Drug Enforcement Administration, U.S. Department of Justice, Washington, DC, 1997. Office of National Drug Control Policy (2003, February). *ONDCP Drug Policy Clearing-house fact sheet: Rohypnol.* Washington, DC: Executive Office of the President.

Nonbenzodiazepine Depressants

Just as benzodiazepines represented a great advance over barbiturates, the development of new nonbenzodiazepine drugs has provided better opportunities to treat

zolpidem (ZOL-pih-dem): A nonbenzodiazepine sedative-hypnotic drug, first introduced in 1993, for the treatment of insomnia. Brand name is Ambien.

sleep disorders and anxiety. Prominent examples of this new generation of medications are zolpidem, eszopiclone, buspirone, beta blockers, and, strangely enough, antidepressants.

Zolpidem and Eszopiclone

Zolpidem (brand name: Ambien) is not a benzodiazepine drug, but it binds to a specific subtype of GABA receptors. This is probably why it produces only some of the effects usually associated with benzodiazepines and is especially useful in the short-term treatment of insomnia.

Its strong but transient sedative effects (with a half-life of about two hours) have led to the marketing of zolpidem, since its introduction in 1993, as a sedative-hypnotic rather than an antianxiety agent. Little or no muscle relaxation is experienced.

Introduced in 2004, **eszopiclone** (brand name: Lunesta, formerly known as Estorra) is also a nonbenzodiazepine drug that is prescribed for the treatment of insomnia. As a result of successful clinical trials lasting six months, the FDA has approved Lunesta for an interval of treatment that is longer than the recommended treatment with Ambien. Because its half-life of six hours is longer than that of Ambien, Lunesta has been helpful for people who have difficulty in *staying asleep* during the night as well as difficulty *falling asleep*.[27]

Buspirone

As an antianxiety medication, **buspirone** (brand name: BuSpar) has a number of remarkable features. It has been found to be equivalent to Valium in its ability to relieve anxiety, but unlike the benzodiazepines in general, buspirone shows no cross-tolerance effects when combined with alcohol or other depressants and no withdrawal symptoms when discontinued after chronic use. When compared with benzodiazepines, side effects are observed less frequently and are less troublesome to the patient; approximately 9 percent report dizziness, and 7 percent report headaches. Animals do not self-administer buspirone in laboratory studies, and human volunteers indicate an absence of euphoria.

Buspirone also fails to cause the impairments in motor skills that are characteristic of benzodiazepines. In other words, the relief of anxiety is attainable without the accompanying feelings and behavioral consequences of sedation. Perhaps anxiety and sedation do not have to be intertwined after all. Unlike benzodiazepines, buspirone does not affect GABA receptors in the brain but rather acts on a special subclass of serotonin receptors. Evidently, the influence of buspirone on serotonin produces the antianxiety effects.

Despite its virtues, however, buspirone has a distinct disadvantage: a very long delay before anxiety relief is felt. It may take weeks for the drug to become completely effective. While this feature makes buspirone clearly inappropriate for relieving *acute* anxiety conditions, patients suffering from long-term generalized anxiety disorder find it helpful as a therapeutic drug. An extra benefit of the delay in the action of buspirone is that it becomes highly undesirable as a drug of abuse. Do not expect to see news headlines in the future warning of an epidemic of buspirone abuse.[28]

Beta Blockers

The traditional medical uses of beta-adrenergic-blocking drugs, commonly known as **beta blockers**, include slowing the heart rate, relaxing pressure on the walls of blood vessels, and decreasing the force of heart contractions. The combination of a beta-blocker drug and a diuretic is a frequent treatment for the control of high blood pressure. These drugs are also prescribed for individuals facing an anxiety-producing event, such as performing on the stage or giving a speech. Examples of beta blockers include atenolol (brand name: Tenormin), metoprolol (brand name: Lopressor), and propanolol (brand name: Inderal).

Antidepressants

Another approach in the treatment of panic disorder, post-traumatic stress disorder, and social anxiety disorder has been the use of antidepressant medications—specifically, selective serotonin reuptake inhibitors (SSRIs) such as sertraline (brand name: Zoloft) and paroxetine (brand names: Paxil, Asima).[29]

A Special Alert: The Risks of GHB

Of all the much-publicized club drugs to emerge in recent years, perhaps the most notorious is the CNS depressant **gamma-hydroxybutyrate (GHB)**. First synthesized in the 1960s, GHB is produced naturally in the body in very small amounts, but no one has discovered its function. At one time, GHB was sold in health-food

eszopiclone (es-ZOP-eh-clone): A nonbenzodiazepine sedative-hypnotic, first introduced in 2005, for the treatment of insomnia. Brand name is Lunesta.

buspirone (BYOO-spir-rone): A nonbenzodiazepine antianxiety drug, first introduced in 1986. Brand name is BuSpar.

beta blockers: Medicinal drugs that are traditionally used to treat cardiac and blood pressure disorders. They are also prescribed for individuals who suffer from "stage fright" or anxiety regarding a specific event. Examples include atenolol (brand name: Tenormin), metoprolol (brand name: Lopressor), and propanolol (brand name: Inderal).

gamma-hydroxybutyrate (GHB) (GAM-ma heye-DROX-ee-BYOO-tih-rate): A powerful depressant, often abused to induce euphoria and sedation. When slipped in an alcoholic beverage without the knowledge of the drinker, GHB has been employed as a date-rape drug.

stores and similar establishments. It was considered to have steroid-enhancing and growth-hormone-stimulating effects, leading to interest among bodybuilders (see Chapter 12). Other promotions focused on GHB as a sedative. By 1990, however, numerous reports of GHB-related seizures and comas led the Food and Drug Administration (FDA) to remove GHB from the legitimate market. Since then, the drug has gone underground. The manufacture of GHB is currently controlled by small clandestine laboratories, guided in many instances by formulas available on the Internet, and its sale is maintained by networks of illicit drug distributors.

Acute Effects

Present-day GHB abuse focuses on its ability to produce euphoria, an "out-of-body" high, in conjunction with lowering of inhibitions. Frequently, a combination of GHB and alcohol can produce a lack of consciousness in about fifteen minutes and subsequent amnesia about the experience. The notoriety of GHB as a "date-rape" drug stems from its being colorless, odorless, and virtually tasteless. As a result, it can be slipped easily into alcoholic beverages without the knowledge of the drinker.[30]

Protective Strategies for Women

The vulnerability of women to being drugged with GHB while consuming alcohol in a club or bar is considerable (Portrait), but a number of protective strategies can be employed to minimize the risk.

- Watch the person who pours you a drink, even if he or she is a friend or a bartender. Even better, do not drink what you cannot open or pour yourself. Avoid punch bowls and shared containers. Never accept a drink offered to you by a stranger.

- Do not leave a drink alone—not while you are dancing, using the restroom, or making a telephone call. If you have left it alone, toss it out.

- Appoint a designated "sober" friend to check up on you at parties, bars, clubs, and other social gatherings.

- If a friend seems extremely drunk or sick after a drink and has trouble breathing, call 911 immediately.

- If you have been slipped GHB, the drug will take effect within ten to thirty minutes. Initially, you will feel dizzy or nauseated or will develop a severe headache. You can be incapacitated rapidly. This is the time when having a nondrinking friend nearby is crucial.

- If you wake up in a strange place and believe that you have been sexually assaulted while under the influence of GHB, do not urinate until you have been admitted to a hospital. There is an approximately twelve-hour window of opportunity to detect GHB through urinanalysis.

A test strip created by Drink Safe Technology is now available that can detect not only GHB but also Rohypnol and ketamine. A straw can be used to place a few drops of one's drink on the test strip. If the liquid turns blue, there is a positive result. Unfortunately, when the drink contains dairy products, an accurate detection cannot be made. Bar coasters have been developed that incorporate this particular test strip. Never forget, however, that the original and all-time leading date-rape drug is alcohol itself.[31]

Inhalants through History

The mind-altering effects of substances inhaled into the lungs have been known since the beginnings of recorded history. Burnt spices and aromatic gums were used in worship ceremonies in many parts of the ancient world; exotic perfumes were inhaled during Egyptian worship as well as in Babylonian rituals. Inhalation effects also

PORTRAIT

PORTRAIT   Patricia White, GHB, and the "Perfect" Crime

Patricia White, a forty-seven-year-old mother of three, was at a party celebrating the birthday of her boss, Lorenzo Feal. According to testimony later given by White, as she was about to leave the party, Feal handed her a bottle of water. She took a gulp. A few hours later, White woke up in Feal's bed, naked and nauseated. She had been drugged and raped. Doctors at the emergency department of the local hospital found traces of GHB in her system, and Feal was eventually convicted of using an anesthetic substance in perpetuating White's rape.

A prosecuting attorney has called GHB "ideal for predators and tough for prosecutors" because it is so easily concealed in a drink. Without toxicological evidence, it is difficult to prove that the rape victim had not given consent to sex. Perhaps GHB should really be called an "acquaintance-rape and date-rape drug."

In 1994, when GHB was relatively new, only 56 GHB-related emergency department "mentions" were reported through the DAWN system (see Chapter 1). By 2002, that number had grown to 3,300. Colleges and universities, as well as commercial bars, have become justifiably alarmed. The Drug Enforcement Administration (DEA) has collaborated with the Rape, Abuse, and Incest National Network (RAINN) in an effort to promote a heightened awareness of GHB and other "predatory" drugs such as Rohypnol.

Patricia White now counsels GHB rape victims and speaks out publicly about her personal story. In the case of GHB, the more you know about this drug, the safer you are.

Source: Smalley, Suzanne (2003, February 3). "The perfect crime": GHB is colorless, odorless, leaves the body within hours—and is fueling a growing number of rapes. *Newsweek*, p. 52. Substance Abuse and Mental Health Services Administration (2003). Emergency Department Trends from the Drug Abuse Warning Network, Final Estimates 1995–2002. Rockville, MD: Substance Abuse and Mental Health Services, Table 3.30.

---

figured prominently in the famous rites of the oracle at Delphi in ancient Greece, where trances induced by the inhaling of vapors led to mysterious utterances that were interpreted as prophecies. We know now, from archeological studies, that limestone faults underneath the temple at Delphi once caused petrochemical fumes to rise to the surface. The oracle was probably inhaling ethylene, a sweet-smelling gas that produces an out-of-body sense of euphoria.[32]

It was not until the latter part of the eighteenth century that reports about the inhalation of specific drugs began to appear. The two most prominent examples were cases involving *nitrous oxide* and *ether*. These anesthetic drugs were first used as surgical analgesics in the 1840s, but they had been synthesized decades earlier. From the very start, the word had spread of recreational possibilities.

Nitrous Oxide

In 1798 at the precocious age of nineteen, the British chemist Sir Humphry Davy began formal investigations of a newly-synthesized gas called **nitrous oxide**. He immediately observed the pleasant effects of this "laughing gas" and proceeded to give nitrous oxide parties for his literary and artistic friends. By the early 1800s, recreational use of nitrous oxide became widespread both in England and the United States as a nonalcoholic avenue to drunkenness. In the 1840s, public demonstrations were held in cities and towns, as a traveling show, by entrepreneurs eager to market the drug commercially.

It was at such an exhibition in Hartford, Connecticut, that a young dentist, Horace Wells, got the idea for using nitrous oxide as an anesthetic. One of the intoxicated participants in the demonstration had stumbled and fallen, receiving in the process a severe wound to the leg. Seeing that the man showed no evidence of being in pain despite his injury, Wells was sufficiently impressed to try out the anesthetic possibilities himself. The next day, he underwent a tooth extraction while under the influence of nitrous oxide. He felt no pain during the procedure, and nitrous oxide has been a part of dental practice ever since, although controversy exists about its routine use as an anesthesia.[33]

During the 1960s, nitrous oxide inhalation reappeared as a recreational drug. Tanks of compressed nitrous oxide were diverted for illicit use, and health professionals, like their counterparts one hundred years

nitrous oxide (NIGH-trus OX-ide): An analgesic gas commonly used in modern dentistry. It is also referred to as laughing gas.

A GRAND EXHIBITION

OF THE EFFECTS PRODUCED BY INHALING

NITROUS OXIDE, EXHILERATING, OR

LAUGHING GAS!

WILL BE GIVEN AT *The Masonic Hall*

Saturday EVENING, *15th* 1845.

50 GALLONS OF GAS will be prepared and administered to all in the audience who desire to inhale it.

MEN will be invited from the audience, to protect those under the influence of the Gas from injuring themselves or others. This course is adopted that no apprehension of danger may be entertained. Probably no one will attempt to fight.

THE EFFECT OF THE GAS is to make those who inhale it, either

LAUGH, SING, DANCE, SPEAK OR FIGHT, &c. &c.

according to the leading trait of their character. They seem to retain consciousness enough not to say or do that which they would have occasion to regret.

N. B. The Gas will be administered only to gentlemen of the first respectability. The object is to make the entertainment in every respect, a genteel affair.

Those who inhale the Gas once, are always anxious to inhale it the second time. There is not an exception to this rule.

No language can describe the delightful sensation produced. Robert Southey, (poet) once said that "the atmosphere of the highest of all possible heavens must be composed of this Gas."

For a full account of the effect produced upon some of the most distinguished men of Europe, see Hooper's Medical Dictionary, under the head of Nitrogen.

The History and properties of the Gas will be explained at the com-

Public demonstrations of nitrous oxide ("laughing gas") inhalation were popular entertainments in the first half of the nineteenth century.

earlier, were reportedly hosting nitrous oxide parties. Small cartridges of nitrous oxide called **whippets**, generally used by restaurants to dispense whipped cream, became available through college campus "head shops" and mail-order catalogs. The customary pattern of nitrous oxide abuse was to fill a balloon from these cylinders and inhale the gas from the balloon. The result was a mild euphoric high that lasted for a few minutes and a sense of well-being that lingered for several hours. Sometimes, there would be a loss of consciousness for a few seconds and an experience of "flying." Once

whippets: Small canisters containing pressurized nitrous oxide.

hypoxia (high-POX-ee-ah): A deficiency in oxygen intake.

ether (EE-ther): An anesthetic drug, first introduced to surgical practice by William T. Morton in the 1840s. It is highly flammable.

consciousness returned, there was the possibility of sensory distortions, nausea, or vomiting. Ordinary cans of commercial whipped cream, in which nitrous oxide is the propellant gas, currently provide easy access to this inhalant.

Nitrous oxide itself is a nontoxic gas, but its inhalation presents serious risks. As with any euphoriant drug, the recreational use of nitrous oxide can be extremely dangerous when a person is driving under its influence. In addition, if nitrous oxide is inhaled through an anesthetic mask and the mask is worn over the mouth and nose, without being combined with oxygen, the consequences can be lethal. Nitrous oxide dilutes the air that a person breathes. Unless there is a minimum of 21 percent oxygen in the mixture, reproducing the 21 percent oxygen content in the air, a lack of oxygen (called **hypoxia**) will produce suffocation or irreversible brain damage.[34]

Ether

Like nitrous oxide, **ether** came into use well before its anesthetic effects were appreciated by the medical profession. It was introduced by Friedrich Hoffmann at the beginning of the 1700s, under the name Anodyne, as a liquid "nerve tonic" for intestinal cramps, toothaches, and other pains. Whether it was swallowed or inhaled (it evaporated very quickly), ether also produced effects that resembled intoxication from alcohol. In fact, during the mid-1800s, when the combination of a heavy tax on alcohol and a temperance campaign in England and Ireland forced people to consider alternatives to alcoholic beverages, both ether drinking and ether inhalation became quite popular. It was used for the same purpose later in the United States during the Prohibition years and in Germany during World War II when alcohol was rationed. Ether's flammability, however, made its recreational use highly dangerous.[35]

Glue, Solvent, and Aerosol Inhalation

The abuse of nitrous oxide and ether may have a relatively long history, but the more familiar reports of inhalation abuse involving glue and solvent chemicals have appeared only since the late 1950s.

Some of the common products that have been subject to abuse includes glues, paint thinners, lighter fluid, and stain removers. In addition, many aerosol products are inhalable: hair sprays, deodorants, vegetable lubricants for cooking, and spray paints. Unfortunately, new products are continually being introduced for genuinely practical uses, with little awareness of (or little regard for) the consequences should someone inhale their ingredients on a recreational basis (Table 11.5). Significant problems are also associated with occupational exposure to solvent vapors. In a study reported in 1999, 125 pregnant women who had been exposed to solvent products at the workplace were studied over a nine-year period. There was a thirteen times greater risk of birth defects among the exposed group, relative to controls. These women included factory workers, laboratory technicians, artists, printing industry workers, chemists, and painters.[36]

TABLE 11.5

Household products with abuse potential and their ingredients

HOUSEHOLD PRODUCT	POSSIBLE INGREDIENTS
Glues, plastic cements, and rubber cements	Acetates, acetone, benzene, hexane, methyl chloride, toluene, trichloroethylene
Cleaning solutions	Carbon tetrachloride, petroleum products, trichloroethylene
Nail polish removers	Acetone
Lighter fluids	Butane, isopropane
Paint sprays, paint thinners, and paint removers	Acetone, butylacetate, methanol, toluene, methyl chloride
Other petroleum products	Acetone, benzene, ether, gasoline, hexane, petroleum, tetraethyl lead, toluene
Typewriter correction fluid	Trichloroethylene, trichlorethane
Hair sprays	Butane, propane
Deodorants, air fresheners	Butane, propane
Whipped cream propellants	Nitrous oxide

Source: Schuckit, Marc A. (2000). *Drug and alcohol abuse: A clinical guide to diagnosis and treatment.* New York: Kluwer Academic/Plenum, p. 222. Sharp, Charles W., and Rosenberg, Neil L. (1997). Inhalants. In Joyce H. Lowinson, Pedro Ruiz, Robert B. Millman, and John G. Langrod (Eds.), *Substance abuse: A comprehensive textbook* (3rd ed.). Baltimore: Williams and Wilkins, p. 248.

The Abuse Potential of Inhalants

Commercial glues, solvents, and aerosol sprays are prime candidates for drug abuse for a number of reasons. First, because they are inhaled into the lungs, the feeling of intoxication occurs more rapidly than with orally administered alcohol. "It's a quicker drunk," in the words of one solvent abuser.[37] The feeling is often described as a "floating euphoria," similar to the effect of alcohol but with a shorter course of intoxication. The high is over in an hour or so, and the hangover is considered less unpleasant than that following alcohol consumption. Second, the typical packaging of inhalant products makes them easy to carry around and conceal from others. Even if they are discovered, many of the products are so common that it is not difficult to invent an excuse for having them on hand.

Finally, most inhalants are easily available in hardware stores, pharmacies, and supermarkets, where they can be bought cheaply or stolen. Among some inhalant abusers, shoplifting these products from open shelves becomes a routine practice. Inhalants are even more widely available than alcohol in poor households; liquor may be in short supply but gasoline, paints, and aerosol products are usually to be found around the house or garage.[38] All these factors contribute to the considerable potential for inhalant abuse.

Acute Effects of Glues, Solvents, and Aerosols

The fumes from commercial inhalant products fall into the general category of depressant drugs, in that the central nervous system is inhibited after they are inhaled. Brain waves, measured objectively through an electroencephalograph (EEG), slow down. Subjectively, the individual feels intoxicated within minutes after inhalation. The most immediate effects include giddiness, euphoria, dizziness, and slurred speech, lasting from fifteen to forty-five minutes. This state is followed by one to two hours of drowsiness and sometimes a loss of consciousness. Along with these effects are occasional experiences of double vision, ringing in the ears, and hallucinations.[39]

The Dangers of Inhalant Abuse

Inhalant abuse often involves concentrations of glue and solvent products that are fifty to a hundred times greater than the maximum allowable concentration of exposure in industry. The health of the inhalant abuser, therefore, is obviously at risk (Help Line).

Help Line

The Signs of Possible Inhalant Abuse

- Headaches and dizziness
- Light sensitivity (from dilation of the pupils)
- Reddened, irritated eyes and rash around the mouth
- Double vision
- Ringing in the ears (tinnitus)
- Sneezing and sniffling
- Coughing and bad breath
- Nausea, vomiting, and loss of appetite
- Diarrhea
- Chest pains
- Abnormal heart rhythm (cardiac arrhythmia)
- Muscle and joint aches

- Slurred speech and unsteady muscle coordination
- Chemical odor or stains on clothing or body
- Rags, empty aerosol cans and other containers
- Plastic and paper bags found in closets and other hidden places

Where to go for assistance:

www.inhalant.org

The web site is sponsored by the National Inhalant Prevention Coalition, Austin, Texas.

Sources: Fox, C. Lynn, and Forbing, Shirley E. (1992). *Creating drug-free schools and communities.* New York: HarperCollins, p. 37. Schuckit, Marc A. (1995). *Drug and alcohol abuse: A clinical guide to diagnosis and treatment* (4th ed.). New York: Plenum Medical Book Co., p. 219.

The dangers of inhalant abuse lie not only in the toxic effects of the inhaled compound on body organs but also in the behavioral effects of the intoxication itself. Inhalant-produced euphoria includes feelings of recklessness and omnipotence. There have been instances of young inhalant abusers leaping off roof tops in an effort to fly, running into traffic, lying on railroad tracks, or incurring severe lacerations when pushing their hand through a glass window that has been perceived as open. The hallucinations that are sometimes experienced carry their own personal risks. Walls may appear to be closing in, or the sky may seem to be falling. Ordinary objects may be perceived to be changing their shape, size, or color. Any one of these delusions can lead to impulsive and potentially destructive behavior.[40]

There are also significant hazards related to the ways in which inhalants are administered. Solvents are sometimes inhaled from a handkerchief or from the container in which they were originally acquired ("huffing"), but glues and similar vaporous compounds are often squeezed into a plastic bag and inhaled while the bag is held tightly over the nose and mouth ("bagging"). Potentially, a loss of consciousness

can result in hypoxia and asphyxiation. Choking can occur if there is vomiting while the inhaler is unconscious. In an early investigation in the 1960s of nine documented deaths attributed to glue inhalation, at least six were caused specifically by a lack of oxygen.[41] Another danger lies in the inhalation of Freon, a refrigerant gas so cold that the larynx and throat can be frozen upon contact.

The toxic effects of inhalant drugs themselves depend on the specific compound, but the picture is complicated by the fact that most products subject to inhalant abuse contain a variety of compounds, and, in some cases, the list of ingredients on the product label is incomplete. Therefore, we often do not know whether the medical symptoms resulted from a particular chemical or from its interaction with others. Nonetheless, there are specific chemicals that have known health risks. The most serious concern involves sudden-death cases, brought on by cardiac dysrhythmia, that have been reported following the inhalation of propane and butane, which are commonly used as propellants for many commercial products.

Besides butane and propane, other inhalant ingredients that present specific hazards are *acetone, benezene, hexane, toluene,* and *gasoline.*

- *Acetone:* **Acetone** inhalation causes significant damage to the mucous membranes of the respiratory tract.
- *Benzene:* Prolonged exposure to **benzene** has been associated with carcinogenic (cancer-producing)

acetone (ASS-eh-tone): A chemical found in nail polish removers and other products.

benzene: A carcinogenic (cancer-producing) compound found in many solvent products, representing a serious health risk when inhaled.

disorders, specifically leukemia, as well as anemia. Benzene is generally used as a solvent in waxes, resins, lacquers, paints, and paint removers.

- *Hexane:* The inhalation of **hexane**, primarily in glues and other adhesive products, has been associated with peripheral nerve damage leading to muscular weakness and muscle atrophy. There is a latency period of a few weeks before the symptoms appear.

- *Toluene:* **Toluene** inhalation through glue sniffing has been associated with a reduction in short-term memory, anemia, and a loss of hearing, as well as dysfunctions in parts of the brain that result in difficulties in movement and coordination. Toluene also has been implicated as a principal factor in cases of lethal inhalation of spray paints and lacquers, though it is difficult to exclude the contribution of other solvents in these products.

- *Gasoline:* Concentrated vapors from gasoline can be lethal when inhaled. Medical symptoms from gasoline inhalation are also frequently attributed to gasoline additives that are mixed in the fuel. The additive **triorthocresyl phosphate (TCP)**, in particular, has been associated with spastic muscle disorders and liver problems. Lead content in gasoline is generally linked to long-term CNS degeneration, but fortunately leaded gasoline is no longer commonly available in the United States. On the other hand, present-day gasoline mixtures contain large amounts of toluene, acetone, and hexane to help achieve the "anti-knock" property that lead had previously provided.[42]

Patterns of Inhalant Abuse

Among all the psychoactive drugs, inhalants are associated most closely with the young—and often the very young. For those who engage in inhalant abuse, these compounds frequently represent the first experience with a psychoactive drug, preceding even alcohol or tobacco. Overall, inhalant abuse ranks fourth highest in drug experimentation among secondary school students, surpassed only by alcohol, tobacco, and marijuana (in that order). Most of those who engage in inhalant abuser, however, are younger than secondary school age; often they are between eleven and thirteen years old.

A group of abandoned Brazilian children inhale glue from bags in Rio de Janeiro. The dazed expression is a typical sign of inhalant intoxication.

The University of Michigan survey of 2009 found that about one out of seven eighth-grade students (15 percent) had used inhalants at some previous time. About 8 percent reported that they had used inhalants within the past year, and 4 percent within the past month. Inhalants are the only class of drugs for which the incidence of usage in the eighth grade significantly *exceeds* the incidence in the tenth and twelfth grades.

Evidently, awareness of this form of drug-taking activity is quite extensive in the later elementary and middle school student population. According to a recent survey, almost two-thirds of ten- to seventeen-year-olds know the meaning of "huffing" and report that they were about twelve years of age when they first became aware of classmates abusing inhalants. The common knowledge of inhalant abuse in this age group and a recent decline in the proportion of eighth-grade students who believe that it is dangerous to use inhalants may account for the upsurge in prevalence rates, since the mid-1990s.[43]

hexane: A dangerous compound present in many glues and adhesive products. Inhalation of these products has been associated with muscular weakness and atrophy.

toluene (TOL-yoo-ene): A compound in glues, cements, and other adhesive products. Inhalation of these products results in behavioral and neurological impairments.

triorthocresyl phosphate (TCP) (tri-OR-thoh-CREH-sil FOS-fate): A gasoline additive. Inhalation of TCP-containing gasoline has been linked to spastic muscle disorders and liver problems.

Drugs... in Focus

Resistol and *Resistoleros* in Latin America

In the cities of Central and South America, the street children are referred to as *resistoleros*, a name derived from their frequent habit of sniffing a commercial brand of shoemaker's glue called Resistol. Granted, many cases of inhalant abuse among the hundreds of thousands of children in Latin America do not specifically involve Resistol; nevertheless, the frequency of Resistol abuse and the fact that Resistol dominates the market in commercial solvent-based adhesives have focused attention on the company that manufactures it, the H. B. Fuller Company of St. Paul, Minnesota.

Concern for the welfare of these children also has spotlighted a thorny ethical issue: Should a corporation accept the social responsibility when widespread abuse of its product exists, either in the United States or elsewhere in the world? Testor Corporation in 1969 added a noxious ingredient to discourage abuse of its model-kit glue; in 1994, a German chemical company marketing a Resistol rival halted its distribution in this region. For its part, Fuller did modify the formulation of Resistol in 1992, replacing the sweet-smelling but highly toxic toluene with a slightly less toxic chemical, cyclohexane. However, it continues to sell Resistol, claiming that its legitimate uses benefit the economies of regions where it is marketed. Moreover, the company has funded community programs for homeless children throughout Central America and has limited its Resistol marketing efforts to large industrial customers rather than marketing to small retailers. Unappeased, foes continue to press Fuller to discontinue the product entirely.

Note: There is no association between Resistol glue and Resistol Western Hats or any corporation-related sponsorships such as the Resistol Arena in Mesquite, Texas.

Source: Henriques, Diana B. (1995, November 26). Black mark for a "good citizen." Critics say H. B. Fuller isn't doing enough to curb glue-sniffing. *New York Times*, Section 3, pp. 1, 11.

In other cultures and under different circumstances, inhalant abuse affects even younger children and a greater proportion of them. In Mexico City, among street children as young as eight or nine who live without families in abandoned buildings, rates of inhalant abuse are extremely high; 22 percent report engaging in some form of solvent inhalation on a daily basis. Inhalant abuse is reported to be commonplace among street children in Rio de Janeiro and other major cities in Central and South America as well as Asia (Drugs . . . in Focus).[44]

Inhalant abuse, on an experimental basis, is not restricted by social or geographic boundaries. Chronic inhalant abuse, however, is overrepresented among the poor and those youths suffering emotional challenges in their lives and seeking some form of escape. Studies of young inhalant abusers show high rates of delinquency, poor school performance, and emotional difficulties. They often come from disorganized homes in which the parents are actually or effectively absent or else engage in abuse of alcohol or some other substance themselves.[45] High prevalence rates for inhalant abuse exist among such disparate groups as Latino children in a rural community in the Southwest, American Indian children on a U.S. reservation, and white children in an economically disadvantaged neighborhood in Philadelphia.

Whatever the ethnic identity of the chronic inhalant abuser, a critical factor is peer influence. Most studies indicate that glue, solvent, or aerosol inhalation is generally experienced in small groups, often at the urging of friends or relatives. Young inhalant abusers tend to be more alienated than others at this age, and feelings of alienation lead youths to others who are also alienated, thus creating a cluster of peers who engage in this form of drug-taking behavior. One survey among American Indian youth, for example, found that when friends strongly encouraged inhalant use or did not try to stop it, 84 percent of the sample reported having tried inhalants and 41 percent reported having used them recently. In contrast, when friends discouraged inhalant use or were perceived as applying strong sanctions against it, only 19 percent reported having tried inhalants and only 3 percent had used them recently.[46]

The Dependence Potential of Chronic Inhalant Abuse

The long-term effects of inhalant abuse are not well documented, because inhalant abuse frequently does not extend over more than a year or two in a person's life and may occur only sporadically. There have been reports of cases showing a tolerance to the intoxicating effects of glues and gasoline. Although it is difficult to determine the dosages that are involved with these tolerance effects, it appears that individuals exposed only to low concentrations for brief periods of time or high levels on an occasional basis do not show tolerance to the inhalants.

Inhalant dependence occurs frequently. Inhalant abusers have reported feeling restless, irritable, and anxious when prevented from inhaling glues, solvents, or aerosols. Physiological withdrawal symptoms are only rarely observed among inhalant abusers but are frequently observed among animals in laboratory studies, so the question of whether physical dependence exists has yet to be definitively answered.[47]

A Gateway for Future Substance Abuse?

The young age at which inhalant abuse occurs leads to the question of whether there is a causal link between inhalant abuse and later abuse of other drugs. Without a doubt, some youths will subsequently replace inhalants with alcohol, marijuana, and other recreational drugs, but the experience of inhalants cannot be considered to lead on a pharmacological level to other drug experimentation or long-term abuse. This is how one author has put it:

> The socially and emotionally healthy juvenile casually experimenting with solvent sniffing does not bear any greater potential for heroin addiction than had he not sniffed solvents. Conversely, the disturbed youth from a broken home, who is frequently exposed to pushers, probably bears the same high risk of ultimate narcotic abuse whether or not he sniffs glue. Regardless of surrounding circumstances, however, any significant resort to intoxicating substances in childhood should be carefully noted as a potential warning of a growing emotional disturbance or as a predictor of a future drug-dependent personality.[48]

A similar "gateway argument" with respect to marijuana was reviewed in Chapter 10.

Responses of Society to Inhalant Abuse

> Sniffing gasoline or paint is a grubby, dirty, cheap way to get high. Inhalant users are, therefore, likely to be the social rejects, the emotionally disturbed, the disadvantaged minorities, the maladjusted, as well as angry and alienated. There is nothing attractive, exciting, or appealing about inhalant use or inhalant users . . .[49]

Certainly, the concern about inhalant abuse takes a backseat to more widely publicized concerns about cocaine, methamphetamine, and heroin abuse or the recent abuse of club drugs. Despite the relatively low priority given to inhalant abuse, however, steps have been taken to reduce some of its hazards. One major approach has been to restrict the availability and sales of glues to young people, a strategy that, as you might predict, has met with mixed success. Some U.S. cities have restricted sales of plastic cement unless it is purchased with a model kit, but such legislation is largely ineffective when model kits themselves are relatively inexpensive. As with the official restriction of sales of alcohol and tobacco to minors, young people can find a way around these laws.

The Testor Corporation, a leading manufacturer of plastic cement for models, took more direct action in 1969 by incorporating **oil of mustard** into the formula. This additive produces severe nasal irritation similar to the effect of horseradish while not affecting its use as a glue or the effect on the user who does not inhale it directly. Other brands of glues and adhesives, however, may not contain oil of mustard and so could still be available for abuse, and additives in general would not be desirable for certain products that are used for cosmetic purposes.

In an additional step taken to reduce inhalant abuse, concentrations of benzene in many household products sold in the United States have been reduced or eliminated, though it is difficult to determine the exact composition of solutions merely by inspecting the label. Standards for products manufactured and sold in foreign countries are typically far less stringent.[50]

---

oil of mustard: An additive in Testor brand hobby-kit glues that produces nasal irritation when inhaled, thus reducing the potential for inhalant abuse.

SNIFFING CORRECTION FLUID CAN STOP YOUR HEART.

If you use IT to get high, you're inhaling poisons that do direct brain damage. No way. Before your heart stops. ☆ Drug Prevention Partnership
1-800-269-4237

Poster images represent a growing national effort to prevent inhalation abuse.

Beyond the difficulty in identifying the toxicity of specific solvent compounds, there is the overriding general problem of the enormous variety and easy availability of solvent-containing products. As one researcher has lamented, "If sales of gold paint or paint thinner are curtailed, people may choose to use typewriter correction fluid, or shoe polish or nail polish remover, or hundreds of other items that have legitimate uses in everyday life."[51]

amyl nitrite (AY-mil NIGH-trite): An inhalant drug that relaxes smooth muscle and produces euphoria. Clinically useful in treating angina pain in cardiac patients, it is also subject to abuse.

butyl nitrite (BYOO-til NIGH-trite): An inhalant drug, similar in its effects to amyl nitrite. It is commonly abused as it induces feelings of euphoria.

Ultimately, some sort of educational strategy must be coordinated that is targeted at children in the elementary grades in school and their parents at home. Different countries have differing educational approaches, ranging from nonalarmist, low-key programs to those urging absolute abstinence, and it is not clear which strategy is most effective in controlling inhalant abuse. A National Inhalants and Poisons Awareness Week is currently held each year in March to promote greater efforts to inform the public about this problem. A 2002 survey conducted by the Partnership for a Drug-Free America has shown that only a small fraction of the parents of teens who have tried inhalants are aware of that fact. On the treatment side, special guidelines are currently being developed for a variety of inhalant-abuse populations—not only the adolescents engaging in transient inhalant abuse but also those individuals who are twenty to twenty-nine years old, have a five-year or longer history of inhalant exposure, and have sustained possible brain damage as a result.[52]

In the meantime, attention has been directed toward the abusive inhalation of two specific products, amyl nitrite and butyl nitrite, which affect a different population from the one traditionally associated with glue, solvent, or aerosol inhalants. Like nitrous oxide and ether, these nitrites have been around for some time, but their abuse began more recently.

Amyl Nitrite and Butyl Nitrite Inhalation

Amyl and butyl nitrites were first identified in the nineteenth century. When inhaled, they produce an intense vasodilation, a relaxation of smooth muscle, a fall in blood pressure, and an increase in heart rate. Since 1867, **amyl nitrite** has been used medically, on a prescription basis, in the treatment of angina pain in heart patients and as an antidote to cyanide poisoning. **Butyl nitrite** produces similar therapeutic effects but has never been used on a clinical basis.

News of the recreational potential of nitrite inhalation began to spread in the 1960s and reached a peak in the 1970s, particularly within the gay community, as it was recognized that the vasodilation of cerebral blood vessels produced a euphoric high, anal sphincter muscles were relaxed, and vasodilation of genital blood vessels enhanced sexual pleasure (Table 11.6). By 1979, more than 5 million people in the United States were using amyl or butyl nitrites more than once a week. Since then, there has been a substantial decline in their popularity.[53]

TABLE 11.6

A chronology of nitrite inhalation abuse

DATE	EVENT	DATE	EVENT
1859	Flushing of skin with amyl nitrite first described	1977	Nitrite inhalation predominant among gay men
1867	First therapeutic use of amyl nitrite for angina pain	1979	More than 5 million people estimated to have used nitrites more than once per week
1880s	Butyl nitrite studied but not used clinically		19 cases of Kaposi's sarcoma found in retrospect
1960	Amyl nitrite prescription requirement eliminated by FDA	1980	56 cases of Kaposi's sarcoma reported
1963	First reports of recreational use of nitrites	1981	Increased suspicions of a link between nitrite use and Kaposi's sarcoma
1960s	Widespread recreational use of nitrites among young adults	1985	Concerns about AIDS and HIV infection beginning to receive widespread media attention
1969	Amyl nitrite prescription requirement reinstated	1990s to present	Association between nitrite inhalation and Kaposi's sarcoma is discredited
1970	Street brands of butyl nitrite beginning to be widely available		Nitrite inhalation abuse greatly reduced among heterosexual populations
1974	Popper craze beginning		
1976	$50 million sales reported in nitrites in one U.S. city		

Source: Updated from Newell, Guy R., Spitz, Margaret R., and Wilson, Michael B. (1988). Nitrite inhalants: Historical perspective. In Harry W. Haverkos and John A. Dougherty (Eds.), *Health hazards of nitrite inhalants* (NIDA Research Monograph 83). Rockville, MD: National Institute of Drug Abuse, p. 6.

Patterns of Nitrite Inhalation Abuse

Amyl nitrite is often referred to as "poppers" or "snappers" because it is commonly available in a mesh-covered glass ampule and there is a popping sound as the ampule is broken and the vapors of the nitrite are inhaled as they are released into the air. It is quick-acting, with vasodilatory effects appearing within thirty seconds. Light-headedness, a flushing sensation, blurred vision, and euphoria last for about five minutes, followed by headache and nausea. Butyl nitrite follows a similar time course in its effects and is available in pornography shops and mail-order catalogs.

Cases of nitrite inhalation have also been found among both heterosexual and gay adolescents, for whom the primary attraction is a feeling of general euphoria. The University of Michigan survey began looking at prevalence rates for nitrite inhalation in 1979. In that year, approximately 11 percent of high school seniors reported having tried nitrite inhalants at least once in their lifetime. By 2003, the rate had dropped substantially to less than 1 percent.[54]

Quick Concept Check 11.2

Understanding the History of Inhalants

Check your understanding of the history of inhalant drugs by indicating whether a particular substance was used (a) first recreationally, then as an application in medicine; (b) first as an application in medicine, then recreationally; or (c) recreationally, with no known application in medicine.

1. amyl nitrite
2. hexane
3. nitrous oxide
4. toluene
5. ether
6. benzene

Answers: 1. b   2. c   3. a   4. c   5. a   6. c

Summary

Barbiturates

- Introduced in 1903 and in use until approximately 1960, the primary sedative-hypnotics (drugs that produce sedation and sleep) belonged to the barbiturate family of drugs.

- Barbiturates are typically classified by virtue of how long their depressant effects are felt, from long acting (example: phenobarbital) to intermediate acting (examples: butalbarbital and amobarbital) to short acting (examples: pentobarbital and secobarbital).

- A major disadvantage of barbiturates is the potential of a lethal overdose, particularly when combined with other depressants such as alcohol. In addition, barbiturate withdrawal symptoms are very severe and require careful medical attention.

Nonbarbiturate Sedative-Hypnotics

- Methaqualone (Quaalude) was introduced in the 1960s as an alternative to barbiturates for sedation and sleep. Unfortunately, this drug produced undesirable side effects and became subject to widespread abuse. It is no longer available as a licit drug.

The Development of Antianxiety Drugs

- Beginning in the 1950s, a major effort was made by the pharmaceutical industry to develop a drug that would relieve anxiety (tranquilize) rather than merely depress the CNS (sedate).

- Meprobamate (Miltown) was introduced in 1955 for this purpose, though it is now understood that the effects of this drug result more from its sedative properties than its ability to relieve anxiety.

Benzodiazepines

- The introduction of benzodiazepines, specifically diazepam (Valium) and chlordiazepoxide (Librium), in the early 1960s, was a significant breakthrough in the development of antianxiety drugs. These drugs selectively affect specific receptors in the brain instead of acting as general depressants of the nervous system.

- In general, benzodiazepines are safer drugs than barbiturates, when taken alone. When taken in combination with alcohol, however, dangerous synergistic effects are observed.

- Benzodiazepines produce their effects by binding to receptors in the brain that are sensitive to the inhibitory neurotransmitter gamma-aminobutyric acid (GABA).

- Social problems concerning the taking of benzodiazepine drugs during the 1970s centered on the widespread misuse of the drug. Prescriptions were written too frequently and for excessive dosages.

Nonbenzodiazepine Depressants

- Recently developed nonbenzodiazepines have provided better opportunities to treat sleep disorders and anxiety. Two examples are zolpidem and buspirone.

- Zolpidem (brand name: Ambien) and eszopiclone (Lunesta) have been useful as a sedative-hypnotic in the treatment of insomnia. They have strong but transient sedative effects and produce little or no muscle relaxation.

- Buspirone (brand name: BuSpar) has been useful as an antianxiety medication that does not cause sedation.

- Beta blockers, traditionally used to treat cardiac and blood pressure disorders, have been prescribed for individuals who are facing an anxiety-producing event, such as performing on the stage or speaking in public.

- Certain antidepressants called selective serotonin reuptake inhibitors (SSRIs) have been successful in treating a variety of anxiety disorders.

The Risks of GHB

- Gamma-hydroxybutyrate (GHB) is a CNS depressant, first used by bodybuilders because of the possibility that it had growth-hormone-stimulating effects. Today, GHB is an illicit drug, available only through clandestine channels.

- As with Rohypnol, the depressant effects of GHB have made it attractive as a club drug. Its involvement as a potential date-rape drug has raised very serious concerns.

Inhalants through History

- Nitrous oxide was first investigated in 1798 and became a major recreational drug in the early 1800s. It is still used recreationally, but its primary application is for routine anesthesia in dentistry.

- Ether is another anesthetic drug, first introduced in the 1840s. It has also been used as a recreational drug, particularly in times when alcohol availability has been severely reduced.

Glue, Solvent, and Aerosol Inhalation

- Present-day inhalant abuse involves a wide range of commercial products: gasoline, glues and other adhesives, household cleaning compounds, aerosol sprays, and solvents of all kinds.

- These products are usually cheap, readily available, and easily concealed, and their intoxicating effects when inhaled are rapid. All these factors make inhalants prime candidates for abuse.
- The principal dangers of inhalant abuse lie in the behavioral consequences of intoxication and in the possibility of asphyxiation when inhalants are abused via an airproof bag held over the nose and mouth.
- Specific toxic substances contained in inhalant products include acetone, benzene, hexane, toluene, and gasoline.

Patterns of Inhalant Abuse

- Inhalant abuse respects no social or geographic boundaries, although prevalence rates are particularly high among poor and disadvantaged populations.
- Research studies indicate the presence of psychological dependence rather than physical dependence in inhalant abuse behavior.

- Tolerance effects are seen for chronic inhalant abusers when the inhalant concentration is high and exposure is frequent.

Responses of Society to Inhalant Abuse

- Concern about the dangers of inhalant abuse has led to restriction of the sale of model-kit glues to minors and to a modification of the formulas for model-kit glue in an attempt to lessen the likelihood of abuse.
- So many products currently on the open market contain volatile chemicals that a universal restriction of abusable inhalants is practically impossible. Therefore, prevention efforts regarding inhalant abuse are critical elements in reducing this form of drug-taking behavior.

Amyl Nitrite and Butyl Nitrite Inhalation

- Two types of inhalants, amyl nitrite and butyl nitrite, appeared on the scene in the 1960s, reaching a peak in the late 1970s. Although they are often identified with gay men, populations of heterosexual adolescents and young adults have also engaged in this form of inhalant abuse.

Key Terms

acetone, p. 258
amobarbital, p. 243
amyl nitrite, p. 262
antianxiety drugs, p. 243
barbiturate, p. 243
benzene, p. 258
benzodiazepines, p. 248
beta blockers, p. 253
buspirone, p. 253

butyl nitrite, p. 262
chloral hydrate, p. 247
chlordiazepoxide, p. 248
diazepam, p. 248
ether, p. 256
eszopiclone, p. 253
gamma-hydroxybutyrate (GHB), p. 253
hexane, p. 259

hypoxia, p. 256
inhalants, p. 243
meprobamate, p. 248
methaqualone, p. 247
nitrous oxide, p. 255
oil of mustard, p. 261
pentobarbital, p. 243
phenobarbital, p. 243

REM-sleep rebound, p. 245
secobarbital, p. 243
sedative-hypnotics, p. 243
toluene, p. 259
triorthocresyl phosphate (TCP), p. 259
whippets, p. 256
zolpidem, p. 252

Endnotes

1. Quotation from Silverstein, Alvin, Silverstein, Virginia, and Silverstein, Robert (1991). *The addictions handbook.* Hillside, NJ: Enslow Publishers, p. 51.
2. Palfai, Tibor, and Jankiewicz, Henry (1991). *Drugs and human behavior.* Dubuque, IA: W. C. Brown, p. 203.
3. Jacobs, Michael R., and Fehr, Kevin O'B. (1987). *Drugs and drug abuse: A reference text* (2d ed.). Toronto: Addiction Research Foundation, pp. 183–194.
4. Palfai and Jankiewicz, *Drugs and human behavior,* p. 213.
5. Jacobs and Fehr, *Drugs and drug abuse,* p. 189.
6. Kauffman, Janice F., Shaffer, Howard, and Burglass, Milton E. (1985). The biological basics: Drugs and their effects. In Thomas E. Bratter and Gary G. Forrest (Eds.), *Alcoholism and substance abuse: Strategies for clinical intervention.* New York: Free Press, pp. 107–136.
7. Sleeping pills and antianxiety drugs (1988). *The Harvard Medical School Mental Health Letter, 5* (6), 1–4.
8. Griffiths, Roland R.; Lukas, Scott E.; Bradford, L. D.; Brady, Joseph V.; and Snell, Jack D. (1981). Self-injection of barbiturates and benzodiazepines in baboons. *Psychopharmacology, 75,* 101–109.

9. Griffiths, Roland R., Bigelow, George, and Liebson, Ira (1979). Human drug self-administration: Double-blind comparison of pentobarbital, diazepam, chlorpromazine, and placebo. *Journal of Pharmacology and Experimental Therapeutics, 210,* 301–310.

10. Johnston, Lloyd D.; O'Malley, Patrick M.; Bachman, Jerald G.; and Schulenberg, John E. (2009, Decembeer 14). Teen marijuana use tilts up, while some drugs decline in use. University of Michigan News Service, Ann Arbor, Tables 1 and 2.

11. Carroll, Marilyn, and Gallo, Gary (1985). *Quaaludes: The quest for oblivion.* New York: Chelsea House.

12. Julien, Robert M. (2001). *A primer of drug action* (9th ed.). New York: Worth, p. 138.

13. Berger, Philip A., and Tinklenberg, Jared R. (1977). Treatment of abusers of alcohol and other addictive drugs. In Jack D. Barchas, Philip A. Berger, Roland D. Caranello, and Glen R. Elliott (Eds.), *Psychopharmacology: From theory to practice.* New York: Oxford University Press, pp. 355–385.

14. Leavitt, Fred (1982). *Drugs and behavior* (2nd ed.). New York: Wiley.

15. Rickels, Karl (1981). Benzodiazepines: Clinical use patterns. In Stephen I. Szara and Jacqueline P. Ludford (Eds.), *Benzodiazepines: A review of research results 1980* (NIDA Research Monograph 33). Rockville, MD: National Institute on Drug Abuse, pp. 43–60.

16. Substance Abuse and Mental Health Services Administration. Benzodiazepines in drug abuse-related emergency department visits: 1995–2002 (2004, April). *The DAWN Report.* Rockville, MD: Center for Substance Abuse Treatment, Substance Abuse and Mental Health Services Administration, pp. 1–4. Lickey, Marvin E., and Gordon, Barbara (1991). *Medicine and mental illness.* New York: Freeman, p. 280. Tanaka, Einosuke (2002). Toxiological interactions between alcohol and benzodiazepines. *Journal of Toxicology—Clinical Toxicology, 40,* 69–75.

17. Cumming, R.G., and LeCouteur, D.G. (2003). Benzodiazepines and risk of hip fractures in older people: A review of the evidence. *CNS Drugs, 17,* 825–837. Salzman, Carl (1999). An 87-year-old woman taking a benzodiazepine. *Journal of the American Medical Association, 281,* 1121–1125.

18. Rickels, Karl; Case, W. George; Downing, Robert W.; and Winokur, Andrew (1983). Long-term diazepam therapy and clinical outcome. *Journal of the American Medical Association, 250,* 767–771.

19. Longo, Lance P., and Johnson, Brian (2000). Addiction: Part I. Benzodiazepines—Side effects, abuse risk and alternatives. *American Family Physician, 61,* 2121–2128.

20. Mohler, H., and Okada, T. (1977). Benzodiazepine receptors in rat brain: Demonstration in the central nervous system. *Science, 198,* 849–851. Squires, Richard F., and Braestrup, Claus (1977). Benzodiazepine receptors in rat brain. *Nature, 266,* 732–734.

21. Nelson, John, and Chouinard, Guy (1996). Benzodiazepines: Mechanisms of action and clinical indications. In Andrius Baskys and Gary Remington (Eds.). *Brain mechanisms and psychotropic drugs.* Boca Raton, FL: CRC Press, pp. 213–238.

22. Löw, Karin; Crestani, Florence; Keist, Ruth; Benke, Dietmar; Brünig, Ina; et al. (2000). Molecular and neuronal substrate for the selective attenuation of anxiety. *Science, 290,* 131–134.

23. Griffiths, Roland R., and Ator, Nancy A. (1981). Benzodiazepine self-administration in animals and humans: A comprehensive literature review. In Stephen I. Szara and Jacqueline P. Ludford (Eds.), *Benzodiazepines: A review of research results, 1980* (NIDA Research Monograph 33). Rockville, MD: National Institute on Drug Abuse, pp. 22–36.

24. Julien, Robert M. (1998). *A primer of drug action* (8th ed.). New York: Freeman, pp. 106–107.

25. Lickey and Gordon, *Medicine and mental illness,* p. 278.

26. Lagnaouli, Rajaa; Moore, Nicholas, Dartigues, Jean François; Fourrier, Annie; and Bégaud, Bernard (2001). Benzodiazepine use and wine consumption in the French elderly. *British Journal of Clinical Pharmacology, 52,* 455–456. Pimlott, Nicholas J. G.; Hux, Janet E.; Wilson, Lynn M.; Kahan, Meldon; Li, Cindy; et al. (2003). Educating physicians to reduce benzodiazepine use by elderly patients: A randomized controlled trial. *Canadian Medical Association Journal, 168,* 835–839.

27. Gershell, Leland (2006). From the analyst's couch: Insomnia market. *Nature Reviews and Drug Discovery, 5,* 15–16.

28. Julien, *A primer of drug action* (9th ed.), pp. 169–171.

29. Kent, J. M., Coplan, J. D., and Gorman, J. M. (1998). Clinical utility of the selective serotonin reuptake inhibitors in the spectrum of anxiety. *Biological Psychiatry, 44,* 812–824.

30. Dyer, J. E. (2000). Evolving abuse of GHB in California: Bodybuilding drug to date-rape drug. *Journal of Toxicology—Clinical Toxicology, 38,* 184. Office of National Drug Control Policy (1998, October). *ONDCP Drug Policy Information Clearinghouse fact sheet: Gamma hydroxybutyrate (GHB).* Washington, DC: Executive Office of the President.

31. Information regarding bar coasters courtesy of Drink Safe Technology, Wellington, Florida. Office of National Drug Control Policy, *ONDCP Drug Policy Information Clearinghouse fact sheet: Gamma hydroxybutyrate (GHB).*

32. Broad, William J. (2002, March 19). For Delphic oracle, fumes and visions. *New York Times,* pp. F1, F4. Preble, Edward, and Laury, Gabriel V. (1967). Plastic cement: The ten cent hallucinogen. *International Journal of the Addictions, 2,* 271–281.

33. Gillman, Mark A., and Lichtigfeld, Frederick J. (1997). Clinical role and mechanisms of action of analgesic nitrous oxide. *International Journal of Neuroscience, 93,* 55–62. Nagle, David R. (1968). Anesthetic addiction and drunkenness. *International Journal of the Addictions, 3,* p. 33.

34. Layzer, Robert B. (1985). Nitrous oxide abuse. In Edmond I. Eger (Ed.), *Nitrous oxide/N$_2$O.*

New York: Elsevier, pp. 249–257. Morgan, Roberta (1988). *The emotional pharmacy.* Los Angeles: Body Press, pp. 212–213.

35. Nagle, Anesthetic addiction and drunkenness, pp. 26–30.

36. Khattak, Sohail; K-Moghtader, Guiti; McMartin, Kristen; Barrera, Maru; Kennedy, Debbie; and Koren, Gideon (1999). Pregnancy outcome following gestational exposure to organic solvents. *Journal of the American Medical Association,* 281, 1106–1109.

37. Cohen, Sidney (1977). Inhalant abuse: An overview of the problem. In Charles W. Sharp and Mary Lee Brehm (Eds.), *Review of inhalants: Euphoria to dysfunction* (NIDA Research Monograph 15). Rockville, MD: National Institute on Drug Abuse, p. 7.

38. Ibid., pp. 6–8.

39. Schuckit, Marc A. (1995). *Drug and alcohol abuse: A clinical guide to diagnosis and treatment* (4th ed.). New York: Plenum Medical Book Co., pp. 217–225. Sharp, Charles W., and Rosenberg, Neil L. (1997). Inhalants. In Joyce H. Lowinson, Pedro Ruiz, Robert B. Millman, and John G. Langrod (Eds.), *Substance abuse: A comprehensive textbook.* Baltimore: Williams and Wilkins, pp. 246–264.

40. Abramovitz, Melissa (2003, October). The dangers of inhalants. *Current Health* 2, pp. 19–21. Winger, Gail, Hofmann, Frederick G., and Woods, James H. (1992). *A handbook on drug and alcohol abuse: The biomedical aspects* (3d ed.). New York: Oxford University Press, pp. 90–91.

41. Brecher, Edward M., and the editors of *Consumer Reports* (1972). *Licit and illicit drugs.* Boston: Little, Brown, p. 331.

42. Brands, Bruna, Sproule, Beth, and Marshman, Joan (1998). *Drugs and drug abuse: A reference text.* Toronto: Addiction Research Foundation, pp. 469–471. Bruckner, James V., and Peterson, Richard G. (1977). Toxicology of aliphatic and aromatic hydrocarbons. In Charles W. Sharp and Mary L. Brehm (Eds.), *Review of inhalants: Euphoria to dysfunction* (NIDA Research Monograph 15). Rockville, MD: National Institute on Drug Abuse, pp. 124–163. Garriott, James C. (1992). Death among inhalant abusers. In Charles W. Sharp, Fred Beauvais, and Richard Spence (Eds.), *Inhalant abuse: A volatile research agenda* (NIDA Research Monograph 129). Rockville, MD: National Institute on Drug Abuse, pp. 171–193.

43. Edwards, Ruth W., and Oetting, E. R. (1995). Inhalant use in the United States. In Nicholas Kozel, Zili Sloboda, and Mario De La Rosa (Eds.), *Epidemiology of inhalant abuse: An international perspective* (NIDA Research Monograph 148). Rockville, MD: National Institute on Drug Abuse, pp. 8–28. Johnston, O'Malley, Bachman, and Schulenberg, Teen marijuana use tilts up, Tables 1, 2, and 3. Preboth, Monica (2000, February 15). Prevalence of inhalant abuse in children. *American Family Physician,* p. 1206.

44. Howard, Matthew O.; Walker, R. Dale; Walker, Patricia S.; Cottler, Linda B.; and Compton, Wilson M. (1999). Inhalant use among urban American Indian youth.

Addiction, 94, 83–95. Kin, Foong, and Navaratnam, Vis (1995). An overview of inhalant abuse in selected countries of Asia and the Pacific region. In Nicholas Kozel, Zili Sloboda, and Mario De La Rosa (Eds.), *Epidemiology of inhalant abuse: An international perspective* (NIDA Research Monograph 148). Rockville, MD: National Institute on Drug Abuse, pp. 29–49. Leal, Hermán; Mejía, Laura; Gómez, Lucila; and Salina de Valle, Olga (1978). Naturalistic study on the phenomenon of inhalant use in a group of children in Mexico City. In Charles W. Sharp and L. T. Carroll (Eds.), *Voluntary inhalation of industrial solvents.* Rockville, MD: National Institute on Drug Abuse, pp. 95–108. Medina-Mora, María Elena, and Berenzon, Shoshana (1995). Epidemiology of inhalant abuse in Mexico. In Nicholas Kozel, Zili Sloboda, and Mario De La Rosa (Eds.), *Epidemiology of inhalant abuse: An international perspective* (NIDA Research Monograph 148). Rockville, MD: National Institute on Drug Abuse, pp. 136–174. Surratt, Hilary L., and Inciardi, James A. (1996). Drug use, HIV risks, and prevention/intervention strategies among street youths in Rio de Janeiro, Brazil. In Clyde B. McCoy, Lisa R. Metsch, and James A. Inciardi (Eds.), *Intervening with drug-involved youth.* Thousand Oaks, MI: Sage Publications, pp. 173–190.

45. Hofmann, Frederick G. (1983), *A handbook on drug and alcohol abuse: The biomedical aspects* (2nd ed.). New York: Oxford University Press, p. 134. Howard, Matthew O., and Jenson, Jeffrey M. (1998). Inhalant use among antisocial youth: Prevalence and correlates. *Addictive Behaviors,* 24, 59–74. Mackesy-Amiti, Mary Ellen, and Fendrich, Michaeal (1999). Inhalant abuse and delinquent behavior among adolescents: A comparison of inhalant users and other drug users. *Addiction,* 94, 555–564.

46. Oetting, E. R., Edwards, Ruth W., and Beauvais, Fred (1988). Social and psychological factors underlying inhalant abuse. In Raquel A. Crider and Beatrice A. Rouse (eds.), *Epidemiology of inhalant abuse: An update* (NIDA Research Monograph 85). Rockville, MD: National Institute on Drug Abuse, pp. 172–203.

47. Hofmann, *Handbook on drug and alcohol abuse,* pp. 138–139. Karch, *The pathology of drug abuse,* p. 432. Korman, Maurice (1977). Clinical evaluation of psychological factors. In Charles W. Sharp and Mary Lee Brehm (Eds.), *Review of inhalants: Euphoria to dysfunction* (NIDA Research Monograph 15). Rockville, MD: National Institute on Drug Abuse, pp. 30–53.

48. Hofmann, *Handbook on drug and alcohol abuse,* p. 134.

49. Oetting, Edwards, and Beauvais, Social and psychological factors, p. 197.

50. Sharp, Charles W. (1977). Approaches to the problem. In Charles W. Sharp and Mary Lee Brehm (Eds.), *Review of inhalants: Euphoria to dysfunction* (NIDA Research Monograph 15). Rockville, MD: National Institute on Drug Abuse, pp. 226–242.

51. Kerner, Karen (1988). Current topics in inhalant abuse. In Raquel A. Crider and Beatrice A. Rouse (Eds.), *Epidemiology of inhalant abuse: An update* (NIDA

Research Monograph 85). Rockville, MD: National Institute on Drug Abuse, p. 20.

52. Draft of National Inhalant Prevention Coalition guidelines for inhalant abuse treatment (2003). Information courtesy of the National Inhalant Prevention Coalition, Austin, Texas. Office of National Drug Control Policy (2003, February). *Inhalants: Drug Policy Information Clearinghouse fact sheet*. Washington, DC: White House Office of National Drug Control Policy. Substance Abuse and Mental Health Services Administration (2003). *Inhalants: Substance abuse treatment advisory*. Rockville, MD: Center for Substance Abuse Treatment, Substance Abuse and Mental Health Services Administration.

53. Newell, Guy R., Spitz, Margaret R., and Wilson, Michael B. (1988). Nitrite inhalants: Historical perspective. In Harry W. Haverkos and John A. Dougherty (Eds.), *Health hazards of nitrite inhalants* (NIDA Research Monograph 83). Rockville, MD: National Institute on Drug Abuse, pp. 1–14.

54. Johnston, Lloyd D., O'Malley, Patrick M., Bachman, Jerald G., & Schulenberg, John E. (2010). *Monitoring the Future: National survey results on drug use, 1975–2009. Volume II: College students and adults ages 19–50, 2009*. Bethesda, MD: National Institute on Drug Abuse, Table 2-2.

chapter 12

Performance-Enhancing Drugs and Drug Testing in Sports

Have I used steroids? You bet I did. Did steroids make me a better baseball player? Of course they did. If I had it all to do over again, would I live a steroid-enriched life? Yes, I would. Do I have any regrets or qualms about relying on chemicals to help me hit a baseball so far? To be honest, no, I don't.

—José Canseco, Juiced (2005)

I'm here to take my medicine . . . I knew we weren't taking Tic Tacs.

—Alex Rodriguez (2009)
On admitting steroid use during the 2001–2003 baseball seasons[1]

After you have completed this chapter, you should have an understanding of

- The history of performance-enhancing drugs in sports
- How anabolic steroids work
- The health risks of steroid abuse
- Patterns of steroid abuse
- Performance-enhancing nonsteroid hormones
- Dietary supplements marketed as performance-enhancing aids
- Nonmedical use of stimulant medication in baseball
- Present-day drug testing in amateur and professional sports
- Current drug-testing techniques in sports, business, and criminal justice
- The social context of performance-enhancing drugs

She was disappointed, and she has every right
to be. I couldn't tell her how so sorry I was.

—*Mark McGwire* (2010)
On apologizing to Roger Maris's widow prior
to admitting steroid use during the 1990s[2]

In a world where running a hundredth of a second faster can mean the difference between a gold medal and a silver, where throwing a javelin a few centimeters farther, hitting a baseball 20 feet farther, or lifting a kilogram more can make you either the champion or an also-ran, temptations abound. In this high-pressure world, athletes are continually on the lookout for a winning edge. The advantage formula may involve a new technique in training, a new attitude toward winning, or a special diet. Or it could involve the use of performance-enhancing drugs.

We are used to hearing the (often belated) public confessions of sports celebrities regarding their past use of performance-enhancing drugs, specifically their use of anabolic steroids. These public displays of contrition have put the records of their lifetime careers in question forever, along with our respect for their athletic achievements. They are (or were) our heroes.

We tend to view performance-enhancing drug use in sports as simply inappropriate. To most people, their behavior represents a betrayal of our trust in their honesty and society's assumption of fair play. In fact, on the basis of federal legislation enacted in 1990 and strengthened in 2004, their actions are more than inappropriate; they are illegal. The nonmedical possession of the most potent category of performance-enhancing drugs, namely anabolic steroids and chemical precursors to anabolic steroids, is a criminal offence.

In 1990, as a response to increasing awareness of the abuse of anabolic steroids both in and out of competitive sports, Congress passed the Anabolic Steroid Control Act, reclassifying anabolic steroids as Schedule III controlled substances. Jurisdiction was transferred from the Food and Drug Administration (FDA) to the Drug Enforcement Administration (DEA). As a result of this legislation, pharmacies are permitted to fill anabolic-steroid prescriptions only up to a maximum of five times. Penalties for violating the law can result in a five-year prison term and a $250,000 fine for illegal nonmedical sales, and a one-year term and a $1,000 fine for nonmedical possession. Penalties are doubled for repeated offenses or for selling these drugs to minors. States are permitted to draft their own laws regarding the definition of anabolic steroids and to set sentencing guidelines for steroid offenders. Although most states follow the federally mandated Schedule III classification, New York lists steroids in Schedule II, and Alaska does not schedule them at all. In some states, possession of small quantities of steroids is regarded as a misdemeanor; other states regard it as a felony. In most but not all states, first-time offenses do not result in imprisonment, unless there are aggravating circumstances such as possession of large quantities or evidence of intent to sell or distribute the drugs.

Anabolic steroid distribution, like the distribution of other restricted drugs in the United States, has become an enormous black-market enterprise. With their use commonly referred to as being "on the juice," these drugs are channeled principally through people associated with body-building gyms and through Internet web sites that frequently change the identity of a company's location in an effort to stay one step ahead of the law. Some Internet-based suppliers include a warning on their web sites, "Due to their profound effects and potencies, it is recommended to seek the guidance of a physician prior to use," to protect themselves from criminal liability, though no customer would voluntarily divulge his or her steroid abuse, much less seek medical guidance. It is estimated that the illicit anabolic steroid market is valued at between $300 million to $400 million each year, with the drugs smuggled into the United States from Europe, Canada, and Mexico.[3]

How did performance-enhancing drugs, particularly anabolic steroids, gain such popularity? Far from being a new phenomenon, performance-enhancing drugs have been a factor in competitive sports for centuries. As we will see, however, the problem of performance-enhancing drugs goes beyond the world of competitive sports. A growing number of young people are using these drugs simply because they want to look better by developing the musculature of their bodies. The serious dangers in such drug-taking behavior, whether the motivation lies in competitive drive or in personal vanity, are major problems that need to be examined closely.

Drug-Taking Behavior in Sports

The first recorded athletic competition, the ancient Olympic Games in Greece, is also the place where we find the first recorded use of psychoactive drugs in sports. As early as 300 B.C., Greek athletes ate hallucinogenic mushrooms either to improve their performance in the competition or to achieve some kind of mystical connection to the gods. Later, Roman gladiators and charioteers used stimulants to sustain themselves longer in competition, even when injured by their opponents.

In the modern era, drugs continued to be a factor in athletic competitions. By the end of the nineteenth century, world-class athletes were experimenting with a variety of stimulant and depressant drugs, including cocaine, caffeine, alcohol, nitroglycerine, opiates, strychnine, and amphetamines. In 1886, while competing in a cross-country race, a Welsh cyclist died of a combination of opiates and cocaine (now referred to as a speedball), the first drug-related death ever recorded in sports. During the 1904 Olympics, U.S. marathoner Tom Hicks collapsed after winning the race and lost consciousness. When he was revived, doctors were told that he had taken a potentially lethal mixture of strychnine (a CNS stimulant when administered in low doses) and brandy.[4]

With the introduction of anabolic steroid drugs specifically patterned after the male sex hormone testosterone, a new element entered the arena of competitive sports. Here was a class of drugs that did more than alter the behavior or experience of the athlete; *these drugs actually altered the structure of the athlete's body.*

Anabolic steroid drugs had been studied since the 1930s as a treatment for anemia (low red blood cell count) and for conditions that caused muscles to waste away. Following the end of World War II, steroid drugs were administered to people who were near death from starvation and weight loss. It quickly became apparent, however, that steroids could be useful when given to otherwise healthy individuals as well. As pharmaceutical companies began to introduce dozens of new body-building drugs based on the testosterone molecule, it was natural that information about anabolic steroids would come to the attention of athletes, as well as their coaches and trainers. No legal barrier to their use would exist for several decades.

What Are Anabolic Steroids?

To understand how testosterone-based steroids produce **ergogenic** (performance-enhancing) changes, we first have to recognize that testosterone itself has two primary effects on the human body. The first and most obvious effect is **androgenic** (literally, "man-producing"), in that the hormone promotes the development of male sex characteristics. As testosterone levels rise during puberty, boys acquire an enlarged larynx (resulting in a deeper voice), body hair, and an increase in body size, as well as genital changes that make them sexually mature adults. The second effect is **anabolic** (upward-changing), in that it promotes the development of protein and, as a result, an increase in muscle tissue. Muscles in men are inherently larger than muscles in women because of the anabolic action of testosterone in the male body.

Steroid drugs based on alterations in the testosterone molecule are therefore called **anabolic-androgenic steroids**. The goal, however, has been to develop drugs that emphasize the anabolic function while retaining as little of the androgenic function as possible. For that reason, they are most often called simply **anabolic steroids**. Unfortunately, as we will see, it has not been possible to develop a testosterone-derived drug without at least some androgenic effects (Table 12.1)

It is important that anabolic steroids not be confused with **adrenocortical steroids**, drugs that are patterned after glucocorticoid hormones secreted by the adrenal glands. The major drug of this latter type is cortisone (brand name, among others: Hydrocortone injection or tablets). The molecular structure of these drugs qualifies them to belong to the steroid family, but there is no relationship to testosterone or any testosterone-like effects. Adrenocorticoidal steroids are useful in the medical treatment of tissue inflammation; in sports, they reduce the inflammation associated with muscle injuries. Their effect on muscle development can be viewed as catabolic (downward-changing), in that muscles tend to weaken as a result, so their long-term use is unlikely to be a desirable option for athletes.[5]

---

ergogenic (ER-go-JEN-ik): Performance-enhancing.

androgenic (AN-droh-JEN-ik): Acting to promote masculinizing changes in the body.

anabolic (AN-ah-BALL-ik): Acting to promote protein growth and muscle development.

anabolic-androgenic steroids: Drugs that promote masculinizing changes in the body and increased muscle development.

anabolic steroids: Drugs patterned after the testosterone molecule that promote masculinizing changes in the body and increased muscle development. The full name is anabolic-androgenic steroids.

adrenocortical steroids: A group of hormones secreted by the adrenal glands. Their anti-inflammatory action makes them useful for treating arthritis and muscle injuries.

TABLE 12.1

Anabolic steroids currently available in the United States

TYPE OF STEROID	GENERIC NAME	BRAND NAME
Oral	danazol	Danocrine
	drostanolone	Masteron
	methandrostenolone	Dianabol
	methyltestosterone	Android, Testred, Virilon
	oxyandrolone	Oxandrin
	oxymetholone	Android-50, Anadrol
	stanozolol	Winstrol V
	boldanone undecylenate	Equipoise, EquiGan, Equidren
	norbolethone	(never marketed)
Intramuscular injection	nandrolone decanoate	Deca-Durabolin IM
	nandrolone phenprionate	Durabolin IM
	testosterone cyprionate	Virilon IM
	testosterone enantrate	Delatestryl IM
Transdermal patch	testosterone	Androderm transdermal system, Testoderm transdermal system

Note: Anabolic steroids are Schedule III controlled substances. As such, they are considered illicit drugs under federal guidelines when not obtained with a medical prescription and restricted to medical use along with other Schedule III controlled substances. Several "brand names" marketed for performance-enhancing purposes are combinations of various forms of steroids.

Sources: National Institute on Drug Abuse (2000, April). Anabolic steroids. *Community drug alert bulletin.* Bethesda, MD: National Institute on Drug Abuse. *Physicians' desk reference* (61st ed.) (2007). Montvale, NJ: Medical Economics Company. Shipley, Amy (2003, March 23). Drug testers have designs on new steroid. *Washington Post,* p. D1.

Anabolic Steroids at the Modern Olympic Games

By the time of the 1952 Olympic Games in Helsinki, athletes were well acquainted with performance-enhancing drugs. Legally available amphetamines (see Chapter 8), in particular, were commonplace, particularly in events that emphasized speed and endurance. Among events requiring strength and size, anabolic steroids were seen to be perfectly suited for gaining a competitive advantage.

It is debatable which country first used anabolic steroids. U.S. athletic officials have claimed that Soviet weight-lifting champions were using steroids in international competitions in 1954; British officials have claimed that a U.S. hammer thrower used steroids prior to 1954. Whoever has the dubious honor of being first, steroid use became the norm by the 1956 Olympic Games in Melbourne for both men and women athletes.

Steroid use was clearly out in the open during the 1968 Olympic Games in Mexico City. An estimated one-third of the entire U.S. track and field team, not merely the strength-event and field-event competitors but the sprinters and middle-distance runners as well, were using anabolic steroids. The controversy did not concern the appropriateness or morality of taking steroids, only which particular steroids worked best. Strength-event athletes were taking at least two to five times the therapeutic recommendations (based on the original intent of replacing body protein). The following year, an editor of *Track and Field News* dubbed anabolic steroids "the breakfast of champions." In 1971, one U.S. weight lifter commented to a reporter in reference to his Soviet rival,

> *Last year the only difference between me and him was I couldn't afford his drug bill. Now I can. When I hit Munich [in 1972] I'll weigh in at about 340, or maybe 350. Then we'll see which is better, his steroids or mine.*[6]

In the meantime, the masculine features of many female athletes from eastern European countries in the 1960s and 1970s, not to mention the number of Olympic records that were suddenly broken, prompted many observers to ask whether they were either men disguised as women or genetic "mistakes." Questions about the unusually deep voices of East German women swimmers prompted their coach, at one point, to respond: "We came here to swim, not to sing."

From information that has come to light since then, we now know that the effects were chiefly due to large doses of steroids. Until the late 1980s, the East German government was conducting a scientific program specifically to develop new steroid formulations that would benefit their national athletes and, at the same time, would be undetectable by standard screening procedures. In 2000, the principal physician in the

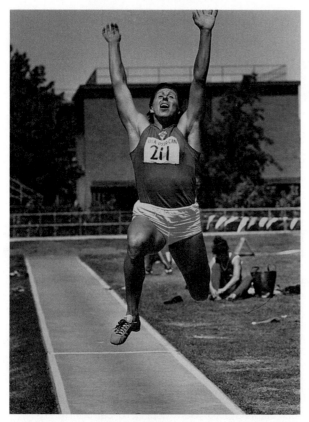

Russian pentathlon champion Nadezhda Tkachenko was one of several world-class female athletes in the 1970s who later tested positive for anabolic steroids.

Since 2009, the World Anti-Doping Code, has been in effect. The Code includes an agreed-upon list of prohibited performance-enhancing drugs and performance-enhancing methods in international sports competitions, testing procedures for their use, and specific penalties for violations. Under the auspices of the World Anti-Doping Agency (WADA), rules and regulations have been formally accepted by more than 200 National Olympic Committees, as well as by professional leagues (such as the National Basketball Association and the National Hockey League) representing the United States in the Olympic Games and other international competitions. Despite these steps toward controlling the impact of performance-enhancing drugs in international competitions, however, drug-related scandals in sports continue. (Drugs . . . in Focus).

Anabolic Steroids in Professional and Collegiate Sports

The wholesale use of anabolic steroids in international athletics in the 1950s soon filtered down to sports closer to home. Beginning in the early 1960s, trainers in the National Football League began to administer anabolic steroids to their players. By the 1970s and 1980s, virtually

East German Swimming Federation at the time when these steroids were being administered was convicted on charges that from 1975 to 1985 the program caused bodily harm to more than four dozen young female swimmers.[7]

The 2000 Olympic Games in Sydney, Australia, instituted the strictest drug-testing procedures to date for all competing athletes, including a new screening for EPO, a drug that enhances endurance by increasing red blood cells. For the first time, a specific phrase was inserted into the Olympic Oath, recited by all athletes at the beginning of the games: ". . . committing ourselves to a sport without doping and without drugs." Unfortunately, accusations of illegal performance-enhancing drug use and expulsions of athletes continued to plague the 2004 Summer Olympic Games in Athens as well as the 2006 Winter Olympic Games in Torino, Italy, as they had in previous ones since the 1950s.

Following the Salt Lake City Olympics in 2002, workers cleaning a home rented to Austrian Nordic cross-country ski team found empty blood packs and transfusion equipment. The equipment was suspected to have been used for "blood packing," a technique in which an athlete freezes his or her own blood, thaws it prior to an athletic event, and injects it to increase oxygen-carrying red blood cells and enhance performance. Two nonmedalist Austrian skiers were later judged disqualified and their scores stricken from the record.

Drugs... in Focus

Disqualified by Your DNA?

Since the 1964 Winter Olympic Games in Innsbruck, Finland's gold-medalist cross-country skier Eero Mantyranta had been rumored to be using performance-enhancing drugs in competition, even though he never failed a drug test. Decades later, DNA technology has made it possible for Mantyranta to be exonerated of any suspicion of wrongdoing. It turns out that Mantyranta had a naturally occurring genetic mutation that produced increased levels of erythropoietin (EPO), a hormone that regulates red blood cells in the body. Since 2000, synthetic forms of EPO have been among the many steroid and nonsteroid drugs screened for in the Olympic Games. In the drug testing administered in today's competitions, Mantyranta would have failed the test and would have been required to submit his DNA to prove himself innocent of "blood doping."

Advancement in gene therapy techniques may in the future lead to all sorts of ergogenic mischief. It is conceivable that we might be able to alter the EPO gene so as to increase the number of red blood cells carrying oxygen to muscles, the vascular endothelial growth factor (VEGF) gene so as to increase the number of blood vessels, or the short form of the angiotensin-converting enzyme (ACE) gene so as to increase the performance of "fast-twitch" muscles necessary for sudden bursts of speed. On the one hand, increasing EPO levels might help people who are anemic, increasing VEGF levels might help people with clogged arteries and other circulatory diseases, and increasing ACE levels might help people suffering from chronic fatigue. On the other hand, for healthy athletes, the procedure would be, in effect, "gene doping."

As investigations of the human genome continue, it may become possible to specify sets of naturally occurring gene mutations that result in unusually high levels of athletic prowess. Would the identification of these mutations in future world champions justify a potential disqualification by virtue of their DNA? Today, the burden of proof is on officials to establish that an athlete is guilty of using a banned ergogenic substance. In the future, the burden of proof might be on the athlete to establish his or her innocence. How would athletes prove that their DNA had not been intentionally modified? Some interesting questions to ponder.

Sources: Begley, Sharon (2002, February 18). Science of speed. *Newsweek*, pp. 56–58. Cooke, Robert (2002, June 18). Fixed genes, fixed games? *Newsday*, pp. D1, D5. Pincock, Stephen (2005). Gene doping. *Lancet, 366,* 518–519. Sokolove, Michael (2004, January 18). The lab animal: Elite athletes always have and always will pursue every competitive advantage—health and the law be damned. Is genetic manipulation next? *New York Times Magazine*, pp. 28–33. Sweeney, H. Lee (2004, July). Gene doping. *Scientific American*, pp. 37–43.

---

all the NFL teams were familiar with these drugs. Estimates of how many players were on anabolic steroids varied from 50 to 90 percent. We will never know the full extent of the practice, but it was certainly substantial.

Several professional football players remarked at the time that their steroid use had begun while they were playing on collegiate teams, and indeed, football players in several colleges and universities during the 1980s were implicated in steroid use. Football players were not alone in this regard. Use of anabolic steroids had found its way into other collegiate and even high school sports of all kinds, including track and field, baseball, basketball, gymnastics, lacrosse, swimming, volleyball, wrestling, and tennis. It is fair to say that until the late 1980s, when screening procedures became commonplace, there was no sport, professional or amateur, for which the use of anabolic steroids was not an accepted element in athletic training.[8]

Performance-Enhancing Drug Abuse and Baseball

Record-breaking home-run performances in the late 1990s and early 2000s raised suspicions that these achievements in baseball were due not solely to athletic prowess but to some pharmacological assistance as well. Yet, until then, major league baseball had stood apart from other professional sports in the United States and sports organizations around the world by failing to establish self-regulatory policies (as opposed to regulatory policies imposed by federal or state governments) regarding steroid abuse and the use of other performance-enhancing drugs.

In 2004, a prominent track coach, two executives of BALCO, a nutritional supplements laboratory in California, and Barry Bonds's personal trainer were indicted on charges of illegally distributing steroids and other performance-enhancing drugs to dozens of professional athletes in baseball and other sports. In a subsequent development, a New York Mets clubhouse assistant pleaded guilty to having supplied performance-enhancing drugs to dozens of current and former major league baseball (MLB) players and their associates beginning in 1995 until 2005, and subsequently laundering the proceeds (see Chapter 5) from these transactions.

Under intense pressure from public opinion and from government officials, MLB players agreed in early 2005 to a policy of steroid testing that was more in line with those of the National Football League and the National Basketball Association. In late 2005, MLB penalties for steroid use were stiffened (Drugs . . . in Focus). Testing procedures and penalties for the use of amphetamine and other stimulants, previously omitted from consideration in the earlier agreement, were added (see page 283).

It has become evident, unfortunately, that drug testing in MLB has failed to eliminate the use of performance-enhancing drugs. In 2007, a major investigation, under the direction of former U.S. senator and federal prosecutor George J. Mitchell, concluded that MLB policies had reduced the use of steroids but that other nonsteroid performance-enhancing drugs, particularly human growth hormone, had increased in popularity and were widely used. The revelations about MLB players, including some of the most prominent names in baseball, having tested positive to performance-enhancing drugs, seem to have no end in sight.[9]

Drugs... in Focus

Suspension Penalties for Performance-Enhancing Drug Use in Sports

The 2005 agreement on regulations against steroid use in major league baseball (MLB) included a ban on "all substances regarded now, or in the future, by the federal government as steroids" as well as human growth hormone and steroid precursor hormones such as androstenedione. Suspension penalties for positive-test infractions under these new regulations are shown in comparison to previous MLB regulations and those of other U.S. and international athletic organizations.

	POSITIVE TEST				
	First	*Second*	*Third*	*Fourth*	*Fifth*
Major League Baseball					
Pre-2005	counseling	15 days	25 days	50 days	1 year
Late 2005	50 games	100 games	lifetime suspension, with right of reinstatement after two years		
Minor League Baseball	15 days	30 days	60 days	1 year	lifetime
National Football League	4 games	6 games	1 year	1 year	1 year
National Basketball Association	5 games	10 games	25 games	25 games	25 games
National Hockey League			—no testing for steroids—		
World Anti-Doping Association (Olympic sports)	2 years	lifetime			

Source: Curry, Jack (2006, November 16). Baseball lacks stiffer penalties for steroid use. *New York Times*, pp. A1, D2. NFL will ban amphetamines as enhancers (2006, June 28). *Newsday*, p. A53.

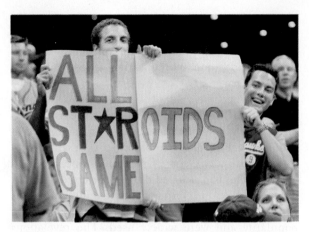

Fans expressed their opinion on steroid use at Major League Baseball's All-Star Game in 2002. Between 5 and 7 percent of MLB players tested positive for anabolic steroids when randomized screening was conducted during spring training in 2003. Steroid testing began in earnest in 2005.

Whether or not aided by performance-enhancing drugs, massive development of musculature continues to be a prized asset in competitive bodybuilding.

The Hazards of Anabolic Steroids

One of the problems in evaluating the adverse effects of steroid abuse is that the dosage levels can vary over an enormous range. Since nonmedical steroid use is illegal, it is virtually impossible to know the exact dosage levels or even the exact combinations of steroids a particular individual may be taking. It is estimated that a "typical" body builder on anabolic steroids may be taking in a minimum of three to ten times the therapeutic doses recommended for the medical use of these drugs, but in some cases, the estimates have gone as high as a hundred to a thousand times the recommended therapeutic dose.[10]

Effects on Hormonal Systems

At these huge dosages, anabolic steroids are literally flooding into the body, upsetting the delicate balance of hormones and other chemicals that are normally controlled by testosterone. The primary effect in men is for the testes gland to react to the newly increased testosterone levels in the blood by producing *less* testosterone

gynecomastia (GUY-neh-coh-MAST-ee-ah): An enlargement of the breasts.

priapism (PRY-ah-pih-zem): A condition marked by persistent and frequently painful penile erections.

on its own. In other words, the gland is getting the incorrect message that its services are no longer needed. As a result, the testicles shrink, and a lower sperm count leads to sterility, reversible for most men but irreversible in a small number of cases. Paradoxically, the male breasts enlarge (a condition called **gynecomastia**) because steroids break down eventually into estradiol, the female sex hormone. Other related consequences include frequent, sustained, and often painful penile erections (a condition called **priapism**) and an enlargement of the prostate gland. Severe acne, particularly on the shoulders and back, results from an increase in the secretions of the sebaceous glands in the skin. Other testosterone-related effects include two changes in hair growth patterns: increased facial hair growth and accelerated balding on the top of the head.

Some athletes have attempted to counter these undesirable hormonal effects by combining anabolic steroids with human chorionic gonadotropin (HCG), a hormone that ordinarily stimulates the testes to secrete testosterone. In theory, this strategy can work, but the dosages have to be carefully controlled, something that self-medicating athletes are unlikely to do. Repeated HCG treatments actually can have the opposite effect from the one that is intended, making matters worse rather than better. In addition, HCG itself has its own adverse effects, including headaches, mood swings, depression, and retention of fluids.[11]

Among women taking anabolic steroids, the dramatically increased levels of testosterone in bodies that normally have only trace amounts produce major physiological changes, only some of which return to normal

TABLE 12.2

Reported side effects of anabolic steroids in ten women

EFFECT	NUMBER REPORTING THE EFFECT	REVERSIBLE AFTER END OF USE
Lower voice	10	no
Increased facial hair	9	no
Enlarged clitoris	8	no
Increased aggressiveness	8	yes
Increased appetite	8	unknown
Decreased body fat	8	unknown
Diminished or stopped menstruation	7	yes
Increased sexual drive	6	yes
Increased acne	6	yes
Decreased breast size	5	unknown
Increased body hair	5	no
Increased loss of scalp hair	2	no

Note: The ten women were all weight-trained athletes.

Sources: Strauss, Richard H., and Yesalis, Charles E. (1993). Additional effects of anabolic steroids in women. In Charles E. Yesalis (Ed.), *Anabolic steroids in sport and exercise*. Champaign, IL: Human Kinetics Publishers, pp. 151–160. Strauss, Richard H., Ligget, M. T., and Lanese R. R. (1985). Anabolic steroid use and perceived effects in ten weight-trained women athletes. *Journal of the American Medical Association, 253*, 2871–2873.

when steroids are withdrawn. Table 12.2 lists the major reversible and irreversible effects among women.

Effects on Other Systems of the Body

Given the fact that the liver is the primary means for clearing drugs from the body (see Chapter 1), it is not surprising that large doses of anabolic steroids take their toll on this organ. The principal result is a greatly increased risk of developing liver tumors. The type of liver tumors that are frequently seen in these circumstances are benign (noncancerous) blood-filled cysts, with the potential for causing liver failure. In addition, a rupture in these cysts can produce abdominal bleeding, requiring life-saving emergency treatment. Fortunately, these liver abnormalities are reversible when steroids are withdrawn from use.

There is evidence from animal studies that increased steroid levels in the body can produce high blood pressure and high cholesterol levels, as well as heart abnormalities. Whether cardiovascular effects present a problem for steroid abusers, however, is not well established, and the often-publicized cardiovascular risks associated with anabolic steroids may be exaggerated. It is extremely difficult to determine whether the small number of documented cases of heart-disease-related deaths among steroid abusers have been specifically linked to chronic intake of steroid drugs.[12]

Psychological Problems

Stories abound of mood swings and increased aggressiveness, often referred to by athletes as "roid rage," when taking anabolic steroids. Numerous anecdotal reports force us to consider the possibility that real psychological changes are going on.[13] As an example, this is how one sportswriter recalled the unusual behavior of the professional football player Lyle Alzado during the 1980s:

> I was covering the Los Angeles Raiders when Alzado, who had played previously with the Denver Broncos and Cleveland Browns, joined [the team] in 1982. In 1984, I was talking to one of his teammates across the Raiders' dressing room, when Alzado, with no provocation, picked up his gray metal stool and threw it in my direction, shouting something about "reporters in the locker room." Shaken, I asked several players who knew him best what was bugging him. They said Alzado probably just had a steroid injection and to stay out of his way. Good advice.[14]

Beyond the well-publicized anecdotal reports, however, more rigorous laboratory investigations into the relationship between anabolic steroid use and psychological problems are needed to provide a better understanding of the phenomenon. In a double-blind study, a group of male volunteers were randomly administered intramuscular injections of either testosterone cyprionate or a placebo over a period of twenty-five weeks. All of them were screened for current or prior psychological problems. One subgroup was engaged in weight training but had no prior history of steroid use. A second subgroup had no training experience and had not used steroids. A third group reported a history of steroid use but had refrained from any use for a minimum of three months prior to the beginning of the study.

The results showed that, on average, testosterone significantly increased manic behavior and feelings of aggressiveness, but the individual reactions were quite variable. Only eight of the fifty men in the study showed any mood changes at all. Two of them showed marked symptoms. One of these men experienced an aggressive outburst at work and, on one occasion, reacted to being cut off in traffic by following the person in his car for several miles. The other man developed extreme euphoria and reported a decreased need for sleep. Six other study participants showed more moderate changes. One man in this category found himself wanting to beat up his opponent in a college sports competition, even though he had never had such aggressive feelings before in the course of a game. All of the other participants in the study showed minimal or no effects, and in no case was there an incident of actual violent behavior. Neither previous steroid use nor regular weight training was associated with the symptoms observed in the men responding to testosterone.

Because the study used a double-blind design, neither the experimenters nor the men being studied knew whether they were being injected with testosterone or a placebo (see Chapter 1); half of the men started with the active drug condition, and half started with the placebo condition. Therefore, in interpreting the results, we can eliminate any possible influences of expectations and preconceptions about what different behaviors and experiences might result from anabolic steroids. On the basis of this information, mood changes and aggressiveness seem genuinely to result from an elevation in testosterone levels, although the reactions of people taking anabolic steroids are far from uniform. Extrapolating from the available research literature on this issue, it has been estimated that somewhere between 2 and 20 percent of men will develop mood-related psychological problems from anabolic steroid use.

However, it is important to realize that experimental studies *underestimate* the extent of the phenomenon in the real world. In the study reported here, the maximum dosage of testosterone was 600 mg per week. In actual practice, steroid abusers often take drugs that boost testosterone to as much as 1,000 to 1,500 mg per week, levels that far exceed those that can be safely studied in the laboratory. As a consequence, the percentage of individuals developing significant mood changes and behavioral problems is likely to be much higher, and the changes and problems themselves can be expected to be substantially greater.[15]

Special Problems for Adolescents

In 2009, the University of Michigan survey reported that between 1 and 2 percent of eighth graders, tenth graders, and high school seniors had used anabolic steroids in their lifetime. During puberty, a particularly crucial process among boys is growth of the long bones

of the body, which results in an increase in height. Anabolic steroids suppress growth hormones; as a result, muscular development is enhanced but overall body growth is stunted. Among girls, testosterone-related drugs delay the onset of puberty, making the body shorter, lighter, and more "girl-like" while enhancing the user's overall strength. On a psychological level, feelings of euphoria and aggression that adolescents experience while using anabolic steroids can be replaced by lethargy, loss of confidence, and depression when these drugs are discontinued (Portrait).[16]

Patterns of Anabolic Steroid Abuse

Some anabolic steroids can be taken orally and others through intramuscular injections, but abusers often administer a combination of both types in a practice called *stacking*. Hard-core abusers may take a combination of three to five different pills and injectables simultaneously, or they may consume any steroid that is available ("shotgunning"), with the total exceeding a dozen. In addition to the complications that result from so many different types of steroids being taken at the same time, multiple injections into the buttocks or thighs, with 1.5-inch needles (called "darts" or "points"),

PORTRAIT

Steve T.—Steroids and Getting the Look

Steve T. isn't his real name. But his story is not only real but undoubtedly a recognizable one to young men in nearly every American community where the importance of personal appearance has managed to outweigh physical risks and criminal prosecution.

Steve was not an aspiring athlete or competitive bodybuilder. The drug-testing program at his school would not have affected him in any way. He was simply a sixteen-year-old suburban teenager, short of stature and self-confidence and convinced that muscles would make the difference. "I wanted people to notice me," he said. In particular, he wanted the girls to notice him.

It began with hours pumping weights at home and poring over muscle web sites on the Internet. One day, he asked for a "shortcut" at a gym he had joined. Soon, he was injecting $150 doses of testosterone on a regular basis. In the meantime, Steve packed on twenty pounds of muscle and finally got all the attention he had always craved from his friends and from girls. He could now bench-press 180 pounds with ease and curl 100 pounds "For a little guy, I was really putting it up," he said. He ignored the acne that spread across his back.

Steve was also getting careless. Afraid to keep his steroids at home, he would take them to school. When they were discovered, school officials notified the police and Steve was arrested for possession of a controlled substance. While charges were reduced to a misdemeanor offense, the real punishment came later when a family physician noted a low sperm count. His mother was convinced that Steve's growth had been stunted. "I was scared," he said. "I kept saying to myself: 'I don't belong here [in this predicament]. I'm not a bad kid.'"

Steve canceled his gym membership and set his sights on turning his life around. Working out was no longer so important to him. Currently, he has a girlfriend and claims that he is off steroids. His parents still worry.

Source: Bruchey, Samuel (2004, December 19). Steroids in the suburbs. *Newsday*, pp. A3, A48–A49.

---

are painful and inevitably leave scars. If these needles are shared, as they frequently are, the risk of hepatitis or HIV contamination is significant.

Steroid abusers often engage in a practice called *cycling*, in which steroids are taken for periods lasting from four to eighteen weeks, the "on" periods being separated by "off" periods of abstinence. Unfortunately, when the drugs are withdrawn, the newly developed muscles tend to "shrink up," throwing the abuser into a panic that his or her body is losing the gains that have been achieved. In addition, abstinence from steroids can lead to signs of depression, sleep problems, lack of appetite, and general moodiness. All these effects encourage a return to steroids, frequently in even larger doses, and generate a craving for the euphoria that the person felt while taking them.

A variation of the cycling pattern is the practice of *pyramiding*. An individual starts with low doses of steroids, gradually increases the doses over several weeks prior to an athletic competition, and then tapers off entirely before the competition itself in an attempt to escape detection during drug testing. However, pyramiding leads to the same problems during withdrawal and abstinence as cycling, except that the symptoms occur during the competition itself.

A major problem associated with steroid abuse is the potential for an individual to believe that his or her physique will forever be imperfect. In a kind of "reverse anorexia" that has been called **muscle dysmorphia**, some body builders continue to see their bodies as weak and small when they look at themselves in the mirror despite their greatly enhanced physical development. Peer pressure at the gyms and clubs is a factor in never being satisfied with the size of one's muscles, but it is becoming apparent that societal pressures play a role as well. In the case of males, it is interesting to examine the evolution of the design of G.I. Joe action figures over the years, from the original toy introduced in 1964 to the incarnation introduced in 1998 (Figure 12.1). Just as the Barbie doll has been criticized as setting an impossible ideal for the female body among girls, male-oriented action figures can be criticized on the same basis for boys.[17]

> **muscle dysmorphia (dis-MORF-ee-ah):** The perception of one's own body as small and weak and one's musculature as inadequately developed, despite evidence to the contrary. Also known as megorexia, the condition of muscle dysmorphia is a form of body dysmorphic disorder.

FIGURE 12.1

The muscular development of the G.I. Joe action figure has increased dramatically since its introduction in 1964. The estimated bicep circumference for a six-foot man, based on dimensions of the action figure, more than doubled from 1964 to 1998.

Source: As G.I. Joe bulks up, concern for the 98-pound weakling (1999, May 30). *New York Times,* p. D2.

Prevention Programs for Steroid Dependence

It has been estimated that between 13 and 18 percent of those who have taken steroids show signs of physical and psychological dependence, in that they are unable to control or cut down on them, take more steroids than they intended, develop a tolerance to them, or take them to relieve or avoid undesirable withdrawal symptoms (Help Line).[18]

Help Line
The Symptoms of Steroid Abuse

For Both Sexes

1. Rapid increases in strength and/or size beyond what you would expect in a relatively short time. Putting on ten to twenty pounds of solid muscle within a period of a few weeks or so should be a major warning.

2. Involvement in activities in which steroid abuse is known to be condoned or encouraged

3. Sudden increases in appetite and preoccupation with changes in one's physical condition

4. Recent appearance of acne, particularly on the upper back, shoulders, and arms

5. Premature male-pattern baldness, including a rapidly receding hairline or loss of hair from the top rear of the head

6. A puffy appearance in the face as if the individual is retaining water

7. An increase in moodiness or unusual shifts in mood

8. A reddening of the face, neck, and upper chest, appearing as if one is constantly flushed

9. A yellowing of the skin or the whites of the eyes, stemming from a disturbance in liver function

For Men

1. An enlargement of the breasts, often accompanied by protruding nipples

2. An increase in sexual interest and a tendency to display that interest more aggressively

For Women

1. A lowering of the vocal range

2. Smaller or flatter breasts (see Table 12.2)

Where to go for assistance:

www.nida.nih.gov/Infofacts/Steroids.html

The National Institute on Drug Abuse sponsors a vast array of web sites related to drug use and abuse. This web site on steroid abuse includes a comprehensive list of potential adverse effects of anabolic steroids.

Source: Wright, James E., and Cowart, Virginia S. (1990). *Anabolic steroids:* Altered states. Carmel, IN: Benchmark Press, pp. 71–91.

In light of the potential for steroid dependence and the adverse effects of acute steroid use, prevention programs have been instituted to address the problems of steroid abuse, particularly among adolescents. The most prominent example, developed by Linn Goldberg at Oregon Health Sciences University in Portland, is called the Adolescents Training and Learning to Avoid Steroids (ATLAS) program. Young athletes, team coaches, and team captains receive instruction on both sides of the issue—the desirable effects as well as the adverse effects of steroid use. This approach is taken because a failure to acknowledge potential benefits reduces the credibility of the intervention.

Evaluations of the ATLAS program have shown that program participants were better informed than a control group about proper exercise, had a better understanding of the harmful effects of steroids, developed a more negative attitude toward others who used steroids, and were more likely to engage in healthful eating habits. They also showed a 53 percent reduction in new use of anabolic steroids after one year as well as a 63 percent reduction in the intention to use these drugs in the future.

Another prevention and education program originating at the Oregon Health and Science University, called Athletes Targeting Healthy Exercise and Nutrition Alternatives (ATHENA), is specifically oriented toward female athletes, addressing issues such as the connection between disordered eating behaviors and use of body-shaping and performance-enhancing drugs. The program promotes healthful sports nutrition and strength-training alternatives, as well as the training needed to make healthy choices in sports and throughout their lives.[19]

Counterfeit Steroids and the Placebo Effect

As with many illicit drugs, some products marketed to look like anabolic steroids are not the real thing. The problem here is that athletes are notoriously superstitious and easily leave themselves open to placebo effects. On the one hand, in the case of anabolic steroids, the effects on muscle development are usually so dramatic that it is difficult to mistake the response as simply a result of a placebo effect. On the other hand, some performance-enhancing drugs have far more subtle effects, and psychological factors can end up playing a greater role. Consider the clever strategy a baseball trainer claims to have used for the St. Louis Cardinals in the 1960s:

In 1964, I devised a yellow RBI pill, a red shutout pill, and a potent green hitting pill. Virtually every player on the team took them, and some wouldn't go out on the field until they took my pills. They worked so well that we won the pennant. We used them again in 1967 and 1968 and also won the pennant. They worked because I never told them that the pills were placebos.[20]

In relating his own experience with steroids, MLB superstar Alex Rodriguez spoke of the placebo effect:

I'm not sure what the benefit was . . . I will say this: when you take any substance, especially in baseball, it's half mental and half physical. If you take this glass of water and say you're going to be a better baseball player, if you believe it, you probably will be. I certainly felt more energy, but it's hard to say.[21]

Nonsteroid Hormones and Performance-Enhancing Supplements

Certainly anabolic steroids have dominated the performance-enhancing drug scene, but other products have been promoted as having performance-enhancing properties. They include human growth hormone, androstendione, and creatine.

Human Growth Hormone

One illicit alternative, **human growth hormone (hGH)**, has become increasingly popular, according to experts in this field, because it is more widely available and cheaper than in previous years, in contrast to the ever more costly illicit steroids. Those who take this pituitary hormone, however, face the increased risk of developing a significant side effect called **acromegaly**, a condition resulting in a coarse and misshapen head, enlarged hands and feet, and damage to various internal organs.

Prior to 1985, hGH was obtained from the pituitary glands of human cadavers, but now genetically engineered hGH (brand names: Protropin and Humatrope)

> **human growth hormone (hGH):** A naturally occurring hormone promoting growth, particularly in the long bones of the body.
>
> **acromegaly (A-kroh-MEG-ah-lee):** A condition resulting in structural abnormalities of the head, hands, and feet, as well as damage to internal organs.

is available, having been approved by the FDA for the treatment of rare cases of stunted growth in children. Although the distribution of these drugs is controlled by their manufacturers as carefully as possible, supplies manage to get diverted for illicit use. The half-life of hGH itself is about 30 minutes, but special processing in synthetic hGH compounds extends its half-life much longer, making it detectable for several hours after use.

Testimony in 2008 that prominent major league baseball players had used hGH for performance-enhancing purposes revealed the abuse potential of this hormone in professional sports. It is doubtful, however, that its reputation for performance enhancement is justified, according to a major review of more than forty studies of hGH in healthy athletes conducted between 1966 and 2007. The conclusion is that hGH use increases lean body mass, but the increased bulk does not raise levels of strength or endurance. Indeed, hGH produces higher levels of lactate in muscle tissue, leading to fatigue; hGH users are more likely than others to develop joint pain and carpal tunnel syndrome. In the absence of scientific evidence of any performance-enhancing effects, it has been suggested that reports by athletes that hGH helped to increase their athletic performance are probably due to a placebo effect. Nonetheless, despite hGH's dubious value, hGH screening, capable of differentiating naturally produced hGH from synthetic hGH, became a fixture of drug testing at the 2008 Summer Olympic Games in Beijing. Due to its relatively short half-life, athletes tested positive only if the drug had been injected in the previous twelve to twenty-four hours. No major hGH-related scandals occurred in the 2010 Winter Olympic Games in Vancouver, although with the number of urine and blood tests exceeding 2000, it will take up to eight years to determine whether any participating athlete violated anti-doping regulations.[22]

Dietary Supplements as Performance-Enhancing Aids

As recently as ten to twenty years ago, fitness-oriented young people might have taken only basic vitamins and minerals to help them build muscle mass or improve

androstenedione (AN-dro-steen-DYE-own): A dietary supplement, acting as a metabolic precursor to testosterone and used as an ergogenic agent.

cardiovascular performance. Today, the fitness market is inundated with a growing number of dietary supplement products with presumed performance-enhancing properties; sales of such products exceed $2 billion each year in the United States. They are sold under short, appealing names such as Adenergy and Lean Stack alongside impressive before-and-after photographs or under long, pseudoscientific names like Vaso XP Xtreme Vasodilator and Xenadrine-NRG that are accompanied by complex molecular diagrams.

> A product called Aftermath, for example, boasts that it can help "swell your muscles to grotesque size" and eliminate the chance of "dooming yourself to girlyman status." Xpand Nitric Oxide Reactor, a drink mix that comes in tropical berry and piña colada flavors, offers bodybuilders "the most unbelievable muscular and vascular pumps you have ever experienced."[23]

Because dietary supplements are not classified by the FDA as drugs (see Chapter 1), they can be marketed and sold without a prescription. Except in rare instances, there is no regulatory authority over their purity, safety or effectiveness.

A prominent example of a dietary supplement used for performance-enhancing purposes is **androstenedione**. Technically speaking, androstenedione is not an anabolic steroid because it is not based on the specific structure of testosterone itself. Nonetheless, it is testosterone-related because it is a naturally occurring metabolic precursor to testosterone. In other words, the body converts androstenedione to testosterone via the action of specific enzymes in the liver. At the recommended daily dose of 300 mg, androstenedione has been found to increase testosterone levels by an average of 34 percent above normal. Despite the increase in testosterone, however, no change in body composition or strength is observed when its effect is compared to that of placebo controls. There is no evidence that androstenedione promotes muscle protein synthesis at these dosage levels.[24]

Androstenedione rose to prominence in the late 1990s when it became public that St. Louis Cardinals baseball player Mark McGwire had been taking the supplement during his phenomenal 1998 hitting season (seventy home runs, far eclipsing the previous record). A storm of controversy ensued, with some commentators suggesting that McGwire's record be disallowed because of his androstenedione use. Although it had been banned by the National Football League and other professional and amateur sports organizations, androstenedione was not banned in major league baseball at the time, so McGwire's use of it was not illegal. The publicity surrounding McGwire's use of androstenedione and its easy availability were blamed for a 30 percent increase among eighth-grade boys and a 75 percent increase among tenth-grade boys in the use of anabolic steroids from 1998 to 2000.

In 2005, the FDA banned the over-the-counter sale of androstenedione (Andro) and other testosterone precursors. By this time, the Anabolic Steroid Control Act of 2004 had expanded the Schedule III classification (see Chapter 2) to include androstenedione and other testosterone precursors, along with anabolic steroids themselves. In early 2010, it was disclosed that androstenedione had not been the only performance-enhancing drug in McGwire's life. He admitted what had been long suspected, that during the 1990s he had used anabolic steroids as well. While he has denied that his home-run record-breaking achievements could be attributed to steroid use, it will never be known whether performance-enhancing drugs did indeed enhance his performance.[25]

Another dietary supplement marketed as a performance-enhancing agent is **creatine** (brand names: Creatine Fuel, Muscle Power, and many other products), a nonprotein amino acid synthesized in the kidney, liver, and pancreas from L-arginine, glycine, and L-methionine. Ingestion of creatine has been found to enhance the retention of water by muscle cells, causing them to expand in size. One hypothesis is that water retention might stimulate protein synthesis and increase muscle mass as a result, but there is no evidence from controlled studies that this is the case. Although creatine appears to enhance performance in repetitive bouts of high-intensity cycling, the weight gain experienced by creatine users makes it undesirable for runners or swimmers. Short-term use of creatine has been found to produce muscle cramping, and its long-term adverse effects have not been fully explored.[26]

Nonmedical Use of Stimulant Medication in Baseball

Earlier in the chapter, we cited nineteenth-century examples of world-class athletes experimenting with stimulants in attempts to achieve some level of performance enhancement in their sport. More than a century later, stimulants have continued to be an attractive option. Amphetamines were officially banned from major league baseball in 2005, but before that time, amphetamine use may have been a mainstay for players to stay focused and ward off fatigue in a grueling and lengthy competitive season. According to a professional baseball team psychiatrist, testifying in congressional hearings in 2008, "Amphetamines are the real performance-enhancing drugs that people should always have been worried about."

It is therefore not surprising that since 2005, some players have attempted to circumvent the amphetamine ban by taking stimulant medications intended for the treatment of attention deficit/hyperactivity disorder (ADHD). In 2007, 103 therapeutic-use exemptions for ADHD were approved for MLB players—a suspiciously high number considering that only 28 players had received such approval in 2006. Whether these exemptions reflected a fourfold increase in the incidence of ADHD symptoms over a single year or an effort to benefit from the performance-enhancing effects of stimulant drugs, without violating the amphetamine ban, continues to be a matter of concern to MLB management as well as baseball fans (see Drugs . . . in Focus, Chapter 8, page 188).[27]

Current Drug-Testing Procedures and Policies

Since the mid-1960s, organizers of major athletic competitions have attempted to develop effective screening procedures to prevent the use of performance-enhancing drugs from giving one competitor an unfair advantage over another. Needless to say, these procedures have neither proved perfect nor served as an effective deterrent for drug use among athletes. We are used to hearing about championship events accompanied by reports of an athlete disqualified from competing or denied the honor of winning because he or she tested positive for a particular banned substance. Ironically, the present status of drug testing as a fact of life in modern sports has brought with it a new form of contest, pitting the skill and ingenuity of the laboratory scientist whose job it is to detect the presence of performance-enhancing drugs against the skill and ingenuity of the athlete in devising ways to use them without detection (Drugs . . . in Focus).[28]

This section looks at drug-testing techniques designed to detect not only performance-enhancing

creatine (CREE-ah-teen): A dietary supplement available for ergogenic uses.

Drugs... in Focus

THG and the War on Performance-Enhancing Drugs

In June 2003, Donald H. Catlin, director of the Olympic drug-testing laboratory at the University of California at Los Angeles, received an unexpected package. According to an attached note written by a track coach who wished to remain anonymous, the test tube inside the package contained the residue of an undetectable anabolic steroid from a used syringe. Catlin had suspected for several years that designer-type steroids were being used by both amateur and professional athletes, but these drugs had remained undetected by standard testing procedures. Within three months, the drug in question was identified as tetrahydrogestrinone (THG), which has a chemical structure resembling that of steroids such as gestrinole, which is used as a therapy for gynecological problems, and trenbolone, which is used by ranchers to increase the beef content of cattle.

THG had been undetectable because the substance would ordinarily disintegrate during standard drug screening. When Catlin's laboratory succeeded in stabilizing THG, its "chemical fingerprint" became obvious. By September, a test for THG was developed and ready to be used to screen 550 refrigerated urine samples obtained from athletes at the U.S. track and field championships held three months earlier, as well as samples forwarded from international track and field competitions. As a result, two U.S. track and field champions—1,500-meter runner Regina Jacobs and shot-putter Kevin Troth—tested positive for THG, as did other athletes in the United States and the United Kingdom.

In 2004 two executives of the nutritional supplement laboratory in California where THG was made were indicted, as were the personal trainer of San Francisco Giants star Barry Bonds and a prominent track-and-field coach. They were charged with illegally distributing steroids and other performance-enhancing drugs to dozens of professional athletes in football, baseball, and track and field. Whether athletes testing positive for THG eventually will be disqualified remains to be determined, along with the question of how widely used THG might be in the present-day sports world. The scope of THG use is expected to become clearer in the future as international sports federations undertake retrospective tests of frozen urine samples collected during championship events that occurred in the past few years.

Despite the negative publicity of the THG scandal, some view these developments in a positive light. According to Gary I. Wadler, an expert on drug testing in sports, "There is no question that this is a real blow to the integrity of sport, but there's a silver lining to the black cloud." Wadler has noted that the United States Anti-Doping Association quickly shared the THG data with the World Anti-Doping Agency (WADA), which then distributed the findings to sports organizations throughout the world.

To some, increased public attention to the problems of performance-enhancing drugs might help to make doping in sports as socially unacceptable as drinking and driving. Others, however, view the THG scandal from a darker perspective—as merely a small victory in an unending game of pharmacological "cat and mouse."

Sources: Ashley, Steven (2004, February). Doping by design. *Scientific American*, pp. 22–23. Curry, Jack (2004, February 13). Four indicted in a steroid scheme that involves top pro athletes. *New York Times*, pp. A1, D3. Kondro, Wayne (2003). Athletes' "designer steroid" leads to widening scandal. *The Lancet, 362,* 1466. Longman, Jere, and Drape, Joe (2003, November 2). Decoding a steroid: Hunches, sweat, and vindication. *New York Times*, pp. 1, 26. Schnirring, Lisa (2003). Experts see silver lining in THG scandal. *Physician and Sportsmedicine, 31,* 16–17. Quotation on page 16.

drugs that are relevant to sports but also a wider range of illicit drugs, such as heroin, cocaine, and marijuana. Within some sports organizations, such as the National Collegiate Athletic Association (NCAA), drug tests are conducted not only for the presence of performance-enhancing drugs but also for the presence of drugs that have no particular performance-enhancing benefits. In the case of marijuana, for example, the proper description for its effects with regard to athletic competitions might be *ergolytic* ("performance-reducing"). The policy is defended on the premise that athletes are likely to be exposed to illicit substances, and no collegiate athlete should be permitted to compete while engaging in illegal activity.

The Forensics of Drug Testing

Present-day drug-testing procedures begin with a urine sample from the individual in question. The advantages lie in the ease and noninvasiveness of collecting urine, the ease with which urine can be analyzed for specific factors, and the fact that drugs or their metabolites (by-products) are usually very stable in frozen urine. Therefore, it is possible to provide long-term storage of positive samples, in case the results are disputed. The disadvantages are that many perceive urine collection to be a humiliating experience, a dehydrated athlete may find it difficult to urinate immediately after competing, and there may be ways to tamper with the urine sample prior to testing.

The two major urinalysis methods are the **enzyme immunoassay (EIA)** technique and a procedure combining **gas chromatography and mass spectrometry (GC/MS)**. In both methods, the collected urine is divided into two samples prior to being sent off to the laboratory so that if the analysis of one sample yields a positive outcome, the analysis can be repeated on the other sample. This reanalysis procedure is usually required if an individual appeals the original test result.[29]

With the EIA method, a separate test must be run on each particular drug that is being screened. First, at an earlier time, the substance to be tested for (THC or cocaine, for example) has been injected into an animal, eliciting specific immunological antibodies to that substance. The antibodies are then purified into a testing substrate. The combination of the collected urine and the testing substrate will yield a specific reaction if the urine contains the banned substance. A popular commercial testing kit for screening major controlled substances (opiates, amphetamines, cocaine, benzodiazepines, and marijuana), called **EMIT (enzyme multiplied immunoassay technique)**, has been marketed by Syva Laboratories, a subsidiary of Syntex Corporation in Palo Alto, California, since the early 1970s. This kit is relatively inexpensive and can be used to screen large numbers of urine samples. It is so widely available that its trademark name, EMIT, is often used to mean any form of EIA method.

With the GC/MS method, the urine is first vaporized and combined with an inert gas and then passed over a number of chemically treated columns. Through the process of gas chromatography, technicians are able to identify the presence of a banned substance by the different colorations that are left on the columns. After this has been done, the gas is ionized (converted into an electrically active form) and sent through an electric current and magnetic field that separates out each of the different ions (electrically charged particles) in the gas. Through the process of mass spectrometry, a particular "fingerprint," or "signature," of each chemical substance can be detected and measured. The GC/MS technique is regarded as more definitive than the EIA technique, but it is considerably more expensive and

time-consuming. It is also the only testing procedure that adequately screens for anabolic steroids.[30]

Until the late 1990s, urinanalysis was the sole means for drug testing. Since then, however, there has been increasing interest in oral fluid testing. In this procedure, a collection pad is placed between the lower cheek and gum for two to five minutes. The collection pad is then sealed and later analyzed by EIA. The sensitivity and specificity of the results (see the next section) are comparable to those obtained through urinalysis. As with positive urinanalysis tests, a confirmation of positive oral fluid results is made by GC/MS.

Currently available FDA-approved drug-testing systems using oral fluid samples can now provide test results in approximately fifteen minutes. The advantages over traditional urinalysis are obvious. Samples are analyzed on-site rather than having to be sent to laboratories. Specimen collection can be performed face-to-face (literally) with the donor, with little risk of sample substitution, dilution, or adulteration. Embarrassment on the part of the donor is eliminated as are privacy concerns.[31]

Sensitivity and Specificity

As you might imagine, two general questions can be posed with regard to drug-testing methods.

- What is the *sensitivity* of the test? The sensitivity is determined by the likelihood that a specimen containing drugs (or drug metabolites) will test positive. This outcome is referred to as a "true positive." If a drug test has a high degree of sensitivity, then there will be very few "false negatives." If a test is sensitive, the subject will seldom test negative when drug-taking behavior has actually occurred.

- What is the *specificity* of the test? The specificity is determined by the likelihood that a drug-free (or drug metabolite-free) specimen will test negative. This outcome is referred to as a "true negative." If a drug test has a high degree of specificity, then there will be very few "false positives."

enzyme immunoassay (EIA): One of the two major drug-testing techniques for detecting banned substances or drugs.

gas chromatography/mass spectrometry (GC/MS): A drug-testing technique based on the combination of gas chromatography and mass spectrometry.

EMIT (enzyme multiplied immunoassay technique): A commercial testing kit for screening major controlled substances, based on enzyme immunoassay analysis.

National concern about drug abuse in all its forms has caused us to consider an increased level of drug testing in our society. Here is an editorial cartoonist's comment on the extent to which this policy might be applied.
© Tribune Media Services, Inc. All Rights Reserved. Reprinted with permission.

In other words, sensitivity indicates the ability of the test to correctly report the presence of drugs. Specificity indicates the ability of the test to correctly report the absence of drugs. In this regard, the GC/MS test is more sensitive and specific than the EIA test.

Frequently, the GC/MS analysis is performed as a confirmation of a positive EIA test. Nonetheless, false positives can occur even with the GC/MS test. Eating a poppy seed roll prior to drug testing or taking quinolone antibiotic medications such as ofloxacin (brand name: Floxin) and ciprofloxacin (brand name: Cipro), for example, has resulted in false-positive indications of opiate use. Therapeutic levels of ibuprofen (brand names: Advil, Motrin, and Nuprin, among others) have resulted in false-positive indications of marijuana smoking. In addition, the passive inhalation of marijuana smoke can leave sufficient levels of THC metabolites to result in false-positive indications of marijuana smoking, though the density of smoke that needs to be present for this to happen makes it unlikely that individuals would be completely unaware that they were being exposed to marijuana.[32]

Masking Drugs and Chemical Manipulations

Two specific tactics have been employed to disguise the prior use of anabolic steroids so that the outcome of a drug test becomes, in effect, a false negative; both are now relatively obsolete. The first strategy was to take the antigout drug probenecid (brand name: Benemid). Available since 1987, it does mask the presence of anabolic steroids, but it is now on the list of banned substances for competitive athletes and is easily detected by GC/MS techniques. The second strategy was to

increase the level of epitestosterone in the body. The standard procedure for determining the present or prior use of anabolic steroids is to calculate the ratio of testosterone against the level of epitestosterone, a naturally occurring hormone that is usually stable at relatively low levels in the body. International athletic organizations now use the standard of a 4:1 ratio (formerly 6:1) or higher as indicating steroid use. If epitestosterone is artificially elevated, the ratio can be manipulated downward so as to indicate a false-negative result in drug testing. However, suspiciously high levels of epitestosterone can now be detected by GC/MS techniques, so this form of manipulation is no longer successful.[33]

Pinpointing the Time of Drug Use

It is important to remember that a positive result in a drug test indicates merely that the test has detected a minimal level of a drug or its metabolite. It is difficult to determine *when* that drug was introduced into the body or *how long* the drug-taking behavior continued. In the case of urinalysis testing, the time it takes for the body to get rid of the metabolites of a particular drug varies considerably, from a few hours to a few weeks (Table 12.3). In the case of oral-fluid (saliva) drug testing, the window of detection may be different, depending on the drug of interest. Opiates and cocaine are detected within two to three days of ingestion; THC in marijuana is detected within a period ranging from one hour after ingestion to fourteen hours later. Because THC metabolites are excreted into the urine for several days or in some cases for several weeks, oral-fluid testing for marijuana is better suited for determining when marijuana has been last used. In effect, the "window of detection" is narrower. If the interval between use and testing has been longer than fourteen hours or so but shorter than a few days, urinanalysis would pick up a positive result, but oral-fluid testing would not.[34]

Owing to the expense of randomized drug-testing programs, not every institution can afford the costs. Large corporations may be able to budget for potentially thousands of tests for preemployment screening purposes, but relatively few colleges and considerably fewer high schools are able to establish the level of funding needed to test their student populations. Even if the costs were lower, it is questionable whether illicit drug-taking behavior would be reduced in the long run as a result. Interestingly, recent evidence indicates that the prospect of randomized drug testing in schools fails to act as a deterrent among

TABLE 12.3

Detection periods for various drugs in urinalysis tests

DRUG	DETECTION PERIOD	DRUG	DETECTION PERIOD
alcohol	1/2 to 1 day	opiates and opiate-like drugs	
amphetamines and derivatives	1–7 days	Dilaudid	2–4 days
barbiturates		Darvon	6–48 hours
amobarbital, pentobarbital	2–4 days	heroin or morphine	2–4 days
phenobarbital	up to 30 days	methadone	2–3 days
secobarbital	2–4 days	phencyclidine (PCP)	
benzodiazepines	up to 30 days	casual use	2–7 days
cocaine		chronic, heavy use	several months
occasional use	6–12 hours	Quaalude	2–4 days
repeated use	up to 48 hours	anabolic steroids	
marijuana (THC)		fat-soluble injectables	6–8 months
casual use up to 4 joints per week	5–7 days	water-soluble oral types	3–6 weeks
daily use	10–15 days	over-the-counter cold medications	48–72 hours
chronic, heavy use	1–2 months	containing ephedrine derivatives as decongestants	

Sources: *Allen and Hanbury's athletic drug reference* (1994). Durham, NC: Clean Data, p. 19. Inaba, Darryl S., and Cohen, William E. (1989). *Uppers, downers, all arounders.* Ashland, OR: Cinemed, p. 206.

students. University of Michigan researchers in 2003 found virtually identical rates of illicit drug use in schools that had drug-testing programs and schools that did not. This general finding was replicated in a study reported in 2008. The deterrent effect of drug testing on illicit drug use in schools clearly has not been demonstrated.[35]

It is also worth considering the following fact regarding abusers of steroids and related performance-enhancing drugs: Individuals who are no longer students in a public institution or participants in an organized athletic program do not need to fear a positive drug test because they will never be required to undergo any form of drug testing, random or otherwise.

The Social Context of Performance-Enhancing Drugs

Anabolic steroids and other performance-enhancing agents are quite different from many of the abused drugs covered in previous chapters in that they affect the way we look and how we compare ourselves to others rather

Quick Concept Check 12.2

Understanding Drug Testing

Check your understanding of present-day drug-testing results by indicating whether the following statements are true.

1. EIA results are more sensitive than GC/MS results. ☐ yes ☐ no

2. The anti-gout drug probenecid (Benemid) is an effective way of achieving a false-positive result. ☐ yes ☐ no

3. The time of marijuana smoking is one conclusion that drug testing has great difficulty in determining. ☐ yes ☐ no

4. Athletes are generally very cooperative in achieving the least number of false-negative outcomes. ☐ yes ☐ no

5. Anabolic steroid screening is presently mandated by the International Olympic Committee for winners of Olympic events. ☐ yes ☐ no

Answers: 1. no 2. no 3. yes 4. no 5. yes

than the way we feel. Charles E. Yesalis, one of the leading experts in steroid abuse, has put it this way:

> If you were stranded on a desert island, you might use cocaine if it were available, but nobody would use steroids. On a desert island, nobody cares what you look like and there is nothing to win. We are the ones who have made the determination that appearance and winning are all important. We're telling kids in our society that sports is more than a game. Until we change those signals, for the most part, we might as well tell people to get used to drug use.[36]

The future of the fight against anabolic steroid abuse is, in part, staked to whether we can change the winner-take-all mentality of our culture.

The pressure to be number one exists in all areas of athletic competition. Temptations to secure a competitive edge, however, extend to the corporate world and academia as well. A growing acceptance of stimulants as "brain steroids" (Chapter 8) reflects our modern-day culture.

Unfortunately, there seems to be little cause for optimism. Numerous surveys taken among young athletes and nonathletes alike indicate that the social signals are crystal clear and they are more than willing to take up the challenge, despite the risks. They have typically been asked variations on the following question: "If you had a magic drug that was so fantastic that if you took it once you would win every competition you would enter, from the Olympic decathlon to Mr. Universe, for the next five years, but it had one minor drawback—it would kill you five years after you took it—would you still take the drug?" More than half of those polled answered "yes" to this question.[37]

There is a more general sense of competition that goes beyond dreams of athletic achievement. It is apparent that an idealized body image is part of today's standard for a sense of sexuality and social acceptance. This standard will not be news at all to women, but it is a fairly recent development in men. The temptations of steroid use as a way of accelerating the effects of weight training are increasing in our culture. One high school senior has said, "The majority now are guys that don't do it for sports. They do it for girls. For the look." Another senior has remarked on a different kind of lifter in weight rooms and gyms: the vanity bodybuilder (see Portrait on page 279). As he expressed it, "We notice a lot of kids now; they just want this certain type of body—with the abs and the ripped chest—and they want it quick."[38] Exercise physiologist David Pearson has remarked on the social pressures involved:

> The teenage years are the skinniest and most awkward, and the idea of being the skinniest kid in the locker room is absolutely terrifying to a teenage boy.[39]

Internet web sites deliver mixed messages, promoting anabolic steroids as well as steroid precursors such as androstenedione with the promise "You'll get huge!" while saying on the labels of their products that people younger than age eighteen should not take them.

Summary

Drug-Taking Behavior in Sports

- The use of performance-enhancing (ergogenic) drugs in athletic competition has a long history, dating from the original Olympic Games in ancient Greece.

- In the modern era, the principal type of performance-enhancing drugs has been anabolic steroids.

These synthetic drugs are all based on variations of the testosterone molecule.

- Since the late 1980s, anabolic steroids have been popular with body builders as well as competitive athletes. This latter group typically takes steroids in enormous quantities and administers them in a largely unsupervised fashion.

- Recently, great concerns have been raised about anabolic steroids and other performance-enhancing drugs, in major league baseball.

The Hazards of Anabolic Steroids

- The hazards of steroid use include liver tumors, mood swings, and increased aggressiveness.
- For men, the effects include lower sperm count, enlargement of the breasts, atrophy of the testicles, baldness, and severe acne. For women, masculinizing changes occur, only some of which are reversible when steroids are withdrawn.

Patterns of Anabolic Steroid Abuse

- Since 1990 anabolic steroids have been classified as Schedule III controlled substances, making their possession and sale without a specific medical prescription illegal. In 2004, steroid precursors were added to the category of Schedule III controlled substances. These drugs are now distributed through illicit black-market channels.
- It has been estimated that between 13 and 18 percent of those who have taken steroids show signs of physical and psychological dependence.

Nonsteroid Hormones and Performance-Enhancing Supplements

- Human growth hormone (hGH) is a nonsteroid hormone that has been used for performance-enhancing purposes.

- Two dietary supplements, androstenedione and creatine, have been prominent recently as performance-enhancing aids.

Nonmedical Use of Stimulant Medication in Baseball

- Although amphetamines were officially banned in major league baseball (MLB) in 2005, for a long time players had been taking amphetamines to stay focused and ward off fatigue.
- In 2007, an unusually large number of MLB players reported taking stimulant medications for ADHD treatment, raising suspicions that this was an effort to circumvent prohibitions against nonmedical stimulant use.

Current Drug-Testing Procedures and Policies

- Drug-testing procedures, chiefly for those in organized athletics, have become increasingly sophisticated in their ability to detect the presence of banned substances.
- Two major techniques, based either on urine or on oral-fluid (saliva) samples, are enzyme immunoassay (EIA) and a combination of gas chromatography and mass spectrometry (GC/MS).
- The ultimate goal of drug-testing procedures is to make it impossible to yield either a false-negative or false-positive result. A sensitive test yields few false negatives and a specific test yields few false positives.

Key Terms

acromegaly, p. 281
adrenocortical steroids, p. 271
anabolic, p. 271
anabolic-androgenic steroids, p. 271
anabolic steroids, p. 271

androgenic, p. 271
androstenedione, p. 282
creatine, p. 283
EMIT (enzyme multiplied immunoassay technique), p. 285

enzyme immunoassay (EIA), p. 285
ergogenic, p. 271
gas chromatography/mass spectrometry (GC/MS), p. 285

gynecomastia, p. 276
human growth hormone (hGH), p. 281
muscle dysmorphia, p. 279
priapism, p. 276

Endnotes

1. Kepner, Tyler (2009, February 18). "We weren't taking Tic Tac." As team looks on, Rodriguez details his use of steroids. *New York Times*, pp. B1, B15. Quotation on p. B1.
2. Kepner, Tyler (2010, January 12). McGwire admits steroid use in 1990s, his years of magic. *New York Times*, pp. B10, B14. Quotation on p. B10.
3. DEA leads largest steroid bust in history (2005, December 15). Drug Enforcement Administration, U.S. Department of Justice. National Institute on Drug Abuse (2000, April).

Anabolic steroids. *Research report series*. Bethesda, MD: National Institute on Drug Abuse. Collins, Rick (2003, January 5). Federal and state steroid laws. Posted on the web site of Collins, McDonald, and Gann, P. C., Attorneys-at-law, Nassau County and New York, NY, www.steroidlaw.com.
4. Dolan, Edward F. (1986). *Drugs in sports* (rev. ed.). New York: Franklin Watts, pp. 17–18. Meer, Jeff (1987). *Drugs and sports*. New York: Chelsea House, pp. 2, 61–75.

Taylor, William N. (1991). *Macho medicine: The history of the anabolic steroid epidemic*. Jefferson, NC: McFarland and Co., pp. 3–16. Wadler, Gary I., and Hainline, Brian (1989). *Drugs and the athlete*. Philadelphia: F. A. Davis, pp. 3–17.

5. Bhasin, Shalender; Storer, Thomas W.; Berman, Nancy; Callegari, Carlos; Clevenger, Brenda; et al. (1996). The effects of supraphysiologic doses of testosterone on muscle size and strength in normal men. *New England Journal of Medicine, 335,* 1–7. Lombardo, John (1993). The efficacy and mechanisms of action of anabolic steroids. In Charles E. Yesalis (Ed.), *Anabolic steroids in sport and exercise.* Champaign, IL: Human Kinetics Publishers, p. 100.

6. Scott, Jack (1971, October 17). It's not how you play the game, but what pill you take. *New York Times Magazine*, p. 41.

7. Catlin, Don H., and Murray, Thomas H. (1996). Performance-enhancing drugs, fair competition, and Olympic sport. *Journal of the American Medical Association, 276,* 231–237. Maimon, Alan (2000, February 6). Doping's sad toll: One athlete's tale from East Germany. *New York Times*, pp. A1, A6. Yesalis, Charles E., Courson, Stephen P., and Wright, James (1993). History of anabolic steroid use in sport and exercise. In Yesalis, *Anabolic steroids*, pp. 1–33.

8. Litsky, Frank (2003, March 6). International drug code is adopted. *New York Times*, p. D5. Longman, Jere (2003, October 24). Steroid is reportedly found in top runner's urine test. *New York Times*, p. D2. Macur Juliet (2008, October 9). Beijing Games blood samples to be retested for new drug. *New York Times*, pp. B17, B20. Starr, Mark (2003, November 3). Blowing the whistle on drugs: A raid on a California laboratory threatens to blemish America's athletes—again. *Newsweek*, pp. 60–61. Vecsey, George (2002, March 1). More curious material in skiing's closet. *New York Times*, pp. D1, D4. World Anti-Doping Association, Montreal. W.W.F.'s McMahon indicted (1993, November 19). *New York Times*, p. B12. Yesalis, Courson, and Wright, History of anabolic steroid use, pp. 40–42.

9. Curry, Jack (2006, June 8). A new front in baseball's drug war. Player's testimony points to holes in testing policy. *New York Times*, pp. D1, D5. Curry, Jack (2005, November 16). Baseball backs stiffer penalties for steroid use. *New York Times*, pp. A1, D2. Fainaru-Wada, Mark and Williams, Lance (2006). *Game of shadows: Barry Bonds, Balco and the steroids scandal that rocked professional sports.* New York: Gotham Books. Kepner, Tyler (2009, July 31). A stain keeps spreading. *New York Times*, pp. B10, B11. Schmidt, Michael S., and Macur, Juliet (2010, August 30). Clemens enters not guilty plea. *New York Times*, p. B14. Vecsey, George (2008, January 16). Spring training and the syringe generation. *New York Times*, pp. D1, D3.

10. Council on Scientific Affairs (1990). Medical and non-medical uses of anabolic-androgenic steroids. *Journal of the American Medical Association, 264,* 2923–2927.

Hartgens, Fred, and Kuipers, Harm (2004). Effects of androgenic-anabolic steroids in athletes. *Sports Medicine, 34,* 513–554. Perry, Paul J.; Lund, Brian C.; Deninger, Michael J.; Kutscher, Eric C.; and Schneider, Justin (2005). Anabolic steroid use in weightlifters and bodybuilders: An Internet survey of drug utilization. *Clinical Journal of Sport Medicine, 15,* 326–330.

11. Friedl, Karl E. (1993). Effects of anabolic steroids on physical health. In, *Anabolic steroids*, pp. 107–150. Galloway, Gantt P. (1997). Anabolic-androgenic steroids. In Joyce H. Lowinson; Pedro Ruiz; Robert B. Millman; and John G. Langrod (Eds.). *Substance abuse: A comprehensive textbook* (3rd ed.). Baltimore: Williams & Wilkins, pp. 308–318.

12. DiPaolo, Marco; Agozzino, Manuela; Toni, Chiara; Luciani, Allesandro Bassi; et al. (2005). Sudden anabolic steroid abuse–related death in athletes. *International Journal of Cardiology, 114,* 114–117. Friedl, *Effects of anabolic steroids*, pp. 116–131. Hartgens and Kuipers, Effects of androgenic-anabolic steroids in athletes, pp. 536–540. Maravelias, C.; Dona, A.; Stefanidou, M.; and Spiliopoulou, C. (2005). Adverse effects of anabolic steroids in athletes: A constant threat. *Toxicology Letters, 158,* 167–175. Urhausen, A., Albers, T., and Kindermann, W. (2004). Are the cardiac effects of anabolic steroid abuse in strength athletes reversible? *Heart, 90,* 496–501.

13. Su, Tung-Ping; Pagliaro, Michael; Schmidt, Peter J.; Pickar, David; Wolkowitz, Owen; et al. (1993). Neuropsychiatric effects of anabolic steroids in male normal volunteers. *Journal of the American Medical Association, 269,* 2760–2764.

14. Greenberg, Alan (1991, June 29). Alzado has a serious message to kids about steroids: Don't use them. *Hartford (CT) Courant*, cited in Jim Ferstle (1993), Evolution and politics of drug testing. In Charles E. Yesalis (Ed.), *Anabolic steroids*, p. 276.

15. Pope, Harrison G., Jr., Kouri, Elena M., and Hudson, James I. (2000). Effects of supraphysiologic doses of testosterone on mood and aggressiveness in normal men: A randomized controlled trial. *Archives of General Psychiatry, 57,* 133–140. Stocker, Steven (2000). Study provides additional evidence that high steroid doses elicit psychiatric symptoms in some men. *NIDA Notes, 15* (4), pp. 8–9. Trenton, Adam J., and Currier, Glenn W. (2005). Behavioural manifestations of anabolic steroid use. *CNS Drugs, 19,* 571–595.

16. Adler, Jerry (2004, December 20). Toxic strength. *Newsweek*, pp. 45–52. Bahrke, Michael S. (1993). Psychological effects of endogenous testosterone and anabolic-androgenic steroids. In Charles E. Yesalis (Ed.), *Anabolic steroids in sport and exercise*. Champaign, IL: Human Kinetics Publishers, pp. 161–192. Doff, Wilson (2005, March 10). After a young athlete's suicide, steroids called the culprit. *New York Times*, pp. A1, D8. Estrada, Manuel, Varshney, Anurag, and Ehrlich, Barbara E. (2006). Elevated testosterone induces apoptosis in neuronal cells. *Journal of Biological Chemistry, 281,* 25492–25501. Johnston,

Lloyd D.; O'Malley, Patrick M.; Bachman, Jerald G.; and Schulenberg, John E. (2009, December 14). Teen marijuana use tilts up, while some drugs decline in use. University of Michigan News Service, Ann Arbor, Table 1. Longman, Jere (2003, November 26). An athlete's dangerous experiment: Using steroids enhanced his physique, but he died trying to stop. *New York Times*, pp. D1, D4.

17. Pope, Harrison G.; Gruber, Amanda J.; Choi, Priscilla; Olivardia, Roberto; and Phillips, Katherine A. (1997). Muscle dysmorphia: An underrecognized form of body dysmorphic disorder. *Psychosomatics*, 38, 548–557. Wroblewska, Anna-M. (1997). Androgenic-anabolic steroids and body dysmorphia in young men. *Journal of Psychosomatic Research*, 42, 225–234.

18. Bahrke, Michael S., Yesalis, Charles E., and Brower, Kirk J. (1998). Anabolic-androgenic steroid abuse and performance-enhancing drugs among adolescents. *Sport Psychiatry*, 7, 821–838. Beel, Andrea, Maycock, Bruce, and McLean, Neil (1998). Current perspectives on anabolic steroids. *Drug and Alcohol Review*, 17, 87–103. Kashkin, Kenneth B., and Kleber, Herbert D. (1989). Hooked on hormones? An anabolic steroid addiction hypothesis. *Journal of the American Medical Association*, 262, 3166–3169. Monaghan, Lee F. (2000). *Bodybuilding, drugs, and risk*. New York: Routledge. Perry, Lund, Deninger, Kutscher, and Schneider, Anabolic steroid use. Schrof, Joanne M. (1992, June 1). Pumped up. *U.S. News and World Report*, pp. 55–63.

19. Goldberg, Linn; Mackinnon, David P.; Elliot, Diane L.; Moe, Esther L.; Clarke, Greg; and Cheong, JeeWon (2000). The Adolescents Training and Learning to Avoid Steroids program. *Archives of Pediatrics and Adolescent Medicine*, 154, 332–338. Information courtesy of the Oregon Health and Science University, Portland, 2008. Moe, Esther L.; Goldberg, Linn D.; MacKinnon, David P.; and Cheong, JeeWon (1999). Reducing drug use and promoting healthy behaviors among athletes: The ATLAS program. *Medical Science Sports Exercise*, 31 (5), S122.

20. Quotation by Bob Bauman (1992). In Bob Goldman and Rochald Klatz, *Death in the locker room II: Drugs and sports*. Chicago: Elite Sports Medicine Pubications, pp. 10–11.

21. Kepner, "We weren't taking Tic Tacs." Quotation from Alex Rodriguez on p. B15.

22. Interlandi, Jeneen (2008, February 25). Myth meets science. *Newsweek*, p. 48. Juhn, Mark S. (2003). Popular sports supplements and ergogenic aids. *Sports Medicine*, 33, 921–939. Liu, Hau; Bravata, Dena M.; Olkin, Ingram; Friedlander, Anne; et al. (2008). Systematic review: The effects of growth hormone on athletic performance. *Annals of Internal Medicine*, 148, 747–748. Macur, Juliet (2008, June). Who has the horse tranquilizers? *Play*, p. 18. Macur, Juliet (2008, October 9). Olympic blood samples to be retested. *New York Times*, p. B17. Macur, Juliet

(2010, February 28). No doping scandals at Games, but time will tell. *New York Times*, Sportspage 9.

23. Tuller, David (2005, January 18). For sale: "muscles" in a bottle. *New York Times*, pp. F5, F10. Quotation on p. F5.

24. Androstenedione (2001). *PDR for nutritional supplements* (1st ed.). Montvale, NJ: Medical Economics, pp. 26–28. Juhn, Popular sports supplements. Leder, Benjamin Z.; Longcope, Christopher; Catlin, Don H.; Ahrens, Brian; and Schoenfeld, Joel S. (2000). Oral androstenedione administration and serum testosterone concentrations in young men. *Journal of the American Medical Association*, 283, 779–782.

25. Denham, Bryan E. (2006). The Anabolic Steroid Control Act of 2004: A study in the political economy of drug policy. *Journal of Health and Social Policy*, 22, 51–78. Kepner, Tyler (2010, January 12). McGwire admits steroid use in 1990s, his years of magic. *New York Times*, pp. B10, B14. Mravic, Mark (2000, February 21). Ban it, bud. *Sports Illustrated*, pp. 24, 26.

26. Buford, Thomas W.; Kreider, Richard B.; Stout, Jeffrey R.; et al. (2007). International Society of Sports Nutrition position stand: Creatine supplementation and exercise. *Journal of the International Society of Sports Nutrition*, 4, 6. Creatine (2001). *PDR for nutritional supplements* (1st ed.). Montvale, NJ: Medical Economics, pp. 114–117. Freeman, Mike (2003, October 21). Scientist fears athletes are using unsafe drugs: Discovery of an undetected steroid confirms suspicions. *New York Times*, p. D2. Gregory, Andrew J. M., and Fitch, Robert W. (2007). Sports medicine: Performance-enhancing drugs. *Pediatric Clinics of North America*, 54, 797–806.

27. Schmidt, Michael S. (2008, January 16). Baseball is challenged on rise in stimulant use. *New York Times*, pp. A1, A16. Quotation on page A16. Schmidt, Michael S. (2009, January 10). Baseball officials give report on amphetamine use among players. *New York Times*, p. D5.

28. Hamilton, Martha McNeil (2003, February 23). Beating drug screening builds cottage industry. Evaders change faster than testing technology. *Houston Chronicle*, p. 2.

29. Wadler and Hainline, *Drugs and the athlete*, pp. 201–202.

30. Hatton, Caroline K. (2007). Beyond sports-doping headlines: The science of laboratory tests for performance-enhancing drugs. *Pediatric Clinics of North America*, 54, 713–733. Meer, *Drugs and sports*, pp. 92–95.

31. Alternate specimen testing policies may be set soon (2005, September). *Occupational Health and Safety*, p. 26. Cone, Edward J.; Presley, Lance; Lehrer, Michael; Seiter, William; Smith, Melissa; et al. (2002). Oral fluid testing for drugs of abuse: Positive prevalence rates by Intercept immunoassay screening and GC-MS-MS confirmation and suggested cutoff concentrations. *Journal of Analytical Toxicology*, 26, 540–546.

32. *Allen and Hanbury's athletic drug reference* (1994). Durham NC: Clean Data, pp. 65–66. Baden, Lindsey R.; Horowitz, Gary; Jacoby, Helen; and Eliopoulos, George M. (2001).

Quinolones and false-positive urine screening for opiates by immunoassay technology. *Journal of the American Medical Association, 286,* 3115–3119. Struempler, Richard E. (1987, May/June). Excretion of codeine and morphine following ingestion of poppy seeds. *Journal of Analytical Toxicology, 11,* 97–99. Wadler and Hainline, *Drugs and the athlete,* pp. 208–209.

33. Catlin, Don;Wright, Jim, Pope, Harrison, and Liggett, Mariah (1993). Assessing the threat of anabolic steroids: Sportsmedicine update. *The Physician and Sportsmedicine, 21,* 37-44.

34. Rosenberg, Ronald (2000, October 12). Citgo to use Avitar drug tests, job applicants to undergo new saliva-based exam. *Boston Globe,* p. C3.

35. Brookman, Richard R. (2008). Unintended consequences of drug and alcohol testing in student athletes. *AAP (American Academy of Pediatrics) Grand Rounds, 19,* 15–16. Yamaguchi, Ryoko, Johnston, Lloyd D., and O'Malley, Patrick M. (2003). Relationship between student illicit drug use and school drug-testing policies. *Journal of School Health, 73,* 159–164.

36. Quotation from Charles E. Yesalis. In Wright, James E, and Cowart, Virginia S. (1990). *Anabolic steroids: Altered States.* Traverse City, MI: Cooper Publishing, p. 196. Schwerin, Michael J.; Corcoran, Kevin J.; Fisher, Leslee; Patterson, David; Askew, Waide; et al. (1996). Social physique anxiety, body esteem, and social anxiety in bodybuilders and self-reported anabolic steroid users. *Addictive Behaviors, 21,* 1–8.

37. Goldman, Bob, and Klatz, Ronald (1992). *Death in the locker room II: Drugs and sports.* Chicago: Elite Sports Medicine Publications, pp. 23–24. McHenry, Christopher R. (2007, December). Presidential address to the American Association of Endocrine Surgeons: The illicit use of hormones for enhancement of athletic performance: A major threat to the integrity of organized athletic competition. *Surgery,* 785-792. Shermer, Michael (2008, April). The doping dilemma. *Scientific American,* pp. 82–89.

38. Egan, Timothy (2002, November 22). Body-conscious boys adopt athlete's taste for steroids. *New York Times,* pp. A1, A24. Quotations on p. A24. Kolata, Gina; Longman, Jere; Weiner, Tim; and Egan, Timothy (2002, December 2). With no answers on risks, steroid users still say "yes." *New York Times,* pp. A1, A19. Pope, Harrison G., Jr., Phillips, Katherine A., and Olivardia, Roberto (2002). *The Adonis complex: How to identify, treat, and prevent body obsession in men and boys.* New York: Simon and Schuster. Roosevelt, ax (2010, January 14). When the gym isn't enough. *New York Times,* pp. E1, E8.

39. Kilgannon, Corey (2001, May 27). Strong Island: More youngsters seek great physiques, and risky ways to get them. *New York Times,* Section 14 (Long Island), pp. 1, 9. Quotation on p. 9. Kolata, With no answers on risks, steroid users still say "yes.", pp. A1, A10. Morgan, Richard (2002). The men in the mirror. *Chronicle of Higher Education, 49,* A53–A54.

PART THREE

Legal Drugs in Our Society

chapter 13

Alcohol: Social Beverage/Social Drug

I was invited to address a convention of high school teachers on the topic of drug abuse. When I arrived at the convention center to give my talk, I was escorted to a special suite, where I was encouraged to join the executive committee in a round of drug taking—the drug was a special high-proof single-malt whiskey. Later, the irony of the situation had its full impact. As I stepped to the podium under the influence of a psychoactive drug (the whiskey), I looked out through the haze of cigarette smoke at an audience of educators who had invited me to speak to them because they were concerned about the unhealthy impact of drugs on their students. The welcoming applause gradually gave way to the melodic tinkling of ice cubes in liquor glasses, and I began. They did not like what I had to say.

—*John P. J. Pinel,* Biopsychology (2003)

After you have completed this chapter, you should have an understanding of

- How alcoholic beverages are produced
- Alcohol use through history
- The history of alcohol regulation from Prohibition to taxation
- Patterns of alcohol consumption
- The pharmacology of alcohol
- Acute physiological and behavioral effects of alcohol
- Alcohol and health benefits
- Strategies for responsible alcohol consumption

Pinel's experience in this opening vignette sums up the central problem facing American society in its dealings with alcohol use and abuse: the frequent failure to acknowledge that alcohol is indeed a psychoactive drug.[1] You may have heard someone remark, "He drinks a little too much, but at least he's not doing drugs." In the eyes of many people, an alcoholic drink is wrongly assumed to be simply a social beverage. In actuality, it is a social drug.

We can see this problem reflected in a number of ways. Those who design college courses that cover drug abuse and its effect on society, perhaps the one you are taking right now, feel obliged to entitle the course "Drugs and Alcohol." Would you personally have expected to cover the effects of alcohol in a course simply called "Drugs" in your college catalog? Chances are that you would not.

Even the U.S. federal government perpetuates the distinction, with separate agencies for alcohol abuse (the National Institute on Alcohol Abuse and Alcoholism, NIAAA) and the abuse of other drugs (the National Institute on Drug Abuse, NIDA). This bureaucratic partitioning admittedly has historical roots, and it can be argued that there are valid reasons to continue the division from a management or budgetary point of view, but it has inadvertently reinforced the unfortunate and inaccurate notion that alcohol is somehow a substance that stands apart from (or worse, is nothing like) other drugs of potential abuse.

In recognition of the immense impact that alcohol use and alcohol abuse have on us individually and our society, two chapters are devoted to alcohol-related issues. This chapter considers alcohol specifically as a drug, with a unique history and tradition and its own

set of acute risks. The next chapter turns to an examination of alcohol's long-term effects, specifically the potential problems of chronic alcohol abuse and alcoholism. We begin by considering the nature of alcohol itself.

What Makes an Alcoholic Beverage?

Creating **ethyl alcohol**, through a process known as **fermentation**, is a remarkably easy thing to do. Almost every culture in the world, at one time or another, has stumbled on the basic recipe. All you need is organic material with a sugar content (honey, grapes, berries, molasses, rye, apples, corn, sugar cane, rice, pumpkins, to name some examples) left undisturbed in a warm container for a time, and nature does the work. Microscopic yeast cells, floating through the air, land on this material and literally consume the sugar in it, so that, for every one sugar molecule consumed, two molecules of alcohol and two molecules of carbon dioxide are left behind as waste. The carbon dioxide bubbles out, and what remains is an alcoholic beverage, less sweet than the substance that began it all but with a new, noticeable kick. Basic fermentation results in a beverage with an alcohol content of between 12 and 16 percent, best exemplified by standard grape wine.

The process of fermenting starchy grains such as barley to produce beer, called **brewing**, is somewhat more complicated. The barley is first soaked in water until it sprouts, producing an enzyme that is capable of breaking down the starch into sugar. It is then slowly dried, the sprouts are removed, and the remainder (now called **barley malt**) is crushed into a powder. The barley malt is combined with water, corn, and rice to form a mixture called a **mash**. The water activates the enzyme so that the starches convert into sugars. The addition of yeast to the mash starts the fermentation process and produces an alcohol content of approximately 4.5 percent. The dried blossoms of the hop plant, called *hops*, are then added to the brew for the characteristic pungent flavoring and aroma.

Relying on fermentation alone gives an alcohol concentration of about 15 to 16 percent at best. An alcohol content above this level starts to kill the yeast and, in doing so, stops the fermentation process. To obtain a higher alcoholic content, another process, called **distillation**, must occur.

Distillation involves heating a container of some fermented mixture until it boils. Because alcohol has a lower boiling temperature than water, the vapor

ethyl alcohol: The product of fermentation of natural sugars. It is generally referred to simply as *alcohol*, though several types of nonethyl alcohol exist.

fermentation: The process of converting natural sugars into ethyl alcohol by the action of yeasts.

brewing: The process of producing beer from barley grain.

barley malt: Barley after it has been soaked in water, sprouts have grown, sprouts have been removed, and the mixture has been dried and crushed to a powder.

mash: Fermented barley malt, following liquification and combination with yeasts.

distillation: A process by which fermented liquid is boiled and then cooled, so that the condensed product contains a higher concentration of alcohol than before.

produced has a higher alcohol-to-water ratio than the original mixture. This alcohol-laden vapor is then drawn off into a special coiled apparatus (often referred to as a *still*), cooled until it condenses back to a liquid, and poured drop by drop into a second container. This new liquid, referred to as **distilled spirits** or simply *liquor*, has an alcohol content considerably higher than 16 percent, generally in the neighborhood of 40 to 50 percent.

It is possible through further distillations to achieve an alcohol content of up to 95 percent. At this point, however, the alcohol content of distilled spirits is commonly described not by percentage but rather by the designation "proof." Any proof is twice the percentage of alcohol: An 80-proof whiskey contains 40 percent alcohol; a 190-proof vodka contains 95 percent alcohol.

The three basic forms of alcoholic beverages are wine, beer, and distilled spirits. Table 13.1 shows the sources of some well-known examples.

> **distilled spirits:** The liquid product of distillation, also known as *liquor*.

TABLE 13.1

Prominent alcoholic beverages and their sources

BEVERAGE	SOURCE	BEVERAGE	SOURCE
Distilled spirits		**Wines**	
Brandy	Distilled from grape wine, cherries, or peaches	Red table wine	Fermented red grapes with skins
		White table wine	Fermented skinless grapes
Liqueur or cordial	Brandy or gin, flavored with blackberry, cherry, chocolate, peppermint, licorice, etc. Alcohol content ranges from 20% to 55%	Champagne	White wine bottled before all of the yeast is gone so that remaining carbon dioxide produces a carbonated effect
Rum	Distilled from the syrup of sugar cane or from molasses	Sparkling wine	Red wine prepared like champagne or with carbonation added
Scotch whiskey	Distilled from fermented corn and barley malt	**Fortified wines**	Wines whose alcohol content is raised or fortified to 20% by the addition of brandy—for example, sherry, port, Marsala, and Madeira
Rye whiskey	Distilled from rye and barley malt		
Blended whiskey	A mixture of two or more types of whiskey		
Bourbon whiskey	Distilled primarily from fermented corn	**Wine-like variations**	
Gin	Distilled from barley, potato, corn, wheat, or rye, and flavored with juniper berries	Hard cider	Fermented apples
		Sake	Fermented rice
Vodka	Approximately 95% pure alcohol, distilled from grains or potatoes and diluted by mixing with water	**Beers**	Types of beer vary depending on brewing procedures.
		Draft beer	Contains 3–6% alcohol
Tequila	Distilled from the fermented juice of the maguey plant	Lager beer	Contains 3–6% alcohol
		Ale	Contains 3–6% alcohol
Grain neutral spirits	Approximately 95% pure alcohol, used either for medicinal purposes or diluted and mixed in less-concentrated distilled spirits	Malt liquor	Contains up to 8% alcohol

Source: Adapted from Becker, Charles E., Roe, Robert L., and Scott, Robert A. (1979). *Alcohol as a drug: A curriculum on pharmacology, neurology, and toxicology.* Huntington, NY: Robert Krieger Publishing, pp. 10–12.

Alcohol Use through History

Historians point out that fermented honey, called *mead*, was probably the original alcoholic beverage, dating from approximately 8000 B.C. Beer, requiring more effort than simple fermentation, came on the scene much later; the Egyptians established the first official brewery about 3700 B.C. At that time, beer was quite different from the watery forms we know today. It more closely resembled bread than a beverage, and the process of producing beer was closer to baking than to brewing.[2]

Evidence of the development of wine comes from references to its sale in the Code of Hammurabi, King of Babylonia, recorded about 1700 B.C. Wine-making itself, however, appears to have begun more than three thousand years before that. Excavations of an ancient village in modern-day Iran have revealed the remains of wine-stained pottery dating back to as early as 5400 B.C.[3]

The first documented distillation of alcohol was the conversion of wine into brandy during the Middle Ages, at a medical school in Salerno, Italy. With an emphasis on its medicinal applications, the new beverage became known in Latin as **aqua vitae** ("the water of life"). People quickly caught on to its inebriating possibilities, and brandy was the primary distilled liquor in Europe until the middle of the seventeenth century. At that time the Dutch perfected the process of distilling liquor and flavoring it with juniper berries. A new alcoholic beverage was born: gin.

The enormous popularity of gin throughout Europe marked a crucial point in the history of alcohol's effect on European society. Because it was easily produced, cheaper than brandy, and faster-acting than wine, gin became attractive to all levels of society, particularly the poorer classes of people. By the mid-1700s, alcohol abuse was being condemned as a major societal problem, and concerns about drunkenness had become a public issue.

Although gin affected life in many parts of Europe, it was in English cities that the gin epidemic became a genuine crisis. By 1750, gin consumption in England had grown to twenty-two times the level in 1685, and the social devastation was obvious. In London, infant mortality rose during this period, with only one of four baptized babies between 1730 and 1749 surviving to the age of five, despite the fact that mortality rates were falling in the countryside. In one section of the city, as many as one in every five houses was a gin shop.

Consumption of other distilled spirits introduced during this period, such as rum and whiskey, added to the

---

aqua vitae (AH-kwa VEYE-tee): A brandy, the first distilled liquor in recorded history.

GIN LANE.

The social chaos of "Gin Lane" in London, as interpreted in this engraving by William Hogarth (1697–1764). Notice the falling baby in the foreground as a symbol of rampant child neglect during this time.

overall problem, but gin was undoubtedly the prime culprit. The epidemic of gin drinking in England during the first half of the eighteenth century illustrates how destructive the introduction of a potent and easily available psychoactive drug into an urban society already suffering from social dislocation and instability can be. The consequences in many ways mirrored the introduction of crack cocaine into the ghettos of the United States during the 1980s.[4]

Alcohol in Nineteenth Century America

From its earliest days as a nation to the nineteenth century, alcohol use was a fact of life in America.[5] Not surprisingly, therefore, the social focus of American communities was the tavern. Not only did taverns serve as public dispensers of alcoholic beverages, but they also served as centers for local business dealings and town politics. Mail was delivered there; travelers could stay the night; elections were held there. As an institution, the tavern was as highly regarded, and as regularly attended, as the local church.[6]

By today's standards, it is difficult to imagine the extent of alcohol consumption that was going on during the early decades of American history. In 1830, the average per capita intake was an immoderate five drinks a day, roughly four times the level of consumption today. It was common to take "whiskey breaks" at 11 A.M. and 4 P.M. each day (except Sunday), much as we take coffee breaks today. As far as types of liquor were concerned, rum was the favorite in New England and along the North Atlantic coast, but elsewhere whiskey was king. George Washington himself went into the whiskey business at Mount Vernon in 1797, eventually establishing the largest whiskey distillery of his time.[7]

The Rise of the Temperance Movement

In the late 1700s, prominent physicians, writers, and scientists began to consider the adverse effects of alcohol consumption and tried to formulate some kind of social reform to mitigate them. The goal at that time was to reduce the consumption of distilled spirits (liquor) only. It was a temperate attitude toward drinking (hence the phrase "**temperance movement**") rather than an insistence on the total prohibition of alcohol in all forms.

In the United States, where the temperance movement was to be stronger than anywhere else, its most influential spokesman was Benjamin Rush, a physician, Revolutionary War hero, and signer of the Declaration of Independence. In his 1785 pamphlet, "An Inquiry into the Effects of Ardent Spirits on the Human Mind and Body," Rush vividly described the range of mental and physical dangers associated with excessive alcohol consumption, focusing on the specific dangers of liquor to the citizens of a new democracy:

> Strong liquor is more destructive than the sword. The destruction of war is periodic, whereas alcohol exerts its influence upon human life at all times and in all seasons . . . A nation corrupted by alcohol can never be free.[8]

Rush's efforts did not have a major impact on the drinking habits of American society during his lifetime, but they would serve as an inspiration to political and religious groups around the country who saw alcohol consumption in social and moral terms. In their view, drunkenness led to poverty, a disorderly society, and civil disobedience. In short, it was unpatriotic at best and subversive at worst. When we hear the phrase "demon rum," we have to recognize that many Americans during the

Even though this 1874 engraving shows a temperance crusader in full battle regalia, relatively few temperance activists resorted to physical violence.

nineteenth century took the phrase quite literally. Liquor was demonized as a direct source of evil in the world.

The temperance point of view toward liquor, like any other form of scapegoating, spread like wildfire. In 1831, the American Temperance Society reported that nearly 2 million Americans had renounced strong liquor and that more than eight hundred local societies had been established. With characteristic succinctness, Abraham Lincoln observed, in an 1842 address before a national temperance organization, that prior to the temperance era, the harm done by alcohol was considered to be a result of the "abuse of a very good thing," whereas his contemporaries now viewed the harm as coming "from the use of a bad thing."[9] By the 1850s, twelve U.S. states (about one-third of the nation at the time) and two Canadian provinces had introduced legislation forbidding the sale of "alcoholic" (distilled) drink.

temperance movement: The social movement in the United States, beginning in the nineteenth century, that advocated the renunciation of alcohol consumption.

Whether or not they were justified in doing so, temperance groups took credit for a drastic change that was occurring in the levels of alcohol consumption in the United States. From 1830 to 1850, consumption of all types of alcohol plummeted from an annual per capita level of roughly 7 gallons to roughly 2 gallons, approximately today's consumption level. It is quite possible that this decline encouraged the temperance movement to formulate its ultimate goal, a prohibition of alcohol consumption in any form.

The Road to National Prohibition

A major development in the temperance movement was the formation in 1880 of a women's organization called the Woman's Christian Temperance Union (WCTU). Almost from the beginning, its primary target was a highly visible fixture of late-nineteenth-century masculine American life: the saloon. These establishments were now vilified as the source of all the troubles alcohol could bring. It is not difficult to imagine how the saloon would have been seen as a significant threat to American women in general.

> Bars appeared to invite family catastrophe. They introduced children to drunkenness and vice and drove husbands to alcoholism; they also caused squandering of wages, wife beating, and child abuse; and, with the patron's inhibitions lowered through drink, the saloon led many men into the arms of prostitutes (and not incidentally, contributed to the alarming spread of syphilis).[10]

No wonder the WCTU hated the saloon, and no saloon in the country was safe from their "pray-in" demonstrations, vocal opposition, and in some cases violent interventions. Their influence eventually extended into every aspect of American culture. The WCTU and other anti-alcohol forces, such as the newly formed Anti-Saloon League and National Prohibition Party, were soon electing congressional candidates who pledged to enact national legislation banning alcohol consumption throughout the land.

The Beginning and Ending of a "Noble Experiment"

In December 1917, Congress passed a resolution "prohibiting the manufacture, sale, transportation, or importation of intoxicating liquors," the simple wording that would form the basis for the Eighteenth Amendment to the U.S. Constitution. (Notice that it did not forbid purchase or use of alcohol.) The Volstead Act of 1919 set up the enforcement procedures. By the end of the year, the necessary thirty-six states had ratified the amendment, and Prohibition took effect in January 1920.

Despite its lofty aims, Prohibition was doomed to failure. In the countryside, operators of illegal stills (called "moonshiners" because they worked largely at night) continued their production despite the efforts of an occasional half-hearted raid by Treasury agents (known as "revenooers"). The major cities became centers of open defiance. Liquor, having been smuggled into the country, flowed abundantly as saloons turned into speakeasies and operated in violation of the law.

The early years of Prohibition did, however, show positive effects in the area of public health. Alcohol-related deaths, cirrhosis of the liver, mental disorders, and alcohol-related crime declined in 1920 and 1921, but in a few years, the figures began to creep up again, and the level of criminal activity associated with illegal drinking was clearly intolerable.[11] By the end of the decade, it was obvious for the vast majority of Americans that the "noble experiment" (as it was called at the time) was not working.

In 1933, President Franklin D. Roosevelt, having campaigned on a platform to repeal the Volstead Act, signed the necessary legislation that became the Twenty-first Amendment; ratification was swift. Alcohol was restored as a legal commodity and its regulation was returned once more to local authorities. Over the years, the states gradually repealed prohibition laws. Mississippi, in 1966, was the last state to do so.

Present-Day Alcohol Regulation by Taxation

One immediate benefit of repealing Prohibition was the return of federal revenue from taxes on alcohol. Indeed, the impact on a struggling national economy hard hit by the Depression had been one of the arguments advanced by the repeal movement. In 1933 alone, such excise taxes brought in $500 million, which was used to finance social programs during the Depression.

The concept of collecting taxes on the basis of alcohol consumption dates back to the very beginning of the United States as a nation. In 1794, the newly formed U.S. Congress passed a law imposing an excise tax on the sale of whiskey. After a short-lived Whiskey Rebellion in which President Washington had to order federal militia to subdue Appalachian farmers who had refused to pay the new tax, the practice of taxing alcohol was accepted and has continued to the present day as a legal way of raising tax money.

Taxes on alcohol sales have been an indirect mechanism for regulating the consumption of alcohol by increasing its price, not unlike taxes on tobacco products (see Chapter 15). More than $8 billion each year is collected from federal excise taxes on alcohol. Total annual revenues exceed $18 billion, when additional excise taxes imposed by all U.S. states and some local communities are included. Today, alcoholic beverages are one of the most heavily taxed consumer products. Approximately 42 percent of the retail price of an average bottle of distilled spirits, for example, is earmarked for federal, state, or local taxes.[12]

It has been proposed that alcohol taxes be set high enough to begin to offset the total societal costs resulting from alcohol abuse. This approach would place a type of "user fee" on the consumption of alcohol. However, there is the possibility that raising alcohol prices by additional taxation might lead to the development of a black market for alcohol purchases, little change in alcohol consumption, and a net decline in tax revenues.[13]

The stainless steel tanks of the world's largest wine maker, the Ernest and Julio Gallo Winery, are located in Modesto, California. Nearly 900 million gallons of wine are produced by E. & J. Gallo each year, accounting for approximately one of every three bottles of wine sold annually in the United States.

Patterns of Alcohol Consumption Today

It has been theorized that the earliest systems of agriculture in human history were born of the desire to secure a dependable supply of beer.[14] If this is so, then alcohol, commercialization, and economics have been linked from the very beginning. Today, of course, alcohol is not merely a big business, but an enormous business. Americans spend more than $140 billion on the purchase of alcoholic beverages each year, and the alcohol industry spends about $1.4 billion advertising its products. More than one-third of this advertising budget is typically devoted to television commercials for beer.[15]

Binge drinking among college students and other young adults is a common social ritual as well as a continuing social concern.
© 2006, McGraw-Hill Higher Education. Reproduced with permission of The McGraw-Hill Companies.

Overall Patterns of Alcohol Consumption

How much do Americans actually drink? The estimated annual per capita consumption of pure alcohol for adults in the United States is approximately 2.3 gallons (8.7 liters). This level of consumption amounts to about three-fourths of an ounce per day.[16]

How many alcoholic drinks does this estimated daily amount add up to? To answer this question, it is important first to consider the amount of pure alcohol that is contained in each of four basic types of alcoholic beverages (Drugs . . . in Focus). A person consumes a single half-ounce of alcohol when drinking any of the following alcoholic beverages:

- One 5-ounce glass of wine
- One 12-ounce bottle or can of beer
- One 12-ounce bottle of wine cooler
- One shot (1.5-ounce size) of 80-proof liquor

All these quantities are approximately equal to about one-half ounce in terms of pure alcohol, and they are often referred to as "standard drinks."

Drugs... in Focus

Multiple Ways of Getting a Standard Drink

A standard alcoholic drink is any drink that contains about 14 grams of pure alcohol (about 0.5 fluid ounce). All of the following seven alcoholic drinks should be considered equivalently as a standard drink.

12 oz of beer or wine cooler	8–9 oz of malt liquor 8.5 oz shown in a 12 oz glass that, if full, would hold about 1.5 standard drinks of malt liquor	5 oz of table wine*	3–4 oz of fortified wine (such as sherry or port) 3.5 oz shown	2–3 oz of cordial, liqueur, or aperitif 2.5 oz shown	1.5 oz of brandy (a single jigger)	1.5 oz of spirits (a single jigger of 80-proof gin, vodka, whiskey, etc.) Shown straight and in a highball glass with ice to show level before adding mixer †
12 oz	8.5 oz	5 oz	3.5 oz	2.5 oz	1.5 oz	1.5 oz

There are so many variations in the quantity of an alcoholic beverage being served that it can be confusing to determine to how many standard drinks are actually being consumed. Here are some examples of how the number of standard drinks can multiply when quantities increase:

- For beer or wine cooler, the approximate number of standard drinks in
    - 12 oz = 1
    - 16 oz = 1.3
    - 22 oz = 2
    - 40 oz = 3.3
- For malt liquor, the approximate number of standard drinks in
    - 12 oz = 1.5
    - 16 oz = 2
    - 22 oz = 2.5
    - 40 oz = 4.5
- For table wine, the approximate number of standard drinks in
    - a standard 750 mL (25 oz) bottle = 5
- For 80-proof spirits, or "hard liquor," the approximate number of standard drinks in
    - a mixed drink = 1 or more†
    - a pint (16 oz) = 11
    - a fifth (25 oz) = 17
    - 1.75 L (59 oz) = 39

*In recent years it has been common for wines to contain an alcohol concentration of 16 percent. In these instances, 5 ounces of wine would be equivalent to 0.80 ounces of alcohol, which is 33 percent higher than when a 12 percent wine is considered. Another way of thinking about this is that for a drink of wine with 16 percent alcohol concentration to be equivalent to a 12-ounce can of beer or a typical shot of liquor, the quantity of wine consumed should be reduced to approximately 4 ounces. In this chapter, however, we will retain the concept of 5 ounces of wine as representing a standard drink, since it is traditional that alcohol equivalencies are calculated on this basis.

†It can be difficult to estimate the number of standard drinks served in a single mixed drink made with hard liquor. Depending on factors such as the type of spirits and the recipe, one mixed drink can contain from one to three or more standard drinks.

Source: National Institute on Alcohol Abuse and Alcoholism (2005). *Helping patients who drink too much: A clinician's guide.* Bethesda, MD: National Institute on Alcohol Abuse and Alcoholism, p. 12.

Based on these equivalencies, the average alcohol consumption in the United States can be approximated as about 1.5 "standard drinks" per day. Bear in mind, however, that a "standard drink" may not be the drink you consume, so it is not necessarily the appropriate unit to use when computing your own personal level of alcohol consumption. Draft beer, for example, is typically dispensed in large glasses that exceed 12 ounces in capacity. A mixed drink in a bar might contain a quantity of liquor that exceeds a standard amount, if the bartender is particularly generous. In either of these circumstances, an individual can be misled into believing that he or she is consuming an "average" amount (in terms of drinks) when, in fact, the quantity of alcohol being consumed is considerably larger. Another consideration when looking at statistics based on population averages is the obvious fact that not everyone is "average." There is an enormous disparity in terms of how much alcohol each person actually consumes during a given year. Some people drink no alcohol at all, whereas others drink heavily. *In fact, 80 percent of the total amount of alcohol consumed in the United States each year is consumed by only the 30 percent of Americans who drink and only 20 percent of the population in general.* Drugs . . . in Focus (see below) provides a demonstration that illustrates the uneven pattern of alcohol consumption in the United States today.

Drugs... in Focus

Visualizing the Pattern of Alcohol Consumption in the United States

To appreciate the uneven pattern of alcohol consumption in the population, try the following demonstration:

Assemble ten people and ten bottles of beer (preferably empty).

Separate three people who hold nothing. They represent the 30 percent of the population that does not drink alcohol at all.

Separate five people; together they hold two bottles. They represent the 50 percent of the population that drinks 20 percent of the total alcohol supply.

Separate the ninth person; this person holds two bottles. This individual represents the 10 percent of the population that drinks another 20 percent of the total alcohol supply.

Separate the tenth person; this person holds a six-pack of bottles. This individual represents the 10 percent of the population that drinks 60 percent of the total alcohol supply.

The Moral of the Story

Twenty percent of the entire population (the ninth and tenth persons in this demonstration) drink 80 percent of the total alcohol consumed in the United States each year. Of those who drink some alcohol, two-sevenths (roughly 30 percent) of them drink 80 percent of the total alcohol consumed each year, while five-sevenths (roughly 70 percent) of them drink the remaining 20 percent. These figures correspond to those expressed in the text.

A Tale of 10 Beers and 10 People

3 drink none

5 share 2 beers

1 drinks 2

1 drinks 6

Source: Kinney, G. Jean (2006). *Loosening the grip: A handbook of alcohol information*, 8th ed. New York: McGraw-Hill, p. 30.

Looking at the types of alcohol consumed in the United States, beer consumption represents 67 percent of overall alcoholic consumption and a disproportionate share of heavy alcohol drinking. When five or more 12-ounce beers are consumed in a day, there is a stronger association with alcohol-related problems than when there are comparable consumption levels of wine or liquor. We can conclude that beer is the most problematic form of alcohol consumption in the United States today.[17]

The Demographics of Alcohol Consumption

Not surprisingly, the prevalence of moderate alcohol consumption in college (assessed in terms of those having a drink in the last thirty days) is substantially higher than levels encountered in high school, although. the establishment of twenty-one as the mandated legal drinking age in all U.S. states has delayed the occurrence of *peak* consumption levels to the junior or senior year. Among young adults, *binge drinking*—defined for men as having five or more alcoholic drinks and for women as having four or more alcoholic drinks over a period of two hours—rises sharply from age eighteen, peaks at ages twenty-one to twenty-two, and then steadily declines over the next ten years. The prevalence of daily drinking also rises from levels encountered in high school but remains relatively stable afterward, through age thirty-two.

An extensive series of surveys conducted from 1993 to 2005 on American college campuses have shown a fairly consistent picture of the drinking patterns of college students in the United States over this period of time. Here are the general findings:

■ Overall, approximately 44 percent of college students report having engaged in binge drinking during the two weeks prior to the administration of the survey— 41 percent of the women and 49 percent of the men. About one in five students abstains from alcohol, whereas one in four is a frequent binge drinker. About half of college students (48 percent) report that drinking to get drunk is an important reason for drinking. Three students in ten (29 percent) report being intoxicated three or more times in a month.

■ College students who drank alcohol at some time over the past year frequently report alcohol-related problems while at college. One in four students report that their drinking had a negative impact on their academic performance. Problems included missing a class, failing behind on course assignments, doing poorly on exams or papers, and receiving lower grades overall.

■ One in five students report that, while intoxicated, they engaged in unplanned sexual activity or engaged in unprotected sex. One in three students report that they had done something they regretted while intoxicated.

The surveys have also shed light on the negative impact of alcohol consumption among college students on *nondrinkers* (defined as either abstainers or nonbinge drinkers). These situations, called secondhand effects (because the individuals themselves were not intoxicated but were affected by those who were), are analogous to the problems of secondhand smoking, which will be examined in Chapter 15. Three in 10 college students (29 percent) report that they were insulted or humiliated by another student who had been drinking. One in five students (19 percent) report having experienced an unwanted sexual advance.

It is estimated that approximately 1,700 college students between the ages of 18 and 24 die each year from alcohol-related unintentional injuries, principally as a consequence of motor vehicle accidents. The trend toward lower levels of high-risk drinking on college campuses will be reviewed in Chapter 16 in the context of overall substance abuse prevention.[18]

Looking at the early years of teenage drinking, we find that alcohol use has been extensive by the eighth

Drugs... in Focus

When Is a Binge Not a Binge?

Since the first survey conducted by the Harvard School of Public Health on alcohol consumption among college students in 1993, the term "binge drinking" has become synonymous in the public mind with the behavior of drinking alcohol with the intention of getting drunk. It is commonly defined in the case of men as having consumed five or more alcoholic drinks on a single occasion (typically within a two-hour interval) or four drinks or more in the case of women. This definition has been referred to as the "5/4 criterion."

Recently, however, some clinicians and researchers in the alcohol abuse field have objected to this term as misleading. While acknowledging that consuming a series of alcoholic drinks on a single occasion should be considered a form of risky behavior that brings with it a host of adverse consequences, they contend that the concept of a "binge" should be restricted to an extended bout of drinking or other substance use (often operationalized as lasting at least two days) in which the person neglects other activities so as to drink or use other psychoactive substances. Indeed, this is the traditional sense of the word.

The *Journal of Studies on Alcohol* presently requires that authors of all submitted manuscripts refrain from the term "binge" unless it refers to an extended period of intoxication, prolonged use, and a giving up of usual activities. Any behavior defined by the 5/4 criterion, as expressed in guidelines for authors of articles in this journal, should be referred to as "heavy episodic drinking" or "heavy episodic use." Other researchers in the field refer to the alcohol-related behavior commonly reported among college students as "episodic high-risk drinking." It may not be nearly as catchy a phrase as "binge drinking," and it is certainly

less convenient for writers of newspaper headlines, but this term is nevertheless more accurate as a description of the phenomenon. Proponents of this terminology argue that the alcohol consumption pattern of behavior among college students is (1) typically restricted to going out and getting drunk one night on a weekend, from once a week to once a month or less often, (2) cyclical in nature, with the highest frequency occurring early in a semester, though it peaks following exam times, home football weekends, and during spring breaks, and (3) strongly determined by living in a college environment, in that it ends for practically all students when they graduate from college and move on.

In the meantime, the 5/4 criterion for binge drinking has the public health community divided. While the Centers for Disease Control and Prevention in Atlanta will continue to define the term "binge drinking" in the 5/4 manner for the foreseeable future, the National Institute on Alcohol Abuse and Alcoholism (NIAAA), the leading federal agency for research on alcohol abuse prevention and treatment, will not. The best advice when perusing the alcohol literature might be to examine carefully the way in which "binge drinking" is defined in a particular article.

Sources: Brower, Aaron M. (2002). Are college student alcoholics? *Journal of American College Health, 50,* 253–255. DeJong, William (2003). Definitions of binge drinking. *Journal of the American Medical Association, 289,* 1635. Naimi, Tim; Brewer, Bob; Mokdad, Ali; Denny, Clark; Serdula, Mary; and Marks, Jim (2003). In reply: Definitions of binge drinking. *Journal of the American Medical Association, 289,* 1636. Wechsler, Henry, and Kuo, Meichun (2000). College students define binge drinking and estimate its prevalence: Results of a national survey. *Journal of American College Health, 49,* 57–64.

---

grade. In fact, among young people who report some alcohol consumption between the ages of twelve and twenty, *the average age when drinking began is fourteen years.* In the 2009 University of Michigan survey, 37 percent of eighth graders reported that they had consumed alcohol, and 17 percent reported that they had been drunk sometime in their lives. Fortunately, these figures are down significantly from those found in earlier surveys. However, approximately 8 percent of students at this age reported consuming more than five drinks on a single occasion in the previous two weeks, a pattern of behavior that is only slightly down from that reported in 1991.

The major challenge in reducing underage alcohol use is the fact that underage drinkers continue to have access to alcoholic beverages, despite the legal restrictions on alcohol sales. Studies show that more than 40 percent of the estimated 11 million underage drinkers, defined as persons aged twelve to twenty who drank in the past 30 days, were provided free alcohol by adults twenty-one or older. About 6 percent of underage drinkers were given alcohol by their parents in the past month. A majority (54 percent) reported drinking alcohol in someone else's home, and 30 percent drank in their own home.[19]

The Pharmacology of Alcohol

Alcohol is a very small molecule that is moderately soluble in fat and highly soluble in water—all characteristics that make it easily absorbed through the gastrointestinal tract once it is ingested, without needing any digestion. About 20 percent of it is absorbed into the bloodstream directly from the stomach, whereas the remaining 80 percent is absorbed from the upper portion of the small intestine.

On entering the stomach, alcohol acts initially as an irritant, increasing the flow of hydrochloric acid and pepsin, chemicals that aid digestion. Therefore, in small amounts, alcohol can help digest a meal. In large amounts, however, alcohol irritates the stomach lining. This is a concern for those already having stomach problems; preexisting ulcers are worsened by drinking alcohol, and heavy alcohol drinking can produce ulcers.

The irritating effect on the stomach explains why the alcohol proceeds on to the small intestine more quickly when alcohol concentrations are high. The stomach is simply trying to get rid of its irritant. Over time, the chronic consumption of alcohol can produce an inflammation of the stomach (gastritis) or the pancreas (pancreatitis).

Because the small intestine assumes the lion's share of the responsibilities and acts extremely rapidly (more rapidly than the stomach), the rate of total alcohol absorption is based largely on the condition of the stomach when the alcohol arrives and the time required for the stomach to empty its contents into the small intestine. If the stomach is empty, an intoxicating effect (the "buzz") will be felt very quickly. If the stomach is full, absorption will be delayed as the alcohol is retained by the stomach along with the food being digested, and the passage of alcohol into the small intestine will slow down.

Besides the condition of the stomach, there are other factors related to the alcohol itself and the behavior of the drinker that influence the rate of alcohol absorption. The principal factor is the concentration of alcohol in the beverage being ingested. An ounce of 80-proof (40 percent) alcohol will be felt more quickly than an ounce of wine containing 12 percent alcohol, and of course the level of alcohol in the blood will be higher as well. Also, if the

---

oxidation: A chemical process in alcohol metabolism.

alcohol dehydrogenase (AL-co-haul DEE-high-DRAW-juh-nays): An enzyme in the stomach and liver that converts alcohol into acetaldehyde.

acetaldehyde (ASS-ee-TAL-duh-hide): A by-product of alcohol metabolism, produced through the action of alcohol dehydrogenase.

---

alcoholic beverage is carbonated, as are champagne and other sparkling wines, the stomach will empty its contents faster and effects will be felt sooner. Finally, if the alcohol enters the body at a rapid pace, such as when drinks are consumed in quick succession, the level of alcohol in the blood will be higher because the liver cannot eliminate it fast enough. All other factors being equal, a bigger person requires a larger quantity of alcohol to have equivalent levels accumulating in the blood, simply because there are more body fluids to absorb the alcohol, thus diluting the overall effect.[20]

The Breakdown and Elimination of Alcohol

Its solubility in water helps alcohol to be distributed to all bodily tissues, with those tissues having greater water content receiving a relatively greater proportion of alcohol. The excretion of alcohol is accomplished in two basic ways. About 5 percent will be eliminated by the lungs through exhalation, causing the characteristic "alcohol breath" of heavy drinkers. Breathalyzers, designed to test for alcohol concentrations in the body and used frequently by law-enforcement officials to test for drunkenness, work on this principle. The remaining 95 percent is eliminated in the urine, after the alcohol has been biotransformed into carbon dioxide and water.[21]

The solubility of alcohol in fat facilitates its passage across the blood-brain barrier (see Chapter 1). As a result, approximately 90 percent of the alcohol in the blood reaches the brain almost immediately. Unfortunately, alcohol passes the blood-placenta barrier with equal ease, so alcohol intake by women during pregnancy affects the developing fetus. As a result, fetal alcohol levels are essentially identical to those of the mother who is drinking.[22] This important matter will be discussed in the next chapter, when we consider a type of mental and physical retardation called *fetal alcohol syndrome*.

The body recognizes alcohol as a visitor with no real biological purpose. It contains calories but no vitamins, minerals, or other components that have any nutritional value. Therefore, the primary bodily reaction is to break it down for eventual removal, through a process called **oxidation**. This biotransformation process consists of two basic steps. First, an enzyme, **alcohol dehydrogenase**, breaks down alcohol into **acetaldehyde**. This enzyme is present in the stomach, where about 20 percent of alcohol is broken down prior to absorption into the bloodstream, and in the liver, where the remaining 80 percent is broken down from accumulations in the blood. Second, another enzyme, **acetaldehyde dehydrogenase**, breaks down acetaldehyde in the liver into **acetic acid**. From there, further oxidation results in oxygen, carbon dioxide, and calories of energy.

The entire process is determined by the speed with which alcohol dehydrogenase does its work, and for a given individual, it works at a constant rate, no matter how much alcohol needs to be broken down. *Imagine a bank at which only one teller window stays open, no matter how long the line of customers grows, and you will understand the limitations under which the body is operating.*

The specific rate of oxidation is approximately 100 milligrams of alcohol per hour per kilogram of body weight. To put this in perspective, 8 grams of alcohol will be broken down in an hour if you weigh 176 pounds (80 kilograms), and 5 grams of alcohol will be broken down in an hour if you weigh 110 pounds (50 kilograms). Certain conditions and circumstances, however, can alter this basic biotransformation rate (Drugs . . . in Focus).

---

acetaldehyde dehydrogenase (ASS-ee-TAL-duh-hide DEE-high-DRAW-juh-nays): An enzyme in the liver that converts acetaldehyde to acetic acid in alcohol metabolism.

acetic acid (a-SEE-tik ASS-id): A by-product of alcohol metabolism, produced through the action of acetaldehyde dehydrogenase.

Drugs... in Focus

Gender, Race, and Medication: Factors in Alcohol Metabolism

Since enzymes play such a critical role in alcohol breakdown, it is important to consider factors that alter the levels of these enzymes. As mentioned in Chapter 4, two of these factors are gender and ethnicity. In general, women have about 60 percent less alcohol dehydrogenase in the stomach than men; thus their oxidation of alcohol is relatively slower, even when different body weights have been taken into account.

In addition, about 50 percent of all people of Asian descent have a genetically imposed lower level of acetaldehyde dehydrogenase in the liver. As a consequence, acetaldehyde builds up, causing nausea, itching, facial flushing, and cardiac acceleration. The combination of these symptoms, often referred to as *fast-flushing*, makes alcohol consumption very unpleasant for many Asians.

It would be reasonable to expect then that those who experienced fast-flushing would drink less alcohol than those who do not. This is true when you look at the population at large. For Japanese American college students who have to contend with peer pressure to drink, however, the relationship between the physiological response and the quantity of alcohol consumed is not nearly as strong. For them, environmental factors encourage alcohol consumption, despite their genetically determined predisposition to get sick. In a similar way, the social life of Japanese businessmen has promoted alcohol consumption, even though many get sick as a result. Unfortunately, accepting an offer from one's boss to go out drinking is part of the social networking required for corporate advancement.

Medications also can influence alcohol breakdown by altering levels of alcohol dehydrogenase in the stomach. Aspirin, for example, when taken on a full stomach, reduces enzyme levels by one-half, causing more alcohol to accumulate in the blood. Among women, aspirin has a greater inhibiting effect than among men, so it is possible that enzyme levels may be reduced to nearly zero if a woman is taking aspirin prior to drinking alcoholic beverages. Gastric ulcer medications also inhibit alcohol dehydrogenase and thus increase the physiological impact of alcohol. Any combination of these factors appears to produce additive effects. (See Table 13.3 on page 309 for other examples of alcohol–medication interactions.)

Sources: Edenberg, Howard J. (2007, Winter). The genetics of alcohol metabolism: Role of alcohol dehydrogenase and aldehyde dehydrogenase variants. *Alcohol Research and Health,* 5–37. Frezza, Mario; DiPadova, Carlo; Pozzato, Gabrielle; Terpin, Maddalena; Baraona, Enrique; and Lieber, Charles S. (1990). High blood alcohol levels in women: The role of decreased gastric alcohol dehydrogenase activity and first-pass metabolism. *New England Journal of Medicine, 322,* 95–99. Nakawatase, Tomoko V., Joe, and Sasao, Toshiaki (1993). The association between fast-flushing response and alcohol use among Japanese Americans. *Journal of Studies on Alcohol, 54,* 48–53. Roine, Risto; Gentry, Thomas; Hernandez-Muñoz, Rolando; Baraona, Enrique; and Lieber, Charles S. (1990). Aspirin increases blood alcohol concentrations in humans after ingestion of ethanol. *Journal of the American Medical Association, 264,* 2406–2408. Scott, Denise M., and Taylor, Robert E. (2007, Winter). Health-related effects of genetic variations of alcohol-metabolizing enzymes in African Americans. *Alcohol Research and Health,* 18–21.

In terms of alcoholic beverages, the oxidation rate for adults in general is approximately one-third to one-half ounce of pure alcohol an hour. If you sipped (not gulped) slightly less than the contents of one 12-ounce bottle of beer, one 5-ounce glass of wine, or any equivalent portion of alcohol (see Drugs . . . in Focus, page 300) very slowly over an hour's time, the enzymes in the stomach and liver would keep up, and you would not feel intoxicated. Naturally, if you consume larger amounts of alcohol at faster rates of consumption, all bets are off.[23]

It is no secret that alcohol consumption is conducive to the accumulation of body fat, most noticeably in the form of the notorious beer belly. It turns out that alcohol does not have significant effects on the biotransformation of dietary carbohydrates and proteins, so a drinking individual who consumes a healthy diet does not have to worry about getting enough nutrients. Alcohol does, however, reduce the breakdown of fat, so dietary fat has a greater chance of being stored rather than expended. Over time, the

accumulation of fat in the liver is particularly serious because it eventually interferes with normal liver function. This potentially life-threatening medical condition involving the liver will be examined in the next chapter as one of the major adverse effects of chronic alcohol consumption.[24]

Measuring Alcohol in the Blood

Alcohol levels in the blood, like levels of any drug, vary considerably not only by virtue of how much is ingested and how long ago but also as a result of differences in an individual's body size and relative proportions of body fat. Consequently, we have to consider a specific ratio referred to as the **blood-alcohol concentration (BAC)** when assessing physiological and psychological effects (an alternative term is blood-alcohol level [BAL]).

The BAC refers to the number of grams of alcohol in the blood relative to 100 milliliters of blood, expressed as a percentage. For example, 0.1 gram (100 milligrams) of alcohol in 100 milliliters of blood is represented by a BAC of 0.10 percent. Table 13.2 (below) shows the BAC levels that can be estimated

blood-alcohol concentration (BAC): The number of grams of alcohol in the blood relative to 100 milliliters of blood, expressed as a percentage.

TABLE 13.2

When are you drunk? Calculating your blood-alcohol concentration (BAC) level

STANDARD DRINKS

WEIGHT (LB)	1	2	3	4	5	6	7	8	9	10
100	.029	.058	.088	.117	.146	.175	.204	.233	.262	.290
120	.024	.048	.073	.097	.121	.145	.170	.194	.219	.243
140	.021	.042	.063	.083	.104	.125	.146	.166	.187	.208
160	.019	.037	.055	.073	.091	.109	.128	.146	.164	.182
180	.017	.033	.049	.065	.081	.097	.113	.130	.146	.162
200	.015	.029	.044	.058	.073	.087	.102	.117	.131	.146
220	.014	.027	.040	.053	.067	.080	.093	.106	.119	.133
240	.012	.024	.037	.048	.061	.073	.085	.097	.109	.122

CAUTION   DRIVING IMPAIRED   LEGALLY DRUNK

Alcohol is "burned up" by your body at .015% per hour, as follows:

Hours since starting first drink	1	2	3	4	5	6
Percent alcohol burned up	.015	.030	.045	.060	.075	.090

To calculate your BAC level correctly, you must consider the number of standard drinks you have consumed, your body weight, and how much time has passed since the first drink. Note that a BAC level of .10% or higher has been, until recently, the standard for drunk driving in most U.S. states. All U.S. states have now adopted the .08% standard.

Source: Updated from *A primer of drug action*, 8th ed., by Robert M. Julien, M.D. © 2001 Worth Publishers. Used with permission.

from one's body weight, number of standard drinks consumed, and hours elapsed since starting the first drink.

From these figures, BAC levels typically are considered in terms of three broad categories of behavior: caution (0.01 to 0.05 percent), driving impaired (0.05 to 0.08 percent), and legally drunk (in all U.S. states, 0.08 percent and higher). In effect, you need to compute the accumulated BAC levels for your specific body weight after having a specific number of drinks, and then subtract 0.015 percent BAC for each hour since the drinking occurred.[25]

Effects of Alcohol on the Brain

Alcohol is clearly a CNS depressant drug, though it is often misidentified as a stimulant. The reason for this confusion is that alcohol, at low doses, first releases the cerebral cortex from its inhibitory control over subcortical systems in the brain, a kind of double-negative effect. In other words, alcohol is depressing an area of the brain that normally would be an inhibitor, and the result is the illusion of stimulation. The impairment in judgment and thinking (the classic features of being drunk) stems from a loosening of social inhibitions that enable us, under non-alcoholic circumstances, to be relatively thoughtful about the consequences of our actions, as well as relatively civil and well behaved.[26]

As the BAC level increases, the depressive action of alcohol extends downward to lower regions of the brain. Eventually, an inhibition of the respiratory centers in the medulla becomes a distinct possibility, leading to asphyxiation (a loss of breathing). The effect of alcohol at the neuronal level is less well understood, but the picture is starting to emerge. At present, the leading candidate for a mechanism is the GABA receptor in the brain. This receptor contains three locations: one sensitive specifically to the neurotransmitter GABA, one sensitive to barbiturates, and one sensitive to a type of antianxiety medication (see Chapter 11). The last location is also sensitive to alcohol, and the research suggests that alcohol acts at this site, making it more difficult for the neuron to be stimulated.[27]

More worrisome than alcohol's depressive effects on the brain, however, is its ability to set up a pattern of psychological dependence. Since the late 1980s, evidence has accumulated that the reinforcing action of alcohol is a result of its influence on dopamine-releasing neurons in the nucleus accumbens of the brain (see Chapter 4). The fact that alcohol shares this effect with other abused drugs, including heroin, cocaine, and nicotine, suggests the possibility that treatments for one form of drug abuse might also be effective for others. Chapter 14 will describe the recent research concerning the use of naltrexone, an opiate antagonist, in the treatment of chronic alcohol abuse.[28]

Acute Physiological Effects

Alcohol can produce a number of immediate physiological effects; they will be examined here. The physiological effects resulting from *chronic* alcohol consumption will be covered in the next chapter.

Toxic Reactions

First and foremost, we have to be aware that death by asphyxiation can happen if BAC levels are elevated, generally when they reach 0.50 percent. In general, the therapeutic index for alcohol, as measured by the LD50/ED50 ratio (see Chapter 2), is approximately 6. This figure is not very high, and caution is strongly advised; the risks of being the "big winner" in a drinking contest should be weighed very carefully. On the one hand, to achieve a lethal BAC level of 0.50 percent, a 165-pound man needs to have consumed approximately twenty-three drinks over a four-hour period.[29] On the other hand, consuming ten drinks in one hour, a drinking schedule that achieves a BAC level of 0.35 percent, puts a person in extremely dangerous territory. We need to remember that LD50 is the *average* level for a lethal effect; there is no way to predict where a particular person might be located on the normal curve!

Fortunately, two mechanisms are designed to protect us to a certain degree. First, alcohol acts as a gastric irritant so the drinker often feels nauseated and vomits. Second, the drinker may simply pass out, and the risk potential from further drinking becomes irrelevant. Nonetheless, there are residual dangers in becoming unconscious; vomiting while in this state can prevent breathing, and death can occur from asphyxiation (Help Line).

Heat Loss and the Saint Bernard Myth

Alcohol is a peripheral dilator, which means that blood vessels near the skin surface enlarge, leading to a greater amount of blood shunted to the skin. The effect gives you the feeling that your skin is warm, which is most likely the basis for the myth that alcohol can keep you warm in freezing weather. In truth, however, peripheral dilation causes core body temperature to decrease. In other words, alcohol produces a greater loss in body heat than would occur without it. So if you are marooned in the snow and you see an approaching Saint Bernard with a cask of brandy strapped to its neck, politely refuse the offer. It will not help and could very well do you harm. (But feel free to hug the dog! That will certainly help.)

Diuretic Effects

As concentration levels rise in the blood, alcohol begins to inhibit **antidiuretic hormone (ADH)**, a hormone that normally acts to reabsorb water in the kidneys prior to elimination in the urine. As a result, urine is more diluted and, because large amounts of liquid are typically being consumed at the time, more copious. Once blood alcohol concentrations have peaked, however, the reverse occurs. Water is now retained in a condition called

antidiuretic hormone (ADH): A hormone that acts to reabsorb water in the kidneys prior to excretion from the body.

antidiuresis: A condition resulting from excessive reabsorption of water in the kidneys.

antidiuresis, resulting in swollen fingers, hands, and feet. This effect is more pronounced if salty foods (peanuts or pretzels, for example) were eaten along with the alcohol.

The inhibition of ADH during the drinking of alcoholic beverages can be a serious concern, particularly following vigorous exercise when the body is already suffering from a loss of water and fluid levels are low. Therefore, the advice to the marathoner, whose body may lose more than a gallon of water over the course of a warm three-hour run, is to celebrate the end of the race not with a beer but with nonintoxicating liquids such as Gatorade or similar mineral-rich drinks.[30]

Effects on Sleep

It might seem tempting to induce sleep with a relaxing "nightcap," but in fact the resulting sleep patterns are adversely affected. Alcohol reduces the duration of a phase of sleep called rapid eye movement (REM) sleep (see Chapter 11). Depending on the dose, REM sleep can be either partially or completely suppressed during the night. When alcohol is withdrawn, REM sleep rebounds and represents a higher percentage of total sleep time than before alcohol consumption began. As a result, individuals sleep poorly and experience nightmares.[31]

Effects on Pregnancy

The consumption of alcohol during pregnancy, even in moderation, greatly increases the risk of retardation in the development of the fetus (a very serious condition called fetal alcohol syndrome, see Chapter 14), and reducing the incidence of this behavior has been a major public health objective since the mid-1990s. From data averaged over 2007 and 2008, it has been estimated that about 11 percent of pregnant women consume alcohol, exposing approximately one in nine fetuses to alcohol *in utero*. National public health goals for the United States in 2010 (see Chapter 17) have included reducing this percentage to 6 percent. In an effort to attain this objective, brief interventions to help pregnant women achieve abstinence from alcohol have been developed. In one program of this kind, women were five times more likely to have abstained by the third trimester of pregnancy, relative to controls, after a 10–15 minute counseling session in a walk-in center.[32]

Interactions with Other Drugs

A major concern in alcohol drinking is the complex interaction of alcohol with many drugs. As noted in Chapter 2, the DAWN reports of emergency department admissions and deaths show an extremely high incidence of medical crises arising from the combination of alcohol not only with prescribed medications but also with virtually all the illicit drugs on the street. Opiates and opiate-like drugs, marijuana, and many prescription medicines interact with alcohol such that the resulting combination produces effects that are either the sum of the parts or greater than the sum of the parts. In other cases, the ingestion of medications with alcohol significantly lessens the medication's benefits. Anticoagulants, anticonvulsants, and monoamine oxidase inhibitors (used as antidepressant medications) fit into this second category. Table 13.3 shows a partial listing of major therapeutic drugs that interact with alcohol and have undesirable, if not dangerous, outcomes.

TABLE 13.3

A partial listing of possible drug-alcohol interactions

GENERIC DRUG (BRAND NAME OR TYPE)	CONDITION BEING TREATED	EFFECT OF INTERACTION
chloral hydrate (Noctec)	Insomnia	Excessive sedation that can be fatal; irregular heartbeat; flushing
glutethimide (Doriden)	Insomnia	Excessive sedation; reduced driving and machine-operating skills
antihypertensives (Apresoline, Diuril)	High blood pressure	Exaggeration of blood pressure–lowering effect; dizziness on rising
diuretics (Aldactone)	High blood pressure	Exaggeration of blood pressure–lowering effect; dizziness on rising
antibiotics (penicillin)	Bacterial infections	Reduced therapeutic effectiveness
nitroglycerin (Nitro-bid)	Angina pain	Severe decrease in blood pressure; intense flushing; headache; dizziness on rising
warfarin (Coumadin)	Blood clot	Decreased anti–blood clotting effect, easy bruising
insulin	Diabetes	Excessive low blood sugar; nausea; flushing
disulfiram (Antabuse)	Alcoholic drinking	Intense flushing; severe headache; vomiting; heart palpitations; could be fatal
methotrexate	Various cancers	Increased risk of liver damage
phenytoin (Dilantin)	Epileptic seizures	Reduced drug effectiveness in preventing seizures; drowsiness
prednisone (Deltasone)	Inflammatory conditions (arthritis, bursitis)	Stomach irritation
various antihistamines	Nasal congestion	Excessive sedation that could be fatal
acetaminophen (Tylenol)	Pain	Increased risk of liver damage

Sources: National Institute on Alcohol Abuse and Alcoholism (1995, January). Alcohol alert: Alcohol–medication interactions. No. 27, PH355. Bethesda, MD: National Institute on Alcohol Abuse and Alcoholism. National Institute on Alcohol Abuse and Alcoholism (2007, Revised). Harmful interactions: Mixing alcohol with medicines. NIH Publication No. 03-5349. Bethesda, MD: National Institute on Alcohol Abuse and Alcoholism.

The complete list is so long that it is fair to say that, whenever any medication is taken, the individual should inquire about possible interactions with alcohol.

Hangovers

About four to twelve hours after heavy consumption of alcohol, usually the next day, unpleasant symptoms of headache, nausea, fatigue, and thirst may occur; these are collectively known as a *hangover*. At least one such experience has been undergone by 40 percent of all men and 27 percent of all women over the age of eighteen.[33] Why these symptoms occur is not at all clear. The probable explanations at present focus on individual aspects of a hangover, though it is likely that several factors contribute to the total phenomenon.

One factor, beyond the simple fact of drinking too much, is the type of alcohol that has been consumed. Among distilled spirits, for example, vodka has a lower probability of inducing hangovers than whiskey. A possible reason is the relatively lower amount of **congeners**. These substances in alcoholic beverages, including trace amounts of nonethyl alcohol, oils, and other organic matter, are by-products of the fermentation and distillation processes and give the drinks their distinctive smell, taste, and color. A common congener is the tannin found in red wines. Although no harm is caused by congeners in minute concentrations, they are still toxic substances, and they probably contribute to hangover symptoms.[34]

Other possible factors include traces of nonoxidized acetaldehyde in the blood, residual irritation in the stomach, and a low blood sugar level rebounding from the high levels induced by the previous ingestion of alcohol. The feeling of swollenness from the antidiuresis, discussed earlier, may contribute to the headache pain. The thirst may be due to the dehydration that occurred the night before.

Acute Behavioral Effects

The consumption of alcoholic beverages is so pervasive in the world that it seems almost unnecessary to comment on how it feels to be intoxicated by alcohol. The

behavioral effects of consuming alcohol in more than very moderate quantities range from the relatively harmless effects of exhilaration and excitement, talkativeness, slurred speech, and irritability to behaviors that have the potential for causing great harm: uncoordinated movement, drowsiness, sensorimotor difficulties, and stupor.[35] Some of the prominent behavioral problems associated with acute alcohol intoxication will be examined in this section.

Blackouts

A **blackout** is an inability to remember events that occurred during the period of intoxication, even though the individual was conscious at the time. For example, a drinker having too much to drink at a party drives home, parks the car on a nearby street, and goes to bed. The next morning, he or she has no memory of having driven home and cannot locate the car. This phenomenon is different from "passing out," which is a loss of consciousness from alcoholic intoxication. In the case of blackouts, consciousness is never lost.

Owing to the possibility of blackouts, drinkers can be easily misled into thinking that because they can understand some information given to them during drinking, they will remember it later. The risk of blackouts is greatest when alcohol is consumed very quickly, forcing the BAC to rise rapidly. In a recent e-mail survey of college students to learn more about their experiences with blackouts, approximately half of those who had ever consumed alcohol reported having experienced a blackout at some point in their lives and 40 percent reported having had at least one experience in the twelve months prior to the survey.[36]

Driving Skills

There is no question that alcohol consumption significantly impairs the ability to drive or deal with automobile traffic, particularly among young people. In 2009, of the 33,808 traffic fatalities that occurred in the United States, approximately 11,000 of them (about 32 percent) were alcohol-related. To put this statistic in perspective, there were approximately 30 alcohol-impaired driving fatalities every day during that year (one instance every 48 minutes).[37]

Most of these alcohol-related fatalities resulted from conditions in which drivers had a BAC of 0.08 percent or higher, the minimum standard for legal intoxication in all U.S. states, but there were also a number of fatalities resulting from a BAC below that level. It is important

---

congeners (KON-jen-ers): Nonethyl alcohols, oils, and other organic substances found in trace amounts in some distilled spirits.

blackout: Amnesia concerning events occurring during the period of alcoholic intoxication, even though consciousness had been maintained at that time.

Every community has its tragic stories of preventable deaths due to drunk driving. Alcohol is also recognized as a major factor in more than 800 boating fatalities in the United States each year.

to recognize that driving is impaired with BAC levels as low as 0.20 to 0.40 percent—well below the "driving while intoxicated" (DWI) threshold.

All these statistics could be viewed as correlational and not necessarily proof of a causal relationship between alcohol and automobile accidents, were it not for the data from laboratory-based experiments showing a clear deterioration of sensorimotor skills following the ingestion of alcohol. Reaction times are slower, the coordination necessary to steer a car steadily is hampered, and the ability to stay awake when fatigued is impaired, but the major way that alcohol impairs driving ability is by reducing the drinker's awareness of peripheral events and stimuli.[38] One researcher in this area has expressed the deficit in this way:

> The overwhelming majority of accidents involving alcohol are not accidents in which tracking is the prime error. Contrary to what most people think, it isn't that people are weaving down the road, which is a sign of very high blood alcohol levels; it's that they have failed to see something. They go through a red light, they fail to see a pedestrian or a motorcyclist, they fail to see that the road is curving. Their perceptual and attentive mechanisms are affected very early, after just one drink. These are the things that are the prime causes of accidents.[39]

Unfortunately, it is the weaving behavior, or other extreme examples of driving impairments, that most often signals the police to stop a car for a possible DWI violation; other alcohol-based impairments frequently go unnoticed until it is too late.

Preventing Alcohol-Related Traffic Fatalities

Increasing the minimum age for alcoholic consumption from eighteen to twenty-one, mandated throughout the United States since 1988, has had a major impact on the likelihood of traffic fatalities among young people. During the early 1980s, when changes in the minimum age were taking place state by state, it was possible to anticipate the improvements that could be made. On average, fatal nighttime accidents involving eighteen- and nineteen-year-old drivers decreased 13 percent between 1975 and 1984 in twenty-six states that had raised the minimum drinking age during that interval. A decrease of 16 percent in nighttime accidents in Michigan following the change in the drinking law was maintained six years later.[40]

With the minimum legal drinking age now set at twenty-one years and the minimum BAC level for intoxication lowered to 0.08 percent, there is reason to be cautiously optimistic. According to estimates made by the National Highway Traffic Safety Administration, the reduction of the minimum BAC level to 0.08 percent has saved five hundred lives each year on the nation's highways. More than 700 lives of persons aged eighteen, nineteen, or twenty have been saved each year as a result of laws setting twenty-one as the minimum drinking age. Since 1998, a nationwide minimum level of intoxication for drivers younger than twenty-one years of age has been set at a BAC level of 0.02 percent.[41]

Educational programs in schools and communities emphasizing the advantage of using "designated drivers" as well as public education and lobbying groups such as Mothers Against Drunk Driving (MADD) and Students Against Drunk Driving (SADD) have had positive effects. This chapter's Portrait feature highlights the origins and current aspirations of MADD.

A major goal in reducing alcohol-related fatalities on the road is to prevent an intoxicated individual from getting behind the wheel in the first place. We cannot prevent any intoxicated individual from driving a car, but we can at least try to prevent an individual who has had a previous DUI arrest from driving while intoxicated. The most widely used technology for preventing such a situation is known as an ignition interlock device. When activated by the detection of a minimum BAC level in the breath of the driver, the ignition interlock will prevent the car from starting (Figure 13.1). In 2007, New Mexico became the first state to require ignition interlocks to be installed after a first DWI offense; alcohol-related fatalities decreased 11 percent in the first year. When, in 2004, Maryland mandated that the system be installed after several DWI arrests, fatalities were

PORTRAIT

Candace Lightner—Founder of MADD

In 1980, Candace Lightner's thirteen-year-old daughter, Cari, was killed by a hit-and-run intoxicated driver in California. The driver had been out of jail on bail for only two days, a consequence of another hit-and-run drunk-driving crash, and he had three previous drunk-driving arrests and two previous convictions. He was allowed to plea bargain to vehicular manslaughter. Although the sentence was to serve two years in prison, the judge allowed him to serve time in a work camp and later a halfway house.

It was appalling to Lightner that drunk drivers, similar to the one who had killed her daughter, were receiving such lenient treatment, with many of them never going to jail for a single day. Lightner quit her job and started an organization that has become a household name: Mothers Against Drunk Driving (MADD).

Since then, MADD has campaigned for stricter laws against drunk driving, and most of the present DWI legislation around the country is a result of its intense efforts. In addition, MADD acts as a voice for victims of drunk-driving injuries and the families of those who have been killed. From a single act of courage, despite enormous grief, Lightner has created an organization that boasts more than 3 million members in the United States, with groups in virtually every state and more than four hundred local chapters.

More recently, MADD has set for itself the goal of reducing the number of all traffic fatalities associated with alcohol drinking. These are some of the group's proposals for change:

1. More effective enforcement of the minimum-drinking-age law.
2. A "0.00 percent BAC" criterion for drivers under twenty-one, making it illegal to drive with *any* measurable level of blood alcohol in any state.
3. Driver's license suspensions for underage persons convicted of purchasing or possessing alcoholic beverages.
4. Alcohol-free zones for youth gatherings.
5. Criminal sanctions against adults who provide or allow alcoholic beverages at events for underage participants.
6. Mandatory alcohol and drug testing for all drivers in all traffic crashes resulting in fatalities or serious bodily injury.
7. Sobriety checkpoints to detect and apprehend alcohol-impaired drivers and to serve as a visible deterrent to drinking and driving.

The most recent initiative of MADD has been its campaign to have ignition interlock systems installed in vehicles driven by individuals convicted of drunk driving (see page 311).

Sources: Information courtesy of Mothers Against Drunk Driving, Dallas, Texas, 2009. Interview with Candace Lightner.

FIGURE 13.1

Recent technologies, such as the ignition interlock device, serve to prevent intoxicated drivers from operating a motor vehicle. The device plugs into the cigarette lighter of the automobile and is hard-wired to the vehicle's ignition system. Before the car can be started, the driver must blow into the mouthpiece of the device and register a BAC level below a certain level. Otherwise, the car will not start. Additionally, periodic breath sampling is required to continue the vehicle's operation.

TABLE 13.4

Blood alcohol concentration at which drivers in different nations are legally drunk.

BAC	0.00+	0.02	0.03	0.05	0.08
COUNTRY	Czech Republic, Slovakia, Hungary	Norway, Poland, Sweden	Japan, China	Argentina, Australia, Costa Rica, Denmark, Finland, France, Italy, Germany, Greece, Netherlands, Peru, Russia, South Africa, Spain, Thailand	Brazil, Britain, Canada, Chile, Ecuador, Ireland, Jamaica, New Zealand, Singapore, United States

Source: Valenti, John (2005, July 13). U.S. lags others in DWI toughness. *Newsday*, p. A15.

reduced by 18 percent. As of mid-2010, 47 states have enacted some form of ignition interlock law, typically during the period of license suspension and/or a specified time before fully re-licensing DWI offenders. In 13 states, ignition interlock devices are mandated even after a first-time DWI offense.[42]

In general, even though we have reason to be cautiously optimistic about reducing alcohol-related traffic fatalities, it is clear that much work remains to be done. The United States presently has one of the most lenient standards for driving while intoxicated among nations in the world (Table 13.4). The number of alcohol-related accidents, particularly among male drivers, whose involvement exceeds that of female drivers by more than 2:1, is far too high. Meanwhile, the drinking-and-driving phenomenon is widespread throughout the population. In 2008, approximately 31 million people—approximately one out of eight adults in the United States—reported that they had been drinking and driving during the past year. It should not be surprising that the peak age of drinking and driving was between 21 and 25, during which one in four reported being intoxicated on the road.[43]

Alcohol, Violence, and Aggression

It is difficult to avoid sweeping generalizations when confronted with statistics about alcohol and violent behavior both in the United States and around the world. In a major study conducted in a community in northwestern Ontario, Canada, and reported in 1991, more than 50 percent of the most recent occasions of physical violence were found to be preceded by alcohol use on the part of the assailant and/or the victims themselves.[44] Other studies show from 50 to 60 percent of all murders being committed when the killer had been drinking. About 40 percent of all acts of male sexual aggression against adult women and from 60 to 70 percent

of male-instigated domestic violence occur when the offender has been drunk; more than 60 percent of all acts of child molestation involve drunkenness.[45]

Researchers have advanced two principal ways of accounting for the linkage between alcohol intoxication and violent behavior. The *disinhibition theory* holds that ingesting alcohol on a pharmacological level impairs normal cortical mechanisms responsible for inhibiting the expression of innate or suppressed aggressive inclinations. The *cognitive-expectation theory* holds that learned beliefs or expectations about alcohol's effects can facilitate aggressive behaviors. The implication is that violence is induced by the act of drinking in combination with one's personal view of how a person is "supposed to respond" rather than by the pharmacological effects of alcohol itself (Drugs . . . in Focus).[46]

Expectations about the consequences of drug-taking behavior or of any behavior at all, as noted in Chapter 3, are studied experimentally through the placebo research design. In the case of the cognitive-expectation theory, it is necessary to use a variation of this design, called the **balanced placebo design**. Subjects are randomly divided into four groups. Two groups are given an alcoholic drink, with one group being told that they are ingesting alcohol and the other that they are ingesting a nonalcohol substitute that tastes and smells like alcohol. Two other groups are given the nonalcohol substitute, with one group being told that they are ingesting this substitute and the other that they are ingesting alcohol.

Studies using the balanced placebo design have shown clearly that beliefs (mind-sets) concerning the

balanced placebo design: An experimental design that distinguishes psychological effects (due to subjective expectations) from physiological effects (due to the pharmacology of the drug).

Alcohol, Security, and Spectator Sports

In 2005, the National Basketball Association (NBA) issued a new set of security guidelines for all thirty teams, including a "Fan Code of Conduct" specifying that "guests will enjoy the basketball experience free from disruptive behavior, including foul or abusive language or obscene gestures." In the words of NBA Commissioner David Stern, "We look at this as an opportunity to remind people that coming to an arena is an opportunity to share an experience of rooting a home team on to victory and booing the opposition, but not doing it in an antisocial way that goes against our civil society."

Acknowledging the connection between disruptive behavior and alcohol, the NBA now bans alcohol sales during the fourth quarter of every game and imposes a 24-ounce limit on the size of alcoholic drinks sold in an arena, with a maximum of two alcoholic drinks per customer. Increased security measures and restrictions on alcohol sales came about after basketball players and fans brawled in the stands and on the court at the end of a game in November 2004 between the Indiana Pacers and the Detroit Pistons. Indiana's Ron Artest went into the seats after being hit by a full cup of beer that had been tossed by a spectator. As a result of the melee, considered to be one

of the most violent episodes in NBA history, Artest was suspended for the rest of the 2004–2005 season, and other players were given suspensions of as many as thirty games. All told, ten players and fans were charged with fighting.

Alcohol consumption has also come under scrutiny during college and professional football games, where binge drinking at tailgating parties and after-game celebrations frequently results in property damage and sometimes leads to injuries or deaths. At the University of Virginia, a tradition that began in the 1980s has seniors individually drinking a fifth of liquor by kick off time at the final game of the football season (the so-called "Fourth-Year Fifth"). This practice was associated with the deaths of eighteen students between 1990 and 2002. Since 1999, a university organization, Fourth-years Acting Responsibly (FAR), has coordinated an annual pledge drive to reduce abusive drinking at the final home game, as part of a campus-wide alcohol-abuse prevention program.

Sources: Eskenazi, Gerald (2005, December 21). For Patriots and Jets, a sobering experience. *New York Times*, p. D3. Football, tailgating parties, and alcohol safety (2005, October 1). *The NCADI Reporter*. Bethesda, MD: National Clearinghouse for Drug Information. NBA issuing sterner security, beer guidelines. *USA Today.com*, accessed May 8, 2005.

effects of drinking are more influential in determining a subject's behavior than the more direct physiological effects of the alcohol. In other words, *what they are told they are consuming is more important than what they consume* (Drugs . . . in Focus). Unfortunately, for a true test of the cognitive-expectation theory, a balanced placebo design cannot be used with BAC levels above 0.035 percent because subjects who drink larger quantities are no longer fooled by the deception, and most alcohol-associated acts of violence occur with BAC levels at least six times higher.[47]

Sex and Sexual Desire

If they were asked, most people would say that alcohol has an enhancing or aphrodisiac effect on sexual desire and performance. The actual effect of alcohol, however, is more complex than what we commonly believe. In fact, it is because of these beliefs that people are frequently

more susceptible to the expectations of what alcohol *should* do for them than they are to the actual physiological effects of alcohol.

To examine the complex relationship between alcohol and sex, we need to turn again to studies using the balanced placebo design. The general results from such studies are quite different for men and women. Among men, those who expected to be receiving low levels of alcohol had greater penile responses, reported greater subjective arousal, and spent more time watching erotic pictures, *regardless of whether they did indeed receive alcohol*. When alcohol concentrations rise to levels that reflect genuine intoxication, however, the pharmacological actions outweigh the expectations, and the overall effect is definitely inhibitory. Men who are drunk have less sexual desire and a decreased capacity to perform sexually.

In contrast, expectations among women play a lesser role. They are more inclined to react to the pharmacological properties of alcohol itself, but the direction

Drugs... in Focus

Caffeine, Alcohol, and the Dangers of Caffeinated Alcoholic Drinks

Despite the popular notion that caffeine has a "sobering" effect on an alcohol-intoxicated state of mind, the truth is often quite the opposite. It appears to be a factor of one's expectations. In one study, subjects were told either that caffeine would have a significant "sobering" effect when they were intoxicated with alcohol or that caffeine would have no effect. The participants who were led to expect counteracting effects of alcohol-induced impairments in behavior actually displayed a *greater* level of impairment than those who were led to expect no such counteraction.

Misconceptions about the effect of caffeine on alcohol-impaired behavior have serious ramifications, particularly in light of the recent popularity of caffeinated alcoholic drinks.

Beverages such as Four Loko and Joose combine caffeine with an alcohol content of between 6 and 12 percent. Since the caffeine masks (but does not counteract) the effects of alcohol, the drinker is fooled into thinking that more alcohol can be consumed. An increasing number of ED-visits among drinkers of caffeinated alcoholic products have occurred, and in some cases elevated BAC levels have approached the lethal dose range with respect to alcohol toxicity. As noted above, an expectation that the caffeine in a caffeinated alcohol drink would make you less impaired will tend to exacerbate an already dangerous situation.

Sources: Fillmore, Mark T., Roach, Emily, L., and Rice, Julietta T. (2002). Does caffeine counteract alcohol-induced impairment? The ironic effects of expectancy. *Journal of Studies on Alcohol, 63,* 745–754. Goodnough, Abby (2010, October 27). Doctors point to caffeinated alcoholic drinksí dangers. *New York Times,* pp. A12, A14.

---

of their response depends on whether we are talking about subjective or physiological measures. For women receiving increasing alcohol concentrations, measures of subjective arousal increase but measures of vaginal arousal decrease. The pattern of their responses mirrors Shakespeare's observation in *Macbeth* that alcohol "provokes the desire, but it takes away the performance," a comment originally intended to reflect only the male point of view.[48]

Alcohol and Health Benefits

The documented health benefits of moderate levels of alcohol consumption over the last thirty years of research have presented a major dilemma among medical and public health professionals. The crux of the dilemma is that moderate amounts of alcohol can possibly save your life, while immoderate amounts can possibly destroy it. As one writer has expressed it, "Alcohol has become the sharpest double-edged sword in medicine."

It started as an observation that did not seem to make sense. Epidemiological studies of French and other European populations who consumed large amounts of butter, cheese, liver, and other animal fats—a diet

Quick Concept Check 13.2

Understanding the Data from Balanced Placebo Designs

Check your understanding of the balanced placebo design by indicating whether the following experimental results reflect (a) psychological effects, (b) physiological effects, or (c) a combination of psychological and physiological effects.

- Scenario 1: Subjects felt sexy after receiving low doses of drug X, regardless of whether they knew what they were receiving.
- Scenario 2: Subjects felt sexy if they received low doses of drug X but were told that they did not receive it and also felt sexy if they did not receive low doses of drug X but were told that they did.
- Scenario 3: Subjects felt sexy after being told they would receive low doses of drug X, regardless of whether they actually received it.

Answers: Scenario 1. b Scenario 2. c Scenario 3. a

A modern-day medical dilemma: Health benefits of moderate alcohol consumption versus the potential for alcohol abuse. (By permission of Mike Luckovich and Creators Syndicate, Inc.)

associated with elevated cholesterol and an elevated risk for coronary failure—found that these populations had a remarkably low incidence of coronary heart disease. The answer seemed to be that relatively more alcohol was consumed along with their dietary food. The "French paradox" was resolved when later research showed that alcohol increases high-density lipoprotein (HDL) cholesterol (the so-called good cholesterol) levels in the blood, with HDL acting as a protective mechanism against a possible restriction of blood flow through arteries. The greatest benefit was seen in those individuals who had high concentrations of low-density lipoprotein (LDL) cholesterol (the so-called bad cholesterol) and therefore had the greatest risk for coronary heart disease. It was estimated that consumption of approximately 8 ounces of wine (a bit less than two standard drinks) per day resulted in a 25 percent reduction in the risk of coronary heart disease.

A natural substance in red wine known as *resveratrol* has been identified as a possible factor in explaining the health benefits of drinking red wine. Mice administered resveratrol in very large quantities were higher in endurance levels, relative to controls, and were less susceptible to the elevations in glucose and insulin that normally result from eating a high-fat diet. However, these animals received a daily dosage of resveratrol far larger than a human would ingest from drinking wine, so the question of whether this substance is a key factor remains unsettled. Human intake of resveratrol at comparable dosages would have a significant potential for acute toxicity (Chapter 2).[49]

The benefits evidently extend beyond coronary heart disease. Moderate alcohol intake reduces the risk of diabetes mellitus, reduces the risk of stroke, and reduces the risk of dementia (possibly by reducing the incidence of mini-strokes or by boosting concentrations of vitamin B_6, which is essential for the formation of essential brain chemicals). A recent study indicates that moderate alcohol consumption can also lower the risk of rheumatoid arthritis by up to 50 percent.[50]

Of course, the key to the health benefits of alcohol consumption lies in moderation. Moderate drinking has been defined as taking no more than one drink per day for women and no more than two drinks per day for men. The newest (2000) Dietary Guidelines for Americans, released by the U.S. Department of Agriculture and the U.S. Department of Health and Human Services, acknowledge the effect of alcohol in reducing the risk of coronary heart disease but limits the recommendation of moderate drinking to men over age forty-five and women over age fifty-five, a subpopulation that carries an elevated risk for the disease.

Despite the weight of evidence tilting toward the potential health benefits of alcohol, the medical field remains divided on the question of whether to encourage patients who do not drink alcohol to start at a moderate level of consumption. In some cases, moderate intake is not advisable. Even one drink per day slightly increases the risk for breast cancer in women, and in no circumstances should alcohol be consumed during pregnancy. Some public health researchers are concerned that an endorsement of moderate alcohol drinking may open up a range of possible risks, in effect giving alcohol a kind of "halo effect" that might be confusing to the public. Besides, an argument can be made that moderate alcohol drinking is simply a behavior that coincides with a healthful lifestyle in the first place, rather than a behavior that actually makes you healthy.[51]

Strategies for Responsible Drinking

This chapter has focused on the various negative consequences of alcohol consumption on physiological responses and behavior. Yet we need to remember that there are very large numbers of people who drink alcoholic beverages and avoid the adverse effects that have been detailed here. An overwhelming proportion of the population, for example, drinks on occasion, enjoy the experience, and have never engaged in any violent or aggressive acts. They drink in moderate amounts, according to the federal guidelines for diet and nutrition. In addition, they avoid situations (such as driving) in which alcohol consumption would impair their performance and endanger their lives. The issue of responsible drinking is an important one; it may not be easy for us to accomplish but, fortunately, guidelines exist that make it easier (Help Line).[52]

At the same time, it is important to remember that, regardless of how it is consumed, alcohol remains a drug with a significant potential for dependence. It is easy to get hooked. As it has been said, people may plan to get drunk, but no one plans to be an alcoholic. The problems surrounding chronic alcohol abuse and alcoholism are examined in the next chapter.

Help Line

Guidelines for Responsible Drinking

- **Know how much you are drinking.** Measure your drinks. Beer is often premeasured (unless you are drinking draft beer from a keg), but wine and liquor drinks frequently are not. Learn what a 5-ounce quantity of wine or a 1½-ounce shot of liquor looks like and use these measures to guide your drinking.

- **Choose beer or wine over liquor.** Beer especially will make you feel fuller more quickly, with a smaller intake of alcohol. But be careful. A 12-ounce beer is equivalent in alcohol content to a 5-ounce glass of wine or a 1-shot drink of liquor.

- **Drink slowly.** One drink an hour stays relatively even with your body's metabolism of the alcohol you consume. Sipping your drinks is a good strategy for slowing down your consumption. If you are a man, you'll look cool; if you are a woman, you'll look refined.

- **Don't cluster your drinking.** If you are going to have seven drinks during a week, don't drink them all on the weekend.

- **Eat something substantial while you are drinking.** Protein is an excellent accompaniment to alcohol. Avoid salty foods because they will make you thirstier and more inclined to have another drink.

- **Drink only when you are already relaxed.** Chronic alcohol abuse occurs more easily when alcohol is viewed as a way to relax. If you have a problem, seek some nondrug alternative.

- **When you drink, savor the experience.** If you focus on the quality of what you drink rather than the quantity you are drinking, you will avoid drinking too much.

- **Never drink alone.** Drinking is never an appropriate answer to social isolation. Besides, when there are people around, there is someone to look out for you.

- **Beware of unfamiliar drinks.** Some drinks, such as zombies and other fruit and rum drinks, are deceptively high in kinds of alcohol that are not easily detected by taste.

- **Never drive a car after having had a drink.** Driving impairment begins after consumption of very low quantities of alcohol.

- **Be a good host or hostess.** If you are serving alcohol at a party, do not make drinking the focus of activity. Do not refill your guests' glasses. Discourage intoxication and do not condone drunkenness. Provide transportation options for those who drink at your party. Present nonalcoholic beverages as prominently as alcoholic ones. Prior to the end of the party, stop serving alcohol and offer coffee or other warm nonalcoholic beverages and a substantial snack, providing an interval of nondrinking time before people leave.

- **Support organizations that encourage responsible drinking.** If you are on a college campus, get involved with the local chapter of BACCHUS (Boost Alcohol Consciousness Concerning the Health of University Students). If there is no chapter, start one.

Where to go for assistance:

www.indiana.edu/~engs/hints/holiday.html

This web site on sensible, moderate, and responsible alcohol consumption and party hosting is adapted from Engs, R.C. (1987). *Alcohol and other drugs: Self responsibility.* Bloomington, IN: Tichenor Publishing.

Sources: Gross, Leonard (1983). *How much is too much? The effects of social drinking.* New York: Random House, pp. 149–152. Hanson, David J., and Engs, Ruth C. (1994). Drinking behavior: Taking personal responsibility. In Peter J. Venturelli (Ed.), *Drug use in America: Social, cultural, and political perspectives.* Boston: Jones and Bartlett, pp. 175–181. *Managing alcohol in your life.* Mansfield, MA: Steele Publishing and Consulting.

What Makes an Alcoholic Beverage?

- Drinkable alcohol is obtained from the fermentation of sugar in some natural products such as grapes, apples, honey, or molasses. The result is some form of wine.

- Beer is obtained from barley, after the starch has first been converted into sugar, fermented along with other grains and hops, and aged.

- To obtain very strong alcoholic beverages, it is necessary to boil the fermented liquid and condense it later by cooling. This process, called distillation, results in alcohol concentrations of up to 95 percent, and the products are known as distilled spirits or liquors.

Alcohol Use through History

- The history of alcohol use dates back many thousands of years; the process of fermentation is very simple and its discovery was probably accidental.

- Distillation techniques were perfected during the Middle Ages, with brandy being the first distilled spirit. In later centuries, gin gained popularity in Europe, as did whiskey in the United States.

- Serious concern about the adverse consequences of chronic alcohol abuse arose in the late 1700s and took root in the United States as a temperance movement. This movement addressed primarily the drinking of distilled spirits.

- The differentiation among forms of alcohol drinking became blurred during the nineteenth century, as temperance advocates began to promote a total ban on alcohol consumption. National Prohibition was the law in the United States from 1920 to 1933.

- Since the end of Prohibition, government regulation has been carried out chiefly through education and the taxation of alcohol.

Patterns of Alcohol Consumption Today

- The demographics of alcohol consumption reveal a large disparity in the drinking habits of the population. About a third do not drink at all, and only about 30 percent of those who drink account for 80 percent of all the alcoholic beverages consumed in the United States.

- Peak alcohol consumption occurs at ages twenty-one to twenty-two.

The Pharmacology of Alcohol

- Alcohol is a very small molecule, easily soluble in both water and fat. Its absorption into the bloodstream is extremely rapid. The breakdown of alcohol is handled by two special enzymes in the stomach and liver.

- The rate of alcohol biodegradation is constant, so alcohol can leave the body only at a specific pace, no matter what the quantity taken in.

- The effective level of alcohol in the body is measured by the blood-alcohol concentration (BAC) level, which adjusts for differences in body weight and the time since ingestion of the last alcoholic beverage.

Effects of Alcohol on the Brain

- Although alcohol affects several neurotransmitters in the brain, it is presently agreed that the principal effect is stimulation of the GABA receptor.

- Generally, the neural effect of alcohol proceeds downward, beginning with inhibition of the cerebral cortex, then that of lower brain regions. Inhibition of respiratory systems in the medulla, usually accomplished at BAC levels in the neighborhood of 0.50 percent, results in asphyxiation and death.

Acute Physiological Effects

- Alcohol at very high levels produces life-threatening consequences and at moderate levels produces a loss of body heat, increased excretion of water, an increase in heart rate and constriction of coronary arteries, disturbed patterns of sleep, and serious interactions with other drugs.

Acute Behavioral Effects

- On a behavioral level, serious adverse effects include blackouts, significant impairment in sensorimotor skills such as driving an automobile, and an increased potential for aggressive or violent acts. Particular attention has been directed toward these problems within a college student population.

- The relationship between alcohol consumption and sexual desire and performance is a complex one, with differences being observed for men and women.

Alcohol and Health Benefits

- The accumulated evidence of medical research has indicated that there is a reduced risk for coronary heart disease and stroke with moderate consumption of alcohol. Possible health benefits include a reduction of risk for diabetes, dementia, and rheumatoid arthritis.

- Moderate alcohol consumption has been defined as no more than one drink per day for women and no more than two drinks per day for men. There should be zero tolerance for alcohol consumption among pregnant women.

Strategies for Responsible Drinking

- Despite the potential for alcohol consumption to produce adverse effects, most people can drink alcohol in a responsible way that avoids these harmful consequences. However, the risk of alcohol dependence is always present.

Key Terms

acetaldehyde, p. 304
acetaldehyde dehydrogenase, p. 305
acetic acid, p. 305
alcohol dehydrogenase, p. 304
antidiuresis, p. 308

antidiuretic hormone (ADH), p. 308
aqua vitae, p. 296
balanced placebo design, p. 313
barley malt, p. 294
blackout, p. 310

blood-alcohol concentration (BAC), p. 306
brewing, p. 294
congeners, p. 310
distillation, p. 294
distilled spirits, p. 295
ethyl alcohol, p. 294

fermentation, p. 294
mash, p. 294
oxidation, p. 304
temperance movement, p. 297

Endnotes

1. Pinel, John P. J. (2003). *Biopsychology* (5th ed.). Boston: Allyn and Bacon, p. 381.
2. Warren, Kenneth R., and Hewitt, Brenda G. (2010). NIAAA: Advancing alcohol research for 40 years. *Alcohol Research and Health*, 33, 5–17.
3. Gibbons, Boyd (1992, February). Alcohol: The legal drug. *National Geographic Magazine*, pp. 2–35. McGovern, Patrick E.; Glusker, Donald L.; Exner, Lawrence J.; and Voigt, Mary M. (1996). Neolithic resinated wine. *Nature*, 381, 480–481. Roueché, Berton (1963). Alcohol in human culture. In Salvatore P. Lucia (Ed.), *Alcohol and civilization*. New York: McGraw-Hill, pp. 167–182. Vallee, Bert L. (1998, June). Alcohol in the western world. *Scientific American*, pp. 80–85.
4. Sournia, Jean-Charles (1990). *A history of alcoholism*. Cambridge, MA: Basil Blackwell, pp. 14–50. U.S. Department of Health, Education, and Welfare (1978). *Perspectives on the history of psychoactive substance use*, pp. 67–75.
5. Grimes, William (1993). *Straight up or on the rocks: A cultural history of American drink*. New York: Simon and Schuster, p. 36. Musto, David F. (1996, April). Alcohol in American history. *Scientific American*, pp. 78–83.
6. Lender, Mark E., and Martin, James K. (1982). *Drinking in America: A history*. New York: Free Press, pp. 13–14.
7. First in war, peace—and hooch, by George! (2000, December 7). *Newsday*, p. A86. Grimes, *Straight up*, p. 51.
8. Quoted in Sournia, Jean-Charles (1990). *A history of alcoholism*. Cambridge, MA: Basil Blackwell, p. 29.
9. Lincoln, Abraham (1842/1989). Address to the Washingtonian Temperance Society of Springfield, Illinois. *Speeches and writings, 1832–1858*. New York: Library of America, p. 84.
10. Lender, Mark E., and Martin, James R. (1982). *Drinking in America: A history*. New York: Free Press, p. 107. Okrent, Daniel (2010). *Last call: The rise and fall of Prohibition*. New York: Scribner.
11. Blocker, Jack S. (2006, February). Did Prohibition really work? Alcohol prohibition as a public health innovation. *American Journal of Public Health*, pp. 233–243. Lerner, Michael A. (2007). *Dry Manhattan*, Cambridge, MA: Harvard University Press. Musto, David F. (1996, April). Alcohol in American history. *Scientific American*, pp. 78–83. Sournia, *History of alcoholism*, p. 122.
12. Alcohol and Tobacco Tax and Trade Bureau, U.S. Department of the Treasury, Washington, DC. U.S. Department of Health and Human Services (2000). *Alcohol and health* (Tenth Special Report to the U.S. Congress). Rockville, MD: National Institute on Alcohol Abuse and Alcoholism, p. 370.
13. U.S. Department of Health and Human Services (2000). *Alcohol and health*, pp. 341–354.
14. Gibbons, Alcohol, p. 7.
15. Garfield, Craig F., Chung, Paul J., and Rathouz, Paul J. (2003). Alcohol advertising in magazines and adolescent readership. *Journal of the American Medical Association*, 289, 2424–2429. Hanson, Glen R., and Li, Ting-Kai (2003). Public health implications of excessive alcohol

consumption. *Journal of the American Medical Association, 289*, 1031–1032. National Association of Convenience Stores (2008). That's the spirit—U.S. alcohol sales growing. www.nacsonline.com. US top five beer companies ranked by prime-time network television advertising outlays in dollars with the top three network TV programs ranked by beer ad expenditures. *Adweek* (2003, April 21), p. SR14.

16. Statistics on 2007 consumption levels from the National Institute on Alcohol Abuse and Alcoholism, Bethesda, MD.

17. Center for Science in the Public Interest (2003, December 16). Press release: "Alcohol facts" label proposed for beer, wine, and liquor. Center for Science in the Public Interest, Washington, DC. Rogers, John D., and Greenfield, Thomas K. (1999). Beer drinking accounts for most of the hazardous alcohol consumption reported in the United States. *Journal of Studies on Alcohol, 60*, 732–739.

18. Busteed, Brandon (2010, March 19). Is high-risk drinking at college on the way out? *Chronicle of Higher Education*, p. A76. Denizet-Lewis, Benoit (2005, January 5). Band of brothers. *New York Times Magazine*, pp. 32–33, 52, 73–74. Heeren, Timothy; Zakocs, Ronda C.; and Kopstein, Andrea (2002). Age of first intoxication, heavy drinking, driving after drinking and risk of unintentional injury among U.S. college students. *Journal of Studies on Alcohol, 63*, 136–144. Hingson, Ralph W., Zha, Wenxing, and Weitzman, Elissa R. (2009). Magnitude of and trends in alcohol-related mortality and morbidity among U.S. college students ages 18–24, 1998–2005. *Journal of Studies on Alcohol and Drugs, Supplement No. 16*, 12–20. National Institute on Alcohol and Alcohol Abuse (2007). *What colleges need to know now: An update on college drinking research.* Bethesda, MD: National Institute on Alcohol and Alcohol Abuse. National Institute on Alcohol and Alcohol Abuse (2010). Statistical snapshot of college drinking. Bethesda, MD: National Institute on Alcohol and Alcohol Abuse. Wechsler, Henry, and Nelson, Toben F. (2008). What we have learned from the Harvard School of Public Health College Alcohol Study: Focusing attention on college student alcohol consumption and the environmental conditions that promote it. *Journal of Studies on Alcohol and Drugs, 69*, 1–10.; Wechsler, Henry; Lee, Jae Eun; Kuo, Meichun; Seibring, Mark; Nelson, Toben F.; et al. (2002). Trends in college binge drinking during a period of increased prevention efforts: Findings from four Harvard School of Public Health College Alcohol Study Surveys: 1993–2001. *Journal of American College Health, 50*, 203–217. Zernike, Kate (2005, March 15). A 21st-birthday drinking game can be a deadly rite of passage. *New York Times*, pp. A1, A13.

19. Johnston, Lloyd D.; O'Malley, Patrick M.; Bachman, Jerald G.; and Schulenberg, John E. (2009, December 14). Teen marijuana use tilts up, while some drugs decline in use. Ann Arbor: University of Michigan News Service, Figures 1 and 4. Substance Abuse and Mental Health Services Administration (2008, June 26). News release: New nationwide report estimates that 40 percent of

underage drinkers received free alcohol from adults over 21. Rockville, MD: Substance Abuse and Mental Health Services Administration. Substance Abuse and Mental Health Services Administration (2008, August 28). Underage alcohol use: Where do young people drink? *The NSDUH Report.* Rockville MD: Office of Applied Studies, Substance Abuse and Mental Health Administration. Windle, Michael, and Zucker, Robert A. (2010). Reducing underage and young adult drinking: How to address critical drinking problems during this developmental period. *Alcohol Research and Health, 33*, 29–44.

20. U.S. Department of Health and Human Services (1990). *Alcohol and health.* (The Seventh Special Report to the U.S. Congress). Rockville, MD: National Institute on Alcohol Abuse and Alcoholism.

21. Dubowski, Kurt M. (1991). *The technology of breath-alcohol analysis.* Rockville, MD: National Institute on Alcohol Abuse and Alcoholism.

22. Julien, Robert M. (2000). *A primer of drug action* (9th ed.). New York: Worth, p. 95.

23. National Institute on Alcohol Abuse and Alcoholism (2007, April). Alcohol alert: Alcohol metabolism: An update. No. 72. Rockville, MD: National Institute on Alcohol Abuse and Alcoholism. Julien, *A primer of drug action*, pp. 91–97.

24. Suter, Paolo M., Schutz, Yves, and Jequier, Eric (1992). The effect of ethanol on fat storage in healthy subjects. *New England Journal of Medicine, 326*, 983–987.

25. Hawks, Richard L., and Chiang, C. Nora (1986). Examples of specific drug assays. In Richard L. Hawks and C. Nora Chiang (Eds.), *Urine testing for drugs of abuse* (NIDA Research Monograph 73). Rockville, MD: National Institute on Drug Abuse, p. 103. Julien, *A primer of drug action*, pp. 91–97.

26. Levinthal, Charles F. (1990). *Introduction to physiological psychology* (3rd ed.). Englewood Cliffs, NJ: Prentice Hall, pp. 181–184.

27. U.S. Department of Health and Human Services (1994). *Alcohol and health.* (The Eighth Special Report to the U.S. Congress). Bethesda, MD: National Institute on Alcohol Abuse and Alcoholism, pp. 4–6, 4–7.

28. Koob, G. F.; Rassnick, S.; Heinrichs, S.; and Weiss, F. (1994). Alcohol, the reward system and dependence. In B. Jansson, H. Jörnvall, U. Rydberg, L. Terenius, and B. L. Vallee (Eds.), *Toward a molecular basis of alcohol use and abuse.* Basel: Birkhäuser-Verlag, pp. 103–114. Rosenbloom, Margaret J, and Pfefferbaum, Adolf (2008), Magnetic resonance imaging of the living brain. Evidence for brain degeneration among alcoholics and recovery with abstinence. *Alcohol Research and Health, 31*, 362–376.

29. Grilly, David M. (2006). *Drugs and human behavior* (5th ed.). Boston: Allyn and Bacon, p. 144.

30. Luks, Allan, and Barbato, Joseph (1989). *You are what you drink.* New York: Villiard, pp. 42–43.

31. National Institute on Alcohol Abuse and Alcoholism (1998, July). Alcohol alert: Alcohol and sleep. No. 41. Bethesda, MD: National Institute on Alcohol Abuse and Alcoholism.

32. O'Connor, Mary J., and Wahley, Shannon E. (2007). Brief intervention for alcohol use by pregnant women. *American Journal of Public Health*, 97, 252–258. Substance Abuse and Mental Health Services Administration (2009). *Results from the 2008 National Survey on Drug Use and Health: National findings.* Rockville, MD: Office of Applied Studies, Substance Abuse and Mental Health Services Administration, p. 33.

33. Schuckit, Marc A. (1989). *Drug and alcohol abuse: A clinical guide to diagnosis and treatment* (3rd ed.). New York: Plenum, p. 62.

34. Wiese, Jeffrey G., Shlipak, Michael G., and Browner, Warren S. (2000). The alcohol hangover. *Annals of Internal Medicine*, 232, 897–902.

35. Victor, Maurice (1976). Treatment of alcohol intoxication and the withdrawal syndrome: A critical analysis of the use of drugs and other forms of therapy. In Peter G. Bourne (Ed.), *Acute drug emergencies: A treatment manual.* New York: Academic Press, p. 199.

36. Luks and Barbato, *You are what you drink*, pp. 52–53. White, Aaron M., Jamieson-Drake, David W., and Swartzwelder, H. Scott (2002). Prevalence and correlates of alcohol-induced blackouts among college students: Results of an e-mail survey. *Journal of American College Health*, 51, 117–131.

37. National Highway Traffic Safety Administration (2010, August). Highlights of 2009 motor crashes. Washington, DC: National Center for Statistics and Analysis, National Highway Traffic Safety Administration.

38. Hoyer, William J., Semenec, Silvie C., and Buchler, Norbou E. G. (2007). Acute alcohol intoxication impairs controlled search across the visual field. *Journal of Studies on Alcohol and Drugs*, 68, 748–758. National Institute on Alcohol Abuse and Alcoholism (1996, January). Alcohol Alert: Drinking and driving. No. 31, PH362. Bethesda, MD: National Institute on Alcohol Abuse and Alcoholism.

39. Gross, Leonard (1983). *How much is too much: The effects of social drinking.* New York: Random House, p. 29. Quotation of Dr. Herbert Moskowitz.

40. National Institute on Alcohol Abuse and Alcoholism (2001, April). Alcohol alert: Alcohol and transportation safety. No. 52. Bethesda, MD: National Institute on Alcohol Abuse and Alcoholism. Wagenaar, Alexander C., O'Malley, Patrick M., and LaFond, Colette (2001). Lowered legal blood alcohol limits for young drivers: Effects on drinking, driving, and driving-after-drinking behaviors in 30 states. *American Journal of Public Health*, 91, 801–803.

41. National Highway Traffic Safety Administration (2009, June). Lives saved in 2008 by restraint use and minimum drinking age laws. *Traffic Safety Facts.* Washington, DC: National Center for Statistics and Analysis, National Highway Traffic Safety Administration U.S. Department of Health and Human Services (1990). *Alcohol and health*, pp. 216–217. Wald, Matthew L. (2006, November 20). A new strategy to discourage driving drunk. *New York Times*, pp. A1, A20.

42. Wald, A new strategy, pp. A1, A20.

43. Hingson, Ralph; Heeren, Timothy; Zakocs, Ronda; Winter, Michael; and Wechsler, Henry (2003). Age of first intoxication, heavy drinking, driving after drinking and risk of unintentional injury among U.S. college students. *Journal of Studies on Alcohol*, 64, 23–31. National Highway Traffic Administration (1999, March). The relationship of alcohol safety laws to drinking drivers in fatal crashes. Washington, DC: U.S. Department of Transportation. Substance Abuse and Mental Health Services Administration (2009). *Results from the 2008 National Survey on Drug Use and Health: Detailed tables.* Rockville, MD: Office of Applied Studies, Substance Abuse and Mental Health Services Administration, Table 3.4.

44. Abbey, Antonia; Zawacki, Tina; Buck, Philip O.; Clinton, A. Monique; and McAuslan, Pam (2004). Sexual assault and alcohol consumption: What do we know about their relationship and what types of research are still needed? *Aggression and Violent Behavior*, 9, 271–303. Haggård-Grann, Ulrika; Hallqvist, Johan; Långström, Niklas; and Möller, Jette (2006). The role of alcohol and drugs in triggering criminal violence: A case-crossover study. *Addiction*, 101, 100–108. Pernanen, Kai (1991). *Alcohol in human violence.* New York: Guilford Press, pp. 192–193.

45. Collins, James J., and Messerschmidt, Pamela M. (1993). Epidemiology of alcohol-related violence. *Alcohol Health and Research World*, 17, 93–100. Goode, Erich (2008). *Drugs in American society* (7th ed.). New York: McGraw-Hill, pp. 343–346. National Institute on Alcohol Abuse and Alcoholism (1997, October). Alcohol alert: Alcohol, violence, and aggression. No. 38. Bethesda, MD: National Institute on Alcohol Abuse and Alcoholism.

46. Giancola, Peter R. (2000). Executive functioning: A conceptual framework for alcohol-related aggression. *Experimental and Clinical Psychopharmacology*, 8, 576–597. Giancola, Peter R. (2002). Alcohol-related aggression in men and women: The influence of dispositional aggressivity. *Journal of Studies on Alcohol*, 63, 696–708. Norris, Jeanette; David, Kelly Cue; George, William H.; Martell, Joel; and Heiman, Julia R. (2002). Alcohol's direct and indirect effects on men's self-reported sexual aggression likelihood. *Journal of Studies on Alcohol*, 63, 688–695.

47. Foran, Heather M., and O'Leary, K. Daniel (2008). Alcohol and intimate partner violence: A meta-analytic review. *Clinical Psychology Review*, 28, 1222–1234. Pernanen, Kai (1993). Research approaches in the study of alcohol-related violence. *Alcohol Health and Research World*, 17, 101–107.

48. Abel, Ernest L. (1985). *Psychoactive drugs and sex.* New York: Plenum Press, pp. 19–54. Cooper, M. Lynne (2006). Does drinking promote risky sexual behavior? A complex answer to a simple question. *Current Directions in Psychological Science*, 15, 19–23. Testa, Maria, Vanzile-Tamsen, Carol, and Livingston, Jennifer A. (2004). The role of victim and perpetrator intoxication on sexual assault outcomes. *Journal of Studies on Alcohol*, 65, 320–329.

49. Rimm, Eric B. (2000). Moderate alcohol intake and lower risk of coronary heart disease: Meta-analysis of effects on lipids and haemostatic factors. *Journal of the American Medical Association, 283,* 1269. Wade, Nicholas (2006, November 2). Yes, red wine holds answer. Check dosage. Zuger, Abigail (2002, December 31). The case for drinking (all together now: in moderation). *New York Times,* pp. F1, F6. Quotation on p. F1.

50. Howard, Andrea A., Arnsten, Julia H., and Gourevitch, Marc N. (2004). Effect of alcohol consumption on diabetes mellitus: A systematic review. *Annals of Internal Medicine, 140,* 211–219. Källberg, Henrik; Jacobsen, Soren; Bengtsson, Camilla; Pdersen, Merete; Padyukov, Leonid; et al. (2009). Alcohol consumption is associated with decreased risk of rheumatoid arthritis: Results from two Scandinavian case-control studies. *Annals of the Rheumatic Diseases, 68,* 222–227. Mukamal, Kenneth J.; Conigrave, Katherine M.; Mittleman, Murray A.; Carmargo, Carlos A., Jr.; Stampfer, Meir J.; et al. (2003). Roles of drinking pattern and type of alcohol consumed in coronary heart disease in men. *New England Journal of Medicine, 348,* 109–118. Mukamal, Kenneth J.; Kuller, Lewis H.; Longstreth, W. T.; Mittleman, Murray A; and Siscovick, David S. (2003). Prospective study of alcohol consumption and risk of dementia in older adults. *Journal of the American Medical Association, 289,* 1405–1413. Reynold, Kristi; Lewis, L. Brian; Nolen, John David L.; Kinney, Gregory L.; Sathya, Bhavani; et al. (2003). Alcohol consumption and risk of stroke: A meta-analysis. *Journal of the American Medical Association, 289,* 579–588.

51. Alcohol Policies Project, Center for Science in the Public Interest (2000). Victory for public health: New U.S. guidelines on alcohol consumption drop positive spin on drinking. Washington, DC: Center for Science in the Public Interest. The Gallup Organization (2005, July 22). Fewer young adults drinking to excess. Gallup Organization, Princeton, NJ. Goldberg, Ira (2003). To drink or not to drink. *New England Journal of Medicine, 348,* 163–164. Klatsky, Arthur (2003, February). Drink to your health? *Scientific American,* pp. 75–81. Rabin, Roni Caryn (2009, June 19). Alcohol's good for you? Some scientists doubt it. *New York Times,* pp. D1, D6.

52. Darby, William, and Heinz, Agnes (1991, January). *The responsible use of alcohol: Defining the parameters of moderation.* New York: American Council on Science and Health, pp. 1–26.

chapter 14

Chronic Alcohol Abuse and Alcoholism

When you live in an alcoholic family, you lie in bed some-times and imagine how things could be different. You dream that you could actually invite your friends over to hang out at your house. You dream that the family car wouldn't get its fenders bashed in on a regular basis. You dream that the money you made mowing lawns didn't end up missing from your room. You dream that you didn't have to plead with them to quit drinking—time after time. You dream that enlisting in the military isn't just a way of getting out of the house. You dream that your life is nor-mal, except that you have no idea what normal is.

—Thoughts of a teenager in an alcoholic family[1]

After you have completed this chapter, you should have an understanding of

- Problems surrounding the definition of alcoholism
- The history of attempts to regulate chronic alcohol abuse
- Physiological effects of chronic alcohol abuse
- Patterns of chronic alcohol abuse
- Special problems among the elderly
- Family dynamics in alcoholism
- Genetic and environmental influences in alcoholism
- Approaches to treatment for alcoholism
- Chronic alcohol abuse and alcoholism in the workplace

Chronic abuse of alcohol has been called the hidden addiction. There is no need to get out on the street and find a drug dealer; for many people, it is remarkably easy to conceal their problem (at least in the beginning) from family and friends. Alcohol consumption is so tightly woven into the social fabric of our lives that it may be difficult to catch on that an individual is drinking too much too often. All too frequently, chronic abuse of alcohol has been treated as a genteel affair, rarely with the same degree of concern as that associated with the chronic abuse of other drugs. Yet from a pharmacological point of view, it is the same, and we have to realize that fact. This chapter will deal with the very serious consequences of this condition on almost 20 million Americans and their families, as well as for society at large.

Alcoholism: Stereotypes, Definitions, and Criteria

Close your eyes and try to imagine what an alcoholic looks like. You might form an image of someone, probably male, homeless, and dirty, perhaps with a bottle of cheap wine in his hands, living from day to day in a state of deteriorating health, with no one caring about him except a social worker or police officer or, inevitably, the medical examiner. But you would be imagining less than 5 percent of all alcoholics; more than 95 percent of them look quite different. They have jobs, a home, and a family. The demographics of alcoholism include every possible category. Alcoholics can be fourteen or eighty-four years of age, male or female, professional or blue-collar. They can be urbanites, suburbanites, or rural residents in any community.

What aspects of their behavior tie them all together, allowing us to describe their condition with a single label? Because of the wide diversity of alcoholics, it has been difficult to come up with one encompassing definition of alcoholism. Instead, we rely on a set of criteria—basically a collection of signs, symptoms, and behaviors that help us make the diagnosis. A single individual may not meet all of these criteria, but if he or she fulfills enough of them, we decide that the standard has been met.

The criteria adopted here focus on four basic life problems that are tied to the consumption of alcohol:

> **alcoholism:** A condition in which the consumption of alcohol has produced major psychological, physical, social, or occupational problems.
>
> **symptomatic drinking:** A pattern of alcohol consumption aimed at reducing stress and anxiety.

(1) problems associated with a preoccupation with drinking, (2) emotional problems, (3) vocational, social, and family problems, and (4) problems associated with physical health. Notice that these criteria make no mention of the cause or causes of alcoholism and reflect only its behavioral, social, and physical consequences. In short, we are recognizing that **alcoholism** is a complex phenomenon with psychological-behavioral components (criteria 1 and 2), social components (criterion 3), and a physical component (criterion 4).

Problems Associated with a Preoccupation with Drinking

The dominant characteristic of alcoholics is their preoccupation with the act of drinking and their incorporation of drinking into their everyday lives. An alcoholic may need a drink prior to a social occasion to feel "fortified." With increasing frequency, such a person sees alcohol as a way of dealing with stress and anxiety. Drinking itself becomes a routine, no longer a social, affair. The habit of taking a few drinks upon arriving home from work each day is an example of **symptomatic drinking**, in which alcohol is viewed specifically as a way of relieving tension. Also increasing is the incidence of unintentional states of severe intoxication and blackouts of events surrounding the time of drinking, a condition quite different from "passing out" from a high BAC level. One such occurrence may not be a particularly critical sign, but recurrences definitely are.[2]

Traditionally, alcoholism is associated with consumption of a large quantity of alcohol. This sounds pretty obvious and is true of most alcoholics, but we still have to be careful about overgeneralizing. There are significant differences in the way alcoholics consume their alcohol. Not all of them drink alone or begin every day with a drink. Many of them drink on a daily basis, but others are spree or binge alcoholics who might become grossly intoxicated on occasion and totally abstain from drinking the rest of the time.[3]

Another feature often attributed to alcoholics is loss of control over their drinking. The alcoholic typically craves a drink and frequently engages in compulsive behavior related to alcohol. There may be a stockpiling of liquor, taking a drink or two before going to a party, or feeling uncomfortable unless alcohol is present. The alcoholic may be sneaking drinks or having drinks that others do not know about, such as surreptitiously having an extra drink or two in the kitchen out of the sight of the party guests.[4] Particularly when the alcoholic is trying to abstain from alcohol or to reduce the quantity of alcohol consumed, his or her thoughts

The typical alcoholic American

Doctor, age 54

Farmer, age 35

Unemployed, age 40

College student, age 19

Counselor, age 38

Retired editor, age 86

Dancer, age 22

Police officer, age 46

Military officer, age 31

Student, age 14

Executive, age 50

Taxi driver, age 61

Homemaker, age 43

Bricklayer, age 29

Computer programmer, age 25

Lawyer, age 52

There's no such thing as typical. We have all kinds.
10 million Americans are alcoholic.
It's our number one drug problem.

Alcoholism affects such a diverse group of people that it is virtually impossible to make generalizations about the typical profile of an alcoholic. Here are sixteen examples of individuals with whom many people might not have immediately associated the term "alcoholic." Note the example in the extreme upper right of the picture.

become focused on the possibility of drinking or on ways to rationalize it.[5]

Yet professionals disagree about whether all alcoholics are necessarily out of control with respect to alcohol. As discussed later in the chapter, this controversy has major implications for choosing the treatment approach in cases of alcohol abuse. If it is true that even a small amount of alcohol will propel a recovering alcoholic back to alcohol abuse, then a primary focus of treatment should be on no drinking at all, better known as absolute **abstinence**. If it is not true, then there is the possibility of controlled drinking without the fear of "falling off the wagon." The well-known alcohol treatment program Alcoholics Anonymous, for example, functions under the assumption that an alcoholic must never drink again, even in minute quantities, if recovery is to be sustained.

Emotional Problems

Given that alcohol is a depressant drug on the central nervous system, it should not be surprising that chronic alcohol intake produces depressive symptoms. Serious depressions and thoughts of suicide frequently occur in the midst of heavy drinking. However, only about 15 percent of individuals who meet the criteria for alcohol dependence (see page 328) have experienced major depression either before the onset of their alcoholic condition or during extended periods of abstinence. Therefore, it is reasonable to conclude that the depressive symptoms are alcohol-induced. Alcoholics are no more likely than others in the general population to have suffered an episode of major depression.[6]

Vocational, Social, and Family Problems

No one questions the potential problems that chronic alcohol abuse can bring to the maintenance of a job or career, social relationships, and a stable family life. These three areas frequently intertwine, and trouble in one usually exacerbates trouble in the others. A job loss puts stress on marital and family relationships, just as marital and family difficulties put stress on occupational performance.

Numerous clinical studies support the idea of increased domestic instability in the lives of alcoholics,

---

abstinence: The avoidance of some consumable item or behavior.

enablers: Individuals whose behavior consciously or unconsciously encourages another person's continuation in a pattern of alcohol or other drug abuse.

---

but the true extent of these problems is difficult to assess. Family violence, for example, is frequently examined through cases seen in treatment or social service programs. As a result, these agencies may interpret the domestic behavior of a father not known to have a drinking problem differently from that of a father with a history of alcoholism. A man who drinks heavily and abuses his children may be more likely to be "counted" as an alcoholic than a nonabusive father who consumes just as much alcohol. It is much easier to assess the likelihood of domestic violence or decline in job performance due to acute intoxication than it is to evaluate the influence of chronic abuse of alcohol. Even so, there is no doubt that the cumulative effects of alcoholism on family dynamics are devastating.[7]

Physical Problems

There is also no question that chronic alcohol consumption has a destructive effect on the body. Not surprisingly, a principal site of damage is the brain. Neuroimaging procedures, such as CT and MRI brain scans, reveal a consistent link between heavy drinking and physical shrinkage of brain matter, particularly in the cerebral cortex, cerebellum, and regions associated with memory and other cognitive functions. These neurological changes are observed even in the absence of other alcohol-related medical conditions such as chronic liver disease.[8]

Hiding the Problems: Denial and Enabling

The major life problems that serve as rough criteria for determining the condition of alcoholism are often not recognized by alcoholics themselves because of their tendency to deny that their drinking has any influence on their lives or the lives of people around them. When in denial, the alcoholic can be extremely sensitive to any mention of problems associated with drinking. A hangover the next day, for example, is seldom discussed because it would draw attention to the fact that drinking has occurred.[9]

Denial also can be manifest among the people around the alcoholic. Members of an alcoholic's family, for example, may try to function as if life were normal. Through their excuse making and efforts to undo or cover up the frequent physical and psychological damage the alcoholic causes, they inadvertently prevent the alcoholic from seeking treatment or delay that treatment until the alcoholism is more severe. These people are referred to as **enablers** because they enable the alcoholic to

Help Line

A Self-Administered Short Michigan Alcoholism Screening Test (SMAST)

The Michigan Alcoholism Screening Test (MAST), twenty-four questions to be answered in ten to fifteen minutes, is designed as a structured interview instrument to detect alcoholism. A shorter thirteen-question version (SMAST-13), shown here, has approximately the same level of reliability and validity. Score one point for each response that matches the one in parentheses. According to the authors of the test, a total score of 0 or 1 indicates a nonalcoholic, 2 a possible alcoholic, and 3 or more an alcoholic.

1. Do you feel you are a normal drinker? (By normal we mean you drink less than or as much as most other people.) (NO)
2. Does your wife, husband, a parent, or other near relative ever worry or complain about your drinking? (YES)
3. Do you ever feel guilty about your drinking? (YES)
4. Do friends or relatives think you are a normal drinker? (NO)
5. Are you able to stop drinking when you want to? (NO)
6. Have you ever attended a meeting of Alcoholics Anonymous? (YES)
7. Has drinking ever created problems between you and your wife, husband, a parent, or other near relative? (YES)
8. Have you ever gotten into trouble at work because of drinking? (YES)
9. Have you ever neglected your obligations, your family, or your work for two or more days in a row because you were drinking? (YES)
10. Have you ever gone to anyone for help about your drinking? (YES)
11. Have you ever been in a hospital because of drinking? (YES)
12. Have you ever been arrested for drunken driving, driving while intoxicated, or driving under the influence of alcoholic beverages? (YES)
13. Have you ever been arrested, even for a few hours, because of other drunken behavior? (YES)

Sources: Barry, Kristen L., and Fleming, Michael F. (1993). The Alcohol Use Disorders Identification Test (AUDIT) and the SMAST-13: Predictive validity in a rural primary care sample. *Alcohol and Alcoholism, 28*, 33–42. Selzer, Melvin L., Vinokur, Amiram, and van Rooijen, Louis (1975). A self-administered Short Michigan Alcoholism Screening Test (SMAST). *Journal of Studies on Alcohol, 36*, 117–126.

function as an alcoholic as opposed to a sober person. Both processes of denial and enabling present major difficulties not only in establishing problem-oriented criteria for diagnosing alcoholism but also in introducing necessary interventions. Denial and enabling are clearly relevant processes in the area of alcoholism, but it is not difficult to see that they present problems with regard to *any* form of substance abuse (see Chapter 16).

Help Line provides a useful self-survey for identifying the signs of potential alcoholism.

Alcohol Abuse and Alcohol Dependence: The Health Care Professional's View

As you can see, the criteria commonly employed in determining the presence of alcoholism are at times quite murky, and often there are nearly as many counterexamples to each of the criteria as there are examples.

The American Psychiatric Association, through its *Diagnostic and Statistical Manual, Text Revision*, fourth edition (DSM-IV-TR), has attempted to put together as many common features as possible and has established two basic syndromes. It is important to understand these technical definitions, because professionals in the field of alcoholism commonly use the DSM-IV-TR either in their research or in clinical practice.[10]

The first syndrome, referred to as **alcohol abuse**, is characterized as either (1) the continued use of alcohol for at least one month despite the knowledge of having a persistent or recurring physical problem or some difficulty in social or occupational functioning, or (2) the recurring use of alcohol in situations (such as driving) when alcohol consumption is physically hazardous.

alcohol abuse: A syndrome characterized primarily by the continued use of alcohol despite the drinker's knowledge of having a persistent physical problem or some social or occupational difficulty.

The second syndrome, referred to as **alcohol dependence**, is characterized as alcohol abuse that involves any three of the following seven circumstances:

- Consuming greater alcohol in amounts or over a longer period than the person intends
- A persistent desire, or one or more unsuccessful attempts, to cut down or control drinking
- A great deal of time spent drinking or recovering from the effects of drinking
- Alcohol consumption continuing despite knowledge that drinking either causes or exacerbates recurrent physical or psychological problems

- Important social, occupational, or recreational activities given up or reduced because of alcohol
- Marked tolerance or the need to drink more than before to achieve previous levels of intoxication
- Symptoms of alcohol withdrawal or the consumption of alcohol to relieve or avoid withdrawal symptoms

Obviously, individuals who fit the second definition are considered more greatly impaired than those who fit the first. That distinction also was true with regard to the more general criteria for substance abuse and substance dependence (see Chapter 1). According to the DSM-IV-TR standards, approximately 8.5 percent of U.S. adults, about one in twelve, are either alcohol abusers or alcohol dependent.

As you might expect, the highest percentages of "heavy drinkers" are found among people eighteen to twenty-five years old. The "heavy drinker" category is defined as having consumed five or more alcoholic drinks on the same occasion on at least five different days within the previous month. The incidence among those eighteen to twenty-five years old has been estimated to be about 15 percent, with a peak incidence of 20 percent at age twenty-one.[11]

Physiological Effects of Chronic Alcohol Use

Let's look at what we know about the consequences of long-term (chronic) consumption of alcohol over and above the acute effects that were discussed in the last chapter.

Tolerance and Withdrawal

As with other CNS depressants, alcohol consumption over a period of time will result in a tolerance effect. On a metabolic level, alcohol dehydrogenase activity during tolerance becomes higher in the stomach and liver, allowing the alcohol to leave the body somewhat faster; on a neural level, the brain is less responsive to alcohol's depressive effects.[12] Therefore, if the level of alcohol consumption remains steady, an individual feels less of an effect.

As a result of tolerance and the tendency to compensate for it in terms of drinking a greater quantity, the chronic alcohol abuser is subject to increased physical risks. There are serious behavioral risks as well; for example, an alcohol-tolerant drinker may consider driving with a BAC level that exceeds the standard for

alcohol dependence: A syndrome in which alcohol abuse involves a variety of significant physical, psychological, social, and behavioral problems.

drunk driving, thinking that he or she is not intoxicated and hence not impaired. A person's driving ability, under these circumstances, will be substantially overestimated.

An alcohol-dependent person's abrupt withdrawal from alcohol can result in a range of serious physical symptoms beginning from six to forty-eight hours after the last drink, but estimates as to how many people are typically affected vary. Among hospitalized patients, only 5 percent appear to show withdrawal symptoms, whereas studies of alcoholics using outpatient facilities have estimated the percentage to be as high as 18. Although the exact incidence may be somewhat unclear, there is less disagreement aboutwhat takes place. Physical withdrawal effects are classified in two clusters of symptoms.

The first cluster, called the **alcohol withdrawal syndrome**, is the more common of the two. It begins with insomnia, vivid dreaming, and a severe hangover; these discomforts are followed by tremors (the "shakes"), sweating, mild agitation, anxiety (the "jitters"), nausea, and vomiting, as well as increased heart rate and blood pressure. In some patients, there are also brief tonic-clonic (grand mal) seizures, as the nervous system rebounds from the chronic depression induced by alcohol. The alcohol withdrawal syndrome usually reaches a peak from twenty-four to thirty-six hours after the last drink and is over after forty-eight hours.

The second cluster, called **delirium tremens (DTs)**, is much more dangerous and is fortunately less common. The symptoms include extreme disorientation and confusion, profuse sweating, fever, and disturbing nightmares. Typically, there are also periods of frightening hallucinations, when the individual might see snakes or insects on the walls, ceiling, or his or her skin. These effects generally reach a peak three to four days after the last drink. During this time, there is the possibility of life-threatening events such as heart failure, dehydration, or suicide, so it is critical for the individual to be hospitalized and under medical supervision at all times. The current medical practice for treating individuals undergoing withdrawal is to administer antianxiety medication (see Chapter 15) to relieve the symptoms. After the withdrawal period has ended, the dose levels of the medication are gradually reduced and discontinued.[13]

Liver Disease

Chronic consumption of alcohol produces three forms of liver disease. The first of these is a **fatty liver**, resulting from an abnormal concentration of fatty deposits inside liver cells. Normally, the liver breaks down fats adequately, but when alcohol is in the body the liver breaks down the alcohol at the expense of fats. As a result, fats accumulate and ultimately interfere with the functioning of the liver. The condition is fortunately reversible, if the drinker abstains. The accumulated fats are gradually metabolized, and the liver returns to normal.

The second condition is **alcoholic hepatitis**, an inflammation of liver tissue causing fever, jaundice (a yellowing of the skin), and abdominal pain, resulting at least in part from a lower functioning level of the immune system. It is also reversible with abstinence, though some residual scarring may remain.

The third and most serious liver condition is **alcoholic cirrhosis**, characterized by the progressive development of scar tissue that chokes off blood vessels in the liver and destroys liver cells by interfering with the cell's utilization of oxygen. At an early stage, the liver is enlarged from the accumulation of fats, but at later stages it is shrunken as liver cells begin to degenerate (Figure 14.1). Though abstinence helps to prevent further liver degeneration when cirrhosis is diagnosed, the condition is not reversible except by liver transplantation surgery.

Prior to the 1970s, alcoholic cirrhosis was attributed to nutritional deficiencies that are often associated with an alcoholic's diet. We know now that, although nutritional problems play a role, alcohol itself is toxic to the liver. After a pattern of heavy alcohol consumption of many years, it is possible to develop cirrhosis, even when nutrition is adequate. A major cause of liver cell damage is the toxic accumulation of free radicals, molecule fragments that are by-products of acetaldehyde (Chapter 13).

alcohol withdrawal syndrome: The more common of two general reactions to the cessation of alcohol consumption in an alcoholic. It is characterized by physiological discomfort, seizures, and sleep disturbances.

delirium tremens (DTs): The less common of two general reactions to the cessation of drinking in an alcoholic. It is characterized by extreme disorientation and confusion, fever, hallucinations, and other symptoms.

fatty liver: A condition in which fat deposits accumulate in the liver as a result of chronic alcohol abuse.

alcoholic hepatitis (AL-co-HAUL-ik hep-ah-TIE-tus): A disease involving inflammation of the liver as a result of chronic alcohol abuse.

alcoholic cirrhosis (AL-co-HAUL-ik seer-OH-sis): A disease involving scarring and deterioration of liver cells as a result of chronic alcohol abuse.

FIGURE 14.1

The dramatic difference between a healthy liver (top) and a cirrhotic liver (bottom).

Cirrhosis and other forms of chronic liver disease are collectively ranked as the twelfth leading cause of death in the United States, claiming more than 27,000 lives each year. Most deaths occur in people forty to sixty-five years old. Daily drinkers are at a higher risk of developing cirrhosis than binge drinkers, though this risk may be the result of the relatively larger quantity of alcohol consumed over a long period of time. Generally, patients showing liver damage have been drinking for ten to twenty years. Only 10 to 20 percent of all heavy drinkers develop cirrhosis, however, in contrast to 90 to 100 percent who show evidence of either fatty liver or hepatitis. There may be a genetic predisposition to cirrhosis that puts a subgroup of alcoholics at increased risk.[14]

Cardiovascular Problems

About one in every four alcoholics develops cardiovascular problems owing to the chronic consumption of

> **alcoholic dementia (AL-co-HAUL-ik dih-MEN-chee-ah):** A condition in which chronic alcohol abuse produces cognitive deficits such as difficulties in problem solving and memory.

alcohol. The effects include inflammation and enlargement of the heart muscle, poor blood circulation to the heart, irregular heart contractions, fatty accumulations in the heart and arteries, high blood pressure, and stroke.[15]

Cancer

Chronic alcohol abuse is associated with the increased risk of several types of cancers—in particular, cancers of the pharynx and larynx. Nearly 50 percent of all such cancers are associated with heavy drinking. If alcohol abusers also smoke cigarettes, the increased risk is even more dramatic. An increased risk of liver cancer is also linked to chronic alcoholic abuse, whether or not cirrhosis is present as well. In addition, alcohol consumption is associated with breast cancer in women. There is either a weaker association or no association at all with cancers of the stomach, colon, pancreas, or rectum.

Alcohol is not technically considered a carcinogen (a direct producer of cancer), so why the risks are increased in certain cancer types is at present unknown. It is possible that the increased risk is a combined result of alcohol enhancing the carcinogenic effects of other chemicals and, as is true with the development of hepatitis, alcohol depressing the immune system. With a reduced immune response, the alcoholic may have a lowered resistance to the development of cancerous tumors.[16]

Dementia and Wernicke-Korsakoff Syndrome

Chronic alcohol consumption can produce longer-lasting deficits in the way an individual solves problems, remembers information, and organizes facts about his or her identity and surroundings. These cognitive deficits are commonly referred to collectively as **alcoholic dementia** and are associated with structural changes in brain tissue. Specifically, there is an enlargement of brain ventricles (the interior fluid-filled spaces within the brain), a widening of fissures separating sections of cerebral cortex, and a loss of acetylcholine-sensitive receptors. The combination of these effects results in a net decrease in brain mass, as indicated in CT and MRI brain scans, and a decline in overall intelligence, verbal learning and retention, and short-term memory, particularly for middle-aged and elderly alcoholics.

Some 50 to 75 percent of all detoxified alcoholics and nearly 20 percent of all individuals admitted to state mental hospitals show signs of alcohol-related dementia. Through abstinence, it is possible to reverse some of the cognitive deficits and even some of the abnormalities in the brain, depending on the age of the alcoholic when treatment begins. As you might suspect, younger alcoholics respond better than older ones.[17]

A more severe form of cognitive impairment related to chronic alcohol consumption is a two-part disease referred to as **Wernicke-Korsakoff syndrome**. In *Wernicke's encephalopathy* or simply *Wernicke's disease*, the patient shows confusion and disorientation, abnormal eye movements, and difficulties in movement and body coordination. These neurological problems arise from a deficiency in vitamin B_1 (**thiamine**), a nutrient required for neurons in the brain to consume glucose. Extreme alcoholics may go days or weeks at a time eating practically nothing and receiving calories exclusively from drinking alcoholic beverages.

As a result of thiamine deficiency, large numbers of neurons die in areas of the brain specifically concerned with thinking and movement. About 15 percent of patients with Wernicke's disease, however, respond favorably to large amounts of thiamine supplements in combination with abstinence from alcohol, restoring their previous level of orientation, eye movements, and coordination.

In some cases, Wernicke's disease patients, whether or not they recover from confusion and motor impairments, also display a severe form of chronic amnesia and general apathy called *Korsakoff's psychosis*. Such patients cannot remember information that has just been presented to them and have only a patchy memory for distant events that occurred prior to their alcoholic state. They frequently attempt, through a behavior called **confabulation**, to compensate for their gaps in memory by telling elaborate stories of imagined past events, as if trying to fool others into thinking that they remember more than they actually do.

Thiamine deficiency is linked to Korsakoff's psychosis as well. After being treated with thiamine supplements, about 20 percent of patients completely recover their memory and 60 percent partially recover it. Yet the remaining 20 percent, generally the most severely impaired patients and those with the longest history of alcohol consumption, show little or no improvement and require chronic institutionalization.[18]

Fetal Alcohol Syndrome (FAS)

The disorders just reviewed generally have been associated with consumption of large quantities of alcohol over a long period of time. In the case of the adverse effects of alcohol during pregnancy on unborn children, we are dealing with a unique situation. First of all, we need to recognize the extreme susceptibility of a developing fetus to conditions in the mother's bloodstream. In short, if the mother takes a drink, the fetus takes one, too. And to make matters worse, the fetus does not have sufficient levels of alcohol dehydrogenase to break down the alcohol properly; thus the alcohol stays in the fetus's system longer than in the mother's. In addition, the presence of alcohol coincides with a period of time in prenatal development when critical processes are occurring that are essential for the development of a healthy, alert child.

Although it has long been suspected that alcohol abuse among pregnant women might present serious risks to the fetus, a specific syndrome was not established until 1973, when Kenneth L. Jones and David W. Smith described a cluster of characteristic features in children of alcoholic mothers that is now referred to as **fetal alcohol syndrome (FAS)**.[19] Their studies, and research conducted since then, have shown clearly that alcohol is **teratogenic;** that is, it produces specific birth defects in offspring by disrupting fetal development during pregnancy, even when differences in prenatal nutrition have been accounted for. Later in life, FAS children show deficits in short-term memory, problem solving, and attentiveness.

The face of a child with fetal alcohol syndrome, showing the wide-set eyes and other features that are characteristic of this condition.

Wernicke-Korsakoff syndrome (VERN-ih-kee KOR-sa-kof SIN-drohm): A condition resulting from chronic alcohol consumption, characterized by disorientation, cognitive deficits, amnesia, and motor difficulty.

thiamine (THY-ah-meen or THY-ah-min): Vitamin B_1.

confabulation: The tendency to make up elaborate past histories to cover the fact that long-term memory has been impaired.

fetal alcohol syndrome (FAS): A serious condition involving mental retardation and facial-cranial malformations in the offspring of an alcoholic mother.

teratogenic (TER-ah-tuh-JEN-ik): Capable of producing specific birth defects.

Present-day diagnoses of FAS are made on the basis of three groups of observations: (1) prenatal or postnatal growth retardation in which the child's weight or length is below the 10th percentile, (2) evidence of CNS abnormalities or mental retardation, and (3) a characteristic skull and facial appearance that includes a smaller-than-normal head, small wide-set eyes, drooping eyelids, a flattening of the vertical groove between the mouth and nose, a thin upper lip, and a short upturned nose. If only some of these characteristics are observed, the condition is referred to as **fetal alcohol effect (FAE)**.

fetal alcohol effect (FAE): A cognitive deficiency in the offspring of an alcoholic mother. It is regarded as less serious than fetal alcohol syndrome.

The incidence of FAS is approximately 0.5 to 3 cases per thousand live births in the general U.S. population, but the rates vary greatly within that population. Incidence is generally higher among Native Americans within the United States.[20]

We do not know at present how alcohol causes FAS or FAE, except that the greatest risk is in the first trimester of pregnancy, especially the third week of gestation when craniofacial formation and brain growth are prominent developmental milestones. Concentrated periods of drinking during this time appear to be very damaging to the fetus. For example, if two mothers consumed a similar overall quantity of alcohol during their pregnancies, but Mother A consumed one drink on each of seven days in a week and Mother B consumed all seven drinks on two weekend evenings, then Mother B would have incurred a far greater risk to her child than Mother A (Help Line).[21]

Help Line

The TWEAK Alcoholism Screening Instrument for Pregnant Women

One of the difficulties in getting information about possible alcoholic behavior is the tendency for the individual to deny that alcohol abuse is going on. It is especially important to find out whether pregnant women are engaging in this behavior. The following is a brief screening questionnaire, called the TWEAK, that provides personal information about drinking problems, without asking about them in a direct fashion. There are five basic questions (one question for each letter in the acronym TWEAK); the first question is presented in two alternative forms. The choice of whether to ask Question 1a or Question 1b is left to the health professional collecting the information.

1a. How many drinks does it take before you begin to feel the first effects of alcohol? (T—it asks about tolerance in terms of an initial state of intoxication)

1b. How many drinks does it take before the alcohol makes you fall asleep or pass out? Or, if you never drink until you pass out, what is the largest number of drinks you have? (T—it asks about tolerance in terms of an extreme level of intoxication)

2. Have your friends or relatives worried or complained about your drinking in the past year? (W—it asks about the extent of worry about one's drinking)

3. Do you sometimes take a drink in the morning when you first get up? (E—it refers to an "eye opener")

4. Are there times when you drink and afterward you can't remember what you did or said? (A—it refers to amnesia or a blackout episode)

5. Do you sometimes feel the need to cut down on your drinking? (K—it refers to the need to cut down on the level of alcohol consumption)

Three drinks or more is considered a positive answer to Question 1a; five drinks or more is considered a positive answer to Question 1b. Positive answers count for two points in Questions 1 and 2, and one point each in Questions 3, 4, and 5. A score of 3 or more, out of a maximum of 7, is interpreted as an indication of a possible alcohol problem.

Researchers have found that TWEAK scores can accurately identify up to 77 percent of women who are problem drinkers (an indication of the sensitivity of the questionnaire) and up to 93 percent of women who are not (an indication of the specificity of the questionnaire). Other short surveys are available, but they do not differentiate the two groups as well as the TWEAK. Using this instrument is a major step toward preventing FAS by identifying those women whose drinking during pregnancy will have potentially adverse effects on the developing fetus.

Sources: Bradley, Katharine A.; Boyd-Wickizer, Jodie; Powell, Suzanne H.; and Burman, Marcia L. (1998). Alcohol screening questionnaires in women: A critical review. *Journal of the American Medical Association, 280,* 166–171. Chan, W. K.; Pristach, E. A.; Welte, J. W.; and Russell, M. (1993). Use of the TWEAK test in screening for heavy drinking in three populations. *Alcoholism: Clinical and Experimental Research, 17,* 1188–1192. Copyright 1993 by Williams and Wilkins. Reprinted with permission. National Institute on Alcohol Abuse and Alcoholism (2002, April). Alcohol alert: Screening for alcohol problems—an update. No. 56. Rockville, MD: National Institute on Alcohol Abuse and Alcoholism.

Although not all alcoholic mothers give birth to babies with FAS or FAE, the research findings are clear: Risks are greatly increased when excessive drinking is taking place. Although an occasional drink may have minimal effects, no one has determined a "safe" level of drinking during pregnancy that would make this behavior risk-free. The objective of prevention, therefore, is to educate women to the dangers of drinking at any level and to encourage complete abstinence from alcohol (as well as other psychoactive drugs) during pregnancy. Since 1989, all containers of alcoholic beverages must contain two warning messages, one of which is that "according to the Surgeon General, women should not drink alcoholic beverages during pregnancy because of the risk of birth defects."

Fortunately, the public is aware of the problem and the number of women who consume alcohol during pregnancy has declined over the last twenty-five years. In some instances, it has been possible to reduce prenatal exposure to alcohol through broad social change. For example, in 1978, a change in social policy among members of a Southwestern Plains Native American tribe, shifting the distribution of mineral-rights income toward social programs on the reservation, resulted in the prevalence rate for FAS decreasing from fourteen per thousand live births to none at all. A combined prevalence rate of FAS and FAE decreased from twenty-seven per thousand live births to five. The potential influence of sociocultural factors in altering alcohol consumption patterns needs to be examined closely in all high-risk populations.[22]

The bad news, however, is that the rates of alcohol consumption among several other high-risk populations in the United States, such as pregnant smokers, unmarried women, women under the age of twenty-five, and women with the fewest years of education, remain substantial despite the fact that about 90 percent of women are aware of the potential harm. Ten percent of pregnant women nationwide continue to consume alcohol. Unfortunately, FAS and FAE continue to be the third leading cause of mental retardation not only in the United States but in the entire Western world, exceeded only by Down syndrome and spina bifida. The fact that the development of alcohol-related fetal defects is entirely preventable makes the incidence of these conditions all the more tragic.[23]

Patterns of Chronic Alcohol Abuse

When we consider the range of direct and indirect costs to society that result from chronic abuse of alcohol, the price we pay is enormous. These costs include the expense of treatment for alcoholism and of medical intervention for alcohol-related diseases, lost productivity from absenteeism and decreases in worker performance, treatment for alcohol-related injuries, and the lost value of future earnings of individuals who die prematurely because of alcoholism. The total costs in the United States are estimated to be about $200 billion annually, even without taking into consideration the incalculable costs of human suffering that are associated with an estimated 85,000 alcohol-related deaths.[24]

The Demographics of Alcoholism

As mentioned earlier, alcoholics can be found in every age, gender, racial, ethnic, and religious group, and in all socioeconomic levels and geographic regions of the country. Nonetheless, large differences in prevalence exist within these categories. For example, men outnumber women in the incidence of alcoholism by about six to one, with men tending to be steadier from day to day in their consumption of alcohol and women tending to abstain from drinking for lengths of time and to binge once they start drinking again. Overall, women are more vulnerable to alcohol-related organ damage. Whether this higher risk results from differences in the pattern of drinking or from differences in the way alcohol is processed in a woman's body is at present unknown.[25]

Figure 14.2 shows a state-by-state analysis of alcohol-related problems as measured by alcohol consumption level.[26] Some of the other demographic differences were examined in Chapter 13.

Alcohol Abuse among the Elderly

There is a widely held misconception that alcohol abuse is not much of a problem with the elderly. On the basis of careful studies addressing the problem of chronic alcohol abuse among the elderly, it has been estimated that approximately 9 percent of the elderly population have alcohol problems, as indicated by consuming four or more drinks in a single day or more than thirty per month. An analysis of Medicare records has indicated that more people over the age of sixty-five are hospitalized each year for alcohol-related problems than for heart attacks.[27]

One of the reasons for the underreporting of this problem is that we typically use the quantity of alcohol consumed as a primary index of alcoholism, and alcohol consumption does indeed decline with age. Yet, because of the changes in alcohol biotransformation over a lifetime, three drinks consumed at age sixty can be equivalent in their effects to four times as many

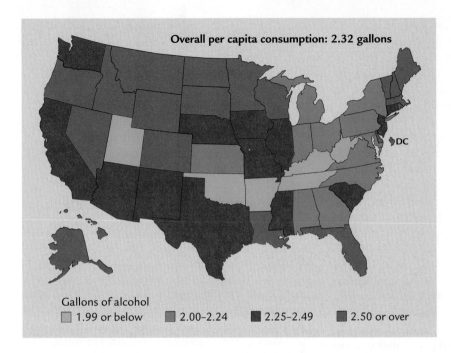

FIGURE 14.2

Annual per capita alcohol consumption in gallons for the U.S. population fourteen years and older by state in 2008.

Source: LaValle, Robin, and Yi, Hsiao-ye. (2010, August). *Surveillance Report 90. Apparent per capita alcohol consumption: National, state and regional trends, 1977–2008.* Bethesda, MD: National Institute on Alcohol Abuse and Alcoholism, Division of Epidemiology and Prevention Research, Alcohol Epidemiologic Data System, Figure 5.

drinks for someone at age twenty. In addition, the indications of social and occupational problems, traditionally part of the criteria for alcoholism, are often irrelevant for an elderly drinker. There would be no incidence of drunk driving if the person is no longer driving, no job supervisor to notice a decline in work performance, and frequently no spouse to complain of social difficulties. Finally, the occurrence of blackouts or symptoms of Wernicke-Korsakoff syndrome may be misdiagnosed simply as an indication of senility or the onset of Alzheimer's disease.

A number of problems particularly affect the elderly who chronically abuse alcohol. One problem is the risk of the alcohol interacting with the many medications that the elderly typically take. Another is the risk of complications for already existing medical conditions, such as gastrointestinal bleeding, hypertension and cardiac arrhythmias, osteoporosis, depression, and cognitive impairment–related disorders.

There is growing recognition that treatment programs for alcoholism ought to be tailored to the special needs of the elderly; frequently the traditional treatment programs that benefit much younger individuals do not work well with older people. Many seniors were brought up in an era when highly negative attitudes toward drinking prevailed, so if they are drinking themselves, they feel stigmatized and resist treatment. On a brighter note, however, it has been found that, when treatment programs are designed specifically with the elderly in mind, older alcoholics often respond well to treatment.[28]

The Family Dynamics of Alcoholism: A Systems Approach

Alcoholism, like any form of drug abuse, is an especially traumatizing experience for the families involved. For every one person who has a problem with alcohol, there are, on average, at least four others who are directly affected on a day-to-day basis. It is therefore important to examine some of these effects on particular family members. Since the 1950s, a **systems approach** has advocated looking at how the alcoholic and other members of the family interact.[29] We discussed one of these aspects earlier in the chapter in connection with the adverse effects of enabling behavior on the alcoholic. Another important aspect related to an alcoholic's family is the possibility of codependency.

Since the early 1980s, the concept of **codependency** has gained widespread attention as a way of understanding people who live on a day-to-day basis with an

systems approach: A way of understanding a phenomenon in terms of complex interacting relationships among individuals, family, friends, and community.

codependency: The concept that individuals who live with a person who has an alcohol (or other drug) dependence suffer themselves from difficulties of self-image and impaired social independence.

alcoholic or any individual with a drug dependence. Definitions vary but most identify four essential features. In members of the family of an alcoholic, therapists have observed (1) an overinvolvement with the alcoholic, (2) obsessive attempts to control the alcoholic's behavior, (3) a strong reliance upon external sources of self-worth, through the approval of others, and (4) an attempt to make personal sacrifices in an effort to improve the alcoholic's condition.[30]

If people in a relationship with a codependent act badly, the codependent believes that he or she is responsible for their behavior. Because codependency is considered to be a learned pattern of thinking rather than an innate trait, the goal of therapy is to teach the codependent person to detach himself or herself from the alcoholic and begin to meet his or her own needs rather than being controlled by the value judgments of others.[31]

Some professionals, however, have questioned the validity of the codependency concept. They have argued that by labeling a person a codependent, the therapist is promoting feelings of helplessness or victimization in these individuals that might not have existed before. Indeed, the idea of codependency might diminish the person's incentive to begin efforts to take control over his or her life by reinforcing the feeling that he or she is "doomed to suffer." Critics also have pointed out that actual patterns of codependency may not be specific to particular individuals but rather are common to practically everyone. Codependency simply may simply reflect the problems of living in modern society, only now we have found language to describe our tendency to explain our own failures by blaming other people.[32]

Children of an Alcoholic Parent or Parents

Considering the immense impact that our parents have in our lives, it is understandable that an alcoholic family has distinct negative consequences on the psychological development of the children in that family. As a result, **children of alcoholics (COAs)** have a higher statistical risk of becoming alcoholics than do children of nonalcoholics. Whether this increased risk is genetically or environmentally based is a complex issue that will be reviewed in the next section.

An equally important and independent risk factor, may be the specific behavioral and physiological reactions a person has to alcohol itself. Men who at age twenty have a relatively low response to alcohol, in that they need to drink more than other people to feel intoxicated, carry a higher risk of becoming alcoholic by the time they are thirty, regardless of their pattern of drinking

at an earlier age and regardless of their parents' drinking. Sons of alcoholics having a low response to alcohol have a 60 percent chance of becoming alcoholics, compared with a 42 percent chance for sons of alcoholics in general. Sons of nonalcoholics having a low response to alcohol have a 22 percent chance of becoming alcoholics, compared with an 8 to 9 percent chance for sons of nonalcoholics in general.

The combination of these two risk factors—family history and a low response to alcohol—is obviously the worst scenario for a development of alcoholism, at least in males. Nonetheless, we should remember that a large proportion of people still *do not* become alcoholics, even with both risk factors present. The question of what protective factors may account for the resilience of high-risk individuals with regard to alcoholism is a major subject of current research.[33]

The Genetics of Alcoholism

For centuries, alcoholism has appeared to run in families. Today, this casual observation has led to a specific question: To what extent is alcoholism genetically determined (through the genes of the parents) and to what extent is it environmentally determined (through the living conditions in which the offspring have been brought up)? One approach is to examine the inheritance pattern in a family tree. It is impossible, however, to tease out the separate genetic (nature) and environmental (nurture) factors from information of this kind.

For more precise answers, one option is to turn to cases of adoption in which children can be compared with either their biological or their adoptive parents. In 1981, an extensive research study in Sweden looked at the adoption records of approximately three thousand children who had alcoholic biological parents but lived with nonalcoholic adoptive parents. The results showed that a larger percentage of these children become alcoholics than would be seen in the general population. The greater incidence was present even when the children had been raised by their adoptive parents immediately after being born, indicating that a strong genetic component was operating.

There were, however, two subgroups among those children who eventually became alcoholics. One subgroup, called *Type 1 alcoholics*, developed problem

> **children of alcoholics (COAs):** Individuals who grew up in a family with either one or two alcoholic parents.

drinking later in life and generally functioned well in society. In addition to a genetic predisposition toward alcoholism, there was for this subgroup a strong environmental factor as well. Whether the child was placed in a middle-class or poor adoptive family influenced the final outcome. A second subgroup, called *Type 2 alcoholics*, developed alcoholism earlier in life and had significant antisocial patterns of behavior. A strong genetic component was operating in this subgroup, and because the socioeconomic status of the adoptive family made no difference in the outcome, we can conclude that environmental factors played a negligible role. Table 14.1 gives a more complete picture of the characteristics associated with Type 1 and Type 2 alcoholics.[34]

The study of twins is another source of information about the genetic and environmental influences in alcoholism. Probably the most important piece of data is the **concordance rate** for alcoholism in pairs of identical twins—that is, how likely one member of a pair is to be alcoholic if the other member is. The concordance rate has been found to be only 58 percent. If genetics were the whole story in determining the incidence of alcoholism, the concordance rate would have been 100 percent.

If we look closely at the type of alcoholic involved and whether the alcoholic is male or female, the data from twin studies are similar to those found in the adoption research. For example, the concordance rate for identical twins has been found to be significantly higher than the concordance rate for fraternal twins when one member of the pair is a male alcoholic whose drinking problems started in adolescence (in other words, a Type 2 alcoholic). For female and male alcoholics whose drinking problems started after adolescence (the Type 1 subgroup), a comparison of concordance rates shows that genetic factors played a lesser role.[35]

In the course of the continuing exploration of the human genome, a number of genes on several different chromosomes have been found to be involved in increasing the risk for alcohol dependence or influencing the tendency to consume alcohol in the first place. As these genes become more clearly identified, new drug-based treatments will probably be developed.[36]

TABLE 14.1

Two types of alcoholics

CHARACTERISTICS	TYPE 1	TYPE 2
Usual age at onset	(late onset) after 25	(early onset) before 25
Inability to abstain	infrequent	frequent
Fights and arrests when drinking	infrequent	frequent
Psychological dependence (loss of control)	infrequent	frequent
Guilt and fear about alcoholism	frequent	infrequent
Novelty-seeking personality	low	high
Tendency to use alcohol to escape negative feelings	high	low
Tendency to use alcohol to achieve positive feelings	low	high
Gender	male and female	male only
Extent of genetic influences	moderate	high
Extent of environmental influences	high	low
Serotonin abnormalities in the brain	absent	present

Source: Updated from Cloninger, C. Robert (1987). Neurogenetic adaptive mechanisms in alcoholism. *Science, 236,* 410–416.

concordance rate: The likelihood that one member of a twin or family relation will have a condition if the other member has it.

The Concept of Alcoholism as a Disease

In contrast to the days when alcoholism was considered a moral failure or worse, the majority opinion today is that alcoholism is best characterized as a disease and that the alcoholic should be treated rather than punished. This viewpoint, by the way, was advanced as early as the 1780s by Benjamin Rush (see Chapter 13). Over the years, the concept of alcoholism as a disease has evolved, principally through the writings of E. M. Jellinek in the late 1940s. Jellinek proposed that alcohol dependence progressed through a natural sequence of stages, much as a physical illness develops.[37] In more recent interpretations, the disease concept has moved away from the idea that all alcoholics follow a common path (many of Jellinek's ideas have not been confirmed) to a more general focus on the biological factors that might differentiate alcoholics from nonalcoholics. In addition, the disease concept has led to the idea that the alcoholics are fundamentally out of control and that abstinence is the only answer to their recovery.[38]

Since 1957, the American Medical Association has defined alcoholism as a disease, and numerous other health organizations have adopted a similar position. As reasonable as this position might sound, the disease concept has created something of a dilemma among professionals concerned with the treatment of alcohol abuse. It places the burden on physicians to deal with the alcoholic through medical interventions, and unfortunately the medical profession is frequently ill equipped to help. A study in 2000, for example, found that 94 percent of a group of primary care physicians failed to make a correct diagnosis of early-stage alcohol abuse when presented with symptoms typical of this condition. Only a small percentage, approximately one out of five, considered themselves "very prepared" to diagnose alcoholism in the first place.[39]

Important legal considerations also cloud this issue. Can we say, for example, that an alcoholic is legally absolved from a crime or a legal obligation because he or she is afflicted with this disease? These and related issues will be explored later in the chapter in Drugs . . . in Focus (page 342).

Approaches to Treatment for Alcoholism

Alcoholism, as should be clear at this point, is a study in diversity, and it makes sense that there might be some advantage in matching alcoholics with certain characteristics to specific forms of treatment. One treatment program might be best suited for one subgroup, another for another subgroup. As reasonable as this hypothesis sounds, however, a major study begun in the late 1980s and completed in 1997 showed little or no benefit in patient–treatment matching. Apparently, no one treatment approach was overwhelmingly superior to others.[40] In this section, we will examine forms of alcoholism treatment as classified into two broad areas: biological interventions, which involve medications, and psychosocial interventions, such as Alcoholics Anonymous and other self-help programs.

Biologically Based Treatments

The use of **disulfiram** (brand name: Antabuse) is based on the idea that if a drug induces an aversive reaction in alcoholics when alcohol is consumed, then consumption will be avoided and the problems of alcoholism will be reduced. Disulfiram, taken orally as a pill once each day,

inhibits alcohol dehydrogenase, allowing acetaldehyde to build up in the bloodstream. As a result, individuals who consume alcohol in combination with disulfiram experience a flushing of the face, rapid heart rate and palpitations, nausea, and vomiting. These effects are brought on not only by consuming alcoholic beverages but also by ingesting alcohol in other forms such as mouthwashes and cough mixtures, and even by the absorption of aftershave lotions and shampoos through the skin.

Clearly the symptoms caused by a combination of disulfiram and alcohol can be a powerful short-term deterrent to alcoholic drinking, but the question is whether this kind of aversion therapy is an effective treatment over the long run. Careful studies in which disulfiram has been administered to large numbers of alcoholics indicate that it is not effective when it is the sole treatment. One major problem is that alcoholics must take the drug regularly every day, and because disulfiram does nothing to reduce the alcoholic's craving for alcohol, compliance rates are low. The consensus among professionals in this field is that disulfiram can be useful in a subgroup of higher-functioning alcoholics with exceptionally high motivation to quit drinking; for others, disulfiram can be useful as a transitional treatment until other support programs are in place.[41]

A more direct approach to treatment than aversion therapy is to reduce the actual craving for alcohol on a physiological level. As noted in Chapter 13, evidence suggests that alcohol dependence is related to neural activity in the same dopamine-releasing receptors in the nucleus accumbens that have been implicated in heroin craving as well as in craving for cocaine and nicotine. This parallel to heroin dependence suggests that opiate receptor antagonists in this region of the brain, such as **naltrexone** (brand name: ReVia) and **nalmefene** (brand name: Revex), should be useful in alcohol-dependence treatment.

---

disulfiram (dye-SULL-fih-ram): A medication that causes severe physical reactions and discomfort when combined with alcohol. Brand name is Antabuse.

naltrexone (nal-TREX-ohn): A long-lasting opiate antagonist for the treatment of alcoholism. Brand name is ReVia. Brand name for an extended-release injectable form is Vivitrol

nalmefene (nal-MEH-feen): A long-lasting opiate antagonist for the treatment of alcoholism. Brand name is Revex.

An extended-release injectable form of naltrexone (brand name: Vivitrol), administered on a monthly basis, was FDA-approved in 2006. The obvious advantage is that individuals do not have to remember to take their medication on a daily basis. Problems associated with individuals skipping their medication are eliminated, and there can be a more intensive concentration on the counseling component of recovery. The advantage of an extended-release naltrexone for treating alcohol dependence parallels that of extended-release formulations of buprenorphine (Subutex, Suboxone) for treating heroin abuse (Chapter 7).

An alternative approach in treating alcohol dependence has been to focus on the regulation of GABA, in a manner similar to the way gamma vinyl-GABA (Vigabatrin) is used for cocaine-abuse treatment (Chapter 8). **Acamprosate** (brand name: Campral) was FDA-approved in 2004 for this purpose. Recent studies have shown the usefulness of topiramate (brand name: Topamax), an antiepileptic and migraine-alleviating medication, for treating alcohol dependence. Still another approach has focused on the role of serotonin levels in the brains of alcoholics. Since early-onset (Type 2) alcoholism differs from late-onset (Type 1) alcoholism owing to its association with serotonin abnormalities in the brain (see Table 14.1), a drug that reduces serotonin levels such as **ondansetron** (brand name: Zofran), typically used as an antinausea medication, should be beneficial in treating this subgroup. This prediction has been confirmed. Among Type 2 alcoholics, Zofran has significantly reduced their drinking behavior and provided a longer period of abstinence.[42]

Alcoholics Anonymous

The best-known treatment program for alcoholism is **Alcoholics Anonymous (AA)**. Founded in 1935, this organization was conceived basically as a fellowship of alcoholics who wish to rid themselves of their problem drinking by helping one another maintain sobriety. The philosophy of AA is expressed in the famous Twelve Steps (Table 14.2). Members must have acknowledged that they were "powerless over alcohol" and that their lives had become unmanageable, and must have turned their will and their lives over "to the care of God *as we understood Him.*" As the steps indicate, there is a strong spiritual component to the AA program, although the

---

TABLE 14.2

The famous Twelve Steps of Alcoholics Anonymous

1. We admitted we were powerless over alcohol—that our lives had become unmanageable.
2. Came to believe that a Power greater than ourselves could restore us to sanity.
3. Made a decision to turn our will and our lives over to the care of God *as we understood Him.*
4. Made a searching and fearless moral inventory of ourselves.
5. Admitted to God, to ourselves, and to another human being the exact nature of our wrongs.
6. Were entirely ready to have God remove all these defects of character.
7. Humbly asked Him to remove our shortcomings.
8. Made a list of all persons we had harmed and became willing to make amends to them all.
9. Made direct amends to such people wherever possible, except when to do so would injure them or others.
10. Continued to take moral inventory and when we were wrong, promptly admitted it.
11. Sought through prayer and meditation to improve our conscious contact with God *as we understood Him*, praying only for knowledge of His will for us and the power to carry that out.
12. Having had a spiritual awakening as a result of these steps, we tried to carry this message to alcoholics, and to practice these principles in all our affairs.

Source: The Twelve Steps are reprinted and adapted with permission of Alcoholics Anonymous World Services, Inc. Permission to reprint this material does not mean that AA has reviewed or approved the contents of this publication, nor that AA agrees with the views expressed herein. AA is a program of recovery from alcoholism *only.* Use of Twelve Steps in connection with programs and activities that are patterned after AA, but that address other problems, does not imply otherwise.

---

acamprosate (A-cam-PRO-sate): A GABA-related drug for the treatment of alcoholism. Brand name is Campral.

ondansetron (on-DANS-eh-tron): A serotonin-related drug for the treatment of alcoholism. Brand name is Zofran.

Alcoholics Anonymous (AA): A worldwide organization devoted to the treatment of alcoholism through self-help groups and adherence to its principles, which include absolute abstinence from alcohol.

An anonymous group of men and women at a typical Alcoholics Anonymous (AA) meeting.

organization vigorously denies that any religious doctrine prevails (Portrait).

AA functions as a type of group therapy with each member oriented toward a common goal: the maintenance of abstinence from alcohol despite a powerful and continuing craving for it. All meetings are completely anonymous (only first names are used in all communications), and the proceedings are dominated by members recounting their personal struggles with alcohol, their efforts to stop drinking, and their support for fellow alcoholics in their own struggles. New members are encouraged to pair up with a sponsor, typically a more experienced AA member who has successfully completed the Twelve Steps and can serve as a personal source of support on a day-to-day basis. According to AA, no

PORTRAIT

Bill W. and Dr. Bob—Founders of Alcoholics Anonymous

When they met in the spring of 1935, the backgrounds of William Griffith Wilson (left) and Dr. Robert Smith (right), could not have been more different, but they shared an important problem. They were both alcoholics, and their lives had come apart because of it. Wilson had gone from being a successful businessman, whose investments on Wall Street during the 1920s had made him rich, to a penniless failure after losing his entire fortune in the 1929 crash. Whether rich or poor, he had been a drunk, but his poverty made the condition worse. In 1934 Wilson was admitted to Towns Hospital in New York City and agreed to subject himself to the "belladonna cure," a treatment based on his receiving morphine and the powerful hallucinogen belladonna. Under the influence of this combination of drugs, Wilson experienced "his spiritual awakening." He later wrote,

In the wake of my spiritual experience there came a vision of a society of alcoholics. If each sufferer were to carry the news of the scientific hopelessness of alcoholism to each new prospect, he might be able to

lay every newcomer wide open to a transforming spiritual experience.

For several months following his new-found mission in life, Wilson sought out drunks to "work on." On a trip to Akron, Ohio, where he was seeking a new job, he was introduced by mutual friends to a proctologist and surgeon named Dr. Robert Smith.

Smith's alcoholism had wrecked a distinguished medical career, and in 1935, he was in severe financial straits. Wilson's determination combined with Smith's desperation led to their taking on the task of keeping each other sober and helping others do the same. On June 10, 1935 (the official date of the founding of Alcoholics Anonymous), Smith took his last drink. By 1939, Wilson had finished writing the Twelve Steps and an extended explanation of the AA philosophy, known today as the "Big Book." Wilson and Smith had discovered that they were most successful in keeping alcoholics abstinent when the latter attended meetings on a regular basis and were assured of complete privacy

and anonymity. Wilson became Bill W., and Smith became Dr. Bob.

It was not until the 1940s that AA began to be nationally known. The *Saturday Evening Post*, one of the leading magazines of the day, gave AA its first real publicity break, publishing an article about the organization that generated an avalanche of responses and a dramatic increase in membership. During this time, a prayer was composed that would eventually be repeated millions of times in AA meetings throughout the world: "God grant me the serenity to accept the things I cannot change, the courage to change the things I can, and the wisdom to know the difference."

Sources: Alcoholics Anonymous comes of age: A brief history of AA (1959). New York: Alcoholics Anonymous World Services. Alibrandi, Lucinda A. (1982). The fellowship of Alcoholics Anonymous. In E. Mansell Pattison and Edward Kaufman (Eds.), *The encyclopedic handbook of alcoholism*. New York: Gardner Press, p. 979. Cheever, Susan (2004). *My name is Bill*. New York: Simon and Schuster.

Drugs... in Focus

The Sociology of Alcoholics Anonymous

Alcoholics Anonymous (AA) is arguably the most success-ful treatment program in history. Here is a selection of excerpts from a major analysis by Mariana Valverde and Kimberly White-Mair into the sociological aspects of AA that, in their judgment, have led to this accomplishment:

- Practice-driven rather than theory-driven activity

  AA does have some theories; for instance, members almost universally believe that "once an alcoholic, always an alcoholic." Nevertheless, it is a fundamentally pragmatic organization, and its basis of unity is not a set of beliefs but rather a set of practices: the twelve steps and the twelve traditions, plus the organisational practices that have evolved in group meetings over the years. (p. 394)

  Activity is the key term here: AA, although driven by beliefs and dogmas to an extent perhaps not recognized by most of its members, is nevertheless an anti-intellectu-al, and particularly anti-scientific, organization. (p. 399)

- A fellowship, not a movement

  AA describes itself not as a movement but as "a fellow-ship," and it positively refuses to engage in political and social change, to lobby for or against legislation, or to participate in the public arena in any way . . . The explicit refusal of a public image, unusual in the context of American philanthropic or spiritual organi-zations, is best explained, we argue, as a reaction to the old temperance movement. (p. 395)

  If AA had set itself squarely against the liquor industry, it probably would have melted into oblivion, given the historical defeat of the temperance movement and the rise in the post–World War II period of a culture of consumerism. (p. 396)

- Beyond outward sobriety to inner peace

  The ultimate goal of AA is not the already ambitious one of helping people stop drinking: it is the even more ambitious one of helping people achieve inner peace. . . . Sobriety is thus more than the absence of drinking: it is difficult to define but is nevertheless a pos-itively existing state. (pp. 397–398)

- Gaining power through powerlessness

  . . . AA indirectly subverts the neoliberal discourse of per-sonal entrepreneurship and perpetual improvement. . . . AA members are perpetually in recovery, always working on their souls, but they do not imagine they will ever re-make themselves from scratch. (p. 401)

- Telling one's story without confessing your sins

  AA is one of the many movements in today's world that relies heavily on autobiographical narratives. First-person accounts of movement from alcoholism to sobriety form a large part of the Big Book, and open group meetings have at least one or two autobiograph-ical segments. . . . In group meetings, the key feature distinguishing "telling one's story" from confession is that the people listening do not either interpret or judge the speaker. (p. 403)

- Appealing to "my" Higher Power, not necessarily "your" Higher Power

  In meetings, people talk not about "the" Higher Power but rather about "my" Higher Power—as in the phrase heard at a meeting, "my Higher Power must have a sense of humour. . . ." The proliferation of individual-ized higher powers would suggest that today's AA mem-bers believe in guardian angels without believing in a God that guarantees the truth of angels . . . (p. 405)

- Building a life on a twenty-four-hour cycle

  One [technique] is the custom of celebrating months or years of sobriety with commemorative tokens, a round of applause, and sometimes even a party—a technique that rewards long-term abstinence. But the other technique, embodied in the "one day at a time" slogan, counteracts the tendency of "oldtimers" to feel superior. Although long-term abstention is prized, AA members sometimes say that the person with the longest sobriety is "whoever woke up the earliest that morning." (p. 406)

- Anonymity at all costs

  . . . Anonymity is perhaps less essential now to protect the individual—in some circles, being a recovering alcoholic is no longer stigmatized, and may even bring some cachet—but rather that the group does not succumb to the temptation of money, fame, and power that have crippled other organizations. [An AA mem-ber writes]: "Anonymity keeps us focused on principles rather than personalities. There are no 'stars' in AA. . . . External anonymity is thus clearly linked to one of AA's key traditions, namely the refusal to own property." (pp. 401–402)

Source: Valverde, Mariana, and White-Mair, Kimberly (1999). "One day at a time" and other slogans for everyday life: The ethical practices of Alcoholics Anonymous. *Sociology, 33,* 393–410.

alcoholic is ever cured but is only recovering and the process of recovery continues throughout that person's life. In this view, alcoholism is a disease, and relapse from sobriety can occur at any moment. The question of whether an alcoholic is totally unable to control his or her drinking is examined in a later section.

AA has grown to more than 114,000 groups and more than 2 million members worldwide, although it is difficult to get a precise count because the organization is deliberately structured very loosely. Perhaps more important than its size is the powerful impact AA has had not only on the way we deal with alcoholism but also on the way we consider treatment for any compulsive behavior in general. Over the years, the twelve-step program has become a generic concept, as the precepts and philosophy of AA have been widely imitated. There are chapters of Gamblers Anonymous, Nicotine Anonymous, Narcotics or Cocaine Anonymous, and Overeaters Anonymous, all based on the AA model. In addition, there are two specialized fellowship organizations, Al-Anon for relatives and friends of alcoholics and Alateen for teenagers living with an alcoholic family member. These programs adopt a twelve-step approach to identifying and dealing with the dysfunctionality of an alcoholic family.

Despite its stature as the preeminent approach to treatment there are relatively few scientific appraisals of the overall effectiveness of AA. One of the principal obstacles to evaluation is the anonymity guaranteed to all members, which makes it difficult to conduct well-controlled follow-up studies on how well AA members are doing. Nonetheless, AA is widely regarded in the field of alcohol rehabilitation as a beneficial self-help approach, particularly when it is combined with other treatments such as individual counseling and medical interventions.[43] It has been pointed out that AA employs four factors that are widely shown to be effective in preventing relapse in alcohol dependence: (1) the imposition of external supervision, (2) the substitution of dependence on a group activity for dependence on drug-taking behavior, (3) the development of caring relationships, and (4) a heightened sense of spirituality.[44] Drugs . . . in Focus on page 342 examines the success of AA from a sociological perspective.

SMART Recovery

In contrast to AA, the self-help program **SMART Recovery** assumes that people do not need to believe they are "powerless over alcohol" or submit to "a Power greater than ourselves" (phrases taken from the Twelve Steps) to recover from alcoholism. Instead, the dominant philosophy is that individuals have the power themselves to overcome anything, including drinking. Unlike AA, SMART Recovery discourages labeling in general; a person is not required to call himself or herself an alcoholic to achieve success in recovery. The strategy is based on rational emotive behavior therapy (REBT), an approach developed by the psychologist Albert Ellis that emphasizes rooting out irrational thoughts, emotions, and beliefs that prevent the achievement of personal goals.

Another major difference is that SMART Recovery insists on professional involvement in its program, with a professional adviser (often a clinical psychologist) helping members learn the fundamentals of REBT. No reference is made to God or a higher power; the objective is "NHP (no higher power) sobriety." The goal is that within a year and a half members will be able to maintain sobriety without going to meetings. In contrast, AA members are encouraged to continue going to meetings for the rest of their lives.

Since 1990, there has been increased interest in secular (nonreligious) approaches to self-help alcoholism treatment such as that practiced by SMART Recovery. Other examples include Men for Sobriety (MFS), Women for Sobriety (WFS), Moderation Management (MM), and Secular Organization for Sobriety (SOS). Nonetheless, recent research has indicated that alcoholics benefit from participation in AA programs, regardless of their religious beliefs (Drugs . . . in Focus).[45]

Controllable or Uncontrollable Drinking

One of the most intensely debated questions in the field of alcoholism treatment has been whether it is possible for alcoholics to achieve a level of "controlled drinking" without falling back into a state of alcohol dependence. On one side are well-entrenched organizations such as

SMART Recovery: A treatment program for abuse of alcohol and other drugs that emphasizes a nonspiritual philosophy and a greater sense of personal control in the abuser. SMART stands for "Self-Management And Recovery Training."

Drugs... in Focus

The Non-Disease Model of Alcoholism

Despite the "official" description of alcoholism as a disease by the American Medical Association and many international health organizations, the concept of alcoholism as a disease remains controversial and continues to attract vigorous criticism. As Erich Goode has put it, the non-disease theorists assert that alcoholics (as well as other substance abusers) are ". . . not 'sick,' but are rational, problem-solving human beings attempting to carve out a meaningful existence in a harsh and seemingly unyielding environment." Others have warned that the disease model encourages alcoholics to assume a passive stance, depending solely on the advances of modern medicine to save the day, and that acceptance of the disease model often leads to making excuses for one's behavior rather than changing it. As a one-liner expresses it, "There's nothing wrong with being an alcoholic, if you're doing something about it."

The "disease versus non-disease" debate has inevitable consequences for the ways in which we choose to respond to the problem. Non-disease theorists view the prevailing majority opinion as unfortunately leading to a marginalization of alcoholics, reducing them to a small group of afflicted, biologically predestined individuals, rather than seeing these people in the context of the way all of us behave to one degree or another. In the words of non-disease advocate Stanton Peele, this attitude fosters a "coercive, one-size-fits-all . . . disease treatment system of hospitals, Alcoholics Anonymous, and the twelve steps, which are increasingly administered within the framework of the law enforcement system." He views the disease model as leading to the assumption that all drinking must cease (a position held by AA), instead of to the encouragement of controlled levels of drinking, as advocated by Moderation Management (MM). He also argues that, without the disease model of alcoholism and other drug abuse, it is possible to focus on "the larger question of why some people seek to close off their experience through a comforting but artificial and self-consuming relationship with something external to themselves. In itself, the choice of object is irrelevant to this universal process of becoming dependent."

Sources: Goode, Erich (1999). *Drugs in American society* (5th ed.). New York: McGraw-Hill College, quotation on p. 350. Kinney, Jean (2003). *Loosening the grip: A handbook of alcohol information* (7th ed.). St. Louis: Mosby, pp. 318–322. Peele, Stanton (1995). Assumptions about drugs and the marketing of drug policies. In W. K. Bickel and R. J. DeGrandpre (Eds.), *Drug policy and human nature.* New York: Plenum, pp. 199–220, first quotation on p. 214. Peele, Stanton, and Brodsky, Archie (1975). *Love and addiction.* New York: Taplinger Publishing, second quotation on p. 55.

Alcoholics Anonymous (AA) and the National Institute on Alcohol Abuse and Alcoholism, as well as many other organizations that assert that alcoholism is an irreversible disease, that abstinence is the only answer, and that even the slightest level of alcohol consumption will trigger a cascade of problems that the alcoholic is constitutionally incapable of handling. On the other side are groups, represented in greater numbers in Canada and Europe than in the United States, asserting that uncontrolled drinking is a reversible behavioral disorder and that for many alcoholics the promotion of total abstinence as a treatment goal is a serious obstacle to their success in rehabilitation. The organization Moderation Management (MM) is an example of this type of therapeutic approach.

Research studies using carefully randomized assignment of alcoholic subjects to either an abstinence-oriented treatment or a controlled-drinking one have shown that long-term results are comparable for either group. This is not to say that the prospects are wonderful for either of them; the odds are still higher against long-term recovery from alcoholism than for it, no matter what the treatment. But it does appear that controlled drinking can occur.

How many alcoholics can manage to achieve a continued level of nonproblem drinking? Percentages vary from 2 to 10 to 15, though the lower figure is probably more accurate for those individuals with severe alcoholic difficulties. Perhaps a more important point is that no one knows how to predict whether an alcohol

Quick Concept Check 14.2

Understanding Alcoholics Anonymous

Check your understanding of the principles and philosophy of Alcoholics Anonymous by indicating whether each of the following statements would be subscribed to by Alcoholics Anonymous.

1. I have always had the power to control my drinking. ☐ yes ☐ no

2. I must put myself in the hands of a Higher Power if I am to be sober for the rest of my life. ☐ yes ☐ no

3. It is possible to be cured of alcoholism. ☐ yes ☐ no

4. I am capable of having a drink once in a great while without slipping back into alcoholism. ☐ yes ☐ no

5. The more meetings I attend, the better chance I have of remaining sober. ☐ yes ☐ no

Answers: 1. no 2. yes 3. no 4. no 5. yes

abuser will be one of that small number of successful controlled drinkers. Obviously, most alcoholics are convinced that they will be the lucky ones.[46]

Chronic Alcohol Abuse and Alcoholism in the Workplace

It has been estimated that about 10 percent of the people in the American work force (12.8 million workers) have been at work either under the influence of alcohol or with a hangover at least once in the previous 12 months. The prevalence rates of alcohol impairment at the workplace are higher among men than women, higher for white employees than minority employees, higher for younger than older employees, and higher for unmarried than married employees. Alcohol impairment is also most frequently reported by individuals in the arts/entertainment/sports/media industries, food preparation and service jobs, and building and grounds maintenance occupations. Individuals with jobs that would be seriously affected if alcohol impairment were present, such as workers in construction/extraction industries and transportation/material-moving industries, do not show a significantly higher prevalence rate of alcohol impairment at work than the work force at large.[47]

Given the adverse impact of chronic alcohol abuse on a range of workplace behaviors, it makes sense that corporations, hospitals, the armed services, and other large organizations should benefit by establishing workplace programs specifically designed for employees who need help. Two major efforts address this problem. The first is employer-sponsored **employee assistance programs (EAPs)**, and the second is union-supported **member assistance programs (MAPs)**. EAPs have been established as a way of increasing the productivity of the organization, whereas MAPs are oriented toward enhancing the welfare of the individual worker.

In either case, a major thrust of workplace interventions has been to change the culture of drinking within the organization. For example, problems arise because employees tend to drink heavily in order to conform to workplace drinking norms. Within a heavy drinking culture, employees are more likely to use alcohol to cope with stress and feelings of alienation. Gender harassment, characterized by behaviors directed at female employees that convey hostile and degrading attitudes toward women, is associated with the proportion of male employees identified as heavy or "at-risk" drinkers, and the association is stronger when alcohol consumption is considered a common pattern of behavior during lunch or other meal breaks. In other words, a permissive, alcohol-oriented culture at work exacerbates an already serious workplace problem.

Workplace EAPs and MAPs will be examined in Chapter 16 in the larger context of treatment for the abuse of alcohol and other drugs.[48]

---

employee assistance programs (EAPs): Corporate or institutional programs for workers or employees to help them with alcohol or other drug-abuse problems.

member assistance programs (MAPs): Institutional programs for workers or employees to help them with alcohol or other drug-abuse problems, set up by established unions within the organization and tailored to meet the needs of union members.

Summary

Alcoholism: Stereotypes, Definitions, and Criteria

- Alcoholism is a multidimensional condition that is typically defined in terms of four major criteria: (1) problems associated with a preoccupation with drinking, (2) emotional problems, (3) vocational, social, and family problems, and (4) physical problems. Not all criteria have to be met, however, for alcoholism to be diagnosed.

Alcohol Abuse and Alcohol Dependence

- According to health professionals, alcohol abuse is defined in terms of (1) persistent physical, social, or occupational problems that have become associated with alcohol use and (2) recurring use of alcohol in physically hazardous situations. Alcohol dependence is defined in terms of uncontrolled alcohol intake, unsuccessful efforts to reduce alcohol use, life problems, and alcohol tolerance and withdrawal.

- According to criteria set by the American Psychiatric Association, an estimated 8.5 percent of U.S. adults can be classified either as alcohol abusers or as alcohol dependent.

Physiological Effects of Chronic Alcohol Abuse

- Physical effects of alcoholism include tolerance and withdrawal, liver disease, cardiovascular disease, cancer, and neurological disorders such as Wernicke-Korsakoff syndrome.

- A particular concern is the development of fetal alcohol syndrome (FAS) in the offspring of alcoholic mothers.

Patterns of Chronic Alcohol Abuse

- Alcoholics can be found in every age, gender, racial, ethnic, and religious group and in all socioeconomic and geographic categories. Nonetheless, men outnumber women in the incidence of alcoholism by about six to one, although women are more vulnerable to alcohol-related organ damage. The elderly tend to be an underreported group with respect to alcoholism.

- A systems approach to alcoholism examines the complex interacting relationships among individuals, family, friends, and community. The concept of codependency has helped shed light on the specific effects of alcoholism on spouses and other family members. The children of alcoholics (COAs) carry an increased risk of becoming alcoholic as a result of a vulnerability toward alcoholism that is genetically or environmentally based, or both.

The Genetics of Alcoholism

- Studies of adoptions and twins have provided information about the relative influences of genetics and environment on the development of alcoholism.

- A distinction has been made between a male or female alcoholic with drinking problems occurring late in life (Type 1) and a male alcoholic with drinking problems occurring in adolescence (Type 2). The latter subgroup appears to have a greater genetic component in the inheritance pattern.

The Concept of Alcoholism as a Disease

- The majority position with respect to alcoholism is that it should be considered a disease and that alcoholics should be treated rather than punished. Since 1957, the American Medical Association has supported this idea.

- Unfortunately, recent surveys of primary-care physicians indicate that the medical profession is frequently ill prepared to diagnose alcoholism or supervise effective treatment.

Approaches to Treatment for Alcoholism

- Approaches include biologically based treatments and psychosocial treatments such as the self-help programs of Alcoholics Anonymous (AA).

- Objections to certain aspects of the AA philosophy have promoted the growth of other self-help organizations, such as Moderation Management (MM) and SMART Recovery.

- Debate continues as to whether alcoholics can sustain a controlled amount of alcohol without losing ground in one's recovery. Only a small proportion of alcoholics are successful in doing so.

- Corporations and other large organizations have instituted employee assistance programs (EAPs), and unions have instituted member assistance programs (MAPs), to help workers with problems of alcohol abuse or other forms of drug abuse.

Key Terms

abstinence, p. 326
acamprosate, p. 338
alcohol abuse, p. 327
alcohol dependence, p. 328
alcoholic cirrhosis, p. 329
alcoholic dementia, p. 330
alcoholic hepatitis, p. 329
Alcoholics Anonymous
(AA), p. 338
alcoholism, p. 324

alcohol withdrawal
syndrome, p. 329
children of alcoholics
(COAs), p. 335
codependency, p. 334
concordance rate, p. 336
confabulation, p. 331
delirium tremens
(DTs), p. 329
disulfiram, p. 337

employee assistance
programs (EAPs), p. 343
enablers, p. 326
fatty liver, p. 329
fetal alcohol effect (FAE),
p. 332
fetal alcohol syndrome
(FAS), p. 331
member assistance programs
(MAPs), p. 343

nalmefene, p. 337
naltrexone, p. 337
ondansetron, p. 338
SMART Recovery, p. 341
symptomatic drinking, p. 324
systems approach, p. 334
teratogenic, p. 331
thiamine, p. 331
Wernicke-Korsakoff
syndrome, p. 331

Endnotes

1. Based upon Kinney, Jean (2006). *Loosening the grip: A handbook of alcohol information*. New York: McGraw-Hill, p. 215.
2. Goodwin, Donald W., and Gabrielli, William F. (1997). Alcohol: Clinical aspects. In Joyce H. Lowinson, Pedro Ruiz, Robert B. Millman, and John G. Langrod (Eds.), *Substance abuse: A comprehensive textbook*. Baltimore: Williams & Wilkins, pp. 142–148. Hoff, Ebbe Curtis (1974). *Alcoholism: The hidden addiction*. New York: Seabury Press, pp. 75–88. Kinney, *Loosening the grip*, pp. 66–92.
3. Hofmann, Frederick G. (1983). *A handbook on drug and alcohol abuse* (2nd ed.). New York: Oxford University Press, p. 99.
4. Hoff, *Alcoholism*, pp. 78–79.
5. Drobes, David J., and Thomas, Suzanne E. (1999). Assessing craving for alcohol. *Alcohol Research and Health*, 23, 179–186.
6. Conner, Kenneth R.; Yue, Li; Meldrum, Sean; Duberstein, Paul R.; and Conwell, Y. (2003). The role of drinking in suicidal ideation: Analysis of Project MATCH data. *Journal of Studies on Alcohol*, 64, 402–408. Schuckit, Marc A. (2000). *Drug and alcohol abuse: A clinical guide to diagnostic and treatment* (5th ed.). New York: Kluver Academic/Plenum, pp. 54–97.
7. Maiden, R. Paul (1997). Alcohol dependence and domestic violence: Incidence and treatment implications. *Alcohol Treatment Quarterly*, 15, 31–50. U.S. Department of Health and Human Services (1990). *Alcohol and health* (Seventh Special Report to the U.S. Congress). Rockville, MD: National Institute on Alcohol Abuse and Alcoholism, p. 174.
8. National Institute on Alcohol Abuse and Alcoholism (2000, April). Alcohol Alert: Imaging and alcoholism: A window on the brain. No. 47. Rockville, MD: National Institute on Alcohol Abuse and Alcoholism.
9. Fishbein, Diana H., and Pease, Susan E. (1996). *The dynamics of drug abuse*. Needham Heights, MA: Allyn and Bacon, pp. 122–124.
10. American Psychiatric Association (2000). *Diagnostic and statistical manual of mental disorders* (4th ed.). *Text Revision*. Washington, DC: American Psychiatric Association, pp. 213–214.
11. Grant, Bridget F.; Stinson, Frederick S.; Dawson, Deborah A.; Chou, S. Patricia; Dufour, Mary C.; et al. (2004). Prevalence and co-occurrence of substance use disorders and independent mood and anxiety disorders. *Archives of General Psychiatry*, 61, 807–816. National Institute on Alcohol Abuse and Alcoholism (1995, October). Alcohol Alert: Diagnostic criteria for alcohol abuse and dependence. No. 30. Bethesda, MD: National Institute on Alcohol Abuse and Alcoholism.
12. Schuckit, *Drug and alcohol abuse*, pp. 79–80.
13. Becker, Howard (2008). Alcohol dependence, withdrawal, and relapse. *Alcohol Research and Health*, 31, 348–361.
14. Centers for Disease Control and Prevention (2009, April 17). Deaths: Final data for 2006. *National Vital Statistics Reports*, 57, p. 1, Table 13. Lieber, Charles S. (2001). Alcohol and hepatitis C. *Alcohol Research and Health*, 25, 245–254. Szabo, Gyongyi, and Mandrekar, Pranoti (2010). Alcohol and the liver. *Alcohol Research and Health*, 33, 87–96.
15. Mukamal, Kenneth J.; Tolstrup, Janne S.; Friberg, Jens; Jensen, Gorm; and Gronbaek, Morton (2005). Alcohol consumption and risk of atrial fibrillation in men and women. *Circulation*, 112, 1736–1742.
16. Bagnardi, Vincenzo, Blangliardo, Marta, and LaVecchia, Carlo (2001). Alcohol consumption and the risk of cancer: A meta-analysis. *Alcohol Research and Health*, 25, 263–270. Molina, Patricia E.; Happel, Kyle I.; Zhang, Ping; Kolls, Jay K.; and Nelson, Steve (2010). Alcohol and the immune system. *Alcohol Research and Health*, 33, 97–108. Smith-Warner, Stephanie A.; Spiegelman, Donna; Shiaw-Shyuan, Yuan; Van den Brandt, Piet A.; Folsom, Aaron R.; et al. (1998). Alcohol and breast cancer in women: A pooled analysis of cohort studies. *Journal of the American Medical Association*, 279, 535–540.

17. National Institute on Alcohol Abuse and Alcoholism (2001, July). Alcohol Alert: Cognitive impairment and recovery from alcoholism. No. 53. Rockville, MD: National Institute on Alcohol Abuse and Alcoholism. U.S. Department of Health and Human Services (1990). *Alcohol and health*, pp. 123–124.

18. McEvoy, Joseph P. (1982). The chronic neuropsychiatric disorders associated with alcoholism. In E. Mansell Pattison and Edward Kaufman (Eds.), *Encyclopedic handbook of alcoholism*. New York: Gardner Press, pp. 167–179.

19. Golden, Janet (2005). *Message in a bottle: The making of fetal alcohol syndrome*. Cambridge, MA: Harvard University Press. Jones, Kenneth L., and Smith, David W. (1973). Recognition of the fetal alcohol syndrome in early infancy. *Lancet*, 2, 999–1001. Sokol, Robert J., Delaney-Black, Virginia, and Nordstrom, Beth (2003). Fetal alcohol spectrum disorder. *Journal of the American Medical Association*, 290, 2996–2999. Thomas, Jennifer, Warren, Kenneth, and Hewitt, Brenda G. (2010). Fetal alcohol spectrum disorders: From research to policy. *Alcohol Research and Health*, 33, 118–126.

20. Ma, Grace X.; Toubbeh, Jamil; Cline, Janette; and Chisholm, Anita (1998). Fetal alcohol syndrome among Native American adolescents: A model prevention program. *Journal of Primary Prevention, 19*, 43–55. Morbidity and Mortality Weekly Report (2002). Fetal alcohol syndrome—Alaska, Arizona, Colorado, and New York, 1995–1997. *Journal of the American Medical Association*, 288, 38–40. U.S. Department of Health and Human Services (2000). *Alcohol and health*, pp. 283–299.

21. National Institute on Alcohol Abuse and Alcoholism (2000, December). Alcohol Alert: Fetal alcohol exposure and the brain. No. 13. Bethesda, MD: National Institute on Alcohol Abuse and Alcoholism. U.S. Department of Health and Human Services (2000). *Alcohol and health*, pp. 300–322.

22. May, Philip A. (1991). Fetal alcohol effects among North American Indians. *Alcohol Health and Research World, 15*, 239–248. National Institute on Alcohol Abuse and Alcoholism (2004, July). Alcohol Alert: Alcohol—An important women's health issue. Bethesda, MD: National Institute on Alcohol Abuse and Alcoholism. U.S. Department of Health and Human Services (2000). *Alcohol and health*, pp. 323–336.

23. Carroll, Linda (2003, November 4). Alcohol's toll on fetuses: Even worse than thought. *New York Times*, pp. F1, F6. Centers for Disease Control and Prevention (2004, December 24). Alcohol consumption among women who are pregnant or who might become pregnant—United States, 2002. *Morbidity and Mortality Weekly Report*, 1178–1181. Floyd, R. Louise; O'Connor, Mary J.; Sokol, Robert J.; Bertrand, Jacquelyn; and Cordero, José F. (2005). Recognition and prevention of fetal alcohol syndrome. *Obstetrics and Gynecology, 106*, 1059–1064.

24. Mokdad, Ali H.; Marks, James S.; Stroup, Donna F.; and Gerberding, Julie L. (2004). Actual causes of death in the United States, 2000. *Journal of the American Medical Association*, 291, 1238–1245.

25. Cloninger, C. Robert (1987). Neurogenetic adaptive mechanisms in alcoholism. *Science, 236*, 410–416. National Institute on Alcohol Abuse and Alcoholism (1999, December). Alcohol Alert: Are women more vulnerable to alcohol's effects? No. 46. Rockville, MD: National Institute on Alcohol Abuse and Alcoholism.

26. LaValle, Robin, and Yi, Hsiao-ye. (2010, August). *Surveillance Report 90. Apparent per capita alcohol consumption: National, state and regional trends, 1977–2008*. Bethesda, MD: National Institute on Alcohol Abuse and Alcoholism, Division of Epidemiology and Prevention Research, Alcohol Epidemiologic Data System, Figure 5.

27. Merrick, Elizabeth L.; Horgan, Constance M.; Hodgkin, Dominic; Garrick, Deborah W.; et al. (2008). Unhealthy drinking patterns in older adults: Prevalence and associated characteristics. *Journal of the American Geriatrics Society, 56*, 214–223.

28. Brody, Jane E. (2002, April 2). Hidden plague of alcohol abuse by the elderly. *New York Times*, p. F7. Fleming, Michael F.; Manwell, Linda B.; Barry, Kristen L.; Adams, Wendy; and Stauffacher, Ellyn A. (1999). Brief physician advice for alcohol problems in older adults: A randomized community-based trial. *Journal of Family Practice, 48*, 378–384. Graham, Kathryn; Della Clarke, Christine B.; Carver, Virginia; Dolinki, Louise; Smythe, Cynthia; et al. (1996). Addictive behaviors in older adults. *Addictive Behaviors, 21*, 331–348. Substance Abuse and Mental Health Services Administration (2007, January/February). Treatment for older adults: What works best? *SAMHSA News*, pp. 1–5.

29. DiNitto, Diana M., and McNeece, C. Aaron (1994). *Chemical dependency: A systems approach*. Englewood Cliffs, NJ: Prentice-Hall, pp. 214–239.

30. Doweiko, Harold E. (1993). *Concepts of chemical dependency* (2nd ed.). Pacific Grove, CA: Brooks-Cole, p. 265.

31. Whitfield, Charles L. (1997). Co-dependence, addictions, and related disorders. In Lowinson et al. (Eds.), *Substance abuse: A comprehensive textbook* (3rd ed.). Baltimore: Williams & Wilkins, pp. 672–683.

32. Anderson, S. C. (1994). A critical analysis of the concept of codependency. *Social Work, 39*, 677–685. Doweiko, *Concepts of chemical dependency*, pp. 269–271, 282–284.

33. Erblich, Joel, and Earleywine, Mitchell (1999). Children of alcoholics exhibit attenuated cognitive impairment during an ethanol challenge. *Alcoholism: Clinical and Experimental Research, 23*, 476–482. Hussong, Andrea M., Curran, Patrick J., and Chassin, Laurie (1998). Pathways of risk for accelerated heavy alcohol use among adolescent children of alcoholic parents. *Journal of Abnormal Child Psychology, 26*, 453–466.

34. Cloninger, Neurogenetic adaptive mechanisms. Cloninger, C. Robert, Gohman, M., and Sigvardsson, S. (1981). Inheritance of alcohol abuse: Cross fostering analysis of adopted men. *Archives of General Psychiatry, 38*, 861–868.

35. McGue, Matt, Pickens, Roy W., and Svikis, Dace S. (1992). Sex and age effects on the inheritance of alcohol problems: A twin study. *Journal of Abnormal Psychology*, *101*, 3–17. Substance Abuse and Mental Health Services Administration (2009, June 18). Fathers' alcohol use and substance use among adolescents. *The NSDUH Report*. Rockville MD: Office of Applied Studies, Substance Abuse and Mental Health Services Administration.

36. Foroud, Tatiana, Edenberg, Howard J., and Crabbe, John C. (2010). Genetic research: Who is at risk for alcoholism? *Alcohol Research and Health*, *33*, 64–75. Nurnberger, John I., and Bierut, Laura Jean. (2007, April). Seeking the connections: Alcoholism and our genes. *Scientific American*, pp. 46–53.

37. Jellinek, E. M. (1960). *The disease concept of alcoholism*. New Haven, CT: Hillhouse Press. Vaillant, George E. (1995). *The natural history of alcoholism revisited*. Cambridge, MA: Harvard University Press.

38. George, William H., and Marlatt, G. Alan. (1983). Alcoholism: The evolution of a behavioral perspective. In Marc Galanter (Ed.), *Recent developments in alcoholism*. Vol. 1. New York: Plenum, pp. 105–138.

39. Maltzman, Irving (1994). Why alcoholism is a disease. *Journal of Psychoactive Drugs*, *26*, 13–31. National Center on Addiction and Substance Abuse at Columbia University (2000, May). *Missed opportunity: National survey of primary care physicians and patients on substance abuse*. New York: National Center on Addiction and Substance Abuse at Columbia University.

40. Fuller, Richard K., and Hiller-Sturmhöfel, Susanne (1999). Alcoholism treatment in the United States. *Alcohol Research and Health*, *23*, 69–77.

41. Banys, Peter (1988). The clinical use of disulfiram (Antabuse): A review. *Journal of Psychoactive Drugs*, *20*, 243–261.

42. Flannery, B. A.; Poole, S. A.; Gallop, R. J.; and Volpicelli, J. R. (2003). Alcohol craving predicts drinking during treatment: An analysis of three assessment instruments. *Journal of Studies on Alcohol*, *64*, 120–126. Johnson, Bankole A.; Rosenthal, Norman; Capece, Julie A.; Wiegand, Frank; Mao, Lian; et al. (2007). Topiramate for treating alcohol dependence: A randomized controlled trial. *Journal of the American Medical Association*, *298*, 1641–1651. Scott, Lesley J.; Figgitt, David P.; Keam, Susan J.; and Waugh, John (2005). Acamprosate: A review of its use in the maintenance of abstinence in patients with alcohol dependence. *CNS Drugs*, *19*, 445–464. Substance Abuse and Mental Health Services Administration (2007, May/June). Treating alcohol dependence: Naltrexone advisory. *SAMHSA News*, p. 14.

43. Hopson, Ronald E., and Beaird-Spiller, Bethany (1995). Why AA works: A psychological analysis of the addictive experience and the efficacy of Alcoholics Anonymous. *Alcoholism Treatment Quarterly*, *12*, 1–17. Morgenstern, Jon; Bux, Donald; LaBouvie, Erich; Blanchard, Kimberly A.; and Morgan, Thomas J. (2002). Examining mechanisms of action in a 12-step treatment: The role of 12-step cognitions. *Journal of Studies on Alcohol*, *63*, 665–672. White, William H. (1998). *Slaying the dragon: The history of addiction treatment and recovery in America*. Bloomington, IL: Chestnut Health Systems, pp. 127–177.

44. Forcehimes, Alyssa A. (2004). *De Profundis*: Spiritual transformations in Alcoholics Anonymous. *Journal of Clinical Psychology/In Session*, *60*, 503–517. How effective is Alcoholics Anonymous? (2003, December). *Harvard Medical Letter*, p. 7.

45. Ellis, Albert, and Velten, Emmett (1992). *When AA doesn't work for you: Rational steps to quitting alcohol*. Fort Lee, NJ: Barricade Press. Kaskutas, Lee A. (1996). A road less traveled: Choosing the "Women for Sobriety" program. *Journal of Drug Issues*, *26*, 77–94. Schmidt, Eric (1996). Rational recovery: Finding an alternative for addiction treatment. *Alcoholism Treatment Quarterly*, *14*, 47–57. SMART Recovery (2004). *SMART Recovery handbook*. Mentor, OH: SMART Recovery®. Winzelberg, Andrew, and Humphreys, Keith (1999). Should patients' religiosity influence clinicians' referral to 12-step self-help groups? Evidence from a study of 3,018 male substance abuse patients. *Journal of Consulting and Clinical Psychology*, *67*, 790–794.

46. Goode, Erich (1999). *Drugs in American society* (5th ed.). Boston: McGraw-Hill College, p. 194. Hester, Reid K., and Miller, William R. (1989). Self-control training. In Reid K. Hester and William R. Miller (Eds.), *Handbook of alcoholism treatment approaches*. New York: Pergamon Press, pp. 141–149. Miller, William R. (1989). Increasing motivation for change. In Reid K. Hester and William R. Miller (Eds.), *Handbook of alcoholism treatment approaches*. New York: Pergamon Press, pp 67–80. Quotation on p. 77. Sobell, Mark B., and Sobell, Linda C. (1978). *Behavioral treatment of alcohol problems: Individualized therapy and controlled drinking*. New York: Plenum.

47. Frone, Michael R. (2006). Prevalence and distribution of alcohol use and impairment in the workplace: A U.S. national survey. *Journal of Studies on Alcohol and Drugs*, *67*, 147–156.

48. Bachrach, Samuel B., Bamberger, Peter A., and McKinney, Valerie M. (2007). Harassing under the influence: The prevalence of male heavy drinking, the embeddedness of permissive workplace drinking norms, and the gender harassment of female coworkers. *Journal of Occupational Health Psychology*, *13*, 232–250. Substance Abuse and Mental Health Services Administration (2009, April 9). Alcohol treatment: Need, utilization, and barriers. *The NSDIH Report*. Rockville, MD: Office of Applied Studies, Substance Abuse and Mental Health Services Administration. Osilla, Karen C.; Zellmer, Steven P.; Larimer, Mary E.: Neighbors, Clayton; and Marlatt, G. Alan (2008). A brief intervention for at-risk drinking in an employee assistance program. *Journal of Studies on Alcohol and Drugs*, *69*, 14–20.

chapter 15

Nicotine and Tobacco Use

I know the old joke. Mark Twain said that quitting smoking was easy and that he should know because he had done it a thousand times.

Well, I should know too. It seems that I've tried to quit a *million* times. I realize it's not good for me; I'm no fool. But somehow I keep on smoking. My fellow smokers and I cluster on the sidewalk outside our offices in the mornings and the afternoons, standing out there in the rain and the cold. I feel like an outcast of society, day in and day out. Someday I'll stop, but in the meantime I will just have to contend with the disapproving glances—and the feelings of failure.

—*Anonymous*

After you have completed this chapter, you should have an understanding of

- The present-day tobacco industry
- The main culprits: carbon monoxide, tar, and nicotine
- Nicotine as a stimulant drug
- Nicotine and smoking dependence
- Adverse health consequences of smoking
- Patterns of tobacco use in the United States
- Global issues in the control of tobacco use
- Strategies for people who want to stop smoking

In some ways, our attitudes toward tobacco have not changed very much over the years. In the sixteenth century, when tobacco was first introduced to the Western world, smoking behavior was considered personally objectionable, yet strangely alluring. The same is true today. And judging from the opening quotation, people in the twenty-first century have as much difficulty quitting as they did in Mark Twain's time.

In other ways, however, the times have definitely changed. For almost fifty years, until the mid-1960s, lighting up and smoking a cigarette was an unquestioned sign of sophistication. There was little or no public awareness that harm would come of it, a possibility that was concealed for decades by the major tobacco companies. It was an era before surgeon general's reports, National Smoke-out Days, and smoke-free restaurants, hotels, and public buildings.

Today, it is no longer a matter of debate that tobacco smoking is a major health hazard, not only to the person doing the smoking but also to society at large. These concerns are based not on public attitudes that can shift over time but on solid scientific fact. It is also no longer a matter of debate that the main psychoactive ingredient in tobacco, nicotine, is a major dependence-producing drug. Even the tobacco companies now concede that their product is dangerous.

Yet, at the same time, the reality is that tobacco products are legally sanctioned commodities with an economic significance, both to the United States and to the world. Banning tobacco products would lead us into a Prohibition era comparable to or perhaps exceeding in social upheaval the one experienced with respect to alcohol in the last century. How did we arrive at this point, and what lies ahead? This chapter will explore what we now know about the effects of tobacco smoking and other forms of tobacco consumption, the impact these behaviors have had on U.S. society and the world, and the ways in which we have dealt with the issue of tobacco over the years. It also will consider current approaches to helping people who choose to stop smoking, and prevention strategies to encourage young people not to start smoking in the first place.

Tobacco Use through History

Shortly after setting foot on the small island of San Salvador on October 12, 1492, Christopher Columbus received from the inhabitants a welcoming gift of large, green, sweet-smelling tobacco leaves. Never having seen tobacco before, Columbus did not know what to make of this curious offering, except to observe in his journal that the leaves were greatly prized by the "Indians." In the first week of November, two members of the expedition ventured to the shores of Cuba, searching at Columbus's insistence for the great khan of Cathay (China). They found no evidence of the khan but did return with reports of natives who apparently were "drinking smoke."

Before long, Columbus's men were "tobacco drinking" as well. One sailor in particular, Rodrigo de Jerez, became quite fond of the practice. He was, in fact, history's first documented European smoker, though he lived to regret it. When Rodrigo returned to Spain, he volunteered to demonstrate the newfound custom to his neighbors, who instead of being impressed thought that anyone who could emit smoke from the nose and mouth without burning had to be possessed by the Devil. A parish priest turned Rodrigo over to the Inquisition, which sentenced him to imprisonment for witchcraft. He spent several years in jail, presumably without a supply of tobacco. Rodrigo therefore also may be remembered as the first European smoker to quit cold turkey.[1]

In 1560, the year historians mark as the year tobacco was officially introduced to Europe, a Spanish physician brought some tobacco plants back from the New World and presented them to King Philip II of Spain. Suddenly, the practice of smoking tobacco through long, elaborate pipes became fashionable among European aristocracy.

Not everyone was enthusiastic about this new fad. In 1604, predating a modern-day surgeon general's report by more than 350 years, King James I of England wrote, "A Counter-blaste to Tobacco," a lengthy treatise condemning tobacco use. Referring to tobacco as a "stinking weede," he characterized smoking as "a custom loathsome to the eye, hateful to the nose, harmful to the brain, [and] dangerous to the lung." In the first recorded comment on its potential for causing dependence, the king observed that "he that taketh tobacco saith he cannot leave it, it doth bewitch him."

Politics, Economics, and Tobacco

Elsewhere in the world, during the early seventeenth century, the condemnation of tobacco became extreme. In Russia, officials established penalties for smoking that included whipping, mutilation, exile to Siberia, and death. Turkey, Japan, and China tried similar tactics, but, not surprisingly, tobacco use continued to spread.[2]

By the end of the seventeenth century even the fiercest opponents of tobacco had to concede that it was here to stay. A sultan of Turkey in 1648 became a smoker himself, and naturally, penalties for tobacco use vanished overnight; Czar Peter the Great in 1689 pledged to open up Russia to the West, and tobacco suddenly became a welcome symbol of modernism; Japan and China stopped trying to enforce a prohibition that citizens obviously did not want. Even England's James I put aside his personal dislike for tobacco and quickly recognized the attractive prospect of sizable revenue from taxes imposed on this popular new commodity.[3]

Snuffing and Chewing

One form of tobacco use observed by the early Spanish explorers was the practice of grinding a mixture of tobacco into a fine powder (**snuff**), placing or sniffing a pinch of it into the nose, and exhaling it with a sneeze. By the 1700s, this custom, called **snuffing**, overtook smoking as the dominant form of tobacco use. Among French aristocrats, both men and women, expensive snuffs, perfumed with exotic scents and carried in jeweled and enameled boxes, became part of the daily routine at the court in France and then in the rest of Europe. Sneezing was considered to clear the head of "superfluous humours," invigorate the brain, and brighten the eyes. In an era when bad smells were constant features of daily living, snuffing brought some degree of relief, not to mention a very effective way of sending nicotine to the brain (see Chapter 1).

Because of their dominance in the rapidly expanding tobacco market, the English colonies in America, particularly Virginia, prospered greatly. England enjoyed a profitable tobacco trade, but you might say that its development of colonial tobacco growing eventually backfired. In 1777, when Benjamin Franklin was sent as an envoy to France to gain support against the British in the American War for Independence, a key factor in his success was an offer to deliver prime Virginia tobacco in return for French money. The French agreed, and the rest is history. Had it not been for American

tobacco, there might not have been a United States of America at all.[4]

In the United States, snuffing was soon replaced by a more rough-and-ready method for using tobacco: chewing. The practice was not totally new; early Spanish explorers had found the natives chewing tobacco as well as smoking it from the earliest days of their conquest, though North American tribes preferred smoking exclusively. Chewing tobacco had the advantage of freeing the hands for work, and its low cost made it a democratic custom befitting a vigorous new nation in the nineteenth century. However, the need to spit out tobacco juices on a regular basis raised the tobacco habit to unimaginable heights of gross behavior. It was enough to make the objections to smoke and of possible fire fade into insignificance; now the problem was a matter of public health. Tobacco spitting became a major factor behind the spread of infectious diseases such as tuberculosis. Adding to this unsavory picture was the likelihood that a man's accuracy in targeting the nearest spittoon was inevitably compromised by his level of alcohol consumption, which was setting all-time records during this period (see Chapter 13). A present-day baseball dugout seems, by comparison, to be a model of decorum.

Cigars and Cigarettes

By the time of the American Civil War, the fashion in tobacco use began to shift once more, as its overall popularity continued to soar. Although the plug of tobacco suitable for chewing was still a major seller and would remain so until the early twentieth century, two new trends emerged, particularly in the growing industrial cities.

The first trend was the popularity of smoking **cigars** (commonly known as "seegars"), tight rolls of dried tobacco leaves. New innovations in curing (drying) tobacco leaves had produced a milder and lighter-quality leaf that was more suitable for smoking than the older forms that had been around since the colonial period. North Carolina, with its ideal soil for cultivating this type of tobacco, began to dominate as the tobacco-growing center of the United States; it continues to do so today. With the advent of cigars, tobacco consumers could combine the feeling of chewing (since the cigar remained in the mouth for a relatively long period of time) and the effects of ingesting tobacco smoke. Pioneers heading west could indulge in foot-long cigars called "stogies," named after the Conestoga wagons that they rode during the long and tedious journey.

The second trend was the introduction of **cigarettes**, rolls of shredded tobacco wrapped in paper.

---

snuff: A quantity of finely shredded or powdered tobacco. Modern forms of snuff are available in either dry or moist forms.

snuffing: The ingestion of snuff either by inhalation or by absorption through tissue in the nose.

cigars: Tightly rolled quantities of dried tobacco leaves.

cigarettes: Rolls of shredded tobacco wrapped in paper, today usually fitted at the mouth end with a filter.

They had become popular among British soldiers returning from the Crimean War in 1856, who had adopted the practice from the Turks. Europe took to cigarettes immediately, but the United States proved a harder sell. Part of the problem was the opposition of a well-entrenched U.S. cigar industry, which did not look kindly on an upstart competitor. Cigar makers did not discourage the circulation of rumors that the cigarette paper wrapping was actually soaked in arsenic or white lead, that cigarette factory workers were urinating on the tobacco to give it an extra "bite," or that Egyptian brands were mixed with crushed camel dung.[5]

An even greater marketing challenge than unsubstantiated rumors was the effeminate image of cigarette smoking itself. A cigarette was looked upon as a dainty, sissy version of the he-man cigar; cigars were fat, long, and dark, whereas cigarettes were slender, short, and light. Well into the beginning of the twentieth century, this attitude persisted. This is what John L. Sullivan, champion boxer and self-appointed defender of American masculinity, thought of cigarettes in 1904:

> Who smokes 'em? Dudes and college stiffs—fellows who'd be wiped out by a single jab or a quick undercut. It isn't natural to smoke cigarettes. An American ought to smoke cigars . . . It's the Dutchmen, Italians, Russians, Turks, and Egyptians who smoke cigarettes and they're no good anyhow.[6]

The public image of the cigarette eventually would change dramatically; until then, cigarette manufacturers had to rely instead on a powerful marketing advantage: low cost. In 1881, James Bonsack patented a cigarette-making machine that transformed the tobacco industry. Instead of producing at most 300 cigarettes an hour by hand, three machine operators could now turn out 200 a minute, or roughly 120,000 cigarettes a day. This is a snail's pace compared to the present state-of-the-art machines capable of producing more than 10,000 cigarettes a minute, but in those days, the Bonsack machine was viewed as an industrial miracle. Cigarette prices by the end of the 1800s were as cheap as twenty for a nickel.[7]

Tobacco in the Twentieth Century

At the beginning of the twentieth century, Americans could choose from a variety of ways to satisfy their hunger for tobacco. Cigars and pipes were still the dominant form of tobacco use, but the future favored the cigarette for two basic reasons.

First, a growing number of women began to challenge the idea of masculine dominance, and smoking tobacco was one of the privileges of men that women now wanted to share. Not that women smoking was met with immediate acceptance; in one famous case in 1904, a New York City woman was arrested for smoking in public. Nonetheless, as smoking among women became more common, the mild-tasting, easy-to-hold cigarette was the perfect option for them. By the 1920s, advertising slogans such as "Reach for a Lucky instead of a sweet" (a clever effort to portray cigarette smoking as a weight-control aid) as well as endorsements by glamorous celebrities were being designed specifically for the women's market. A second factor was World War I, during which time cigarettes were a logical form of tobacco to take along to war. Times of tension have always been times of increased tobacco use. When the war was over, the cigarette was, in the words of one historian, "enshrined forever as the weary soldier's relief, the worried man's support, and the relaxing man's companion."[8]

Cigarettes really came into their own in the 1920s, with the introduction of heavily advertised brand names and intense competition among American tobacco companies. Cigarette sales in the United States increased from $45 billion in 1920 to $80 billion in 1925 and $180 billion by 1940.[9]

To encourage male cigarette smokers, advertisements drew heavily on an association with baseball players. What is arguably the most famous and most valuable baseball card, depicting 1909 baseball player Honus Wagner, was actually included in a packet of cigarettes, long before baseball cards became associated with bubble gum.

Health Concerns
and Smoking Behavior

A combination of promotion through mass-media advertising and the endorsement of smoking by sports celebrities and glamorous people in the entertainment industry enabled the tobacco industry, now dominated by cigarettes, to increase its volume of sales from the 1940s to the 1980s by a steady 9 billion cigarettes each year. The peak in domestic sales was reached in 1981, when approximately 640 billion were sold. Owing to the increase in population, however, per capita consumption in the United States had peaked in 1963 at approximately 4,300 cigarettes per year (roughly twelve cigarettes per day).

Beginning in 1964, per capita consumption began a steady decline to the present level of approximately 2,100 cigarettes per year (roughly six cigarettes per day). The year of the turnaround coincided with the U.S. surgeon general's first report on smoking and health. For the first time, the federal government asserted publicly what had been suspected for decades: that tobacco smoking was linked to cancer and other serious diseases. From the standpoint of tobacco use in America, surgeon general's reports issued from 1964 to 2006 resulted in a number of developments in smoking behavior.

- In the month or so immediately after the first report was released, there was a dramatic drop (approximately 25 percent) in per capita consumption levels. Although succeeding months in 1964 showed a bounce upward, most likely reflecting the fact that many people who tried to quit had only temporary success, the long-term trend in U.S. tobacco consumption from that point on would never be upward again.

- As evidence of health risks accumulated, restrictions on public consumption were instituted. In 1971, all television advertising for tobacco was banned, and in 1984, a rotating series of warning labels (already on all packages of tobacco products since 1966) was required on all print advertisements and outdoor billboards.

- There was a significant change in the type of cigarette smoked by the average smoker. In the 1950s, more and more cigarette smokers chose to smoke *filtered as* distinct from *unfiltered* cigarettes, in an effort to ingest less of the toxins in tobacco. By the 1990s,

about 95 percent of all smokers were using filtered brands. However, after the introduction of filtered cigarettes, the industry *changed* the formulation of the tobacco to a stronger blend with an increased tar content. As a result of a stronger "filter blend" formula in the cigarette, **sidestream smoke**, the smoke directly inhaled by a nonsmoker from a burning cigarette, ended up more toxic when originating from a filtered cigarette than it was from an unfiltered one. In principle, a cigarette filter should have allowed a flow of air through small holes in the filter itself. Because a smoker typically held the cigarette with the fingers covering these holes, however, little or no filtering was accomplished. In the meantime, filtered cigarettes increased tobacco company profits. Filters were only paper and therefore cost considerably less than filling the same space with tobacco.

- As a consequence of the surgeon general's assertion that tar and nicotine were specifically responsible for increased health risks from smoking, new "light" and "mild" cigarette brands were introduced that were low in tar and nicotine (T/N), and the Federal Trade Commission began to issue a listing of tar and nicotine levels in major commercial brands. As later surgeon general's reports indicated, however, smokers cancelled out the benefits of switching to low T/N brands by varying the manner in which they smoked a low T/N cigarette. Smokers took more puffs, inhaled more deeply, and smoked more of the cigarette when it has a lower T/N level so as to maintain the same amount of nicotine (the same number of nicotine "hits"). Moreover, a greater number of low T/N cigarettes had to be smoked in order to satisfy the smoker's needs. In 2010, tobacco companies changed the branding labels to acknowledge that "light" or "mild" brands were no less harmful than regular brands. Marlboro Lights, for example, became Marlboro Gold, and, Marlboro Ultra Lights became Marlboro Silver.

- In 2007, it was confirmed that cigarette manufacturers had increased the nicotine concentrations in tobacco from 1997 to 2005 by 11 percent and also had modified certain design features of the cigarettes themselves to increase the number of puffs per cigarette during smoking. In the "medium/mild" market category, nicotine levels more than doubled from 1998 to 2005 in nonmetholated cigarettes and rose by 22 percent in mentholated cigarettes (Drugs . . . in Focus, page 353). Whether tobacco companies will be required to make modifications in their products, bringing nicotine levels back to 1997 levels, under new regulations (see next section) remains uncertain.[10]

sidestream smoke: Tobacco smoke that is inhaled by nonsmokers from the burning cigarettes of nearby smokers. Also referred to as environmental tobacco smoke.

Drugs... in Focus

African Americans, Smoking, and Mentholated Cigarettes

It has long been puzzling that African Americans tend to smoke fewer cigarettes than white smokers but carry a higher risk of tobacco-related disorders such as lung cancer and heart disease. One factor that has been used as an explanation is the relatively slower rate of nicotine metabolism among African Americans following cigarette smoking (Chapter 1). African Americans may be taking in and retaining relatively more nicotine per cigarette and, as a result, may not need to smoke as many cigarettes per day to take in an equivalent dose of nicotine.

Recent studies have indicated that a major factor might be the menthol in certain brands of cigarettes. More than 60 percent of African American smokers prefer mentholated brands such as Newport and Kool over nonmentholated brands such as Marlboro and Camel, almost the complete opposite to the pattern of brand preferences among white smokers. Menthol allows smokers to take in more smoke and possibly hold it in longer, essentially canceling any benefit of choosing a "light" or "ultralight" brand to smoke. Relative to other smokers, African Americans who smoked menthol cigarettes had higher levels in their saliva of a specific nicotine by-product. The finding that smokers of mentholated cigarettes are almost twice as likely to relapse after attempts to quit smoking, compared to smokers of nonmentholated cigarettes, is consistent with the relatively higher levels of nicotine intake likely to occur when one is smoking mentholated brands.

The growing evidence of the effect of menthol content in cigarettes on smoking behavior and the implications with regard to smoking cessation have led some to demand that tobacco companies be required to report how much menthol is contained in various cigarette brands, as they now do for levels of nicotine and tars. Others have even called for mentholated cigarettes to be banned altogether. These actions might be required as part of future FDA regulations over tobacco products, as authorized by the Tobacco Control Act of 2009.

Sources: Celebucki, Carolyn C.; Wayne, Geoffrey, F.; Connolly, Gregory N.; Pankow, James F.; and Chang, Elsa I. (2005). Characterization of measured menthol in 48 U.S. cigarette sub-brands. *Nicotine and Tobacco Research, 7,* 523–531. Mustonen, Tanu K.; Spencer, Stacie M.; Hoskinson, Randall A.; Sachs, David P. L.; and Garvey, Arthur J. (2005). The influence of gender, race, and menthol content on tobacco exposure measures. *Nicotine and Tobacco Research, 7,* 581–590. Pletcher, Mark J.; Hulley, Benjamin J.; Houston, Thomas; Kiefe, Catarina; Benowitz, Neal; et al. (2006). Menthol cigarettes, smoking cessation, atherosclerosis, and pulmonary function. *Archives of Internal Medicine, 166,* 1915–1922. Samet, Jonathan, and Wipfli, Heather (2009). Unfinished business in tobacco control. *Journal of the American Medical Association, 302,* 681–682. Substance Abuse and Mental Health Services Administration (2009, November 19). Use of menthol cigarettes. *The NSDUH Report.* Rockville, MD: Substance Abuse and Mental Health Services Administration.

Tobacco Today: An Industry on the Defensive

The tobacco industry in the United States, since the early 1990s, has faced continuing challenges from federal governmental agencies as well as individuals and groups who have sued tobacco companies for damages resulting from the ingestion of their tobacco products. As a result, the legal and economic status of the tobacco industry has been altered significantly.

Two major events occurred that would forever change the image of tobacco use in American society. In 1993, the U.S. Environmental Protection Agency (EPA) announced its conclusion from available research that **environmental tobacco smoke (ETS)**, the sidestream smoke in the air that is inhaled by nonsmokers as a result of tobacco smoking, causes lung cancer. Since then, most U.S. states, cities, and communities have enacted laws mandating smoke-free environments in all public and private workplaces, unless ventilated smoking rooms have been provided. It is now commonplace for restaurants, hotels, and other commercial spaces to

environmental tobacco smoke (ETS): Tobacco smoke in the atmosphere as a result of burning cigarettes; also called sidestream or secondary smoke.

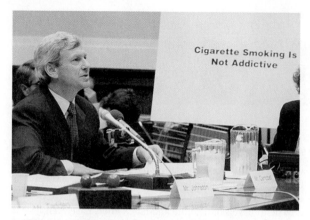

In 1994, tobacco industry executives testified before a congressional committee in defense of cigarette smoking and other tobacco use. In 1999, the Phillp Morris company formally reversed its earlier position that smoking was not addictive.

be completely smoke-free. In 1994, congressional hearings were held on allegations that during the 1970s tobacco companies had suppressed data obtained in their own research laboratories regarding the hazards of cigarette smoking.

The Philip Morris company has issued a statement, formally admitting that there is "overwhelming medical and scientific consensus that cigarette smoking causes cancer, heart disease, emphysema, and other serious diseases" and that "cigarette smoking is addictive, as that term is most commonly used today." This stance can be viewed as a complete reversal of the industry's 1994 congressional testimony regarding tobacco use.

The Tobacco Settlement of 1998

In 1998, the major American tobacco corporations entered into an agreement with all fifty U.S. states to resolve claims that the states should be compensated for the costs of treating people with smoking-related illnesses. Under the terms of the settlement, the tobacco industry agreed to pay the states approximately $246 billion in annual installments over twenty-four years. The tobacco industry also agreed to refrain from marketing tobacco products to those under eighteen and to pay $24 million annually over ten years for a research foundation dedicated to finding ways to reduce smoking among youths. In contrast to earlier proposed settlements, however, tobacco corporations under this agreement would not be penalized if levels of underage smoking did not decline over that period of time. In addition, the settlement did not prevent individuals or groups of

individuals from suing tobacco corporations in separate actions.

Unfortunately, the 1998 tobacco settlement had a mixed effect on smoking behavior. By and large, compensation funds awarded to the states were used to keep taxes down or pay off debt, rather than support tobacco use prevention programs. In 2007, only three states (Maine, Delaware, and Colorado) had funded programs at the minimum levels recommended (but not required) by the U.S. Centers for Disease Control and Prevention. Since then, funding for prevention programs has been reduced even further as states contend with their own budget deficits. On the other hand, an increase in cigarette prices imposed by tobacco companies to finance the settlement, as well as higher excise taxes imposed by U.S. states, made cigarettes more expensive, especially for young people with relatively little money to spend (Figure 15.1). The decline in cigarette smoking in this age group since 1998 has been attributed, in part, to the economics of tobacco product purchases. Today, every smoker knows how expensive cigarette smoking can be. As of mid-2010, New York has the highest state tax on cigarettes ($4.35), resulting in an average cost of $11.21 for a pack of cigarettes purchased in New York City.[11]

The Tobacco Control Act of 2009

In June 2009, a new era in the history of governmental relations with the tobacco industry began, with the enactment of the federal Family Smoking and Tobacco Control Act, giving the FDA for the first time sweeping regulatory authority over tobacco products sold in the United States. The immediate effects of the legislation include creation of a new FDA Center for Tobacco Products to oversee the science-based regulation of tobacco products, the banning of candy-flavored cigarettes, full disclosure of ingredients and additives in tobacco products, aggressive moves to stop youth-focused marketing, and new graphic warning labels highlighting the health risks of smoking.[12]

Tobacco Regulation and Global Economics

As will be discussed later in this chapter, many other nations have substantially higher prevalence rates for cigarette smoking, and their governments have taken far fewer steps toward instituting policies to reduce smoking behavior. For American tobacco corporations, an expanding global marketplace for American cigarettes has given them the opportunity for an increase in profits

Cigarette Purchases on the Internet

The economic difference can be dramatic. A carton of Marlboro Full Flavor Kings ordered online from a web site in Paducah, Kentucky, might cost approximately $35, including shipping. No state sales tax is charged, and the state excise tax amounts to 3 cents per pack. In New York City, the same carton would cost $30 in city and state taxes alone. The significance of the price difference has produced a rapidly expanding industry that witnessed an annual online cigarette sales increase in a single year from $1.2 billion in 2002 to $2.2 billion in 2003.

The Internet as a smoker's haven may be on the decline. Several states have passed laws barring both online and mail-order sales of cigarettes, in an attempt to protect the economic interests of both traditional merchants and the states themselves. Most web sites have no mechanism by which one can verify that the purchaser meets the minimum age to buy cigarettes in the first place. In California, online retailers are now required to verify the age of the customer by matching names, addresses, and dates of birth to government records. If a tobacco retailer does not collect California excise tax at the time of a California resident's purchase, the outside surface of the shipping container must include a notification that the state has been informed of the sale and that the customer is responsible for reporting such purchases on his or her tax returns.

Regulation of Internet cigarette sales is viewed as a major step toward the reduction of underage smoking. Nonetheless, online cigarette sales remain a significant problem worldwide, particularly in regions in which traditional tobacco sales, through local retail vendors, have been restricted.

Sources: Phan, Monty (2003, June 19). Law smokes out online cigarette sales. *Newsday*, A46. Ribisi, Kurt M., Williams, Rebecca S., and Kim, Annice E. (2003). Internet sales of cigarettes to minors. *Journal of the American Medical Association, 290*, 1356–1359. Tedeschi, Bob (2003, February 24). E-commerce report: Pressure grows from states to restrict and tax a smoker's haven—the Internet. *New York Times*, p. C7. World Health Organization (2008). The tobacco atlas (3rd ed.). Geneva, Switzerland: World Health Organization, pp. 60–61.

from foreign sales that has largely compensated for the financial losses from a decline in domestic sales. In a larger sense, cigarette sales abroad represent a major component of overall U.S. foreign trade. In recent years, U.S. exports of tobacco products have exceeded imports by billions of dollars, creating a significant trade surplus. Therefore, the U.S. trade deficit (defined as an excess of imports over exports) would be worse than it is today were it not for the export of tobacco products to other nations (Drugs. . .in Focus).[13]

What's in Tobacco?

When a smoker inhales from a lit cigarette, the temperature at the tip rises to approximately 1,700 degrees Fahrenheit (926 degrees centigrade), as oxygen is drawn through the tobacco, paper, and other additives. This accounts for the bright glow as a smoker inhales from a cigarette. At this intense heat, more than four thousand separate compounds are oxidized and released through cigarette smoke. The smoker inhales the result as **mainstream smoke**, usually screened through the cigarette filter and cigarette paper. As mentioned earlier, the sidestream smoke that is released from the burning cigarette tip itself is unfiltered, and because it is a product of a slightly less intense burning process occurring between puffs, more unburned particles are contained in the smoke.

In general, we can speak of two components in tobacco smoke. The **particulate phase**, consisting of small particles (one micrometer or larger in diameter) suspended in the smoke, includes water droplets, nicotine, and a collection of compounds that will be referred to collectively as **tar**. The particles in tar constitute the

mainstream smoke: The smoke inhaled directly from cigarettes or other tobacco products.

particulate phase: Those components of smoke that consist of particles.

tar: A sticky material found in the particulate phase of tobacco smoke and other pollutants in the air.

primary source of carcinogenic compounds in tobacco. The second component is the **gaseous phase**, consisting of gas compounds in the smoke, including carbon dioxide, carbon monoxide, ammonia, hydrogen cyanide, acetaldehyde, and acetone. Among these gases, carbon monoxide is clearly the most toxic.

This diverse collection of physiologically active toxins is quite unique to tobacco. One way of putting it is to say that the fifty thousand to seventy thousand puffs per year that a one-pack-a-day cigarette smoker takes in amount to a level of pollution far beyond even the most polluted urban environment anywhere in the world.[14] The following sections will focus on three of the most important compounds in tobacco smoke: carbon monoxide, tar, and nicotine.

Carbon Monoxide

As most people know, **carbon monoxide** is an odorless, colorless, tasteless, but extraordinarily toxic gas. It is formed when tobacco burns because the oxidation process is incomplete. In that sense, burning tobacco is similar to an inefficient engine, like a car in need of a tune-up. The danger in carbon monoxide is that it easily attaches itself to hemoglobin, the protein inside red blood cells, occupying those portions of the hemoglobin molecule normally reserved for the transport of oxygen from the lungs to the rest of the body. Carbon monoxide has about a two hundred times greater affinity for hemoglobin than does oxygen, so oxygen does not have much of a chance. Carbon monoxide is also more resistant to detaching itself from hemoglobin, so there is an accumulation of carbon monoxide over time.

The ultimate result of carbon monoxide is a subtle but effective asphyxiation of the body from a lack of oxygen. Generally, people who smoke a pack a day accumulate levels of carbon monoxide in the blood of 25 to 35

parts per million blood components (p.p.m.), with levels of 100 p.p.m. for short periods of time while they are actually smoking. Of course, greater use of tobacco produces proportionately higher levels of carbon monoxide. Carbon monoxide is the primary culprit in producing cardiovascular disease among smokers, as well as in causing deficiencies in physiological functioning and behavior.[15]

Tar

The quantity of tar in a cigarette varies from levels of 12 to 16 mg per cigarette to less than 6 mg. It also should be noted that the last third of each cigarette contains 50 percent of the total tar, making the final few puffs far more hazardous than the first ones.

The major problem with tar lies in its sticky quality, not unlike that of the material used in paving roads, which causes it to adhere to cells in the lungs and the airways leading to them. Normally, specialized cells with small, hair-like attachments called **cilia** are capable of removing contaminants in the air that might impede the breathing process. These cilia literally sweep the unwanted particles upward, in a process called the **ciliary escalator**, to the throat, where they are typically swallowed, digested, and finally excreted from the body through the gastrointestinal system. Components in tar alter the coordination of these cilia so that they can no longer function effectively. The accumulation of sticky tar on the surface of the cells along the pulmonary system permits carcinogenic compounds that normally would have been eliminated to settle on the tissue. As will be discussed later, the resulting cellular changes produce lung cancer, and similar carcinogenic effects in other tissues of the body produce cancer in other organs.[16]

Nicotine

Nicotine is a toxic, dependence-producing psychoactive drug found exclusively in tobacco. It is an oily compound varying in hue from colorless to brown. A few drops of pure nicotine, about 60 mg, on the tongue would quickly kill a healthy adult, and it is commonly used as a major ingredient in insecticides and pesticides of all kinds. Cigarettes, however, contain from 0.5 to 2.0 mg of nicotine (depending on the brand), about 20 percent of which is actually inhaled and reaches the bloodstream. This means that 2 to 8 mg of nicotine is ingested per day for a pack-a-day smoker, and 4 to 16 mg of nicotine for a smoker of two packs a day.[17]

gaseous phase: The portion of tobacco smoke that consists of gases.

carbon monoxide: An extremely toxic gas that prevents blood cells from carrying oxygen from the lungs to the rest of the body.

cilia: Small hair cells.

ciliary escalator: The pushing back of inhaled foreign particles which might interfere with breathing, upward from the air passages into the throat, where they can be swallowed and excreted through the gastrointestinal tract.

nicotine: The prime psychoactive drug in tobacco products.

Inhaled nicotine from smoking is absorbed extremely rapidly and easily passes through the blood-brain barrier, as well as through the blood-placental barrier in pregnant women, in a few seconds. The entire effect is over in a matter of minutes. By the time a cigarette butt is extinguished, the levels of nicotine in the blood have peaked, and its breakdown and excretion from the body are well underway. The elimination half-life of nicotine is approximately two to three hours.

The speed of nicotine absorption ordinarily would be much slower if it were not for the presence of ammonia as an additive in the tobacco blend. The combination of nicotine and ammonia changes the naturally acidic nicotine into an alkalinic free-base form that more easily passes from body tissues into the bloodstream. As a result, ammonia increases the availability of nicotine in the blood, much as the addition of alkaline materials such as baking soda converts cocaine into crack cocaine (see Chapter 4). The information that ammonia had been introduced into the manufacture of cigarette tobacco during the 1970s, in an apparent effort to increase the "kick" of nicotine, came to light in 1995 and was confirmed by tobacco industry documents released in 1998.[18]

The primary effect of nicotine is to stimulate CNS receptors that are sensitive to acetylcholine (see Chapter 4). These receptors are called *nicotinic receptors* because they are excited by nicotine. One of the effects of activating them is the release of adrenalin, which increases blood pressure and heart rate. Another effect is to inhibit activity in the gastrointestinal system. At the same time, however, as most smokers will tell you, a cigarette is a relaxing factor in their lives. Part of this reaction may be due to an effect on the brain that promotes a greater level of clear thinking and concentration; another part may be related to the fact that nicotine, at moderate doses, serves to reduce muscle tone so that muscular tightness is decreased. Research has shown that cigarette smoking helps to sustain performance on monotonous tasks and to improve short-term memory. We can assume that it is the nicotine in cigarettes and other tobacco products that is responsible because nicotine tablets have comparable behavioral effects.[19]

The Dependence Potential of Nicotine

Historically, the dependence potential of nicotine has been demonstrated at times in which the usual availability of tobacco has suddenly been curtailed. In Germany following the end of World War II, for example, cigarettes were rationed to two packs a month for men and one pack a month for women. This "cigarette famine" produced dramatic effects on the behavior of German civilians. Smokers bartered their food rations for cigarettes, even under the extreme circumstances of chronic hunger and poor nutrition. Cigarette butts were picked from the dirt in the streets by people who admitted that they were personally disgusted by their desperate behavior. Some women turned to prostitution to obtain cigarettes. Alcoholics of both sexes testified that it was easier to abstain from drinking alcohol than from smoking.[20]

It is now known that nicotine stimulates the release of dopamine in the nucleus accumbens, the same area of the brain responsible for the reinforcing properties of opiates, cocaine, and alcohol. In addition, several behavioral factors combine with this physiological effect to increase the likelihood that a strong dependence will be created. One of these factors is the speed with which smoked nicotine reaches the brain. The delivery time has been estimated as five to eight seconds. Another factor is the wide variety of circumstances and settings surrounding the act of smoking that later come to serve as learned rewards. A smoker may find, for example, that the first cigarette with a cup of coffee in the morning (a source of another psychoactive drug, caffeine) is strongly reinforcing.[21]

The Titration Hypothesis of Nicotine Dependence

There is considerable evidence that smokers adjust their smoking behavior to obtain a stable dose of nicotine from whatever cigarettes they are smoking, an idea called the **titration hypothesis**. When exposed to cigarettes of decreasing nicotine content, smokers smoke a greater number of them to compensate and increase the volume of each puff. When they inhale more puffs per cigarette, a greater interval of time elapses before they light up another one. If they are given nicotine gum to chew, the intensity of their smoking behavior declines, even though they have not been told whether the gum contains nicotine or is a placebo. All these studies indicate that experienced smokers arrive at a consistent "style" of smoking that provides their bodies with a relatively constant level of nicotine.[22]

titration hypothesis: The idea that smokers will adjust their smoking of cigarettes in such a way as to maintain a steady input of nicotine into the body.

Tolerance and Withdrawal

First-time smokers often react to a cigarette with a mixture of nausea, dizziness, and vomiting. These effects typically disappear as tolerance develops in the nicotinic receptors in the brain. Other physiological effects, such as increases in heart rate, tremors, and changes in skin temperature, show weaker tolerance effects or none at all.

The strongest dependence-related effect of cigarette smoking can be seen in the symptoms of withdrawal that follow the discontinuation of smoking. Within about six hours after the last cigarette, a smoker's heart rate and blood pressure decrease. Over the next twenty-four hours, common symptoms include headache, an inability to concentrate, irritability, drowsiness, and fatigue, as well as insomnia and other sleep disturbances. Most striking of all are the strong feelings of craving for a cigarette. Ex-smokers can attest to cravings that slowly diminish but nonetheless linger on for months and, in some cases, for years.[23]

Nicotine dependence is the central factor in the continuation of smoking behaviors. The level of dependence is significant, even when compared with dependence levels of illicit drugs available on the street. In a study of people who smoked and were also in some form of drug-abuse treatment, 74 percent judged the difficulty of quitting smoking to be at least as great as the difficulty in stopping their drug of choice. One in three considered it "much harder" to quit smoking.[24]

Health Consequences of Tobacco Use

The adverse health consequences of tobacco use can be classified in three broad categories: cardiovascular disease, respiratory disease, and cancer. In addition, there are special health difficulties that smoking can raise for women and hazards from using smokeless tobacco. An enormous literature on the adverse effects of tobacco use has grown steadily since the original surgeon general's report in 1964, although even by that time more than thirty thousand research studies had been conducted on the question.

Beyond all the research reports are the sheer numbers of people who are affected. In the United States alone, of the estimated half-million deaths each year that are attributed to substance abuse of one kind or another, approximately 443,000 are specifically tied to tobacco use or second-hand smoke from tobacco use. This figure is higher than the total number of American casualties during World War II (Drugs . . . in Focus). The public health community considers these deaths premature deaths because they were entirely preventable; these people would have been alive if their behaviors had been different.

The numbers are simple, and staggering: Smoking-related deaths account for nearly one out of every five deaths in the United States every year, more than 1,200 deaths each day. It has been estimated that a person's life expectancy is shortened by fourteen minutes every

Drugs... in Focus

Visualizing 400,000 to 440,000 Annual Tobacco-Related Deaths

The estimated annual death toll due to tobacco-related diseases is staggering but often difficult to visualize. In 2009, the following U.S. cities had populations in the neighborhood of this number. Imagine the disappearance of the entire population in any of these cities each year, or all of them in five years.

- Virginia Beach, Virginia (pop. 433,575)
- Miami, Florida (pop. 433,136)
- Cleveland, Ohio (pop. 431,363)
- Oakland, California (pop. 409,184)
- Raleigh, North Carolina (pop. 405,791)

Source: United States Census Bureau, July 1, 2009 estimates.

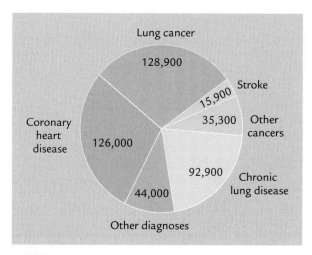

FIGURE 15.1

The distribution of approximately 443,000 U.S. deaths attributed each year to tobacco use or secondhand smoke from tobacco use.

Source: Centers for Disease Control and Prevention (2008, November 14). Cigarette smoking-attributable morbidity, years of potential life lost, and productivity losses—United States, 2000–2004. *Morbidity and Mortality Weekly Report, 57,* 1226–1228.

time he or she smokes a cigarette. Smoking two packs a day for twenty years reduces one's estimated lifespan by approximately eight years. Unlike alcohol, which presents no significant health hazards when consumed in moderation, tobacco is a dangerous product *when used as intended* (Figure 15.1).[25]

Cardiovascular Disease

Cardiovascular disease includes a number of specific conditions. Some of these diseases are **coronary heart disease (CHD)**, in which the heart is damaged by the restriction of blood flow through narrowed or blocked coronary arteries; **arteriosclerosis**, in which the walls of arteries harden and lose their elasticity; **atherosclerosis**, in which fatty deposits inside arteries impede blood flow; and **ischemic stroke**, in which interruption or reduction in blood flow causes damage to the brain. In all these diseases, cigarette smoking increases the risk dramatically.

We know now that smoking is responsible for approximately 30 percent of all CHD deaths. The risk of CHD doubles if you smoke and quadruples if you smoke heavily. On average, smoking also raises the risk of a sudden death (such as from a fatal heart attack) by two to four times, with the degree of risk increasing as a

direct function of how many cigarettes are smoked per day. To put it even more bluntly, it has been estimated that unless smoking patterns change dramatically in the future, about 10 percent of all Americans now alive may die prematurely from some form of heart disease as a result of their smoking behavior.[26]

These statistics are strengthened by our understanding of how cigarette smoking actually produces these dangerous cardiovascular conditions. The major villains are nicotine and carbon monoxide. Nicotine, as a stimulant drug, increases the contraction of heart muscle and elevates heart rate.

At the same time, nicotine causes a constriction of blood vessels, leading to a rise in blood pressure, and also increases *platelet adhesiveness* in the blood. As a result of a greater adhesiveness, platelets clump together and increase the risk of developing a blood clot. When a clot forms within coronary arteries, a heart attack can occur; a clot traveling into the blood vessels of the brain can produce a stroke. Finally, nicotine increases the body's serum cholesterol and fatty deposits, leading to the development of atherosclerosis.

While nicotine is doing its dirty work, carbon monoxide makes matters worse. A lack of oxygen puts further strain on the ability of the heart to function under already trying circumstances.[27]

Respiratory Diseases

The general term **chronic obstructive pulmonary disease (COPD)** refers to several conditions in which breathing is impaired because of some abnormality in the air passages either leading to or within the lungs. Although only 20 percent of smokers in the United

coronary heart disease (CHD): Disease that damages the heart as a result of a restriction of blood flow through coronary arteries.

arteriosclerosis (ar-TEER-ee-oh-scluh-ROH-sis): A disease in which blood flow is restricted because the walls of arteries harden and lose their elasticity.

atherosclerosis (ATH-er-oh-scluh-ROH-sis): A disease in which blood flow is restricted because of the buildup of fatty deposits inside arteries.

ischemic (iz-SKEE-mic) stroke: A disease in which there is an interruption of or reduction in blood flow to the brain, causing paralysis, sensory loss, cognitive deficits, or a combination of neuropsychological effects.

chronic obstructive pulmonary disease (COPD): A group of diseases characterized by impaired breathing due to an abnormality in the air passages.

States develop COPD, 80 to 90 percent of all COPD cases are the result of smoking. Historically, COPD has been viewed as "a man's disease," but since 1980 the death rate in women has tripled, and since 2000, more women than men have died or been hospitalized each year as a result of COPD. With the exception of a rare genetic defect, smoking is the only established cause of clinically significant COPD.

Two examples of COPD are **chronic bronchitis**, in which excess mucus builds up in air passages, leading to an inflammation of bronchial tissue, and **emphysema**, in which air sacs in the lungs are abnormally enlarged and the air sac walls either become inelastic or rupture, leading to extreme difficulty in inhaling oxygen and exhaling carbon dioxide. In the case of advanced emphysema, more than 80 percent of a patient's energy is required merely to breathe. These two diseases account for more than 100,000 deaths each year, and many additional thousands are forced to lead increasingly debilitating lives, gasping and struggling each day to breathe.

Pulmonary damage, however, is not limited to adults who have been smoking for many years. Cigarette smoking is also associated with airway obstruction and slower growth of lung function in younger populations. Adolescents who smoke five or more cigarettes a day are 40 percent more likely to develop asthma and 30 percent more likely to have symptoms of wheezing but not asthma than those who do not smoke. Among smokers, girls show a greater loss of pulmonary function than boys, even though boys report that they smoke more cigarettes.[28]

Lung Cancer

At the beginning of the twentieth century, lung cancer was a rare disease. Its steady increase in the United States as well as the rest of the world since then has occurred in direct proportion to the growing prevalence of cigarette smoking and other tobacco use. Today, nearly 87 percent of the more than approximately 223,000 new cases of lung cancer in the United States in 2010 have been determined by the American Cancer Society to be due to smoking. Although there has been a steady

decline in deaths due to lung cancer among American males overall since 1990, there remains an approximately 35 percent greater mortality rate among African American males due to smoking relative to white males. In general, males who are currently smoking incur a risk of lung cancer that is about twenty-three times higher than the risk for nonsmokers.

Another important change has occurred over the years with respect to the incidence of lung cancer among women. Like COPD, lung cancer was once considered to be limited largely to male smokers. More recently, however, increasing numbers of women have contracted lung cancer as a result of their increased level of cigarette smoking. The age-adjusted mortality rate for women is still about one-half that for men, but the decline in mortality rates seen among men since 1990 has yet to be realized among women. Since 1988, lung cancer has exceeded breast cancer as the leading cause of cancer deaths among women (Figure 15.2). In general, females who are currently smoking incur a risk of lung cancer that is about thirteen times higher than that for nonsmokers.

These facts about lung cancer become even more tragic when you consider that the overall five-year survival rate after initial diagnosis of lung cancer (for all stages of cancer combined) is only 15 percent. Lung cancer patients have an approximately 50 percent chance of living five years when the disease is still localized at the time of diagnosis, but only 15 percent of lung cancers are diagnosed at this early stage.

As discussed earlier in the chapter, the exposure to tar in cigarette smoke disrupts the indispensable action of ciliary cells in the bronchial tubes leading to the lungs. Without their protective function, the lungs are open to attack. Several carcinogenic compounds in the smoke can now enter the lungs and stimulate the formation of cancerous growths, **carcinomas**, in lung tissue. One of these compounds, *benzopyrene*, has been found to cause genetic mutations in cells that are identical to the mutations observed in patients who have developed carcinomas in their lungs. This finding is important because it establishes a causal link between a specific ingredient in tobacco smoke and human cases of cancer.[29]

Other Cancers

Certainly lung cancer is the best-known and most common example of smoking-related cancers, but other organs are affected in a similar way. In the United States, approximately 30 percent of cancer deaths *of all types* have been linked to smoking. It has been estimated that smokers increase their risk by two to twenty-seven times for cancer of the larynx, thirteen times for mouth

---

chronic bronchitis: A respiratory disease involving inflammation of bronchial tissue following a buildup of excess mucus in air passages.

emphysema (EM-fuh-SEE-mah): An enlargement of air sacs in the lungs and abnormalities in the air sac walls, causing great difficulty in breathing.

carcinomas (CAR-sih-NOH-mas): Cancerous tumors or growths.

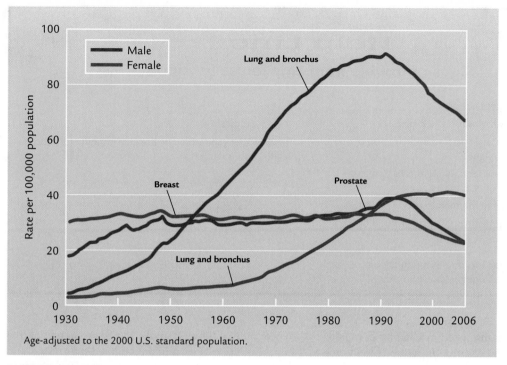

Rate per 100,000 population

- Male
- Female

Lung and bronchus

Breast

Prostate

Lung and bronchus

Age-adjusted to the 2000 U.S. standard population.

FIGURE 15.2

Age-adjusted death rates from lung and bronchus cancer and other cancers among males and females in the United States, 1930–2006.

Sources: Statistics from the American Cancer Society, Atlanta, GA. Modified and reprinted by the permission of the American Cancer Society (2010). *Cancer facts and figures 2010.* Atlanta, GA: American Cancer Society, Inc., pp. 2–3.

or lip cancer, two to three times for bladder cancer, two times for pancreatic cancer, and five times for cancers of the kidney or uterine cervix.[30]

Despite a widespread belief to the contrary, using smokeless tobacco, in the form of chewing tobacco or snuff, does not prevent the user from incurring an increased risk of cancer. Continuing contact with tobacco in the mouth has been shown to produce precancerous cell changes, as revealed by **leukoplakia** (white spots) and **erythroplakia** (red spots) inside the mouth and nasal cavity. Even though smokeless tobacco obviously avoids the problems associated with tobacco smoke, it does not prevent the user from being exposed to carcinogens, specifically a class of compounds called **nitrosamines** that are present in all tobacco products. As a result of federal legislation enacted in 1986, all forms of smokeless tobacco must contain, on the package, a set of specific warnings that these products may cause mouth cancer as well as gum disease and tooth loss (Help Line). To reinforce the idea that grave dangers lurk in smokeless tobacco, one of these warnings reads: "This product is not a safe alternative to cigarette smoking."

Special Health Concerns for Women

Tobacco use presents specific health risk for women. Women who smoke have a more than three times greater risk of dying from stroke due to brain hemorrhaging and an almost two times greater risk of dying from a heart attack. Added to these concerns is the toxic interaction of tobacco smoke with birth control pills. If a woman is using birth control pills as well, the risk increases to twenty-two times and twenty times, respectively.

The higher risk of low birth weight and physical defects in the newborn due to the mother's smoking

leukoplakia (LOO-koh-PLAY-kee-ah): Small white spots inside the mouth and nasal cavity, indicating precancerous tissue.

erythroplakia (eh-RITH-ro-PLAY-kee-ah): Small red spots inside the mouth and nasal cavity, indicating precancerous tissue.

nitrosamines (nih-TRAW-seh-meens): A group of carcinogenic compounds found in tobacco.

during pregnancy was discussed in Chapter 2. In addition, there is a specific elevation in systolic blood pressure at about 2 months of age among infants whose mothers smoked during pregnancy.[31] Even though there has been a decline in smoking in recent years among pregnant women, more than one in six pregnant women (17 percent) have smoked in the past month, with more of them smoking in their first trimester of pregnancy (22 percent) than in their second or third trimester (14 percent and 15 percent, respectively).

The Hazards of Environmental Smoke

In the early days of development of methods for detecting the effects of nicotine in the bloodstream, scientists were puzzled to find traces of a nicotine metabolite in nonsmokers. They suspected at first that there was some flaw in their analysis but later had to conclude that their measurements were indeed accurate. Nonsmokers testing positive had shared car rides or workplaces with smokers shortly before their tests. Today, a large body of evidence indicates not only the presence of tobacco smoke compounds in the bodies of nonsmokers but also the adverse consequences that such "involuntary smoking" can provoke. In other words, environmental tobacco smoke is a significant health hazard even to people who are not actively smoking.

Approximately 85 percent of the smoke in an average room where people are smoking cigarettes is generated by sidestream smoke, and about three-fourths of the nicotine originating from these cigarettes ends up in the atmosphere. In some cases, the carcinogens released in environmental tobacco smoke (ETS) are so potent that they are dangerous even in their diluted state. For example, N-nitrosamine (an example of a group of carcinogens mentioned earlier in connection with smokeless tobacco) is so much more concentrated in sidestream smoke than in mainstream smoke that nonsmokers end up inhaling as much of it after one hour in a very smoky room as will a smoker after smoking ten to fifteen cigarettes.[32]

The U.S. surgeon general's report on involuntary exposure to tobacco smoke in 2006 has confirmed previous data on this question and extended its conclusions to the following:

- For nonsmoking adults, exposure to environmental smoke raises the risk of heart disease by 25 to 30 percent in both men and women. The risk of lung cancer is increased by 20 to 30 percent among nonsmokers who live with a smoker.
- Environmental smoke is a cause of sudden infant death syndrome (SIDS), accounting for 430 deaths per year in the United States. The risk is higher for children whose mothers were exposed to tobacco smoke during pregnancy and for children exposed during infancy.
- Among children of parents who smoke in the home, there is an increased risk of lower respiratory illnesses such as bronchitis, middle ear disease, wheezing, and childhood asthma.

It is estimated that environmental smoke exposure accounts for 46,000 premature deaths from heart disease and 3,400 premature deaths from cancer among adults in the United States each year. Although the proportion of nonsmokers has declined substantially as a result of publicity about the hazards of ETS and extensive smoking bans and restrictions, more than 126 million Americans remain subject to exposure at some time in their lives.[33]

Patterns of Smoking Behavior and Use of Smokeless Tobacco

In 1965, about 40 percent of all American teenagers and adults smoked cigarettes, and it is estimated that more than 50 percent did in the 1940s. In 2009, however, according to the National Survey on Drug Use and Health, approximately 23 percent of people aged twelve or older smoked a cigarette within the past month, qualifying as current smokers. Although this percentage is significantly less than it was, it still represents a very large number of people. Extrapolating to the U.S. population, a 23 percent prevalence rate corresponds to nearly 60 million Americans. American Indians and Alaska natives are more likely to smoke than any other group in the United States, with 33 percent of adults defined as smokers. In contrast, individuals of Asian descent are the least likely to smoke, with just 11 percent report

having smoked a cigarette in the past month (Drugs. . .in Focus).

There has been only a small decline in the percentage of American adult smokers in the last few years. Among college students, thirty-day prevalence rates increased from 1990 to 1999, but have since then declined by 50 percent. In 2009, about 18 percent of college students had smoked cigarettes within the previous month, a lower proportion than the national average. About 13 percent of tenth graders in 2009 and 20 percent of high school seniors reported cigarette smoking within the previous month. **If high school seniors have not begun smoking at this point in their lives, it is unlikely that they will do so in the future.**[34]

The Youngest Smokers

In the 2009 University of Michigan survey, approximately 20 percent of eighth graders reported that they had tried cigarettes in their lifetime and about 7 percent reported smoking at least once in the previous month. These figures are down substantially from the 49 and 21 percent figures, respectively, reported as recently as 1996. Approximately 3 percent of eighth graders smoked on a daily basis in 2009, and about 1 percent smoked at least a half a pack a day, once again down substantially from 10 and 4 percent, respectively, in 1996.

In previous Michigan surveys, the peak years for starting to smoke have been reported to be in the sixth and seventh grade, though a significant number of eighth graders qualifying as regular smokers have said that they had started earlier. About 16 percent have reported that they had begun prior to the sixth grade; in fact, about 8 percent have reported that they had started prior to the fifth grade. In general, it has been estimated that between 80 and 90 percent of regular smokers began to smoke by the age of eighteen.[35]

Attitudes toward Smoking among Young People

Adolescent attitudes toward cigarette smoking have changed dramatically in the early years of the twenty-first century. In general, young people in middle school and high school have become less accepting of cigarette smoking. About 87 percent of eighth graders, for example, reported in 2009 their disapproval of someone smoking a pack of cigarettes per day and 60 percent reported that people engaging in such behavior would present "great risk" of harming themselves physically or otherwise.

Drugs... in Focus

Smoking in Movies and Movie Ratings

Concerns about the influence of the media on young people with respect to various forms of drug-taking behavior have recently turned to the issue of cigarette smoking in movies. In May 2007, the Motion Picture Association of America (MPAA) announced a significant change in its movie rating system. Previously, the portrayal of teenage smoking in a movie, along with sexual situations, violence, and adult language, would be a factor in deciding whether a movie merited an R rating (which requires those under 17 to be accompanied by a parent or adult guardian). Now, the Film Ratings Board would consider *any* portrayal of smoking in a movie, not just teenage smoking, in their rating decision, unless smoking was central to the movie's historical content. Depictions that glamorized smoking or movies that featured pervasive smoking could receive a higher rating than PG-13, according to the new standards. The MPAA made the following statement:

> Clearly, smoking is increasingly an unacceptable behavior in our society. There is broad awareness of smoking as a unique public health concern due to nicotine's highly addictive nature, and no parent wants their child to take up the habit. The appropriate response of the rating system is to give more information to parents on this issue.

Media reporters quickly came up with "WARNING: Smoking may be hazardous to your movie rating."

Antismoking organizations, however, were not entirely satisfied with the MPAA announcement. According to the Campaign for Tobacco-Free Kids, the new policy fell short "of the real change needed to reduce youth exposure to smoking in the movies." They pointed out that the Film Ratings Board would only "consider smoking" in their decisions. "Meaningful, objective standards that produce measurable reductions in smoking in the movies" had not been established.

Meanwhile, trends are mixed with respect to smoking in the movies. A recent study of popular movies from 1991 to 2009 has indicated that smoking in movies declined since 2005. In 2009, more than half of the 145 top-grossing movies had no smoking scenes at all. However, almost half of the 10 top-grossing movies of 2009 contained tobacco imagery, including movies with a PG-13 rating.

Sources: Cieply, Michael (2007, May 11). Puffing away that PG rating: Smoking to join sex and violence in determining ratings for movies. *New York Times*, pp. C1, C4. Los Angeles Times (2010, August 20). Fewer smokers on TV, in film. *Newsday*, p. A45. Press release. Motion Picture Association of America, Hollywood, California. May 10, 2007. Press release. Campaign for Tobacco-Free Kids, Washington, DC. May 10, 2007.

Interestingly, adolescent attitudes toward the *social* aspects of smoking have become more negative as well. About half of tenth and twelfth graders agree with the statement "I strongly dislike being near people who are smoking." Between 75 and 80 percent of them prefer to date nonsmokers. About six out of ten view smoking as a behavior that reflects poor judgment on the part of those who smoke. The continuing disinclination toward dating smokers over recent years has been observed equally among males and females.[36] As Lloyd D. Johnston of the University of Michigan has observed:

> It now appears that taking up smoking makes a youngster less attractive to the great majority of the opposite sex, just the opposite of what cigarette advertising has been promising all these years. I think this is something that teens need to know, because it may be the most compelling argument for

> why they should abstain from smoking or, for that matter, quit if they have already started.[37]

Since 1997, all fifty U.S. states have been required to establish eighteen as the minimum age at which tobacco products can be purchased. Vendors have been required to verify the age of purchasers up to the age of twenty-seven as a means for reducing the access of young people to tobacco. In some U.S. states, efforts are under way to raise the minimum age for tobacco purchases to nineteen or twenty-one, and other states have this higher minimum age already in effect. Any upward change from the national standard reduces the incidence of high school seniors buying cigarettes for their younger friends.

With regard to standards set in federal regulations on underage smoking, compliance rates on the part of tobacco retail vendors nationwide reached 90 percent

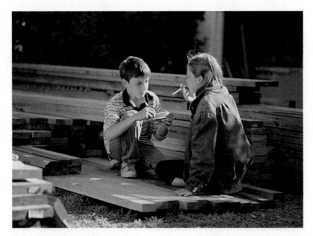

Cigarette smoking among minors is a continuing social and public-health problem.

Use of Smokeless Tobacco

Smokeless tobacco is ingested, as the name implies, by absorption through the membranes of the mouth rather than by inhalation of smoke into the lungs (Table 15.1, page 366). The two most common forms are the traditional loose-leaf chewing tobacco (brand names include Red Man and Beech Nut) and moist, more finely shredded tobacco called **moist snuff** or simply snuff (brand names include Copenhagen and Skoal). Snuff, by the way, is no longer sniffed into the nose, as in the eighteenth century, but rather placed inside the cheek or alongside the gum under the lower lip. Some varieties of snuff are available in a small absorbent-paper sack (like a tea bag) so that the tobacco particles do not get stuck in the teeth. The practice is called "dipping."

According to the 2009 University of Michigan survey, about 4 percent of eighth graders, 7 percent of tenth

in 2008, which was substantially higher than the 60 percent rate reported in 1996. However, about 59 percent of eighth graders said in 2009 that cigarettes were fairly easy or very easy to get. This percentage is significantly lower than percentages reported in the 1990s, but it still reflects relatively easy access (Drugs. . .in Focus).[38]

moist snuff: Damp, finely shredded tobacco, placed inside the cheek or alongside the gum under the lower lip.

Drugs... in Focus

Reducing Youth Access to Tobacco: The Synar Amendment, 1992

In 1992, Congress enacted the Alcohol, Drug Abuse, and Mental Health Administration Reorganization Act with an amendment sponsored by Representative Mike Synar of Oklahoma. The amendment aimed at decreasing youth access to tobacco by mandating a number of important changes in the way young people purchase tobacco products and in the practice of commercial tobacco distribution operations. Specifically, the Synar Amendment required

- The enactment of state laws prohibiting any manufacturer, retailer, or distributor of tobacco products from selling or distributing such products to any individuals younger than age 18.

- Annual, unannounced inspections in a way that provides a sampling of tobacco sales outlets that are accessible to minors.

- Each state to reduce its retail violation rate (RVR), referring to the rate at which tobacco products were sold to individuals younger than eighteen years of age, to 20 percent or less by 2003.

How have we done since then? In 1997, the average RVR nationwide was 40.1 percent; in 2008, it was 9.9 percent. In 2008, 46 out of the 50 states and the District of Columbia had achieved an RVR below 15 percent; 26 had achieved an RVR below 10 percent. California, Hawaii, New Hampshire, and Texas have been cited as states with the best records in complying with Synar Amendment objectives. At the same time, however, the relatively high percentage of eighth graders reporting that they had "relatively easy" access to tobacco products suggests that they are getting cigarettes through family members or older friends.

Source: Substance Abuse and Mental Health Services Administration (2008). *FFY 2008 annual Synar reports: Youth tobacco sales.* Rockville, MD: Substance Abuse and Mental Health Services Administration.

TABLE 15.1

Forms of smokeless tobacco

TYPE	DESCRIPTION
Chewing tobacco	
Loose-leaf	Made of cigar-leaf tobacco, sold in small packages, heavily flavored or plain
Fine-cut	Similar to loose-leaf but more finely cut so that it resembles snuff
Plug	Leaf tobacco pressed into flat cakes and sweetened with molasses, licorice, maple sugar, or honey
Twist	Made of stemmed leaves twisted into small rolls and then folded
(Chewing tobacco is not really chewed but rather held in the mouth between the cheek and lower jaw.)	
Snuff	
Dry, moist, sweetened, flavored, salted, scented	
(A pinch of snuff, called a *quid*, is typically tucked between the gum and the lower lip. Moist varieties are currently the most popular.)	

Source: Adapted from Popescu, Cathy (1992). The health hazards of smokeless tobacco. In Kristine Napier (Ed.), *Issues in tobacco*. New York: American Council on Science and Health, pp. 11–12.

graders, and 8 percent of high school seniors had used smokeless tobacco within the previous thirty days. Although 80 percent disapprove of others using smokeless tobacco, only about 40 percent perceive great risk in this form of tobacco use. In general, prevalence rates are higher for males than for females, and higher for the southern region of the United States than for the Northeast, Midwest, or West.[39]

Currently, the form of smokeless tobacco showing the most consistent gains in recent sales is moist snuff; some brands are sold in cherry or wintergreen flavors. As with cigarette tobacco, variations in the alkalinity of different brands of moist snuff allow for different percentages of the nicotine in the tobacco to be absorbed through the membranes of the mouth. Thus, snuff users typically start with brands that release relatively low levels of nicotine and then "graduate" to more potent brands. The most potent brand on the current market, Copenhagen, is also the best-selling snuff in the United States.[40]

Despite continuing warnings that smokeless tobacco presents great risk to one's health, its popularity persists. As we have noted, although smokeless tobacco presents no immediate danger to the lungs, there are substantial adverse effects on other organs of the body. At the very least, regular use of smokeless tobacco increases the risk of gum disease, damage to tooth enamel, and eventually the loss of teeth. More seriously, the direct contact of the tobacco with membranes of the mouth allows carcinogenic nitrosamines to cause tissue changes that can lead to oral cancer. Delay in the treatment of oral cancer increases the likelihood of the cancer spreading to the jaw, pharynx, and neck. When swallowed, saliva containing nitrosamines can produce stomach and urinary tract cancer. Moreover, all the negative consequences of ingesting nicotine during tobacco smoking are also present in the use of smokeless tobacco. In 2009, Altria, the leading tobacco company in the United States began an aggressive marketing campaign for Marlboro *Snus*, a smokeless tobacco product, with the slogan: "When smoking isn't your option, reach for Marlboro Snus." It remains uncertain whether Altria's argument to FDA regulators that smokeless tobacco represents a less harmful alternative to cigarettes will prevail.[41]

Cigars

For a brief time in the 1990s, there was a resurgence in the popularity of cigars, spurred on by images of media stars, both male and female, who had taken up cigar smoking as the tobacco use of choice. The cigar suddenly was fashionable.

By the end of the decade, however, the cigar-smoking craze had "gone up in smoke." This was partly because of changing market conditions for imported cigars, but a major contributing factor was increasing recognition that cigars could not be regarded as a safe alternative to cigarettes.[42] Cigar smoke is more alkaline than cigarette smoke, so the nicotine content in cigars can be absorbed directly through tissues lining the mouth rather than requiring inhalation into the lungs. In addition, due to the tar content, the risk of lung cancer is five times higher for those who smoke cigars than for nonsmokers, eight times higher for those smoking three or more cigars per day, and eleven times higher for those inhaling the smoke of cigars. Regular cigar smokers have a doubled risk, relative to nonsmokers, for cancers of the mouth, throat, and esophagus; they also incur a 45 percent higher risk of COPD and a 27 percent higher risk of coronary heart disease (Portrait). Major cigar manufacturers have now agreed to place warning labels on their products, alerting consumers to the risk of mouth and throat cancer, lung cancer and heart disease, and to the hazards to fertility and unborn children.[43]

PORTRAIT

Sigmund Freud—Nicotine Dependence, Cigars, and Cancer

Probably the best-known photograph of Sigmund Freud, founder of psychoanalysis and one-time proponent of cocaine use (see Chapter 8), shows him with a cigar in hand. Given the fact that Freud typically smoked twenty cigars each day, it is not surprising that he did not set it aside merely to have his picture taken. But there is a story behind this photograph, a lesson about the power of smoking over the will to stop and the tragic health consequences when the will succumbs.

In 1923, at the age of sixty-seven, Freud noted sores on his palate and jaw that failed to heal, a sign of oral cancer. Surgery was indicated and fortunately proved successful in removing the cancerous tissue. This would be only the first of thirty-three surgical

operations on the jaw and oral cavity that Freud was to endure for the remaining sixteen years of his life. As the leukoplakia and finally genuine carcinomas returned to his mouth, he was repeatedly warned by specialists that his practice of smoking cigars was the root of his problems and that he must stop. Despite these warnings, Freud kept on smoking.

Freud tried very hard to stop; indeed, sometimes he would not smoke for a few weeks at a time. In addition to his problems with cancer, he suffered from chest pains called "tobacco angina." In 1936, the angina became acutely painful and as his biographer, Ernest Jones, has noted, "It was evidently exacerbated by nicotine, since it was relieved as soon as he stopped smoking."

By this time, Freud's jaw had been entirely removed and an artificial jaw substituted in its place. He was almost constantly in pain, often could not speak, and sometimes could not eat or swallow. Despite the agony, Freud still smoked a steady stream of cigars until he finally died at the age of eighty-three.

Here was a man whom many consider to be one of the intellectual giants of the twentieth century. Yet the giant was a slave to his cigars.

Source: Brecher, Ruth; Brecher, Edward; Herzog, Arthur; Goodman, Walter; Walker, Gerald; and the Editors of *Consumer Reports* (1963). *The Consumer Union's report on smoking and the public interest.* Mount Vernon, NY: Consumer Union, pp. 91–95.

Tobacco Use around the World

Since the seventeenth century, the practice of tobacco smoking has spread throughout the world, but until the 1980s the behavior itself outside the United States had been largely independent of American tobacco corporations. Today, the picture has changed dramatically. Between 1985 and 1994 alone, U.S. cigarette exports to Japan increased 700 percent and to South Korea increased 1200 percent. In the late 1990s, American-made cigarettes moved into significant markets in Eastern Europe and Russia, where smoking prevalence rates are substantially higher than those in the United States (Figure 15.3, page 368). Presently, U.S. tobacco exports total more than $6 billion each year.

Unfortunately, the prevalence rate of smoking in many foreign countries far exceeds that of the United States, coupled with substantially less public concern for the consequences of smoking on health. In the Russian Federation, Kenya, South Korea and China, for example, more than 60 percent of all adult men smoke cigarettes. In Japan, as in many nations of the world, no-smoking sections in restaurants and offices are uncommon; approximately half a million outdoor vending machines allow minors to purchase cigarettes easily, and

there is little or no governmental opposition to smoking in general.[44]

Clearly, tobacco use on a global scale presents one of the most significant public health challenges we face in the twenty-first century. According to the World Health Organization (WHO), an estimated 5.4 million people worldwide die each year from tobacco-related diseases, and this figure is projected to increase to more than 810 million by 2030. In the twentieth century, tobacco smoking contributed to the deaths of 100 million people worldwide. During the twenty-first century, the death toll could rise as high as a billion people.

Making matters worse, global approaches to reducing the deadly effects of tobacco use are discouragingly weak or absent. Approximately 40 percent of countries in the world still allow smoking in hospitals and schools; only 5 percent of the world's population lives in a country that imposes a comprehensive national ban on tobacco advertising. Only 5 percent of the world's population, too, lives in a country in which full services to treat tobacco dependence are widely available.[45]

In recognition of the enormous health crisis that exists at present and the potential calamity that looms in the future, a Framework Convention on Tobacco Control

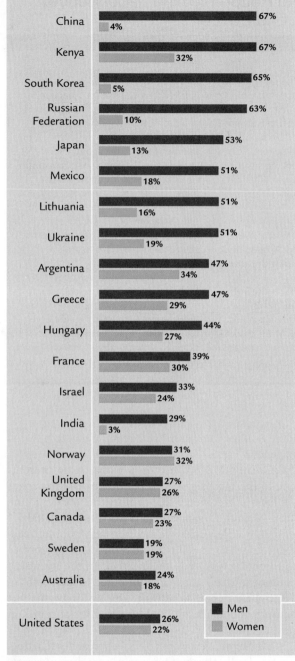

FIGURE 15.3

Smoking rates for men and women over fifteen years old in twenty countries, including the United States.

Note: As a consequence of differences in criteria and age range, percentages for the United States differ slightly from data in the National Household Survey on Drug Use and Health.

Source: Mackay, Judith, and Eriksen, Michael (2002). *The tobacco atlas.* Geneva, Switzerland: World Health Organization, Table A. Reprinted with permission.

has been signed by more than 170 members of the World Health Organization, an agency of the United Nations. Implementation of the tobacco-use reduction initiates in the agreement is voluntary, however, and progress on a global level has been slow. A major reason is that governments around the world collect more than $200 billion dollars each year in taxes imposed on tobacco sales. In some cases, governments are dependent on these tax revenues to sustain their economies. In other cases, governments receive direct profits from state-owned tobacco corporations.[46]

Quitting Smoking: The Good News and the Bad

There is no question that tobacco use of any kind is harmful to your health as well as your wallet, and it is indeed hard to quit once you have started. But there's some good news with respect to the consequences of quitting.

The Good News: Undoing the Damage

Given the grim story of all the documented health risks associated with tobacco, it is at least reassuring to know that if a smoker does succeed in quitting, some of the damage can be undone. Here are the benefits:

- Within eight hours—Carbon monoxide levels in the blood drop to normal.
- Within twenty-four hours—Chances of a heart attack decrease.
- Within two weeks to three months—Circulation improves. Lung function increases by up to 30 percent.
- Within one to nine months—Coughing, sinus congestion, fatigue, and shortness of breath decrease. Cilia regain normal function in the lungs and become increasingly able to handle mucus, clean the lungs, and reduce infection.
- Within one year—Excess risk of coronary heart disease is half that of a smoker.
- Within five to ten years—Risk of stroke is reduced to that of a nonsmoker.
- Within ten years—Lung cancer death rate is about half that of a continuing smoker.
- Within fifteen years—Risk of coronary heart disease is equal to that of a nonsmoker.[47]

The Bad News: How Hard It Is to Quit

The advantages of quitting are real and most people are aware of them, but the fact remains that, in the words of the surgeon general's report in 1988, "The pharmacologic and behavioral processes that determine tobacco addiction are similar to those that determine addiction to drugs such as heroin and cocaine."[48] It may be easy to quit smoking for a short while but it is very difficult to avoid a relapse, as any former or present smoker will tell you (Help Line).

About one-third of all smokers in the United States try to quit each year, the vast majority of them without any treatment, but only about 3 to 5 percent succeed with their initial attempt. Nonetheless, about half of all smokers do eventually manage to achieve long-term abstinence from the nicotine in tobacco products, but only after an average of eight attempts at quitting.

Research studies on smoking cessation indicate that there are no gender differences with regard to the likelihood that a person will quit smoking for one to four years, though men are more likely than women to have been abstinent for five years or more. The fact that a higher level of smoking is consistently related to a lower level of education and family income makes it vital that smoking-cessation programs be available to those who ordinarily would not be able to afford them.[49]

The options available to smokers who want to quit are numerous. In addition to behaviorally oriented social support groups (Smokers Anonymous, SmokeEnders, Smoke-Stoppers), counseling either in person or through telephone "quitlines," hypnosis, acupuncture, and specific prescription drugs can help reduce the withdrawal symptoms and feelings of nicotine craving. One example is a sustained-release form of the antidepressant drug bupropion. Originally marketed as a treatment for depression under the name Wellbutrin, it was approved by the FDA in 1997 for use as an aid for smoking cessation and was renamed Zyban when marketed for this purpose. It is recommended that Zyban be taken daily for a week prior to the last cigarette to allow drug levels to build up in the bloodstream and buffer the loss of nicotine when smoking stops. About 44 percent of individuals taking Zyban have refrained from smoking after seven weeks, and 23 percent remain smoke-free after one year—roughly twice the percentage among those who receive a placebo. Since 1999, the costs of all prescription medications and quit-smoking programs have been tax-deductible as medical expenses.[50]

In 2006, a twice-daily tablet called Chantix became available in the United States as a nicotine-free stop-smoking medication. Clinical trials of Chantix have shown that users have a rate of abstinence from tobacco of 22 percent, compared to 16 percent among those

---

Help Line

Ten Tips on How to Succeed When Trying to Quit Smoking

- Choose a quit date and stick to it.
- Remember that you are dependent, physiologically and psychologically, on nicotine and that the first few days without cigarettes will be the hardest.
- Change the habits that are associated with smoking. If you have had a cigarette with your morning coffee, drink orange juice instead.
- Tell all the people you know that you are quitting and ask for their support.
- Drink lots of water and brush your teeth frequently to rid yourself of the taste of tobacco.
- Never carry matches or a lighter with you. Put away your ashtrays or fill them with something else.
- Spend time with people who don't smoke.
- Keep a supply of sugarless gum, celery sticks, or hard candy on hand to use as a cigarette substitute.

- If you have an uncontrollable urge to light up, take ten deep breaths instead. Hold the last breath, then exhale slowly, and tell yourself you have just had a cigarette.
- Think about all the money you are saving by not buying cigarettes. A simple calculation will convince you that the amount saved in five years from just a moderate level of smoking (say half a pack a day) can be more than $5,000.
- Get in touch with your local Department of Health Services or call the National Cancer Institute Quitline at 877-44U-QUIT.

Source: Information gathered from American Cancer Society (2008). *Guide to quitting smoking.* Atlanta, GA: American Cancer Society.

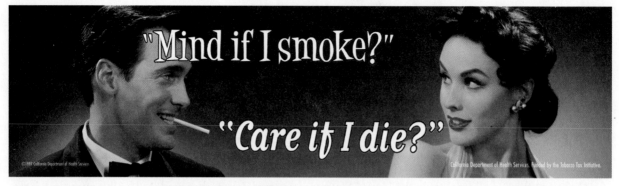

Part of California's antismoking campaign, this billboard focuses on the dangers of environmental tobacco smoke. Researchers have found that an approach based on the smoker's potential decline in social attractiveness reduces the desire among adolescents to start smoking. In 2005, state health officials announced that smoking rates among adolescents and adults in California had declined sharply since the inception of the anti-tobacco campaign in 1990.

taking Zyban. Forty-eight percent of long-time, one-pack-per-day smokers quit after a twelve-week treatment with Chantix, compared to 33 percent among Zyban patients. Successful long-term abstinence may require multiple treatments.[51]

Nicotine Gums, Patches, Sprays, and Inhalers

The long-term goal in quitting smoking is to withdraw from dependence-producing nicotine altogether and to be totally free of any hazard associated with tobacco. In the meantime, however, it is possible to employ an alternative route of ingestion for nicotine that avoids inhaling carbon monoxide and tar into the lungs. Chewing gum containing nicotine (brand name: Nicorette), available since the early 1970s as a prescription drug, is now marketed on a nonprescription basis. Transdermal nicotine patches are marketed on a nonprescription basis as well. Prescription nicotine-substitute options include a nasal spray (brand name: Nicotrol NS) and an oral inhalation system (brand name: Nicotrol Inhaler) in which nicotine is inhaled from a cartridge through a plastic mouthpiece, and lozenges (brand name: Commit).[52]

The Role of Physicians in Smoking Cessation

Owing to the fact that tobacco use is the leading cause of preventable death in the United States, it is clear that physicians must play a critical role in addressing the issue of tobacco use in their patients as part of an intervention to help them quit smoking. Suggestions for

a greater role of the physician in this regard have been dubbed the "Five A's":

- *Ask about tobacco use.* Identify and document tobacco-use status for every patient at every visit.
- *Advise to quit.* In a clear, strong, and personalized manner, urge every tobacco user to quit.
- *Assess willingness to make a cessation attempt.* Is the tobacco user willing to make a cessation attempt at this time?
- *Assist in cessation attempt.* For the patient willing to make a cessation attempt, use counseling and pharmacotherapy to help him or her quit.
- *Arrange follow-up.* Schedule follow-up contact, preferably within the first week after the cessation date.[53]

A recent study suggests that when physicians tell smokers their "lung age," as determined by the age of an average healthy nonsmoker with a comparable level of breathing strength, smokers evidently get the message. They are twice as likely to quit, compared to smokers who are not informed of this fact. Unfortunately, however, the campaign encouraging physicians or other health professionals to communicate any sort of quit-smoking information to patients has a long way to go. It has been estimated that as many as 42,000 additional lives in the United States would be saved each year if 90 percent of smokers were advised by a health professional to quit and were offered medication or other assistance to do so. Presently, only 28 percent of smokers receive such services. Meanwhile, a disturbingly high percentage of physicians worldwide continue to be smokers themselves (Figure 15.4).[54]

FIGURE 15.4

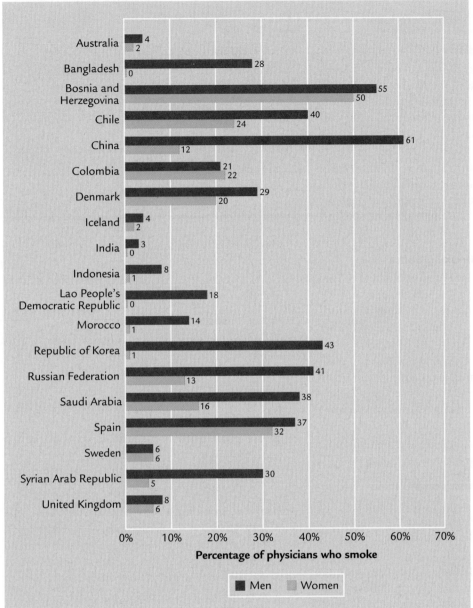

Percentages of physicians who smoke, worldwide

Source: World Health Organization (2002). *The tobacco atlas.* Geneva: Switzerland: World Health Organization, p. 25.

A Final Word on Quitting

When these efforts to quit on one's own have failed, alternative approaches need to be considered. Health professionals emphasize that if one treatment strategy does not work out, the smoker should try another. The long-term consequences of failure are just too great.

The best option, of course, is never to start in the first place, which brings us back to the teenage years, when virtually all adult smokers pick up the habit. The challenge as we progress further into the twenty-first century will be to maintain the communication of effective messages that prevent the initiation of cigarette smoking as well as other forms of tobacco use by young people (see Chapter 16).[55]

Summary

Tobacco Use through History

- Tobacco use originated among the original inhabitants of North and South America, and its introduction to Europe and the rest of the world dates from the first voyage of Columbus. Europeans used tobacco initially in the form of pipe smoking and later in the form of snuff.

- In the nineteenth-century United States, the most popular form was tobacco chewing and later cigar smoking. It was not until the late nineteenth century and early twentieth century that cigarette smoking became popular.

Health Concerns and Smoking Behavior

- The 1964 surgeon general's report, the first official statement on the connection between smoking and adverse health consequences, produced a general reversal in the previously climbing per capita consumption of cigarettes.

- Since 1964, the surgeon general's reports have solidified the position that nicotine is a clearly addicting component of tobacco and that tobacco use, whether in a smoked or smokeless form, causes significant health risks.

- Since 1964, there has been increased use of filtered, low-tar, and low-nicotine cigarettes.

Tobacco Today: An Industry on the Defensive

- Since the early 1990s, most U.S. states, cities, and communities have enacted laws mandating smoke-free environments in all public and private workplaces. It is now typical for restaurants, hotels, and other commercial spaces to be at least partially smoke-free.

- Additional pressure on the tobacco industry has come from proposals to increase the federal excise tax on tobacco products.

- Increased public pressure since the mid-1990s has resulted in a greatly limited marketing approach for tobacco products, particularly with respect to sales to young people.

- In 1998, the major American tobacco corporations entered into a $246 billion settlement agreement with all fifty U.S. states to resolve claims that the states should be compensated for the costs of treating people with smoking-related illnesses.

- In 2009, the Family Smoking and Tobacco Control Act was signed into law, authorizing the FDA to regulate tobacco products sold in the United States.

What's in Tobacco?

- The principal ingredients consumed during the smoking of tobacco are nicotine, tar, and carbon monoxide.

- The smoker inhales smoke in the form of mainstream smoke (through the cigarette itself) and sidestream smoke (released from the cigarette tip into the air).

The Dependence Potential of Nicotine

- Nicotine ingestion produces both tolerance effects and physical withdrawal symptoms. A prominent feature of nicotine withdrawal is the strong craving to return to tobacco use.

- Smokers typically adjust their smoking behavior to obtain a stable dose of nicotine.

Health Consequences of Tobacco Use

- Tobacco smoking produces an increased risk of cardiovascular disease such as coronary heart disease and stroke, lung cancer and other forms of cancer, and respiratory diseases such as chronic bronchitis and emphysema.

- In addition to the hazards to the smoker through the inhalation of mainstream smoke, there are hazards to the developing fetus when the mother is smoking and hazards to nonsmokers who inhale environmental tobacco smoke.

Patterns of Smoking Behavior and Use of Smokeless Tobacco

- In 2009, the past-month prevalence rate for cigarette smoking in the United States among people 12 years or older was approximately 23 percent.

- The peak years for starting to smoke are in the sixth and seventh grades of school.

- A steady increase in the prevalence of smoking among secondary school students during the 1990s has been reversed. As these young people get older, the prevalence rates for cigarette smoking among college students and young adults are likely to decline.

- A global trend of unabated smoking rates in Asia, Eastern Europe, Russia, and elsewhere threatens the future health of huge populations of people worldwide.

Quitting Smoking: The Good News and the Bad

- Research has clearly shown that when people quit smoking, many health risks diminish rapidly. Unfortunately, nicotine dependence is very strong, and it is difficult to quit smoking. Nonetheless, a wide range of smoking cessation treatments are available, and about 50 percent of smokers eventually succeed in quitting on a permanent basis.

- Present-day approaches to smoking cessation include behavioral treatment programs, hypnosis, acupuncture, and prescription drugs to reduce withdrawal symptoms and craving, as well as a variety of nicotine substitutes.

Key Terms

arteriosclerosis, p. 359
atherosclerosis, p. 359
carbon monoxide, p. 356
carcinomas, p. 360
chronic bronchitis,
    p. 360
chronic obstructive
    pulmonary disease
    (COPD), p. 359

cigarettes, p. 350
cigars, p. 350
cilia, p. 356
ciliary escalator, p. 356
coronary heart disease
    (CHD), p. 359
emphysema, p. 360
environmental tobacco
    smoke (ETS), p. 353

erythroplakia, p. 361
gaseous phase, p. 356
ischemic stroke, p. 359
leukoplakia, p. 361
mainstream smoke, p. 355
moist snuff, p. 365
nicotine, p. 356
nitrosamines, p. 361
particulate phase, p. 355

sidestream smoke, p. 352
snuff, p. 350
snuffing, p. 350
tar, p. 355
titration hypothesis, p. 357

Endnotes

1. Brooks, Jerome E. (1952). *The mighty leaf: Tobacco through the centuries.* Boston: Little, Brown, pp. 11–14. Fairholt, Frederick W. (1859). *Tobacco: Its history and associations.* London: Chapman and Hill, p. 13.

2. Brooks, *The mighty leaf*, pp. 74–80. White, Jason M. (1991). *Drug dependence.* Englewood Cliffs, NJ: Prentice-Hall, pp. 32–33.

3. Austin, Gregory A. (1978). *Perspectives on the history of psychoactive substance use.* Rockville, MD: National Institute on Drug Abuse, pp. 1–12.

4. Brooks, *The mighty leaf*, p. 181. Lehman Brothers (1955). *About tobacco.* New York: Lehman Brothers, pp. 18–20.

5. Kluger, Richard (1996). *Ashes to ashes: America's hundred-year cigarette war, the public health, and the "unabashed" triumph of Philip Morris.* New York: Knopf, p. 14. Tate, Cassandra (1989). In the 1800s, antismoking was a burning issue. *Smithsonian, 20* (4), 111.

6. Quotation originally in Bain, John, and Werner, Carl (1905). *Cigarettes in fact and fancy.* Boston: H. M. Caldwell. Cited in Brooks, *The mighty leaf*, p. 259.

7. Kluger, *Ashes to ashes*, pp. 16–20. Lehman Brothers, *About tobacco*, pp. 24–27. Slade, John (1992). The tobacco epidemic: Lessons from history. *Journal of Psychoactive Drugs, 24*, 99–109.

8. Lehman Brothers, *About tobacco*, p. 30.

9. Ibid., p. 31.

10. Connolly, Gregory N.; Alpert, Hillel R.; Wayne, Geoffrey F.; and Koh, Howard (2007, January). Trends in smoke nicotine yield and relationship to design characteristics among popular U.S. cigarette brands 1997–2005. A report of the Tobacco Research Program, Harvard School of Public Health, Boston. Federal Trade Commission Report to Congress (1992). Pursuant to the Federal Cigarette Labeling and Advertising Act, p. 31. U.S. Department of Health and Human Services (1991). *Strategies to control tobacco use in the United States: A blueprint for public health action in the 1990s* (NIH Smoking and Tobacco Control Monograph No. 1). Bethesda, MD: National Cancer Institute. Wilson, Duff (2010, February 19). Coded to obey law, lights become Marlboro Gold. *New York Times*, pp. B1, B5.

11. Campaign for Tobacco Free Kids, American Heart Association, American Lung Association, and American Cancer Society Cancer Action Network (2007, December 17). *A broken promise to our children. The 1998 State Tobacco Settlement nine years later.* Washington, DC: Campaign for Tobacco Free Kids. Madore, James T. (2010, June 22). State OKs tobacco fix for budget gap. *Newsday*, pp. A4–A5, National Women's Health Information Center (2009, December 19). States slash funding for tobacco prevention programs. Washington, DC: National Women's Health Information Center, U.S. Department of Health and Human Services.

12. Office of the Press Secretary, The White House (2009, June 22). Fact sheet: The Family Smoking Prevention and Tobacco Control Act of 2009. Washington, DC: Office of the President. Samet, Jonathan, and Wipfli, Heather (2009). Unfinished business in tobacco control. *Journal of the American Medical Association, 302*, 681–682.

13. Alcoholic beverages and tobacco (1997, September 11). *Standard and Poor's Industry Surveys*, p. 10. Lok, Corie (2002, August 5). Hitting teen smokers where it hurts: In the wallet. *Newsweek*, p. 47. Wilgoren, Jodi (2002, July 17). Facing new costs, some smokers say "enough." *New York Times*, p. A14.

14. Centers for Disease Control and Prevention (2008). Smoking and tobacco use: Frequently asked questions. Atlanta, GA: Centers for Disease Control and Prevention. Payne, Wayne A., Hahn, Dale B, and Lucas, Ellen B. (2009). *Understanding your health* (10th ed.). New York: McGraw-Hill, p. 270.

15. Schlaadt, Richard G. (1992). *Tobacco and health.* Guilford, CT: Dushkin Publishing, p. 41.

16. Gahagan, Dolly D. (1987). *Switch down and quit: What the cigarette companies don't want you to know about smoking.* Berkeley, CA: Ten Speed Press, p. 44. Payne and Hahn, *Understanding your health*, pp. 273–275.

17. Jacobs, Michael R., and Fehr, Kevin O'B. (1987). *Drugs and drug abuse: A reference text* (2nd ed.). Toronto: Addiction Research Foundation, pp. 417–425. Julien, Robert M. (2005). *A primer of drug action* (10th ed.). New York: Worth, pp. 233–234

18. Meier, Barry (1998, February 23). Cigarette maker manipulated nicotine, its records suggest. *New York Times*, pp. A1, A15. Pankow, J. F.; Mader, B. T.; Isabelle, L. M.; Luo, W. T.; et al. (1997). Conversion of nicotine and tobacco smoke to its volatile and available free-base form through the action of gaseous ammonia. *Environmental Science & Technology*, 31, 2428–2433.

19. Julien, Robert A *primer of drug action*, pp. 234–238. Phillips, Sarah, and Fox, Pauline (1998). An investigation into the effects of nicotine gum on short-term memory. *Psychopharmacology*, 140, 429–433. Schuckit, Marc A. (2000). *Drug and alcohol abuse: A clinical guide to diagnosis and treatment* (5th ed.). New York: Kluwer Academic/Plenum, pp. 262–264.

20. Brecher, Edward M., and the editors of *Consumer Reports* (1972). *Licit and illicit drugs.* Boston, Little, Brown, pp. 220–228. DiFranza, Joseph R. (2008, May). Hooked from the first cigarette. *Scientific American*, pp. 82–87.

21. Pontieri, Francesco E.; Tanda, Gianluigi; Orzi, Francesco; and DiChiara, Gaetano (1996). Effects of nicotine on the nucleus accumbens and similarity to those of addictive drugs. *Science*, 382, 255–257. Risso, Francesca; Parodi, Monica; Grilli, Massimo; Molfino, Francesca; et al. (2004). Chronic nicotine causes functional upregulation of ionotropic glutamate receptors mediating hippocampal noradrenaline and stratal dopamine release. *Neurochemistry International*, 44, 293–301.

22. Herning, Ronald I., Jones, Reese T., and Fischman, Patricio (1985). The titration hypothesis revisited: Nicotine gum reduces smoking intensity. In John Grabowski and Sharon M. Hall (Eds.), *Pharmacological adjuncts in smoking cessation* (NIDA Research Monograph 53). Rockville, MD: National Institute on Drug Abuse, pp. 27–41. Jarvik, Murray E. (1979). Biological influences on cigarette smoking. In Norman A. Krasnegor (Ed.), *The behavioral aspects of smoking* (NIDA Research Monograph 26). Rockville, MD: National Institute on Drug Abuse, pp. 7–45.

23. Jarvik, Biological influences, pp. 25–29. Schuckit, *Drugs and alcohol abuse*, pp. 264–265.

24. Koslowski, Lynn T.; Wilkinson, Adrian; Skinner, Wayne; Kent, Carl; Franklin, Tom; and Pope, Marilyn. (1989). Comparing tobacco cigarette dependence with other drug dependencies. *Journal of the American Medical Association*, 261, 898–901.

25. Centers for Disease Control and Prevention (2008, November 14). Cigarette smoking-attributable morbidity, years of potential life lost, and productivity losses— United States, 2000–2004. *Morbidity and Mortality Weekly Report*, 57, 1226–1228.

26. Howard, George; Wagenknecht, Lynne E.; Burke, Gregory L.; Diez-Roux, Ana; et al. (1998). Cigarette smoking and progression of atherosclerosis. *Journal of the American Medical Association*, 279, 119–124. U.S. Department of Health and Human Services, Public Health Service, Office of Smoking and Health (1983). *The health consequences of smoking: Cardiovascular disease* (A report of the surgeon general) Rockville, MD: U.S. Public Health Service, pp. 63–156.

27. Payne, Hahn and Lucas, *Understanding your health*, pp. 272–273.

28. Gold, Diane R.; Wang, Xiaobin; Wypij, David; Speizer, Frank E.; Ware, James H.; et al. (1996). Effects of cigarette smoking on lung function in adolescent boys and girls. *New England Journal of Medicine*, 335, 931–937. Updated from U.S. Department of Health and Human Services, Public Health Service, Office of Smoking and Health (1984). *The health consequences of smoking: Chronic obstructive lung disease* (A report of the surgeon general). Rockville, MD: U.S. Public Health Service, pp. 329–360.

29. American Cancer Society (2010). *Cancer Facts and Figures 2010.* Atlanta, GA: American Cancer Society. Denissenko, Mikhail F.; Pao, Annie; Tang, Moon-Shong; and Pfeifer, Gerd P. (1996). Preferential formation of benzopyrene adducts at lung cancer mutational hotspots in *P53. Science*, 274, 430–432. Landi, Maria T.; Dracheva, Tatiana; Rotunno, Melissa;, Figueroa, Jonine D.; et al. (2008). Gene expression signature of cigarette smoking and its role in lung adenocarcinoma development and survival. *PLoS ONE*, published online February 20, 2008, by the Public Library of Science, San Francisco, CA.

30. Schuckit, *Drug and alcohol abuse*, p. 264.

31. Ebrahim, Shahul H.; Floyd, R. Louise; Merritt II, Robert K; Decoufle, Pierre; and Holtzman, David (2000). Trends in pregnancy-related smoking rates in the United States, 1987–1996. *Journal of the American Medical Association*, 283, 361–366. Geerts, Caroline C.; Grobbee, Diederick E.; van der Ent, Cornelis K; de Jong, Brita M.; et al. (2007). Tobacco smoke exposure of pregnant mothers and blood pressure in their newborns. *Hypertension*, 50, 572–578. Li, Yu-Fen; Langholz, Bryan; Salam, Muhammad T.; and Gilliland, Frank D. (2005). Maternal and grandmaternal smoking patterns are associated with early childhood asthma. *Chest*, 127, 1232–1241.

32. Davis, Ronald M. (1998). Exposure to environmental tobacco smoke: Identifying and protecting those at risk. *Journal of the American Medical Association, 280,* 1947–1949. Ginzel, K. H. (1992). The ill-effects of second hand smoke. In Kristine Napier (Ed.), *Issues in tobacco.* New York: American Council on Science and Health, pp. 6–7.

33. Aligne, C. Andrew; Moss, Mark E.; Auinger, Peggy; and Weitzman, Michael (2003). Association of pediatric dental caries with passive smoking. *Journal of the American Medical Association, 289,* 1258–1264. Fielding, Jonathan E., and Phenow, Kenneth J. (1989). *Health effects of involuntary smoking.* Atlanta, GA: American Cancer Society. In France, adieu to smoking (2008, January). *Newsday,* p. A17. Kawachi, Ichiro; Colditz, Graham A.; Speizer, Frank E.; Manson, JoAnn E.; et al. (1997). A prospective study of passive smoking and coronary heart disease. *Circulation, 95,* 2374–2379. Nafstad, Per; Fugelseth, Drude; Qvigstad, Erik; Zahlsen, Kolbjørn; et al. (1998). Nicotine concentration in the hair of nonsmoking mothers and size of offspring. *American Journal of Public Health, 88,* 120–124. U.S. Department of Health and Human Services, Public Health Service, Office of Smoking and Health (2006). *The health consequences of involuntary exposure to tobacco smoke* (A report of the surgeon general). Rockville, MD: U.S. Public Health Service.

34. Johnston, Lloyd D.; O'Malley, Patrick M.; Bachman, Jerald G.; and Schulenberg, John E. (2009, December 14), Smoking continues gradual decline among U.S. teens, smokeless tobacco threatens a comeback,University of Michigan News Service, Ann Arbor, Table 1. Johnston, Lloyd M.; O'Malley, Patrick M.; Bachman, Gerald G.; and Schulenberg, John E. (2010). *Monitoring the Future: National survey results on drug use, 1975–2009. Volume II. College students and adults ages 19–50, 2009.* Bethesda, MD: National Institute on Drug Abuse, Table 2–3. Substance Abuse and Mental Health Administration (2010). *Results from the 2009 National Survey on Drug Use and Health: Detailed tables.* Rockville, MD: Office of Applied Studies, Substance Abuse and Mental Health Administration, Tables 2-1A, 2-1B, and 2-22B. Wechsler, Henry, Rigotti, Nancy A., and Gledhill-Hoyt, Jeana (1998). Increased levels of cigarette use among college students: A cause for national concern. *Journal of the American Medical Association, 280,* 1673–1678.

35. Centers for Disease Control and Prevention (2003). Tobacco use among middle and high school students—New Hampshire, 1995–2001. *Morbidity and Mortality Weekly Report, 52,* 7–9. Johnston, O'Malley, Bachman, and Schulenberg (2009), Smoking continues gradual decline, Table 1. Johnston, Lloyd D., O'Malley, Patrick M., and Bachman, Jerald G. (2002). *Monitoring the future: National results for adolescent drug use 1975–2001. Volume 1: Secondary school students 2001.* Bethesda, MD: National Institute on Drug Abuse, Table 6–1.

36. Johnston, O'Malley, Bachman, and Schulenberg (2009), Smoking continues gradual decline, Tables 2 and 3.

37. Johnston, Lloyd D., O'Malley, Patrick M., and Bachman, Jerald G. (2002, December 16). Teen smoking declines sharply in 2002, more than offsetting large increases in the early 1990s. University of Michigan News and Information Service, Ann Arbor, pp. 4–5. Quotation by Lloyd D. Johnston, p. 5.

38. Johnston, O'Malley, Bachman, and Schulenberg (2009), Smoking continues gradual decline, Table 2. Rigotti, Nancy A.; DiFranza, Joseph R.; Chang, YuChiao; Tisdale, Thelma; et al. (1997). The effect of enforcing tobacco-sales laws on adolescents' access to tobacco and smoking behavior. *New England Journal of Medicine, 337,* 1044–1057. Substance Abuse and Mental Health Services Administration (2008). *FY 2008 annual Synar reports: Youth tobacco sales.* Substance Abuse and Mental Health Administration.

39. Johnston, O'Malley, Bachman, and Schulenberg (2009), Smoking continues gradual decline, Tables 4, 5, 9, 10, and 11.

40. Freedman, Alix M. How a tobacco giant doctors snuff brands to boost their "kick." (1994, October 26). *Wall Street Journal,* pp. A1, A14.

41. U.S. Department of Health and Human Services, Public Health Service, Office of Smoking and Health (1986). *The health consequences of smokeless tobacco* (A report of the advisory committee to the surgeon general). Rockville, MD: Public Health Service. Wilson, Duff, and Creswell, Julie (2010, January 31). Where there's no smoke, Altria hopes there's fire. *New York Times,* pp. B1, B5.

42. Hamilton, Kendall (1997, July 21). Blowing smoke. *Newsweek,* pp. 54–60.

43. Ackerman, Elise (1999, November 29). The cigar boom goes up in smoke. *Newsweek,* p. 55. Baker, Frank, et al. (2000). Health risks associated with cigar smoking. *Journal of the American Medical Association, 284,* 735–740. Substance Abuse and Mental Health Administration (2001, December 21). *The NHSDA report: Cigar use.* Rockville, MD: Office of Applied Studies, Substance Abuse and Mental Health Administration.

44. Sterngold, James (1993, October 17). When smoking is a patriotic duty. *New York Times,* Sect. 3, pp. 1, 6. Strom, Stephanie (2001, June 13). Japan and tobacco revenue: Leader faces difficult choice. *New York Times,* pp. A1, A14. Tagliabue, John (2005, September 8). The ash may finally be falling from the Gauloise. *New York Times,* p. A4. Watts, Jonathan (1999). Smoking, sake, and suicide: Japan plans a healthier future. *The Lancet, 354,* p. 843. Winter, Greg (2001, August 24). Enticing Third World youth. *New York Times,* pp. C1, C4.

45. Hampton, Tracy (2008, April 2). Global report highlights tobacco use, offers countermeasures for nations. *Journal of the American Medical Association, 299,* 1531–1552.

46. Marsh, Bill (2008, February 24). A growing cloud over the planet. *New York Times,* p. 4. Reeves, Hope (2000, November 5). Blowing smoke: What's one little worldwide antismoking treaty compared to the force of

1.1 billion nicotine-craving cigarette fiends? *New York Times Magazine*, p. 26. Shafey, Omar; Eriksen, Michael, Ross, Hana, and MacKay, Judith (2009). The tobacco atlas (3rd.ed.). Atlanta: American Cancer Society, pp. 22–23. World Health Organization (2008). *WHO report on the global tobacco epidemic 2008: The MPOWER package*. Geneva, Switzerland: World Health Organization.

47. American Cancer Society, Atlanta. Cited in *The world almanac and book of facts 2000* (1999). Mahwah, NJ: Primedia Reference, p. 733.

48. U.S. Department of Health and Human Services, Public Health Service, Office of Smoking and Health (1988). *The health consequences of smoking: Nicotine addiction* (A report of the surgeon general). Rockville, MD: Public Health Service, p. 9.

49. American Legacy Foundation (2003). Factsheet: Quitting smoking. Washington, DC: American Legacy Foundation. Ehrich, Beverly, and Emmons, Karen M. (1994). Addressing the needs of smokers in the 1990s. *The Behavior Therapist*, 17 (6), 119–122. Freudenheim, Milt (2007, October 26). Seeking savings, employers help smokers quit. *New York Times*, pp. A1, A18. Hughes, J. R., Keely, J., and Naud, S. (2004). Shape of the relapse curve and long-term abstinence among untreated smokers. *Addiction*, 99, 29–38. Lichtenstein, Edward, Zhu, Shu-Hong, and Tedeschi, Gary J. (2010, May–June). Smoking cessation quitlines: An underrecognized intervention success story. *American Psychologist*, 253–261. Munafò, Marcus R.; Clark, Taane G.; Johnstone, Elaine C.; Murphy, Michael F. G.; et al. (2004). The genetic basis for smoking behavior: A systematic review and meta-analysis. *Nicotine and Tobacco Research*, 6, 583–597.

50. Ahluwalia, Jasjit S.; Harris, Kari Jo; Catley, Delwyn; Okuyemi, Kolawole S.; and Mayo, Matthew S. (2002). Sustained-release bupropion for smoking cessation in African Americans: A randomized controlled trial. *Journal of the American Medical Association*, 288, 468–474. Benowitz, Neal L. (1997). Treating tobacco addiction—Nicotine or no nicotine? *New England Journal of Medicine*, 337, 1230–1231. Jain, Anjali (2003). Treating nicotine addiction. *British Medical Journal*, 327, 1394–1395. Zickler, Patrick (2003). Genetic variation may increase nicotine craving and smoking relapse. *NIDA Notes*, 18(3), 1, 6.

51. Nides, Mitchell; Oncken, Cheryl; Gonzales, David; Rennard, Stephen; Watsky, Eric J.; et al. (2006). Smoking cessation with varenicline, a selective alpha-4-beta-2 nicotinic receptor partial agonist. *Archives of Internal Medicine*, 166, 1561–1568.

52. Franzon, Mikael, Gustavsson, Gunnar, and Korberly, Barbara H. (2002). Effectiveness of over-the-counter nicotine replacement therapy. *Journal of the American Medical Association*, 288, 3108–3110. Mathias, Robert (2001). Nicotine patch helps smokeless tobacco users quit, but maintaining abstinence may require additional treatment. *NIDA Notes*, 16(1), 8–9. Shiffman, Saul, Dresler, Carolyn M., and Rohay, Jeffrey M. (2004). Successful treatment with a nicotine lozenge of smokers with prior failure in pharmacological therapy. *Addiction*, 99, 83–92.

53. Fiore, Michael C., Hatsukami, Dorothy K., and Baker, Timothy, B. (2002). Effective tobacco dependence treatment. *Journal of the American Medical Association*, 288, 1768–1771. Spangler, John G.; George, Geeta; Foley, Kristie Long; and Crandall, Sonia J. (2002). Tobacco intervention training: Current efforts and gaps in U.S. medical schools. *Journal of the American Medical Association*, 288, 1102–1109.

54. Parkes, Gary; Greenhaigh, Trisha; Griffin, Mark; and Dent, Richard (2008). Effect on smoking quit rate of telling patients their lung age: The Step2quit randomized controlled trial. *British Medical Journal*, 336, 598–600. Partnership for Prevention (2008). New study: Boosting five preventive services would save 100,000 lives each year. Washington, DC: Partnership for Prevention, National Commission on Prevention Priorities. World Health Organization (2002). *The tobacco atlas*. Geneva: Switzerland: World Health Organization, pp. 24–25.

55. Goldman, Lisa K., and Glantz, Stanton A. (1999). Evaluation of antismoking advertising campaigns. *Journal of the American Medical Association*, 279, 772–777. Raising kids who don't smoke (2003), created by Philip Morris USA Youth Smoking Prevention. Story, Louise (2007, January 2). Kicking an addiction, with real people. *New York Times*, p. C7. Two questions to identify future smokers (2008, July 15). *New York Times*, p. F6.

chapter 16

Prevention and Treatment: Drug Policy and Intervention

After you have completed this chapter, you should have an understanding of

- Primary, secondary, and tertiary prevention as three levels of intervention

- The concept of resilience in substance abuse prevention

- Substance abuse prevention in the context of public health

- Approaches to substance abuse prevention that have failed in the past

- Successful school-based substance abuse prevention programs

- Community-based prevention and the impact of mass media

- The importance of family systems in substance abuse prevention

- Substance abuse prevention in the workplace

- Substance abuse treatment programs and the concept of stages of change

I would lie about everything, and I lied to everybody. I was so good at it because it was so easy to do. My parents were in major denial, and I played off of that. What is all that drug stuff in my room? Oh, I'm just holding it for a friend. It would get me so angry that the lies worked so well with them. They would never call me on anything.

It became a way of life. But after a while I got sick and tired of all the lying. And I started to think about the possibility that I might be dead at an early age. Half of my friends are now dead; the other half are in jail. That's why

I'm here to get help. I had to change somehow. It really just came down to that.

—A seventeen-year-old recovering drug abuser, explaining why he came to Daytop Village

In this final chapter, we turn to drug-control policies and interventions related to prevention and treatment. Before we begin, however, it is important to be reminded once again that drug-taking behavior encompasses a wide range of potentially abusable substances. They include illicit drugs, alcohol, and nicotine as well as prescription and nonprescription medications. Unfortunately, as a result, we are presented with a challenge in coming up with a single phrase for prevention or treatment that incorporates all the possibilities that drug-taking behavior can entail. For example, the awkward phrase *alcohol, tobacco, and other drug (ATOD) prevention* has been used to describe prevention strategies for illicit drugs, alcohol, and tobacco. In this chapter, we will use a more concise phrase—*substance abuse prevention*—and focus primarily on prevention strategies related to the abuse of illicit drugs and alcohol. As we will see, the principles of effective substance abuse prevention are applicable (and effective substance abuse prevention programs have been adapted) to a host of life-style situations, including tobacco use, the nonmedical use of prescription and nonprescription medications, and a number of high-risk social behaviors such as adolescent delinquency, unsafe driving, and unsafe sex.

Levels of Intervention in Substance Abuse Prevention

Substance abuse prevention takes place at primary, secondary, and tertiary levels of intervention. Each level of intervention has its own target population and specific goals. As we will see, primary prevention, secondary prevention, and tertiary prevention populations vary according to the extent of prior drug use.

- In **primary prevention**, efforts are directed to those who have not had any experience with drugs or those who have been only minimally exposed. The objective is to prevent substance abuse from starting in the first place, "nipping the problem in the bud" so to speak. Targets in primary prevention programs are most frequently elementary school or middle school youths, and intervention usually occurs within a school-based curriculum or specific educational program, though community involvement is encouraged. For example, a primary prevention program would include the development of peer-refusal skills that students can use when offered marijuana, alcohol, or cigarettes (that is, teaching "ways to say no").

- In **secondary prevention**, the target population has already had some experience with alcohol, nicotine, and other drugs. The objective is to limit the extent of substance abuse (reducing it, if possible), prevent its spread of abuse behavior beyond the drugs already encountered, and teach strategies for the responsible use of alcohol if the legal minimum age has been met. Ordinarily, those individuals receiving secondary-prevention efforts are older than those involved in primary-prevention programs. High school students who are identified as alcohol or other drug users, for example, may participate in a program that emphasizes social alternatives to drug-taking behavior (after-school programs, sports, etc.) to drug-taking behavior. College students may focus on the skills necessary to restrict their behavior to the moderate use of alcohol, the significant dangers of combining drinking and driving, and the signs of chronic alcohol abuse. Secondary prevention efforts are consistent with the philosophy of Harm Reduction rather than Zero Tolerance of drug-taking behavior (Drugs . . . in Focus).

- In **tertiary prevention**, the objective is to ensure that an individual who has entered treatment for some form of substance abuse or substance dependence problem becomes drug-free after treatment has ended and does not revert to former patterns of drug-taking behavior. Successful prevention of relapse is the ultimate indication that the treatment has taken hold. Issues related to tertiary prevention will be reviewed later in the chapter.

In the case of primary prevention, we are assuming that the target population for these interventions may have been exposed to drug-taking behavior in other

primary prevention: A type of intervention in which the goal is to forestall the onset of drug use by an individual who has had little or no previous exposure to drugs.

secondary prevention: A type of intervention in which the goal is to reduce the extent of drug use in individuals who have already had some exposure to drugs.

tertiary (TER-shee-eh-ree) prevention: A type of intervention in which the goal is to prevent relapse in an individual following recovery in a drug-treatment program.

Drugs... in Focus

Harm Reduction as a National Drug-Abuse Policy

To say that we are waging a "war on drugs" is, in effect, communicating how serious we are in dealing with the problems of drug abuse in the United States. Using the metaphor of warfare, we recognize that there is an acknowledged enemy (drug misuse and abuse), there are victims or casualties (us), there are resources at our disposal to fight the necessary battles (federal and state governments, communities, parents, etc.), and there is a high price to pay (billions of dollars of federal funds each year).

The implications of this real-life struggle, such as our overall strategy and ultimate goals, are also drawn in metaphorical terms. Do we want total victory and complete annihilation of the enemy? Or do we want some kind of negotiated settlement, some type of compromise that gives us some semblance of peace and tranquility? If it is the former, then we require a total elimination, often expressed as "zero tolerance" of abuse drug-taking behavior in America. If it is the latter, then we require a good deal less. We desire, in that case, only a reduction of the harmful consequences of abusive drug-taking behavior, knowing fully well that a total elimination is unrealistic and perhaps unattainable. The second alternative is referred to as the Harm Reduction approach. Whether we choose a harm-reduction approach or an approach based on zero tolerance is the essence of our deliberation on a national drug-abuse policy.

The harm-reduction approach in drug policy has its historical roots in the libertarian philosophy of the nineteenth-century philosopher John Stuart Mill, who argued that the state did not have the duty to protect individual citizens from harming themselves. As Mill expressed it,

> The only purpose for which power can be rightfully executed over any member of a civilized community, against his will, is to prevent harm to others. His own good, either physical or moral, is not a sufficient warrant . . . Over himself, over his own body and mind, the individual is sovereign.

It is evident, however, that drug-taking behavior does indeed harm other people. The question, according to those advocating a harm-reduction strategy, is to look for policies that reduce the harm that drugs do, both directly to the drug user and indirectly to others.

Examples of the Harm Reduction approach include needle-exchange programs to lower the incidence of HIV infection among intravenous drug abusers (see Chapter 2), methadone maintenance programs for the treatment of heroin abusers (see Chapter 7), efforts to reduce the incidence of driving while under the influence of alcohol (see Chapter 13), and the use of nicotine patches to avoid the effects of cigarette smoking such as emphysema and lung cancer (see Chapter 15). A more controversial application of the Harm Reduction approach is the suggestion that we should attempt to reduce the level of heavy drug use down to a level of occasional use, rather than no use at all.

With regard to cigarette smoking and marijuana use, there is an indication that some teenagers may already be "harm reducing." In the University of Michigan survey, high school seniors engaging in occasional marijuana smoking and occasional cigarette smoking indicated a higher perceived risk of "regular substance use" than did high school seniors engaging in heavy use, even though there was no difference in the perceived risk of "occasional substance use." In other words, occasional users may have been moderating their behavior to minimize the harmful effects they associated with heavy drug-taking behavior. Whether a prevention program that emphasizes the risks of heavy drug use, as opposed to emphasizing the risks of any level of use, is the more successful strategy in reducing significant levels of drug-taking behavior is a question that advocates of the Harm Reduction approach will be investigating in the future with great interest.

Sources: Denning, Patt (2003). *Over the influence: The harm reduction guide for managing drugs and alcohol.* New York: Guilford Press. Des Jarlais, Don C. (2000). Prospects for a public health perspective on psychoactive drug use. *American Journal of Public Health, 90,* 335–337. How did we get here? History has a habit of repeating itself (2001, July 28–August 3). *Economist,* pp. 4–5. Quotation of John Stuart Mill on page 5. Levinthal, Charles F. (2003). Question: Should harm reduction be our overall goal in fighting drug abuse? *Point/Counterpoint: Opposing perspectives on issues of drug policy.* Boston: Allyn and Bacon, pp. 70–73. Marlatt, G. Alan (Ed.) (2002). *Harm reduction: Pragmatic strategies for managing high-risk behaviors.* New York: Guilford Press. Resnicow, Ken; Smith, Matt; Harrison, Lana; and Drucker, Ernest (1999). Correlates of occasional cigarette and marijuana use. Are teens harm reducing? *Addictive Behaviors, 24,* 251–266.

people but have not had significant drug experiences of their own. We recognize that the potential for young people to engage in drug use themselves is substantial, and only through effective primary prevention can we keep that potential from turning into reality. It is increasingly clear that the *age of onset* for drug-taking behavior of any kind is a key factor in determining problems later in life, particularly with respect to licit drugs. For example, a young person who begins drinking before the age of fifteen is twice as likely to develop a pattern of alcohol abuse and four times as likely to develop alcohol dependence as an individual who begins drinking at the age of twenty-one. In general, if the age of onset can be delayed significantly or even moderately, it may be possible to reduce the incidence of substance abuse or dependence over one's lifetime.[1]

In the case of secondary prevention, we are concentrating on the life-style of a somewhat older population,

and our goal is to minimize the problems associated with drug-taking behavior, assuming that some level of that behavior already exists. Emphasis is placed on social alternatives to behaviors involving alcohol and other drugs among high school students. At the college level, the moderate use of alcohol, the avoidance of alcohol binging in particular, and education about the personal risks of some of the newer club drugs and the nonmedical use of prescription medications, are all elements in a program of secondary prevention.

Strategies for Substance Abuse Prevention

The U.S. federal agency specifically charged with prevention programs is the Center for Substance Abuse Prevention (CSAP), a division of the Substance Abuse and Mental Health Services Administration (SAMHSA), which is in turn a division of the U.S. Department of Health and Human Services. According to CSAP guidelines, substance abuse prevention is accomplished through two principal efforts. The first is the promotion of constructive life-styles and norms that discourage substance abuse. The second is the development of social and physical environments that facilitate drug-free life-styles and act as a buffer against the development of substance abuse behaviors.

You may recall from Chapter 4 that two groups of factors play a major role in predicting the extent of drug-taking behavior in a given individual: (1) risk factors that increase the likelihood of drug-taking behavior and (2) protective factors that decrease it. You can think of the goals of substance abuse prevention in those terms. The optimal substance abuse prevention program effectively reduces the impact of risk factors in an individual's life and, at the same time, enhances the impact of protective factors.

Resilience and Primary Prevention Efforts

Successful primary prevention programs are built around the central idea that an individual is less inclined to engage in substance abuse if the protective factors in his or her life are enhanced and the risk factors are diminished. Only then can a young person be resilient enough to overcome the temptations of alcohol, tobacco, and other drugs. **Resilience**, defined as the inclination to resist the effect of risk factors through the action of protective factors, can be a make-or-break element in one's

Quick Concept Check 16.1

Understanding Levels of Intervention in Substance Abuse Prevention Programs

Check your understanding of the three basic levels of intervention in drug-abuse prevention by matching the following five scenarios with (a) primary, (b) secondary, or (c) tertiary prevention.

1. Midnight basketball sessions keep teenagers from drinking on weekends out of boredom.

2. Young children receive lessons on how to refuse the offer of drugs from a friend or acquaintance.

3. A child learns about "good drugs" and "bad drugs" in the first grade.

4. A man learns how to live without cocaine following a successful cocaine treatment program.

5. College students organize a "responsible drinking" program on campus.

Answers: 1. b 2. a 3. a 4. c 5. b

---

resilience: The inclination to resist the negative impact of risk factors in a person's life through the positive impact of protective factors. Sometimes referred to as resiliency.

social development. The promotion of positive social skills and the encouragement of a proactive rather than a passive approach to problem solving enhance the "buffering effect" of protective factors with respect to drug-taking behavior and other forms of deviant behavior. Since a young population is the principal target for primary prevention, programs are customarily implemented in the school. To be most effective, however, it is necessary to incorporate aspects of a young person's life outside of school. In a later section, we will turn to primary prevention programs that involve the community at large.[2]

Measuring Success in a Substance Abuse Prevention Program

Evaluating the success or failure of a substance abuse prevention program is more complicated than people often think. In the public mind, a school-based substance abuse prevention program might be considered successful, for example, if it enjoys support from parents, administrators, and teachers. There might be a long list of testimonials in which participants attest to their belief that they have benefitted from the program. It might be also considered successful if there is evidence of a change in a child's view toward drug use or a change in a child's stated inclination to engage in drug use in the future.

However gratifying these outcomes might be to the community and however persuasive they might be to the general public, they do not get to the core issue: Is the prevalence of substance abuse reduced as a result of the program? *The goal of any prevention program, particularly a primary prevention program aimed at young people, is to lower the numbers of new drug users or to delay the first use of alcohol and tobacco closer to an age at which young people are considered adults.* To be considered "evidence-based," primary prevention programs must be evaluated against a control group that did not receive the intervention; otherwise, it is impossible to determine whether the effect of the program itself was greater than that of doing nothing at all. Positive change *per se* is not enough. For example, if drug use among eighth graders has declined as a result of a prevention program but this decline is not greater than the decline among eighth graders in the control group, then the prevention program is essentially ineffective. Secondary prevention programs are judged to be effective by a similar comparison against a control group. When successful prevention programs are reviewed later in this chapter, their effectiveness will have been measured by this rigorous "yardstick" of performance. The effectiveness of substance abuse treatment programs must be evaluated in the same way.

Substance Abuse Prevention in the Context of National Drug-Control Policy

The overall national policy for the control of drug use in the United States is coordinated by the White House Office of National Drug Control Policy (ONDCP). It is clear that two of the three priorities established by the ONDCP as components of a national drug-control strategy pertain specifically to substance abuse prevention.[3]

- *Priority I—Stopping drug use before it starts.* Primary prevention programs, to be reviewed in this chapter, are essentially the first line of defense against substance abuse problems among young people. As we will see, effective school-based prevention programs do exist, but the overall effectiveness is enhanced when there is a combination of education and community action.

- *Priority II—Healing America's drug users.* Efforts toward substance abuse treatment and tertiary prevention of drug-taking behavior have been substantial. In 2003, for example, a federal "voucher program" was instituted for people in need of treatment for services that could be obtained in a variety of contexts, including emergency departments in hospitals, health clinics, the criminal justice system, schools, or the faith community. In addition, drug court programs have been expanded to provide treatment, mandatory drug testing, and vigorous aftercare services to help sustain drug-abuse recovery. Despite these programs, however, a wide disparity exists between those who need substance abuse treatment and those who receive it (Portrait).

- *Priority III—Disrupting the market.* Attacking the economic basis of the drug trade, from the cultivation of raw materials for illicit drugs and drug trafficking on domestic and international levels to the sale of illicit drugs at the local level, forms the "supply side" approach to the drug-abuse problem. Chapter 6 specifically addressed attempts to reduce the influx and distribution of illicit drugs. Chapters 13 and 15 addressed efforts to reduce the sale of alcohol and tobacco to individuals below legally defined age limits.

Substance Abuse Prevention and Public Health Policy

It is important to recognize that a drug-free life constitutes a major element in a healthy life and, in turn, a healthy

PORTRAIT

Dr. A. Thomas McLellan: Reframing National Drug Policy

Administrators in the Office of National Drug Control Policy have traditionally been recruited from positions of authority, military or otherwise. So when President Obama announced in early 2009 Dr. A. Thomas McLellan as his choice for deputy director, it sent a clear signal that the decades-long approach to substance abuse and dependence in America was about to change.

Dr. McLellan was no ordinary governmental appointee. A professor of psychiatry at the University of Pennsylvania School of Medicine, author of more than 400 papers on substance dependence, and author of two of the most practical and widely used methods of assessing the severity of substance dependence and potential success of treatment, Dr. McLellan had the academic credentials to examine national drug policy with fresh and unbiased eyes.

Dr. McLellan also had a unique personal story. Three months prior to his appointment, his son had died of a drug overdose, a mixture of antianxiety medication and Scotch. Another son was in residential treatment for alcohol and cocaine dependence. Married to a recovering cocaine abuser, Dr. McLellan had been surrounded by substance abuse and dependence in life as well as in his work. His family was a personal battlefield that mirrored the nation's own struggle with drug-taking behavior.

The task of reframing and reformulating national drug policy is formidable. Dr. McLellan understands that only one in ten individuals who need treatment actually receives it. He wants to triple the number in treatment, integrating treatment programs into the primary health care system. He understands that up to two-thirds of the budget for drug control goes to law enforcement and antitrafficking

projects. He wants the budget redirected to prevention and treatment.

According to Dr. McLellan, we should no longer be fighting a "war on drugs," by which he implies that the government should stop waging battle against its citizens. Instead, the focus should be redirected toward substance abuse prevention and treatment, with an emphasis on full community involvement. His supporters are many, but so are his detractors. Even so, in the words of Dr. Nora D. Volkow, director of the National Institute on Drug Abuse (see Portrait in Chapter 3), "This is an extraordinary moment of opportunity."

Sources: Clark, Jared C. (2009, December). Kicking the national drug habit. *Monitor on Psychology*, pp. 36-38. Kershaw, Sarah (2009, December 8). Addiction on 2 fronts: Work and home. *New York Times*, p. D1. Quotation on p. D1.

society. Figure 16.1 shows dramatically how substance abuse impacts the nation's health in general. As you can see, about one-half of all preventable deaths in the United States are accounted for by the abuse of alcohol products (7 percent), tobacco products (38 percent), or illicit drugs (2 percent). Each year, an estimated 537,000 deaths are attributed to these three circumstances (Drugs . . . in Focus).[4]

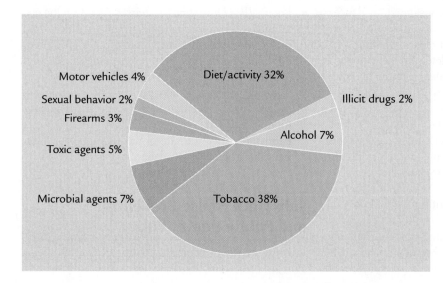

FIGURE 16.1

The relative incidence of preventable deaths annually in the United States.

Source: Mokdad, Ali H.; Marks, James S.; Stroup, Donna F.; and Gerberding, Julie L. (2004). Actual causes of death in the United States, 2000. Journal of the American Medical Association, 291, 1238–1245, Table 2.

Drugs... in Focus

The Public Health Model and the Analogy of Infectious Disease Control

The idea that reducing the negative consequences of drug-taking behavior is a desirable goal for the enhancement of the overall health of society is often referred to as the Public Health Model. As Avram Goldstein, a prominent drug-abuse researcher and policy analyst, has pointed out, the problems of reducing drug-taking behavior have many similarities to wresting control over an infectious disease. A virus, for example, infects some people who are relatively more susceptible than others (in other words, there are risk factors), while some people will be relatively immune (in other words, there are protective factors). Public health measures can be established to reduce or eradicate the virus (just as we attempt to reduce the supply of illicit drugs from reaching the consumer); specific vaccinations can be discovered to increase a person's resistance to the virus (just as we search for effective primary prevention programs in drug abuse).

We can carry the analogy further. Medical treatment for an infectious disease is considered uncontroversial and necessary for two reasons. First, we are alleviating the suffering of the infected individual; second, we are reducing the pool of infection to limit the spread to others. Analogously,

drug-abuse treatment is desirable to relieve the negative consequences of drug abuse, as well as reduce the social influence of drug abusers on nondrug abusers in our society. Goldstein asks a provocative question:

> There are individuals who contribute to the AIDS epidemic by having promiscuous sexual contacts without taking elementary precautions. Are those behaviors, which contribute to the spread of infectious disease, really different in principle from that of pack-a-day cigarette smokers who will not try to quit, despite all the evidence of physical harm to themselves and their families?

There is certainly no consensus on how the problem of drug abuse should be conceptualized. Some have objected to the implications of the Public Health Model, arguing that it ignores the moral and ethical choices that are made in establishing a pattern of drug-taking behavior. You may recognize a similar controversy, discussed in Chapter 14, regarding the question of whether alcoholism should be considered a disease.

Sources: Goldstein, Avram (1994). *Addiction: From biology to drug policy.* New York: Freeman. Quotation on p. 10. Jonas, Steven (1997). Public health approaches. In Joyce H. Lowinson, Pedro Ruiz, Robert B. Millman, and John G. Langrod (Eds.), *Substance abuse: A comprehensive textbook.* Baltimore, MD: Williams & Wilkins, pp. 775–785.

In addition, the monetary impact is immense, with the estimated costs of substance abuse exceeding $1 trillion each year. Some of these costs are incurred through accidents, crime, academic underachievement from underage drinking ($64 billion), drug-related hospital emergency visits ($4 billion), incarceration of individuals committing drug-law offenses ($30 billion), alcohol-related workplace injuries and absenteeism ($28 billion), and DWI-related collisions on highways ($230 billion). More than eighteen dollars could be saved for every dollar spent on effective school-based prevention programs.[5] It should not be surprising that when the U.S. Public Health Service established in the 1990s a comprehensive, national health promotion and disease prevention agenda in a program called Healthy People 2000 (now updated to Healthy People 2020), a major component concerned behaviors related to substance abuse.[6]

Lessons from the Past: Prevention Approaches That Have Failed

When deciding how to solve a problem, it always helps to look at what has *not* worked in the past. That way, we can avoid wasting time, effort, and money on nonsolutions. In the general opinion of health professionals and researchers, the following efforts have been largely unsuccessful with regard to primary prevention, when positioned as the major thrust of a particular program. Nonetheless, some of these approaches have been incorporated successfully as one of several components within an overall effective package.

Reducing the Availability of Drugs

It is reasonable to expect that problems of illicit drug abuse could be prevented if the availability of these drugs were reduced or eliminated altogether. This is essentially the "supply/availability" argument in drug prevention and constitutes approximately 64 percent of the federal budget on drug control each year.[7]

According to the economic principle of supply and demand, however, a decline in supply or availability works to produce an increase in value and an increase in demand. If one accepts the first viewpoint, then reductions in supply or availability should help prevent drug-taking behavior because the cost of the drug would be too high for people to obtain it. If one accepts the second viewpoint, then such reductions should exacerbate the situation; people would want the drug even more than before. Which theoretical viewpoint is operating with respect to illicit drugs (or with respect to alcohol, tobacco, and other licit drugs) is a point of contention among health professionals both inside and outside the government.

The United States has adopted the policy of reducing the supply or availability of illicit drugs as part of an overall national drug-control strategy, but how successful have we been? Have we been able, for example, to reduce the production of illicit drugs around the world and their influx into the United States? Unfortunately, drug cultivation (such as the harvesting of opium, coca leaves, and marijuana) and the exportation of processed illicit drugs from their points of origin are so deeply entrenched in many regions of the world and the resourcefulness of drug producers is so great that our global efforts have been frustratingly inadequate. As we noted in Chapter 6, a production crackdown in one region merely serves to create a marketing vacuum which another region quickly fills. Moreover, efforts to control international drug trafficking have been embarrassingly unsuccessful, despite well-publicized drug busts, arrests, and seizures. It is estimated that only a small fraction of illicit drugs is interdicted (intercepted) at U.S. borders.[8]

With respect to alcohol, a strategy of reduced availability has been implemented on a nationwide basis since 1984 by prohibiting young people under the age of twenty-one from buying alcoholic beverages (see Chapter 13). Prior to this time, some states had adopted this policy but neighboring states had not. It was possible, therefore, to compare alcohol consumption rates and the incidence of alcohol-related automobile accidents. In one such study, the percentage of teenage, nighttime, single-vehicle accident fatalities in Massachusetts was found to have declined in 1979 (the year the legal drinking age in that state was raised to twenty-one) to a significantly greater degree than in New York, which at that time still had a minimum drinking age of eighteen. That was the good news.

The bad news was that levels of alcohol consumption in this age range stayed the same. Therefore, although one particular consequence of immoderate alcohol use (drunk driving) was reduced as a *secondary* prevention intervention, the prevalence of alcohol use itself was unaffected as a primary prevention intervention. As we are all aware, underage drinking still is widespread; minors still find opportunities to drink and to drink in excess. The fact that minimum-age requirements have only a limited effect on drinking among minors reinforces the complexity of designing primary prevention programs based on reduced drug availability.[9]

Punitive Measures

There is a common expectation, when policies related to law enforcement and the criminal justice system are considered, that individuals would be less inclined to use and abuse illicit drugs if they were afraid of being arrested, prosecuted, convicted, and incarcerated. The available statistics show that this threat has little effect as a deterrent. The enticements of many psychoactive drugs are extremely powerful, and the imposition of harsh penalties has frequently been delayed or inconsistent. Mandatory minimum-sentencing laws (see Chapter 6) have resulted in a clogged judicial system and vastly overcrowded prisons, without making any noticeable dent in the trafficking in or consumption of illicit drugs. Although the enforcement of these penalties may be defended in terms of an overall social policy toward illicit drugs, it has evidently failed as an effective means for either primary or secondary prevention.[10]

Scare Tactics and Negative Education

In the late 1960s, the suddenly widespread use of marijuana, amphetamines, barbiturates, LSD, and other hallucinogens, first among students on college campuses and later among youth at large, spawned a number of hastily designed programs based on the arousal of fear and exaggerated or blatantly inaccurate information about the risks involved. They were the products of panic rather than careful thought.

As might be imagined, such efforts turned young people *off* precisely at the time when they were turning themselves on to an array of exotic and seemingly innocuous drug-taking experiences. Professionals have called these misguided efforts the "reefer madness approach," an allusion to the government-sponsored movie of the 1930s that attempted to scare people away from experimenting with marijuana (see Chapter 10). These programs accomplished little, except to erode even further the credibility of the adults in the eyes of youths who often knew (or thought they knew) a great deal more about drugs and their effects than their elders.[11]

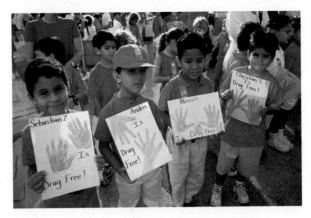

Elementary school children display their handprint art projects. Designations of drug-free pledges are prominent features of many school-based drug abuse prevention programs.

Objective Information Approaches

At the opposite end of the emotional spectrum are programs designed to present information about drugs and their potential dangers in a straightforward, non-judgmental way. Unfortunately, evaluations of this "just the facts, ma'am" approach have found that youths exposed to such primary prevention programs are no less likely to use drugs and sometimes are *more* likely to use drugs later in their lives. These programs tend to increase their curiosity about drugs in general, obviously something the program planners want to avoid.[12]

Despite these failures, however, it would be a mistake to dismiss the informational aspect of any substance abuse prevention program completely out of hand, particularly when the information is presented in a low-fear atmosphere.[13] The overall value of an informational approach appears to depend on whether the target population consists of high-risk or low-risk children. The evidence indicates that when low-risk young people are presented with drug-related information, they really understand the dangers and the chances of remaining drug-free are increased. High-risk youth, on the other hand, may not be so easily dissuaded and additional interventions appear to be necessary.[14]

Magic Bullets and Promotional Campaigns

A variety of antidrug promotional materials such as T-shirts, caps, rings, buttons, bumper stickers, posters, rap songs, school assembly productions, books, and brochures are available and frequently seen as "magic bullets" that can clinch success in

substance abuse prevention programs. Their appeal lies in their high visibility; these items send a clear signal to the public at large, ever eager for signs that the drug-abuse problem might easily go away, that something is being done. Yet, although they may be helpful in deglamorizing drug-taking behavior and providing a forum for young people to express their feelings about drugs, promotional items are inadequate by themselves to reduce substance abuse overall. They do, however, remain viable components of more comprehensive programs that will be examined later in the chapter.[15]

Self-Esteem Enhancement and Affective Education

In the early 1970s, several substance abuse prevention programs were developed that emphasized the affective or emotional component of drug-taking behavior rather than specific information about drugs. In the wake of research that showed a relationship between drug abuse and psychological variables such as low self-esteem, poor decision-making skills, and poor interpersonal communication skills, programs were instituted that incorporated role-playing exercises with other assignments designed to help young people get in touch with their own emotions and feel better about themselves.

This effort, called **affective education**, was an attempt to deal with underlying emotional and attitudinal

affective education: An approach in ATOD prevention programs that emphasizes the building of self-esteem and an improved self-image.

factors rather than specific behaviors related to drug use (in fact, alcohol, tobacco, and other drugs were seldom mentioned at all). Affective education was based on the observation that drug users had difficulty identifying and expressing emotions such as anger and love. In a related set of programs called **values clarification**, moral values were actively taught to children, on the assumption that they frequently had a poorly developed sense of where their life was going and lacked a "moral compass" to guide their behavior.

Difficulties arose, however, when parents, community leaders, and frequently educators themselves argued that the emphasis of affective education on values clarification was inappropriate for public schools. There was concern that a system of morality was being imposed on students without respecting their individual backgrounds and cultures. This kind of instruction, it was felt, was more suited for faith-based education settings.[16]

Above and beyond these social considerations, neither affective education nor values clarification was effective in preventing drug-taking behavior. Some researchers have recently questioned the basic premise that self-esteem is a major factor at all. As a result, affective issues are no longer viewed as central considerations in primary or secondary substance abuse prevention. Nonetheless, they can be found as components in more comprehensive prevention programs, discussed later, that have been more successful.[17]

Hope and Promise: Components of Effective School-Based Prevention Programs

One of the major lessons to be learned from evaluations of previous substance abuse prevention efforts is that there is a far greater chance for success when the programs are multifaceted than when they focus on only a single aspect of drug-taking behavior. The following are elements of school-based, substance abuse prevention programs that have been shown to work.

---

values clarification: An approach in ATOD prevention programs that teaches positive social values and attitudes.

peer-refusal skills: Techniques by which an individual can resist peer pressure to use alcohol, tobacco, or other drugs.

Peer-Refusal Skills

A number of school-based programs developed during the 1980s have included the teaching of personal and social skills as well as techniques for resisting various forms of social pressure to smoke, drink, or use other drugs (often referred to as **peer-refusal skills**). The emphasis is directed toward an individual's relationships with his or her peers and the surrounding social climate. Rather than simply prodding adolescents to "just say no," these programs teach them *how to do so* when they find themselves in uncomfortable social circumstances.

Primary prevention programs using peer-refusal skill training have been shown to reduce the rate of tobacco smoking, as well as the rates of alcohol drinking and marijuana smoking, by 35 to 45 percent, considerably better than any change observed in control groups. With respect to tobacco smoking, this approach has been even more effective for young people identified as being in a high-risk category (in that their friends or family smoked) than for other students.[18]

Anxiety and Stress Reduction

Adolescence can be an enormously stressful time, and drug-taking behavior is frequently seen as a way to reduce feelings of anxiety, particularly when an individual has inadequate coping skills to deal with that anxiety. It is therefore useful to learn techniques of self-relaxation and stress management and to practice the application of these techniques to everyday situations.

Social Skills and Personal Decision Making

Peer-refusal skills are but one example of a range of assertiveness skills that allow young people to express their feelings, needs, preferences, and opinions directly and honestly, without fearing that they will jeopardize their friendships or lose the respect of others. Learning assertiveness skills not only helps advance the goals of primary prevention but also fosters positive interpersonal relationships throughout life. Tasks in social skills training include the ability to initiate social interactions (introducing oneself to a stranger), offer a compliment to others, engage in conversation, and express feelings and opinions. Lessons generally involve a combination of instruction, demonstration, feedback, reinforcement, behavioral rehearsal, and extended practice through behavioral homework assignments.

A related skill is the ability to make decisions in a thoughtful and careful way. Emphasis is placed on the identification of problem situations, the formulation of goals, the generation of alternative solutions, and the consideration of the likely consequences of each. Lessons also focus on identifying persuasive advertising appeals and exploring counterarguments that can defuse them. Primary prevention programs that employ a social skills training approach have been shown to reduce by 42 to 75 percent the likelihood that a young person will try cigarette smoking and to reduce by 56 to 67 percent the likelihood that a nonsmoker will be a regular smoker in a one-year follow-up.[19]

An Example of an Effective School-Based Prevention Program

Substance abuse prevention professionals are in general agreement that the most effective programs should be comprehensive in nature, with special emphasis on the teaching of specific social decision-making skills such as resisting peer pressure to engage in drug-taking behavior.[20] An example of a successful school-based prevention effort is the Life Skills Training (LST) program, developed by Gilbert Botvin at the Cornell University Medical College in New York City. Three LST programs have been designed with developmentally appropriate content for young people in elementary school, middle school, and high school, respectively. The elementary school program can be taught either during the third grade or over the course of the fourth, fifth, and sixth grades. The middle school program is taught over the course of the seventh, eighth, and ninth grades. The high school program is taught in one year, either as a stand-alone program or as a maintenance program in conjunction with earlier sessions in middle school. The major elements of the LST programs are

- A *cognitive component* designed to provide information about the short-term consequences of using alcohol, tobacco, and other drugs. Unlike traditional prevention approaches, LST includes only minimal information on the long-term health consequences of drug-taking behavior. Evidently, it is not useful to tell young people about what might happen when they are "old." Instead, information is provided concerning immediate negative effects, the impact on social acceptability, and actual prevalence rates among adults and adolescents. This last element of the lesson is to counter the myth that drug-taking behavior is the norm in their age group—the misconception that "everyone's doing it."
- A *decision-making component* designed to facilitate critical thinking and independent decision making.

Students learn to evaluate the role of the media in shaping behavior as well as to formulate counterarguments and other cognitive strategies to resist advertising pressures.

- A *stress-reduction component* designed to help students develop ways to lessen anxiety. Students learn relaxation techniques and cognitive techniques to manage stress.
- A *social skills component* designed to teach social assertiveness and specific techniques for resisting peer pressure.
- A *self-directed behavior-change component* designed to facilitate self-improvement and encourage a sense of personal control and self-esteem. Students are assigned to identify a skill or behavior that they would like to change or improve and to develop a long-term goal over an eight-week period and short-term objectives that can be met week by week.

Originally designed as a smoking-prevention program, LST presently focuses on issues related to the entire spectrum of drug-taking behavior. Over a period of as long as six years following exposure to the program, participants have been found to have a 50 to 75 percent lower incidence of alcohol, tobacco, and marijuana use, a 66 percent lower incidence of multiple-drug use, a 25 percent lower incidence of pack-a-day cigarette smoking, and a lower incidence of inhalant, opiate, and hallucinogen use, relative to controls.[21] Reductions in drug use have been seen among inner-city minority students as well as among white middle-class youths, an encouraging sign that these primary prevention strategies can have a positive influence on adolescents from varying social backgrounds. In effect, as Botvin has expressed it, LST and similar programs work "in cities and towns and villages across the United States without having to develop separate intervention approaches for each and every different population."[22]

LST programs also exert positive influences in a number of high-risk social behaviors beyond simply drug-taking behavior. Reductions in violence and delinquency have been observed among sixth-grade LST participants, relative to controls. There has also been a reduction in risky driving behaviors among adolescent participants. Young adults who have participated in LST programs engage in a reduced level of HIV-risk behaviors, as indicated by multiple sex partners, frequency of intercourse while drunk or high, and recent high-risk substance use (for example, administration by needle injection). These studies illustrate the long-term protective results of effective primary and secondary prevention programs for a range of life decisions. Similar programs emphasizing life skills and other forms of social development have been reported to have equivalent success.[23]

Drug Abuse Resistance Education (DARE)

The Drug Abuse Resistance Education program, commonly known as DARE, is undoubtedly the best-known school-based primary prevention program in the United States and perhaps the world. It was developed in 1983 as a collaborative effort by the Los Angeles Police Department and the Los Angeles United School District to bring uniformed police officers into kindergarten and elementary grade classrooms to teach basic drug information, peer-refusal skills, self-management techniques, and alternatives to drug use.

The DARE program expanded quite rapidly. Today, it has been established in all fifty U.S. states, in all Native American schools administered by the Bureau of Indian Affairs, in U.S. Department of Defense schools worldwide, and in school systems in many foreign countries. There are also teacher-orientation sessions, officer–student interactions at playgrounds and in cafeterias, and parent-education evenings.[24]

Responses to Project DARE from teachers, principals, students, and police officers are typically enthusiastic, and it is clear that the program has struck a responsive chord over the years for a public that has pushed for active prevention programs in the schools. Part of this enthusiasm can be seen as arising from the image of police departments shifting their emphasis from exclusively "supply reduction" to a more proactive social role in "demand reduction."

Yet, despite its success in the area of public relations, the research-based evidence supporting the effectiveness of DARE in achieving genuine reductions in drug use is weak. In general, children who participated in the DARE program have a more negative attitude toward drugs one year later than children who did not, as well as a greater capability to resist peer pressure and a lower estimate of how many of their peers smoked cigarettes. However, there are no significant differences between DARE and non-DARE control groups. There is little evidence for differences in drug use, drug attitudes, or self-esteem when young people are measured ten years after administration of the DARE program.[25]

The DARE program has also been criticized for advocating that children be questioned about possible drug offenders in their families. A DARE lesson called "The Three R's: Recognize, Resist, Report" encourages them to tell friends, teachers, or police if they find drugs at home. Critics of DARE have viewed this and related elements of the program as a mechanism for turning young children into informants.[26]

Why DARE remains popular when its effectiveness and questionable practices have been consistently challenged is an interesting question. Some health professionals in this field theorize that the popularity of DARE results, in part, from the perception among parents and DARE supporters that it *appears* to work, through a process of informally comparing children who go through DARE with unfounded assumptions about children who do not:

> *The adults rightly perceive that most children who go through DARE do not engage in problematic drug use. Unfortunately, these individuals may not realize that the vast majority of children, even*

Quick Concept Check 16.2

Understanding Substance Abuse Prevention Strategies

Check your understanding of substance abuse prevention strategies by deciding whether the following approaches would or would not be effective (in and of themselves) in reducing drug or alcohol use or delaying its onset, based on the available research.

	WOULD BE EFFECTIVE	WOULD NOT BE EFFECTIVE
1. Scare tactics	☐	☐
2. Life skills training	☐	☐
3. Peer-refusal skills training	☐	☐
4. Values clarification	☐	☐
5. Objective information	☐	☐
6. Anxiety reduction and stress management	☐	☐
7. Assertiveness training	☐	☐
8. Training in problem solving and goal setting	☐	☐

Answers: 1. would not   2. would   3. would   4. would not   5. would not   6. would   7. would   8. would *without any intervention, do not engage in problematic drug use . . . That is, adults may believe that drug use among adolescents is much more frequent than it actually is. When the children who go through DARE are compared to this "normative" group of drug-using teens, DARE appears effective.*[27]

In 2001, in response to the criticism leveled against its lack of impact on drug use, the DARE program was modified to become "enhanced DARE." In this new approach, more emphasis has been placed on student interaction and on providing more opportunities for children to participate rather than being lectured by police officers.[28] In effect, DARE administrators have adopted many of the basic components of effective school-based prevention programs such as LST.

Community-Based Prevention Programs

Community-based prevention programs offer several obvious advantages over those restricted to schools. The first is the greater opportunity to involve parents and other family members, religious institutions, and the media as collaborative agents for change. The most important factor here is the comprehensive nature of such programs. They draw on multiple social institutions that have been demonstrated to represent protective factors in an individual's life, such as the family, religious groups, and community organizations. In addition, corporations and businesses can be contributing partners, in both a financial and a nonfinancial sense. Undoubtedly, we are in a better position to tackle the complexities of drug-taking behavior through the use of multiple strategies rather than a single approach.

Components of an Effective Community-Based Program

Typically, many of the prevention components that have been incorporated into the schools are also components of community-based programs, such as the dissemination of information, stress management, and life skills training. Other approaches can be handled better in a community setting. For example, although schools can promote the possibility of alternative student activities that provide positive and constructive means for addressing feelings of boredom, frustration, and powerlessness (activities such as Midnight Basketball and Boys and Girls Clubs), the community is in a better position than the schools to actually provide these activities.

There is also a greater opportunity in the community to elicit the involvement of significant individuals to act as positive role models, referred to as **impactors**, and to enlist the help of the mass media to promote antidrug messages in the press and on television. In addition, community-based programs can be more influential in promoting changes in public policy that foster opportunities for education, employment, and self-development.[29]

Alternative-Behavior Programming

It is easier to say no to drugs when you can say yes to something else. In community-based prevention programs, a major effort is made to provide the activities and outlets that steer people away from the high-risk situations. Because adolescents spend a majority of their time outside school, and it is outside school that the preponderance of drug-taking behavior occurs, community programs have the best chance of providing the necessary interventions. In fact, high-risk adolescents are the least likely even to be attending school on the days that prevention efforts are delivered.[30]

Table 16.1 gives a sampling of alternative behaviors corresponding to a particular individual's interests and needs. One way of thinking about alternative-behavior programming is that a person is trading a negative dependence (on alcohol, tobacco, or other drugs) that causes harm on a physical or psychological level for a positive dependence that causes no harm and taps into pleasures from within.

In a 1986 review of its effectiveness based on well-controlled research studies, alternative-behavior programming was identified as being highly successful for at-risk adolescents such as illicit drug users, juvenile delinquents, and students having problems in school. On the basis of these evaluations, the general view is that alternative-behavior programming can work and deserves to have a place in comprehensive prevention programs.[31]

The Influence of Media

In the words of a major 2005 study analyzing the lifestyles of eight- to eighteen-year-olds, young people today live "media-saturated lives, spending an average of nearly 6½ hours a day with media." Since about one-fourth of the time they are engaged in media multitasking (reading, listening to music, text messaging with friends,

---

impactors: Individuals in the community who function as positive role models to children and adolescents in ATOD prevention programs.

TABLE 16.1

Alternative behaviors to drug use: Needs and motives

LEVEL OF EXPERIENCE	NEEDS AND MOTIVES	ALTERNATIVES
Physical	Physical satisfaction, more energy	Athletics, dance/exercise, hiking, carpentry, or outdoor work
Sensory	Stimulation of sensory experience	Sensory awareness training, amusement park rides
Emotional	Relief from anxiety, mood elevation, emotional relaxation	Individual counseling, group therapy
Interpersonal	Peer acceptance, defiance of authority figures	Confidence training, sensitivity groups, helping others in distress
Social/environmental	Promotion of social change or identification with a subculture	Social service; community action; helping the poor, aged, handicapped; environmental activism
Intellectual	Escape from boredom, curiosity, or inclination to explore one's own awareness	Reading, creative games, memory training, discussion groups
Creative/aesthetic	Increase in one's creativity or enjoyment of images and thoughts	Nongraded instruction in visual arts, music, drama, crafts, cooking, gardening, writing, singing
Philosophical	Discovery of the meaning of life, organization of a belief system	Discussions, study of ethics or other philosophical literature
Spiritual/mystical	Transcendence of organized religion, spiritual insight or enlightenment	Study of world religions, meditation, yoga
Miscellaneous	Adventure, risk taking, "kicks"	Outward Bound survival training, meaningful employment

Source: Adapted from Cohen, Allan Y. (1972). The journey beyond trips: Alternatives to drugs. In David E. Smith and George R. Gay (Eds.), *It's so good, don't even try it once: Heroin in perspective.* Englewood Cliffs, NJ: Prentice Hall, pp. 191–192.

for example), they are actually crowding about 8 hours of media into each day—the equivalent of a full-time job. These individuals (who have been dubbed "Generation M" to reflect the dominance of media in their lives) are the first generation to have grown up with easy access to computers and particularly the Internet.[32]

Because of the unprecedented media access available at home (frequently in the privacy of their bedrooms), it is important to evaluate the impact of media messages on drug-taking behavior in their lives and the potential for media exposure to promote primary prevention. It has been estimated that young people are exposed to more than eighty explicit references to substance use per day in the course of listening to popular music. A statistical relationship has been identified between the amount of exposure among young people ten to fourteen years old to alcohol drinking in popular movies and early-onset teen drinking, even after controlling for variables such as socioeconomic status, personality characteristics, school performance, and gender. In other words, exposure to alcohol use in movies can be viewed as an independent risk factor for drinking behavior in this population.[33]

Traditionally, anti-drug messages have been largely confined to public-service announcements, brief commercials, and limited program series. Even so, the potential impact can be substantial. A prominent example is a series of memorable and persuasive anti-drug advertisements on TV, on the radio, in print, and in other media sources, sponsored by the Partnership for a Drug-Free America (PDFA), a nonprofit coalition of professionals in the communications industry whose mission is to reduce demand for drugs in America. In the early 1990s, a number of PDFA spots targeted inner-city youths living in high-risk drug-use environments, and a 1994 study indicated that these messages had a significant effect in promoting increasingly anti-drug attitudes, particularly among African American children attending schools in areas where many families had incomes below the poverty line.[34]

Unfortunately, Internet media have undermined these efforts. A rapidly growing number of Internet web

sites are devoted to information about marijuana cultivation, drug paraphernalia, and illicit drug use in general. These pro-drug outlets have proliferated since the
advent of online services. Making matters worse, the
percentage of adolescents reporting that they remember
seeing or hearing substance abuse prevention messages
has declined.[35]

An Example of an Effective Community-Based Prevention Program

An intensive and coordinated program of preventive services and community-based law enforcement has been
designed by the National Center on Addiction and Substance Abuse at Columbia University in New York,
called CASASTART. (The first part of the acronym
refers to the center that designed it, and the latter part
stands for "Striving Together to Achieve Rewarding
Tomorrows.") The target population for the program is
defined as children between eight and thirteen years of
age who have at least four risk factors for substance
abuse problems. These risk factors may involve school
(such as poor academic performance, in-school behavior problems, or truancy), family (such as poverty, violence at home, or a family member involved with gangs,
drug use or sales, or a criminal conviction within five
years), or the individual child (such as a history of
known or suspected drug use or sales, past arrest, gang
membership, or being a victim of child maltreatment).

In the CASASTART program, a case manager serving fifteen children and their families coordinates a variety of services, including social support, family and
educational services, after-school and summer activities,
mentoring, incentives, and juvenile justice intervention.
The objective is to build resilience in the child,
strengthen families, and make neighborhoods safer for
children and their families. Relative to controls,
CASASTART children have been found to be 60 percent less likely to sell drugs, 20 percent less likely to
have used drugs in the past thirty days, 20 percent less
likely to commit a violent act, and more likely to be
promoted to the next grade in school.[36]

Family Systems in Primary and Secondary Prevention

It can be argued that family influences form the corner-
stone of any successful substance abuse prevention program; we will see the significant impact of the family on

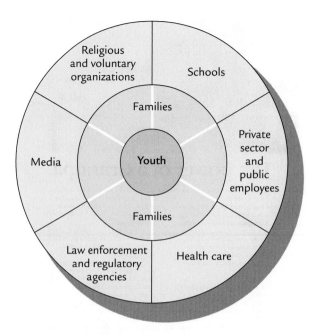

FIGURE 16.2

A schematic of various factors that impact upon young
people in substance abuse prevention.

Source: Adapted from Fields, Richard (1998). *Drugs in per-
spective* (3rd ed.). Dubuque, IA: WCB McGraw-Hill, p. 309.
Reprinted with permission of the McGraw-Hill Companies.
Copyright 1998.

substance abuse treatment, later in the chapter. In effect,
the family is the first line of defense against substance
abuse (Figure 16.2). Reaching the parents or guardians
of youths at greatest risk, however, is a difficult task. Too
often, substance abuse prevention programs are attended
by those parents or guardians who do not really need the
information; those who need the information the most—
parents who are in denial, too embarrassed, or out of control themselves—are notably absent. Other parents or
guardians may need and genuinely want to participate,
but they may have difficulty attending because of lack of
child care at home, lack of transportation, scheduling
conflicts with their employment, or language differences.
Several of the factors that discourage their attendance are
the same factors that increase the risk of substance abuse
among their children.[37]

Special Role Models in Substance Abuse Prevention

Although obstacles exist, comprehensive substance abuse
prevention programs strive to incorporate parents
or guardians, as well as other family members such as

The power of a Grandpa.

Children have a very special relationship with Grandma and Grandpa. That's why grandparents can be such powerful allies in helping keep a kid off drugs.

Grandparents are cool. Relaxed. They're not on the firing line every day. Some days a kid hates his folks. He never hates his grandparents. Grandparents ask direct, point-blank, embarrassing questions you're too nervous to ask:

"Who's the girl?"

"How come you're doing poorly in history?"

"Why are your eyes always red?"

"Did you go to the doctor? What did he say?"

The same kid who cons his parents is ashamed to lie to Grandpa. Without betraying their trust, a loving, understanding grandparent can discuss the danger of drugs openly with the child he adores. And should.

• The average age of first-time drug use among teens is 13. Some kids start at 9.

• 1 out of 4 American kids between 9 and 12 is offered illegal drugs. 22% of these kids receive the offer from a friend. And 10% named a family member as their source.

• Illegal drugs are linked to increased violence in many communities, to AIDS, to birth defects, drug-related crime, and homelessness.

As a grandparent, you hold a special place in the hearts and minds of your grandchildren. Share your knowledge, your love, your faith in them. Use your power as an influencer to steer your grandchildren away from drugs.

If you don't have the words, we do. We'll send you information on how to talk to your grandkids about drugs. Just ask for your free copy of *Keeping Youth Drug-Free*. Call 1-800-788-2800 or visit our websites, www.projectknow.com or www.drugfreeamerica.org.

Grandma, Grandpa. Talk to your grandkids. You don't realize the power you have to save them.

Office of National Drug Control Policy
Partnership for a Drug-Free America

Communication between grandparents and grandchildren can be an important tool in substance abuse prevention.

grandparents, into the overall effort. The reason lies in the variety of special roles they play in influencing children:

- As role models, parents or guardians may drink alcoholic beverages, smoke, or drink excessive amounts of caffeinated coffee, not thinking of these habits as drug-taking behaviors. They can learn to avoid sending their children signals about abstinence that are inconsistent at best, hypocritical at worst.

- As educators or resources for information, they can help by conveying verbal messages about health risks that are accurate and sincere.

- As family policymakers and rule setters, they can convey a clear understanding of the consequences of drug-taking behaviors. If a parent or guardian cannot or will not back up family rules with logical and consistent consequences, the risk increases that rules will be broken.

- As stimulators of enjoyable family activities, parents or guardians can provide alternative-behavior programming necessary to steer youths away from high-risk situations.

- As consultants against peer pressure, parents or guardians can help reinforce the peer-refusal skills of

their children. Children and adolescents frequently report that a strongly negative reaction at home was the single most important reason for their refusing alcohol, tobacco, and other drugs from their peers.

Parental Communication in Substance Abuse Prevention

In recognition of the importance of parental communication in efforts to reduce substance abuse, the program "Parents: The Antidrug" has been a dominant feature in

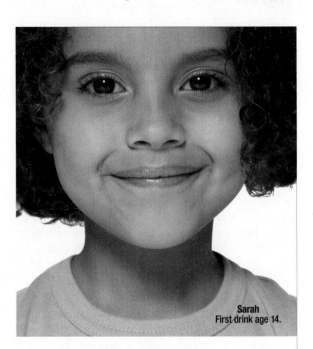

Sarah
First drink age 14.

START TALKING
BEFORE THEY
START DRINKING

www.stopalcoholabuse.gov

Kids who drink before age 15
are 5 times more likely to have
alcohol problems when they're adults.

SAMHSA
Substance Abuse & Mental Health
Services Administration

Ad Council

An outdoor public-service announcement urges parents to begin a dialogue early about the short-term and long-term dangers of underage drinking. Parents generally underestimate the extent of alcohol use in their children and find it hard to decide how or when to begin this important conversation.

A Test Kit for Drugs in the Home: Whom Can You Trust?

In 1995, a drug detection company introduced a commercial kit capable of testing for illicit drugs in the home. Marketed for parents who wish to check for possible drug abuse among their children, the kit consists of a 3-inch premoistened pad that can be wiped across desk tops, telephones, books, clothing, or other items. The pad is mailed to the company, where an analysis for the presence of cocaine, crack cocaine, heroin, methamphetamine, LSD, marijuana, and PCP is performed. The testing destroys the sample, so it cannot be used later in any court proceedings. The results of the analysis are then mailed to the parents.

The fact that the test kit is designed to be used by parents with or without their children's knowledge has raised a number of controversial issues. On the one hand, the kit is promoted as a potent new weapon in the battle against the increased levels of drug abuse among young people. From this point of view, parents are now able to get early help for their children before drug-abuse problems become too great. On the other hand, the kit can be viewed as a new weapon in the battle of the generations. Detractors argue that it sets up an atmosphere of distrust between parents and their children.

What do you think? If you were a parent, would you consider this new testing kit as a step forward or a step backward in the effort to prevent drug abuse in your family?

Sources: Kit to test for drugs at home (1995, March 29). *Newsday*, p. A8. Winslow, Olivia, and Lam, Chau (1995, March 30). Test fuels drugs debate. *Newsday*, pp. A6, A51.

---

public-service announcements in recent years.[38] The need for better lines of communication between parents and teenagers is illustrated in a PDFA survey. When asked whether they talked to their teenagers about drugs at least once, 98 percent of parents reported that they had done so, but only 65 percent of teenagers recalled such a conversation. Barely 27 percent of teenagers reported learning at lot at home about the risks of drug use, even though virtually all of their parents said they had discussed the topic. Justifiably, anti-drug media campaigns have focused on parent–child communication skills, specifically on the difficulty many parents have in talking to their children about sensitive subjects such as drugs and the role of drug-taking behavior in their children's social lives.[39] Drugs . . . in Focus examines an option that may be necessary, however, when family communication breaks down.

The Triple Threat: Stress, Boredom, and Spending Money

Substance abuse prevention in young people can sometimes be simpler and more straightforward than we realize. A recent survey of teenagers aged twelve to seventeen measured the effects of three circumstances on the likelihood that a teenager would engage in some form of substance abuse: (1) the degree of stress they feel they are under, (2) the frequency with which they are bored, and (3) the amount of money they have to spend in a typical week. High-stress teens (one-fourth of teens interviewed) were twice as likely as low-stress teens (a little more than one-fourth of teens interviewed) to smoke, drink, get drunk, and use illicit drugs. Teens reporting that they were frequently bored were 50 percent more likely than not-often-bored teens to engage in these behaviors. Teens with $25 or more a week in spending money were nearly twice as likely as teens with less spending money to smoke, drink, and use illicit drugs, and they were more than twice as likely to get drunk. Combining two or three of these risk factors (high stress, frequent boredom, and too much spending money) made the risk of smoking, drinking, and illicit drug use three times higher than when none of these characteristics was present.[40]

Yes, You: Substance Abuse Prevention and the College Student

Effective substance abuse programs among college students present an unusual challenge, in that we are hardly speaking of a homogeneous population. U.S. college students represent all racial, ethnic, and socioeconomic groups and are likely to come from all parts of the world. They include undergraduate and graduate students, full-time and part-time students, residential students and commuters, students of traditional college age and students who are considerably older. Each of these groups has a different perspective on drug-taking behavior, different opportunities for drug-taking behavior, and different life experiences.

In particular, there are marked differences in the objectives of a prevention program for those under twenty-one years of age and for those who are older. In the former group, the goal may be "no use of" (or abstinence from) alcohol, tobacco, and other drugs, whereas in the latter group the goal may be the low-risk (that is, responsible) consumption of alcohol and no use of tobacco and other drugs. The term "low-risk consumption" refers to a level of use restricted by considerations of physical health, family background, pregnancy risk, the law, safety, and other personal concerns.

With respect to alcohol, secondary prevention guidelines might stipulate that pregnant women, recovering alcoholics those with a family history of alcoholism, people driving cars or heavy machinery, people on medications, and those under the age of twenty-one should not drink alcohol at all. But even though the distinction between under-twenty-one and over-twenty-one preventive goals is applicable in many community-oriented programs, it is an especially difficult challenge for prevention efforts on a college campus where the target population contains both subgroups so closely intermingled.[41]

Changing the Culture of Alcohol and Other Drug Use in College

A major challenge with regard to prevention programs at colleges and universities comes from the widely regarded expectation that heavy alcohol drinking, as well as some illicit drug use, during the college years represents something of a rite of passage. College alumni (and potential benefactors) frequently oppose the implementation of drug and alcohol crackdowns, arguing that "we did it when we were in school."[42] Moreover, the 2009 University of Michigan survey indicated that by the end of high school about 72 percent of all students have consumed alcoholic beverages, 57 percent have been drunk at least once, and

42 percent have smoked marijuana. Therefore, we cannot say that use of these drugs is a new experience for many college students.[43] Given this prior exposure, it is not surprising that further experimentation and more extensive patterns of drug-taking behavior will occur. There is a compelling argument for secondary and tertiary prevention programs to be in place at this point.

The emphasis on most campuses is on the prevention and control of alcohol problems (Drugs . . . in Focus). However, it is less common for college administrators to focus on the problems associated with drugs other than alcohol. Frequently, the only policy in place involves punitive action if a student-athlete tests positive for an illicit drug. And although no-smoking campuses are the norm, few if any programs are in place to help reduce the level of tobacco use among college students.

Substance Abuse Prevention on College Campuses

On the positive side, college campuses have the potential to be ideal environments for comprehensive substance abuse prevention programs because they combine features of both school and community settings. Here are some suggested strategies for prevention on the college campus:

- Develop a multifaceted prevention program of assessment, education, policy, and enforcement. Involve students, faculty, and administrators in determining the degree of availability and demand for alcohol and other drugs on campus and in the surrounding community and initiate public information and education efforts.

- Incorporate alcohol and other drug education into the curriculum. Faculty members can use drug-related situations as teachable moments, include drug topics in their course syllabi, and develop courses or course projects on issues relating to alcohol and other drugs.

- Ensure that hypocrisy is not the rule of the day. Substance abuse prevention is not a goal for college students only but is a larger issue that affects all members of the academic community, including faculty and administration.

- Encourage environments that reduce the pressures to engage in drug-taking behavior. Foster more places

Drugs... in Focus

Alcohol 101 on College Campuses

A familiar experience among many students entering college for the first time is referred to by public health officials as the "college effect"—defined as an increase in drinking and negative behaviors associated with it (Chapter 13). One increasingly popular approach intended to minimize this phenomenon is a three-hour web-based online course called AlcoholEdu, developed by Outside the Classroom, Inc. More than 500 colleges and universities nationwide are currently participating in this program.

AlcoholEdu is oriented toward responsible drinking behavior rather than abstinence. Topics include an understanding of blood alcohol concentrations, activities that increase the likelihood of blacking out, discredited remedies for hangovers, as well as an appreciation of the alcohol beverage industry's role in fostering the image of alcohol consumption as a means for advancing social and interpersonal relationships. Participants are given an exam that tests their knowledge of the information provided in the course.

Colleges and universities have varying policies regarding students taking AlcoholEdu. Some require students to complete and pass the course with a minimum score on the exam prior to the first day of classes or prior to registering for the next semester. Others convey an expectation that the AlcoholEdu should be completed and warn that severe consequences will be imposed for those students who fail to finish the course and commit an alcohol violation in the future. There are early indications that student participation in AlcoholEdu results in significantly fewer negative consequences of drinking, such as missing class, attending class with a hangover, blacking out, and abusive behavior. Intensive studies of effectiveness, both short-term and long-term, however, need to be carried out.

In the meantime, additional programs addressing a wider range of alcohol problems on campuses have been developed. AlcoholEdu for Sanctions is an intervention program suited for students who have violated academic policies on alcohol, aimed at reducing recidivism rates. Alcohol Innerview is a brief motivational intervention tool for students who have experienced alcohol problems or are in alcohol-abuse counseling. AlcoholEdu for Parents is designed to support parents with college-age children in fostering conversations that can help shape healthy decisions about alcohol use at college.

Recent developments in online prevention programs by Outside the Classroom, Inc. include MentalHealthEdu, raising campus community awareness of college student mental-health issues, and SexualAssaultEdu, focusing on relationships and decision making to reduce the incidence of sexual assaults on campus.

Sources: Fact sheet on alcohol issues, University of Colorado at Boulder (2004, August 11). Boulder, CO: Office of News Services, University of Colorado. Kesmodel, David (2005, November 1). Schools use web to teach about booze. *Wall Street Journal Online.* Outside the Classroom (2008), www.outsidetheclassroom.com.

---

where social and recreational activities can take place spontaneously and at hours when the most enticing alternative may be the consumption of alcohol and other drugs. A recent promising sign is the growing popularity of drug-free dormitories on many college campuses, where student residents specifically choose to refrain from using alcohol, tobacco, and other drugs.[44]

The seriousness of the drug-taking behavior on college campuses could not be demonstrated more clearly than in the context of alcohol drinking among members of college fraternities. A statement in a 1994 decision of the Arizona Supreme Court expressed this concern in no uncertain terms:

> We are hardpressed to find a setting where the risk of an alcohol-related injury is more likely than from under-age drinking at a university fraternity party the first week of the new college year.[45]

Since 2000, when one in five fraternity chapters in the United States began to phase in a policy forbidding alcohol of any kind anywhere in the fraternity house, even in rooms of members who were of legal drinking age, there has been a steady upward trend in the number of alcohol-free fraternity (and sorority) houses around the country.[46]

This Bed's For You.

Spring break in the ER, instead of on the beach?

There's no view of the beach and the food is terrible. You don't want your spring break to end in an emergency room.

Yet every year, that's where more and more students are winding up.

Alcohol poisoning. Car wrecks. Falls from balconies. Fistfights. Rape.

Why? Statistics show that half of male students – and 40 percent of females – drink

on spring break until they vomit or pass out. The average male student consumes 18 drinks daily. The average female downs 10.

The alcohol and tour industries are urging you on with free beer, all-you-can-drink parties, booze cruises and endless happy hours.

Don't fall for it. Enjoy a fun, safe spring break. And remember. Nobody looks good in a hospital robe.

This message is sponsored by **A Matter of Degree**
The National Effort to Reduce High-Risk Drinking Among College Students

AMOD is a project of the American Medical Association and campus-community partnerships across America • www.alcoholpolicysolutions.net

This ad, sponsored by the American Medical Association (AMA), appeared in college newspapers in 2004 in a campaign to discourage binge drinking, just prior to Spring Break. In 2007, the AMA called on the National Collegiate Athletic Association (NCAA) to eliminate alcohol advertising during radio and television broadcasts of college sports. The NCAA currently limits alcohol-related commercials to one minute per broadcast and encourages "responsibility themes and messages."

---

employee assistance programs (EAPs): Corporate-based services designed to identify and counsel employees with personal problems that are connected to substance abuse or dependence and to provide referrals to community agencies where these individuals can get further help.

member assistance programs (MAPs): Corporate-based services similar to employee assistance programs (EAPs) that are sponsored and supervised by labor unions.

Prevention and Treatment in the Workplace

According to statistics from the 2009 National Survey on Drug Use and Health (see Chapter 2), more than 66 percent of current illicit drug users were employed either full-time or part-time, as were 74 percent of adult binge drinkers and persons reporting heavy alcohol use. Workers have reported being put in danger, having been injured, having to work harder or re-do work, or having to cover for a co-worker as a result of a fellow employee's drinking. Small businesses are particularly disadvantaged by worker substance abuse.

The 1988 Drug-free Workplace Act requires that all companies and businesses receiving any U.S. federal contracts or grants provide a drug-free workplace. Specifically, all U.S. federal agencies have been mandated to establish **employee assistance programs (EAPs)** in order to identify and counsel workers with personal problems associated with substance abuse or dependence and to provide referrals to community agencies where these individuals can get further help. Nongovernmental organizations have since been encouraged (but not required) by the act to establish EAP services as well. As a result, though not technically required to do so, steadily increasing numbers of American businesses have set up EAPs and are becoming committed to treatment as well as prevention. Traditionally, the emphasis in EAPs (as well as in union-supported **member assistance programs, or MAPs**) has been on problems resulting from alcohol abuse, understandable given that this category represents such a large proportion of substance abuse in general (Chapter 14). In recent years, EAPs and MAPs have expanded their services to focus on psychological problems that do not necessarily concern substance abuse.

Even a modest amount of treatment that results from an EAP or MAP intervention has proven to be beneficial to both the employee and the employer. In one study, heavy drinkers who received brief intervention over a two-month period had significantly fewer accidents, hospital visits, and other events related to problem drinking during the following year. The cost of each brief intervention was $166 per employee, and the medical savings to the employee amounted to $523.[47]

Specifically, organizations must initiate a comprehensive and continuing program of drug education and awareness. Employees must also be notified that the distribution, possession, or unauthorized use of controlled substances is prohibited in that workplace and that actions will be taken against any employee violating these rules. Supervisors are advised to be especially alert to changes in a worker that might signal early or progressive stages in the abuse of alcohol and/or other drugs. These signals include chronic absenteeism, a sudden change in physical appearance or behavior, spasmodic work pace, unexpectedly lower quantity or quality of work, partial or unexplained absences, a pattern of excuse-making or lying, the avoidance of supervisors or coworkers, and on-the-job accidents or lost time from such accidents.

In effect, achieving a drug-free workplace is made possible by a combination of secondary prevention and tertiary prevention interventions.

The Economic Costs of Substance Abuse in the Workplace

High-profile instances of on-the-job accidents involving the effects of either illicit drugs or alcohol are often given as examples of the scope of substance abuse in the workplace and the need for workplace drug testing. In 1991, for example, a New York subway operator crashed his train near a station in lower Manhattan, resulting in five deaths and 215 injuries. The operator admitted that he had been drinking prior to the crash, and his BAC level was measured at 0.21 percent, more than twice the legal limit of 0.10 percent in New York at that time. In 1987, a Conrail train brakeman and an engineer were found to be responsible for a collision that resulted in sixteen deaths and 170 injuries. Drug testing revealed traces of marijuana in their systems.

There are two reasons why such examples do not accurately reflect the impact of alcohol and other drug abuse in the workplace. First, the likelihood of an adverse effect is not adequately reflected in news reports, any more than the impact of drug toxicity on our society can be assessed by reading the news stories of public figures and celebrities who have died of drug overdoses (Chapter 2). Second, in many cases, we are limited in determining the extent to which we can connect drug use with the tragic consequences of an accident because some drugs leave metabolites in the system long after they have stopped producing behavioral effects. As in the case of the Conrail incident, the continued presence of marijuana metabolites for weeks after marijuana use (see Chapter 12) can make the positive test results irrelevant.

We must turn instead to estimates gathered from other sources of information. Unfortunately, these estimates are "soft," having large margins of error. Even so, they leave little doubt that the abuse of alcohol and other drugs has a major impact on workplace productivity.

On the basis of its own studies, CSAP estimates that, relative to nonabusers, abusers of alcohol and other drugs are

- 5 times more likely to file a workers' compensation claim
- 3.6 times more likely to be involved in an accident on the job
- 5 times more likely to be personally injured on the job
- 3 times more likely to be late for work
- 2.2 times more likely to request early dismissal from work or time off
- 16 times more likely to take sick leave

Overall, the estimated costs from productivity lost as a result of such behavior amount to $60–$100 billion each year.[48]

Drug Testing in the Workplace

By executive order of President Reagan in 1986, preemployment drug screening was mandated for all federal

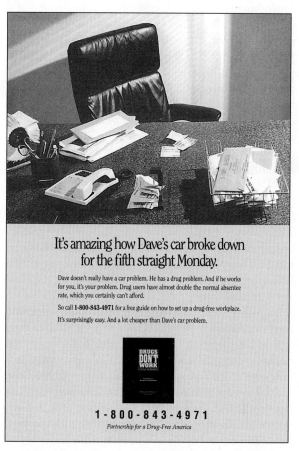

It's amazing how Dave's car broke down for the fifth straight Monday.

Dave doesn't really have a car problem. He has a drug problem. And if he works for you, it's your problem. Drug users have almost double the normal absentee rate, which you certainly can't afford.

So call 1-800-843-4971 for a free guide on how to set up a drug-free workplace. It's surprisingly easy. And a lot cheaper than Dave's car problem.

DRUGS DON'T WORK IN YOUR WORKPLACE

1 - 8 0 0 - 8 4 3 - 4 9 7 1

Partnership for a Drug-Free America

Drug and alcohol problems are major sources of worker absenteeism and decreased workplace productivity.

employees as well as periodic, random schedules of drug testing afterward. (It is not known whether the president at the time or subsequent presidents since 1986 have been included in this requirement.) Federal statutes have not required drug testing for employees other than those working for the federal government. In 1996, 81 percent of employers reported having a drug-testing program in place. By 2004, however, an American Management Association survey reported that the percentage had gone down considerably. Approximately 62 percent of all companies tested for illicit drugs; 55 percent conducted testing as part of the job application process, and 44 percent conducted testing among current employees on a periodic basis. Surveys have not been conducted more recently but the chances are that there has been a further decline.[49]

While it is easy to understand the rationale for drug testing in the workplace in the overall scheme of drug prevention, the procedure has raised a number of important issues regarding individual rights. Is the taking of a urine sample a violation of a person's freedom from "unreasonable search and seizure" as guaranteed by the Fourth Amendment to the U.S. Constitution? It turns out that if the government requires it, the decision rests on the question of whether there is reasonable or unreasonable cause for the drug testing to occur. In cases in which a threat to public safety is involved, the cause has been ruled as reasonable. However, if a private business requires it, the legal rights of employees are somewhat murky. An employee typically accepts his or her job offer with the assumption and agreement that periodic monitoring of drug use will take place, but whether this understanding is a form of implied coercion is an open question.

If you lose your job as a result of testing positive in a drug test, has there been a violation of your right to "due process" as guaranteed by the Fifth Amendment? The courts have ruled that this right would be violated only if the method of drug screening were unreliable, if the analysis and reporting were carried out in an unreliable manner, or if it could not be shown that the presence of any one of the screened substances had a relationship to job impairment. In general, screening methods are not perfectly reliable, the handling of drug tests is not perfectly controlled, and the relationship between drug use and a decline in job performance is not perfectly clear, but drug tests have nonetheless been judged to have met reasonable standards and the practice is allowed. The bottom line is that drug testing, despite its obvious infringements on individual privacy, has become a fact of life in corporate America.[50]

Nonetheless, despite the increasing acceptance of drug testing as a tool for drug-abuse prevention in the workplace, there will always be questions about the impact on workers themselves. For example, the possibility of false positives (when an individual tests positive but has not been using a particular drug) or false negatives (when an individual who, on the basis of prior drug use, should test positive for a particular drug, but does not do so) during drug testing can present unfortunate consequences. Consider this possible preemployment screening scenario:

> Suppose that the EMIT test were 100 percent effective in spotting drug users (it is not) and that it has a false-positive rate of 3 percent (which is not unreasonable). In a group of 100 prospective employees, one person has recently taken an illegal drug. Since the test is 100 percent effective, that person will be caught, but three other people (the 3 percent false-positive rate) will also. Therefore, 75 percent of those who fail the test are innocent parties.[51]

Another problem is that companies are not required to follow up a positive EMIT test result with another more sensitive method, such as one using the GC/MS procedure (Chapter 12). Some companies allow for retesting in general, but most do not.

The Impact of Drug-Free Workplace Policies

Given the adverse effects of drug abuse on productivity, we should expect to see substantial economic and personal benefits when drug-free workplace policies are in place. In one well-documented case, a program developed by the Southern Pacific Railroad Company in the 1980s, extensive drug testing was required for all employees who had been involved in a company accident or rule violation. As a result, the annual number of accidents decreased from 911 to 168 in three years and the financial losses from such accidents decreased from $6.4 million to $1.2 million. During the first few months of the new testing program, it was found that 22–24 percent of employees who had experienced some human-factor-related accident tested positive for alcohol or other drugs, a figure that fell to 3 percent three years later.[52]

It makes sense that substance abuse prevention programs would have the greatest impact in companies within the transportation industry, owing to the close relationship between drug-induced impairments in performance and the incidence of industrial accidents. Beyond this application, however, it is widely recognized that a similar impact, if not one as dramatic in magnitude, can be demonstrated in any business setting. The reasons relate to the basic goals of prevention, as discussed earlier: deterrence and rehabilitation. The practice of testing for illicit drug use in the workplace functions as an effective deterrent among workers because the likelihood is strong that illicit drug use will be detected. Substance abuse treatment programs in the workplace can function as an effective rehabilitative tool because those workers who might otherwise not receive help with drug-abuse problems will be referred to appropriate agencies for treatment services.[53]

Multicultural Issues in Prevention and Treatment

In the case of substance abuse prevention messages and administration of substance abuse treatment programs, it is important to remember that information intended to reach individuals of a specific culture passes through a series of **sociocultural filters**. Understanding this filtering process is essential to providing effective substance abuse prevention and treatment programs.

Latino Communities

A good example of the need to recognize sociocultural filters is the set of special concerns associated with communicating drug-related information to Latinos, a diverse group representing more than 13 percent of the U.S. population and expected to represent more than 25 percent by 2050. The following insights concerning elements of the Latino community can enhance the chances of success in Latino-targeted prevention and treatment initiatives.

- Because of the importance Latinos confer on the family and religious institutions, prevention and treatment efforts should be targeted to include the entire family and, if possible, its religious leaders. Prevention and treatment efforts will be most effective when counselors reinforce family units and value them as a whole.

- Prevention programs are needed to help Latino fathers recognize how important their role or example is to their sons' and daughters' self-image regarding alcohol and other drugs. Because being a good father is part of *machismo*, it is important that the men become full partners in parenting. Mothers should be encouraged to learn strategies for including their husbands in family interactions at home.

- Because a Latina woman with alcohol or other drug problems is strongly associated with a violation of womanly ideals of purity, discipline, and self-sacrifice, educational efforts should concentrate on reducing the shame associated with her reaching out for help.

One particular web site that addresses the needs of the Latino community (www.nlcatp.org) is sponsored by the National Latino Council on Alcohol and Tobacco Prevention (NLCATP).[54]

African American Communities

Another set of special concerns exists with regard to communicating drug-related information in African American communities. Some basic generalizations have proven helpful in optimizing the design of prevention and treatment programs.

- African American youths tend to use drugs other than alcohol after they form social attitudes and adopt behaviors associated with delinquency. The most common examples of delinquency include drug dealing, shoplifting, and petty theft. With regard to the designing of media campaigns, it is the deglamorization of the drug dealer that appears to be most helpful in primary prevention efforts among African American youths.

- Drug use and social problems are likely to be interrelated in primarily African American neighborhoods. The effects of substance abuse are intensified when other factors exist, such as high unemployment, poverty, poor health care, and poor nutrition.

- Several research studies have shown that most African American youths, even those in low-income neighborhoods, do manage to escape from the pressures to use alcohol and other drugs. The protective factors of staying in school, solid family bonds, strong religious beliefs, high self-esteem, adequate coping strategies, social skills, and steady employment all build on one another to provide resilience on the part of high-risk children and adolescents. As noted before, prevention programs developed with protective factors in mind have the greatest chance for success.[55]

Substance Abuse Treatment: The Journey to Recovery

A person's early days in recovery might be compared to a climber's first step up a great mountain. There's a lot of work ahead. As time passes, healing occurs

sociocultural filters: A set of considerations specific to a particular culture or community that can influence the reception and acceptance of public information.

not only for the person in recovery but also for relatives, coworkers, business associates, and the community at large. At its core, the philosophy of recovery embraces and encourages an individual's capacity for change and personal transformation. But that change does not happen overnight. Challenges can and often do crop up every step of the way.[56]

Individuals who seek help in a treatment program have typically been "jolted" by some external force in their lives. They may have no other option except imprisonment for drug offenses; they may be at risk of losing their job because their supervisor has identified an unproductive pattern of behavior; a spouse may have threatened to leave if something is not done; a friend may have died from a drug overdose or a drug-related accident. Any of these crises or others similar to them can force the question and the decision to seek treatment.

The prospect of entering a treatment program is probably the most frightening experience the abuser has ever had in his or her life. Treatment counselors frequently hear the questions "Couldn't I just cut down?" and "Couldn't I just give up drugs temporarily?" and "How will I be able to take the pain of withdrawal?" and "How will I be able to stand the humiliation?" Far from stalling tactics, these questions represent real fears and significant obstacles to taking the crucial first steps to recovery.[57]

Substance Abuse Treatment through Stages of Change

Rehabilitation from substance abuse and dependence has three major goals. First, the long decline in physical and psychological functioning that has accumulated over the years must be reversed. Drugs take a heavy toll on the user's medical condition and his or her personal relationships. Second, the use of all psychoactive substances must stop, not simply the one or two causing the immediate problem, and not merely for a limited period of time. Thus, the motivation to stop using alcohol and other drugs and to remain abstinent on a permanent basis must be strong, and it must stay strong.

precontemplation stage: A stage of change in which the individual may wish to change but either lacks the serious intention to undergo change in the foreseeable future or is unaware of how significant his or her problem has become.

contemplation stage: A stage of change in which the individual is aware that a problem exists and is thinking about overcoming it but has not yet made a commitment to take action.

Third, a life-style free of alcohol and other drugs must be rebuilt, from scratch if necessary. This frequently means giving up the old friends and the old places where drugs were part of an abuser's life, and finding new friends and places that reinforce a drug-free existence. A determination to stay clean and sober requires avoiding high-risk situations, defined as those that increase the possibility of relapse.

Unfortunately, it is hard to ascertain the success rates of substance abuse and dependence treatment options. Relatively few treatment programs allow outside evaluators to determine whether or not treatment has conferred a genuine benefit. The need for evidence-based treatment strategies is no less urgent than the need for evidence-based prevention strategies and the judgment of effectiveness must be made in the same way. A major public official in the field of substance abuse treatment has expressed the lack of proper evaluation of treatment outcomes: "You're discharged [after 60 visits or 60 days] and everyone's crying and hugging and feeling proud—and you're supposed to be cured."[58]

However uncertain the outcome of substance abuse treatment, there is little disagreement about the process an individual must follow to reach a level of recovery: There are five distinct "stages of change" through which the recovering individual must pass.[59] These stages are (1) precontemplation, (2) contemplation, (3) preparation, (4) action, and (5) maintenance. The following is a description of each stage in detail.

- *Precontemplation.* Individuals who are in the **precontemplation stage** may *wish* to change but lack the serious intention to undergo change in the foreseeable future or may be unaware of how significant their problems have become. They may be entering treatment at this time only because they perceive that a crisis is at hand. They may even demonstrate a change in behavior while the pressure is on, but once the pressure is off, they revert to their former ways. It is often difficult for a counselor to deal with a drug abuser during the precontemplation stage because the abuser still feels committed to positive aspects of drug use. A principal goal at this point is to induce inconsistencies in the abuser's perception of drugs in general.

- *Contemplation.* In the **contemplation stage**, individuals are aware that a problem exists and are thinking about overcoming it but have not yet made a commitment to take action. At this point, drug abusers may struggle with the prospect of the tremendous amount of effort and energy needed to overcome the problem. Counselors can help them by highlighting the negative aspects of drug use, making reasonable assurances about the recovery process, and building the self-confidence necessary to change.

■ *Preparation*. Individuals in the **preparation stage** are those who are seriously considering taking action in the next thirty days and have unsuccessfully taken action over the past twelve months. Alcohol abusers or tobacco smokers may at this point set a "quit date," and a heroin abuser may make a firm date to enter a therapeutic community within the next month. Because drug abusers are fully capable of stating a clear commitment to change at the preparation stage, counselors can begin to discuss the specific steps in the recovery process, strategies for avoiding problems or postponements, and ways to involve friends and family members.

■ *Action*. The **action stage** is the point at which individuals actually modify their behavior, their experiences, and their environment in an effort to overcome their problem. Drug use has now stopped. This is the most fragile stage; abusers are at a high risk of giving in to drug cravings and experiencing mixed feelings about the psychological costs of staying clean. If they successfully resist these urges to return to drug use, the counselor should strongly reinforce their restraint. If they slip back to drug use temporarily and then return to abstinence, the counselor should praise their efforts to turn their life around. An important message to be conveyed at this stage is that a fundamental change in life-style and a strong support system of friends and family will reduce the chances of relapse.

■ *Maintenance*. Individuals in the **maintenance stage** have been drug-free for a minimum of six months. They have developed new skills and strategies to avoid backsliding and are consolidating a life-style free of drugs. Here, the counselor must simultaneously acknowledge the success that has been achieved and emphasize that the struggle will never be totally over. The maintenance stage is ultimately open-ended, in that it continues for the rest of the ex-user's life. Therefore, it may be necessary to have booster sessions from time to time so that the maintenance stage is itself maintained.

Rather than thinking of these stages as a linear progression, it is more accurate to think of them as points along a spiral (Figure 16.3); a person will probably recycle through the stages many times before he or she is totally rehabilitated. Unfortunately, relapse is the rule rather than the exception in the process of recovery.

preparation stage: A stage of change in which the individual seriously considers taking action to overcome a problem in the next thirty days and has unsuccessfully taken action over the past twelve months.

action stage: A stage of change in which the individual actually modifies his or her behavior and environment to overcome a problem.

maintenance stage: A stage of change in which the individual has become drug-free for a minimum of six months and has developed new skills and strategies that reduce the probability of relapse.

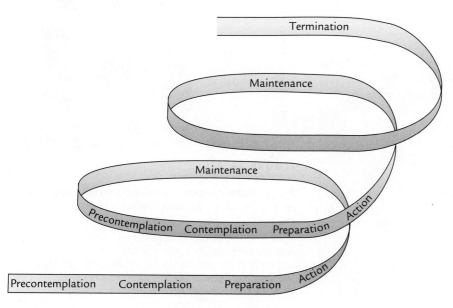

FIGURE 16.3

A spiral model of the stages of change in the recovery from drug abuse and dependence.

Source: Prochaska, James O., DiClemente, Carlo C., and Norcross, John C. (1992). In search of how people change: Applications to addictive behaviors. *American Psychologist, 47,* 1104. Copyright © 1992 by the American Psychological Association. Reprinted with permission.

Stages of Change for Other Problems in Life

If the stages of change listed above seem vaguely familiar to you, even without a drug-related problem, it is no accident. Problems may take many different forms, but the difficulties that we face when we confront these problems have a great deal in common. We may wish to lose weight, get more exercise, stop smoking, end an unhappy relationship, seek out a physician to help with a medical condition, or any of a number of actions that might lead toward a healthier and more productive life.

We only have to witness the popularity of New Year's Eve resolutions to appreciate the fact that our desire to take steps to change is part of being human. And yet, we often feel frustrated when our good intentions do not prevail and those New Year's Eve resolutions are left unfulfilled. You may find it helpful to look at your own personal journey toward resolving a problem in your life in terms of the five stages of change.[60]

Needing versus Receiving Substance Abuse Treatment

According to U.S. government estimates in 2009, approximately 7.8 million people aged twelve or older needed treatment for an illicit drug problem, but only 19 percent of them received drug-abuse treatment at a specialty substance-abuse facility in the past twelve months. With respect to those identified as having a need for alcohol-abuse treatment, the picture was even worse. In 2009, approximately 19 million people aged twelve or older needed treatment for an alcohol use problem, but only 9 percent of them received it. All told, approximately 23 million people needed treatment for a problem with use of an illicit drug or alcohol use, and only 11 percent received it. Figure 16.4 shows, in

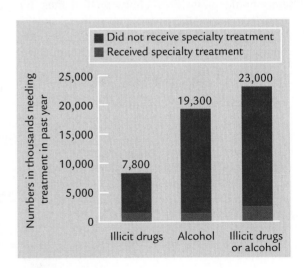

FIGURE 16.4

The gap between treatment needed and treatment received among individuals over the age of twelve in the United States.

Source: Substance Abuse and Mental Health Services Administration (2010). *Results from the 2009 National Survey on Drug Use and Health: National findings.* Rockville, MD: Office of Applied Studies, Substance Abuse and Mental Health Services Administration, pp. 84, 87.

visual terms, the wide gap between treatment needed and treatment received. The disparity between need and receipt of treatment is even greater among the Hispanic population in the United States.

Only a small percentage of people needing treatment in 2009 for a problem with use of either an illicit drug or alcohol, but who did not receive it, personally felt a need to seek help. Of the approximately 6.4 million individuals who needed treatment for *an illicit drug problem* but did not receive it, only about 490,000 of them (8 percent) personally felt a need to seek help. Of the approximately 18 million individuals who needed treatment for *an alcohol use problem* but did not receive it, only about 676,000 of them (4 percent) personally felt a need to seek help. About three-fourths of the people in this latter group made no effort at all to receive treatment.[61]

What can be done to reduce this disparity between treatment needed and treatment received? First, more work must be done to increase the number of substance abusers who recognize that they need to seek treatment and understand that treatment will not have a negative impact in their lives. An encouraging new program called Screening, Brief Intervention, and Referral to Treatment (SBIRT) might help in getting individuals into treatment at an early stage and with less resistance. The program creates a system within community and/or medical settings—including physician offices, hospitals, educational institutions and mental health centers—that screens for and identifies individuals with or at-risk for problems related to substance use. The screening determines the severity of substance use and identifies the appropriate intervention. There is a brief intervention with the community setting, followed by referral to more extensive services if needed. The intent is to make interventions in a relatively non-threatening manner and to increase the numbers of individuals who are motivated to seek out treatment.[62]

Second, more work must be done to provide accessible and affordable substance-abuse treatment for those individuals who want it and are willing to seek it out. Fortunately, affordable substance abuse treatment in the United States took a major step forward through the enactment of the Mental Health Parity and Addiction Equity Act of 2008. In the past, Americans seeking help for psychological problems (including problems related to substance abuse) were reimbursed differently from Americans seeking help with medical conditions. After January 2010, individuals seeking treatment for substance use or a mental-health disorder no longer faced unfair and arbitrary restrictions on their benefits coverage, relative to coverage for other forms of health treatment.

It is estimated that approximately 113 million Americans have been the beneficiaries of this new legislation. It will be particularly helpful in promoting substance abuse substance-abuse treatment. More than 37 percent of individuals in need of treatment have reported that they did not receive it, even though they made the effort, because they had no health insurance coverage and they could not afford the cost.[63]

A Final Note: For Those Who Need Help . . .

Throughout our lives, we will need to confront the reality that licit and illicit substance abuse represents a significant factor in our personal health and the public health of our communities. From everything that has been reviewed in this introduction to drug-taking behavior in today's society and its ramifications for the criminal justice system, it is clear that as decision makers we need all the help we can get.

Fortunately, information and guidance are all around us. For local referral sources for treatment programs, check out the Yellow Pages of your telephone book under "Alcoholism Information" or "Drug Abuse and Addiction Information." There are also numerous web sites on the Internet that are specifically designed to provide assistance with any problem associated with substance abuse. The most comprehensive source of substance abuse prevention and treatment information is the National Clearinghouse for Alcohol and Drug Information (NCADI). Educational materials about virtually every aspect of drug use, misuse, or abuse can be ordered free by calling 800-729-6686 or accessing NCADI's web site at www.health.org. For residents of Canada, the Canadian Centre on Substance Abuse is a useful source of help; you can reach it by calling 613-235-4048 or accessing its web site at www.ccsa.ca. For residents of the United Kingdom, the following web sites are available: www.talktofrank.com and www.drugs.homeoffice.gov.uk/drug-strategy.

Good luck to you all.

Summary

Levels of Intervention in Substance Abuse Prevention

- Substance abuse prevention efforts fall into three basic levels of intervention: primary, secondary, and tertiary.

- Primary prevention focuses on populations that have had only minimal or no exposure to drugs. Secondary prevention focuses on populations whose drug experience has not yet been associated with serious long-term problems. Tertiary prevention focuses on populations who have entered treatment; the goal is to prevent relapse.

Strategies for Substance Abuse Prevention

- The U.S. federal agency specifically charged with prevention programs is the Center for Substance Abuse Prevention (CSAP), a division of the Substance Abuse and Mental Health Services Administration (SAMHSA), which is in turn a division of the U.S. Department of Health and Human Services.

- The overall strategy for substance abuse prevention is to minimize the risk factors in a person's life with respect to drug-taking behavior and maximize the protective factors. The inclination to resist the effects of risk factors for drug-taking behavior through the action of protective factors is referred to as resilience.

- In order to be "evidence-based," primary and secondary prevention programs must be evaluated against a control group that did not receive the intervention. Positive change *per se* is not enough for a judgment of success.

- The overall national policy for the control of drug use in the United States is coordinated by the White House Office of National Drug Control Policy (ONDCP). In a recent formulation of this policy, three priorities have been established as components of a national strategy: stopping drug use before it starts through primary prevention, healing America's drug users through tertiary prevention, and disrupting the market through efforts to reduce the availability of illicit drugs.

- The federal program, Healthy People 2020, has set specific objectives with regard to aspects of personal health, including those that pertain to substance use.

Lessons from the Past: Prevention Approaches That Have Failed

- Several strategies have been largely unsuccessful in meeting the goals of substance abuse prevention. They include the reliance on supply/availability reduction, punitive judicial policies, scare tactics, objective information, and affective education.

Hope and Promise: Components of Effective School-Based Prevention Programs

- Effective school-based programs have incorporated a combination of peer-refusal skills training, relaxation and stress management, and training in social skills and personal decision making.

- The Life Skills Training program is an example of a comprehensive program that incorporates several of these school-based components for effective substance abuse prevention. The Drug Abuse Resistance Education (DARE) program, in its original form, has been shown to be of little effectiveness in primary prevention, though later versions have incorporated many of the components that have been demonstrated to be effective.

Community-Based Prevention Programs

- Community-based programs make use of a broader range of resources, including community leaders and public figures as positive role models, opportunities for alternative-behavior programming, and the mass media.

- Recent efforts by the media have had a major impact on the image of drug-taking behavior in both high-risk populations and others in the community.

- CASASTART is an example of a community-based program that incorporates intensive community-wide components of substance abuse prevention.

Family Systems in Primary and Secondary Prevention

- Community-based prevention programs are increasingly mindful of the importance of the family, particularly parents, as the first line of defense in prevention efforts.

- A major emphasis in primary and secondary prevention programs has been on the special roles of parents, grandparents, guardians, and other family members. Improved lines of communication within the family are crucial elements.

Yes, You: Substance Abuse Prevention and the College Student

- On college campuses, substance abuse prevention programs are incorporating features of both school-based and community-based approaches. There is a compelling argument for the need to change the culture of alcohol and other drug use in college.

- Substance abuse prevention programs should involve faculty and administrators, as well as students, in an overall comprehensive strategy. College fraternities have taken important strides toward an alcohol ban in fraternity houses, even when members are of legal drinking age.

Substance Abuse Prevention and Treatment in the Workplace

- The 1988 Drug-free Workplace Act mandated that any company or business receiving U.S. federal contracts or grants provide a drug-free workplace. This is carried out through a comprehensive and continuing program of drug education and awareness. It is estimated that substance abuse costs as much as $60-$100 billion each year.
- One element of most drug-free workplace programs is an employee assistance program (EAP), serving to help workers with abuse problems. Where unions exist, member assistance programs (MAPs) supplement and complement the work of EAPs.
- Frequently, substance abuse prevention efforts in the workplace entail drug testing among employees, either as a prescreening procedure for new job applicants or as a continuing program for all employees.

Multicultural Issues in Prevention and Treatment

- Special cultural considerations need to be made when communicating about substance abuse with specific population subgroups such as Latino and African American individuals.

Substance Abuse Treatment and the Journey to Recovery

- The road to recovery can be understood in terms of five distinct "stages of change." These stages are precontemplation, contemplation, preparation, action, and maintenance. It is possible to cycle through these stages many times in a kind of spiraling pattern before long-term recovery is attained.
- The five stages of change are applicable to the resolution of most life problems, not just those associated with substance abuse.

Needing versus Receiving Substance Abuse Treatment

- According to U.S. government estimates, more than 7 million people aged twelve or older need treatment for an illicit drug problem; approximately 19 million people need treatment for an alcohol problem. Only a small fraction, however, have received treatment at a specialized facility—or, indeed, at any facility—in the past twelve months.
- Of those individuals who have needed treatment for problems with illicit drug or alcohol use but have not received it, fewer than 10 percent personally felt the need to seek it out. Major reasons for not seeking treatment include the lack of financial means to pay for treatment services and inadequate health insurance coverage. The Mental Health Parity and Addiction Equity Act of 2008 allows individuals in substance abuse treatment to receive reimbursement on a par with treatment for medical conditions.

A Final Note: For Those who Need Help . . .

- The most comprehensive source for substance abuse treatment information in the United States is the National Clearinghouse for Alcohol and Drug Information (NCADI). Similar information sources exist in Canada, the United Kingdom, and most other nations.

Key Terms

action stage, p. 401
affective education, p. 385
contemplation stage, p. 400
employee assistance
    programs (EAPs), p. 396

impactors, p. 389
maintenance stage, p. 401
member assistance programs
    (MAPs), p. 396
peer-refusal skills, p. 386

precontemplation stage,
    p. 400
preparation stage, p. 401
primary prevention, p. 378
resilience, p. 380

secondary prevention,
    p. 378
sociocultural filters, p. 399
tertiary prevention, p. 378
values clarification, p. 386

Endnotes

1. Grant, Bridget F., and Dawson, Deborah A. (1997). Age at onset of alcohol use and its association with DSM-IV alcohol abuse and dependence: Results from the National Longitudinal Alcohol Epidemiological Survey. *Journal of Substance Abuse, 9,* 103–110. Grant, Bridget F., and Dawson, Deborah A. (1998). Age of onset of drug use and its association with DSM-IV drug abuse and dependence: Results from the National Longitudinal Alcohol Epidemiological Survey. *Journal of Substance Abuse, 10,* 163–173.

2. Brook, Judith S., and Brook, David W. (1996). Risk and protective factors for drug use. In Clyde B. McCoy, Lisa R. Metsch, and James A. Inciardi (Eds.), *Intervening with drug-involved youth.* Thousand Oaks, CA: Sage Publications, pp. 23–44. Clayton, Richard R., Segress, Melissa J.H., and Caudill, Crystal A. (2008) Prevention of substance abuse. In Marc Galanter and Herbert D. Kleber (Eds.), *Textbook of substance abuse treatment* (4th ed.). Washington, DC: American Psychiatric Publishing, pp. 681–688. Glantz, Meyer D., and Johnson, Jeannette, L. (Eds.) (2003). *Resilience and development: Positive life adaptations.* New York: Kluwer Academic/Plenum. Wong, Maria M.; Nigg, Joel T.; Zucker, Robert A.; Puttler, Leon I.; et al. (2006). Behavioral control and resiliency in the onset of alcohol and illicit drug use: A prospective study from preschool to adolescence. *Child Development, 77,* 1016–1033.

3. Biglan, Anthony; Mrazek, Patricia J.; Carnine, Douglas; and Flay, Brian R. (2003). The integration of research and practice in the prevention of youth problem behaviors. *American Psychologist, 58,* 433–441. Office of National Drug Control Policy (2010, February). *National drug control budget: FY 2011 funding highlights.* Washington, DC: White House Office of National Drug Control Policy.

4. Mokdad, Ali H.; Marks, James S.; Stroup, Donna F.; and Gerberding, Julie L. (2004). Actual causes of death in the United States, 2000. *Journal of the American Medical Association, 291,* 1238–1245. Mokdad, Ali H.; Marks, James S.; Stroup, Donna F.; and Gerberding, Julie L. (2005). Correction: Actual causes of death in the United States, 2000. *Journal of the American Medical Association, 293,* 298.

5. Califano, Joseph A., Jr. (2007). High society: How substance abuse ravages America and what to do about it. New York: PublicAffairs. Center for Substance Abuse Prevention (2009). Substance abuse prevention dollars and cents: A cost-benefit analysis. Rockville, MD: Substance Abuse and Mental Health Services Administration.

6. Public Health Service (October–November 2009). Healthy People 2020: Public meeting. 2009 draft objectives. Bethesda, MD: Public Health Service.

7. Office of National Drug Control Policy, *National drug control strategy,* Table 1.

8. Goode, Erich (2008). *Drugs in American society* (7th ed.). New York: McGraw-Hill College, pp. 400–403. National Drug Intelligence Center (2008). *National drug threat assessment 2009.* Washington, DC: U.S. Department of Justice, pp. 25–32.

9. Hingson, Ralph W.; Scotch, Norman; Mangione, Thomas; Meyers, Allan; Glantz, Leonard; et al. (1983). Impact of legislation raising the legal drinking age in Massachusetts from 18 to 21. *American Journal of Public Health, 73,* 163–170.

10. Goode, *Drugs in American society,* pp. 385–417. Greenhouse, Linda (2007, December 11). Justices restore judges' control over sentencing. *New York Times,* pp. A1, A28. Peters, Jeremy W. (2009, March 11). Legislation to overhaul Rockefeller drug laws advances swiftly. *New York Times,* p. 20. Steinberg, Neil (1994, May 5). The law of unintended consequences. *Rolling Stone,* pp. 33–34.

11. Funkhouser, Judith E., and Denniston, Robert W. (1992). Historical perspective. In Mary A. Jansen (Ed.), *A promising future: Alcohol and other drug problem prevention services improvement* (OSAP Prevention Monograph 10). Rockville, MD: Office of Substance Abuse Prevention, pp. 5–15.

12. Flay, Brian R., and Sobel, Judith L. (1983). The role of mass media in preventing adolescent substance abuse. In Thomas J. Glynn, Carl G. Leukenfeld, and Jacqueline P. Ludford (Eds.), *Preventive adolescent drug abuse.* Rockville, MD: National Institute on Drug Abuse, pp. 5–35.

13. Williams, R., Ward, D., and Gray, L. (1985). The persistence of experimentally induced cognitive change: A neglected dimension in the assessment of drug prevention programs. *Journal of Drug Education, 15,* 33–42.

14. Meeks, Linda, Heit, Philip, and Page, Randy (1994). *Drugs, alcohol, and tobacco.* Blacklick, OH: Meeks Heit Publishing, p. 201.

15. Ibid., p. 202.

16. McBride, Duane C., Mutch, Patricia B., and Chitwood, Dale D. (1996). Religious belief and the initiation and prevention of drug use among youth. In Clyde B. McCoy, Lisa R. Metsch, and James A. Inciardi (Eds.), *Intervening with drug-involved youth.* Thousand Oaks, CA: Sage Publications, pp. 110–130.

17. Schroeder, Debra S., Laflin, Molly T., and Weis, David L. (1993). Is there a relationship between self-esteem and drug use? Methodological and statistical limitations of the research. *Journal of Drug Issues, 22,* 645–665. Yuen, Francis K. O., and Pardeck, John T. (1998). Effective strategies for preventing substance abuse among children and adolescents. *Early Child Development and Care, 145,* 119–131.

18. Best, J. Allan; Flay, Brian R.; Towson, Shelagh M. J.; Ryan, Katherine B.; et al. (1984). Smoking prevention and the concept of risk. *Journal of Applied Social Psychology, 14,* 257–273. Pandina, Robert J., Johnson, Valerie L.,

and White, Helene R. (2010). Peer influences on substance use during adolescence and emerging adulthood. In Lawrence M. Scheier, (Ed.), Scheier, *Handbook of drug use etiology: Theory, methods, and empirical findings*. Washington, DC: American Psychological Association, pp. 383–402.

19. Botvin, Gilbert J., and Griffin, Kenneth W. (2010). Advances in the science and practice of prevention: Targeting individual-level etiological factors and the challenge of going to scale. In Lawrence M. Scheier, (Ed.), *Handbook of drug use etiology: Theory, methods, and empirical findings*. Washington, DC: American Psychological Association, pp. 631–650. Botvin, Elizabeth M. (1992). School-based and community-based prevention approaches. In Joyce H. Lewisohn, Pedro Ruiz, and Robert B. Millman (Eds.), *Substance abuse: A comprehensive textbook* (2nd ed.). Baltimore: Williams & Wilkins, pp. 910–927.

20. Culpers, Pim (2002). Effective ingredients of school-based drug prevention programs: A systematic review. *Addictive Behaviors*, 27, 1009–1023. Faggiano, Fabrizio; Vigna-Tagliante, Federica; Versino, Elizabetta; Zambon, Alberto, and Lemma, Patrizia (2005). School-based prevention for illicit drugs' use. *Cochrane Database of Systematic Reviews*, Issue 2. Article No.: CD003020. DOI: 10.1002/14651858.CD0030.pub2.

21. Botvin, Gilbert J.; Baker, Eli; Dusenbury, Linda; Botvin, Elizabeth M.; and Diaz, Tracy (1995). Long-term follow-up results of a randomized drug abuse prevention trial in a white middle-class population. *Journal of the American Medical Association*, 273, 1106–1112. Botvin, Gilbert J.; Epstein Jennifer A.; Baker, Eli; Diaz, Tracy; and Ifill-Williams, Michelle (1997). School-based drug abuse prevention with inner-city minority youth. *Journal of Child and Adolescent Substance Abuse*, 6, 5–19. Botvin, Gilbert J., and Tortu, Stephanie (1988). Preventing adolescent substance abuse through life skills training. In Richard M. Price, Emory L. Cowen, Raymond P. Lorion, and Julia Ramos-McKay (Eds.), *Fourteen ounces of prevention: A casebook for practitioners*. Washington, DC: American Psychological Association, pp. 98–110.

22. Mathias, Robert (1997, March/April). From the 'burbs to the 'hood . . . This program reduces student's risk of drug use. *NIDA Notes*, pp. 1, 5–6. Quotation on p. 6.

23. Beets, Michael W.; Flay, Brian R.; Vuchinich, Samuel; Snyder, Frank J.; Acock, Alan; et al. (2009). Use of a social and character development progam to prevent substance use, violent behaviors, and sexual activity among elementary-school students in Hawaii. *American Journal of Public Health*, 99, 1438–1445. Botvin, Gilbert J.; Griffin, Kenneth W., and Nichols, Tracy D. (2006). Preventing youth violence and delinquency through a universal school-based prevention approach. *Prevention Science*, 7, 403–408. Griffin, Kenneth W., Botvin, Gilbert J., and Nichols, Tracy D. (2006). Effects of a school-based drug abuse prevention program for adolescents on HIV risk behaviors in young adulthood. *Prevention Science*, 7,

103–112. Griffin, Kenneth W., Botvin, Gilbert J., and Nichols, Tracy D. (2004). Long-term follow-up effects of a school-based drug abuse prevention program on adolescent risky driving. *Prevention Science*, 5, 207–212.

24. Cavazos, Lauro F. (1989). *What works: Schools without drugs*. Washington, DC: U.S. Department of Education, p. 38.

25. Clayton, Richard R., Cattarello, Anne M., and Johnstone, Bryan M. (1996). The effectiveness of Drug Abuse Resistance Education (Project DARE): 5-year follow-up results. *Preventive Medicine*, 25, 307–318. Lynam, Donald R.; Milich, Richard; Zimmerman, Rick; Novak, Scott P.; Logan, T. K.; et al. (1999). Project DARE: No effects at 10-year follow-up. *Journal of Consulting and Clinical Psychology*, 67, 590–593.

26. Miller, Joel (2004). Bad trip: *How the war against drugs is destroying America*. New York: Nelson Thomas.

27. Lynam, Project DARE, p. 593.

28. Zernike, Kate (2001, February 15). Antidrug program says it will adopt a new strategy. *New York Times*, pp. A1, A29.

29. Gardner, Margo, Barajas, R. Gabriela, and Brooks-Gunn, Jeanne (2010). Neighborhood influences on substance use etiology: Is where you live important? In Lawrence M. Scheier, (Ed.), *Handbook of drug use etiology: Theory, methods, and empirical findings*. Washington, DC: American Psychological Association, pp. 423–442. Snyder, Leslie B., and Nadorff, P. Gayle (2010). Youth substance use and the media. In Lawrence M. Scheier, (Ed.), *Handbook of drug use etiology: Theory, methods, and empirical findings*. Washington, DC: American Psychological Association, pp. 475–492. Wandersman, Abraham, and Florin, Paul (2003). Community interventions and effective prevention. *American Psychologist*, 58, 441–448.

30. Rhodes, Jean E., and Jason, Leonard A. (1991). The social stress model of alcohol and other drug abuse: A basis for comprehensive, community-based prevention. In Ketty H. Rey, Christopher L. Faegre, and Patti Lowery (Eds.), *Prevention research findings: 1988* (OSAP Prevention Monograph 3). Rockville, MD: Office of Substance Abuse Prevention, pp. 155–171.

31. Tobler, Nancy S. (1986). Meta-analysis of 143 adolescent drug prevention programs: Quantitative outcome results of program participants compared to a control group. *Journal of Drug Issues*, 16, 537–567.

32. Ridout, Victoria, Roberts, Donald F., and Foehr, Ulla G. (2005, March). *Generation M: Media in the lives of 8–18-year-olds: Executive summary*. Menlo Park, CA: Kaiser Family Foundation. Quotation on page 6.

33. Masten, Ann S.; Faden, Vivian B.; Zucker, Robert A.; and Spear, Linda P. (2008). Underage drinking: A developmental framework. *Pediatrics*, 121, S235–S251. Primack, Brian; Dalton, Margaret A.; Carroll, Mary V.; Agarwal, Aaron A.; and Fine, Michael J. (2008). Content analysis of tobacco, alcohol, and other drugs in popular music. *Archives of Pediatric and Adolescent Medicine*, 162, 169–175. Sargent, James D.; Wills, Thomas A.; Stoolmiller, Mike; Gibson, Jennifer; and Gibbons,

Frederick X. (2006). Alcohol use in motion pictures and its relation with early-onset teen drinking. *Journal of Studies in Alcohol, 67,* 54–65.

34. Partnership for a Drug-Free America (1994, July 12). Press release: New study shows children in NYC becoming more anti-drug, bucking national trends. Partnership for a Drug-Free America, New York.

35. Office of National Drug Control Policy (2006, July 21). Media campaign fact sheets: Teens and technology fact sheet. National Youth Anti-drug Media Campaign, Office of National Drug Control Policy, Washington, DC. Partnership for a Drug-Free America, New York. Substance Abuse and Mental Health Services Administration (2009, April 3). SAMHSA News Release: National survey finds a decrease in the percentage of adolescents seeing substance use prevention messages in the media. Rockville, MD: Substance Abuse and Mental Health Services Administration.

36. Information courtesy of the Substance Abuse and Mental Health Services Administration, Rockville, MD.

37. Kliewer, Wendy (2010). Family processes in drug use etiology. In Lawrence M. Scheier, (Ed.), *Handbook of drug use etiology: Theory, methods, and empirical findings.* Washington, DC: American Psychological Association, pp. 365–382. National Center on Addiction and Substance Abuse at Columbia University (1999). No safe haven: Children of substance-abusing parents. New York: National Center on Addiction and Substance Abuse. Seizas, Judith S., and Youcha, Geraldine (1999). *Drugs, alcohol, and your children: What every parent needs to know.* New York: Penguin Books.

38. The Ad Council. (2008, March/April). Underage drinking prevention: Alcohol initation rates highest during summer. *PSA Bulletin,* p. 1. Lae, Andrew, and Crano, William D. (2009). Monitoring matters: Meta-analytic review reveals the reliable linkage of parental monitoring with adolescent marijuana use. *Perspectives on Psychological Science, 4,* 578–586. Wooldridge, Leslie Quander (2007, March/April). Ads, billboards highlight younger children. *SAMHSA News,* p. 11.

39. The National Center on Addiction and Substance Abuse at Columbia University (2005, September). The importance of family dinners II. New York: National Center on Addiction and Substance Abuse at Columbia University. The National Center on Addiction and Substance Abuse at Columbia University (2006, August). National Survey of American Attitudes on Substance Abuse XI: Teens and parents. New York: National Center on Addiction and Substance Abuse at Columbia University. Partnership for a Drug-Free America (1998). Partnership attitude tracking survey: Parents say they're talking, but only 27% of teens—1 in 4—are learning a lot at home about the risk of drugs. Partnership for a Drug-Free America (1999). Partnership attitude tracking survey: More parents talking with kids about drugs more often, and appear to be having an impact. Information courtesy of Partnership for a Drug-Free America, New York.

40. The National Center on Addiction and Substance Abuse at Columbia University (2003, August). National Survey American Attitudes on Substance Abuse VIII: Teens and parents. New York: National Center on Addiction and Substance Abuse at Columbia University.

41. Castro, Ralph J., and Foy, Betsy D. (2002). Harm reduction: A promising approach for college health. *Journal of American College Health, 51,* 89–91. Lewis, David C. (2001). Urging college alcohol and drug policies that target adverse behavior, not use. *Journal of American College Health, 50,* 39–41. Weitzman, Elissa R.; Nelson, Toben F.; Lee, Hang; and Wechsler, Henry (2004). Reducing drinking and related harms in college: Evaluation of the "A Matter of Degree" program. *American Journal of Preventive Medicine, 27,* 187–196.

42. Freedman, Samuel G. (2007, September 12). Calling the folks about campus drinking. *New York Times,* p. B6. National Institute on Alcohol Abuse and Alcoholism (2002, October). Changing the culture of campus drinking. *Alcohol Alert,* No. 58. Rockville, MD: National Institute on Alcohol Abuse and Alcoholism.

43. Johnston, Lloyd D.; O'Malley, Patrick M.; Bachman, Jerald G.; and Schulenberg, John E. (2009, December 14). Teen marijuana use tilts up, while some drugs decline in use. Ann Arbor, MI: University of Michigan News Service, Table 1.

44. Office of Educational Research and Improvement (1990). *A guide for college presidents and governing bodies: Strategies for eliminating alcohol and other drug abuse on campuses.* Washington, DC: U.S. Department of Education.

45. Denizet-Lewis, Benoit (2005, January 9). Band of brothers. *New York Times Magazine,* pp. 32–39, 52, 73. Quotation on page 35. Office of Educational Research and Improvement, *A guide for college presidents.*

46. Busteed, Brandon (2010, March 19). Is high-risk drinking at college on the way out? *Chronicle of Higher Education,* p. A76. Crump, Sarah (2008, March 6). Fraternity life without keg parties safer, saner, say Phi Delta Theta guys. www.cleveland.com/lifestyles/2008. Schackner, Bill (2000, August 18). Fraternity houses turn off the taps and sober up. www.post-gazette.com.

47. Center for Substance Abuse Treatment (accessed April 4, 2010). Issue Brief #12 for Employers: What you need to know about substance abuse treatment. Rockville, MD: Substance Abuse and Mental Health Services Administration. Larson, Sharon L.; Eyerman, Joe; Foster, Misty S.; and Gfroerer, Joseph C. (2007). *Worker substance use and workplace policies and programs.* Rockville, MD: Substance Abuse and Mental Health Services Administration, p. 2. Lehman, Wayne E.K.; Farabee, David J., and Bennett, Joel B. (1998). Perceptions and correlates of co-worker substance use. *Employee Assistance Quarterly, 13,* 1–22. Substance Abuse and Mental Health Services Administration (2009). *Results from the 2008 National Survey on Drug Use and Health: National findings.* Rockville, MD: Substance Abuse and Mental Health Services Administration, pp. 35 and 79.

48. Center for Substance Abuse Prevention (1994). *Making the link: Alcohol, tobacco, and other drugs in the workplace*. Rockville, MD: Center for Substance Abuse Prevention. Substance Abuse and Mental Health Services Administration.

49. American Management Association (2004). *AMA 2004 workplace testing survey: Medical testing*. New York: American Management Association, p. 3. Holding Reynolds (2006, July 7). Whatever happened to drug testing? *Time*, retrieved from http://www.time.com/time/nation/article/0,8599,1211429,00.html. Substance Abuse and Mental Health Services Administration (2008, March 15). *Making your workplace drug-free: A kit for employers*. Rockville, MD: Substance Abuse and Mental Health Services Administration.

50. Comerford, Anthony W. (1999). Work dysfunction and addiction. *Journal of Substance Abuse Treatment, 16*, 247–253. Normand, J., Lempert, R., and O'Brien, C. (Eds.) (1994). *Under the influence? Drugs and the American work force*. Washington, DC: National Academy Press.

51. Avis, Harry (1996). *Drugs and life* (3rd ed.). Dubuque, IA: Brown and Benchmark, p. 256.

52. National Transportation Safety Board (1988). *Alcohol/drug use and its impact on railroad safety: Safety study*. Washington, DC: U.S. Department of Transportation.

53. Blum, Terry C., and Roman, Paul M. (1995). *Cost-effectiveness and preventive implications of employee assistance programs*. Rockville, MD: Substance Abuse and Mental Health Services Administration.

54. Hernandez, Lawrence P., and Lucero, Ed (1996). La Familia community drug and alcohol prevention program: Family-centered model for working with inner-city Hispanic families. *Journal of Primary Prevention, 16*, 255–272 El-Guebaly, Nady (2008). Cross-cultural aspects of addiction. In Marc Galanter and Herbert D. Kleber (Eds.), *Textbook of substance abuse treatment* (4th ed.). Washington, DC: American Psychiatric Publishing, pp. 45–52. Office of Substance Abuse Prevention (1990). *The fact is . . . reaching Hispanic/Latino audiences requires cultural sensitivity*. Rockville, MD: National Clearinghouse for Alcohol and Drug Information, National Institute on Drug Abuse. U.S. Census Bureau (2005). *The Hispanic population in the United States: March 2004*. Washington, DC: U.S. Department of Commerce.

55. Hahn, Ellen J., and Rado, Mary (1996). African-American Head Start parent involvement in drug prevention. *American Journal of Health Behavior, 20*, 41–51. Office of Substance Abuse Prevention (1990). *The fact is . . . alcohol and other drug use is a special concern for African American families and communities*. Rockville, MD: National Clearinghouse for Drug and Alcohol Information, National Institute on Drug Abuse.

56. Meeks, Heit, and Page, *Drugs*, p. 219.

57. Connors, Gerard J., Donovan, Dennis J., and DiClemente, Carlo C. (2001). *Substance abuse treatment and the stages of change: Selecting and planning interventions*. New York: Guilford Press. DiClemente, Carlo C., Bellino, Lori E., and Neavins, Tara M. (1999). Motivation for change and alcoholism treatment. *Alcohol Research and Health, 23*, 86–92. Schuckit, Marc A. (1995). *Educating yourself about alcohol and drugs: A people's primer*. New York: Plenum Press, pp. 131–153.

58. Schuckit, *Educating yourself*, pp. 186–216.

59. DiClemente, Carlo C., Garay, Miranda, and Gemmell, Leigh (2008). Motivational enhancement. In Marc Galanter and Herbert D. Kleber (Eds.), *Textbook of substance abuse treatment* (4th ed.). Washington, DC: American Psychiatric Publishing, pp. 361–372. Dijkstra, Arie, Roijackers, Jolanda, and DeVries, Hein (1998). Smokers in four stages of readiness to change. *Addictive Behaviors, 23*, 339–350. Prochaska, James O., DiClemente, Carlo C., and Norcross, John C. (1992). In search of how people change. *American Psychologist, 47*, 1102–1114.

60. Norman, Gregory J.; Velicer, Wayne F.; Fava, Joseph L.; and Prochaska, James O. (1998). Dynamic typology clustering within the stages of change for smoking cessation. *Addictive Behaviors, 23*, 139–153. Prochaska, James O. (1994). *Changing for good*. New York: William Morrow. Velicer, Wayne F.; Norman, Gregory J.; Fava, Joseph L.; and Prochaska, James O. (1999). Testing 40 predictions from the transtheoretical model. *Addictive Behaviors, 24*, 455–469.

61. Markel, Howard (2003, October 21). Treatment for addiction meets barriers in the doctor's office. *New York Times*, pp. F5, F8. Substance Abuse and Mental Health Services Administration, *Results of the 2008 National Survey on Drug Use and Health*, pp. 80–87 and Table G.30. Substance Abuse and Mental Health Services Administration (2009, July 16). Substance use treatment need and receipt among Hispanics. *The NSDUH Report*, Figures 1 and 2.

62. McClellan, A. Thomas (2008). Evolution in addiction treatment concepts and methods. In Marc Galanter and Herbert D. Kleber (Eds.), *Textbook of substance abuse treatment* (4th ed.). Washington, DC: American Psychiatric Publishing, pp. 93–108. Substance Abuse and Mental Health Services Administration (2009, November/December). Screening, brief intervention, and referral to treatment. *SAMHSA News*, 1–2.

63. Parity: What does the new law mean? (2008, November/December). *SAMHSA News*, pp. 1–4. Substance Abuse and Mental Health Services Administration, *Results from 2008 National Survey on Drug Use and Health*, p. 86.

INDEX

Note: Boldface indicates key terms and the pages where they are defined.

Ephedrine, 179
Ephedrine derivatives, 287
Epilepsy
    barbiturates for, 243, 246
    bezodiazepines for, 249
"Episodic high-risk drinking," 303. See also
        Binge drinking
Epitestosterone, 286
EPO (erythropoietin), 274
Equidren, EquiGan, and Equipoise
        (boldanone undecylenate), 272
Ergogenic drugs, 269–70., **271,** 272. *See also*
        Anabolic steroids
    testing procedures and policies, 283–7
Ergot, 196
Ergotism, 196, 197
Ernest and Julio Gallo Winery, 299
Erythroplakia, 361
Erythropoietin (EPO), 274
Erythroxylon coca, 167. See also Cocaine
Escobar, Pablo, 100–1
Estazolam, 249
Estradiol, 276
Estrogen, 11
Eszopiclone, 252–3, **253**
Ether, 255, **256,** 257
Ethnicity. *See* Race and ethnicity
Ethyl alcohol, 294
ETS (environmental tobacco smoke), 353,
        362
Euphoria seekers, 73
Excitation, 70
Excretion of drugs, 13
Expectation effects, 19–20
    cognitive-expectation theory, 313
    secondary deviance and, 79
Extinction, 73

FAE, 332
Family
    alcoholism and, 326, 334–5
    prevention and, 391–3
Family Smoking and Tobacco Control Act
        (2009), 354
FARC, 102
Farley, Chris, 32, 177
FAS, 304
Fast-flushing, 305
Fatty liver, 329
FDA. *See* Food and Drug Administration
        (FDA)
Feal, Lorenzo, 255
Federal agencies involved in interdiction,
        120–3
Federal Bureau of Investigation (FBI), 60
Federal Bureau of Narcotics (FBN), 58, 59,
        221–2
Federal Trade Commission, 352
Fenichel, Otto, 72
Fentanyl, 148, 159, 160
    federal penalties for, 131
Fermentation, 294
Fetal alcohol effect (FAE), 332
Fetal alcohol syndrome (FAS), 331, 331–3
Fisher, Gary, 68
Fitch, Russell, 162
5/4 criterion for binge drinking, 303
Flashbacks, 203, 212–13
Flavored snuff, 366

Fleischl-Marxow, Ernst von, 170
Floxin (ofloxacin), 286
Flunitrazepam, 45, 251–2, 254
    penalties for, 131
Flurazepam, 249
Fly agaric (*Amanita muscaria*), 52, 209
Focalin, 186
Food and Drug Administration (FDA), 31, 62,
        254, 283
    "black box" warning on ADHD
        medications, 186
    dietary supplements, 283
    tobacco control, 354
Food-drug interactions, 15
Football players, steroid use by, 274
Ford, Gerald, 60
Forfeiture, asset, 126–8
Formication, 170, 171
Fortified wines, 295, 300
Fourth Amendment, 398
"Fourth-Year Fifth," 314
Fourth-years Acting Responsibly (FAR), 314
Framework Convention on Tobacco Control
        (2003), 367–8
France
    smoking in, 368
    snuffing in, 350
Franklin, Benjamin, 350
Free-base cocaine, 174, 174
Freelance model of retail drug distribution,
        95
French Connection, 59, 116, 122, 148
French paradox, 316
French Wine Cola, 168
Freon, 258
Freud, Sigmund, 53, 71, 166–7, 170, 367

GABA receptor
    sensitivity to alcohol, 307
    treatment, 338
Galen, Claudius, 142
Gallup Poll
    on LSD use (1967-1971), 201
    on medical marijuana use (2009), 237
Gamblers Anonymous, 341
Gamma aminobutyric acid (GABA), 70
    alcohol sensitivity, 307
    benzodiazepines and facilitation of, 250–1
    nonbenzodiazepine depressants, 252–3
Gamma-hydroxybutyrate (GHB), 36, 62,
        253, 253–4, 255
    penalties for, 131
Gamma-vinyl-GABA (GVG), 178
Gangs
    community policing, 93
    heroin distribution, 152
    Hispanic/Latino and PCP trafficking, 107
    motorcycle, 105, 107–8
Garland, Judy, 32
Gas chromatography and mass spectrometry
        (GC/MS), 285, 286
Gaseous phase, 356
Gasoline, 257, 259
Gasoline inhalation, 259
Gastritis, 304
Gastrointestinal tract, absorption through, 9–10
Gateway hypothesis, 230, 230–1
    association question in, 230–1
    causation question in, 231

developmental sequence, 230
    inhalant abuse and, 261
GC/MS, 285, 286, 287
Gender
    alcohol and sexual desire and, 314
    alcohol consumption and, 303
    alcohol metabolism and, 305
    DAWN statistics by, 34
    drug effect and, 18
    lung cancer and, 360
    opium use and, 144
    respiratory disease in adolescent smokers
        and, 360
    smoking cessation rates, 369
Generic names, 6
Gene therapy, 274
Genetic factors, 68–9
    in alcoholism, 68–9, 335–6
GHB (gamma-hydroxybutyrate), 44, 62
    ED visits for, 36
G.I. Joe action figures, evolution of muscle
        representation on, 279–80
Gin, 295, 296
Giraldo, Greg, 32
Glaucoma, marijuana to treat, 234
Glue inhalation, 256–9, 261, 262
Glutamate, 70
Glutamate receptors, 211, 213
Glutethimide, 309
Goldberg, Linn, 281
Golden Crescent, 98, 148
Golden Triangle, 96, 148
Goldstein, Avram, 383
Goldstein tripartite model of drugs and
        violence, 93
Golub, Andrew, 94
Goode, Erich, 69, 77, 237, 342
Goodman, Benny, 221
Gore, Al, 3
Grain neutral spirits, 295
Grandparents, 392
Grant, Ulysses S., 168
Great Depression, 58
Greece, smoking in, 368
Gums, nicotine, 370
GVG (gamma-vinyl-GABA), 178
Gynecomastia, 276

Hague, conference on opium trade in the
        (1912), 56
Halcion (triazolam), 249
Half-life, elimination, 13
Hallucinations, 194–5. See also
        Hallucinogens
    from inhalants, 257
    LSD vs. schizophrenia, 202
    PCP-induced, 211
hallucinogen persisting perception disorder,
        203
Hallucinogens, 74
Hallucinogens, 193–213, **194.** See also
        Lysergic acid diethylamide (LSD);
        Phencyclidine (PCP)
    botanical sources for, 195
    classifying, 195–6
    DEA seizures 2006-2009, 120
    definitions of, 194–5
    dissociative anesthetic, 211, 212–13
    in early times, 51–2

Infectious disease control, analogy to drug abuse prevention, 383
Inhalants, 75, 242–3, **243**
  abuse potential of, 257
  acute effects of, 257
  amyl nitrite and butyl nitrite, 262–3
  chronic effects of, 261
  dangers of abuse, 257–9
  dependence on, 261
  DMT, 205
  as gateway for future drug abuse, 261
  glue, solvent and aerosol inhalation, 242, 256–9
  history of, 254–6, 263
  household products with abuse potential, 257
  patterns of abuse, 259–61
  signs of abuse, 258
  society's responses to abuse of, 261–2
  sudden deaths from, 258
  use by youth, 38–40
Inhalation, 10–11, 12
Inhalers
  amphetamine, 180
  nicotine, 370
Inhibition, 70
Injection, 10, 12
Inmates. *See* Prisoners
Innocent VIII, Pope, 221
Innovation, as adaptation to anomie, 75
Inpatient treatment for cocaine, 177–8
Inquiry into the effects of ardent spirits on the human mind and body, An (Rush), 297
In rem civil forfeitures, 128
Insomnia
  barbiturates to treat, 246
  benzodiazepine to treat, 251
  non-barbiturates to treat, 247
  nonbenzodiazepine drugs to treat, 252–3
Institute of Medicine, 235
Instrumental use, 6, 7
Insulin, 10, 11–12, 309
Intensification model of drug use and crime, 89
Interactional circumstances, **92**, 92–3
Interdiction, **119**, 119–23
  federal agencies, 120–3
  forty-year chronology of, 122
Internal Revenue Service, 57, 146
International Association of Chiefs of Police, 88
International drug code for sport competitions, 273
International drug regulation, 63–4
International Monetary Fund, 119
Internet
  prescription pain relievers, buying on, 45, 46
  sales of cigarettes on, 355
  steroid suppliers on, 270, 288
Intervention, levels of, 378–80. See also Prevention strategies
Intestinal spasm, 161
Intramuscular (i.m.) injections, **10**, 12
Intranasal administration, **11**
Intravenous (i.v.) injection, **10**, 12
  heroin, 155
Involvement (social bond), 76, 77

Iran, heroin from, 97–8, 148
ischemic stroke, **359**
Isopropane, 257
Israel
  smoking in, 368

Jackson, Michael, 32
Jacobs, Regina, 284
Jamaica, marijuana in, 224
James I of England, King, 349
Japan, smoking in, 367, 368
Japanese Yakuza, 102
Jazz world, marijuana's popularity in, 221
Jellinek, E. M., 336
Jerez, Rodrigo de, 349
Jimsonweed, 196, 210
"Jitters," 329
Johnson, Bruce, 77, 78, 94
Johnston, Lloyd D., 232, 364
Joint, **223.** See also Marijuana
Jones, Ernest, 170, 367
Jones, Kenneth L., 331
Joplin, Janis, 32
Journal of Studies on Alcohol, 303
Jungle, The (Sinclair), 55
Justice, Department of, 92, 235–6
"Just Say No" campaign, 61

Kadian (morphine), 160
Kandel, Denise, 78, 230
Karzai government in Afghanistan, 98
Kennedy, David A., 32
Kenya, 368
Ketalar. *See* Ketamine
Ketamine, 195, **212**, 212–13
  ED visits for, 36, 44
  trafficking, 107
Kindling effect, **172**
Klonopin (clonazepam), 249
Knock and talk, **126**
Korsakoff's psychosis, 331

LAA (lysergic acid amide), 195, 204–5
LAAM (levo-alpha-acetylmethadol), **158**, 158–9
Labeling theory, 78, 78–9
Labor, endorphins and, 151
La Familia cocaine and methamphetamine cartel, 122
Lager beer, 295
Laissez-faire, **53**
L-amphetamine, 180
Language of drug subculture, private, 78
Lao People's Democratic Republic, 371
Laos, 97, 148
Latency period, **13**
Latino groups
  cocaine use, 171
  drug abuse prevention approaches in, 399
  racial profiling, 125
Laudanum, 143
Laughing gas. *See* Nitrous oxide
Laundromats, money laundering originating from, 109
LDL (low-density lipoprotein), 316
Lean Stack, 282
Leary, Timothy, 198, 199, 201, 223
Ledger, Heath, 32
Legalization of drugs, 135–6

Legal status of drugs, 7
Lehder, Carlos, 122
Leo XII, Pope, 168
Lethal dose, **30**, 30–1
  alcohol, 307
  heroin, 154
Lethal emergencies. *See* Deaths
Leukoencephalopathy, 154
Leukoplakia, **361**
Levo-alpha-acetylmethadol, 158
Levoamphetamine (l-amphetamine), 45, 180
Leyva, Arturo Bertrán, 97
Librium (chlordiazepoxide), 248–9, 251
Licit (legal) drugs, **4**
  emergencies related to, 36
Lidocaine, 172
Life Skills Training (LST), 387–8
Lightner, Candace, 312
Limbic system, 72
Limbitrol (chlordiazepoxide and amitriptyline), 249
Lincoln, Abraham, 54
Lipid-soluble, 10
Liqueur, 295
Liquor. *See* Distilled spirits
Lithuania, smoking in, 368
Liver
  alcohol abuse and, 329–30
  cancer of, 330
  fatty, 329
  screening of orally-administered drugs by, 10
  steroid use and, 277
Loperamide, 159
Lopressor (metoprolol), 253
Lorazepam, 249
Los Angeles County Sheriff's Department, "funding raid" by, 129
Low-density lipoprotein (LDL), 316
LSD. *See* Lysergic acid diethylamide (LSD)
LST (Life Skills Training), 387–8
Lucido, Dr. Frank, 234
Lunesta (eszopiclone), 253
Lung cancer, 356, 360, 362
Luteinizing hormone (LH), 228
Lysergic acid amide (LAA), 195, **204**, 204–5
Lysergic acid diethylamide (LSD), 29, 45, 193–203, **194**
  acute effects of, 199–200
  brain and, 201
  chromosomal damage and, 202–3
  cocaine combined with, 174
  creativity and, 202
  criminal or violent behavior and, 203
  cross tolerance between psilocin and, 204
  DAWN report on, 199–200
  dependence and, 201
  ED visits for, 36, 199
  effective dose of, 199
  emergency guidelines for bad trip, 202
  facts and fictions about, 201–3
  history of, 59
  learning techniques to use and enjoy, 77
  mescaline effects compared to, 206
  panic or psychosis produced by, 201–2
  patterns of use, 201
  penalties for, 131
  personality disorder, 74
  production of, 95

Micrograms (mikes), 199
Midazolam, 249
Military, U.S., interdiction by, 122–3
Mill, John Stuart, 379
Miltown (meprobamate), 248
Minor League Baseball, 275
Minor tranquilizers. *See* Antianxiety drugs
Mitchell, George J., 275
Mithradates VI of Pontus, King, 14–15, 17
Mithradatism, 15
Modafinil, 187
Moderation Management (MM), 341, 342
Moist snuff, 365, 366
Money, cocaine-contaminated paper, 176
Money laundering, 108, 108–9
Monitoring the Future (MTF) Study, 37, 38
Monoamine oxidase (MAO) inhibitors, alcohol mixed with, 309
Monroe, Marilyn, 32
Mood, 70
    amphetamines and swings of, 181
    anabolic steroids and swings of, 277–8
"Moonshiners," 298
Moral model, 68
Morning glory seeds, 195, 204–5
Morocco, smoking in, 371
Morphine, 7, 17, 19, 53, **145,** 160–1, 287
    deaths from, 32, 34
    discovery of, 145
    heroin production from, 96
    history of, 145–6
    medical uses of, 160
    possible adverse effects of, 159
    street names for, 155
    tolerance for, 16–17
Morphine-sensitive receptors, 150, 226
Mothers Against Drunk Driving (MADD), 311, 312
Motion Picture Association of America (MPAA), 364
Motorcycle gangs, 105, 107–8
Motor tasks, marijuana's effect on, 225
Motrin (ibuprofen), 286
Movies, depiction of smoking in, 364
MPTP, 155
MS Contin (morphine), 160
"Mules" (couriers), 99, 119–20
Multicultural issues in prevention, 399
Multimodality programs, 159
Multiple substance abuse, 251
Muscle dysmorphia, 279
Muscle Power, 283
Mushrooms. *See Amanita muscaria;* Psilocybin
Muslims, history of hashish and, 220
Musto, David, 59
Myanmar (Burma), 97, 148

Nabilone, 235
Nalmefene, 337
Naloxone, 150, 157, 158
Naltrexone, 140, **152,** 337–8
Nandrolone decanoate, 272
Nandrolone phenprionate, 272
Narcan (naloxone), 150
Narcolepsy, 187
Narcoterrorism in Mexico, 97
Narcotic analgesics, 36

Narcotics, 140–62, **141.** See also Heroin; Morphine; Opiates; Opium
    classification of, 56
    possible adverse effects of, 159
    street names for, 155
    treatment for, 156–9
Narcotics Anonymous, 341
Narcotics Control Act (1956), 59
Nasal decongestants, 187
National Association of Counties, 183
National Basketball Association, 275, 314
National Cancer Institute, 369
National Center on Addiction and Substance Abuse, 391
National Clearinghouse for Alcohol and Drug Information (NCADI), 403
National Collegiate Athletic Association (NCAA), 284
National Commission on Marijuana and Drug Abuse, 237
National Drug Control Policy, Office of, 62, 63, 381
National Drug Control Strategy, Office of, 235
National Drug Threat Assessment (NDTA) Program, 38
National Football League, 273, 275
National Guard, role in drug interdiction, 123
National Highway Traffic Safety Administration, 311
National Hockey League, 275
National Household Survey on Drug Abuse. *See* National Survey of Drug Use and Health (NSDUH) Study
National Inhalants and Poisons Awareness Week, 262
National Institute of Drug Abuse (NIDA), 72, 88, 168, 294
National Institute of Justice, 88
National Institute on Alcohol Abuse and Alcoholism (NIAAA), 294, 303, 342
National Prohibition Party, 298
National Survey of Drug Use and Health (NSDUH) Study, 38
    of 2009, 43, 175, 232, 363, 396
Native American Church of North America, peyote use by, 207
Native Americans
    FAS and FAE among, 332, 333
    inhalant use by, 260
Natural-product names, 6
Nausea
    medical use of marijuana, 234–5
    medical use of morphine, 161
NCAA, 284
NDTA (National Drug Threat Assessment) Program, 38
Needle freaks, 154
Negative education, 384–5
Nembutal (pentobarbital), 244, 247
    death from, 32
Nerve impulse, 70
Ness, Eliot, 56–7
Neurochemical systems in brain, 70–1
Neurons, 70
    nucleus accumbens, 71, 72, 172, 307
    synaptic communication, 70
Neurotransmitters, 70–1, **71**
    cocaine and, 172

Newborns, marijuana smoking during pregnancy and, 228. See also Pregnancy
New York City
    crack abuse, 174
    eras of drug scene in, 94
    subway train crash, 397
NIAAA, 294, 303, 342
Nicorette, 370
Nicotine, 12, **356,** 356–7. *See also* Tobacco
    cigarette content increases from 1997-2005, 352
    dependence on, 357–8, 367
    elimination half-life of, 357
    ethnic differences in metabolism of, 18
    metabolism of, 18, 353
    neurochemical system in brain and, 71
    tolerance, 358
    withdrawal from, 358
Nicotine Anonymous, 341
Nicotine gums, patches, sprays, and inhalers, 370
Nicotinic receptors, 357
Nicotrol Inhaler, 370
Nicotrol NS, 370
NIDA, 72, 88, 168, 294
Niemann, Alfred, 167
Nightshade, 209–10
Nitrite inhalation abuse, 262–3
Nitro-bid (nitroglycerin), 309
Nitroglycerin, 11–12, 309
Nitrosamines, 361
Nitrous oxide, 255, 255–6, 257
Nixon, Richard M., 60
N-nitrosamine, 362
Noctec (chloral hydrate), 309
Norbolethone, 272
Norman's Cay, 122
Norms of drug subculture, 78
Norpinephrine, 70
    ADHD and, 187
    amphetamines and, 180–1
    hallucinogens related to, 195, 206–9
    molecular structure of, 180
North Carolina, tobacco growing in, 350
Norway, smoking in, 368
NSDUH. *See* National Survey of Drug Use and Health (NSDUH) Study
Nucleus accumbens, 71, **71,** 72, 172, 307, 337
Numorphan (oxymorphone), 160
Nuprin (ibuprofen), 286
NyQuil, 47
Nyswander, Marie, 157

Oakland Cannabis Buyers' Cooperative, 234
Objective-information approach to prevention, 385
Office of National Drug Control Strategy, 235
Offshore banks, money laundering through, 109
Ofloxacin, 286
Oil of mustard, 261
Ololuiqui, 204. See also Lysergic acid amide (LAA)
Olympic Games, 270, 272–3, 275, 282, 284
Ondansetron, 338
Operation Casablanca, 122
Operation Golden Flow, 148
Operation Intercept, 122